THIRD EDITION

STRATEGIC MANAGEMENT
IN ACTION

mary coulter

PEARSON

Prentice
Hall

Pearson Education International

Acquisitions Editor: Michael Ablassmeir
VP/Editorial Director: Jeff Shelstad
Assistant Editor: Melissa Yu
Editorial Assistant: Richard Gomes
Media Project Manager: Jessica Sabloff
Marketing Manager: Shannon Moore
Marketing Assistant: Patrick Danzuso
Sr. Managing Editor (Production): Judy Leale
Production Editor: Theresa Festa
Permissions Coordinator: Charles Morris
Manufacturing Buyer: Diane Peirano
Design Director: Maria Lange
Designer: Michael J. Fruhbeis
Interior Design: Michael J. Fruhbeis
Cover Design: Michael J. Fruhbeis
Cover Photo: Photodisc Blue Collection/Getty Images, Inc.
Illustrator (Interior): ElectraGraphics Inc.
Manager, Print Production: Christy Mahon
Composition: Carlisle Communications, Ltd.
Printer/Binder: Courier-Westford/Lehigh

Pearson Education LTD.
Pearson Education Singapore, Pte. Ltd
Pearson Education, Canada, Ltd
Pearson Education–Japan
Pearson Education, Upper Saddle River,
    New Jersey

Pearson Education Australia PTY, Limited
Pearson Education North Asia Ltd
Pearson Educación de Mexico, S.A. de C.V.
Pearson Education Malaysia, Pte. Ltd

10 9 8 7 6 5 4 3 2 1
ISBN 0-13-129388-5

To Ron, Sarah, and Katie

Brief Contents

Contents

CHAPTER 7: CORPORATE STRATEGIES   215

Preface

Welcome to the third edition of *Strategic Management in Action!* This book has increased its user base from edition to edition. I think its popularity is based on my belief that strategic management can (and should be) interesting and exciting, and yet also can be based on sound, current academic theory. I've always felt that there was a distinct need for a strategy book that effectively integrated strategy theory and strategy action, and I wanted to show strategic management "in action." That's the way I approached writing the first edition and that approach continues with this edition.

How is this book different from the other strategic management textbooks on the market? I want to share with you what I feel are its competitive advantages—a term you will be quite familiar with after reading this text! As it did in the first two editions, the book effectively integrates strategy theory and strategy action. As one user so plainly described it: "It's the right stuff compactly and clearly presented." I've tried to show strategic management in action in an exciting and engaging way. How? Through the new features in this edition and the popular features retained from earlier editions.

One new feature in this edition is a chapter box theme called Strategic Managers in Action, which provide descriptions of real people dealing with real strategic issues. Some of these real-life strategic managers include Joel Ronning of Digital River, Philippe Bourguignon of Club Med, and Henrietta Holsman Fore of the United States Mint. Also new to this edition is an appendix on how to do a case analysis. Because case analysis is a major component of the strategic management course at many schools, the information in this appendix should be helpful to a lot of readers.

Other chapter features, which customers say they liked and used frequently, have been retained and updated from earlier editions. One of these features is the chapter-opening Strategic Management in Action mini-case, which highlights dynamic companies facing strategic decisions. Some of these chapter-opening cases include Avon Products, the recorded music industry, Haier Group, and Nike. Another feature continued from the last edition of the book is the Strategic Management in Action boxes, which describe companies and the unique strategies they're using. Some of the companies portrayed include E*Trade Group, FedEx, Hallmark Cards, Cold Stone Creamery, The Salvation Army, and Krispy Kreme. Then, there are the FYI (For Your Information) boxes in every chapter that provide a concise overview of contemporary strategic management topics. For example, some of the topics discussed include the copycat economy, designing desirable workspaces, the human capital index, the rule of three, and ethics in real life. Because the global marketplace is so important to strategic management, there's also a chapter box feature called Strategic Management—the Global Perspective. Some of the companies whose strategies are described include Hyundai Motor Company of India, Magna International, Sony, and Trend Micro. Finally, because strategic decision makers are often faced with ethical dilemmas, there's an ethics dilemma presented in every chapter under the heading of The Grey Zone. These were written to encourage you to think about the ethical implications inherent in strategic decisions. To make these chapter box features more relevant, most include suggestions for further research, review, or discussion. Be prepared—your professor might make assignments from any of these boxed items!

Another feature that was retained was the comprehensive cases. These cases— which include McDonald's Corporation, Starbucks, Southwest Airlines, Ford Motor Corporation, and Dell—cover a range of industries and strategic issues and were written so you can perform a thorough strategic analysis, identify strategic issues, and develop appropriate strategic choices. In addition to the in-book cases, I am writing other comprehensive cases that will be available online through this book's Companion Website found at **www.prenhall.com/coulter**.

Don't you think it would be helpful when you're reading a chapter to know what the important concepts were so you could focus on learning and understanding them? I thought so, too. Continued and improved from the last edition are several pedagogical tools to help you better learn and understand the concepts and theories of strategic management. One tool is the coordinated Learning Outline and Learning Review questions approach. At the beginning of each chapter, you'll find a Learning Outline, which is a unique approach that combines learning objectives and a chapter outline. Throughout the chapter at the end of major sections, you'll find Learning Review boxes that correspond to the Learning Outline and reinforce what you should have learned after reading the material in that section. I think this coordinated approach helps you better focus on understanding and comprehending the important material. The chapter summaries are also an important aspect of this learning approach and are presented in a form called The Bottom Line. I chose this term very carefully because when a company focuses on the bottom line, it's focusing on the things that are the most important to improving its performance. Therefore, this end-of-chapter feature summarizes the important information, including key terms and definitions. In addition to these learning tools, I have also updated the end-of-chapter Building Your Skills exercises, which give you the chance to "practice" various skills that successful strategic managers are going to need in tomorrow's organizations. I also retained the short end-of-chapter cases (I like to call them mini-cases), which provide an opportunity for you to further explore the topics in each chapter by answering questions about the companies being studied. One of those mini-cases is the chapter-opening case. Some of the other companies that you'll find include Getty Images, Panera Bread Company, NASCAR, Eclipse Aviation. AutoZone, and Electronic Arts.

This third edition continues to introduce contemporary strategic management theories and practices including, for example, corporate governance, global outsourcing of jobs, and the Global Entrepreneurship Monitor. Of course, the traditional concepts of strategic management such as competitive advantage, SWOT, corporate growth, and strategy implementation are covered as well.

Another distinguishing feature of *Strategic Management in Action* retained from the second edition is that the discussion of the various strategy levels (functional, competitive, and corporate) covers formulation, implementation, and evaluation in the respective chapters. Other strategy texts cover strategy formulation in one chapter, implementation in another, and then evaluation in another. I felt that this approach made it hard for readers to see and understand the integrative nature of strategy. So, I decided it made more sense (both from the student's perspective in learning the material and from the professor's perspective in presenting the material) to discuss formulation, implementation, and evaluation as each strategy level was being discussed. So, for instance, when discussing functional strategy, you'll find information on how it's formulated, implemented, and evaluated; and likewise for the competitive and corporate levels, as well.

Finally, I want to say that I think this book is unique in the market because of its conversational and highly readable writing style. Although an author's style is difficult to describe (especially your own!), I did write this text in a way that I hope makes strategy and strategic management clear and understandable—yet enjoyable. My teaching philosophy (and I've been teaching for over 25 years now, have won teaching awards at my university, and am consistently ranked toward the top of my department based on student evaluations) has been that learning *can* be fun! So, I write like I teach. But only you, the reader, can ultimately judge how well I've written the material.

I need to thank a number of people for their contributions to this book. Without them, *Strategic Management in Action, 3rd edition* wouldn't be a reality. First of all are my students—current and past. Through my experiences teaching our Strategic Management course (most of them enjoyable!), I've developed my own personal philosophy of what works and what doesn't. I learn things every semester from my students and love when they challenge me on topics (even if I am the textbook author!). And I hope they're learning from me. Then, I'd like to say "Thanks" to my department head Barry Wisdom, and my college dean, Ron Bottin. Thank you very much for your ongoing support and encouragement of my authoring efforts. And then, of course my departmental secretaries, Carole Hale, Anita Looney (who has recently retired and is enjoying herself tremendously), and Jeanne Limp. Thank you for all you do to make my "school" life efficient and easier.

I would also like to recognize the individuals who provided me with intelligent and thorough reviews of the first and second editions of *Strategic Management in Action*. I appreciate your willingness to provide these comprehensive and thought-provoking reviews. I know the third edition is better because of the suggestions each of you has provided. These individuals are

Dr. William P. Anthony Florida State University
Dr. Jeryl L. Nelson, Wayne State College
Jerry Thomas, Arapahoe Community College
Patrick L. Schultz, Texas Tech University
Frederick J. Richards, Sacred Heart University
Dr. A. D. Amar, Seton Hall University
Dr. Augustus Abbey, Morgan State University
Dr. Richard D. Babcock, University of San Francisco
Richard Potter, University of Illinois at Chicago
Jack Wheeler, Indiana Wesleyan University
Don Otto, Lindenwood University
Laurie Dahlin, Worcester State College
Moses Acquaah, University of North Carolina Greensboro

Cliff Relyea, Arkansas State University
Eugene Baten, Central Connecticut State University
Ram Subramanian, Grand Valley State University

Supplements

Instructor's Manual and Test Item File

In the Instructor's Manual each chapter includes learning objectives, lecture outline, references to the relevant PowerPoint slides, and answers and suggestions to all chapter boxed elements and end of chapter mini-cases.

In the Test Item File, there are 55–60 questions with a mix of multiple choice, true/false, and essay questions for each chapter.

Computerized Test Item File

The computerized test item file contains all of the questions in the printed Test Item File, and allows educators to easily create and distribute tests for their courses.

Instructor's Resource Center on CD-ROM

This CD-ROM contains the electronic files for the Instructor's Manual, Test Item File, computerized test item file, and PowerPoint Presentation. The PowerPoint presentation is a comprehensive package of text outlines and figures corresponding to the text, which also includes teaching notes.

Companion Website

The Prentice Hall Companion Website features an interactive online student study guide. Students can access multiple choice, true/false, and Internet-based essay questions that accompany each chapter in the text. This is also where you'll find the additional comprehensive cases for analysis. Faculty resources are also available for download and are password-protected.

Acknowledgments

I'd also like to thank the wonderful people at Prentice Hall, my publisher. As usual, all of you have been just super to work with! A big THANK YOU to my editor, Mike Ablassmeir, Senior Acquisitions Editor for Management. Mike, thanks for all your support and encouragement. I'd also like to especially thank Melissa Yu, Assistant Editor, who is always there to answer my many questions and to calm my many concerns! Thank you, Melissa! Then, there's the person who is responsible for the marketing of my book, Shannon Moore, Executive Marketing Manager. Shannon, what can I say? You are an incredibly hardworking, talented person and my books wouldn't be the successes they are without your help! Thank you . . . thank you . . . thank you! The other people on the Management Team—Jessica Sabloff, Rich Gomes, Tom Nixon— and all the others . . . you guys rock! Thank you for all your hard work to make PH's management list the best there is! I'd also like to thank the hardworking people on the production side. Theresa Festa, Judy Leale, Michael Fruhbeis, Diane Peirano, Jennifer Coker, and Lynn Steines, you have been truly super professionals who helped make *Strategic Management in Action 3rd edition* look as great as it does! Thank you so much!

Next, I'd like to say a special thank you to a good friend and outstanding mentor—Steve Robbins, a textbook author icon! Steve, your friendship and advice continue to mean a lot to me! As I've said before, thanks for taking a chance on me and for showing me the ropes of textbook publishing. I know I'm a better writer because of you! Thanks!

Finally, I can't forget the three people in my life who mean the world to me—my wonderful and truly supportive husband Ron and our bright, beautiful, talented, and truly special daughters Sarah and Katie, both who have become the most amazing young women. Words cannot express how much you guys mean to me! Thank you for being so patient with me when I was focused on writing and for not complaining about the many take-out meals we've consumed and the many times I've not been able to go do something because I had a deadline! You provide that much-needed balance to my life. And what I've been able to do is because of all three of you. Thank you!

Mary Coulter
Southwest Missouri State University

1

Introducing the Concepts

STRATEGIC MANAGEMENT IN ACTION CASE #1

Making Over Avon

As the world's largest direct seller of cosmetics and beauty-related items, Avon Products wants to continue building its global reach.[1] To do so, however, Andrea Jung, chairman and CEO, must continually juggle the strategic challenges of guiding this $6.9 billion company and its worldwide army of almost 4 million sales representatives.

Jung was named Avon's first female CEO in 1999. Since that time, she has overseen some significant strategic initiatives. One of these is the company's $100 million investment in a state-of-the-art product research facility outside of New York City, which is scheduled to open in 2005. Avon had always lagged behind its competitors in R&D (research and development), spending less than 1 percent of sales on R&D. Competitors Estée Lauder Companies and L'Oreal SA were spending over 1.3 percent and 3 percent, respectively. Because this industry is one in which customers are continually looking for new products that look good and that are also good for the skin, R&D is critical. In addition, because Avon is primarily a direct-sales company whose sales representatives pitch new products to customers every two weeks, the importance of investing in new product development becomes even more apparent.

Another of Jung's strategic moves was revamping Avon's stodgy, old-fashioned image through new marketing and advertising. Avon, best known for its troops of mostly middle-aged women selling skin creams to their neighbors from catalogs, needed a serious overhaul of its dated image. Jung ordered a new design for the company's all-important sales brochure. Using heavier, glossier paper that was more visually appealing, the company completely redid its brochure and increased distribution by 6 percent. This meant that its sales brochure would now reach an additional 1 million women every two weeks—a bold strategic move that Jung felt would pay off.

The biggest strategic initiative, though, was Jung's decision to develop and target a new line of cosmetics at young women ages 16 to 24. It was the company's first push into the youth market and a dramatic change from its core customer group that was age 35 and older. Deborah Fine, president of Avon Future, the company division responsible for the new line, said, "We want to capture a younger customer, bring in new reps, and create a new global youth brand." According to Avon, 17 million young women in the United States spend at least $75 billion a year on beauty and fashion. If Avon could capture part of that spending with appealing products, it had the potential to add significantly to its bottom line. With over 300 items available, the new brand, called *mark,* was launched in summer 2003. So far, more than 16,000 young Avon sales representatives have distributed 25 million mark catalogs. Avon plans to go global with the product line in 2004. Jung is confident that the company's new brand will help it "pass the makeup brush" to a new generation of Avon customers. The strategic challenge, obviously, will be to keep mark's customers and sales force excited and hooked. Teens are notoriously fickle; what's hot one day can be passé the next. But Jung, her management team, and the company's global sales force appear to be up for the strategic challenges.

This chapter-opening case illustrates many of the complexities and challenges that today's managers face in doing strategic management; that is, in *managing strategically.* Avon's strategic initiatives have implications for managers and employees throughout the entire organization. Even managers at other cosmetic companies, such as Estée Lauder, L'Oreal, or Mary Kay, will have to decide if and how to respond to Avon's strategic moves. These types of strategic decisions are common in today's competitive environment for organizations of all types and sizes. Understanding how and why employees formulate strategic responses is what this book is about. By studying strategic management in action, you can begin to understand how different employees cope with various strategic issues and challenges. Then, whether you're a local sales representative for Avon in Omaha, a regional marketing manager for Avon in Buenos Aires, or a human resources executive at Avon's headquarters in New York, you would be able to recognize and understand the implications of strategic decisions. How might these decisions affect your own work, and how might they affect what your work group does? What kinds of strategic changes might be necessary?

In this introductory chapter, you'll get a flavor of what strategic management is all about. It's divided into three major sections: why is strategic management important, what is strategic management, and who's involved with it. The one thing you might notice that isn't included is the *how* aspect. But don't worry! That's what the rest of the text covers—how you actually *do* strategic management. First, though, we want to look at why strategic management is important.

WHY IS STRATEGIC MANAGEMENT IMPORTANT?

One thing you may be asking yourself about now is, "Why is this stuff important to organizations and, even more directly, why is it important to me? I'm majoring in accounting, and my career goal is to make partner in one of the big four accounting firms. What do I care about strategic management?" Or you may be a computer major who plans to work on e-business applications for an online retailer. You may feel that strategic management and managing strategically have little to do with you. However, one of the assumptions we make in this book is that *everyone* in an organization plays a role in managing strategically. Because life after school for most of you means finding a job in order to have an income, this means you'll be working for some organization. (Even if you choose to start your own business, managing strategically is important, as we'll discuss in Chapter 8.) The very fact that you'll be working in some organization of some size and type means you'll need to know about strategic management. Why? Because understanding how you can be a more effective and efficient strategic decision maker is important so that you can do your job well and have your work performance valued and rewarded accordingly. However, strategic management also is important for other reasons that pertain more directly to the organization.

One of the most significant reasons it's important to understand strategic management is that whether an organization's employees manage strategically does appear to make a

Corporate Reputations

A nationwide online and telephone survey of over 22,000 people conducted by Harris Interactive provided a listing of the top 30 companies based on their score on a Reputation Quotient (RQ). The RQ measured corporate attributes in the following six dimensions: emotional appeal (how much the company is liked, admired, and respected), social responsibility (perceptions of the company as a good citizen in its dealings with communities, employees, and the environment), products and services (perceptions of the quality, innovation, value, and reliability of its products and services), workplace environment (perception of how well the company is managed, how it is to work for, and the quality of its employees), vision and leadership (how much the company demonstrates a clear vision and strong leadership), and financial performance (perceptions of its profitability, prospects, and risk). Who had the best

corporate reputations? The top 10 in the latest list included Johnson & Johnson, Harley Davidson, Coca-Cola, United Parcel Service, General Mills, Maytag, Eastman Kodak, Home Depot, Dell, and 3M. The next 10 included Sony, FedEx, Microsoft, Procter & Gamble, Disney, PepsiCo, Wal-Mart, Anheuser-Busch, Intel, and General Electric. The remaining companies included Xerox, Southwest Airlines, Hewlett-Packard, IBM, Honda, Target, Toyota, DuPont, Sears, and Cisco Systems. Considering that there are thousands of businesses around the world, what got these companies the distinction of having a "best" corporate reputation? What will keep these companies on such a list? Although there are many things these companies do well, strategic management is one thing they do exceptionally well!

Sources: "Johnson & Johnson Ranks #1 in National Corporate Reputation Survey for the Fourth Consecutive Year," Harris Interactive, **www.harrisinteractive.com**, February 4, 2004; and R. Alsop, "The Best Corporate Reputations in America," Wall Street Journal, September 23, 1999, p. B1.

difference in how well the organization performs. The most fundamental questions in strategy are why firms succeed or fail and why firms have varying levels of performance. These questions have influenced what strategic management researchers have studied over the years.[2] What have researchers found in attempting to answer these questions? Does strategic management make a difference? The overall conclusion of numerous studies is that a small but positive relationship between strategic planning and performance does exist.[3] In other words, it appears that organizations that use strategic management concepts and techniques do have higher levels of performance. If it impacts the organization's performance (one measure being the proverbial "bottom line," or corporate profits), that would appear to be a pretty important reason to know something about strategic management.

Another reason for studying strategic management is that organizations of all types and sizes continually face changing situations. Being able to effectively cope with these uncertainties in the organization's external and internal environments *and* achieve expected levels of performance is a real challenge. However, this is where strategic management comes in. The deliberate structure of the strategic management process "forces" organizational employees to examine all the important aspects of a situation to determine the most appropriate strategic decisions and actions. In fact, some recent studies of the strategy decision process suggest that the *way* strategy is developed also can make a difference in performance. For instance, one study of strategic decision makers found that those who collected information and used analytical techniques made more effective strategic decisions than those who did not.[4] And, that's what strategic management is all about—analyzing the situation and then developing and implementing appropriate strategies. Another study found that organizations that used several approaches to developing strategy outperformed those that used a single approach.[5] These studies provide further verification that the strategic management process can affect organizational performance. What we mean is that some structured, systematic approach to coping with the uncertain environments organizations face is needed, and that's what the strategic management process provides.

Finally, strategic management is important because an organization is composed of diverse divisions, functions, and work activities that need to be coordinated and focused on achieving the organization's goals. The strategic management process fills this purpose. Organizational employees from all of the organization's diverse perspectives—manufacturing to marketing to accounting *and* at all organizational levels—develop, implement, and evaluate strategies that they hope will help the organization perform at desired levels. And, they're using strategic management to coordinate their actions.

Although using the strategic management process to manage strategically is important, keep in mind that it won't solve all of an organization's problems or challenges. However, given the fact that it's becoming increasingly difficult for organizations of all sizes and types to achieve high levels of performance, the structure and order imposed by the strategic management process, at the very least, forces employees to think about the relevant variables.

Learning Review

- How can the strategic management process benefit you as an individual?
- What have studies shown about the relationship between the use of the strategic management process and an organization's performance? What are the implications?
- How does strategic management help an organization cope with changes in its external and internal environments?
- What coordinating role does the strategic management process play?
- Suppose you had to explain to a friend why you're studying strategic management. What would you tell that person?

WHAT IS STRATEGIC MANAGEMENT?

The study of strategic management *is* one of the most exciting of all of the traditional business areas! That's because every decision made by an organization's employees has strategic implications. Whether it's the National Basketball Association looking to expand its market reach globally, Kodak's attempts to become known for its digital technology, your local library's decision to use self-check-out procedures similar to those used at Wal-Mart, or Avon's corporate makeover plans, some aspect of strategic management is involved. One of this book's explicit assumptions is that strategic management isn't simply the responsibility of an organization's top managers. People at *all* organizational levels play a role in developing, implementing, and changing strategy. But, what *is* strategic management? Let's take a closer look.

The Basics of Strategy and Strategic Management

To begin to understand the basics of strategy and strategic management, you need look no further than at what's happened in the discount retail industry. Two of the industry's largest competitors—Wal-Mart and Kmart—have battled for market dominance since 1962, the year both companies were founded. The two chains have other striking similarities as well: store atmosphere, names, markets served, and organizational purpose. Yet, Wal-Mart's performance (financial and otherwise) has far surpassed that of Kmart. Why? That, again, is the most fundamental question in strategy: why firms succeed or fail or why

Sysco Corporation, a Houston-based company, was recognized in 2004 as one of the best-managed companies in America. With just 13 percent market share, Sysco is the largest food-service distributor in North America, delivering supplies to customers ranging from small-town diners to the Hilton chain of hotels. The company's five-year average return on capital is 19.1 percent—the best in its industry sector. How has the company been able to achieve such performance results? One key reason: its strategies for controlling distribution costs. For instance, the company recently invested over $113 million in a mega-warehouse in Virginia that will take deliveries from food manufacturers. From that base, Sysco's fleet of trucks will deliver food supplies to 14 regional Sysco operating companies in the Northeast United States, which in turn directly service customers. Managers claim that this new setup will cut down the amount of time between order and delivery from two weeks to two days.

Source: E. Lambert, "Best Managed Companies in America: Food Markets," Forbes, January 12, 2004, p. 166.

firms have varying levels of performance. Organizations vary in how well they perform because of differences in their strategic positions and differences in how they've used strategic management.[6]

Definition of Strategy

The term *strategy* has been defined in a variety of ways. Early descriptions ranged from strategies as integrated decisions, actions, or plans designed to set and achieve organizational goals to strategy as simply the outcome of the strategy formulation process.[7] We're defining an organization's **strategies** as its goal-directed decisions and actions in which its capabilities and resources are matched with the opportunities and threats in its environment. Let's look at some key parts of this definition. First of all, strategy involves an organization's goals. The chosen strategy (or strategies) should help an organization achieve its goals. But formulating a goal-directed strategy isn't enough. Strategy also involves goal-directed actions—implementing the strategy. In other words, an organization's strategy involves not only *what* it wants to do, but actually *doing* it. Finally, strategies should be designed so they take into account the organization's key internal strengths (capabilities and resources) and external opportunities and threats. This "matching" idea is important to the concept of strategy and strategic management, and you'll see it frequently referred to throughout the book.

Definition of Strategic Management

Strategic management is a process of analyzing the current situation; developing appropriate strategies; putting those strategies into action; and evaluating, modifying, or changing those strategies as needed. The basic activities in strategic management can be described as situation analysis, strategy formulation, strategy implementation, and strategy evaluation. (See Figure 1.1.)

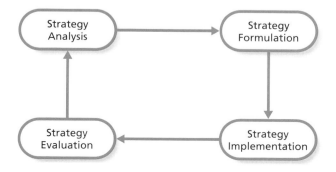

Figure 1.1

Basic Activities of Strategic Management

How is strategic management different from other types of management? Four characteristics set it apart. First, strategic management is, by nature, *interdisciplinary*.[8] It's not like other types of management that focus on specific organizational areas such as human resources, operations, or marketing. Instead, it encompasses all the areas of an organization. Second, strategic management is characterized by its emphasis on the interactions of the organization with its external environment—that is, strategic management has an *external focus*. As organizational employees manage strategically, one important thing they do is look at the external environment to see the positive or negative impact that factors such as the economic situation, competitors, or the changing characteristics of the target market might have on strategic decisions and actions. The third characteristic of strategic management is that it involves the organization's specific resources and capabilities. As organizational employees manage strategically, they're determining what resources the organization has or doesn't have and what it does or doesn't do well. In other words, strategic management has an *internal focus*. Finally, strategic management is characterized by its concern with the *future direction* of the organization. Whether that "future" means weekly manufacturing decisions, yearly financial planning cycles, or significant long-term shifts in the organization's target market, organizational employees are using strategic management. As organizational members determine what they're going to do and how they're going to do it, they do so in light of relevant external and internal factors. Now, think back to the chapter-opening case on Avon. How was strategic management illustrated? According to our description, when Andrea Jung and other managers evaluated the situation (using both external and internal information) and decided what future actions to take, they were using strategic management. Let's examine the specific process by which organizational employees do this.

The Strategic Management Process

A process simply means that there's a series of interrelated and continuous steps that lead to some outcome. In the strategic management process, the series of steps—situation analysis, strategy formulation, strategy implementation, and strategy evaluation—result in a set of strategies the organization uses as it does its business. Figure 1.2 illustrates this process. As organizational members manage strategically, these are the activities they're engaged in. What's involved in each of these steps?

Situation Analysis

Before deciding on an appropriate strategic direction or response, organizational employees need to analyze the current situation. This **situation analysis** entails scanning and evaluating the organizational context, the external environment, and the organizational environment. In Chapter 2, we'll be exploring relevant components of the organizational context,

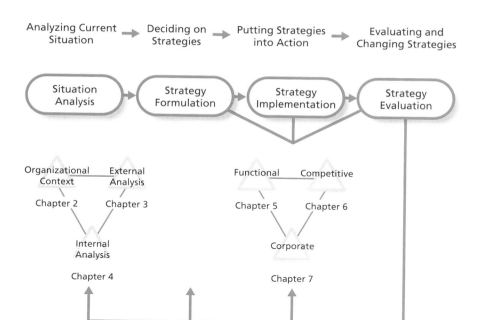

Figure 1.2

Strategic Management in Action

including, for example, the new economy, the role of stakeholders, the dynamics of change, and the role of organizational culture and mission. In Chapter 3, we'll look closely at what an external analysis is and how it is done. Finally, in Chapter 4, we'll study the steps involved in doing an internal analysis and look carefully at an organization's resources, distinctive capabilities, and core competencies. Each of these parts of the strategic management process provides important clues to understanding and evaluating the organization's current situation.

Strategy Formulation

Strategy formulation involves the design and choice of appropriate organizational strategies. In this stage of the strategic management process, the organization's strategies are designed and developed. The typical approach to describing the strategies that are formulated is to look at them from three different organizational levels (see Figure 1.3).

Functional strategies (also called **operational strategies**) are the short-term (less than a year) goal-directed decisions and actions of the organization's various functional areas. What are the organization's functional areas? The most common ones are production–operations (manufacturing), marketing, research and development, human resources, financial–accounting, and perhaps information systems technology and support. But keep in mind that each organization will have its own unique functions. For instance, your university's functional areas might include the various academic departments, student services, facilities management, alumni relations, and athletics. In a retail store, the functional areas might include purchasing, merchandising display, floor sales, personnel, and accounting. We'll discuss the various functional strategies in Chapter 5.

The **competitive strategies** (also called **business unit strategies**) are concerned with how an organization is going to compete in a specific business or industry. For instance, Abercrombie & Fitch competes with American Eagle Outfitters, Gap, J. Crew, and other specialty clothing retailers. Consider our chapter-opening case in which Avon competes with other cosmetics companies. The competitive strategies address what competitive advantages an organization currently has or wants to develop. The various aspects of competitive strategies and competitive moves and actions are explored in Chapter 6.

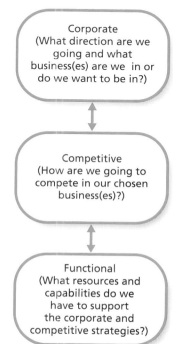

Figure 1.3

Levels of Strategies

Corporate
(What direction are we going and what business(es) are we in or do we want to be in?)

Competitive
(How are we going to compete in our chosen business(es)?)

Functional
(What resources and capabilities do we have to support the corporate and competitive strategies?)

The grocery industry is an extremely competitive one, indeed. And no one knows that better than The Kroger Company (**www.kroger.com**). The early part of the twenty-first century was incredibly difficult for traditional grocers as prices were slashed and a new and aggressive competitor—Wal-Mart—made an all-out push for market share. Talk about the need for some effective competitive strategies! Log on to Kroger's Web site and go to the section on company information. Browse through the store formats, company beliefs, mission, and operations overview. What types of things is Kroger doing to compete in the grocery industry? Make a bulleted list of Kroger's strategies. What do you think of these strategies?

Source: *Kroger,* **www.kroger.com**, *February 9, 2004.*

Corporate strategies are concerned with the broad and more long-term questions of "what business(es) are we in or do we want to be in, and what do we want to do with these businesses?" For instance, FedEx's decision to acquire Kinko's is an example of a corporate strategy. Another example of corporate strategy would be the decisions PepsiCo makes regarding its various divisions—soft drinks (Pepsi Cola), snack foods (Frito Lay), sports/juice drinks (Gatorade and Tropicana), prepared foods (Quaker Oats), and international. Any changes PepsiCo might choose to make in this portfolio of businesses—as it did when it decided to spin off its fast-food division (which included Taco Bell, Pizza Hut, and KFC) as a separate business in the late 1990s—involve changing its corporate strategy. But, what about organizations that don't have a portfolio of different businesses? What does their corporate strategy entail? Corporate strategy in these types of single-business companies is not so much concerned with the optimal mix of corporate business(es) as it is decisions about the future direction of the organization. The various aspects of corporate direction and strategy will be discussed in Chapter 7.

Strategy Implementation

It's not enough for an organization's employees to develop or formulate great strategies. In the next stage of the strategic management process, these strategies have to be implemented. **Strategy implementation** is putting the organization's various strategies into action. The approaches to implementing the various strategies should be considered as the strategies are formulated, so we'll be looking at strategy implementation as we discuss the strategies. In other words, in our discussion of functional strategies, we'll look at how they're formulated *and* implemented, and so on for each level.

Strategy Evaluation

Strategy evaluation is the process of examining how the strategy has been implemented as well as the outcomes of the strategy. An organization's employees should monitor both the actual implementation of the strategy and the performance outcomes of strategies that have been implemented. If these don't measure up to expectations or strategic goals, then the strategy itself or the implementation process may have to be modified or totally changed. Again, because strategy evaluation is inherently part of the whole strategy package, we'll also cover it as we discuss each level of strategy.

Continuing Process of Strategic Management in Action

It's important to recognize that, even though we discuss the strategic management process by isolating each step individually in order to study it, in reality it's a continuous cycle of situation analysis and strategy formulation, implementation, and evaluation. As performance results or outcomes are realized—at *any* level of the organization—organizational members assess the implications and adjust the strategies as needed. Typically, when an organization goes in a new strategic direction or develops a totally new strategy, the strategic management process is followed in sequential order, starting with situation analysis. Otherwise, strategic management in action involves minor and major adjustments to organizational strategies (functional, competitive, and corporate) currently in effect. This may mean starting with strategy evaluation, then doing a situation analysis before proceeding to strategy formulation and implementation. The point is that the way organizations actually function doesn't always happen neatly and logically according to a prescribed sequence, but that doesn't discount the importance of the specific steps in the process.

Learning Review

- What is strategy? Why isn't it just a plan?
- What is the concept of "matching" and why is it important?
- What is strategic management? How is it different from other types of management?
- Describe the strategic management process. Why is it a process?
- What does a situation analysis include?
- Describe the levels of strategy.
- What connections are there between strategy implementation and strategy evaluation?

Looking at Strategic Management's Past

Why look at the history of strategic management? Because it can help us better understand how and why today's managers are practicing strategic management in action and even perhaps get clues as to why organizational performance levels vary. Strategic management's past is quite fascinating, ranging from great historical military battles to current attempts to understand why firms succeed or fail.

Strategy's Military Roots

Although strategic management is a relatively young academic discipline, the concept of strategy can be seen in history in the decisions of and actions taken by military organizations. Historical accounts tell us that a country's military decision makers designed battlefield strategies to gain an edge on the enemy. They would try to exploit the enemy's weak spots and attack them where they were most vulnerable, thus giving the aggressor the best chance of succeeding. Even today, military historians like to analyze great battles in terms of the strategies that each side used and try to interpret why some were successful whereas others failed. And, many popular children's games (such as Battleship, tic-tac-toe, and even checkers) are based on military concepts and designed around the idea of a "strategy." Most involve figuring out what your opponent is doing and taking actions based on that information. The process of analyzing the situation and crafting, implementing, and evaluating an appropriate response is quite common, although we may not think of it specifically in strategy terms.

Academic Origins of Strategic Management[9]

The fields of economics and organization theory provided the earliest academic bases for strategic management. What did the field of economics contribute? Although mainstream

FOR YOUR information

Principles of War

The United States' leading military academies teach the "nine principles of war." These principles have stood the test of time even though the environment of war has changed dramatically. Because the marketplace is often viewed as a "battleground," these principles might be useful in developing an organization's competitive strategy. What are these nine principles?

- **The objective:** Direct every operation toward a clearly defined, decisive, and attainable objective.
- **The offensive:** Seize, retain, and exploit the initiative.
- **Unity of command:** Forces must be under one commander with full authority and responsibility.
- **Mass:** Concentrate combat power at the decisive place and time.
- **Economy of force:** Allocate only the essential minimum of forces to secondary efforts.
- **Maneuver:** Place the enemy in a position of disadvantage through the flexible application of combat power.
- **Surprise:** Strike at the enemy at a time or a place that's unexpected.
- **Security:** Never allow the enemy to acquire an unexpected advantage.
- **Simplicity:** Prepare clear, uncomplicated plans and clear, concise orders to ensure thorough understanding.

Now relate these nine "war" principles to what an organization does as it "battles" in the marketplace for customers. Can they be applied? Explain.

Sources: "Nine Principles of War," Department of Military Science, Worcester Polytechnic Institute, **www.wpi.edu/Academics/Depts/Mi/Sci**, February 9, 2004; and W. C. Finnie, "A Four Cycle Approach to Strategy Development and Implementation," Strategy & Leadership, January–February 1997, p. 28.

economic theory, with its emphasis on rationality, predictability, and similarity, doesn't quite match the realities of strategic management, it did provide an avenue for beginning to explore the role of management decisions and the possibility of strategic choices. In addition, early organizational studies by Frederick Taylor (scientific management), Max Weber (bureaucratic organizations), and Chester Barnard (administrative functions and the organization as an open system) provided important knowledge about efficient and effective organizations and the role that managers played.

Strategic Planning and Strategic Management Emerge[10]

The 1960s were a time when many of society's customs and practices were challenged. This also was true with regards to the way management was being practiced. The universalistic principles of management, which proposed that there was only one correct way to manage in all situations, were being replaced by contingency ideas, which proposed that each organizational situation was different and that the best way of managing depended on the situation. Organization theorists were searching for explanations of organizational differences in functioning and performance. Also during the 1960s, three classic books on strategy—*Strategy and Structure* by Alfred Chandler; *Corporate Strategy* by Igor Ansoff; and a Harvard textbook, *Business Policy: Text and Cases,* by Learned, Christensen, Andrews, and Guth—proved to be instrumental in distinguishing strategic management as a separate academic field and establishing many basic concepts of strategic management.

During the 1970s and 1980s, strategic management became more of a distinct academic field as researchers began studying organizations, managers, and strategies. A dichotomy developed as these researchers tried to understand and describe strategic management.[11] Process researchers studied "how" strategy is formed; that is, the process of strategic management. Content researchers studied the "what," or the content, of a strategic decision. Despite their differences in perspective, both process and content researchers have attempted to establish a relationship between strategic decisions and organizational performance. In addition, strategy researchers have begun looking at the important relationships between strategy content, strategy process, organizational context, and performance. Because explaining and predicting organizational performance is a primary research objective in the field of strategic management, these types of studies continue to provide important clues to how organizational employees can be effective in managing strategically.

STRATEGIC MANAGEMENT
the global perspective

Giant Manufacturing Company Ltd.—which bills itself as "The Global Bicycle Company"—has a name befitting its strategic performance. Located in Taichung, Taiwan, Giant manufactures bicycles that are exported around the world. In fact, over 93 percent of its bicycles are exported. In building its global brand, Giant not only distributed overseas, but also built manufacturing facilities abroad. It selected the Netherlands as one of its manufacturing bases, which people thought was crazy. After all, wages were 50 percent higher in the Netherlands than in Taichung. But,

CEO Antony Lo said that shipping finished bicycles from Taiwan to Europe could take up to two months, so locating there made strategic sense because it allowed the company to react more quickly to customer demands such as color and size changes. Also, by manufacturing in the Netherlands, Giant could avoid strict European Union antidumping duties. What do you think of Lo's strategy?

Sources: *Giant®,* **www.giant-bicycle.com**, February 9, 2004; and W. Royal, "Made in Taiwan," Industry Week, February 15, 1999, pp. 56–70.

- What role has the military played in the development of strategy and strategic management?
- How did economic theory and studies of organizations contribute to strategic management?
- How would strategy process researchers study the chapter-opening case? How about strategy content researchers?
- What have you learned from looking at the history of the development of strategic management?

WHO'S INVOLVED WITH STRATEGIC MANAGEMENT?

As stated earlier, one of the major assumptions of this text is that *all* an organization's employees play an important role in strategic management. Strategic management is just as important for the bank teller at a drive-through facility as it is for the bank's executive vice president who's in charge of commercial loans. Think back to our definition of strategic management—those organizational decisions and actions in which organizational members analyze the current situation; decide on strategies; put those strategies into action; and evaluate, modify, or change strategies—and you can begin to see how each and every employee is involved. The only aspect that differs is the scope or range of the individual's strategic decision making and action. For instance, the bank teller is concerned only with his or her direct work activities in assessing the situation and formulating, implementing, and evaluating specific functional strategies (goal-directed decisions and actions) for dealing with strategic issues that arise at the drive-through facility; the bank's executive vice president does the same either on the competitive or corporate level (or both) with several work areas. Given the importance of each and every employee in strategic management, we need to look at the three major groups who play key roles in the strategic management process: the board of directors, the top management team, and other strategic managers and organizational employees.

The Role of the Board of Directors in Strategic Management

What is a board of directors? For publicly owned business organizations (those whose stocks or shares are sold to the public), the **board of directors** serves as the elected representatives of the company's stockholders. They play a significant role in corporate governance—that is, in governing the decisions and actions of the organization. Corporate governance has become an extremely important issue for today's strategic managers, and we'll discuss it extensively in the last section of this chapter. Table 1.1 lists some responsibilities of a board of directors. The board's legal obligation is to represent the shareholders (stockholders) and protect their interests. Even not-for-profit organizations often have a board of advisers. In fact, your college may have a board of regents (or board of governors or whatever name it has) that evaluates top management decisions and perhaps even makes recommendations as far as future strategic decisions and actions.

The extent to which a board is involved in formulating and implementing strategy has always been a sensitive issue.[12] In the past, the role of the board in the firm's strategy process was often viewed from two opposing perspectives, approving strategy or initiating strategy, as shown in Figure 1.4. In those organizations in which the board acted in an

Table 1.1

Typical Board Responsibilities

- Review and approve strategic goals and plans
- Review and approve organization's financial standards and policies
- Ensure integrity of organization's financial controls and reporting system
- Approve an organizational philosophy
- Monitor organizational performance and regularly review performance results
- Select, evaluate, and compensate top-level managers
- Develop management succession plans
- Review and approve capital allocations and expenditures
- Monitor relations with shareholders and other key stakeholders

Other responsibilities may be assigned depending on the unique culture and needs of the organization.

Source: *Based on K. McG. Sullivan and H. J. Gregory, "Board Self-Assessment," The Corporate Board, November–December 1995, p. 7.*

Figure 1.4

Board Involvement in Strategic Management Process

approving role, the top management team would keep board members informed of strategy, but it was also standard, and accepted, practice for the top managers to keep "ownership" of the strategy and manage it with limited board input regarding specific operational approaches (implementation issues). In fact, the organization's management and board often had unique and different perspectives on strategy. Whereas managers were responsible for turning strategic vision and goals into operational reality, it was believed that the board's responsibility was simply to determine whether the strategies benefited stockholders' interests. However, that's not what we're seeing in today's organizations. Significant changes in legal mandates, investor activism, and corporate strategy have changed the role of many boards in the strategic management process. Today's boards often find themselves taking a much more involved role in the strategic management process by initiating strategies as well as overseeing the implementation and evaluation of those strategies.

The Role of Top Management

There's absolutely no doubt that an organization's top managers play a significant role in the strategic management process. The top organizational manager typically is called the CEO

The Grey Zone

Ethics in Action

Suppose you're in a management position and you're asked by your company's top managers to lie about information you have that's going to be presented to the board. Is lying always wrong, or might it be acceptable under certain circumstances? What, if any, might those circumstances be? What about simply distorting information that's being presented to the board? Is that always wrong, or might it be acceptable under certain circumstances? What circumstances?

strategic MANAGERS *in action*

Michael Weinstein exhibits many of the characteristics of an effective strategic leader. In 1997, along with an investment group, he was involved in the $300 million buyout of Snapple Beverage Corporation from Quaker Oats Company. Long known for its sassy products and advertising, Snapple had "lost its snap" in the corporate environment at Quaker. Weinstein knew that to return the company to the prominence it once had the sagging brand had to be revived. But how? Weinstein said, "We tried to create an atmosphere that was fun and timely. We introduced our first new product two weeks after we bought the company." And the rest is history! In 2000, Cadbury Schweppes bought Snapple for $1 billion and appointed Weinstein to President of Innovation at Cadbury Schweppes Americas Beverage—a pretty good return on investment and a pretty good measure of how successful their strategies were!

Sources: *Hoover's Online*, **www.hoovers.com**, February 9, 2004; and "The Fast 50 Leaders," Fast Company, March 2002, p. 97.

(chief executive officer). This person (Andrea Jung in our chapter-opening case) usually has a top management team composed of other executive or senior managers such as a COO (chief operating officer), CFO (chief financial officer), CIO (chief information officer), and other individuals who may have various titles. Traditional descriptions of the CEO's role in strategic management include being the "chief" strategist, structural architect, and developer of the organization's information and control systems.[13] Other descriptions of the strategic role of the "chief executive" include key decision maker, visionary leader, political actor, monitor and interpreter of environment changes, and strategy designer.[14]

No matter how we characterize top management's job, you can be certain that from their perspective at the upper levels of an organization, it's like no other job in the organization. By definition, they are ultimately responsible for every decision and action of every organizational employee. One important aspect of top management's role in strategy that we need to look at concerns top managers as strategic leaders. As you're probably well aware, leadership is a perennially popular management topic. Libraries and bookstores have numerous books on the subject. Organizational researchers continue to study it in relation to strategic management, because an organization's top managers need to provide effective strategic leadership. What is **strategic leadership**? It's the ability to anticipate, envision, maintain flexibility, think strategically, and work with others in the organization to initiate changes that will create a viable and valuable future for the organization.[15] How can top managers provide effective strategic leadership? Six key dimensions of strategic leadership have been identified, as shown in Figure 1.5.[16] These include determining the organization's purpose or vision, exploiting and maintaining the organization's core competencies, developing the organization's human capital, creating and sustaining a strong organizational culture, emphasizing ethical organizational decisions and practices, and establishing appropriately balanced organizational controls. Each of these strategic leadership dimensions is an important part of the strategic management process, which we'll be discussing in detail in Chapters 2 through 7.

Other Strategic Managers and Organizational Employees

Although an organization's top managers have several important strategic leadership responsibilities in the strategic management process, managers and employees at other levels throughout the organization also are important to the process. What are some of their strategic responsibilities?[17] One is strategy implementation. They're the people putting the strategies into action. They might be supervising the work of others (in the case of a supervisor or manager) or they may be personally performing some of the work as well. For

Figure 1.5

What Effective Strategic Leadership Involves

Source: Based on R. D. Ireland and M. A. Hitt, "Achieving and Maintaining Strategic Competitiveness in the 21st Century: The Role of Strategic Leadership," Academy of Management Executive, February 1999, pp. 43–57.

example, think back to our opening case. Someone had to design the revised sales brochure and see that it was printed. Someone had to oversee the product development process and marketing strategies for the new brand, mark. And, someone had to plan and supervise the building of the new product-research facility. As Avon continues to adjust to its changing environment, new strategies may have to be put into action. That's the role other strategic managers and organizational employees will play.

Organizational employees and managers also are likely to be responsible for evaluating whether the strategies are working. If the strategies aren't achieving the desired levels of performance, then they need to be changed or modified. Although top management may establish the guidelines and policies for evaluating performance, it's the other strategic managers and organizational employees who often do the evaluation and take any necessary actions.

Learning Review

- How are boards of directors involved in the strategic management process?
- Describe the two levels of board involvement in the strategic management process.
- What role do top managers play in strategic management?
- What is strategic leadership?
- List the six key dimensions of strategic leadership.
- What roles do other strategic managers and organizational employees play in strategic management?

STRATEGIC MANAGEMENT IN TODAY'S WORLD

Managing strategically in today's world isn't easy! Here we want to look at three important issues affecting strategic management in today's world: globalization, corporate governance, and e-business.

Globalization

Organizations are no longer constrained by national borders. Over 61 percent of Avon's revenues come from outside North America. Nissan, a Japanese firm, makes cars in Mississippi. Lend Lease Corporation, Australia's leading real estate company, built the Bluewater shopping complex in Kent, England, and has contracts with Coca-Cola to build all the soft-drink maker's bottling plants in Southeast Asia. McDonald's, a U.S. business, sells hamburgers in China. Globalization presents significant business opportunities, and the world has definitely become a global village. However, doing business globally in today's world isn't easy.[18] Strategic decision makers face challenges in two areas: those from the openness associated with globalization and those resulting from significant cultural differences.

The push to go global has been widespread. Advocates praise the economic and social benefits that come from widespread globalization. Yet, globalization has created challenges because of the openness it requires. After the terrorist attacks on the United States on September 11, 2001, some have questioned whether the "openness" of globalization has made countries more sensitive to political and cultural differences and whether these profound differences bring increased threats of additional terrorist attacks by those who misunderstand and disagree. Although globalization is meant to open up trade and break down the geographical barriers separating countries, opening up means being open to both the bad as well as the good. Another challenge of the openness that globalization brings is the economic interdependence of trading countries. If one country's economy falters, it potentially could have a domino effect on other countries with which it does business. So far, however, that hasn't happened. For example, the severe Asian financial crisis in the late 1990s had the potential to totally disrupt economic growth around the globe and bring on a worldwide recession. But it didn't. Why? Because there were mechanisms in place to prevent it from happening—mechanisms that encouraged global trade and averted a potential crisis. One of the most important of these mechanisms is the **World Trade Organization (WTO)**, which is a global organization of 147 countries that deals with the rules of trade among nations.[19] The WTO, founded in 1995, evolved from the General Agreement on Tariffs and Trade (GATT), a trade agreement in effect since the end of World War II. The goal of the WTO is to help organizations conduct business by enacting trade agreements that are negotiated and ratified by the vast majority of the world's trading nations. Although a number of vocal critics have staged visible protests lambasting the WTO, it does appear to play an important role in monitoring and promoting global trade.

It's not just simply the challenges from openness that strategic managers must face. The far more serious challenges come from the intense underlying and fundamental cultural differences between countries—differences that encompass traditions, history, religious beliefs, and deep-seated values. Although globalization has long been praised for its economic benefits, there are those who think that it is simply a euphemism for "Americanization"—that is, the way U.S. cultural values and U.S. business philosophy are said to be slowly taking over the world.[20] At its best, proponents of Americanization hope that others will see how progressive, efficient, industrious, and free U.S. society and businesses are and want to emulate that way of doing things. However, critics claim that this attitude of the "almighty American dollar spreading the American way to every single country" has created numerous problems.[21] Although history is filled with clashes between civilizations, what's unique about this period in time is the speed and ease with which misunderstandings and disagreements can erupt and escalate. The Internet, television and other media, and global air travel have brought the good and the bad of American entertainment, products, and behaviors to every corner of the globe. For those who don't like what Americans do, say, or believe, it can lead to resentment, dislike, distrust, and even outright hatred.

As the world's largest food company, Swiss-based Nestlé has revenues of more than $60 billion a year from the global sales of its over 8,000 brands—brands ranging from Nescafé instant coffee to Purina cat food to KitKat candy bars. Although other food companies have deliberately cut costs in recent years, Nestlé's strategic focus has been on robust sales growth. The result has been lower operating margins than competitors and below-average stock performance. CEO Peter Brabeck-Letmathe has undertaken some strategic changes, including streamlining worldwide operations by improving information technology and centralizing purchasing and other corporate activities, strengthening key segments by acquiring competitors such as Dreyer's Grand ice cream and Ralston Purina pet foods, eliminating less profitable activities such as tomato canning and pasta production, and developing new products such as nutritionally enhanced cosmetics and toothpastes. Brabeck-Letmathe hopes that these new strategies will deliver both the robust sales growth and the cost savings that will give Nestlé the operating margins it desires in this competitive industry. However, as a global company, what types of strategic challenges might Brabeck-Letmathe face in implementing these strategies?

Sources: *Hoover's Online*, **www.hoovers.com**, *February 18, 2004; and C. Matlack, "Nestlé is Starting to Slim Down at Last," Business Week, October 27, 2003, pp. 56–57.*

Being successful at strategic management under such conditions will require incredible cultural and political sensitivity and understanding. Strategic decision makers will need to be aware of how their decisions and actions will be viewed, not only by those who may agree, but, more importantly, by those who may disagree. Organizations will likely have to adjust their strategic approaches to accommodate these diverse views.

Corporate Governance

Enron. Tyco. WorldCom. These are just a few of the notorious names from the corporate scandals that destroyed billions of dollars in shareholder value during a period of approximately 18 months in 2001 and 2002. Because directors at these companies had missed or ignored problems, many of which involved fraudulent accounting schemes, U.S. regulators told businesses that the old style of corporate governance couldn't continue and would have to be reformed. A significant part of that reform was the **Sarbanes-Oxley Act of 2002**, a U.S. federal law designed to protect investors by improving the accuracy and reliability of corporate disclosures, which was enacted on July 30, 2002. With the stroke of a pen, corporate governance has become an important issue that today's strategic decision makers must cope with.

What is **corporate governance**? It's the "determination of the broad uses to which organizational resources will be deployed and the resolution of conflicts among the myriad participants in organizations."[22] In other words, corporate governance involves the mechanisms and approaches that govern the way a corporation uses its resources so that stakeholders' interests are taken into consideration and protected. Two areas in which corporate governance reform was mandated by Sarbanes-Oxley are the role of boards of directors and financial reporting.

The Role of Boards of Directors

The original purpose of a board of directors was to have a group, independent from management, that looked out for the interests of the owners (i.e., the shareholders) who, because of the corporate form of structure, were not involved in the day-to-day management of the organization. What actually happened in many organizations was that board members often enjoyed a cozy relationship in which the board members

Table 1.2

*21st Century Governance
Principles for U.S. Public
Companies*

1. *Interaction:* Sound governance requires effective interaction among the board, management, the external auditor, and the internal auditor.

2. *Board Purpose:* The board of directors should understand that its purpose is to protect the interests of the corporation's stockholders, while considering the interests of other stakeholders (e.g., creditors, employees, etc.).

3. *Board Responsibilities:* The board's major areas of responsibility should be monitoring the CEO, overseeing the corporation's strategy, and monitoring risks and the corporation's control system. Directors should employ healthy skepticism in meeting these responsibilities.

4. *Independence:* The major stock exchanges should define an "independent" director as one who has no professional or personal ties (either current or former) to the corporation or its management other than service as a director. The vast majority of the directors should be independent in both fact and appearance so as to promote arms-length oversight.

5. *Expertise:* The directors should possess relevant industry, company, functional area, and governance expertise. The directors should reflect a mix of backgrounds and perspectives. All directors should receive detailed orientation and continuing education to assure they achieve and maintain the necessary level of expertise.

6. *Meetings and Information:* The board should meet frequently for extended periods of time and should have access to the information and personnel it needs to perform its duties.

7. *Leadership:* The roles of Board Chair and CEO should be separate.

8. *Disclosure:* Proxy statements and other board communications should reflect board activities and transactions (e.g., insider trades) in a transparent and timely manner.

9. *Committees:* The nominating, compensation, and audit committees of the board should be composed only of independent directors.

10. *Internal Audit:* All public companies should maintain an effective, full-time internal audit function that reports directly to the audit committee.

Source: *Corporate Governance Center, Kennesaw State University, March 26, 2002.*

"took care" of the CEO and the CEO "took care" of the board members. This quid pro quo arrangement changed with the passage of Sarbanes-Oxley, and demands on board members of publicly traded companies increased considerably.[23] To help board members do their job better, researchers at the Corporate Governance Center at Kennesaw State University developed 10 governance principles for U.S. public companies that have been endorsed by the Institute of Internal Auditors. These principles are shown in Table 1.2.

Financial Reporting

In addition to expanding the role of board members, Sarbanes-Oxley also calls for more disclosure and transparency of financial information. In fact, senior managers are now required to certify their companies' financial results. And the law must be working! On November 4, 2003, Richard Scrushy, the former HealthSouth Corporation CEO, became the first CEO of a major U.S. company to be indicted for violating the Sarbanes-Oxley Act, which holds top managers personally accountable for their companies' financial reporting.[24] To effectively fulfill their financial reporting responsibilities, strategic managers might want to follow the financial reporting principles also developed by the researchers at the Corporate Governance Center at Kennesaw State University. These seven principles are shown in Table 1.3.

Mitch Caplan, CEO of E*Trade Group Inc., and his board of directors are passionately embracing corporate governance reform, and in some areas have actually gone beyond what the new rules require. For instance, other than Mr. Caplan, all of E*Trade's nine board members are outside directors (i.e., directors who are not organizational employees), which is a highly unusual approach. Mr. Caplan says in response, "Management credibility has to be regained; the walk has to match the talk." The board also thoroughly studied executive compensation packages, overhauled those compensation packages by establishing more specific performance targets, and grilled company executives over lackluster results in certain areas. This is a company that obviously takes corporate governance seriously! What impact are such actions likely to have on the strategic management process and on the people in the company who are managing strategically?

Source: S. Craig, "How One Firm Uses Strict Governance to Fix Its Troubles," Wall Street Journal, August 21, 2003, p. A1.

Table 1.3

21st Century Financial Reporting Principles for U.S. Public Companies

1. *Reporting Model:* The current GAAP financial reporting model is becoming increasingly less appropriate for U.S. public companies. The industrial-age model currently used should be replaced or enhanced so that tangible and intangible resources, risks, and performance of information-age companies can be effectively and efficiently communicated to financial statement users. The new model should be developed and implemented as soon as possible.

2. *Philosophy and Culture:* Financial statements and supporting disclosures should reflect economic substance and should be prepared with the goal of maximum informativeness and transparency. A legalistic view of accounting and auditing (e.g., "can we get away with recording it this way?") is not appropriate. Management integrity and a strong control environment are critical to reliable financial reporting.

3. *Audit Committees:* The audit committee of the board of directors should be composed of independent directors with financial, auditing, company, and industry expertise. These members must have the will, authority, and resources to provide diligent oversight of the financial reporting process. The board should consider the risks of audit committee member stock/stock option holdings and should set audit committee member compensation at an appropriate level given the expanded duties and risks faced by audit committee members. The audit committee should select the external auditor, evaluate external and internal auditor performance, and approve the audit fee.

4. *Fraud:* Corporate management should face strict criminal penalties in fraudulent financial reporting cases. The Securities and Exchange Commission should be given the resources it needs to effectively combat financial statement fraud. The board, management, and auditors all should perform fraud risk assessments.

5. *Audit Firms:* Audit firms should focus primarily on providing high-quality audit and assurance services and should perform no consulting for audit clients. Audit firm personnel should be selected, evaluated, compensated, and promoted primarily based on technical competence, not on their ability to generate new business. Audit fees should reflect engagements' scope of work and risk.

6. *External Auditing Profession:* Auditors should view public accounting as a noble profession focused on the public interest, not as a competitive business. The profession should carefully consider expanding audit reports beyond the current "clean" versus modified dichotomy so as to enhance communication to financial report users.

7. *Analysts:* Analysts should not be compensated (directly or indirectly) based on the investment banking activities of their firms. Analysts should not hold stock in the companies they follow, and they should disclose any business relationships between the companies they follow and their firms.

Source: *Corporate Governance Center, Kennesaw State University, March 26, 2002.*

Strategic Management in an E-Business World

Do you use e-mail to communicate? Can you find an advertisement that doesn't have a Web address in it somewhere? Today's strategic decision makers function in an e-business world. Although critics have questioned the viability of Internet-based companies, especially after the dot-com implosion in 2000 and 2001, e-business is here to stay and offers many strategic advantages.[25]

E-business (electronic business) is a comprehensive term describing the way an organization does its work by using electronic (Internet-based) linkages with its key constituencies (employees, customers, clients, suppliers, and partners). It includes **e-commerce**, which is essentially the sales and marketing component of e-business. Organizations such as Dell (computers) and 1-800-Flowers (floral and other types of gifts) are engaged in e-commerce because they sell items over the Internet.

Not every organization is, or needs to be, a total e-business. Instead, strategic decision makers may choose from three different strategic approaches to e-business. The first approach is an e-business *enhanced* organization, a traditional organization that sets up e-business capabilities, usually e-commerce, while maintaining its traditional structure. Many *Fortune 500* organizations have evolved into e-businesses using this approach. They use the Internet to *enhance* (not replace) their traditional ways of doing business. For instance, the Internet division of Sears, a traditional bricks-and-mortar retailer with thousands of physical stores worldwide, is intended to expand, not replace, the company's main source of revenue.

Another approach to e-business is an e-business *enabled* organization that uses the Internet to perform its traditional business functions better, but not to sell anything. In other words, the Internet *enables* organizational members to do their work more efficiently and effectively. Numerous organizations use electronic linkages to communicate with employees, customers, or suppliers and to support them with information. For instance, Levi Strauss uses its Web site to interact with customers, providing them the latest information about the company and its products, but not to sell the jeans. It also uses an **intranet**, an internal organizational communication system that uses Internet technology and is accessible only by organizational employees, to communicate with its global workforce.

The last approach to e-business involvement is when an organization becomes a *total* e-business. Organizations such as Amazon.com, Yahoo!, and eBay are total e-business organizations. Their whole existence is based on the Internet. Other organizations have evolved into e-business organizations, seamlessly integrating traditional and e-business functions. When an organization becomes a total e-business, there's a complete transformation in the way it does its work.

Concluding Thought

No matter what organizational level you're on, you'll find yourself involved in some way with strategic management. Whether your career goal is to be part of a top management team or whether you plan to apply your technical training in some functional area of the organization, you'll be affected by and have an effect on the organization's strategic management process. This chapter is just the beginning of your exciting journey to understand strategic management!

- How do organizations benefit from globalization?
- What problems does the openness associated with globalization bring?
- What role does the World Trade Organization play in globalization?
- What is the Sarbanes-Oxley Act?
- What is corporate governance and what does it involve?
- How is corporate governance being reformed?
- What is e-business? E-commerce?
- What are the three different strategic approaches to being an e-business?

the bottom line

- Strategic management is important to you individually because you'll be working in some organization and will be evaluated and rewarded on being an effective and efficient strategic decision maker.

- Strategic management is important to organizations because it does appear to make a difference in how well the organization performs; it helps employees decide what to do and how to respond to continually changing situations; and it helps coordinate the diverse divisions, functions, and work activities. However, although strategic management is important, it won't solve all of an organization's problems or challenges.

- An organization's **strategies** are its goal-directed decisions and actions in which its capabilities and resources are matched with environmental opportunities and threats.

- **Strategic management** is a process of analyzing the current situation; developing appropriate strategies; putting those strategies into action; and evaluating, modifying, or changing those strategies as needed.

- The basic activities of strategic management are situation analysis, strategy formulation, strategy implementation, and strategy evaluation.

- Strategic management is different from other types of management because it is interdisciplinary, has an external focus, has an internal focus, and has a future focus.

- The strategic management process consists of **situation analysis** (scanning and evaluating the organizational context, the external environment, and the organizational environment), **strategy formulation** (the design and choice of appropriate organizational strategies), **strategy implementation** (putting the organization's various strategies into action), and **strategy evaluation** (assessing how the strategy has been implemented as well as the outcomes of the strategy).

- In reality, the strategic management process may not always follow the prescribed sequence, but the activities are still completed.

- An organization will have three different types of strategies. **Functional strategies** (also called **operational strategies**) are the short-term goal-directed decisions and actions of the organization's various functional departments. **Competitive strategies** (also called **business unit strategies**) dictate how an organization is going to compete in a specific business or industry. **Corporate strategies** are broad and more long-term and address issues of what businesses the organization is in or wants to be in, what they hope to do with these businesses, and the direction the organization is pursuing.

- Strategic management has its roots in military strategies because military units would try to gain the edge on an enemy, much like an organization does as it tries to gain the edge on competitors.

- Strategic management also has evolved out of the academic fields of economics and organization theory.

- Strategic management as an academic discipline was influenced by work in the 1960s in which researchers looked for explanations of organizational differences in performance and functioning.

- During the 1970s and 1980s, researchers looked at how strategies were formed and implemented (*process* research) and at the relationship between strategic choices and performance (*content* research).

- Although people at *all* organizational levels play a role in strategic management, three main groups can be identified.

- One of these groups is the **board of directors**, the elected representatives of the company's stockholders. Their involvement can range from an initiating role (highest level of involvement) to an approving role (lowest level of involvement).

- Top management is another of these groups. The top management team (CEO and other executive or senior managers) is ultimately responsible for every decision and action of employees.

- One important characteristic of top managers is their **strategic leadership**, the ability to anticipate, envision, maintain flexibility, think strategically, and work with others in the organization to initiate changes that will create a viable and valuable future for the organization.

- Six key dimensions of strategic leadership include determining the organization's purpose or vision, exploiting and maintaining the organization's core competencies, developing the organization's human capital, creating and sustaining a strong organizational culture, emphasizing ethical organizational decisions and practices, and establishing appropriately balanced organizational controls.

- The third important group involved in strategic management is other strategic managers and organizational employees at middle and lower organizational levels. One of their primary tasks is implementation. And, they're also likely to be responsible for strategy evaluation.

- Three important issues affecting strategic management in today's world are globalization, corporate governance, and e-business.

- Although globalization brings both economic and social benefits, the openness of globalization has made countries more vulnerable to political and cultural differences and brought about the increased threat of terrorist attacks by those who don't agree with a country's politics or culture.

- Another challenge brought about by the openness of globalization is the economic interdependence of trading nations.

- The **World Trade Organization (WTO)** is a global organization of 147 countries that deals with the rules of trade among nations.

- Far more serious challenges of globalization are the intense underlying and fundamental cultural differences between countries. Organizations may have to adjust their strategic approaches to accommodate these diverse views.

- A significant part of the corporate governance reform push, the **Sarbanes-Oxley Act of 2002**, a U.S. federal law designed to protect investors by improving the accuracy and reliability of corporate disclosures, was enacted on July 30, 2002.

- **Corporate governance** is the determination of the broad uses to which organizational resources will be deployed and the resolution of conflicts among the myriad participants in organizations.

- Corporate governance reforms have taken place in two ways. First, reforms have altered the role that boards of directors play. Second, the Sarbanes-Oxley Act now requires more financial disclosure and more transparency of financial information.

- **E-business (electronic business)** is a comprehensive term describing the way an organization does its work by using electronic (Internet-based) linkages with its key constituencies (employees, customers, clients, suppliers, and partners).

- E-business includes **e-commerce**, which is the sales and marketing component of e-business.

- Strategic decision makers can choose from three different approaches to e-business.

- An e-business enhanced organization is one that uses e-business (usually e-commerce) to enhance its business while also maintaining its traditional way of doing business.

- An e-business enabled organization is one that uses the Internet to perform its traditional business functions better, but not to sell anything.

- An **intranet**, an internal organizational communication system that uses Internet technology and is accessible only by organizational employees, is often used by e-business enabled organizations.

- A total e-business organization is one whose existence is based on the Internet.

building your skills

1. Research the strategic leader(s) of Coca-Cola, Amazon.com, and Ford Motor Company. Use paper-based sources (business periodicals, books, and so forth) or Web-based information. In a brief paper, describe how each of these strategic leaders fulfills the characteristics of effective strategic leadership (see Figure 1.5).

2. "Making strategy, once an event, is now a continuous process." Explain what you think this statement means.

3. The performance of an organization's board of directors is being scrutinized more closely than ever. Complete the following assignments having to do with boards of directors.

   a. Find a recent listing of the worst boards of directors. (You will have to do a Web search to find these.) Locate financial information on the top three companies on this list. Report what you find. Draw some conclusions about why these boards are cited as being among the worst.

   b. *Fortune* publishes an annual ranking of the most admired companies, both global and American. Choose either category and get the most recent listing of the top 10 admired companies. Look up financial information on the top three companies on the list. Look up information on the boards of directors of these companies. Report what you find. What conclusions might you draw about the role of the board in the strategic management of these most-admired companies?

4. "With respect to business, the Internet represents one of the most important innovations of this generation for firms to cut costs, improve services, and expand markets." Do you agree with this statement? Why or why not? What are the implications for strategic decision makers?

5. The term "business model" became extremely popular during the dot-com craze—everyone was searching for that Web-based business model that promised unimaginable profits. However, as the dot-com craze imploded, the concept lost its luster. But maybe we shouldn't be so quick to dismiss the idea. A good **business model**, which is simply a strategic design for how a company intends to profit from its broad array of strategies, processes, and activities, should answer four questions: (1) Who is our customer? (2) What does the customer value? (3) How do we make money in this business? and (4) What underlying economic logic explains how we can deliver value to customers at an appropriate cost?

   With this in mind, describe the business model used by each of the following companies: eBay, Carnival Cruise Lines, Domino's Pizza, and Dell Computer.

Strategic Management in Action Cases

CASE #1: Making Over Avon

This Strategic Management in Action Case can be found at the beginning of Chapter 1.

Discussion Questions

1. Explain how strategic management and the strategic management process are illustrated in this case.

2. What are some performance measures that Avon's strategic decision makers might use as they evaluate the results of the three major strategic initiatives described in the case?

3. Andrea Jung is Avon's first female CEO, which you might find surprising considering that Avon's target market is overwhelmingly female. Do some research on the number of female CEOs and female board members in U.S. companies. Have these numbers changed over time? What conclusions might you draw from these data?

4. Go to Avon's Web site (**www.avoncompany. com**). What are Avon's vision and mission? How might these statements affect strategic decisions and actions? Check out the company's products. What is the company's number one brand globally? What strategies are being proposed for mark?

CASE #2: Fighting Grime

Look in your pantry, your laundry room, your bathroom, or under your kitchen sink. Chances are you have at least one of the Clorox Company's many cleaning products in your household. The Clorox Company (**www.clorox.com**) manufactures and markets household cleaning and grocery products around the globe. Some of the product names you might recognize include Clorox Bleach, Glad bags, Soft Scrub bathroom cleaner, Tilex shower cleaner, Combat Plus pest control, STP automotive products, Kingsford charcoal, S.O.S. cleaning pads, Hidden Valley Ranch dressings, and many others.

Although most people probably know Clorox from its best-selling bleach products (it's the worldwide leader in the bleach market), Clorox bleach is not even the company's biggest brand. That distinction belongs to the Glad line of food storage and disposal products. The Glad line was part of the acquisition of First Brands Corporation, a $2 billion acquisition, that the Clorox Company completed in January of 1999. In addition to the Glad products, the acquisition brought the STP line of automotive additives and the Scoop Away and Fresh Step litter brands under the Clorox Company's fold. It was a bold strategic move on the part of the Clorox Company.

The Clorox Company's strategic position began to improve in the late 1990s. Much of that success could be traced to G. Craig Sullivan, Clorox's CEO, who was brought on board in the early 1990s. In the early 1990s, Clorox was viewed by its competitors as knowing how to sell bleach, but not much else. There was a complacent and content management team who did an adequate job of strategically managing a tired product line. When Sullivan was hired, his first action was to let go those managers he judged unable to adapt to the new strategic direction he had in mind for Clorox. Half the management team left. His next step was to sell off money-losing operations such as bottled water and restaurant equipment and to acquire grime-fighting brands such as S.O.S. scrubbing pads and Lestoil cleaner that were more in line with Clorox's core products. Then, Sullivan stepped up marketing efforts for the company's existing brands such as Pine Sol and Formula 409 cleansers. But the biggest strategic change of all was the acquisition of First Brands Corporation, an acquisition that increased the Clorox Company's size by almost 50 percent overnight. In the period of one year (the time it took to complete the transaction), Clorox went from a $2.7 billion company with 6,600 employees to a $4 billion company with almost 9,000 employees.

First Brands was a lot like the "old" Clorox Company. It had a stable of solid brands that had stalled or faded from consumers' minds, and thus from their purchases. However, Mr. Sullivan felt that he could make First Brands a better organization. How? A key element of his overall growth strategy was to "dust off" brands that had languished. His strategic formula: Execute. Freshen old brands, extend product lines, improve advertising, and lower costs. Revitalizing product lines was a key to the success of this strategy. Mr. Sullivan also recognized that, in addition to successfully integrating the new businesses, it was important to continue to support and grow the company's base business. For instance, in 2003, the company introduced a totally new addition to its line of bleach products—and it didn't come in a bottle or a jug! It was the first-ever bleach in a pen, the new Bleach Pen Gel, a pen-like tool filled with an all-new gel form of bleach that would "write out" stains in laundry and around the house.

However, not everything the Clorox Company has done has been a success. A line of Hidden Valley salad dressings aimed at children with flavors like pizza and nacho sauce got the thumbs down by kids. And, sales of the company's pest control products continued to decline, resulting in the eventual sale of its insecticides business to another company, Reckitt Benckiser, in April 2003. As one investment analyst said, the company seems to be "willing to cut things off when they're not working."

On December 31, 2003, Sullivan retired as CEO and Chairman of the Clorox Company. He was replaced by Jerry Johnston, who has been with the company since 1981, serving in positions with increasing levels of strategic responsibility over the years. As the new CEO, Johnston said, "I'm honored to have the opportunity to lead the Clorox organization as we build on our strong track record. Clorox is a great company with an excellent portfolio of strong brands and many talented people around the world.

Together, we will remain squarely focused on our goal of delivering healthy, consistent growth." And that will be an enormous strategic challenge! That growth may have to come from international markets where Clorox has a small presence and where one of its major competitors, Colgate-Palmolive, already has an enormous one. Yet, these are strategic challenges that Johnston and the management team at the Clorox Company welcome. After all, if they can effectively fight the grime and dirt found in customers' homes, the war in the marketplace might not seem so bad after all!

Discussion Questions

1. Do you think strategic management has contributed to the Clorox Company's success? Why or why not?

2. Given the information included in this mini-case about the Clorox Company, at what step in the strategic management process do you think it excels? Explain your choice.

3. Using Figure 1.5, evaluate G. Craig Sullivan's strategic leadership.

4. How might Jerry Johnston use strategic management to manage the challenges facing his company?

5. Update the information on the Clorox Company by logging on to the company's Web site (**www.clorox.com**). How big is Clorox now in terms of sales? In terms of number of employees? What new strategies is it pursuing, if any?

Sources: Clorox Company, **www.clorox.com**, February 20, 2004; Associated Press, "Clorox Profit Jumps 22 percent with $109 Million," Hoover's Online, **www.hoovers.com**, February 20, 2004; and D. Canedy, "Resurgence of a Grime Fighter," *New York Times*, March 14, 1999, p. BU1.

CASE #3: In the Zone

Like that other illustrious retail chain started in Arkansas, AutoZone is also known for its clean floors, friendly clerks, and spirited corporate culture featuring a rousing cheer performed by employees. With over 3,200 stores in 48 states and Mexico, AutoZone

is the number one auto parts chain in the United States. The $5.5-billion-a-year company enjoys profit margins of 9.5 percent (almost triple that of Wal-Mart, that other famous Arkansas company) and the highest return on equity of any company in the

S&P 500 retail index. The company appears to be doing for auto parts what Wal-Mart did for discount retailing and what Home Depot did for the do-it-yourself home-remodeling market. Yet, it has nowhere achieved the level of brand recognition that Wal-Mart or Home Depot have. What has contributed to the company's enviable track record?

One important element in AutoZone's success is its attention to detail. It has made its stores appealing to anyone who drives a car. From the hard-core NASCAR buffs and *Fast and Furious* accessorizers to the grandmother looking for new wiper blades, AutoZone is customer-friendly. The company's pledge states: "AutoZoners [that's the name company employees use to refer to themselves] always put customers first. We know our parts and products. Our stores look great. And we've got the best merchandise at the right price." It's a strategic formula that has proven to be a winner for this company.

CEO Steve Odland, a former executive with Quaker Oats, was hired in 2001 by the company's board after frustration over the company's performance in the 1990s. During that time, the company had grown so fast by acquiring other auto parts chains that it had trouble keeping profits up because of the high cost of integrating all those new stores. Odland says, "AutoZone had grown so fast and was so successful all of a sudden, it became a Fortune 500 company almost overnight. We had to bring in the financial discipline a company that size needed." But the financial area wasn't the only area that Odland addressed. He ordered a revamping of the company's marketing with a new "Get in the Zone" theme and concentrated on running ads when customers would be conscious of the comfort in their vehicles—during morning and evening drive times. He focused on the stores' appearance, wanting to get away from that image of a dirty, dark, and greasy "auto parts" store. The shelves in AutoZone stores are neatly stocked with everything you could possibly need for your car, and the stores themselves, sparkling from top to bottom, are arranged for efficient product sales. Finally, Odland started a "Wal-Mart-style squeeze on its suppliers." Because it

was the largest buyer from many auto parts producers, the company already had significant buying power. It just had to exercise that power. The company now consolidates suppliers' shipments into single trucks to speed distribution. It also gives suppliers suggestions on how to drive down their costs. The company's most recent inventory management innovation is a "pay-on-scan" system in which it pays the supplier for a product only after a customer purchases it. AutoZone has proven to be so adept at inventory and supply management that other retailers, including Midas and Firestone, have hired it to stock their stores and repair shops. In fact, in June 2003 Midas contracted with AutoZone to take over its entire supply chain.

Odland and his employees obviously have figured out what it takes to manage strategically. They're "in the zone" and are doing whatever it takes to ensure that they stay there!

Discussion Questions

1. In this brief description of AutoZone, how is strategic management illustrated?

2. What examples of functional strategy do you see? Describe. What factor(s) do you think AutoZone might use in its competitive strategy?

3. AutoZone is committed to "playing it clean" in terms of the way it does business. In fact, in 2003 it was ranked fourth out of 5,000 companies on Institutional Shareholder Services' evaluation of corporate decency. Go to the company's Web site at **www.autozone.com**. Find the section on corporate governance. Describe what the company has done in terms of corporate governance. Evaluate what they're doing.

4. What types of strategic challenges might Odland and the company face as it pursues aggressive growth? How might strategic management help them deal with these challenges?

Sources: AutoZone (**www.autozone.com**), February 20, 2004; and J. Boorstin, "An Auto-Parts Store Your Mother Could Love," *Fortune,* November 10, 2003, pp. 163–168.

Endnotes

1. J. Franklin, "Paddling for Profits," *Latin Trade,* December 2003, p. 24; J. Jusko, "Avon Calling—On Russia," *Industry Week,* December 2003, p. 48; D. Tsiantor, "Avon's Makeover," *Time,* December 2003, *Time Bonus Section—Inside Business,* p. 4; N. Byrnes, "Avon Calling—Lots of New Reps," *Business Week,* June 2, 2003, pp. 53–54; C. H. Deutsch, "In a Dull Economy, Avon Finds a Hidden Gloss," *New York Times,* June 1, 2003, p. BU4; S. Beatty, "Avon Is Set to Call on Teens," *Wall Street Journal,* October 17, 2002, pp. B1; K. Moreno, "UnbeComing," *Forbes,* June 10, 2002, pp. 151–52; and E. Nelson, "Avon Calls on Good-Looking Research," *Wall Street Journal,* May 23, 2002, p. B6.

2. T. C. Powell, "Varieties of Competitive Parity," *Strategic Management Journal,* January 2003, pp. 61–86; and M. Farjoun, "Towards an Organic Perspective on Strategy," *Strategic Management Journal,* July 2002, pp. 561–94.

3. P. J. Brews and M. R. Hunt, "Learning to Plan and Planning to Learn: Resolving the Planning School–Learning School Debate," *Strategic Management Journal,* 20 (1999), pp. 889–913; D. J. Ketchen, Jr., J. B. Thomas, and R. R. McDaniel, Jr., "Process, Content and Context: Synergistic Effects on Performance," *Journal of Management* 22, no. 2 (1996), pp. 231–57; C. C. Miller and L. B. Cardinal, "Strategic Planning and Firm Performance: A Synthesis of More Than Two Decades of Research," *Academy of Management Journal,* December 1994, pp. 1649–65; and N. Capon, J. U. Farley, and J. M. Hulbert, "Strategic Planning and Financial Performance: More Evidence," *Journal of Management Studies,* January 1994, pp. 105–10.

4. J. W. Dean, Jr. and M. P. Sharfman, "Does Decision Process Matter? A Study of Strategic Decision-Making Effectiveness," *Academy of Management Journal,* April 1996, pp. 368–96.

5. S. Hart and C. Banbury, "How Strategy-Making Processes Can Make a Difference," *Strategic Management Journal,* May 1994, pp. 251–69.

6. W. P. Barnett, H. R. Greve, and D. Y. Park, "An Evolutionary Model of Organizational Performance," *Strategic Management Journal,* Winter 1994, pp. 11–28.

7. A. D. Chandler, Jr., *Strategy and Structure: Chapters in the History of the Industrial Enterprise* (Cambridge, MA: MIT Press, 1962); and C. W. Hofer and D. Schendel, *Strategy Formulation: Analytical Concepts* (St. Paul, MN: West Publishing Company, 1978).

8. O. E. Williamson, "Strategy Research: Governance and Competence Perspectives," *Strategic Management Journal,* 20 (1999), pp. 1087–108.

9. R. P. Rumelt, D. E. Schendel, and D. J. Teece, "Fundamental Issues in Strategy," in R. P. Rumelt, D. E. Schendel, and D. J. Teece (eds.), *Fundamental Issues in Strategy: A Research Agenda* (Boston, MA: Harvard Business School Press, 1994), pp. 9–47.

10. R. E. Hoskisson, M. A. Hitt, W. P. Wan, and D. Yiu, "Theory and Research in Strategic Management: Swings of a Pendulum," *Journal of Management,* 25, no. 3 (1999), pp. 417–56; and R. P. Rumelt, D. E. Schendel, and D. J. Teece, *Fundamental Issues in Strategy.*

11. D. J. Ketchen, Jr., J. B. Thomas, and R. R. McDaniel, Jr., "Process, Content and Context."

12. N. Donaldson, "A New Tool for Boards: The Strategic Audit," *Harvard Business Review,* July–August 1995, pp. 99–107.

13. S. Ghoshal and C. A. Bartlett, "Changing the Role of Top Management: Beyond Structure to Process," *Harvard Business Review,* January–February 1995, pp. 86–96.

14. R. Calori, G. Johnson, and P. Sarnin, "CEO's Cognitive Maps and the Scope of the Organization," *Strategic Management Journal,* July 1994, pp. 437–57.

15. R. D. Ireland and M. A. Hitt, "Achieving and Maintaining Strategic Competitiveness in the 21st Century: The Role of Strategic Leadership," *Academy of Management Executive,* February 1999, pp. 43–57.

16. Ibid.

17. S. W. Floyd and P. J. Lane, "Strategizing Throughout the Organization: Managing Role Conflict in Strategic Renewal," *Academy of Management Review,* January 2000, pp. 154–77.

18. J. Guyon, "Brand America," *Fortune,* October 27, 2003, pp. 179–82.

19. World Trade Organization, **www.wto.org**, August 2, 2004.

20. T. Purdum, "Survival of the Fittest," *Industry Week,* October 2003, pp. 23–25; D. Yergin, "Globalization Opens Door to New Dangers," *USA Today,* May 28, 2003, p. 11A; K. Lowrey Miller, "Is It Globaloney?" *Newsweek,* December 16, 2002, pp. E4–E8; L. Gomes, "Globalization Is Now a Two-Way Street—Good News for the U.S.," *Wall Street Journal,* December 9, 2002, p. B1; J. Kurlantzick and J. T. Allen, "The Trouble With Globalism," *U.S. News and World Report,* February 11, 2002, pp. 38–41; and J. Guyon, "The American Way," *Fortune,* November 26, 2001, pp. 114–20.

21. J. Guyon, "Brand America" and "The American Way."

22. C. M. Daily, D. R. Dalton, and A. A. Cannella, Jr., "Corporate Governance: Decades of Dialogue and Data," *Academy of Management Review,* July 2003, p. 371.

23. S. Liebs, "New Terrain," *CFO,* February 2004, pp. 40–47; C. Hymowitz and J. S. Lublin, "Boardrooms Under Renovation," *Wall Street Journal,* July 22, 2003, pp. B1; and D. Salierno, "Boards Face Increased Responsibility," *Internal Auditor,* June 2003, pp. 14–15.

24. M. Roman, "Sarbanes-Oxley's First," *Business Week,* November 17, 2003, p. 52.

25. T. J. Mullaney, H. Gree, M. Arndt, R. D. Hof, and L. Himelstein, "The E-Biz Surprise," *Business Week,* May 12, 2003, pp. 60–68; R. D. Hof and S. Hamm, "How E-Biz Rose, Fell, and Will Rise Anew," *Business Week,* May 13, 2002, pp. 64–72; and "Companies Leading Online," *IQ Magazine,* November–December 2001, pp. 54–63.

2

The Context of Managing Strategically

LEARNING OUTLINE

Managing Strategically and Competitive Advantage

- *Define competitive advantage.*

- *Describe the different perspectives on how to achieve competitive advantage.*

- *Explain what makes organizational resources unique.*

- *Discuss the concept of temporary competitive advantage.*

The Realities of the New Business Environment

- *Describe the three driving forces of the new business environment.*

- *Explain the four implications of the new business environment.*

- *Discuss the three critical success factors for the new business environment.*

- *Differentiate between organizational vision and mission.*

- *Describe the concept of a world-class organization.*

- *Discuss how corporate social responsibility and ethics affect strategic management.*

- *Define organizational learning.*

- *Describe the characteristics of a learning organization.*

- *Explain the 4I organizational learning model.*

Out of Tune

January 1999 might well be described as the month the music died (to paraphrase a popular song lyric). And, if the music didn't actually stop, then, at the very least, it was the date the music industry changed forever.[1] Why? Shawn Fanning, a student at Northeastern University in Boston, launched Napster, the pioneering Internet file-sharing service that introduced people to "free" music downloading. As the music industry was about to discover, the incredible opportunities offered by the Internet had a dark side.

Executives at the "big 5" music companies—Universal Music Group, Sony, EMI, AOL Time Warner, and Bertelsmann—insist that they weren't caught off guard by the digital distribution revolution. In fact, they believed that it would be a great way to market, promote, and sell directly to fans. However, they weren't prepared for the excruciating efforts of trying to figure out the best ways to adapt to the changed environment.

What the music companies faced was an increasing avalanche of downloading by consumers. Because Internet file sharing offered convenience and anonymity, downloaders saw nothing wrong with it and flocked to Napster's Web site. However, what consumers saw as harmless actions would ultimately have a major negative impact on the music industry as CD and album sales plummeted. And the industry decided to fight back the best way it knew how—through the legal system. In December 1999, the Recording Industry Association of America (RIAA)—the trade group representing the U.S. recording industry—sued Napster for contributory copyright infringement. Due to the long appeals process, it was July 2001 before Napster was finally forced out of business. Yet, even with Napster gone, the downloading didn't stop. Other sites, such as Grokster and Kazaa, soon took Napster's place. Obviously, digital distribution was here to stay. Perhaps what the industry needed was a way to work within the changed environment. After all, a report by Forrester Research predicted that by 2008 one third of all music sales would come from downloads. Another industry report said that consumers wanted flexibility, choice, and extras. The challenge for the music companies was to find an acceptable and profitable way to give them what they wanted. And industry participants are rising to the challenge! How?

Apple's iTunes store is one example. The site offers more than 200,000 songs at 99 cents per download. From its debut in summer 2003 to December 2003, more than 25 million downloads were sold, and the music companies received a royalty percentage for each download. Others are joining in. Microsoft, Hewlett-Packard, Sony, and Dell, for example, are opening online music stores in 2004. Start-up label Magnatune is experimenting with download pricing as low as 50 cents per song and $5 per album. Even Napster is back selling music downloads (legally!) as part of Roxio Software. Technology is also creating new markets for music. Music companies are signing agreements with wireless providers for access to popular songs that can be used as cell phone ring tones. In addition to these strategic initiatives, the music industry is continuing its legal pursuit of illegal downloading—this time going after individuals. And the strategy seems to be working. According to a major study published in January 2004, unauthorized online song-swapping in the United States had been cut in half since the record companies started this tactic in the fall of 2003. Also, sales of CDs and singles were down only 3.6 percent in 2003, versus a drop of 12.9 percent in 2002 and 10.3 percent in 2001. Maybe the music companies had finally found the ways to "get in tune" with the realities of this new context.

The difficult challenges faced by the recorded music industry provide a compelling illustration of why it's important to consider, understand, and interpret the context in which an organization's employees do strategic management. A company's strategic decision makers need to know their competitive advantage *and* the dynamic context they're operating in. Why? Because an organization's context determines the "rules" of the game and what actions are likely to work best. Just as the coach of a baseball team analyzes the specific context (factors such as the condition of the playing field, the cohesiveness of the team's players, player injuries, or maybe even the team's current rankings in its division) in deciding what game strategies might work best, so, too, must organizational decision makers be aware of the context within which strategic decisions are made and implemented. For example, the travel industry (airlines and hotels) had been facing a context of decreased travel because of continued terrorism threats and the economic downturn. Aware of these realities, industry executives responded by exploiting technology to make their businesses run more smoothly and efficiently.[2] You can see how the context of managing strategically fits into the overall strategic management process in Figure 2.1.

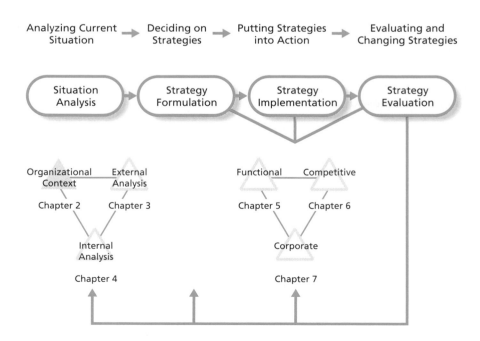

Figure 2.1

Strategic Management in Action

MANAGING STRATEGICALLY AND COMPETITIVE ADVANTAGE

Managing strategically means formulating and implementing strategies that enable an organization to develop and maintain competitive advantage. Competitive advantage is a key concept in strategic management. What is **competitive advantage**? It's what sets an organization apart—in other words, its competitive edge. When an organization has a competitive advantage, it has something that other competitors don't, does something better than other organizations, or does something that others can't. Organizations have long sought a competitive advantage in dynamic environments because it's a necessary ingredient for long-term success and survival. Even not-for-profit organizations (such as governmental agencies, educational institutions, community arts organizations, or social service groups) need something that sets them apart—something unique that they offer in order to stay in business. Getting and keeping competitive advantage is what managing strategically is all about. It's tough to do, and getting tougher. The pursuit of competitive advantage leads to organizational success or failure. Although most prefer success, organizations don't choose to fail. Instead, poor performance typically can be traced to the failure to recognize the impact of important external factors or the failure to capitalize on organizational resources and capabilities. Both of these failures represent different perspectives on what it takes to capture competitive advantage—that is, to manage strategically. The first view suggests organizations look at the impact of important external factors and is called the industrial organization (I/O) view.[3] The second perspective emphasizes exploiting organizational resources in order to develop and maintain competitive advantage and is called the resource-based view.[4] In addition to these two traditional perspectives, there's another contemporary perspective we're calling the guerrilla view of competitive advantage because it proposes that an organization's competitive advantage is temporary and can be gained only by peppering the competitive marketplace with rapid radical surprises.[5] Because there's a serious desire among strategic management researchers and organizational strategists to know where an organization's competitive advantage comes from, we need to look closer at these three perspectives. Table 2.1 summarizes the main points of each of these views.

Table 2.1 Comparison of I/O, Resource-Based, and Guerrilla Views of Competitive Advantage

	I/O View	Resource-Based View	Guerrilla View
Competitive Advantage	Positioning in industry	Possessing unique organizational assets or capabilities	Temporary
Determinants of Profitability	Characteristics of industry; firm's position within industry	Type, amount, and nature of firm's resources	Ability to change and radically surprise competitors with strategic actions
Focus of Analysis	External	Internal	External and internal
Major Concern	Competition	Resources–capabilities	Continual, radical, and chaotic conditions
Strategic Choices	Choosing attractive industry; appropriate position	Developing unique resources and distinctive capabilities	Rapidly and repeatedly disrupting current situation and surprising competitors

strategic MANAGEMENT *in action*

Maybe you've never even heard of the Dictaphone Corporation (**www.dictaphone.com**), but they've been around for over 100 years as a market leader in the voice-recording industry. Dictaphone equipment was once standard issue in offices around the United States. Executives would dictate letters, instructions, or other information and a secretary or administrative assistant would transcribe the tape. However, as the need for voice-recording capabilities changed, so did Dictaphone. Today, its products are no longer stand-alone voice recorders, but instead are part of

enterprise-wide information systems in organizations where voice recordings are an essential part of doing business. The company views the human voice as just another form of data transmission and approaches its markets in that way. Check out the company's Web site. What does it say about the company's strategic direction? How would Porter evaluate Dictaphone's strategic direction?

Sources: Dictaphone, **www.dictaphone.com**, February 23, 2004; and C. H. Deutsch, "Take a Memo: Dictaphone is Still in Business," New York Times, December 27, 1999, p. C1.

The Industrial Organization (I/O) View

The **industrial organization (I/O) view** focuses on the structural forces within an industry, the competitive environment of firms, and how these influence competitive advantage. The best-known proponent of the I/O approach to competitive advantage is Michael Porter of Harvard University. According to Porter, five industry forces (which we'll cover in detail in Chapter 3) determine the average profitability of an industry, which in turn influences the profitability of firms within the industry. His approach emphasizes choosing the "right" industries and within those industries, the most advantageous (or competitive) positions.

The I/O approach proposes that getting and keeping competitive advantage means analyzing external forces and basing strategic decisions on what is happening. Not surprisingly, then, the focus of strategic analysis in the I/O view is external. Because all firms within an industry face essentially the same external forces, a major concern of the I/O view is how the firm stacks up against its competitors. Keep in mind that the I/O view proposes that competitive advantage relates to competitive positioning in the industry. Also, the I/O view suggests that both a firm's position within the industry and the underlying industry characteristics determine its potential profitability. This means that if there are a lot of negative forces in the industry or the firm has a weak position within the industry, then its profitability will be lower than average. But, if the industry is characterized by significant opportunities or the firm has a strong position within the industry, then its profitability will be above average. How do managers make sound strategic choices? According to the I/O view, it's a matter of understanding the nature of an attractive industry and then choosing an appropriate competitive position within that industry.

Although the I/O view makes important contributions to understanding how to manage strategically in order to gain competitive advantage, critics complain that it neglects to tell the whole story. Although Porter's ideas don't ignore the characteristics of individual companies, the emphasis is clearly on understanding what is happening at the industry level. Other researchers believe that a complete understanding of sources of competitive advantage also requires looking at the role a firm's resources play.

Resource-Based View

The **resource-based view (RBV)** takes the approach that a firm's resources are more important than industry structure in getting and keeping competitive advantage. It sees organizations as very different collections of assets and capabilities. No two organizations

Digital River helps companies sell their products on the Web without having to build an e-commerce platform from scratch. This is the third successful company that CEO Joel Ronning has built. One of the things Ronning understands about successful companies is how important employee involvement is. At Digital River, he established an entrepreneurial council—a team of around 50 employees—that generates ideas. This team meets every Friday and operates under the motto that "There are no bad ideas." And the team strictly adheres to that rule. No one can criticize another's ideas in a session. Instead, team members have found that the peer process eventually works, and people figure out on their own when an idea isn't good. In an industry where keeping on top of trends and continually creating new products are critical, Ronning seems to have found an effective solution. And with sales growing at almost 30 percent a year, at least some of those new ideas must be paying off. What type of resource is Ronning's entrepreneurial council? Explain. Evaluate this resource in terms of its uniqueness. What other types of resources would Digital River probably need to do its business?

Sources: *Digital River,* **www.digitalriver.com**, *February 29, 2004; and "Fast Talk," Fast Company, November 2003,* p. 58.

will be alike because they haven't had the same set of experiences, acquired the same assets or capabilities, or built the same organizational cultures. The organization's assets and capabilities will determine how efficiently and effectively it does its work—whether that "work" involves selling hamburgers, providing health care services, or educating students. According to the RBV, certain key assets (resources) will give the firm a sustainable competitive advantage. Therefore, an organization will be positioned to succeed if it has the best and most appropriate resources for its business.

The major organizational concern according to the RBV is resources and capabilities. Competitive advantage will accrue to the organization that possesses unique assets or capabilities. Organizational profitability is determined by the type, amount, and nature of a firm's resources and capabilities. Therefore, managing strategically according to the RBV involves developing and exploiting an organization's unique resources and capabilities. But, what exactly are "resources" and what makes them "unique"?

Resources include all of the financial, physical, human, intangible, and structural/cultural assets used by an organization to develop, manufacture, and deliver products or services to its customers.[6] Financial assets include the financial holdings of the organization (cash reserves, investments, and so forth), the actual and potential debt and equity used by the organization, and any retained earnings. Physical assets include machines, office buildings, manufacturing or sales facilities, raw materials, or any other tangible materials the organization has. Human resources include the experiences, characteristics, knowledge, judgment, wisdom, skills, abilities, and competencies of the organization's employees. Intangible assets include such things as brand names, patents, reputation, trademarks, copyrights, registered designs, and databases. Finally, structural/cultural assets include the organization's history, culture, work systems, organizational policies, working relationships, level of trust, and the formal reporting (organizational) structure being used.

Although every organization has resources, not all of those resources are going to lead to a sustainable competitive advantage. The RBV suggests that resources must be unique to be a source of potential competitive advantage. Figure 2.2 illustrates what makes organizational resources unique. Because these characteristics are important, let's look at them more closely.

Value

An organizational resource is unique if it adds value. What does it mean to "add value"? It means that the resource can be used to exploit external circumstances that are likely to

Figure 2.2

*What Makes Organizational
Resources Unique?*

Source: *Based on Jay B. Barney, "Looking
Inside for Competitive Advantage,"
Academy of Management Executive,
November 1995, pp. 49–61.*

bring in organizational revenues or the resource can be used to neutralize negative external situations that are likely to keep revenue from flowing in. An organization's resources aren't valuable in a vacuum, but only when they exploit those external opportunities or neutralize the threats. As environmental factors such as customer tastes or technology change, resources can become more valuable or less valuable. So, a resource is valuable—that is, it adds value—in the context of what's happening in the external environment.

Rare

For a resource to be rare, ideally no other competing firms should already possess it. If more and more competitors acquire certain resources that have been a source of competitive advantage, then it becomes a less likely source of sustainable competitive advantage for an organization. Keep in mind, though, that even commonly held resources may be valuable if for no other reason than the firm's survival in a competitive environment. But, in order to gain a competitive advantage, a resource should be both valuable *and* rare.

Hard to Imitate

Obviously, if a resource can't be imitated by a competitor, then any revenues it's able to generate are more likely to continue flowing in. Organizations want resources that are hard to imitate. Imitation by competitors can happen in at least two ways: duplication and substitution. Duplication is when a competitor builds the same kind of resources as the firm it's imitating. Substitution is when a firm substitutes some alternative resources for the specific resources currently being used to gain competitive advantage and achieves the same results. So, in order to keep resources unique, you want them to be hard to imitate. Some resources are much harder to imitate than others. For instance, such things as company reputation, employee trust, teamwork, and organizational culture are difficult for competitors to imitate.

Ability to Exploit

Not only must organizational resources be valuable, rare, and hard to imitate, the organization must be able to exploit them. Does the firm have in place the formal structure,

W. L. Gore & Associates (**www.gore.com**) is well known for its high-quality and revolutionary outdoor-wear products and was recently named one of *Fortune*'s "100 Best Companies to Work For." The kinds of innovative efforts exhibited by Gore's associates (not employees) are made possible by a unique organizational culture that unleashes creativity and fosters teamwork. Being an associate at Gore requires a commitment to four basic principles articulated by company founder Bill Gore: fairness to each other and everyone you come in contact with; freedom to encourage, help, and allow other associates to grow in knowledge, skill and scope of responsibility; the ability to make your own commitments and keep them; and consulting with other associates before undertaking actions that could impact the reputation of the company by hitting it "below the waterline." Go to the company's Web site. Do you think Gore's "resources" are unique? Explain and give examples.

Sources: W. L. Gore & Associates, **www.gore.com**, February 23, 2004; R. Levering and M. Moskowitz, "100 Best Companies to Work For," Fortune, January 12, 2004, pp. 56–68; A. Harrington, "Who's Afraid of a New Product? Not W. L. Gore," Fortune, October 27, 2003, pp. 189–191; and D. Anfuso, "Core Values Shape W. L. Gore's Innovative Culture," Workforce, March 1999, pp. 48–53.

systems, policies, procedures, and processes to take full advantage of the resources it has in order to develop a sustainable competitive advantage? In other words, is it organized to exploit the full competitive potential of its resources? Without these abilities in place, it would be difficult for an organization to create and maintain a competitive advantage.

All four of these characteristics—valuable, rare, hard to imitate, and ability to exploit—are important indicators of a resource's chances of being a source of sustainable competitive advantage. The popular business press is filled with stories of companies that have unique and valuable resources they're able to exploit. But, there are also many examples of organizations that have not been able to get and keep a competitive edge because they have no unique resources or they haven't been able to exploit the unique resources they do have. According to the RBV, managing strategically means continually maintaining and building organizational resources—in essence, capitalizing on what can be called the "crown jewels" of the firm. However, a question facing strategic decision makers is this: Do these "crown jewels" (unique resources that are sources of an organization's competitive advantage) remain the same over time? According to our next view of competitive advantage, they do not.

Guerrilla View

What do you think of when you hear the term *guerrilla?* Do you envision quick and overt attacks on an enemy position by a well-trained, competent, and skilled force? That's very much the analogy behind the guerrilla view of competitive advantage. The main premise of the **guerrilla view** is that an organization's competitive advantage is temporary. Why? Because the environment is characterized by continual, radical, and often revolutionary changes. For instance, disruptions in technology, market instabilities, and other types of significant, but unpredictable, changes can challenge strategic managers' attempts at creating a long-term sustainable competitive advantage. (Think back to our chapter-opening case about the music industry.) Under these types of chaotic conditions, it's difficult to develop and maintain a permanent competitive advantage. Instead, successful organizations must be adept at rapidly and repeatedly disrupting the current situation and radically surprising competitors with strategic actions designed to keep them off balance—in other words, acting like a guerrilla unit. And, the successful organization will repeatedly form

What if customers said they no longer needed packages shipped "absolutely, positively overnight?" That's the position FedEx (**www.fedex.com**), the world's largest express transport company and a company that prided itself for being consistently on the cutting edge of product delivery, found itself in. Overnight, its market turned upside down, and the competitive advantage FedEx had developed was no longer valuable. Customers no longer wanted fast, but pricey, delivery service. External changes such as instantaneous e-mail delivery of information, discount carriers that provided package tracking information online, and competitive rivals that copied FedEx's elaborate information system that once distinguished the company have all contributed to its uncertain future. The company's strategic decision makers aren't just sitting back, however. To bolster the number of package pick-up locations, they recently completed the acquisition of Kinko's, the copy king. Take a look at the company's Web site. What other strategic options are they pursuing? Do FedEx's actions reflect the guerrilla view of competitive advantage? Explain.

Sources: *FedEx*, **www.fedex.com**, *February 23, 2004; D. Rynecki, "Does This Package Make Sense?" Fortune, January 26, 2004, p.132; and A. Harrington, "America's Most Admired Companies," Fortune, March 8, 2004, pp. 80–82, and D. A. Blackmon, "Speed Limits," Wall Street Journal, November 4, 1999, p. A1.*

new competitive advantages based on different rules and different asset combinations than the existing strategies being used.

All Three Views Provide Clues to Understanding Competitive Advantage

We know the important role competitive advantage plays in how an organization ultimately performs, so which of these views is most appropriate for understanding competitive advantage? Each view brings a unique perspective to understanding the all-important concept. The I/O view addresses the need to look at the external environment, particularly the industry and competitors, and emphasizes the importance of understanding competitive positioning. The RBV considers the need to look inside the organization for the unique resources and capabilities that can be exploited. This approach continues to be a popular topic for strategic management researchers attempting to clarify why organizations differ in their performance. However, the guerrilla view forces strategic decision makers to recognize that the chaotic nature of the external environment can affect what is considered a competitive advantage and how long that competitive advantage can last.

Realistically speaking, managing strategically involves looking both externally and internally to come up with strategies that have a chance of creating a sustainable competitive advantage, even if for only a brief period of time. In this way, unique resources and capabilities can be "matched" to changing external circumstances. Because the external environment is continually changing (new competitors come and go, customers' tastes change, technology changes, current competitors start a price war, etc.), the source of sustainable competitive advantage—the "edge" an organization has over its competitors—*is* probably found in different places at different points in time. Given these realities, how can strategic managers possibly ever hope to develop a sustainable competitive advantage—that is, manage strategically? The answer is by continually analyzing both the external and internal organizational environments and then taking advantage of any positive changes (or buffering against negative changes) with the organization's unique resources and capabilities. That's the ever-changing, yet constant, challenge for the strategic manager.

One of the most important changes strategic managers must contend with today is the realities of the new business environment. That's what we'll look at next.

- What is competitive advantage and why is it important?
- Describe the important points of the industrial organization (I/O) view.
- Describe the important points of the resource-based view (RBV).
- What makes a resource unique?
- Describe the important points of the guerrilla view.
- Why are all three views important to understanding competitive advantage?

THE REALITIES OF THE NEW BUSINESS ENVIRONMENT

The business context that organizations operate in today is a lot different than what it used to be. It's an important topic to discuss in the context of managing strategically because it establishes the "rules of the game" for doing business. Even not-for-profit organizations feel the impact of these changing realities because they, too, need resources such as labor, technology, and funding to operate. We need to examine important characteristics of this business environment: What forces are "driving" it? What are the implications? And, what will it take to be successful in this context? Figure 2.3 provides an overview.

Drivers of the New Business Environment

What are the driving forces in the twenty-first-century business environment? Three of the most critical ones are (1) the information revolution, (2) technological advances and breakthroughs, and (3) globalization. Let's discuss each more thoroughly.[7]

Figure 2.3

The New Business Environment

All Service All the Time

When Wal-Mart Stores, the largest private employer in the United States and with revenues of over $255 billion, topped the list of *Fortune*'s "Global 500" and *Business Week*'s "Top 25 in Sales," it was the culmination of a major economic shift that had been taking place for years—that is, the shift from producing goods to producing services. Manufacturing's share of U.S. employment, which peaked in 1953 at 35 percent, has been steadily declining ever since. The Bureau of Labor Statistics predicts that for the decade ending in 2010, goods-producing industries will create 1.3 million new jobs, whereas service industries will create 20 million. To put it another way, there are about four times as many people working in service jobs today as there are people working in other kinds of jobs. One explanation for this shift is that as America got richer, consumption became more complicated. With more income to spend, people started purchasing more services—movies and travel, massages and facials, mortgages to buy houses, insurance to protect those houses and possessions, and so on. Economists call this a shift in the demand pattern. It's also a reason why so many of the top global and American companies are service companies. How has the information revolution impacted service businesses? Choose a couple of service businesses and do some research to answer this question.

Sources: "Large and in Charge," Business Week, February 23, 2004, p. 61; "Fortune Global 500," Fortune, July 21, 2003, pp. 97–112; and C. Murphy, "Fortune 500," Fortune, April 15, 2002, pp. 94–98.

The Information Revolution

If there's one driving force that has set the tone for this new business environment, it's the information revolution. *And* not only is this revolution continuing to spread, it's also accelerating. A recent study showed that the supply of new information saved in a single year alone (2002) would fill half a million libraries the size of the Library of Congress.[8] That's a lot of new information! And not only is there more information, but that information is readily available to practically anyone from anywhere on the globe at any hour of the day and pretty much in any format. An investor in Los Angeles at 3 A.M. can check currency exchange rates for the euro or yuan, click on another software program, and e-mail instructions to a broker in London. A shopper in Shanghai with a fondness for maple syrup can indulge that passion by purchasing products from a small retail store in Vermont without ever physically stepping foot in the United States. How? By linking to its virtual storefront on the Web. The almost instant availability of almost any type of information has radically changed the nature of the business environment, which, in turn, affects the context of strategic management.

Information has always been a factor in producing goods and services. Organizations have always used information to design work tools, organizational processes, management systems, and products as they searched for ways to be more efficient and effective. However, today we're seeing information as *the* essential resource of production, not simply as a means to an end. Knowledge is no longer viewed only as a way to make sure other resources are used efficiently. Instead, a fundamental shift has occurred in which knowledge is applied to knowledge itself.[9] Land, labor, and capital have become support factors of production, not the main factors. In this new information context where knowledge is applied to knowledge, strategic decision makers can always use their knowledge to obtain the other necessary resources. The implication of such a profound change is that organizations can no longer simply rely on the traditional factors of production to provide a sustainable competitive advantage, but must now look to how information and knowledge can be exploited. One of the areas in which knowledge and information has had a significant impact is in technology and innovation. That's the next driving force we'll discuss.

Table 2.2

Major Technological Trends

- Technology is starting to pay back with real savings and real productivity gains.
- Innovations are increasingly being commercialized.
- There is an increasing dependence on information and knowledge.
- Technology, especially information technology, is creating deep structural transformations in the economy:
  - Network capabilities mean that everything is connected.
  - Digital technology is making businesses smarter.
  - Digital technology has helped create completely new subindustries.
  - The economy is becoming a "bottom-up" economy.
- Great companies are pioneers and leaders in applying technology.

Technological Advances

All organizations—regardless of size, type, or location—use some form of technology to do their work. What is **technology**? It's the use of equipment, materials, knowledge, and experience to perform tasks. Some industries are, by necessity, more technology intensive than others. (For instance, think of electronics, telecommunications, software, pharmaceuticals, and so forth.) But even organizations such as the American Red Cross, your neighborhood grocery store, utility companies, and steel mills use technology. Technology significantly changed the nature of competition in the last part of the twentieth century. Approaches and tools that may have been effective in the past weren't any more, and new ones were rapidly being developed. Innovations in telecommunications and computer technology, in particular, have had far-reaching effects for strategic managers in all types of organizations.

There's no doubt technology is changing the way we work and the type of work we do.[10] What are some of the major broad technological trends that affect the context of managing strategically? Five trends we need to discuss are summarized in Table 2.2.[11]

The first trend is the realization that technology is starting to result in real savings and real productivity. Many criticize the 1990s as a time when companies spent far too much on computing power and believed too naively in the power of the Web. However, those companies are now starting to digest all of that computing power and figure out realistic ways to harness the power of the Internet, both as a way to run their business and to interact with their customers. Both companies and consumers are learning how to use technology productively. And the payoffs, now just beginning to be realized, will continue.

The increasing payoffs from technology have impacted the competitive protection offered by patents, which brings us to the second major technological trend: the increasing commercialization of innovations. We're defining **innovation** as the process of taking a creative idea and turning it into a product or process that can be used or sold. It's more than just being creative—it's developing, making, and marketing something that can generate revenue. Some experts have cited growing evidence that the U.S. economy is in the early stages of a powerful new wave of innovation. For instance, the number of patent applications received by the U.S. Patent and Trade Office has doubled in a 10-year time span.[12] Although patents traditionally provided many organizations with protection for technological discoveries that were the basis for profitable products or services, this advantage is declining in significance because technological improvements can rapidly replace the technology that's currently protected by the patent and being used to create value.

The third significant trend in technology is something we covered earlier, and that's the increasing dependence on information and knowledge. Because technology—both the creation and use of it—involves knowledge, the importance of knowledge as a resource for sustainable competitive advantage has increased significantly. The implication of this relationship is that as the use of technology increases, so does the need for knowledge. The reverse is true as well—as knowledge increases, so does the use of technology. For instance,

Even the gambling industry has embraced the wonders of technology—especially in player surveillance. For instance, although blackjack may be a simple game, blackjack tables have become quite technologically sophisticated. Casinos now monitor cards using invisible codes, track chips with RFID (radio frequency identification) tags, and scrutinize players using facial recognition software. When players take a seat at the tables, electronic eyes scan faces and compare them with a database of known cheaters. If the database finds a match, the person is escorted out of the casino by security. European casinos pioneered the use of RFID chips, which makes it easier to track inventory, betting patterns, and customer status. U.S. casinos started using these new technology-enhanced chips in 2004. Can you think of some other ways that casinos might use technology in their business? Explain.

Source: D. Terdiman, "The New Deal," Wired, February 2004, p. 38.

even employees on an assembly line now must have more than manual dexterity skills and physical stamina. They need knowledge to run the sophisticated machinery found in today's manufacturing environment.

The fourth major trend from technology, especially information technology, is that it is creating deep structural transformations in the economy. What types of transformations? First, the fact that we have network capabilities—both wired and wireless—means that everything is connected. And work that used to be performed by humans has now become, in many instances, interactions among devices that "talk" with one another, decide what to do, and then do it. For example, airplane navigation used to require a crew member to calculate positions by hand and convey them to the pilot. Now, it's a conversation among an onboard GPS system, stationary-orbit satellites, ground stations, and an aircraft-control system. Architectural design used to be an interaction between a person using pens and paper to physically drawn a design. Now, many times it's a "conversation" with a CAD (computer-aided design) program. The second transformation we're seeing is that digital technology is making businesses smarter. For example, organizations are digitally connected with suppliers, the production process, shipments, and customers. Using technology such as sensor tags, products can be tracked in transit, on the shelf, and even after the sale. The third transformation is that digital technology has helped create completely new subindustries. For instance, the movie business uses digitization to create and manipulate special images, and a whole new industry—digital effects—has sprung up to provide this expertise. The pharmaceutical industry uses digital research in designing new drugs to explore molecular combinations. Many other examples can be provided to show how digital technology has changed practically every industry. The final transformation is an economy that can be described as "bottom up." Through technological advancements, such as the Internet and personal messaging systems, power is shifting away from institutions to individuals. Take, for example, the popularity of Fox Network's reality show *American Idol,* in which the audience decides who "wins." Or look at the success of eBay. Its founder Pierre Omidyar stated, "At eBay the managers don't control the brand or the customer experience—our customers themselves do." That's the reality of this transformed economy.

The final major trend we're seeing from technology is that the great companies (Wal-Mart, General Electric, Southwest Airlines) are leaders in technology. But simply having the latest and best technology isn't the goal of these pioneers. Instead, these great companies realize that technology is a tool—a very powerful tool, needless to say—to enhance their business. They realize that it's not a replacement for understanding the economics of their business and creating a business model that allows them to be the best at what they do, but that it can help them do their work better.

The increasing pace of technological breakthroughs and the importance of continual innovation are quite evident. Within the context of managing strategically, technology and innovation are obviously going to influence an organization's sustainable competitive advantage. The challenge is capturing and exploiting the unique advantages of technology by using the organizational innovation process to create valuable products and processes. What makes these activities even more challenging is that they're occurring globally, not just in the domestic arena. The challenges and opportunities of globalization are the final driving force we're going to look at.

Globalization

In Chapter 1, we discussed how globalization is affecting strategic management. We've been hearing about the concept of globalization for so long now (you undoubtedly hear about it in every business class you take) that it almost seems a cliché. However, it *is* important and continues to be a dominant characteristic of the business environment.[13] More than ever, organizations are going global. The days when all our consumer products—for instance, the shoes we wore, the cars we drove, and the food we ate—were produced in the United States are long gone. Now, it's common for the products we purchase and consume to be provided by a foreign company or by a domestic company that also does business globally. Even small businesses are impacted by the global business environment. How does the context of globalization influence strategic management? Two specific ways are (1) the global marketplace and (2) global competitors.

It's not an understatement to say that the whole world is a potential marketplace. Providing products to meet consumer needs has taken on a global perspective. Potential markets are found all the way from small villages in China to Johannesburg to Moscow to Mexico City, and all points in between. This global marketplace provides significant opportunities for organizations to market their goods and services. Creating sustainable competitive advantage may require looking globally, not just domestically, for customers. But, the global marketplace shouldn't just be viewed as just an outlet for products. It's also a critical source of resources as well. Financial, material, human, and knowledge resources are available globally and should be acquired wherever it strategically makes sense to do so. In other words, geographic boundaries shouldn't constrain an organization's strategic decisions and actions. However, not only does this mean domestic organizations can operate anywhere in the world, it also means foreign organizations—that is, competitors—can, too.

As global markets open, global competition becomes a reality. Competitors can come from anywhere, and they, too, will be looking for a sustainable competitive advantage. Although the rewards of a global market are attractive, competing in a global marketplace is more challenging because now, all of a sudden, you're dealing with competitors who've had their own unique set of experiences and resources, making it much more difficult to understand their strategic approach and intent. However, global competitors don't always have to be a threat to each other. They might find that the most effective strategy for them to achieve a sustainable competitive advantage is to partner together in some type of an arrangement to make or market products. In fact, in Chapter 7, in which we discuss corporate strategy, we'll look at global strategic alliances and how organizations are using such alliances.

Globalization is more than just producing, marketing, and distributing goods and services throughout the world—"It is a new way of thinking."[14] It's solving customers' needs no matter where the customers are. It's segmenting markets on a global basis and sourcing people, capital, technologies, and ideas from anywhere in the world. Globalization has transformed and continues to transform the new business environment.

Each of these driving forces of the new business environment—the information revolution, technological advances, and globalization—is affecting the context within which

information

Outsourcing: The Good, the Bad, and the Ugly

This is a story about the global economy. It's about free markets, politics, and public opinion. And as jobs—especially white-collar jobs—continue to be outsourced, the story hits closer and closer to home.

One of the realities of a global economy is that to be competitive, strategic decision makers must look for the best places to conduct business. If a car can be made more cheaply in Mexico, it should be. If a telephone inquiry can be processed more cheaply in India, it should be. And if programming code can be written more cheaply in China, it should be. Almost any professional job that can be done long distance is up for grabs. There's nothing political or philosophical about the reason for shipping jobs overseas. The bottom line is that it can save companies tons of money. But there's a price to be paid in terms of angry and anxious employees. So, is outsourcing bad?

Critics say "Yes." It's affecting jobs once considered "safe" across a wider range of white-collar work activities. And the outsourcing is taking place at a breathtaking pace. What this means is that the careers college students are preparing for probably won't sustain them in the long run. This structural change in the U.S. economy also means that the workforce is likely to face frequent career changes and downward pressures on wages.

Proponents say "No." Their argument is based on viewing economic development as a ladder with every country trying to climb to the next rung. And it's foolish to think that in the United States we've reached the top of the ladder and there's nowhere else to go. Although people fear that educated U.S. workers will face the same fate as blue-collar workers of the 1970s and 1980s as their jobs shifted to lower-cost countries such as Mexico, the truth is that the United States still has a distinct competitive advantage in innovation. The biggest danger to U.S. workers isn't overseas competition; it's worrying too much about other countries climbing up the economic ladder and not enough about finding that next higher rung.

Who's right? We probably can't answer that question just yet. Only time will tell. However, what we do know is that what we see here with outsourcing is another example of why strategic decision makers need to be aware of the context within which their organizations are doing business. Do some research on outsourcing and come up with arguments for and against it.

Sources: J. Thottam, "Is Your Job Going Abroad?" Time, March 1, 2004, pp. 26–36; M. Gongloff, "Outsourcing: What to Do?" CNN/Money, www.cnnmoney.com, March 1, 2004; L. D. Tyson, "Outsourcing: Who's Safe Anymore?" Business Week, February 23, 2004, p. 26; A. Fisher, "Think Globally, Save Your Job Locally," Fortune, February 23, 2004, p. 60; "The New Job Migration," The Economist, February 21, 2004, p. 11; M. Kripalani, S. Hamm, S. E. Ante, and A. Reinhardt, "Scrambling to Stem India's Onslaught," Business Week, January 26, 2004, pp. 81–82; N. D. Schwartz, "Will 'Made in USA' Fade Away?" Fortune, November 24, 2003, pp. 98–110; O. Thomas, "The Outsourcing Solution," Business 2.0, September 2003, pp. 159–160; R. Meredith, "Giant Sucking Sound," Forbes, September 29, 2003, pp. 58–60; and K. Madigan and M. J. Mandel, "Outsourcing Jobs: Is It Bad?" Business Week, August 25, 2003, pp. 36–38.

strategic decision makers manage strategically. What are the implications of these driving forces for strategic decision makers?

Implications of These Driving Forces

Look back at Figure 2.3 on page 37, and you'll see that there are four major implications arising out of the driving forces of the new business environment. These include continual turbulence and change, the reduced need for physical assets, vanishing distance and compressed time, and increased vulnerability. Let's examine each of these more closely.

Continual Turbulence and Change

Change, and for many organizations, turbulent and chaotic change, is an undeniable reality of today's business environment. *All* organizations must deal with change, if not on a daily basis, then on an increasingly frequent basis. **Change** is defined as any alteration in

the global perspective

Steve Ming-Jang Chang, CEO and president of Trend Micro, Inc., a high-tech transnational company, believes that "borders are so twentieth century." As a provider of computer network antivirus and Internet security software, Trend Micro has spread its executives, engineers, and support staff around the world in order to improve its response time to new virus threats. It's routinely the first to go on the offensive when a new virus strikes, often 30 minutes before market-leader Symantec (maker of the popular Norton Antivirus software) reacts. Although Trend Micro's corporate and financial headquarters are in Tokyo, its computer virus response center is based in Manila (where costs are low), product development is based in Taiwan (where there's a plentiful supply of PhDs), and sales are centered in California's Silicon Valley (where there's easier access to the vast American market). No competitor has such an international reach. The company has been successful because it has set up its business in a way that takes advantage of the realities of today's context.

Sources: *Hoover's Online*, **www.hoovers.com**, February 25, 2004; and S. Hamm, *"Borders Are So Twentieth Century,"* Business Week, September 22, 2003, pp. 68–73.

external environmental factors or internal organizational arrangements. Oftentimes, changes in external conditions or even in internal ones stimulate the need for organizational change. **Organizational change** is defined as any alteration in what an organization does and how it does it. For instance, changes in technology (an external factor) have opened up new avenues for organizations with Web sites where electronic greeting cards can be purchased and sent. Because of this change, the large corporate greeting card companies were forced to rethink their business and make organizational changes. Or consider changing demographic trends (another external factor). The baby boomlet (resulting from the large group of baby boomers who have had and are having children), the increasing Hispanic population, and other demographic changes have forced organizations to alter the types of products they offer, the packaging of these products, and the promotional techniques used to sell these products. Change is the new order of business in today's context.

Reduced Need for Physical Assets

The business environment confronting business organizations even just a few years ago was one in which having a large number of physical assets (manufacturing facilities, office buildings, equipment, inventory, and so forth) was critical for financial success. The more physical assets you had, the more economically powerful you were. However, that's not the case in today's economy. Success in today's economy isn't reliant simply on physical assets. Instead, value can be found in intangible factors such as information, people, ideas, and knowledge. Companies such as General Electric, eBay, Amazon.com, and even Toyota are finding that they can achieve a sustainable competitive advantage with nonphysical assets such as customer database information, online ordering systems, continual product and process innovation, and employee knowledge sharing.

Vanishing Distance and Compressed Time

The impact of physical distance and long time constraints on an organization's strategic decisions and actions have all but disappeared! While geography traditionally played an important role in determining customers and competitors, that's no longer the reality. An organization's potential market can be found anywhere. The limitations once imposed because of physical distance have vanished. The world is your customer, but this also means that the world is your competitor. The opportunities—and challenges—for strategic decision makers have never been greater. In addition, as the limitations of physical space have disappeared, so, too, have the limitations of time. Where it used to take Pony Express riders weeks to deliver information via the mail, we now have the U.S. Postal Service delivering mail in two to three days, and even overnight. But, that time frame, as you know, is even more compressed with electronic mail and interactive Web sites that give us almost instantaneous delivery of information. This instant interactivity (between customer and business, between employees, between companies and suppliers, or between friends and family) has created a context within which an organization must stay on top of changes or find its marketplace advantage temporary, at best. Although it isn't easy to stay on top of changes, it's important. Take Dell, for example. It has been able to hold on to its marketplace advantage by understanding the benefits and challenges of compressed time. The company builds computers directly from buyers' requests. Then, using its lightning-fast inventory and purchasing cycles, Dell builds and ships out computers not long after the customer's order is received. It also uses information from customers' orders to adapt to emerging trends way ahead of the curve.

Vulnerability

Their names are usually quite innocent and often very clever—Blaster, SoBig, Love Bug, BugBear, Coolnow. However, these global computer viruses were very destructive and are just one example of the final implication of the driving forces in today's context—the increased vulnerability that organizations face from interconnectedness and openness.[15] The threat of terrorist attacks, biological attacks, and computer virus attacks should be enough to make strategic decision makers realize that their facilities, employees, and information are vulnerable. Protecting valuable resources against such potential attacks is no longer a "maybe"—it's a strategic certainty, and one that shouldn't be ignored.

Learning Review

- Describe the three major driving forces of the new business environment.
- How is the information revolution affecting the context of managing strategically?
- What is technology?
- What technological trends are affecting the context of managing strategically?
- What is innovation?
- How do global factors impact the context of managing strategically?
- Describe the four major implications of the driving forces of the new business environment.
- Define change. Define organizational change.

Critical Success Factors

Three factors critical to success in this new business environment are listed in Figure 2.3 (p. 37). These factors are (1) the ability to embrace change, (2) creativity and innovation capabilities, and (3) being a world-class organization. Let's look at each of these critical success factors.

1. *Ability to embrace change.* If there's one word that captures the essence of this new business environment, it's *change*—change from technological advances, change from resource vulnerability, or change from information availability. Do you like change? Probably not. Few people enjoy or even seek out change. Most of us think change is annoying, scary, or both. We like order and structure, not chaos. We like

the old and comfortable, not the new or the unknown. But change is a given in this new business environment. Being successful in this kind of turbulent environment means not only being tolerant of change, but seeking it out and embracing it with open arms. Change brings not only opportunities to exploit but challenges in dealing successfully with the changes. In any type of organizational change effort, the caliber of organizational strategic leadership can spell the difference between success and failure.

Strategic decision makers play an important role as change agents. Effective change just doesn't happen by itself. There's got to be someone (or groups of "someones") to initiate and oversee the process. **Change agents** are individuals or groups who strategically manage the formulation, implementation, and evaluation of organizational change efforts. Whether it's major or minor changes in organizational strategy, change "drivers" are needed. Strategic decision makers can play this important role. Ideally, an organization's top-level strategic decision makers provide a sense of long-term direction and offer support and rationale for needed changes.[16] But, strategic leaders at any level of the organization play an important role in managing the change process.

Any type of change is difficult for all involved. (Think about how you react when you find a substitute professor in class one day or if your professor changes the course assignment schedule to accommodate a change in plans. Most of us feel anxious, maybe even angry.) Although strong strategic leadership can't eliminate all the challenges associated with change, it can smooth the process and facilitate successful implementation of the change. Considering the numerous dynamic forces facing today's organizations, strong strategic leadership can play a significant role in providing an appropriate and supportive organizational environment in which employees are encouraged to take responsibility for problems and taking action to solve them.[17]

2. *Creativity and innovation capabilities.* Here's an abbreviated statement of just how critical this factor is: "Create and innovate or fail!" It's that simple. In this dynamic, chaotic world we've described, strategic decision makers must be

FOR YOUR information

The DNA of Corporate Innovation

The members of Innovation Network Inc. (**www.thinksmart.com**) put their heads together and developed the Innovation DNA Model. This model identifies seven dimensions that need to be in place for organizational innovation to take root. These dimensions include: (1) challenge—the bigger the challenge and the passion behind it, the more energy innovation efforts will need; (2) customer focus—all innovation should be focused on creating value for customers, external or internal, and it requires understanding their needs; (3) creativity—everything starts from an idea, and the best way to get ideas is to generate a lot of possibilities; (4) communication—open communication of ideas,

information, and feelings is the lifeblood of innovation; (5) collaboration—innovation is a group process; (6) completion—innovations require "doing," (i.e., decision making, delegating, scheduling, monitoring, and feedback skills), and completed projects should be celebrated; and (7) contemplation—learning from completed projects builds a knowledge base that creates an upward cycle of success. In addition, the organization's culture creates the playing field for all the other elements to happen. Research a company (General Electric, Ford, Microsoft, or pick your own) and assess it on these dimensions. Be sure to document your sources, and be prepared to share your findings with your class.

Sources: *Innovation Network Inc.,* **www.thinksmart.com**, *February 25, 2004; and S. Caudron, "The Economics of Innovation,"* Business Finance, *November 1999, pp. 23–27.*

prepared to create new products and services and adopt state-of-the-art technology if their organizations are to compete successfully and survive. **Creativity**, the ability to combine ideas in a unique way or to make unusual associations between ideas, is an important capability.[18] A creative person or organization develops novel approaches to doing work or unique solutions to problems. But, creativity alone isn't enough. We know from our earlier discussion that innovation is the process of taking a creative idea and then turning it into a product or process that can be used to generate revenue. An innovative organization is characterized by its ability to channel creativity into useful outcomes. Both capabilities, being creative and being innovative, are critical to strategic success in this new business environment.

3. *Being a world-class organization.* Given the importance of creating a sustainable competitive advantage in light of the realities of today's business environment, you'd probably agree that ensuring an organization's long-run survival and success isn't easy. Even not-for-profit organizations face the challenge of managing strategically in such a context. Is there anything strategic decision makers can do to surmount this seemingly overwhelming challenge? One strategic management concept that has considerable potential for helping organizational decision makers meet the challenge is that of the world-class organization.[19] What is a **world-class organization**? It's one that continually acquires and utilizes knowledge in its strategic decisions and actions in order to be the best in the world at what it does. Recall our earlier discussion of the realities of the new business environment with respect to information and knowledge, technology, and increasing globalization, and you can begin to appreciate why being a world-class organization is an important goal. Even if an organization operates in a single geographic location, it should still strive to be the best at what it does in its own little "world" or competitive arena. What characteristics does a world-class organization have? The major ones are shown in Figure 2.4. Although these characteristics are important to becoming a world-class organization, the decision to be a world-class organization starts with developing an organizational vision and mission.

Figure 2.4

Major Characteristics of World-Class Organizations

Source: Based on Richard M. Hodgetts, Fred Luthans, and Sang M. Lee, "New Paradigm Organizations: From Total Quality to Learning to World Class," Organizational Dynamics, Winter 1994, pp. 4–19.

Organizational Vision and Mission

Yes, it's equally important for an organization to have both an organizational vision *and* a mission. Although some view the two as the same concept, we're going to define them as different. An **organizational vision** is a broad comprehensive picture of what a leader wants an organization to become. It's a statement of what the organization stands for, what it believes in, and why it exists. The vision provides a vibrant and compelling picture of the future. It presents a view beyond what the organization "is" to what the organization "could be."[20] You may think that the concept of a vision is simply "fluff"—something that sounds good on paper, but does nothing to improve the organization's performance. Yet, if organizational leaders can articulate a distinct vision, organizational members may be more motivated to contribute increased levels of effort.[21] For instance, at Microsoft Inc. the vision, "A computer on every desk and in every home," which had guided organizational decisions and actions throughout the company's history of explosive growth, was changed to "Empower people through great software anytime, any place, and on any device." The company's strategists broadened the vision statement because of continuing changes in the business environment.

What should organizational vision include? Four components have been identified as important to organizational vision.[22] First is that the vision *be built on a foundation of the organization's core values and beliefs*. These values and beliefs address what's fundamentally important to the organization, whether it's conducting business ethically and responsibly, satisfying the customer, emphasizing quality in all aspects, or being a leader in technology. And, the vision should stress whatever those core values might be. Just how important are values to doing business? A recent survey about corporate values by the American Management Association found that almost 86 percent of the respondents said the values of their organization were specifically stated or written, and 64 percent said that the values were linked to performance evaluations and compensation.[23] Although a statement of values doesn't guarantee success, it can provide employees with a sense of behavioral expectations. For example, if employees know that outstanding customer service is valued by the organization, then they can make decisions and act in ways that champion customer service.

Second, the vision should *elaborate a purpose for the organization*. Every organization—profit or not-for-profit, large or small, local or global—has a purpose, and that purpose should be specified in the organization's vision. That way, all organizational stakeholders are explicitly aware of why this organization exists.

The third component of organizational vision is that it should *include a brief summary of what the organization does*. While the vision shouldn't provide explicit details of what the organization does (this is done in the various mission statements, discussed shortly) it should explain what it's doing to fulfill its purpose. And, this is a good time to say that while

strategic **MANAGEMENT** *in action*

Although many old-line manufacturers dream of transforming themselves into nimble technology companies, Corning Inc. (**www.corning.com**) has actually pulled off this difficult transformation. Maybe you (or older family members or friends) still have Corning baking dishes in your kitchen. The Corning that manufactured those dishes and other glassware still works mostly in glass, but in forms that most people would not recognize. The company has shifted its focus to products such as optical fibers and liquid crystal display screens. In fact, the company states that it has a proud history of "enriching people's lives through research and technological innovation." Go to Corning's Web site, find the company's seven values, and describe them. How will these values affect the way organizational employees manage strategically?

Sources: *Corning Inc.,* **www.corning.com**, *February 25, 2004; A. Carter, "Reigniting Corning," Money,* **www.cnnmoney.com**, *May 2003; J. Kimelman, "Corning May Be Turning a Corner," New York Times, May 4, 2003, Section 3, p. 6; and T. Aeppel, "Corning's Makeover: From Casseroles to Fiber Optics," Wall Street Journal, July 16, 1999, p. B4.*

they're related, there *is* a difference between an organization's purpose and what it does. For example, several organizations may have the purpose of ecological preservation, but the way they carry out that purpose (i.e., what they do) may be different.

The last component of organizational vision is that it should *specify broad goals*. Goals provide a target that all organizational members work toward meeting. Goals also serve to unify organizational members toward a common end. An organization's vision can and should be a guiding force in every decision.

Although organizational vision provides an overall picture of where the organization would like to be in the future, a **mission** is a statement of what specific organizational units do and what they hope to accomplish in alignment with the organizational vision. An organization will have only one vision and potentially several missions (divisional, departmental, project work group, or any number of others) that contribute to the pursuit of the organizational vision. A unit's mission statement provides a focus for unit employees as they make strategic decisions and implement them. Although it's not as comprehensive and broad as the organizational vision, a unit's mission statement still provides an overview of the unit's purpose, what it does, and its goals. Each unit's mission statement also aligns with the organizational vision. Ideally what you have is a broad framework within which organizational members know what they're doing and why they're doing it. The vision and missions also should reflect the organization's commitment to social responsibility and ethical decision making.

Corporate Social Responsibility and Ethics

How much and what type of social responsibility business organizations should pursue has been a topic of heated debate for a number of years. **Corporate social responsibility (CSR)** is the obligation of organizational decision makers to make decisions and act in ways that recognize the interrelatedness of business and society.[24] CSR recognizes the existence of various stakeholders and how organizations deal with them. But, it's in the definition of "who" organizations are responsible to that we find a diversity of opinions.

The traditional view was that corporations existed solely to serve the interests of one stakeholder group—the stockholders.[25] Milton Friedman, the most outspoken advocate of this view, argued that corporate social programs and actions must be paid for in some way and add to the costs of doing business. Those costs either have to be passed on to customers in the form of higher prices or absorbed internally. In either case, profitability suffers

The Grey Zone

Are vision and mission statements just a bunch of empty words? A study of several securities firms and investment banks showed that many hours had been spent crafting elegant mission statements that extolled the virtues of teamwork, integrity, and respect for the individual. Yet, the partners at those firms treated their young analysts like second-class citizens. They gave them work that wasn't commensurate with their skills, were openly impolite to them, and in many instances, were verbally abusive toward them. When these conditions were described to the top decision makers, they said that kind of behavior couldn't be happening—it went against their companies' mission statements. Yet, this type of situation doesn't just occur in securities firms. Could this situation have been prevented? If so, how? If not, why not? How can strategic decision makers make sure that vision and mission statements are more than empty words?

Strategic Management in Action

The Greening of Strategic Management

A number of highly visible global ecological problems and environmental disasters have brought about a new awareness and spirit of environmentalism among strategic decision makers, who increasingly have begun to confront questions about the natural environment and its impact on organizations. This recognition of the close link between an organization's decisions and actions and its impact on the natural environment is referred to as the **greening of management**. As organizations become "greener," we find more and more of them issuing detailed reports on their environmental performance. The Global Reporting Initiative (**www.globalreporting.org**), launched in 1997

as a joint initiative of the Coalition for Environmentally Responsible Economies (CERES) and the United Nations Environment Program, has the goal of enhancing the quality, rigor, and utility of sustainability reporting. To that extent, GRI created its Sustainability Reporting Guidelines. Using the Guidelines, hundreds of companies around the globe report their efforts in promoting environmental sustainability. Check out the GRI Web site. What guidelines does the Global Reporting Initiative suggest? Pick out five of the reporting companies and describe their environmental reports.

Sources: *Global Reporting Initiative*, **www.globalreporting.org**, February 25, 2004; and A. Kolk, "Green Reporting," Harvard Business Review, January–February 2000, pp. 15–16.

because customers might buy less at higher prices or organizational costs would increase. Understand that Friedman didn't say that organizations shouldn't be socially responsible. In fact, he felt they *should* be. But, his argument was that the extent of the responsibility was to maximize shareholder returns.

However, the traditional—and purely economic—perspective of corporate social responsibility has given way to a belief that organizations have a larger societal role to play and a broader constituency to serve than just stockholders alone. Yet, balancing various stakeholder demands is a complicated process because they often have a wide range of needs and conflicting expectations.[26] What this means for managing strategically as a world-class organization is recognizing the commitment to make decisions and to implement those decisions in ways that will enhance the various stakeholder relationships. **Stakeholders** are individuals or groups who have a stake in or are significantly influenced by an organization's decisions and actions and who, in turn, can influence the organization. What types of stakeholders might an organization have to deal with? Figure 2.5 identifies the most common.

Many organizations believe that strong and socially responsible stakeholder relationships make them more competitive.[27] For example, every single day, General Mills ships three semi-trailer trucks full of cereal and other packaged goods to food banks around the United States.[28] The message is loud and clear throughout the company that good corporate citizenship "doesn't end with the bottom line." In fact, performance reviews of top executives include an evaluation of community involvement. Although corporate social responsibility emphasizes the broad picture of an organization's societal interactions, it's also important that these interactions take place in a context of "doing the right thing." That's where the concept of ethics comes in.

Ethics—or more correctly, the lack of ethics—seemed to be all we heard in 2001 and 2002 as news reports surfaced about unbelievable and inexcusable behaviors of executives from Enron, Tyco, Worldcom, ImClone, and other organizations. It's no wonder that when teens were asked in a survey sponsored by Junior Achievement if business leaders were ethical, only 18 percent said "yes."[29] But it's not just corporate executives who must deal with ethical issues. By this time in your life, you've undoubtedly faced numerous ethical dilemmas, both in academics and, if you're employed, at your job. For instance, is it ethical to make a copy of inexpensive computer software for a friend who's short of money or to

Stakeholders *do* play a significant role in the strategies that organizations ultimately choose. For instance, when Ben & Jerry's Homemade, a company well known for its socially responsible approach to doing business, decided to seek a buyer, a group of owners of Ben & Jerry's ice cream shops rallied to make the point that they didn't want a corporate takeover that would pose a threat to the company's image. Another example of the role that stakeholders play in organizational strategies is Procter & Gamble, who after years of protests from animal rights groups, decided to stop animal testing for a broad range of products, including cosmetics, shampoos, detergents, cleansers, and paper goods. McDonald's Corporation also has faced protests from animal rights activists who want the company to demand better treatment of farm animals. And, Gerber and H.J. Heinz, two food processors, have been grilled by Greenpeace, the activist European environmental group, over the use of genetically engineered food. Although these examples illustrate some of the more radical stakeholder demands, all organizations must understand the demands of stakeholders and their impact on strategic choices.

Sources: C. L. Hays, "Shops Rally to the Ben & Jerry's Cause(s)," New York Times, January 25, 2000, p. C2; R. Gibson, "Animal Rights Flare Up as McDonald's Is Torched, PETA Breaks Off Talks," Wall Street Journal, August 13, 1999, p. B8; L. Lagnado, "Strained Peace," Wall Street Journal, July 30, 1999, p. A1; G. Fairclough, "Procter & Gamble Makes Move Away From Animal Tests," Wall Street Journal, July 1, 1999, p. B10; and D. Canedy, "P&G to End Animal Tests for Most Consumer Goods," New York Times, July 1, 1999, p. C2.

Figure 2.5

Potential Organizational Stakeholders

"donate" copies of completed case homework or other assignments to your sorority or fraternity? Or say that you work part time as a telemarketing representative. Is it ethical for you to pressure customers to purchase a product just so you can win a prize? **Ethics** involves the principles that define right and wrong decisions and behavior. In other words, as we live our lives—attend school, work at a job, engage in hobbies, and so forth—certain decisions and behaviors are ethically "right" and certain decisions and behaviors are ethically "wrong." Considering the varied interpretations of right and wrong, you can see what

Ethics in Real Life

An ethics code should be more than great public relations. After all, Enron had a code of ethics, which is kind of ironic considering the behaviors exhibited by many of its top executives. The success—or failure—of corporate ethics programs has less to do with such things as written ethics codes and compliance hotlines, and everything to do with why employees think the programs were established in the first place. For example, George David, CEO of United Technologies Corporation, believes very deeply in the power of a code of ethics, but the company's ethics program entails much more than that. Although the company has a detailed, 16-page code of ethics, including 35 standards of conduct, it's not just having the written code that makes ethics work so well. It's the fact that employees know the behavioral expectations, especially when it comes to ethics. What can strategic decision makers do to make sure their companies' codes of ethics are effective? First, ethics codes should be developed and then communicated regularly and consistently to employees. Second, all levels of management should continually reaffirm the importance of the ethics code and the organization's commitment to it, and consistently discipline those who break it. Finally, top management should set a good example. What they *do* is more important than what they *say*. What do you think of these suggestions? Do you agree? Why or why not? What are the implications of these ideas for managing strategically? Go to United Technology's Web site (**www.utc.com**) and check out the section on ethics. What did you find there that might be helpful to other strategic decision makers?

Sources: J. S. McClenahen, "UTC's Master of Principle," Industry Week, January 2003, pp. 30–36; and "Global Ethics Codes Gain Importance as a Tool to Avoid Litigation and Fines," Wall Street Journal, August 19, 1999, p. B3.

a complex topic ethics is to address. Although we won't get into an extended discussion of the origin of ethics, be aware that ethical considerations should play a role in managing strategically. In fact, some individuals believe that ethics is both a personal and organizational issue and should be part of the strategic management process.[30]

What does this mean for managing strategically? It means recognizing the ethical implications of the outcomes of strategic decisions and actions. It means considering more than just being in compliance with the law as organizational strategies are formulated and implemented. For example, Avon Products Inc. sells its cosmetics products mainly to women. When Avon asked women what their number one health concern was, breast cancer was the overwhelming answer. In response, Avon created its Worldwide Fund for Women's Health. This umbrella organization has spread around the globe. The company's biggest women's health program in this fund is the Breast Cancer Awareness Crusade in the United States. Through this program, the company's sales force educates women about breast cancer by distributing brochures about the disease on their sales visits. In this instance, Avon's strategic decision makers chose to develop and implement a sales strategy that addressed a significant customer concern. Was it the "right" thing to do? Well, Avon's decision makers think so. Not only were they being ethical in their dealings with customers, those customers responded by boosting company sales. Although not every strategic decision will be this broad in scope, the ethical implications for managing strategically are clear: As you're managing strategically, ask yourself what's the "right" thing to do in making this decision or taking this action? (The Grey Zone ethical dilemmas you're seeing in each chapter of this book emphasize the importance of understanding the role of ethics in strategic decision making.)

Organizational Learning

The final aspect of world-class organizations concerns the significant role that organizational learning plays. **Organizational learning** is the intentional and ongoing actions of an organization to continuously transform itself by acquiring information and knowledge and

Communities of Practice

A new organizational approach that promises to radically change knowledge sharing and learning is emerging. It's called a **community of practice**. What is a community of practice? It's a group of people bound together by shared expertise and passion for a joint interest or endeavor. The primary output from the group is "knowledge." This community of practice may actually meet face-to-face or it may be a meeting of the minds via e-mail. It may not have an explicit agenda of items to cover and may not even follow the agenda if it does have one. But, the one thing that characterizes this community of practice is the sharing of experiences and knowledge in free-flowing, creative ways.

What benefits can communities of practice bring to organizations? They have the potential to add value in the following ways: They help drive strategy; they start new lines of business; they solve problems quickly; they transfer and spread best practices among organizational units; they develop professional skills that allow them to act as mentors and coaches; and they help companies recruit and retain talent. So, in many ways, the communities of practice within an organization can serve to build and exchange that all-important knowledge. Find two or three examples of companies that are employing communities of practice. Describe their experiences.

Source: E. Wenger, R. McDermott, and W. M. Snyder, Cultivating Communities of Practice: A Guide to Managing Knowledge (Boston: Harvard Business School Press, 2002).

Table 2.3

Characteristics of a Learning Organization

- Learns continuously, collaboratively, and openly
- Values *how* it learns as well as what it learns
- Invests in staying on top of what's happening in its industry
- Learns faster and smarter than its competitors
- Rewards both "failure" learning (learning from what goes wrong) as well as "success" learning (learning from what goes right)
- Takes risks but doesn't jeopardize organization's basic security
- Encourages organizational members to share information
- Develops and exhibits an organizational culture that promotes learning
- Uses what it learns in developing and implementing strategies

Sources: P. M. Senge, The Fifth Discipline (New York: Doubleday, 1990); and Richard M. Hodgetts, Fred Luthans, and Sang M. Lee, "New Paradigm Organizations: From Total Quality to Learning to World Class," Organizational Dynamics, Winter 1994, pp. 4–19.

---

incorporating these into organizational decisions and actions. A learning organization can either create or acquire new ideas and information and then use these to make decisions and take action. Organizational learning has been shown to be an important means for an organization to gain competitive advantage, and in fact, may be the only sustainable competitive advantage.[31] Table 2.3 lists some of the characteristics of a learning organization. As you can see from this list, a learning organization values all kinds of learning. But most importantly, managers in a learning organization incorporate learning into every aspect of the strategic management process.

How does an organization "learn?" A model called the 4I Organizational Learning Framework provides an explanation.[32] (See Figure 2.6.) The first thing the model illustrates is that organizational learning takes place at three levels throughout the organization: individual, group, and organizational. Within these three levels, four different learning processes occur. *Intuiting* is recognizing patterns or possibilities because of a personal stream of experience. It's a uniquely individual process—organizations do not intuit. *Interpreting* is explaining insights and ideas to yourself and to others. *Integrating* is

Figure 2.6

*The 4I Organizational
Learning Framework*

Source: M. M. Crossan, H. W. Lane, and
R. E. White, "An Organizational Learning
Framework: From Intuition to Institution,"
Academy of Management Review, July
1999, p. 525.

Level	Process
Individual	Intuiting
	Interpreting
Group	Integrating
Organization	Institutionalizing

developing shared understanding among individuals and taking coordinated action. And finally, *institutionalizing* is ensuring that the learning is embedded into the strategy, structures, procedures, and routines of the organization. What this model tells us about organizational learning is that it must take place throughout the organization and entails more than just having good ideas.

Learning and the application of learning by sharing it throughout the organization will be critical to organizational success given the realities of the new economy and the dynamics of change.[33] What's the payoff? Employees who are making strategic decisions in a world-class organization and attempting to create a sustainable competitive advantage in light of the increasingly competitive global environment.

Learning Review

- Describe the three critical factors for succeeding in this new business environment.
- What role do change agents play in managing strategically?
- Differentiate between creativity and innovation.
- What is a world-class organization? Why is the concept important?
- What is organizational vision? What should it include?
- What is a mission?
- What is corporate social responsibility?
- Who are stakeholders and why are they important to managing strategically?
- What is ethics and why is it important to strategic decision makers?
- What is organizational learning?
- What are some characteristics of learning organizations?
- Describe the 4I Organizational Learning Framework.
- Why is the concept of organizational learning important to managing strategically?

- **Managing strategically** means formulating and implementing strategies that allow an organization to develop and maintain competitive advantage.

- **Competitive advantage** is what sets an organization apart; its competitive edge.

- Competitive advantage is a necessary ingredient for an organization's long-term success and survival.

- There are three different views of competitive advantage.

- The **industrial organization (I/O) view**, developed by Michael Porter, focuses on the structural forces within an industry, the competitive environment of firms, and how these influence competitive advantage. This view proposes that getting and keeping competitive advantage means analyzing the external forces and then basing strategic decisions and actions on what is found.

- The **resource-based view (RBV)** proposes that a firm's resources are more important than industry structure in getting and keeping competitive advantage and sees organizations as very different collections of assets and capabilities.

- **Resources** can include all of the financial, physical, human, intangible, and structural/cultural assets used by an organization to develop, manufacture, and deliver products and services to its customers.

- Although every organization has resources, not all of these resources are going to be unique and capable of leading to a sustainable competitive advantage.

- To be unique, resources must add value, be rare, be hard to imitate, and be able to be exploited.

- The **guerrilla view** of competitive advantage proposes that an organization's competitive advantage is temporary because the environment is characterized by continual, radical, and often revolutionary changes.

- All three views (I/O, RBV, and guerilla) provide unique perspectives on understanding competitive advantage.

- The business context that organizations operate in is important because it establishes the rules of the game for doing business.

- The driving forces of this context include the information revolution, technological advances and breakthroughs, and globalization.

- In this new environment, organizations can no longer rely on the traditional factors of production to provide a competitive advantage, but must look to how information and knowledge can be exploited.

- **Technology** is the use of equipment, materials, knowledge, and experience to perform tasks. Technology is changing the way we work and the type of work we do.

- Five technological trends affecting the context of managing strategically include the realization that technology is starting to pay back with real savings and real productivity gains; the increasing commercialization of **innovation** (the process of taking a creative idea and turning it into a product or process that can be used or sold); the increasing dependence on knowledge and information; the increasing recognition that technology, especially information technology, is creating deep structural transformations in the economy; and the realization that great companies are pioneers and leaders in applying technology.

○ Four structural transformations in the economy have been caused by technology: network capabilities mean that everything is connected; digital technology is making businesses smarter; digital technology has helped create completely new subindustries; and technology has transformed the economy to a "bottom-up" economy.

○ Two specific ways that globalization impacts the context of managing strategically are in the global marketplace and through global competitors.

○ There are four implications of these driving forces of the new business environment: continual turbulence and change, reduced need for physical assets, vanishing distance and compressed time, and increased vulnerability.

○ **Change** is any alteration in external environmental factors or internal organizational arrangements.

○ **Organizational change** is any alteration in what an organization does and how it does it. The organization may have to change in response to changes in external or internal factors.

○ Success in today's economy isn't reliant simply on physical assets. Instead, value can be found in intangible factors such as information, people, ideas, and knowledge.

○ Geography no longer is a constraint on customers and competitors. An organization's potential markets and competitors can be found anywhere.

○ The instant interactivity e-mail and interactive Web sites have created a context where an organization needs to stay on top of changes.

○ Organizations also face increased vulnerability of their facilities, employees, and information from the openness and interconnectedness of today's business context.

○ The critical success factors for this new business environment include the ability to embrace change, creativity and innovation capabilities, and being a world-class organization.

○ Being successful in this turbulent environment means seeking out change and embracing it.

○ Strategic decision makers play an important role as **change agents**—individuals or groups who strategically manage the formulation, implementation, and evaluation of organizational change efforts.

○ "Create and innovate or fail!" **Creativity** is the ability to combine ideas in a unique way or to make unusual associations between ideas. However, creativity isn't enough. An organization also needs to be innovative—that is, be able to take that creative idea and turn it into a product or process that can be used to generate revenue.

- A **world-class organization** is one that continually acquires and utilizes knowledge in its strategic decisions and actions in order to be the best in the world at what it does.

- The characteristics of world-class organizations include strong customer focus, continual learning and improvement, flexible organization structure, creative human resource management, egalitarian climate, and significant technological support.

- The decision to be a world-class organization starts with developing an organizational vision and mission.

- **Organizational vision** is a broad comprehensive picture of what a leader wants an organization to become. It's a statement of what the organization stands for, what it believes in, and why it exists.

- The four components of an organizational vision include: it must be built on a foundation of the organization's core values and beliefs; it should create a purpose for the organization; it should include a brief summary of what the organization does; and it should specify broad goals.

- A **mission** is a statement of what the various organizational units do and what they hope to accomplish in alignment with the organizational vision.

- An organization will have one vision and potentially several missions that contribute to the pursuit of the organizational vision.

- **Corporate social responsibility (CSR)** refers to the obligations of organizational decision makers to make decisions and act in ways that recognize the interrelatedness of business and society.

- The traditional view of CSR was that organizations existed to serve the interests of one stakeholder group—the stockholders.

- The current perspective is that organizations have a larger societal role to play and a broader constituency to serve than just stockholders alone.

- Organizations have to recognize the existence of other **stakeholders**—individuals or groups who have a stake in or are significantly influenced by an organization's decisions and actions and who, in turn, can influence the organization.

- One area of CSR that's growing in importance is the **greening of management**, which is a recognition of the close link between an organization's decisions and actions and its impact on the natural environment.

- **Ethics** involves the principles that define right and wrong decisions and behaviors.

- Ethics should be considered in the context of managing strategically.

- **Organizational learning**—the intentional and ongoing actions of an organization to continuously transform itself by acquiring information and knowledge and incorporating these into organizational decisions and actions—plays a significant role in managing strategically.

- A new form of organizational learning is called the **community of practice**, which is a group of people bound together by shared expertise and passion for a joint interest or endeavor.

- Learning organizations are characterized by their focus on learning and sharing that learning.

- Organizational learning takes place at three levels throughout the organization: individual, group, and organizational. Within these three levels, four different learning processes take place. Intuiting is recognizing patterns or possibilities because of personal experience. Interpreting is explaining insights and ideas to yourself and to others. Integrating is developing shared understanding among individuals and taking coordinated action. Institutionalizing is ensuring that the learning is embedded into the strategy, structures, procedures, and routines of the organization.

1. Organizational vision statements can take some interesting directions. For instance, Future Network USA (formerly Imagine Media) developed a purpose statement and underlying values that it believes are the road map for the company's success. Go to the company's Web site (**www.futurenetworkusa.com**) and find its purpose statement and statement of values.

   What do you think of these statements? Do they fit the four components of an organizational vision? How might these statements affect the strategic choices made by the company's strategic decision makers?

2. "Technology is fostering a free flow of information." Using a bulleted list format, write arguments supporting this statement. Then, write arguments against this statement. Be prepared to debate one or both sides in class.

3. Knowledge management is a relatively young science. Here are some suggestions for capturing knowledge and using it effectively: (a) keep it human; (b) focus on useful knowledge or "know-how"; (c) collect artifacts such as Post-it notes and other documents and make these public; (d) avoid an insular, isolated focus; and (e) keep your knowledge fresh. Explain what you think each of these suggestions refers to. As you write your explanations, discuss the implications for strategic decision makers.

4. For each of the following quotes, explain what you think they mean and the implications for understanding the context of managing strategically.

   - "To stay ahead, you must have your next idea waiting in the wings." (Rosabeth Moss Kanter—management professor, consultant, and author)

   - "Time is a river of passing events, and strong is its current; no sooner is a thing brought to sight than it is swept by and another takes its place, and this too will be swept away." (Marcus Aurelius Antoninus)

5. Every year, *Fortune* publishes lists of "America's Most Admired Companies" and "Global Most Admired Companies." Choose one list. Get the most recent one and answer the following questions.

   - Define the key attributes that companies are evaluated on.

   - What companies are in the top 10?

   - Why do you think these companies are at the top of the list? What are they doing differently—that is, how are they managing strategically?

   - What companies are on the bottom 10 list? How are they managing strategically?

   - What could strategic decision makers learn from both groups?

6. The TQM (total quality management) movement encouraged organizational managers to *do it right the first time*. Make it right the first time and you eliminate waste. Finish it right the first time and you save money, time, and customer relationships. Makes sense, doesn't it? However, what if *doing it right the first time* stifles creativity and risk taking? Because breakthrough innovations are rarely well-planned, mistake-free processes, wouldn't an emphasis on *doing it right* suppress going out on a limb to try something different? Maybe *doing it right* isn't as important as *doing it best*. What do you think? Write a paper exploring these concepts.

7. One problem that organizations wanting to become knowledge-based organizations (or learning organizations) need to overcome is *knowledge hoarding,* an old business habit people used to get power, to protect themselves, and to get ahead. Getting people to share information may well be the key managerial issue in the twenty-first century. How would you overcome knowledge hoarding? Make a bulleted list of ideas. Be prepared to present these in class.

8. Social Accountability International (SAI) is a U.S.-based nonprofit organization dedicated to the development, implementation, and oversight of voluntary accountability standards. It works to improve workplaces and combat sweatshops. Every year it awards its Corporate Conscience Awards (CCA), which recognize progressive companies that respect the rights of workers and the community. The CCA honors outstanding social and environmental performance and seeks to encourage widespread adoption of award-winning responsible business practices. Go to SAI's Web site (**www.cepaa.org**) and find the list of the current awardees. Pick two of the award winners and describe what strategic initiatives they're using. What could other companies learn from them?

Strategic Management in Action Cases

CASE #1: Out of Tune

This Strategic Management in Action Case can be found at the beginning of Chapter 2.

Discussion Questions

1. Using Figure 2.3, describe the context confronting the music companies. Was the context totally negative or were there possibly some positive elements? Explain your answer.

2. Evaluate the strategic responses used by the music companies as they coped with the changed environment.

3. Update the information on the music industry. What new developments have taken place? What strategies do the music companies appear to be using in response to these new developments?

4. How would proponents of the I/O view analyze this case? How about proponents of the RBV? How about proponents of the guerrilla view?

CASE #2: In the Know

Buckman Laboratories International (**www.buckman. com**), headquartered in Memphis, Tennessee, manufactures more than 500 specialty chemical products. The company employs over 1,300 people in 22 countries, and its annual revenues exceed $300 million. Although this small, privately held company depends on its research laboratories for the products that bring in its revenues, the whole company itself is a learning laboratory.

What is it about Buckman Labs that attracts executives from AT&T, 3M, Champion International, US West, and other *Fortune* 500 companies, who trek to Memphis to see and learn? They're coming to see how the company stays so fast, global, and interactive. Bob Buckman, Buckman Lab's founder, recognized the power of knowledge and information long before others did. Buckman and his employees began treating knowledge as the company's most important corporate asset back in 1992. They believed that being (and remaining) competitive in a knowledge-intensive global environment required three things: (1) closing the gap between the organization and the customer; (2) staying in touch with each other; and (3) bringing *all* of the company's brainpower together to serve each customer. Buckman was concerned with staying connected, sharing knowledge, and functioning anytime, anywhere, no matter what.

Buckman Labs has organized its employees and their work around its knowledge network, K'Netix®. This global electronic communications network resulted from Buckman's being confined to bed after

rupturing disks in his back. Lying there, unable to stand or even to sit up, Buckman felt isolated and uninformed about what was happening in the company while he was flat on his back. He started thinking about how important information and knowledge were—not just to him, but to *all* of Buckman Labs' employees. What he needed and what his employees needed was a steady stream of information about products, markets, and customers. And this information needed to be easily accessible and easily shared. As an ardent reader of business and management information, Buckman had read a comment from a well-known and well-respected CEO (Scandinavian Airlines' former CEO, Jan Carlzon) that stuck in his mind: "An individual without information cannot take responsibility; an individual who is given information cannot help but take responsibility."

Buckman realized that the way to maximize each of his individual employee's power was to connect each employee to the world. He wrote down what his ideal knowledge transfer system would do. Here's what he wrote: (1) It would be possible for people to talk to each other directly to minimize distortion. (2) It would give everyone access to the company's knowledge base. (3) It would allow each individual in the company to enter knowledge into the system. (4) It would be available 24 hours a day, 7 days a week. (5) It would be easy to use. (6) It would communicate in whatever language was best for the user. (7) It would be updated automatically, capturing questions and answers as a future knowledge base. Such a system would require a total cultural transformation—literally turning the organization upside down by getting employees to be deeply involved with collaborating and sharing knowledge. And that's what Bob Buckman set out to do. However, transforming the company from an old pyramidal, bureaucratic, command-and-control organization to an organization in which every employee would have complete access to information and in which no one would be telling employees what to do all the time wasn't easy.

Getting the physical hardware and software in place to support such a system was only half the battle. Getting employees to use the knowledge base *and* contribute to it were also important. After all, a knowledge-based company is successful only if knowledge is shared among organizational members. What was particularly difficult about this type of cultural transformation was that employees in traditional organizations had always been rewarded on their ability to hoard knowledge and thus gain power. This is how the situation at Buckman Labs was described: "There were people whose file cabinets were filled with everything they knew, and that was the source of their power." But that philosophy had to change if the knowledge system was going to work. Not long after K-Netix® went online, Buckman made his expectations clear: "Those of you who have something intelligent to say now have a forum in which to say it. Those of you who will not or cannot contribute also become obvious. If you are not willing to contribute or participate, then you should understand that the many opportunities offered to you in the past will no longer be available." What ultimately emerged at Buckman Labs has been a mixture of visible incentives and invisible pressure to use the Buckman Knowledge Network.

Because Buckman Labs competes in a variety of businesses, often against competitors three to five times its size, its commitment to knowledge takes on a new urgency. Salespeople need the right answer for each customer, and they need it fast. K'Netix® has made getting answers simple. But the company's commitment to speed, employee interactivity and knowledge sharing, and globalization would not be possible without a recognition of the context within which managing strategically takes place.

Discussion Questions

1. According to Table 2.3, is Buckman Labs a learning organization? Explain.

2. Describe Buckman Labs' strategic approaches in light of the drivers of the new business environment, the implications of these driving forces, and the critical success factors.

3. Go to Buckman's Web site. Answer the following:
   - Find the statement of mission. What is it? What other unique element(s) do you see on Buckman's statement of mission?
   - Locate the company's code of ethics. Summarize some of the company's basic principles.
   - Would you call the company a "green" company? Explain and support your answer.
   - Find the Knowledge Nurture page. What is the Buckman Room? What is the Starter Kit? What is the Library?
   - Find the page that describes K'Netix®. What does it say about the Buckman Knowledge Network?

4. What could other organizations learn from Buckman Labs approach?

Sources: Buckman Laboratories International, **www.buckman.com**, February 24, 2004; S. Thurm, "What Do You Know?" *Wall Street Journal,* June 21, 1999, p. R10; B. P. Sunoo, "How HR Supports Knowledge Sharing," *Workforce,* March 1999, pp. 30–32; G. Rifkin, "Buckman Labs Is Nothing But Net," *Fast Company,* June–July 1996, pp. 118–123; and A. Bruzzese, "Sharing Knowledge Breaks Hierarchy," *Springfield News Leader,* October 17, 1997, p. 7A.

CASE #3: They've Got Game

Although their expertise lies in creating games, it's definitely serious business for the video game industry. For two years straight, U.S. computer and video game revenues surpassed domestic movie box-office receipts. In this industry, where customers are fickle and demanding and competition is intense, one company, Electronic Arts (EA), has prospered. As the world's largest independent video game software maker, EA lives and dies by its innovations. Its product lineup includes over 100 titles, including *Def Jam*

Vendetta, The Sims, Madden NFL Football, The Lord of the Rings, and *Harry Potter.* The company has created over 50 best-sellers (each with more than 1 million copies sold) since 1998. Revenues in 2003 approached $2.5 billion, up almost 44 percent over 2002, the previous best year when revenues were up 30 percent over 2001. Net income in 2003 was up 212 percent, as it also was in 2002. In addition, the company was included on *Fortune's* list of the "100 Best Companies to Work For." It would appear that this is a company that knows its game.

With its record of accomplishment, you wouldn't think there'd be much anxiety or stress at EA. Yet, the reality is that paranoia is a critical part of its success. A top game title takes anywhere from 12 to 36 months to produce and costs between $5 million and $10 million. That's a significant investment risk riding on the company's ability to innovate. John Riccitiello, president and chief operating officer, says, "The forgotten aspect of creativity is discipline." The hard part, and the part that EA relentlessly pursues, "is identifying the right idea, assembling the best development team, solving the inevitable technical problems, creating a game that people want to play, getting all of the work done on schedule, getting it to market at the right time, and knowing how to generate buzz about it in an increasingly crowded market." How does EA do it?

It starts with the discipline of understanding ideas. Game designers try to identify the creative center of a game—what they call the "creative x"—so they understand what the game is about. Then, it's the discipline of understanding the customers by using focus groups to pinpoint desires and likes and dislikes. And it's the discipline of sharing best practices and technologies through the company's intranet library. As one employee said, "If somebody develops a better blade of grass in one game, that grass will be in somebody else's game the next day." Then,

there's the discipline of developing the next generation of creative leaders. The company's "emerging leaders" program gives participants first-hand experience in departments outside their own. And there's the discipline of studying the competition. Employees are encouraged to know the features of competitors' products. Then, it's disciplined project management. Riccitiello says, "If you're working on a game and you miss your deadlines, you won't be working here very long." Although the discipline of creativity is important at EA, you can't overlook the passion of the company's game designers. Nearly everyone at EA grew up playing games. They love what they do and are inspired to look for new and creative challenges, not only for the hard-core gamers, but for the casual gamers as well.

Discussion Questions

1. Describe EA's competitive advantage from each of the three perspectives on competitive advantage.

2. Does EA exhibit the critical success factors for the new business context? Explain.

3. Describe the types of resources EA appears to have. Do you think any of these resources might be unique? Explain.

4. What stakeholders might EA have to be concerned with and how might those stakeholders affect EA's strategic decisions and actions?

Sources: Electronic Arts, **www.ea.com**; Hoover's Online, **www.hoovers.com**, February 29, 2004; R. A. Guth, "Electronic Arts Profit Jumps 57% On Strong Sales of Core Titles," *Wall Street Journal,* January 28, 2004, p. B3; N'Gai Croal, "He's Got Games," *Newsweek,* December 29, 2003–January 5, 2004, p. 101; P. Lewis, "The Biggest Game in Town," *Fortune,* September 15, 2003, pp. 132–142; C. Salter, "Playing to Win," *Fast Company,* December 2002, pp. 80–91; G. L. Cooper and E. K. Brown, "Video Game Industry Update," *Bank of America Equity Research Brief,* June 7, 2002; and M. Athitakis, "Steve Rechtschaffner, Game Wizard," *Business 2.0,* May 2002, p. 82.

Endnotes

1. H. Green, "Downloads: The Next Generation," *Business Week,* February 16, 2004, p. 64; J. Graham, "Lawsuits Help Cut Song-Swapping in USA by Half," *USA Today,* January 5, 2004, p. B2; S. Levy, "Owning the Music," *Newsweek,* December 29, 2003–January 5, 2004, p. 20; B. Acohido, "2004 May See 'Bit of a Gold Rush' for Digital Tunes," *USA Today,* December 30, 2003, p. B1; P. Burrows, "Napster Lives Again—Sort of," *Business Week,* October 20, 2003, pp. 66–68; P. Burrows, R. Grover, and J. Greene, "Tuning Up Like Nobody's Business," *Business Week,* October 13, 2003, p. 42; M. France and R. Grover, "Striking Back," *Business Week,* September 29, 2003, pp. 94–96; L. T. Cullen, "How to Go Legit," *Time,* September 22, 2003, pp. 44–45; S. Levy, "Courthouse Rock," *Newsweek,* September 22, 2003, pp. 38–45; and K. Terrell, "A Nation of Pirates," *U.S. News & World Report,* July 14, 2003, pp. 40–46.

2. H. Baldwin, "The Journey Forward," *IQ Magazine,* June 2003, pp. 38–47.

3. This discussion of industrial/organization perspective is based on K. R. Conner, "A Historical Comparison of Resource-Based Theory and Five Schools of Thought within Industrial Organization Economics: Do We Have a New Theory of the Firm?" *Journal of Management,* 17, no. 1 (1991), 121–54; M. Porter, *Competitive Advantage: Creating and Sustaining Superior Performance* (New York: Free Press, 1985); and M. Porter, *Competitive Strategy: Techniques for Analyzing Industries and Competitors* (New York: Free Press, 1980).

4. This discussion of resource-based view is based on D. G. Hoopes, T. L. Madsen, and G. Walker, "Guest Editors' Introduction to the Special Issue: Why Is There a Resource-Based View? Toward a Theory of Competitive Heterogeneity," *Strategic Management Journal,* October 2003, pp. 889–902; A. M. Rugman and A. Verbeke, "Edith Penrose's Contribution to the Resource-Based View of Strategic Management," *Strategic Management Journal,* August 2002, pp. 769–80; J. B. Barney, "Looking Inside for Competitive Advantage," *Academy of Management Executive,* November 1995, pp. 49–61; J. B. Barney and E. J. Zajac, "Competitive Organizational Behavior: Toward an Organizationally-Based Theory of Competitive Advantage," *Strategic Management Journal,* Winter 1995, pp. 5–9; R. Ashkenas, "Capability: Strategic Tool for a Competitive Edge," *Journal of Business Strategy,* November–December 1995, pp. 13–15; J. B. Black and K. B. Boal, "Strategic Resources: Traits, Configurations, and Paths to Sustainable Competitive Advantage," *Strategic Management Journal,* Summer 1995, pp. 131–38; B. Wernerfelt, "The Resource-Based View of the Firm: Ten Years After," *Strategic Management Journal,* March 1995, pp. 171–74; D. J. Collis, "Research Notes: How Valuable Are Organizational Capabilities," *Strategic Management Journal,* Winter 1994, pp. 143–52; R. Hall, "A Framework Linking Intangible Resources and Capabilities to Sustainable Competitive Advantage," *Academy of Management Journal,* November 1993, pp. 607–18; M. A. Peteraf, "The Cornerstones of Competitive Advantage: A Resource-Based View," *Strategic Management Journal,* March 1993, pp. 179–91; R. Amit and P. J. H. Schoemaker, "Strategic Assets and Organizational Rent," *Strategic Management Journal,* January 1993, pp. 33–46; R. M. Grant, "The Resource-Based Theory of Competitive Advantage: Implications for Strategy Formulation," *California Management Review,* Spring 1991, pp. 114–35; J. B. Barney, "Firm Resources and Sustained Competitive Advantage," *Journal of Management,* 17, no. 1 (1991), pp. 99–120; K. R. Conner, "A Historical-Based Comparison of Resource-Based Theory and Five Schools of Thought within Industrial Organization Economics: Do We Have a New Theory of the Firm?" *Journal of Management,* 17, no. 1, 1991, pp. 121–154; J. B. Barney, "Asset Stocks and Sustained Competitive Advantage: A Comment," *Management Science,* December 1989, pp. 1511–13; I. Dierickx and K. Cool, "Asset Stock Accumulation and Sustainability of Competitive Advantage," *Management Science,* December 1989, pp. 1504–11; R. P. Rumelt, "Towards a Strategic Theory of the Firm," in R. B. Lamb (ed.), *Competitive Strategic Management* (Upper Saddle River, NJ: Prentice Hall, 1984), pp. 556–70; and B. Wernerfelt, "A Resource-Based View of the Firm," *Strategic Management Journal,* 14 (1984), pp. 4–12.

5. This discussion of the guerrilla view is based on G. Hamel and L. Valikangas, "Zero Trauma—the Essence of Resilience," *Wall Street Journal,* September 16, 2003, p. B2; C. A. Lengnick-Hall and J.A. Wolff, "Similarities and Contradictions in the Core Logic of Three Strategy Research Streams," *Strategic Management Journal,* December 1999, pp. 1109–32; V. Rindova and C. J. Fombrun, "Constructing Competitive Advantage: The Role of Firm-Constituent Interactions," *Strategic Management Journal,* August 1999, pp. 691–710; K. M. Eisenhardt and S. L. Brown, "Patching: Restitching Business Portfolios in Dynamic Markets," *Harvard Business Review,* May–June 1999, pp. 72–81; B. Chakravarthy, "A New Strategy Framework for Coping With Turbulence," *Sloan Management Review,* Winter 1997, pp. 69–82; R. A. D'Aveni, *Hypercompetition: Managing the Dynamics of Strategic Maneuvering* (New York: Free Press, 1994); D. J. Collis, "Research Note: How Valuable Are Organizational Capabilities?" *Strategic Management Journal,* Winter Special Issue, 1994, pp. 143–52; and K. M. Eisenhardt, "Making Fast Strategic Decisions in High-Velocity Environments," *Academy of Management Journal,* December 1989, pp. 543–76.

6. J. B. Barney, "Looking Inside for Competitive Advantage," *Academy of Management Executive,* November 1995, pp. 49–61.

7. "10 Driving Principles of the New Economy," *Business 2.0,* March 2000, pp. 191–284; M. J. Mandel, "The New Economy," *Business Week,* January 31, 2000, pp. 73–77; "The Internet Age," *Business Week,* October 4, 1999, pp. 69–202; G. J. Church, "The Economy of the Future," *Time,* October 4, 1999, pp. 77–79; P. Coy and N. Gross, "21 Ideas for the 21st Century," *Business Week,* August 30, 1999, pp. 78–162; C. V. Callahan and B. R. Pasternack, "Corporate Strategy in the Digital Age," *Strategy and Business,* Second Quarter 1999, pp. 10–14; N. D. Schwartz, "The Tech Boom Will Keep on Rocking," *Fortune,* February 15, 1999, pp. 64–80; and D. B. Yoffie and M. A. Cusumano, "Judo Strategy: The Competitive Dynamics of Internet Time," *Harvard Business Review,* January–February 1999, pp. 71–81.

8. R. S. Boyd, "World Choking on a Deluge of Data," *Springfield News Leader,* February 22, 2004, p. 5A.

9. P. F. Drucker, *Post-Capitalist Society* (New York: Harper Business, 1993).

10. S. Kerr and D. Ulrich, "Creating the Boundaryless Organization: The Radical Reconstruction of Organizational Capabilities," *Planning Review,* September–October 1995, pp. 43–62.

11. D. Kirkpatrick, "Why 'Bottom-Up' Is on Its Way Up," *Fortune,* January 26, 2004, p. 54; W. Brian Arthur, "Why Tech Is Still the Future," *Fortune,* November 24, 2003, pp. 119–27; A. M. Webber, "Economic Optimism Rises," *USA Today,* July 15, 2003, p. 13A; and J. Collins, "How Great Companies Tame Technology," *Newsweek,* April 29, 2002, p. 51.

12. Information from the U.S. Patent and Trade Office Web site, **www.uspto.gov**, March 5, 2004; and M. J. Mandel, "You Ain't Seen Nothing Yet," *Business Week,* August 31, 1998, pp. 60–63.

13. S. A. Zahra, "The Changing Rules of Global Competitiveness in the 21st Century," *Academy of Management Executive,* February 1999, pp. 36–42; J. A. Petrick, R. F. Shcere, J. D. Brodzinski, J. F. Quinn, and M. F. Ainina, "Global Leadership Skills and Reputational Capital: Intangible Resources for Sustainable Competitive Advantage," *Academy of Management Executive,* February 1999, pp. 58–69; and H. Thomas, T. Pollock, and P. Gorman, "Global Strategic Analyses: Frameworks and Approaches," *Academy of Management Executive,* February 1999, pp. 70–82.

14. R. W. Oliver, *The Shape of Things to Come: 7 Imperatives for Winning in the New World of Business* (New York: McGraw-Hill Business Week Books, 1999), p. 23.

15. "Workplace Security," Special section of *Wall Street Journal,* September 29, 2003, pp. R1–R7; D. Kirkpatrick, "Taking Back the Net," *Fortune,* September 29, 2003, pp. 117–22; T. Purdum, "Preparing for the Worst," *Industry Week,* January 2003, pp. 53–55; and S. Leibs, "Lesson from 9/11: It's Not about Data," *CFO,* September 2002, pp. 31–32.

16. B. C. Reimann, "The New Strategic Leadership: Driving Change, Getting Results!" *Planning Review,* September–October 1994, pp. 6–8.

17. "People Power: Enlisting the Agents of Change," *Chief Executive,* May 1995, p. 516.

18. This definition is based on T. M. Amabile, "A Model of Creativity and Innovation in Organizations," in B. M. Staw and L. L. Cummings (eds.), *Research in Organizational Behavior,* Vol. 10 (Greenwich, CT: JAI Press, 1988), p. 126.

19. R. M. Hodgetts, F. Luthans, and S. M. Lee, "New Paradigm Organizations: From Total Quality to Learning to World Class," *Organizational Dynamics,* Winter 1994, pp. 4–19.

20. S. F. Marino, "Where There Is No Visionary, Companies Falter," *Industry Week,* March 15, 1999, p. 20; D. I. Silvers, "Vision—Not Just for CEOs," *Management Quarterly,* Winter 1994–1995, pp. 10–14.

21. L. Larwood, C. M. Falbe, M. P. Kriger, and P. Miesing, "Structure and Meaning of Organizational Vision," *Academy of Management Journal,* June 1995, pp. 740–69; and S. L. Oswald, K. W. Mossholder, and S. G. Harris, "Vision Salience and Strategic Involvement: Implications for Psychological Attachment to Organization and Job," *Strategic Management Journal,* July 1994, pp. 477–89.

22. D. I. Silvers, "Vision—Not Just for CEOs."

23. AMA 2002 Corporate Values Survey," American Management Association Web site, **www.amanet.org**, October 30, 2002.

24. D. J. Wood, "Corporate Social Performance Revisited," *Academy of Management Review,* October 1991, pp. 691–718.

25. M. Friedman, *Capitalism and Freedom* (Chicago: University of Chicago Press, 1962).

26. L. D. Lerner and G. E. Fryxell, "CEO Stakeholder Attitudes and Corporate Social Activity in the *Fortune* 500," *Business and Society,* April 1994, pp. 58–81.

27. E. Laise, "A Few Good Companies," *Smart Money,* January 2004, pp. 25–27; and P. W. Roberts and G. R. Dowling, "Corporate Reputation and Sustained Superior Financial Performance," *Strategic Management Journal,* December 2002, pp. 1077–93.

28. M. Conlin, J. Hempel, J. Tanzer, and D. Polek, "The Corporate Donors," *Business Week,* December 1, 2003, pp. 92–96.

29. D. Haralson and A. Lewis, "Teens Question Executives' Ethics," *USA Today,* November 11, 2003, p. 1B.

30. L. T. Hosmer, "Strategic Planning as if Ethics Mattered," *Strategic Management Journal,* Summer 1994, pp. 17–34; L. S. Paine, "Managing for Organizational Integrity," *Harvard Business Review,* March–April 1994, pp. 106–17; and A. E. Singer, "Strategy as Moral Philosophy," *Strategic Management Journal,* March 1994, pp. 192–213.

31. M. M. Crossan and I. Berdrow, "Organizational Learning and Strategic Renewal," *Strategic Management Journal,* November 2003, pp. 1087–1105; V. Dimovski, *Organizational Learning and Competitive Advantage: A Theoretical and Empirical Analysis.* Dissertation, Cleveland State University, March 1994; and A. P. DeGeus, "Planning as Learning," *Harvard Business Review,* March–April, 1988, pp. 70–74.

32. M. M. Crossan, H. W. Lane, and R. E. White, "An Organizational Learning Framework: From Intuition to Institution," *Academy of Management Review,* July 1999, pp. 522–37.

33. S. L. Mintz, "A Knowing Glance," *CFO,* February 2000, pp. 52–61; N. Bontis, "Managing an Organizational Learning System by Aligning Stocks and Flows of Knowledge," *Academy of Management Proceedings,* CD-ROM, BPS, J1–J6.

3

Assessing Opportunities and Threats

DOING AN EXTERNAL ANALYSIS

LEARNING OUTLINE

What Is an External Analysis?

- *Differentiate between external opportunities and threats.*

- *Describe how organizations are open systems.*

- *Distinguish between the environment as information perspective and the environment as source of resources perspective.*

- *Explain how an external analysis is more than just scanning the environment.*

How Do You Do an External Analysis?

- *Describe the components in an organization's specific environment.*

- *Explain each of the forces in Porter's five forces model.*

- *Describe the components in an organization's general environment.*

- *Discuss what types of external information strategic managers need and where they might find this information.*

- *Describe the type of external information managers at different levels might need.*

Why Do an External Analysis?

- *Explain the benefits of doing an external analysis.*

- *Explain the challenges of doing an external analysis.*

Dressing Up

The retail department store industry is one of the toughest industries in which to compete. However, Kohl's Corporation has found a way to succeed.[1] Kohl's is one of the fastest-growing and most successful department store chains in the United States. The company, with 2003 revenues of $9.1 billion (up almost 22 percent over 2002), operates over 600 discount department stores in 38 states. Although most of its stores are located in the Midwest, the company is aggressively moving into the western and southern United States. To continue its retailing successes, it's important that Kohl's understand the changing needs of its customers.

Over the last few years, customers have become disillusioned with the overall shopping experience at many retail establishments. Long checkout lines, missing or vague product information, out-of-stock products, incorrect price tags, and scarce and often unknowledgeable sales staff have made the shopping experience quite unpleasant. Local shopping malls with their anchor department stores have lost much of their popularity with shoppers. Unlike these other retail department stores, Kohl's has followed a different path to meeting its customers' needs.

Kohl's strategic approach is built around convenience and price. The typical Kohl's is a boxlike structure with one floor of merchandise under inexpensive lighting where shoppers use carts as they browse through the simple racks and shelves of clothing, shoes, and home apparel merchandise. The company is especially selective with regards to store location. Everything about the way Kohl's does business—who it sells to and how those customers shop—hinges on where it puts its stores. Its major goal is to set up shop in the heart of "soccer mom country." It typically avoids malls when looking at store sites, believing that its target customers—young mothers—typically don't have the time for a long drive to a mall location and certainly don't want parking hassles when they do go shopping. Kohl's usually goes for free-standing buildings with smaller parking lots in retailing power centers (a retailing destination where several large, specialty brand retailers often locate together) and other kinds of strip malls. For instance, the Kohl's store in Springfield, Missouri, is located adjacent to a Wal-Mart

Super Center, a Home Depot, a McDonald's, a Michael's hobby and crafts store, and a number of casual dining restaurants. The company's target market is women ages 25 to 54 who have children and whose annual household incomes range from $35,000 to $75,000. Even the merchandise selection offered at Kohl's is aimed at this target demographic, selling casual brands (such as Sag Harbor, Villager, Union Bay, Haggar, Jockey, HealthTex, and others) at low prices.

Although Kohl's has done well in a difficult industry, it's facing some serious challenges. Rivals, ranging from J.C. Penney and Sears to Macy's, have copied Kohl's approach. These competitors have made their stores easier to navigate and enhanced their selections of casual brands. Most of all, they've cut prices to counter the advantage of Kohl's locations, trying to lure back shoppers to malls with better prices. Even specialty retailers such as Old Navy (a unit of Gap, Inc.) and American Eagle have shifted from trendy teenage fashion toward clothing that appeals to moms. And on the discount end, Wal-Mart has added national brands and improved the quality of its apparel. These competitor actions and other external trends will keep strategic decision makers at Kohl's on their toes for quite a while!

This chapter-opening case illustrates how strategic decision makers can profit when they pay attention to changes in the external environment and why they must continue to monitor those changes. As the case points out, external environmental factors can significantly affect companies' strategic decisions and actions. Being alert to changing trends in different external factors such as customer tastes and habits, what competitors are doing, and even technology is an important step in formulating effective strategies. In this chapter, we'll look at the process of external analysis by first describing what an external analysis is. Then, we'll look at the details of how to do an external analysis and how to identify positive and negative aspects of the environment. Finally, we'll discuss why doing an external analysis is so important in managing strategically and why managers at all levels of the organization need to know how to understand and analyze what's happening outside the boundaries of their organizations.

WHAT IS AN EXTERNAL ANALYSIS?

After 50-plus years of steady growth, sales of french fries declined almost 10 percent last year.[2] Although fries continue to be a popular side dish when eating out, a 10 percent decline gets the attention of strategic decision makers! Several factors believed to be contributing to the decline include healthier eating habits, the switch to salads, cancer concerns, aging baby boomers, and the growing popularity of nonfried foods. Fast-food companies and potato growers must continue to monitor such trends, which is what external analysis is all about.

An **external analysis** is the process of scanning and evaluating an organization's various external environmental sectors to determine positive and negative trends that could impact organizational performance. It's how strategic managers determine the opportunities and threats that face their organizations. **Opportunities** are positive external trends or changes that may help the organization improve its performance. **Threats**, in contrast, are negative external trends or changes that may hinder the organization's performance. In assessing an organization's current situation, it's important to know what's happening in the external environment so you can design new strategies or change current strategies to take advantage of opportunities and avoid threats. You can see where external analysis fits into the strategic management in action process in Figure 3.1.

Organizations as Open Systems

The fact that an organization interacts with its environment can be traced to the concept of organizations as open systems. Systems theory comes from the physical sciences and

Figure 3.1

Strategic Management in Action

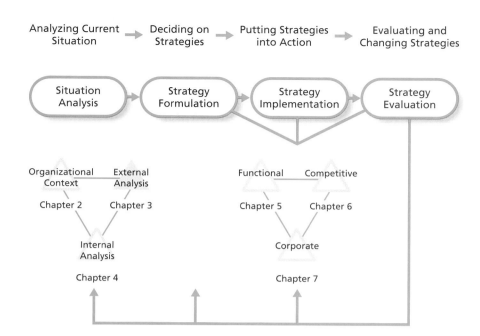

studies of living organisms. Physical scientists view living organisms as systems whose various parts (or subsystems) are interrelated, interdependent, and function as a whole. As an open system, these living organisms interact with their environment by taking in sustenance and other inputs and giving off outputs such as energy, waste, or other by-products. This is similar to what happens in organizations as they take in inputs and process those inputs into outputs. In fact, Chester Barnard, an early management theorist, first suggested back in 1938 that organizations functioned as systems.[3] However, it took several years for Barnard's ideas about organizations as systems to be accepted in mainstream management theory.

Although viewing organizations as systems—and specifically, open systems—seems entirely logical to us today, it wasn't until the late 1950s that various organizational researchers finally saw the wisdom of Barnard's concepts and suggested that organizations could be viewed as systems.[4] In other words, organizations, too, had interrelated and interdependent parts (departments or divisions) that functioned as a whole. Any changes in any subsystem would affect the other subsystems. For instance, if a change is made in marketing, it influences what happens in manufacturing, accounting, human resources, or any other functional area. Also, organizations could be viewed as open systems in much the same way a living organism was an open system. Inputs to be processed have to come from somewhere and the outputs must be distributed somewhere. That "somewhere" is the external environment. Thus, when we say that an organization is an **open system**, we mean that it interacts with and responds to its external environment. As an open system, an organization is impacted by the environment and can also impact that environment. Figure 3.2 shows a simple example of an organization as an open system.

Perspectives on Organizational Environments

As the external environment changes, strategic decision makers may choose to respond to these new, and often vastly different, circumstances. The belief that an organization interacted with its environment has been the catalyst behind attempts by organizational researchers to describe and understand organizational environments and their potential impact on an organization's performance. The various studies of organizational environments can be summarized from two different perspectives: (1) environment as a

Figure 3.2 *Organization as an Open System*

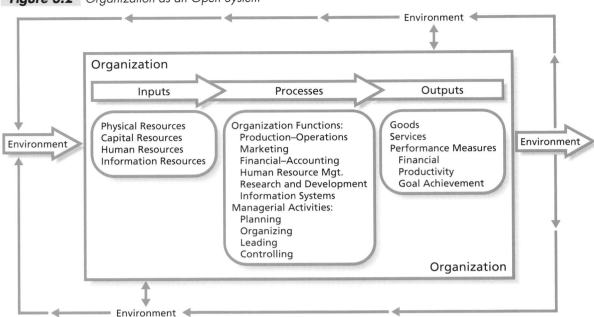

source of information and (2) environment as a source of resources. To help you better understand the impact of the environment on an organization and its ultimate performance, let's look at these perspectives more closely.

Environment as Information Perspective

In this approach to organizational environments, the environment is viewed as a source of information for decision making.[5] A key element of this approach is the idea of **environmental uncertainty**, which is defined as the amount of change and complexity in an organization's environment. What do we mean by these terms? The amount of change occurring in an organization's environment can be characterized as either dynamic or stable. If the organization's environment is changing rapidly, it's classified as a more dynamic one. If changes are minimal or slow in occurring, the environment is a more stable one. For instance, the environmental changes taking place in the oil refining industry are not as rapid as those, say, in the cell phone service industry. Therefore, the cell phone service industry would be considered more dynamic than the oil refining industry. Similarly, if decision makers must monitor a number of components in the environment, that environment is considered to be complex. If the number of environmental components is few, it's a simple environment. The more complex and dynamic the environment, the more uncertain it is, and the more information that decision makers need about the environment to make appropriate decisions. According to this perspective, then, the perceived uncertainty of the environment (amount of change and complexity) dictates the amount and types of information that managers need about that environment. Where do strategic decision makers get that information? They get it from doing an external analysis—in other words, the environment serves as a source of information.

Environment as Source of Resources Perspective

In this approach, the environment is viewed as a source of scarce and necessary resources that are sought by competing organizations.[6] As the environment becomes more "hostile" (i.e., resources become harder to obtain and control), organizations are subjected to greater

Carlos Gutierrez took over the job of CEO at Kellogg Company in April 1999 at a time when the company was struggling with aggressive competitors and changing consumer eating habits. Prior to Gutierrez's appointment as CEO, Kellogg had launched a substantial global expansion and had eliminated about 25 percent of its U.S. salaried workforce. As if these issues weren't enough to deal with, cereal competitor General Mills had closed the gap with Kellogg in U.S. market share and at one point took over the number one spot from Kellogg for a short period of time. So Gutierrez had several significant strategic challenges to deal with. One of the first things he did was respond to the rapidly expanding consumer trend toward healthier breakfast food by acquiring privately held Kashi Company, a natural-cereal and convenience-foods company based in California. Kashi had grown 100 percent during 1999, and consumers were jumping at the opportunity to taste its products made from a blend of

sesame and whole grains. Through this acquisition, Kellogg learned Kashi's trade secrets *and* expanded its presence in the cereal aisle. And the natural-cereal company complemented Kellogg's other natural-foods division, veggie-burger-maker Morningstar Farms, which it got as part of its purchase of Worthington Foods in 1999. But the biggest strategic move for Gutierrez was his acquisition of Keebler Foods Company in March 2001. This acquisition helped Kellogg diversify its product offerings in the United States and fit perfectly into its brand-building strategy. It took a few years, but Gutierrez positioned Kellogg to compete more effectively in the food aisle. Have the strategies worked? Revenues in 2003 were up 6.1 percent and profits were up 9.2 percent in a tough market. How does this example illustrate the environment as information perspective?

Sources: *Hoover's Online*, **www.hoovers.com**, *March 6, 2004; and N. Hudson, "He's Grrreat!" Hispanic Business, January–February 2004, pp. 26–28.*

uncertainty. Given these uncertain conditions, managers look for ways to acquire and control those critical resources. They do so by monitoring the environment and making appropriate decisions based on what they see happening, keeping in mind that the environment is the source of those scarce resources.

The main points of each approach to organizational environments are summarized in Table 3.1. These two different perspectives on how managers can view the organization's environment provide us with a basic understanding of what's involved in an external analysis. Yet, how *can* managers determine what's happening in the external environments? That's where environmental scanning comes in.

ENVIRONMENT AS SOURCE OF INFORMATION

- Environment viewed as source of information
- Environments differ in amount of uncertainty
- Uncertainty is determined by complexity and rate of change
- Reducing uncertainty means obtaining information
- Amount of uncertainty determines amount and types of information needed
- Information obtained by analyzing external environment

ENVIRONMENT AS SOURCE OF RESOURCES

- Environment viewed as source of scarce and valued resources
- Organizations depend on the environment for these resources
- Resources are sought by competing organizations
- Dependency is determined by difficulty of obtaining and controlling resources
- Reducing dependency means controlling environmental resources
- Controlling environmental resources means knowing about the environment and attempting to change or influence it

Table 3.1

Summary of Two Perspectives on Environment

Source: *Based on Richard A. Bettis and Michael A. Hitt, "The New Competitive Landscape," Strategic Management Journal, Summer 1995, pp. 7–19.*

Environmental Scanning and External Analysis

One impression we get from the previous discussion of both perspectives on organizational environments is that it's important for strategic decision makers to engage in environmental scanning—to know what's happening in the external environment, whether we see the environment as a source of information, as a source of scarce resources, or as a source of both. Strategic decision makers must be on the lookout for environmental changes, because their ability to recognize and anticipate environmental changes plays a key role in shaping the organization's future by limiting or opening up strategic options. However, what does it mean to recognize and anticipate environmental changes? It means scanning the environment and evaluating what the various data and trends mean to the organization. Note that it's not enough just to know what's happening in the organization's environment—you also need to *assess,* to evaluate, what this information means for your organization. In other words, you need to do an external analysis and determine the opportunities and threats facing your organization. For example, look back at the chapter-opening case. Based upon their recognition *and* assessment of customer and competitor trends, strategic decision makers at Kohl's chose strategies that appealed to their target market.

Learning Review

- What is an external analysis and what does it show managers?
- How is an organization an open system? How does this relate to external analysis?
- What does each of the perspectives on organizational environments say?
- What is environmental uncertainty and what role does it play in external analysis?
- Why does a manager need to do more than just scan the environment?

HOW DO YOU DO AN EXTERNAL ANALYSIS?

Now that we know *what* an external analysis is, we need to look specifically at *how* you do one. What exactly do managers need to look for when they do an external analysis? Where can you find information about the external environment and how do you evaluate this information? How do managers at different organizational levels do an external analysis? We explore these topics in this section. When you've finished reading this part of the chapter, you should know how to do an external analysis and determine an organization's opportunities and threats.

External Environmental Sectors

It would be very difficult, if not impossible, to do an effective and comprehensive external analysis without some type of outline or format to follow. In other words, what external sectors need to be examined to identify potential opportunities and threats? An organization's external environment includes sectors that are directly relevant to its strategic decisions and sectors that aren't directly relevant but that must be considered. We're going to classify external sectors as being part of the specific environment or part of the general environment. The **specific environment** describes those external sectors that directly impact the organization's strategic decisions by opening up opportunities or threats. It includes customers, competitors, suppliers, and other important industry–competitive variables. (See Figure 3.3.) The **general environment** refers to those external environmental sectors that indirectly affect the organization's strategic decisions and that may pose opportunities or threats. What does the general environment include? It includes

Figure 3.3

An Organization's External
Environment

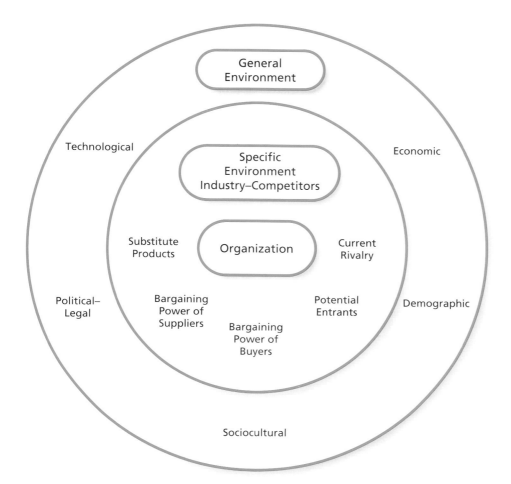

economic, demographic, sociocultural, political–legal, and technological sectors. (See Figure 3.3.) Let's look at each of these environmental sectors. We'll start with the specific environment.

Specific Environment

The specific environment consists of those external sectors that the organization directly interacts with. In other words, the specific environment includes industry and competitive variables. An **industry** can be defined as a group or groups of organizations producing similar or identical products. These organizations also compete for customers to purchase their products and must secure the necessary resources that are converted into products. One frequently used approach for assessing an organization's specific environment is the five forces model developed by Michael Porter.[7] (See Figure 3.4.)

Porter is a renowned strategic management scholar, and his work on industry analysis provides one framework for looking at an organization's specific environment. One assumption of his five forces model is that some industries are inherently more attractive than others; that is, the profit potential for companies in that industry is higher. What influences profit potential? The interaction and strength of these five competitive forces. A strategic decision maker can determine the opportunities and threats in the organization's specific environment by evaluating these five forces. How do you evaluate these five forces

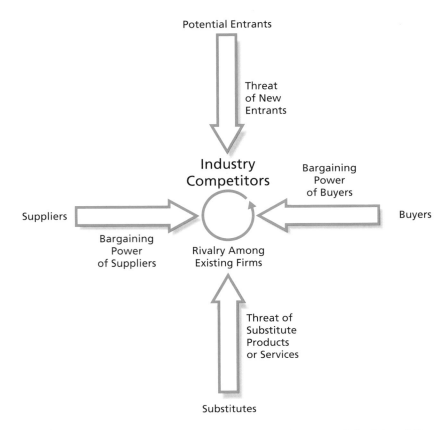

and determine whether they represent opportunities or threats? Let's look carefully at each so you'll know what to look for.

Current Rivalry Among Existing Firms

The existing firms in your industry are your organization's current and direct competitors. These include the organizations already in the industry that produce and market products similar to yours. For instance, in the soft drink industry, Coca Cola, PepsiCo, Cott, Cadbury Schweppes, and Sam's (Wal-Mart's house brand) would be existing firms. In this part of the five forces analysis, we determine the level of rivalry among these current competitors. In other words, how intense is the rivalry? Is it intensely competitive or not? Is it "cutthroat" or "polite"? Are competitors constantly trying to take away customers from each other or do competitors seem to get along with one another? The more intense the rivalry among existing firms, the more that industry profitability, and thus your company's profitability, will suffer.

What affects the level of rivalry? Porter lists eight conditions that contribute to intense rivalry among existing competitors. First is *numerous or equally balanced competitors*. If an industry has a number of competitors, there's a greater likelihood that some of those firms will think they can take competitive actions and no one will notice, thus keeping the industry in constant competitive turmoil. Or, if competitors are equal in terms of size or resources, they'll constantly be jockeying for position, also creating intense competitive action. The second condition is *slow industry growth*. When industry growth has slowed—in other words, consumer demand for our industry's products has leveled off—the "market share pie" isn't getting any bigger. For your company to keep growing means that you're going to have to steal market share away from your competitors. Conditions will be ripe for competitors battling with each other to maintain or increase market share, making the level of rivalry intense. For example, that's what happened in the heavy-duty truck industry when orders for big 18-wheelers declined sharply. Industry competitors such as Navistar International Corporation, Volvo Trucks, PACCAR, DaimlerChrysler, and Renault SA's Mack Truck responded by cutting production with the intent of trimming costs to the bone. When that strategy didn't add to profits, the next step was luring customers from competitors by offering them a better deal. Next is the condition of *high fixed* or *storage costs*. If organizations have high fixed costs, they'll do whatever it takes to operate at capacity and thus spread out those fixed costs over a larger volume. This situation often leads to back-and-forth price cutting by competitors in order to attract customers, which increases competitive rivalry. Also, if the industry's products are difficult or costly to store, companies will want to sell their products as quickly as possible (keeping inventory at the lowest possible levels) and often resort to price cutting to do so. In both instances, price cuts by industry competitors keep profits low. The fourth condition that can lead to intense rivalry is *lack of differentiation* or *switching costs*. If the industry's product is perceived to be a commodity or like a commodity (i.e., not unique in any way), then customers make their purchase decisions largely because of price and service. Both forms of competition lead to intense rivalry. For instance, you might not think that the casual dining industry would face problems of differentiation. After all, industry competitors such as P.F. Chang's, Romano's Macaroni Grill, Olive Garden, and Chili's, have spent significant dollars creating a theme and recreating it in numerous locations. However, it's precisely that endless round of building that's created a problem of differentiation. Every format—American, Italian, Chinese, or Mexican—that's proven successful has been endlessly copied until it's practically impossible to tell the theme restaurants apart. This has created intense competitive rivalry in an attempt to capture consumers' dining-out dollars. Also, if there's no cost (either actual dollars or even the amount of time you'd have to invest to learn about a new product) associated with switching from one competitor's product to another's, then competitive intensity will be high because competitors will be trying to steal customers away from one another. The fifth condition is *capacity must be added in large increments*. In industries where capacity must be added in large increments to be economically feasible, then these capacity additions by competitors can create competitive disruptions. That's because the industry will suffer from overcapacity, which leads to price cutting and intense competitive rivalry. For instance, take the cruise line industry. It used to be that a 1,200-passenger boat was considered enormous. Now, new cruise ships can carry up to 4,400 passengers, and new liner capacity is still being added. If passenger growth slows, there's intense competitive pressure to keep these boats filled. The sixth condition is *diverse competitors*. When competitors differ in their strategic approaches, philosophies, or circumstances, it's hard to judge how competitors are going to act and react as they compete. This diversity increases the level of rivalry. Next is *high strategic stakes,* which means that industry competitors have strong reasons to want to succeed (e.g., CEO's reputation, large dollar investments, etc.) and will do whatever it takes to do so, even so far as sacrificing short-run profitability. If industry competitors feel this way, then rivalry will be high. The last condition is the existence of *high exit barriers*. Porter defines **exit barriers** as "economic, strategic, and emotional factors that keep companies competing in businesses even though they may be earning low or even negative returns on investment."[8] Examples of exit barriers include highly specialized assets that can't be used in other ways or that have low liquidation value; labor agreements that must be honored; or management's unwillingness to leave a business because of pride, fear, or other psychological reasons. If there are high exit barriers, the company is, in a sense, "stuck" in that industry and may use extreme tactics to compete.

One aspect of current rivalry that we need to clarify is "How do you know who your organization's current competitors are?" Obviously, if an industry includes several firms, you may find that not all of those firms are your actual direct competitors or competitors that you'd be concerned with. One solution is to evaluate only the competitors that are

Professional sports are big business, and technology is helping make them even bigger. Interactive technologies are being used in sports arenas to heighten interest among fans. Whereas existing media—visual and audio—bring the action in living color to fans off the field, interactive technologies make it even more up close and intense. Athletes can be outfitted with transmitters embedded in helmets and other equipment that digitize the game, recording speed, movement, and even the force of collisions.

Fans get to experience the action without stepping foot on the field or court. This technology investment can differentiate the various sports franchises and contribute to continuing growth. After all, with continuing consumer interest in sports, strategic decision makers are always looking for strategies that can help differentiate their product.

Source: K. Tan, "Interactive Technology Boosts Sports Business," Wall Street Journal, January 31, 2000, p. B17A.

currently in your organization's strategic group. A **strategic group** is a set of firms with similar strategies, resources, and customers competing within an industry. Strategy researchers have proposed that organizations within a strategic group compete more directly than other organizations that may also be in the industry.[9] For instance, even though Mercedes-Benz and General Motors' Saturn are both in the automobile manufacturing industry, they're not considered direct competitors because they don't use similar strategies, don't have the same customer base, and don't have similar resources. In analyzing the level of current rivalry, it makes sense to look at those organizations whose strategic actions have the most potential to affect your profitability; and that means looking at those competitors in your organization's relevant strategic group.

Potential Entrants

Not only should you be concerned with the opportunities and threats presented by your current competitors, you also need to be on the lookout for others moving into your industry. Why? Because these organizations bring new capacity to the industry, want to gain customers (market share), and perhaps even possess substantial resources that can be used to launch competitive attacks against current competitors. The threat of potential entrants depends on the barriers to entry and the reaction by current competitors to new entrants. **Barriers to entry** are obstacles to entering an industry. When barriers are high or current competitors can be expected to take significant actions to keep newcomers out, then the threat of entry is low. A low threat of potential entrants is positive for an industry because profitability won't be divided up among numerous competitors. What are the major entry barriers? Porter described seven.

1. *Economies of scale.* Economies of scale refers to the cost savings that you get as volume increases. Increasing levels of activity in any of the organization's functions (e.g., production—producing more; marketing—selling more; research and development—innovating more; etc.) can lead to cost savings because the fixed costs are spread out over a larger volume, which drives the cost per unit down. How do economies of scale keep potential entrants out? Strategic decision makers might think twice because they'd either have to come into the industry operating at a large scale and risk retaliation by current competitors or they'd have to come in at a smaller scale and have a cost disadvantage compared with the others.

2. *Cost disadvantages from other than scale.* Established competitors may enjoy cost advantages that potential entrants can't duplicate even if they can operate at large volume. These include factors such as exclusive or protected product technology; favorable access to raw materials; favorable locations; government subsidies; or human resource advantages because of employees' cumulative level of knowledge, learning, and experience.

The Rule of Three

The burger industry has McDonald's, Wendy's, and Burger King. The credit card industry has VISA, MasterCard, and American Express. The athletic footwear industry has Nike, Adidas, and Reebok. What do these industry lists have in common? A phenomenon called the **rule of three**, which argues that competitive forces in an industry, if kept relatively free of government interference or other special circumstances, will inevitably create a situation where three companies dominate.

The premise of the rule of three is that each industry has three large, dominant players; that is, three "full-line generalists" that dominate and hold most of the industry market share. Although there are exceptions (e.g., the soft drink industry with Coca Cola and Pepsi), the rule of three seems to hold true across many different industries. And why three? It seems that two companies tend to lead to monopolistic pricing or mutual destruction, whereas four encourages continual price wars, which can be detrimental. In addition to the big three, there are other firms in the industry that want to be successful. They play the role of "super niche players" by specializing either through product or market segmentation. Finally, there are "ditch dwellers"—

a competitive position held by organizations that are not one of the highly efficient generalist "big three" or one of the highly focused niche players. These firms end up "stuck in the ditch" where competitive position and financial performance are weakest.

This arrangement of generalist firms, specialists, and weak performers has been found to be fairly common across all kinds of industries around the world. For instance, take the discount retail industry. The big three include Wal-Mart, Costco, and Target. The super niche players include Kohl's, TJX (T.J. Maxx and Marshall's), and Walgreen's. In the ditch are Kmart and Mervyn's. In the airline industry, we have the big three (United, American, and Delta), the super niche players (Southwest and Jet Blue), and in the ditch (U.S. Air and Midwest Airlines).

Because the rule of three says that most markets evolve in a cyclical fashion, strategic decision makers must understand where their industry is in that evolutionary process. And that could be an important aspect of analyzing your industry and competition. Think of some other industries and see if the rule of three arrangement is evident.

Sources: J. N. Sheth and R. S. Sisodia, "Competitive Markets and the Rule of Three," Ivey Business Journal, September–October 2002, pp. 1–5; and The Rule of Three: Surviving and Thriving in Competitive Markets (New York: The Free Press, 2002).

3. *Product differentiation.* Current competitors usually have worked hard and spent large sums to establish a specific product identification with customers. If it's strong enough, brand identity differentiates an organization and leads to loyal customers. To overcome this brand loyalty, potential entrants have to spend heavily on customer research, advertising, packaging, and other marketing activities. This can be a significant hurdle for a new competitor wanting to enter an industry. For example, in the sporting goods industry, there's no better differentiator than Sports Authority Inc., the world's largest retail sporting goods chain. Its closest rivals include Dick's Sporting Goods, Wal-Mart, and online retailer, mvp.com. Together, these four competitors have established such strong product differentiation that potential entrants are discouraged from entering the industry.

4. *Capital requirements.* If an organization has to invest significant financial resources in order to compete, this creates a barrier to entry. Potential entrants may think twice about coming into an industry in which high levels of dollars are needed even to be able to compete. Take the ski industry, for example. As customers demanded better amenities at ski sites—good, consistent snow base, groomed trails, comfortable but luxurious accommodations—the capital investment required to satisfy these customer demands rose significantly. Unless potential competitors have that kind of money, they're shut out of the industry.

strategic MANAGEMENT *in action*

The beverage giants (Coke and Pepsi) are at it again. The bottled-water business, long an industry of numerous small regional players, has become an intense battleground for the beverage companies. With the soda business maturing and bottled-water consumption increasing, it's not surprising that Coke and Pepsi want to make a splash in the market. However, they have to cope with the dilemma of getting their water on the shelves without sacrificing space for their cola products. In addition, small regional water bottlers are vulnerable to the giants' marketing tactics. It's an interesting battle. Analyze this situation using the seven barriers to entry from the perspective of the potential entrants *and* from the perspective of current competitors.

Sources: B. McKay, "In a Water Fight, Coke and Pepsi Try Opposite Tacks," Wall Street Journal, April 28, 2002, p. A1; and D. Foust, "Guess Who Wants to Make a Splash in Water," Business Week, March 1, 1999, p. 36.

5. *Switching costs.* Are you familiar with and do you consistently use one word processing package? Maybe it's Word or WordPerfect. What keeps you from using another one or ones? For most of us, it's the time and effort we'd have to invest in learning a new set of commands and keyboard shortcuts. That's an example of **switching costs**—the one-time costs facing the buyer who switches from one supplier's product to another's. These costs don't even necessarily have to be monetary costs. They can be psychological costs associated with change. These switching costs serve as a barrier to entry because the industry's current customers may be reluctant to switch to a new supplier.

6. *Access to distribution channels.* You have a product to sell. You need an outlet or distribution channel for that product. If current competitors have already secured the logical distribution sources, a new entrant is going to have to persuade these sources to accept its product. This may mean you have to give the distributor a price break or set up cooperative advertising arrangements, both of which reduce potential profits. Therefore, closing off access to distribution channels can be a barrier to entry.

7. *Government policy.* If the government imposes laws and regulations (such as licensing requirements, controlling access to raw materials, air/water pollution standards, product safety standards, product testing time requirements, etc.), this can create a barrier to entry. Potential entrants would have to meet these requirements, which often can cost a significant amount.

Learning Review

- What sectors does the specific environment include? How about the general environment?
- What is an industry? How are the organizations in an industry similar? Different?
- What is the five forces model and how is it used?
- What eight factors determine the current level of competitive rivalry?
- What is a strategic group and how does it fit in with the concept of an industry? How does it fit in with the concept of current competitors?
- How do current industry competitors attempt to keep out potential entrants? Why would they want to do so?

Bargaining Power of Buyers

Your buyers are your customers—those individuals or organizations who purchase your products. How can buyers affect industry profitability? If they have a lot of bargaining power, they can force prices down, bargain for higher quality or more services, or they might even play competitors against each other, seeing who will give them the best deal.

What makes a buyer powerful? One factor is that the *buyer purchases large volumes of the seller's product*. The implication in this circumstance is that the customer is more important to the seller than the seller is to the customer. This gives that customer a lot of bargaining power. For instance, Wal-Mart can account for a significant part of many manufacturers' revenues. With this much buying power, Wal-Mart can pretty much dictate selling terms. Another factor that influences a buyer's bargaining power is that the *products purchased by the customer represent a significant portion of its costs or purchases*. In this situation, customers are going to be looking for the best price and will shop around. Customers will also have significant bargaining power if *the products they purchase are standard or undifferentiated*. Here again, a customer will likely play one supplier off against another in an attempt to find the best deal. Another factor that gives buyers greater bargaining power is if they *face few switching costs*. In other words, if there are few switching costs or if switching costs are low, then the customer doesn't feel obligated to stay with the original supplier and can shop around. The buyer may also exert bargaining power if *the buyer earns low profits or has low income levels*. If the customer has low income levels or is earning low profits, the customer is going to look for ways to reduce costs however it can, and that often means reducing the costs of purchasing goods. Another factor that gives the customers bargaining power over the supplier is when *buyers have the ability and resources themselves to manufacture the products they're purchasing from the industry*. If the customer can make the product rather then purchase it, then the customer is in a powerful position to ask for concessions from the supplier. For example, some large businesses that purchase large quantities of electric power from local utilities have threatened to take their business elsewhere unless they get lower rates. Many of these businesses can do just that by either building their own generating plants or persuading a local government to form a municipal system to buy electric power at bulk rates. As customers, these large businesses are exerting power. Buyers also have bargaining power if *the industry's product isn't important to the quality of the buyers' products or services*. What this means is that if the buyers don't need the industry's products to get desired quality levels in their products or services, then the buyer has power to bargain with the industry over prices and services offered. On the other hand, if the industry's product *is* important to the quality of the customer's products, then the customer won't have much bargaining power. Last, buyers have bargaining power if *they have full information* about product demand, actual market prices, and supplier costs. This information gives the customer good ammunition to get the best possible prices from suppliers. The Internet has played a significant role in customers' access to information. Think, for example, of the car industry in which buyers can compare prices and features and bargain for the best deal.

The Grey Zone

How much power do buyers really have? In today's economy, practically anything labeled as "digital" sells. Marketers label products as digital whether they really are or not. Although the term *digital* is defined as anything represented by discrete numerical values instead of approximations, it has become an all-purpose adjective for any product that wants to appear high tech. Movie theaters using old-fashioned reel-to-reel film proclaim themselves as "a digital experience" when they have an expensive sound system. Toasters that use a microprocessor to time browning are labeled digital and sold for twice the price of old-fashioned analog toasters. Is it ethical to call a product digital that really doesn't fit the scientific definition just to get a premium price? Some experts say it's okay because the usage just reaffirms the importance of being digital. What do you think?

Bargaining Power of Suppliers

If your industry's suppliers have bargaining power, they can raise prices or reduce the number of services provided or the quality of products that your industry purchases. An industry's suppliers include any resource providers: raw materials sources, equipment manufacturers, financial institutions, and even labor sources. How can you tell whether your industry's suppliers are powerful? One characteristic to look for is *domination by a few companies and more concentration than the industry.* If suppliers are few in number and are selling to an industry that's fragmented (i.e., the industry has a lot of small and not very powerful companies in it), then the suppliers will usually be able to exert considerable influence over prices, quality, and sales terms. Another characteristic to look for is *whether there any substitute products.* If the supplier has to compete with possible substitutes, then it doesn't have a lot of bargaining power over the industry. But, if there aren't any good substitutes, then the supplier can exert more power over the industry. Suppliers can also exert power when *the industry is not an important customer.* If your industry is just one of many that the supplier sells to, then it could care less whether it keeps you as a customer and is more likely to exert bargaining power. On the other hand, if your industry is an important customer, the supplier will want to protect that relationship and won't try to exert bargaining power. Another characteristic to evaluate is whether *the supplier's product is an important input to your industry.* If it is, then the supplier will have more bargaining power. For example, suppliers of silicon wafers have significant power over the semiconductor industry. Even though silicon is one of the most abundant elements on earth, shortfalls in the availability of silicon wafers affect the ability of chipmakers to satisfy demand for their product. This situation gives suppliers a lot of power over computer chip manufacturers. Also, it's important to know whether *the supplier's products are differentiated or if there are customer switching costs.* If the supplier's products are differentiated or if your industry would experience switching costs, then the supplier is going to be able to exert more power. For example, Department 56 is a well-known manufacturer of miniature ceramic and porcelain buildings used in Christmas decorating. Many of its pieces sell for $50 or more when first issued, but sometimes sell for thousands of dollars after they're no longer available at retail. The company keeps its differentiation strong by eliminating several pieces every year and destroying the molds. When it discovered that some of its dealers (retailers) were discounting the collectibles (a move that Department 56 felt cheapened its image), it terminated their distribution rights as a violation of policy. As a supplier, Department 56 was exerting significant power over the retailers. The final characteristic for determining supplier power is *the supplier's ability to provide the products that your industry is currently providing.* If the supplier can do what your industry does (i.e., produce or market your industry's products) and do it better or cheaper, then this gives the supplier more bargaining power. In other words, if you don't agree to the supplier's terms and conditions, they could start doing what you do and attempt to put you out of business.

Substitute Products

The last of the five industry forces we need to discuss is the threat of substitute products. The best way to evaluate the threat of substitute products is to ask whether there are other industries that can satisfy the consumer need that our industry is satisfying. For instance, take a customer's need for something to drink. If your company is in the cola industry, substitute products, such as fruit drinks, alcoholic beverages, milk or milk-based products, and even mineral water, could come from other industries. Any of these industries could fill the customer's need for something to drink. (Other companies in the cola industry would be your current competitors and would be evaluated as current rivalry.) If there aren't many good substitutes for your industry's product, then this threat isn't very high. However, if there are a few good substitutes, or even several not-so-good substitutes, for your product, then this isn't favorable for your industry's profitability.

Car dealers can't find enough mechanics to do their customers' service work. According to the Bureau of Labor Statistics, dealers will face an annual shortage of over 35,000 technicians through the year 2010. It seems that the stereotypical image of the job as dirty and low paying keeps young people from considering the career. However, this image contradicts the reality that mechanics earn good pay, have job security, and most dealerships have clean and comfortable workplaces. Adding to the problem is that many older mechanics are retiring rather than completing the training needed to work on today's technology-enhanced cars. According to the five forces model, what might the implications of this situation be for industry competitors?

Source: E. Eldridge, "Auto Dealers Face Mechanics Shortfall," USA Today, February 17, 2004, p. B5; **www.usatoday.com**.

By now, you should have a good grasp of what you examine as you look at an organization's specific environment. Porter's five forces model provides one framework for determining the opportunities and threats of the industry and competitive environment. In Table 3.2, you'll find a quick summary of the five forces and what you need to look at as you determine whether the specific industry–competitive environment is favorable or unfavorable.

Industry–Competitive Force	Threat	Opportunity
Current Rivalry		
Numerous competitors	✓	
Few competitors		✓
Equally balanced competitors	✓	
One or a few strong competitors		✓
Industry sales growth slowing	✓	
Industry sales growth strong		✓
High fixed or inventory storage costs	✓	
Low fixed or inventory storage costs		✓
No differentiation or no switching costs	✓	
Significant differentiation or significant switching costs		✓
Large capacity increments required	✓	
Minimal capacity increments required		✓
Diverse competitors	✓	
Similar competitors		✓
High strategic stakes	✓	
Low strategic stakes		✓
High exit barriers	✓	
Minimal exit barriers		✓
Potential Entrants		
Significant economies of scale		✓
No or low economies of scale	✓	
Cost disadvantages from other aspects		✓
No other potential cost disadvantages	✓	
Strong product differentiation		✓
Weak product differentiation	✓	
Huge capital requirements		✓
Minimal capital requirements	✓	
Significant switching costs		✓
Minimal switching costs	✓	
Controlled access to distribution channels		✓
Open access to distribution channels	✓	
Government policy protection		✓
No government policy protection	✓	

Table 3.2

Evaluating the Five Forces

Table 3.2

Continued

Industry–Competitive Force	Threat	Opportunity
Bargaining Power of Buyers		
Buyer purchases large volumes	✓	
Buyer purchases small volumes		✓
Products purchased are significant part of buyer's costs	✓	
Products purchased aren't significant part of buyer's costs		✓
Products purchased are standard or undifferentiated	✓	
Products purchased are highly differentiated and unique		✓
Buyer faces few switching costs	✓	
Buyer faces significant switching costs		✓
Buyer's profits are low	✓	
Buyer's profits are strong		✓
Buyer has ability to manufacture products being purchased	✓	
Buyer doesn't have ability to manufacture products		✓
Industry's products aren't important to quality of buyer's products	✓	
Industry's products are important to quality of buyer's products		✓
Buyers have full information	✓	
Buyers have limited information		✓
Bargaining Power of Suppliers		
Supplying industry has few companies and is more concentrated	✓	
Supplying industry has many companies and is fragmented		✓
There are no substitute products for supplier's products	✓	
There are substitute products for supplier's products		✓
Industry being supplied is not an important customer	✓	
Industry being supplied is an important customer		✓
Supplier's product is an important input to industry	✓	
Supplier's product is not an important input to industry		✓
Supplier's products are differentiated	✓	
Supplier's products aren't differentiated		✓
There are significant switching costs in supplier's products	✓	
There are minimal switching costs in supplier's products		✓
Supplier has ability to do what buying industry does	✓	
Supplier doesn't have ability to do what buying industry does		✓
Substitute Products		
There are few good substitutes	✓	
There are several not-so-good substitutes	✓	
There are no good substitutes		✓

Learning Review

- What makes buyers powerful?
- Why should an industry's competitors be concerned with how much bargaining power customers have?
- What makes suppliers powerful?
- Why should an industry's competitors be concerned with how much bargaining power suppliers have?
- What determines whether substitutes present a threat?
- Why should an industry's competitors be concerned with substitute products?

General Environment

Remember that the general environment includes those external sectors that indirectly influence an organization. The trends in these sectors could have a potential positive impact on the organization (opportunity) or a potential negative impact (threat). However, not everything that happens in these sectors is going to be an opportunity or threat. Many changes that take place won't affect the organization one way or the other. We'll be looking at five main general external sectors: economic, demographic, sociocultural, political–legal, and technological.

Economic

The economic sector encompasses all the macroeconomic data—current statistics, trends, and changes—that reflect what's happening with the economy. It doesn't include the economic statistics of an organization's industry. For instance, industry sales forecasts and trends aren't part of the general economic sector. However, you would look at those statistics in evaluating the industry and competitive environment. So, what *does* the economic sector include? The major economic information that might be important (either positive or negative) includes interest rates; exchange rates and the value of the dollar; budget deficit–surplus; trade deficit–surplus; inflation rates; Gross National Product (GNP) or Gross Domestic Product (GDP) levels and resulting stage of the economic cycle; consumer income, spending, and debt levels; employment–unemployment levels; and workforce productivity. As you examine these economic statistics, you're looking at the current information as well as forecasted trends. You need to determine what impact, if any, these trends will have on your organization. For instance, are rising interest rates good or bad for your organization—in other words, are they opportunities or threats? If the economy is growing moderately, what does this mean for your organization? What if the dollar falls in value against the Chinese yuan or against the euro? Are the implications good or bad? What if workforce productivity has leveled off and is predicted to stay stagnant? What does this mean? Take consumer debt levels. Think for a minute about what industries would be affected positively by increases in consumer debt levels. What industries might suffer? These are the types of questions you need to ask as you evaluate the economic sector for opportunities and threats. And, keep in mind, that industries (and thus the organizations in those industries) will be affected differently by these economic trends and changes. For instance, declining interest rates tend to have a favorable impact on the construction industry, but are less favorable for the bank card industry. Also, keep in mind that every organization in an industry is faced with the same economic trends and changes. That is, the inflation rate doesn't change just because your organization is McDonalds, as opposed to Wendy's. So the ultimate performance of an organization is determined by how it responds to the various economic opportunities and threats—that is, it's determined by the strategies decision makers develop. This is also true for the rest of the general environmental sectors we'll look at.

What if your organization does business globally? How would this change the economic analysis you do? Fortunately, it wouldn't change all that much. The only additional challenge you might face is finding convenient and reliable sources of statistics. However, all of the industrialized, and an increasing number of semi-industrialized countries, collect economic data. The United Nations also collects a variety of economic information about countries. You can find information on GNP or GDP, which provides clues to the stage of the economic cycle and whether the country's economy is growing or contracting. You can also find information on exchange rates, trade figures, interest rates, and inflation rates. Probably the most important economic information you'd want about another country would be inflation rates, interest rates, currency-exchange rates, and consumer income–spending–debt levels. Because these tend to be the most volatile economic factors, upward and downward trends or changes in these figures can significantly affect strategic decisions.

the global perspective

The big names in the global car business—General Motors, Ford, Toyota, and DaimlerChrysler—are excited about India's 1 billion potential drivers. However, it's South Korea's Hyundai Motor Company that has the edge. Hyundai is India's second largest car manufacturer, behind Maruti Udyog, a joint venture between Suzuki Motor and the Indian government that has half the market. Hyundai customized its cars for the Indian market by adapting ideas it got from consumers. For instance, its Atoz model has more headroom, a bigger engine, and better air conditioning to deal with India's unbearably hot summers. And

Hyundai recently introduced its first SUV to the Indian market, the Terracan. As B. V. R. Suddu, president of Hyundai Motor India, says, "Indian consumers don't want to be taken for granted anymore." Do some research on India's economic and demographic trends. (You might try *The World Factbook* available at **www.cia.gov/cia/ publications/factbook**.) What are some of the trends and what implications might these trends have for global companies?

Source: M. Schuman, "How Hyundai Got in the Driver's Seat," Time Global Business, *September 2003, p. A10.*

Demographics

In this general external sector, you'll look at current statistical data and trends in population characteristics. The demographic sector includes the kinds of information that the U.S. Census Bureau gathers: gender, age, income levels, ethnic makeup, education, family composition, geographic location, birth rates, employment status, and so forth. The data collected by the Census Bureau are used by many different types of organizations—government as well as business—in making strategic decisions. As you look at population statistics, what trends do you see in these categories that might affect your organization positively or negatively? For instance, recent census data showed that for the first time in the history of the United States there were more Americans over age 30 than under; that the number of women working outside the home continues to increase and is estimated to reach 65 percent by 2005; that the U.S. population is becoming more educated; and that there are more than 43 million disabled persons (a number that's larger than either the African-American market or the Hispanic market). What strategic implications might these types of population changes have for different organizations?

You might also find it's important to examine the interactions of these variables. For instance, which age group has the fastest-growing incomes? Or, in what geographic locations is there a greater concentration of senior citizens? Or, what is the average level of education of Asian Americans? In fact, one particular population group (another term for this is population *cohort*) that you've probably heard a lot about is the baby boomers. This group typically includes individuals who were born between the years 1946 and 1964. The reason you hear so much about the baby boomers is that there are so many of them. Through every life stage they've entered (going to elementary school, teenage years, climbing the career ladder, and now reaching that midlife threshold age of 50), they've had an enormous impact because of their sheer numbers. Although some experts believe that segmenting markets by age is inappropriate, others say it's a good clue to consumer attitudes and behavior. Other age cohorts besides boomers that have been identified include: the Depression group (born 1912–1921); the World War II group (born 1922–1927); the Postwar group (born 1928–1945); the Generation X, or "zoomers," group (born 1965–1977); and the Generation Y, or baby-boomlet, generation (born 1978–1994). This last group is predicted to be as large as, if not larger than, its boomer parents and might prove to be a source of significant demographic opportunities and threats.

Demographic data can show you these types of population changes and trends. As you can probably guess, this type of information is useful for understanding your current

The New Labels

The traditional categories used by demographers for labeling population groups are being discarded in favor of ones that better reflect the changes taking place in U.S. society. Two powerful demographic forces—aging and diversity—have made many traditional categories irrelevant. Using the latest U.S. Census data and consumer research, Claritas, a San Diego-based firm known for its "geodemographic segmentation," is documenting these important shifts, which include the following:

- *Youth and education trump old money in cities.* The richest city residents are no longer the older and mostly white people.

- *The big money is in the suburbs.* The most affluent population segments are suburban homeowners (couples age 45 and older, middle-age executives with children, and middle-age couples who are usually entrepreneurs).

- *Americans don't need to live in big cities to be urbane.* A number of small urban centers on the edges of large metropolitan areas are home to suburban professionals—wealthy, middle-age couples with two incomes and no kids.

- *Suburbs are going childless.* The aging population is redefining the suburbs as the children of these residents grow up and move out.

- *Young African-American and Hispanic graduates are reviving cities.* These racially and ethnically diverse groups are affluent and socialize across racial lines.

Check out Claritas' Web site (**www.claritas.com**). Click on "You Are Where You Live." Take a look at the different segments (e.g., Microvision, PRIZM, ConneXions, LifeP$YCLE, and so forth) and look at the groups that are identified in those segments. What's your impression? How do you think strategic decision makers might be able to use this information?

Sources: Claritas, **www.claritas.com**, March 3, 2004; and H. El Nasser and P. Overberg, "Old Labels Just Don't Stick in 21st Century," USA Today, December 17, 2003, p. 17A.

customer base and for targeting other potential customers. By examining current and forecasted demographic trends, you can identify positive and negative shifts that you either try to take advantage of or stay away from (i.e., potential opportunities or threats).

Again, what if your organization is currently operating in other countries or is looking to expand globally? How does the need for demographic information change? Obviously, it's going to be important for your organization to have as much demographic information as possible about the global locations you're currently in or thinking about entering. The need for having information about current or potential target customers doesn't change! All industrialized, and most of the larger semi-industrialized countries, collect census information. Also, the United Nations collects a considerable amount of demographic information. However, be aware that in some of the semi-industrialized countries, the collection and statistical analysis of the information might not be as thorough or reliable as census information from the more industrialized nations.

strategic MANAGEMENT *in action*

The nation's fast-growing Hispanic population is attracting the interest of major American corporations. For instance, Kmart has added Mexican-born pop star Thalia to its product line. The "queen of Latin pop" will have her own line of clothing, shoes, and cosmetics. Thalia has a big following among Hispanics in the United States, and Kmart's exclusive line is part of a strategy to win over Hispanic shoppers. What potential drawbacks, if any, might there be to the company's strategy?

Source: J. Muller and W. Zellner, "Kmart Con Salsa—Will It Be Enough?" Business Week, September 9, 2002, p. 46.

Sociocultural

There's more to understanding your current and potential customers than just their physical (demographic) characteristics. You should also know what's going on culturally. In other words, what's your country's culture like and is it changing? What are the traditions, lifestyles, values, attitudes, beliefs, tastes, and patterns of behavior and how are these changing? The sociocultural sector encompasses these aspects. These elements aren't quite as obvious and as easy to determine as the demographic information. Measuring and interpreting people's opinions, values, attitudes, or likes and dislikes tends to be more challenging. However, it's important for strategic decision makers to recognize both the current status and the trends in these types of information. For instance, how would you interpret the results of a *Wall Street Journal* poll that showed 59 percent of the respondents described their lives as busy and 19 percent said their lives were busy to the point of discomfort? What strategic implications (potential opportunities and threats) might this information have?

How can you determine what's happening in the sociocultural sector? Look at the values and attitudes being expressed by people. For instance, we can identify some of the basic values that characterize the U.S. culture, such as individual freedom, the work ethic, and equality of opportunity. These values influence people's behavior in the way they shop, work, raise their families, and otherwise live their lives. People's attitudes also influence their behavior. For example, male shoppers have traditionally relied on catalogs for purchasing hobby, electronic, and automotive items, but not clothing. But, they're willing to use the Internet to buy clothes. This change in attitude would be an opportunity for some industries and a threat for others. Some of the more noticeable attitudinal changes over the last few years (please note that this is by no means an exhaustive list of every relevant social change) would include the increasing fear of crime, violence, and terrorism; more acceptance of gambling and gaming activities; more emphasis on religion and spiritual activities, particularly by baby boomers; and increasing use of technology in schools, homes, and workplaces.

In evaluating this sector, you'd also want to look for changes or trends in people's activities, behavior, and purchases. For example, look at how Kraft, the country's largest food maker, responded to customers' changing attitudes about food. Overall, people were demanding healthier versions of their favorite foods. Citing rising obesity rates, strategic decision makers at Kraft (maker of Oreo cookies, Ritz crackers, Oscar Mayer meats, and Velveeta cheese) decided to scale back calories, salt, and saturated and trans fats in many of its snack food products. Kraft's managers recognized a sociocultural trend, evaluated how they could combat it, and developed alternative products. And Kraft wasn't the only food purveyor to start offering healthier foods. McDonald's switched to vegetable oil to limit the amount of artery-clogging trans fats in its french fries. Pizza Hut brought out a healthier pizza that has half the cheese of regular pizza and more tomato sauce. And Subway decided to make its kids' meals healthier by eliminating the cookie and soft drink in favor of a fruit roll up and a carton of 100 percent juice. Another sociocultural trend that many organizations have recognized and changed marketing strategies to take advantage of is the increasingly diverse U.S. population and the different behaviors, attitudes, and values expressed by these diverse groups. In this sector, then, you're looking for those cultural and behavioral trends and changes that present potential opportunities and threats.

How does the importance of this sector change if you're in different global locations? It doesn't. You're obviously going to want this type of information. However, getting and interpreting this information for different global locations isn't as easy as getting economic and demographic information. That's because there's no standard governmental collection of this type of information. Keep in mind that each country has its own distinctive culture—its own generally accepted traditions, lifestyles, values, attitudes, beliefs, tastes, and patterns of behavior. Your challenge, then, is to understand each country's culture. In addition to knowing the current culture, you'd also want to try to uncover any trends or

Hallmark Cards has been quite successful at "reading" social trends and translating those trends into greeting cards. That's why company strategists, aware of the demographic reality of 78 million baby boomers hitting age 50, created a line of cards (birthday, friendship, thinking of you, anniversary, etc.) designed to "subtly flatter the aging boomer's flagging middle-aged ego"—a line they called "Time of Your Life." They decided to display the line in its own separate section of Hallmark stores and to use advertising displays showing middle-aged people looking youthful in active settings. A Hallmark spokesperson said, "We had done a lot of research showing that baby boomers don't want to get old, but that if it's going to happen, they want to emphasize the positive side of aging." However, what Hallmark failed to understand is that given a choice between shopping in the regular greeting cards section and shopping in a special 50-plus section, potential customers, of course, chose the regular cards. After a miserable two years of sales, the company scrapped the line.

Go to Hallmark's Web site (**www.hallmark.com**). Click on "About Hallmark" and then the "Pressroom." There you'll find a category called "Trends and Products." Click on it. What trends are described there? How might these trends affect strategies at Hallmark?

Sources: *Hallmark,* **www.hallmark.com**, *March 6, 2004; and P. Paul, "Sell It to the Psyche," Inside Business, October 2003, Time Bonus section, p. A2.*

changes—again, so you can determine potential opportunities and threats. For example, how would European consumers' increased willingness to use credit cards affect an organization's strategies? What implications might such a trend have for different industries?

Political–Legal

In this general environmental sector, you'll be looking at the various laws, regulations, judicial decisions, and political forces that are currently in effect at the federal, state, and local levels of government. It might also include regulations enacted by professional associations (such as FASB—the Financial Accounting Standards Board). Some of the more significant federal laws and regulations for businesses and other types of organizations are shown in Table 3.3. You'd also want to keep track of any potential legal, regulatory, and political changes or pending judicial decisions that could impact your organization. For instance, the Occupational Safety and Health Administration (OSHA) has been working to establish ergonomic (jobs and tools designed to fit the physical and psychological limits of workers) guidelines for workplaces, including home offices. What impact might such guidelines have on different industries? What industries would benefit (i.e., be an opportunity)? Which ones might suffer (i.e., be a threat)? Also, a country's political–legal climate can affect the attitudes toward business and how much regulation an industry faces. For instance, deregulation removed a number of operating constraints and created both opportunities and threats for organizations in industries such as trucking, phone service, banking, and others. Other major aspects of the political–legal sector are taxation and minimum wage laws. Obviously, the prevailing laws governing these two areas can have a significant impact on an organization's financial performance. However, it's not only the federal laws and regulations that you have to be aware of. Many states have laws and regulations that present opportunities and threats as well. For instance, as people's attitudes toward gambling and gaming have softened, more and more states have created state-run lotteries and allowed riverboat casinos and other forms of gaming activities to operate. Also, all U.S. states have income tax laws, sales tax laws, or both, which can be sources of opportunities and threats for organizations. Likewise, if they're applicable or could have a significant impact on your organization, you should be aware of any local laws, regulations, or political–legal actions.

Obviously, if your organization is operating in another country, you need to know the relevant laws and regulations and abide by them. In addition, you'd want to stay on top of political changes as far as who or what political party is in power and the likelihood that

Internet Sales Taxes

Taxes. The Internet. The two realities were once worlds apart, but 20 states now have a line on their income tax forms asking filers to declare what sales tax they owe from purchasing products online. By law, residents are supposed to pay sales taxes to their states if they order merchandise by mail or online from businesses based elsewhere. But very few ever followed the rule, especially when it came to Internet sales. This is a controversial political issue that needs to be resolved. Proponents of Internet sales taxes include most state governments and traditional bricks-and-mortar retailers. Opponents include e-tailers and most consumers who purchase on the Internet. It's an interesting debate. Research the issue and come up with a bulleted list of items supporting both sides. Be prepared to take one side and debate it in class. Be sure to look at how organizational strategies might have to change if Internet sales are taxed.

Sources: M. Gormley, "More States Seek Sales Taxes Due on E-Commerce," The Kansas City Star, March 4, 2004, p. C2.; J. Novack, "Uncle Sam Watching the Web," ABC News, www.abcnew.go.com, February 3, 2004; and H. Gleckman, "The Great Internet Tax Debate," Business Week, March 27, 2000, pp. 228–236.

Table 3.3

Examples of Significant Legislation Affecting Organizations

OCCUPATIONAL SAFETY AND HEALTH ACT OF 1970
Requires employers to provide a working environment free from hazards to health.

CONSUMER PRODUCT SAFETY ACT OF 1972
Sets standards on selected products, requires warning labels, and orders product recalls.

EQUAL EMPLOYMENT OPPORTUNITY ACT OF 1972
Forbids discrimination in all areas of employer–employee relations.

WORKER ADJUSTMENT AND RETRAINING NOTIFICATION ACT OF 1988
Requires employers with 100 or more employees to provide 60 days' notice before a facility closing or mass layoff.

AMERICANS WITH DISABILITIES ACT OF 1990
Prohibits employers from discriminating against individuals with physical or mental disabilities or the chronically ill; also requires organizations to reasonably accommodate these individuals.

CIVIL RIGHTS ACT OF 1991
Reaffirms and tightens prohibition of discrimination; permits individuals to sue for punitive damages in cases of intentional discrimination.

FAMILY AND MEDICAL LEAVE ACT OF 1993
Grants 12 weeks of unpaid leave each year to employees for the birth or adoption of a child or the care of a spouse, child, or parent with a serious health condition; covers organizations with 50 or more employees.

NORTH AMERICAN FREE TRADE AGREEMENT OF 1993
Creates a free trade zone between the United States, Canada, and Mexico.

U.S. ECONOMIC ESPIONAGE ACT OF 1996
Makes theft or misappropriation of trade secrets a federal crime.

SARBANES-OXLEY ACT OF 2002
Holds businesses to higher standards of disclosure and corporate governance.

Scientists have known for years that the element silver can kill germs. Now, medical companies are looking at new ways to use silver's antibacterial properties in products such as surgical threads, bandages, and even in the clothing that health care professionals wear. Although corporate giants such as Dow Chemical, DuPont, and Smith & Nephew are pursuing product development in this area, a small Pennsylvania company called Noble Fiber Technologies is leading the pack. It has licensed its brand of silver-coated fibers (called X-Static) to more than 100 manufacturers, including Adidas, Spyder, and Johnson & Johnson. Besides its antibacterial properties, X-Static also acts as an antistatic and a heat conductor, two other chemical properties of silver. In addition to the medical market, X-Static is being used in workout gear. The U.S. Army bought 5.5 million pairs of socks containing X-Static, and five teams in the 2002 Olympics wore uniforms made with X-Static fibers.

Source: S. Kitchens, "Silver Bullet," Forbes, November 10, 2003, pp. 110–12.

new laws and regulations might be enacted. Although political stability is a given in most countries, there still are some where the political situation is volatile and unstable. You should watch these trends as well. Another significant change in the global environment is the various trade alliances among countries. These alliances—such as the North American Free Trade Agreement (NAFTA), the European Union, the Free Trade Area of the Americas (FTAA), and the Association of Southeast Asian Nations (ASEAN)—are easing many of the political and economic restrictions on trade and creating numerous opportunities and threats. These types of global political changes are sources of global political–legal opportunities and threats.

Technological

The last general environmental sector to be analyzed concerns technological trends and changes. Within the technological sector, you'd look for scientific or technological improvements, advancements, and innovations that create opportunities and threats for your organization, especially as they relate to the organization's products or work processes. For instance, communications companies are using the latest technology to explore the untapped portions of the radio spectrum and are moving into such applications as car crash-avoidance radar or using infrared to send data over short lines of sight. Obviously, as technology advances, these types of applications will become commonplace. An even more routine application of technology can be seen in the ways that companies are advertising their products. It's common now to see computerized information kiosks and Internet multimedia pages extolling the virtues of products. The two organizational areas impacted most by technological innovations concern the product and process. In other words, how will technological advancements affect your organization's products (positively or negatively)? Likewise, how will technological advancements affect the way you produce your products (the process)?

One of the biggest technological advancements that's affected organizational work processes has been the continuing computerization of an organization's activities. For example, retailers have direct computer links to suppliers that replenish inventory as needed. Manufacturers have flexible manufacturing systems that allow them to mass customize products. Airlines have Web pages where customers can arrange flight times, destinations, and fares. Most organizational employees communicate by e-mail. In addition, continuing innovations in different scientific and engineering fields such as lasers, robotics, biotechnology, food additives, medicine, consumer electronics, and telecommunications provide numerous opportunities and threats for many different industries. However, keep in mind that the impact of these technological innovations is different for different industries. Some of these improvements may not offer opportunities or threats to your organization, whereas others are significant. For instance, how will technological innovations such as smart cards, 3D computing, and satellite imaging affect different industries? Some other interesting technological trends that have the potential to change life include genetics-based medicines, personalized computers, multifuel automobiles, high-definition TV, home health monitors, smart maps and tracking devices, smart materials, and weight-control and anti-aging products. These are the types of technological changes and trends you'll need to uncover as you do your external analysis.

How would your analysis of the technological sector differ if your organization was operating globally? Obviously, a country's level of technological advancement is going to affect your assessment. Some countries don't have the needed infrastructure to support available technology. For instance, the phone system or telecommunications system may be unreliable or dated. Or, the power (electricity) generation system may be insufficient to support the technological requirements. A country's highway system may be in poor shape or not be conveniently located. Many variables affect whether a given technology will prove to be an opportunity or a threat to your organization in another global location. For example, what would appear to be a dream market—personal computers for China's billion-plus population—has been a nightmare for computer companies. Why? Because the Chinese language would require a keyboard the size of a kitchen table. The challenge for computer companies has been to figure out strategies to deal with this technological barrier. As this example illustrates, however, it's important to assess the potential technological opportunities and threats that face your organization in another country.

Learning Review

- What are the five components of the general environment?
- What are some types of economic information that you might need to consider?
- What does the demographics sector include?
- What types of information are you looking at in the sociocultural sector?
- Describe what the political–legal sector includes.
- What should you look for as you examine the technological sector?
- How would you analyze global general environmental sectors?

Finding Information on the External Environment and Evaluating It

Now that you know what external sectors to look at, how do you know what to look for and where to find information? Let's first discuss what to look for. You should look for specific data, statistics, analyses, trends, predictions, forecasts, inferences or statements made by experts, or other types of evidence of what's happening or predicted to happen in the sectors. You then need to evaluate whether this specific information is good or bad for your organization. Will it help your organization improve its performance currently or in the future or will it hinder its performance? In other words, does the current external environment present opportunities or threats to your organization? How about the changes or trends? These bits and pieces of information about the external environment are used by decision makers as they evaluate current strategies and design future ones.

The approach to finding external information can range all the way from informal, unscientific observations to a formal, systematic search. For many decision makers, it's enough to talk to customers, read industry trade journals or general news magazines, or talk with suppliers' sales representatives. These informal, unscientific information-gathering activities often provide sufficient clues to the trends taking place in certain

Spotting Trends

Spotting trends can be a good skill for strategic decision makers, and there's no more difficult age group to attempt to pin down as far as what they're thinking than teenagers! They may be fickle and unpredictable, but they're an enormous and attractive market because they control significant purchasing power (estimated between $120 billion and $150 billion a year and growing at a 6 percent annual rate). For companies that market products to teens, however, spotting trends is a real art *and* science. How do they do it? One thing they've discovered is that **focus groups** (a marketing research tool in which an informal group of people, with the help of a moderator, discuss a product or service and other marketing issues) don't work with teens. In group settings, teens tend to clam up, joke around, or harass the moderator. Also, asking teens direct questions about their likes and dislikes typically results in useless information. What does work are tactics such as arming teens with disposable cameras and asking them to shoot pictures of things in their lives or asking them to complete drawings that say things like "This is a snapshot of you. Tell us more about you—what you like, wear, listen to, read, say!" Another approach is having teens match a list of products (restaurants, clothes, etc.) with the celebrities they think are likely to be using the products. Others have tried stealth teen sales forces or "buzz agents" that get their friends and family to try products. And some trend spotters have tried "crib chats," in which a researcher goes to kids' houses and videotapes them talking about whatever they're interested in. These approaches to finding information can provide strategic decision makers with significant insights into what elusive teenage minds are thinking.

Sources: M. Wells, "Kid Nabbing," Forbes, February 2, 2004, pp. 84–88; L. Grossman, "The Quest for Cool," Time, September 8, 2003, pp. 48–54; and T. Delaney, "Smells Like Teen Spirit," Smart Money, September 2003, pp. 108–13.

sectors of the external environment, from which strategic decision makers can make effective strategic decisions based on rather limited information. However, a thorough and comprehensive external analysis requires more of a systematic, deliberate search. In fact, having some type of formal external information system is the key to identifying specific opportunities and threats. An **external information system (EIS)** is an information system that provides managers with needed external information on a regular basis. Again, keep in mind that the whole purpose of the external analysis is to identify potential trends and changes that could positively or negatively impact your organization's performance. How often is a "regular" basis—in other words, how often do decision makers need information about external sectors? It depends on how complex and dynamic your organization's environment is. The more complex and dynamic the environment (i.e., the more environmental uncertainty there is), the more often you'd want information about what's occurring. For some organizations in highly complex and very dynamic industries, this might be as often as once a month. For others, gathering and assessing external information twice a year would be enough. In some situations, once a year might be often enough to provide needed external information. No matter how uncertain the external environment is, if decision makers find that their current strategies aren't working (getting desired results), they're going to do something about them. As you know from the strategic management in action model, one of the steps in formulating appropriate strategies is determining opportunities and threats by doing an external analysis. A key concern is where to find information on the various external sectors.

Doing an external analysis isn't as difficult as it may sound! You may feel that you're going to have to spend hours locating and interpreting information. Actually, you're going to find that the problem isn't that there's *not enough* information. The problem is that there's *too much* information. What you have to do, then, is approach it systematically. For each of the external sectors, ask yourself what specific information you think you need, keeping in mind that industries differ in terms of the potential impact of these external trends. For instance, in the economic sector, you may decide that interest rates will have a significant impact on your industry, so you'd want to find out current and forecasted interest rates. If your target customers are teenage girls, you'd probably want to know the demographic and sociocultural trends for this particular group. Study each external sector carefully and identify what information you'll want in order to make intelligent strategic decisions. As a strategic decision maker, you'll come to recognize what external information is truly important to your strategic decisions and what you'll want to concentrate your external analysis on. Rather than describing each and every source of information for the various external sectors (the list would constantly change and could potentially go on and on), Table 3.4 lists some useful information sources on each of the external sectors. Although most of these sources can be found in any library, you might choose to find information online. Some of these sources are listed as well.

Table 3.4

Selected Sources of External Information

INDUSTRY–COMPETITORS
Reports published by industry trade associations
Industry outlooks presented in various business periodicals (*Business Week, Fortune, Forbes, Wall Street Journal*)
Standard & Poor's Industry Surveys: Trends and Projections
Survey of Current Business
Census of Manufacturers
U.S. Industrial Outlook
Predicasts Basebook and Predicasts Forecasts
Moody's Manuals
Market Share Reporter
Encyclopedia of Business Information Sources
Various industry sourcebooks and industry-specific publications

WEB SITES

Hoover's Online	**www.hoovers.com**
New York Stock Exchange	**www.nyse.com**
Investor Home	**www.investorhome.com**
Bloomberg	**www.bloomberg.com**
Yahoo!	**www.yahoo.com**

ECONOMIC
Economic Report of the President
World Fact Book
Economic Indicators
Consumer Confidence Survey
Economic Outlook by U.S. Chamber of Commerce
Economic Times
Standard & Poor's Industry Surveys
International Economic Outlook by Union Bank of Switzerland
Predicasts Forecasts
U.S. Industrial Outlook
World Economic Survey by United Nations
Census of Retail Trade
Census of Manufacturing

WEB SITES

Bureau of Labor Statistics	**stats.bls.gov**
Board of Governors of the Federal Reserve System	**www.bog.frb.fed.us**
EDGAR Database	**www.sec.gov/edgar**
Federal Reserve Bank of New York	**www.ny.frb.org**

Federal Reserve Bank of St. Louis	**www.stls.frb.org**
Export-Import Bank of the United States	**www.exim.gov**
Fedstats	**www.fedstats.gov**
STAT-USA	**www.stat-usa.gov**
Economic Statistics Briefing Room	**www.whitehouse.gov/fsbr/esbr.html**
Census Bureau	**www.census.gov**
U.S. Securities and Exchange Commission	**www.sec.gov**
Wall Street Research Net	**www.wsrn.com**
Statistical Abstract of the United States	**www.census.gov/statab/www/**

DEMOGRAPHIC

U.S. Bureau of the Census publications
Statistical Abstract of the United States
Demographic Yearbook by United Nations
Statistical Abstract of the World
Statistical Yearbook
Productivity Measures for Selected Industries and Government Services

WEB SITES

American Demographics	**www.demographics.com**
BLS	**stats.bls.gov**
Current Population Survey	**www.census.gov**
Fedstats	**www.fedstats.gov**
Statistical Abstract of the United States	**www.census.gov/statab/www/**
STAT-USA	**www.stat-usa.gov**
Census Bureau	**www.census.gov**
Department of Labor	**www.dol.gov**

SOCIOCULTURAL

Publications by U.S. Department of Labor, Bureau of Labor Statistics
Statistical Abstract of the United States
Survey of Consumers by the University of Michigan's Institute of Social Research
Statistical Abstract of the World

WEB SITES

Advertising Age	**www.adage.com**
Fedstats	**www.fedstats.gov**
Generational Research	**tomorrowtoday.biz/generations/**
Trendsetters	**www.trendsetters.com/trendscape/index.html**

POLITICAL–LEGAL

Congressional Reports
Reports published by industry trade associations

WEB SITES

Federal Trade Commission	**www.ftc.gov**
Library of Congress	**lcweb.loc.gov**
OSHA	**www.osha.gov**
Department of State	**www.state.gov**
Environmental Protection Agency	**www.epa.gov**
Findlaw	**www.findlaw.com/index.html**

TECHNOLOGICAL

Inside U.S. Business: A Concise Encyclopedia of Leading Industries
Predicasts Forecasts
Reports published by industry trade associations

Table 3.4

Continued

GLOBAL
The Big Emerging Markets Outlook and Sourcebook
Demographic Yearbook
Statistical Abstract of the World
Statistical Yearbook

WEB SITES

CIA World Factbook	**www.odci.gov/cia/publications/ factbook**
Export-Import Bank of the United States	**www.exim.gov**
U.S. Customs Service	**www.customs.ustreas.gov**
U.S. Department of State	**www.state.gov**
United Nations	**www.un.org**

Responsibilities for External Analysis at Different Managerial Levels

Obviously, an organization's size is going to determine the number of management levels. In small and even some medium-sized organizations, there may be only one or two levels. If your organization is structured like this, it's important that all employees be encouraged to monitor changes in the specific (industry–competitive) environment. In fact, in many smaller organizations, front-line employees often have the most direct interactions with customers and supplier representatives. Depending on the situation, they may even have some contact with competitors. These employees on the "firing line" often hear comments or statements from these outside people. They should be educated about the importance of knowing what's happening in the organization's external environment and should understand the importance of this type of information to strategic decision making. If they hear any comments that appear important or possibly indicate changing circumstances, they should share that information with managers. The managers can then determine if the situation warrants further study and possible strategy changes. If the organization is large enough to have functional area managers, they should be responsible for monitoring any trends or changes in their particular areas that could be potential opportunities or threats. Also, there should be someone in the organization (the owner, general manager, or someone else) who monitors changes in the general environmental sectors. In effect, then, all of the external environmental sectors are monitored and evaluated even in smaller or medium-sized organizations.

In large organizations, it's not possible to do a simple, single external analysis. There are too many organizational levels and too many variables. However, this doesn't mean that you don't do one. Rather, it becomes even more important to involve all levels in monitoring information and making this information available for strategic decision making. Just like smaller organizations, managers at lower (supervisory) levels in large organizations should encourage workers to listen to what customers are saying (compliments or complaints) or to what suppliers' sales representatives are saying. For instance, customer service employees often are an important source of information about changing customer trends. This type of information about the specific environment can point out the need to change strategies, particularly at functional levels. Middle managers should coordinate any external information provided from the different functional departments or divisional units and share this information with other organizational units that might benefit. The role of the middle manager in external analysis is to act more as an information gatherer and disseminator. Also, middle managers might monitor changes in general environmental sectors that are particularly important to their specific circumstances and use this information to make any

needed strategic changes. That leaves top-level managers. Because of their broad perspective on situations, top-level managers see the "whole" picture. As part of establishing the organization's future direction, top-level managers should evaluate external opportunities and threats. Information about possible opportunities and threats (in either the specific or the general environmental sectors) flows up from other organizational levels. If the organization has a strategic planning department responsible for doing external analysis—in other words, a more formalized strategic planning process—this information is probably monitored and compiled there.

No matter what organizational level you're on, you'll be involved in some aspect of external analysis. That's further verification of one of this book's premises—that everyone in the organization is involved in managing strategically.

WHY DO AN EXTERNAL ANALYSIS?

By now, you should have a pretty good feel for what an external analysis is and how one is done, but you still may not be convinced of the necessity for knowing what's happening in your organization's external environment. In this section, we're going to look at *why* you need to do an external analysis. We also want to look at some of the challenges of doing an external analysis.

Benefits of Doing an External Analysis

We've already mentioned that the reason for doing an external analysis is to identify potential opportunities and threats facing your organization. If you didn't examine, monitor, and evaluate the external changes and trends taking place, how could you pinpoint those opportunities and threats? It's not as if these changes would never impact your organization's performance. They would, but instead of being on top of what's taking place, you'd constantly be reacting to changes. By deliberately and systematically analyzing the external environment, you're going to be a **proactive manager**—a manager who anticipates changes and plans for those changes accordingly. In fact, a proactive manager may, at times, be able to influence various external environmental sectors to the organization's benefit (i.e., encourage changes that would affect the organization's performance positively). For instance, lobbying is one way managers can proactively manage their external environment. However, there are other reasons why an external analysis is important.

One reason is that the external analysis provides the information that strategic managers use in planning, decision making, and strategy formulation.[10] Think back to our discussion of the "environment as information" perspective. One real value of studying the external environment is the information it provides. This information is useful to the extent that strategic decision makers can determine ways to take advantage of the positive changes and ways to buffer against or adapt to the negative changes; that is, strategic decision makers can change the organization's strategies. The organization's strategies should be based on information about markets, customers, technology, and so forth.[11] Because an organization's environment is changing continually, having information about the various external sectors is important so that decision makers can formulate strategies that "align" the organization with its environment.

The "environment as source of resources" perspective also provides another reason for doing an external analysis. Your organization's ability to acquire and control needed resources depends on having strategies that take advantage of the environment's abundant resources and strategies that cope with the environment's limited resources.[12] Think back to our description of an organization as an open system. Because the organization depends on the environment as a source of inputs (resources) and as an outlet for outputs, it only makes sense that we'd want to design organizational strategies that allow us to get the resources we need so we can convert those resources into desired outputs. We can do that most effectively by understanding what the environment has to offer.

Another reason for doing an external analysis is the realization that today's external environment is increasingly dynamic. Turbulent market conditions, fragmented markets, less brand loyalty, more demanding customers, rapid changes in technology, and intense global competition are just a few of the realities of today's business environment. And, these types of conditions aren't the exception—they're the norm. All sizes and all types of organizations are facing increasingly dynamic environments. To effectively cope with these significant changes, managers need to examine the environment.[13]

Our final reason for doing an external analysis relates to whether doing so really makes a difference. In other words, what difference does an external analysis really make in the way an organization performs? The answer is that it *does* appear to make a difference. Various research studies generally have shown that in organizations where strategic decision makers did external analyses, performance was higher.[14] Performance was typically evaluated using a financial measure such as return on assets or growth in profitability. The fact that doing an external analysis appears to make a difference in performance results is a pretty good reason for wanting to know how to do one and to actually do it as part of the strategic management process.

Challenges of Doing an External Analysis

You might encounter some problems as you do an external analysis. For one thing, the environment might be changing more rapidly than you realistically can keep up with. For example, in the mid- to late 1990s when Internet usage absolutely exploded, it seemed that technological advances, new competitors, more customers (users), and debates over possible regulations were happening faster than anyone could completely comprehend. This type of rapid change isn't just a characteristic of high-tech industries—it's happening in many industries. So, just keeping track of the current situation and trends or changes can be a challenge.

Another challenge of doing an external analysis is the amount of time it can consume. We've established that systematically examining and evaluating the environment is important; yet it takes time to do it, and most strategic decision makers are busy managing and don't feel they have the time. However, the fact remains that an external analysis *is* an important part of managing strategically. The key is to make the process as efficient and effective as possible. This may mean doing things such as identifying significant external sectors and monitoring those more frequently and other sectors not as frequently; relying on specialized database searches, news clipping services, or even personalized Internet searches to monitor changes in those significant sectors; or even sharing the responsibilities for analyzing the external sectors with others in the organization. After all, many employees interact in some way with the external environment, especially through customer or supplier contacts, and can be encouraged to communicate what they hear or read about.

Finally, we need to point out the shortcomings of forecasts and trend analyses because they are a significant part of the external analysis. Forecasts aren't fact. They're the best predictions that experts have about what they believe is going to happen. For instance, you've probably had the experience of leaving your home without a coat and umbrella after listening to the weather forecast for a sunny, warm day only to be greeted by a cold, pouring rain. Forecasts of business, economic, or attitudinal trends aren't always accurate either. However, the key for strategic decision makers is to be flexible, open, and alert to changing circumstances. Strategic management is an ongoing process. Strategies don't always succeed, for whatever reason. Maybe results fall short because of some internal shortcoming or maybe because the predictions made about external opportunities and threats were inaccurate. Whatever the reason, we change the strategies as needed to take advantage of new information. Therefore, even though forecasts, predictions, and trend analyses aren't always 100 percent accurate, they can provide us with a sense of the strategic direction we need to go. Even given the shortcomings, that's a pretty good reason to continue to look at them.

Learning Review

- What should you be looking for as you examine the specific and general environmental sectors?
- How can managers approach finding external information? How can they determine what approach they need to take?
- What are some information sources for each of the external sectors?
- How does external analysis change for different managerial levels?
- List some benefits of doing an external analysis.
- What are some challenges associated with doing an external analysis?

the bottom line

- An **external analysis** is the process of scanning and evaluating an organization's various external environmental sectors to determine positive and negative trends that could impact organizational performance.

- **Opportunities** are positive external environmental trends or changes that may help the organization improve its performance.

- **Threats** are negative external environmental trends or changes that may hinder the organization's performance.

- The belief that an organization interacts with its environment can be traced back to the concept of organizations as **open systems**, which means that the organization interacts with and responds to its external environment.

- Two perspectives on organizational environments are the environment as a source of information and the environment as a source of resources.

- A key aspect of the environment as information perspective is the concept of **environmental uncertainty**, which is the amount of change and complexity in an organization's environment.

- The more complex and dynamic the environment, the more uncertain it is, and the more information decision makers need to be able to make appropriate decisions.

- The main idea behind the perspective of the environment as a source of resources is that as the environment becomes more hostile (i.e., resources become harder to obtain and control), the more that managers need to monitor the environment and make appropriate decisions based on what they see.

- It's important for strategic decision makers to engage in environmental scanning—to know what's happening in the external environment.

- An organization's environment can be divided into the **specific environment** (those external environmental sectors that directly impact the organization's strategic decisions by opening up opportunities or threats) and the **general environment** (those external environmental sectors that indirectly affect the organization's strategic decisions and may pose opportunities or threats).

- The specific environment includes industry and competitive variables.

- An **industry** is a group or groups of organizations producing similar or identical products and who also compete for customers and resources.

- The five forces model developed by Michael Porter is one way to assess an organization's specific environment.

- The five forces assessed for relevant opportunities and threats are current rivalry among existing firms, potential entrants, bargaining power of buyers, bargaining power of suppliers, and substitute products.

- Eight conditions affect the level of current rivalry: numerous or equally balanced competitors, slow industry growth, high fixed or storage costs, lack of differentiation or switching costs, capacity must be added in large increments, diverse competitors, high strategic stakes, and high **exit barriers** (factors that keep companies competing in businesses even though they may be earning low or even negative returns).

- One way to determine your current rivalry is by looking at your **strategic group**—a set of firms competing within an industry that have similar strategies, resources, and customers.

- The **rule of three** is a phenomenon of industry arrangement that argues that competitive forces in an industry, if kept relatively free of government interference or other special circumstances, will inevitably create a situation where three companies dominate.

- The threat of potential entrants is determined by the **barriers to entry**— obstacles to entering an industry.

- The seven major entry barriers include economies of scale, cost disadvantages from other than scale, product differentiation, capital requirements, **switching costs** (the one-time financial or psychological costs facing a buyer who switches from one product to another), access to distribution channels, and government policy.

- Buyers' bargaining power is determined by the following factors: buyer purchases large volumes of the seller's product, products purchased by the customer represent a significant portion of the buyer's costs or purchases, products purchased are standard or undifferentiated, few switching costs, low profits/income, buyers have the ability and resources to manufacture the products they're purchasing, product isn't important to quality of buyers' products, and availability of full information.

- Suppliers' bargaining power is determined by the following factors: domination by a few companies and more concentration than the buying industry, whether there are substitute products, buying industry is not an important customer, supplier's product is an important input to buying industry, supplier's products are differentiated or there are switching costs, and the supplier's ability to provide products that buying industry is currently providing.

- The threat of substitute products is determined by the availability of a number of good or not-so-good substitutes.

- The general environment includes five main sectors: economic, demographic, sociocultural, political–legal, and technological.

- The economic sector encompasses all the macroeconomic data, including current statistics, trends, and changes, that reflect what's happening with the economy.

- The demographic sector includes data and trends in population characteristics such as gender, age, ethnic makeup, education, family composition, and so forth.

- The sociocultural sector includes information about society's traditions, lifestyles, values, attitudes, beliefs, tastes, and patterns of behavior.

- The political–legal sector includes the various laws, regulations, judicial decisions, and political forces currently in effect at the federal, state, and local levels of government. It may also include regulations enacted by professional associations.

- The technological segment includes scientific or technological improvements, advancements, and innovations in products or processes.

- In doing an external analysis, you should look for specific data, statistics, analyses, trends, predictions, forecasts, inferences or statements made by experts, or other types of evidence of what's happening or predicted to happen in the various external sectors. Then, you must assess whether these changes are good (opportunities) or bad (threats) for your organization.

- One approach to spotting trends is using **focus groups**—a marketing research tool in which an informal group of people, with the help of a moderator, discusses a product or service and other marketing issues.

- The approaches to finding external information can range from informal, unscientific observations to a formal, systematic search.

- Some type of **external information system (EIS)** is necessary. This is an information system that provides managers with needed external information on a regular basis.

- **Competitor intelligence** is one type of environmental scanning that seeks to identify who competitors are, what they're doing, and how their actions will affect your organization.

- Doing an external analysis isn't as difficult as it sounds. Just ask yourself what specific information you think you should know. Study each external sector carefully and identify what information you'll want to make good strategic decisions.

- The size of your organization will affect who does what type of external analysis.

- The benefits of doing an external analysis are as follows: It allows you to be able to pinpoint opportunities and threats; it makes you a **proactive manager**—a manager who anticipates changes and plans for those changes; it provides the information that strategic decision makers use in planning, decision making, and strategy formulation; it allows the organization to better monitor sources of needed resources; it allows strategic decision makers to be better able to cope with the increasingly dynamic environment; and finally, it does appear to make a difference in how well an organization performs.

- The challenges of doing an external analysis are that the dynamic nature of the environment can be hard to keep track of; it can take a lot of time; and forecasts and trend analyses aren't always accurate.

1. Inflation is an economic fact of life. Yet, businesses, consumers, strategic decision makers, and investors nearly everywhere in the developed world are confronting economies with low to no inflation. What are the strategic implications of a low- or no-inflation economy? What industries might find significant opportunities in such an environment? What industries might face significant threats? Explain your choices.

2. Children, aged 6 to 10, are proving to be as picky about their fashions as teenagers are. Although children have always used fashion to fit in with their peers, their desire to match the clothing that's popular among older siblings and even young adults is rising. Their tastes are no longer the cute and innocent (hearts, teddy bears, angels, and bunnies). They want the clothes, jewelry, and shoes that pop music stars and teen actors and actresses are wearing. What are the implications (opportunities and threats) for clothing manufacturers? For retailers (specialty, discount, and department store)?

3. A study for the U.S. Department of Labor completed by the Rand Corporation, a think tank based in Santa Monica, California, showed that in the future the nation's workforce will be smaller, more diverse, more mobile, and more vulnerable to global competition. What implications (positive and negative) do these trends have for organizational strategies?

4. The demographic trend of an aging baby boom generation, combined with stagnating financial markets, has forced many people to delay retirement, creating some interesting strategic scenarios, not only in marketing opportunities and threats, but also in the area of human resources. What opportunities and threats do you see in this convergence of demographic factors? How might these opportunities and threats change for different industries?

5. Understanding an industry's profit pools is an interesting twist in industry analysis. What are *profit pools*? They're the total profits earned in an industry at all points along its value chain. (The value chain consists of all the activities that add "value" to a product or service, from inputs to outputs.) Determining profit pools involves looking at your suppliers' suppliers and their suppliers, as well as at your customers' customers and their customers. By examining all aspects of a product or service from raw material to final destination, proponents of profit pool analysis say that you can identify where the money is actually being made and make better strategic decisions. Do some research on profit pools (another term often used is *profit zones*). Summarize your findings in a bulleted list format. What are the implications of such profit pools (or profit zones) for industry and competitor analysis?

6. Two of the major competitors in the fast food industry—Wendy's and McDonald's—have positioned themselves differently. Wendy's has taken the adult approach, practically ignoring the children's market with its advertising tie-ins and toy giveaways. McDonald's has pursued the kids' market. Think about demographic and sociocultural trends and changes. How would each organization's interpretation of these trends and changes affect its choice of strategy? Which organization do you think is positioned better? Explain your choice.

7. A survey listed the top U.S. values (most important listed first): protecting the family, honesty, stable personal relationships, self-esteem, freedom, friendship, and respecting one's ancestors. What are the strategic implications of such findings? Would these implications change for different industries? If so, how? If not, why not?

Strategic Management in Action Cases

CASE #1: Dressing Up

This Strategic Management in Action Case can be found at the beginning of Chapter 3.

Discussion Questions

1. What external trends were strategic managers at Kohl's having to deal with? In addition to these trends, what other external areas might be important to these managers? How might they keep track of changes?

2. If you were a strategic decision maker at Kohl's headquarters, what types of external information would you want? What if you were a Kohl's store manager? What types of external information would you want?

3. Do you think that Kohl's strategic decision makers have done a good job of scanning and assessing the environment? Explain.

4. What conclusion(s) about opportunities and threats can you draw from this case?

CASE #2: Going After Generation Y

"We are going to own this generation." These words reflect the not-so-subtle philosophy of dELiA*s (**www.delias.com** and Alloy **www.alloy.com**). Together, they have become one of the most formidable forces in Generation Y retailing. (In September 2003, dELiA*s was acquired by rival Alloy, Inc.) If you've never heard of dELiA*s or Alloy, you're probably not a teenager or around them.

These two companies sell a variety of trendy clothing, accessories, and home furnishings to young girls and boys between the ages of 10 to 24 through approximately 70 dELiA*s stores, catalogs, and their Web sites. Alloy's revenues—almost $300 million in 2003—come from selling merchandise through its Web site and from sponsorships and advertising on that Web site. Alloy also owns and operates more than 8,200 display media boards on high school and college campuses. The companies' urban fashions appeal to girls and guys everywhere. And with a database of over 25 million names and 8.5 million registered users on their Web sites, Alloy and dELiA*s have incredible points of contact with large numbers of kids who have significant purchasing power.

The companies attract and keep their target customers in different ways. First, they design and market clothes that parents raise their eyebrows at. Also, their catalogs show these fashions with models who look like regular teenagers, not the glamorous fashion types, which heightens the appeal. And the companies' youthful image isn't just a public persona. Most of the company's employees are under the age of 30. Their phone representatives—who are mostly high school and college students—do more than take orders. They also offer fashion tips and advice. One retailing analyst described the companies as speaking the language of their consumers. They don't use mass-market advertising, which Generation Y consumers tend to distrust. Instead, they get their message out with hot Web sites.

The companies' goal is to become the leading Generation Y media, direct marketing, and marketing services company. Their philosophy is that the business is defined by customers, not by product categories. They foresee a time when they will help their customers get their first credit cards, first car loan, and first mortgage. "We'll follow them and broaden our offerings."

Discussion Questions

1. What general environmental trends, statistics, analyses, and so forth might strategic decision makers at Alloy and dELiA*s be particularly interested in? Where could they find this information?

2. What do you think is meant by the statement that the business is defined by its customers, not by product categories? What implications does this statement have for assessing external opportunities and threats?

3. What types of competitive information might Alloy's and dELiA*s strategic decision makers want? Would the strategic groups concept be useful for such uniquely positioned companies? If so, what companies might you place in their strategic group? If not, what competitors do you think they might have? How did you choose these competitors?

4. Do some research on Generation Y. What are their demographics? How about their sociocultural characteristics? Now, check out dELiA*s Web site and Alloy's Web site. If possible, get a copy of a catalog. How are the companies attempting to appeal to Generation Y? Would you say they're doing a good job of appealing to this generation? How might they have to change their strategies as this generation ages?

Sources: Information on dELiA*s and Alloy from Hoovers Online, **www.hoovers.com**, March 7, 2004; dELiA*s, **www.delias.com**, March 7, 2004; Alloy, **www.alloy.com**, March 7, 2004; and E. Neuborne and K. Kerwin, "Generation Y," *Business Week*, February 15, 1999, pp. 80–88.

CASE #3: Being the Best

As the nation's leading consumer electronics retailer, Best Buy *is* trying to be the best. And by responding to changing trends, it's trying something new in the process—the fourth major evolution in the chain's history.

Best Buy was founded under the name Sound of Music in 1966 as a home and car stereo store by Dick Schulze (who still remains as board chairman), who got fed up working for his father who would never listen to his ideas on how to improve the family's electronics distribution business. However, while chairing a school board in the early 1980s, Schulze realized that his target customer group—15- to 18-year-old males—was declining sharply, and he decided to broaden his product line and target older and more affluent customers by offering appliances and VCRs—the first major evolutionary change. A tornado wiped out his entire store in 1981 (but not the inventory). Schulze decided to spend his entire marketing budget on advertising a huge parking lot sale. The successful sale taught him the importance of strong advertising, wide selection, and low prices—lessons that would serve him well as he built his business. In 1983, Schulze changed the name to Best Buy and began to open larger superstores. The store format change and the fast-rising popularity of VCRs led to rapid growth. The number of stores grew from 8 to 24, and revenues skyrocketed from $29 million to $240 million.

In 1989, Schulze introduced the warehouse-like store format—the second major evolutionary change. By setting up stores so that customers could browse where they wanted, the company was able to reduce the number of employees, a real cost-saver. Larger store formats were introduced in 1994, and the company kept opening new stores. By 1997, the company realized that it had overextended itself with its expansion efforts, the super-sized stores, and costly consumer financing promotions. In response, the company went through a massive makeover, scaling back expansion plans and doing away with its "no money down, no monthly payments, no interest" program.

In 1999, Best Buy went through its third major evolutionary change as digital electronics began to flood the market. Store formats now highlighted digital products and featured stations for computer software and DVD demonstrations. They also decided to branch out into audio and video stores by acquiring the Magnolia Hi-Fi chain of stores and The Musicland Group (Sam Goody Stores, Suncoast, On Cue, and Media Play music stores). This strategy would turn out to be a mistake, and Best Buy sold off that entire subsidiary in June 2003.

In 2004, the company was working on its fourth major evolution—a focus on bundling high-end electronics with service and installation, without giving up the low prices. The strategy is risky. Best Buy's CEO, Brad Anderson admits as much, stating, "Nobody has been able to do this before. If we can only figure out the puzzle." Why are they messing with a successful formula? Because Anderson sees trouble ahead. The company's store base is maturing. Imports are flooding the market and shorter product life cycles are exerting severe price pressures on some of the

Strategic Management in Action

company's most profitable products—digital TVs, cameras, and home entertainment systems. And then there's Wal-Mart. Its share of the electronics market has gone from 6.9 percent in 1996 to 11 percent. Anderson says, "If we do nothing, Wal-Mart will surpass us by the simple fact they're adding more stores than we are each year." Best Buy can't win by "trying to chase the customer out of Wal-Mart." However, Best Buy does feel that if it can't compete on merchandise, it can compete with add-on services. In addition, Best Buy is tapping into private-label goods. It opened an office in Shanghai in September 2003 that will allow it to source products directly. And it's initiated a massive effort to identify and serve its most profitable shoppers (a process it's calling "customer centricity") by upgrading products, adding to staff, and remodeling stores.

Best Buy's strategic moves are not without risk. However, because the retail environment continues to change, doing nothing isn't a feasible option.

Discussion Questions

1. What examples of environmental scanning do you see in this case? What role do you think environmental scanning has played in the company's evolution? What role will it need to play in the company's future?

2. Using Porter's five forces model and the information in the case, do a brief industry–competitive analysis.

3. What types of information do you think Schulze and Anderson might want from each of the five general environmental sectors? (You don't need to look up this information. Just indicate what trends they would probably want to keep track of.)

4. What opportunities and threats do you think are facing this industry?

5. Best Buy is not heavily into global sales (it has stores in Canada). If the company would choose to go international, what types of external information might it need to make such a strategic move?

6. Update the information on Best Buy: number of stores, revenues, profits, and employees. Are these numbers increasing or declining?

Sources: Hoover's Online, **www.hoovers.com**, March 7, 2004; Best Buy, **www.bestbuy.com**, March 7, 2004; M. Tatge, "Fun and Games," *Forbes,* January 12, 2004, pp. 138–144; and E. Williams, "Hollywood and Whine," *Forbes,* March 4, 2002, pp. 38–39.

Endnotes

1. Kohl's, **www.kohls.com**, March 1, 2004; Hoover's Online, **www.hoovers.com**, March 1, 2004; G. Creno, "Mall-shunning Kohl's Fixates on 'Mom Country,'" *Springfield News Leader,* October 19, 2003, p. 5E; R. Berner, "Is Kohl's Coming Unbuttoned?" *Business Week,* July 28, 2003, p. 44; L. Lee, "Thinking Small at the Mall," *Business Week,* May 26, 2003, pp. 94–95; P. Tyre, "Retail's Quick Hit," *Newsweek,* December 2, 2002, p. 41; D. Starkman, "As Malls Multiply, Developers Fight Fiercely for Turf," *Wall Street Journal,* April 19, 2002, p. A1; and A. Merrick, "New Game at Kohl's: Dressing Up," *Wall Street Journal,* March 12, 2002, p. B1.

2. B. Horovitz, "Do You Want Fries with That? Nope," *USA Today,* September 22, 2003, p. B1.

3. C. Barnard, *The Functions of the Executive* (Cambridge, MA: Harvard University Press, 1938).

4. W. R. Dill, "Environment as an Influence on Managerial Autonomy," *Administrative Science Quarterly,* 2 (1958), pp. 409–43; and J. G. March and H. A. Simon, *Organizations* (New York: John Wiley & Sons, 1958).

5. R. L. Tung, "Dimensions of Organizational Environments: An Exploratory Study of Their Impact on Organizational Structure," *Academy of Management Journal,* 22 (1979), pp. 672–93; J. R. Galbraith, *Designing Complex Organizations* (Reading, MA: Addison-Wesley, 1973); R. B. Duncan, "Characteristics of Organizational Environments and Perceived Environment Uncertainty," *Administrative Science Quarterly,* 17 (1972), pp. 313–27; and P. R. Lawrence and J. W. Lorsch, "Differentiation and Integration in Complex Organizations," *Administrative Science Quarterly,* 12 (1967), pp. 1–47.

6. R. Bettis and C. K. Prahalad, "The Visible and the Invisible Hand: Resource Allocation in the Industrial Sector," *Strategic Management Journal,* 4 (1983), pp. 27–43; J. Freeman, "Organizational Life Cycles and Natural Selection Processes," in B. M. Staw and L. L. Cummings (eds.), *Research in Organizational Behavior* (Greenwich, CT: JAI Press, 1982); H. E. Aldrich, *Organizations and Environments* (Upper Saddle River, NJ: Prentice Hall, 1979); J. Pfeffer and G. R. Salancik, *The External Control of Organizations: A Resource Dependence Perspective* (New York: Harper & Row, 1978); H. E. Aldrich and J. Pfeffer, "Environments of Organizations," *Annual Review of Sociology,* 2 (1976), pp. 79–105; S. Mindlin, *Organizational Dependence on Environment and Organizational Structure: A Reexamination of the Aston Group,* unpublished master's thesis, Cornell University, Ithaca, NY, 1974; J. Hage and M. Aiken, "Program Change and Organizational Properties," *American Journal of Sociology,* 72 (1973), pp. 503–79; and March & Simon, *Organizations,* 1958.

7. M. E. Porter, *Competitive Strategy* (New York: The Free Press, 1980).

8. Ibid, p. 20.

9. J. R. Gregg, "Strategic Groups Theory: Past Nuances, Future Frontiers," *Southwest Academy of Management Proceedings,* March 1996, San Antonio, Texas, pp. 29–32; J. R. Barney and R. Hoskisson, "Strategic Groups: Untested Assertions and Research Proposals," *Managerial and Decision Economics,* 11 (1990), pp. 187–98; K. Cool and D. Schendel, "Strategic Group Formation and Performance: The Case of the U.S. Pharmaceutical Industry, 1963–1982," *Management Science,* 33, no. 9 (1987), pp. 1101–24; G. Dess and P. Davis, "Porter's [1980] Generic Strategies as Determinants of Strategic Group Membership and Organizational Performance," *Academy of Management Journal,* 27, no. 3 (1984), pp. 467–88; and M. S. Hunt, *Competition in the Major Home Appliance Industry 1960–1970,* unpublished doctoral dissertation, Harvard University, 1972.

10. B. K. Boyd and J. Fulk, "Executive Scanning and Perceived Uncertainty: A Multidimensional Model," *Journal of Management,* 22, no. 1, 1996, pp. 1–21; and R. L. Daft, et al., "Chief Executive Scanning, Environmental Characteristics, and Company Performance: An Empirical Study," *Strategic Management Journal,* 9 (1988), pp. 123–39.

11. P. F. Drucker, "The Information Executives Truly Need," *Harvard Business Review,* January–February 1995, pp. 54–62.

12. C. S. Korberg and G. R. Ungson, "The Effects of Environmental Uncertainty and Dependence on Organizational Structure and Performance: A Comparative Study," *Journal of Management,* Winter 1987, pp. 725–37.

13. R. S. Achrol and L. W. Stern, "Environmental Determinants of Decision-Making Uncertainty in Marketing Channels," *Journal of Marketing,* February 1988, pp. 36–50.

14. S. Kotha and A. Nair, "Strategy and Environment as Determinants of Performance: Evidence From the Japanese Machine Tool Industry," *Strategic Management Journal,* 16 (1995), pp. 497–518; R. Subramanian et al., "An Empirical Examination of the Relationship Between Strategy and Scanning," *The Mid-Atlantic Journal of Business,* December 1993, pp. 315–30; and Daft, et al., "Chief Executive Scanning, Environmental Characteristics, and Company Performance," 1988.

4

Assessing Strengths and Weaknesses

DOING AN INTERNAL ANALYSIS

LEARNING OUTLINE

What Is an Internal Analysis?

- *Define internal analysis.*

- *Describe the relationship between organizational resources, organizational capabilities, core competencies, and distinctive capabilities.*

- *Explain what organizational strengths and weaknesses are.*

How To Do an Internal Analysis

- *Describe the primary and support activities on the value chain.*

- *Explain what an internal audit is and how it can be used for an internal analysis.*

- *Describe the steps in a capabilities assessment profile.*

- *Explain the criteria that could be used to assess an organization's strengths and weaknesses.*

Why Do an Internal Analysis?

- *Discuss why an internal analysis is important.*

Higher and Higher

You may not be familiar with the Haier Group (sounds like "higher"), but if you've ever shopped for a refrigerator, microwave, or air conditioner at Wal-Mart, Best Buy, Lowe's, or Home Depot, you've undoubtedly seen, if not purchased, the company's products.[1] Haier Group is China's largest home-appliance maker, and CEO Zhang has ambitious goals for the company. Whereas the United States has General Electric, Germany has Mercedes-Benz, and Japan has Sony, China has yet to produce a comparable global competitor. Zhang is hoping to change that. Haier enjoys enviable prestige in China (a survey of "young, fashionable" Chinese ranked Haier as the country's third most popular brand behind Shanghai Volkswagen and Motorola, with Coca-Cola fourth), but Zhang isn't satisfied. He wants to gain worldwide recognition, build the company into China's first global brand, and be listed on the *Fortune* Global 500.

The Haier Group started as the Qingdao Refrigerator Company. When Zhang took charge of the government-controlled company in 1984, his first deed as CEO was to take a hammer and smash 76 refrigerators because of their poor quality. Why? To drive home the point that product quality was going to improve. At that time, the company had only one product and 800 workers. Today, over 30,000 employees make some 13,000 products in 86 different categories, from air conditioners to mobile phones to vacuums and more. And those products are now known around the world for quality and innovation. The Haier Group exports its products to more than 160 countries and regions and has established more than 40,000 global sales outlets. Its annual revenues are closing in on $9 billion. Although Haier is the number one domestic appliance producer in China, it ranks fifth in global appliance sales behind General Electric, Whirlpool, Electrolux, and Siemens.

An important division for the Haier Group is Haier America, its U.S. sales and marketing arm. From its headquarters in New York to its state-of-the-art refrigerator manufacturing facility in South Carolina, Haier America is committed to establishing itself as a powerful U.S. brand known for original products. For instance, one of those products is its popular frog-shaped television console, which also doubles as a nightlight and asks kids to answer math problems before switching itself on. The Haier Ribbit has been so popular that at least one retailer is asking for variations using other popular cartoon characters. Haier America CEO Michael Jemal is working on the licensing deals to make it happen. He says, "We're the new kid on the block, so we have to ask them (the customers) what they want. If we don't have it, we have to build it." Other popular products include its compact refrigerator, wine cooler, and office refrigerator.

Zhang is considered by many to be China's leading corporate executive. In November 2002, he became the first businessman ever elected to the Chinese Communist Party's Central Committee, a major political triumph for the 54-year-old with an MBA from China's University of Science and Technology. Zhang has been described as "a very charismatic business leader and not just in the Chinese perspective. He's emerging as a global business leader." Zhang's plans for pushing his company "higher and higher" rests on his ability to exploit Haier's resources and capabilities as the company relentlessly pursues its goal of becoming a global brand.

What factors would you say have contributed to the success of the Haier Group? What are its strengths? What potential weaknesses might the company have to address? In this chapter, we're going to concentrate on how to determine these important elements by discussing the internal analysis of an organization. Just as we've done in earlier chapters, we'll first look at *what* an internal analysis is, then at *how* you do one, and finally at *why* an internal analysis is an important part of managing strategically.

WHAT IS AN INTERNAL ANALYSIS?

To come up with the most appropriate and effective strategies, it's important to know what the organization can and cannot do particularly well and what assets it has and doesn't have. As part of managing strategically, **internal analysis** is a process of identifying and evaluating an organization's specific characteristics, including its resources, capabilities, and core competencies. An internal analysis provides important information about an organization's specific assets, skills, and work activities—in other words, what's good and what's lacking or deficient. In the strategic management process, internal analysis is the final step in analyzing the current situation. (See Figure 4.1.) One important part of this analysis entails looking at the organization's *current* vision, mission(s), strategic objectives, and strategies. Knowing what an organization is doing currently gives strategic decision makers a beginning understanding of whether strategic changes might be necessary. Further describing *what* an internal analysis is means looking closer at the organization's resources, capabilities, and core competencies.

A Quick Review of Organizational Resources

We've already discussed resources in relation to the resource-based view of achieving a sustainable competitive advantage (look back at Chapter 2 for a more complete description). As you'll recall, resources are simply the assets an organization has for carrying out whatever work activities and processes it's in business to do (making tacos, providing at-home health care, or marketing refrigerators). These resources (or assets) can be financial, physical, human, intangible, and structural–cultural. Financial resources include debt capacity, credit lines, available equity (stock), cash reserves, and any other financial assets. Physical resources include tangible assets such as buildings, equipment and fixtures, raw materials, office supplies, manufacturing facilities, machines, and so forth. Human resources include the experiences, knowledge, judgment, skills, accumulated wisdom, and competencies of

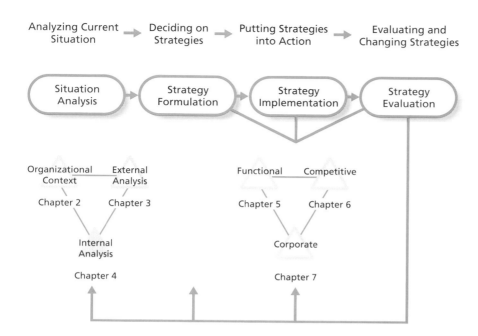

Figure 4.1

*Strategic Management
in Action*

the organization's employees. At Microsoft Corporation, for example, employees' programming skills would be part of its human resources. Intangible resources are such things as brand names, patents, trademarks, databases, copyrights, or registered designs. For instance, Nike's "swoosh" symbol is an intangible resource, as is the Haier brand name and American Express Company's customer database. Finally, structural–cultural resources include such things as organizational history, culture, work systems, policies, relationships, and the formal reporting (organizational) structure being used. For example, 3M Corporation's organizational culture stresses risk taking and innovation by its research scientists and engineers. Because 3M's competitive advantage is based on its ability to continually develop and market innovative products, this type of culture is one of its most important organizational resources.

Although an organization's tangible and intangible resources can be a source of competitive advantage (see Chapter 2 for what it takes for a resource to be unique—that is, capable of leading to a competitive advantage), they play a more important role in determining an organization's capabilities and core competencies. Figure 4.2 illustrates this relationship.

From Resources to Organizational Capabilities

An organization's resources simply are the inputs it needs to perform its work, whether that's making hamburgers, collecting blood plasma, or producing the show *Footloose* at a local community theater. Another way to describe resources is to view them as the organization's "whats"—what it has or owns. A good example to illustrate this is someone who's considered an excellent cook. This cook will own pots and pans, spices, equipment, and other cooking materials (i.e., resources) to be used in preparing delicious meals. Likewise, an organization possesses resources that hopefully can be used to put together a sustainable competitive advantage. Although an organization's resources can be considered its "pantry of goodies," these assets are much more valuable as they're used by organizational members in their work, which is directed at helping the organization reach its goals. By themselves,

Figure 4.2

The Strategic Role of Organizational Resources and Organizational Capabilities

Source: *Based on G. S. Day, "The Capabilities of Market-Driven Companies,"* Journal of Marketing, *October 1994, pp. 37–52.*

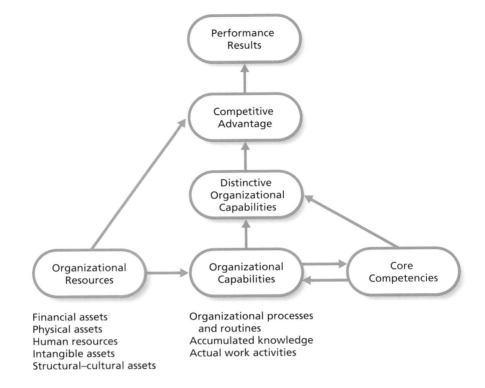

resources aren't productive—think of the cook who has to combine the spices and food using the appropriate equipment to put together those delicious meals. Likewise, organizational resources must be processed or used in some way to get the value out of them. For instance, American Express Company's customer database isn't valuable unless someone knows how to "mine" the database and use the information for making good strategic decisions. As such, the various resources are the inputs for organizational capabilities. **Organizational capabilities** can be defined as the network of organizational routines and processes that determine how efficiently and effectively the organization transforms its inputs (resources) into outputs (products including physical goods and services).[2] **Organizational routines and processes** are the regular, predictable, and sequential patterns of work activities performed by organizational members. The organization itself is a huge and complex network of routines and processes, encompassing such varied work activities as obtaining needed raw materials to establishing various product pricing structures to generating end-of-quarter financial and other statistical reports. Think back to our opening case and what various capabilities—that is, organizational routines and processes—the Haier Group might need as it produces and markets its refrigerators, microwaves, and other appliances.

As organizational members do their work, combining organizational resources within the structure of organizational routines and processes, they accumulate knowledge and experience on how best to capture the value (i.e., get the most) of the resources and turn them into possible core competencies or distinctive organizational capabilities. After all, creating organizational capabilities isn't simply a matter of assembling resources. Instead, capabilities involve complex patterns of coordination between people and between people and other organizational resources.[3] In fact, some organizations never get the hang of it. They're never quite able to develop efficient and effective capabilities and

How might an organization's resources and capabilities have to change when its product must continually change? Hoover's Inc., which was purchased by Dun & Bradstreet in 2003, is managing its resources and capabilities quite well under that scenario. The company sells company, market, industry, and competitive data—covering basic information on 12 million public and private companies and in-depth information on about 40,000 of the world's top business enterprises. To be valuable to its customers, this information must be constantly and continually updated. Its traditional products, *Hoover's Handbooks,* long available in libraries everywhere, have been surpassed by its online offerings. In fact, the majority of its revenues now come from Hoover's Online (**www.hoovers.com**). What are the implications of such a transition from a paper-based information company to an Internet-based information company on needed resources and capabilities? Explain.

Sources: *Hoover's Online,* **www.hoovers.com***, March 8, 2004; and R. A. Oppel, Jr., "A Company Short on Buzz but Long on Results,"* New York Times, *July 21, 1999, p. C1.*

struggle exhaustively to survive in an increasingly dynamic and competitive marketplace. For instance, look at how Wal-Mart and Kmart differ. Both have organizational resources and organizational routines and processes, yet Wal-Mart has been able to develop valuable capabilities and significant competitive advantages while Kmart has struggled. However, even Wal-Mart is finding that the strategic importance of organizational capabilities can change. Just because organizational capabilities were once the source of competitive advantage doesn't mean that those capabilities will continue to be a source of competitive advantage—that is, they don't always lead to a *sustainable* competitive advantage.[4]

In today's dynamic and complex environment, capabilities that are capable of leading to a competitive advantage today may not continue to do so as conditions and competitors change. To recognize and accommodate these new realities, some people have proposed that we need to think in terms of **dynamic capabilities**—an organization's ability to build, integrate, and reconfigure capabilities to address rapidly changing environments.[5] Successful competitors in the global marketplace will be those firms that can demonstrate timely responsiveness, rapid and flexible product innovation, and management expertise in coordinating and redeploying organizational resources and capabilities. However, before any organizational capabilities—dynamic or otherwise—can become a source of competitive advantage, they must be truly distinctive and also contribute to the development of an organization's core competencies.

Learning Review

- What is an internal analysis?
- How is an internal analysis different from an external analysis?
- What kinds of resources might an organization possess? Give examples of each.
- How are resources (assets) valuable to organizations?
- What are capabilities?
- What are organizational routines and processes?
- How are capabilities valuable to organizations?
- What are dynamic capabilities?

From Capabilities to Distinctive Capabilities and Core Competencies

Every organization has capabilities that enable it to do what it's in business to do. Some capabilities will be done poorly and some will be done adequately. However, if the organization is going to develop a sustainable competitive advantage *and* outperform its competition, some capabilities must be performed in a superior or distinct fashion. (Refer back to Figure 4.2.) Thus, **distinctive organizational capabilities** are the special and unique capabilities that distinguish the organization from its competitors. For example, Southwest Airlines has developed distinctive organizational capabilities in organizational processes and routines, including gate turnaround, ticketing, and employee–customer interactions. Although every airline uses these same organizational processes and routines, Southwest has developed distinctive capabilities in these particular areas and has been able to create a sustainable competitive advantage and enjoy outstanding performance results. Other airlines have tried but have not been able to duplicate what Southwest does, making its capabilities truly distinctive. What makes capabilities distinct? Figure 4.3 outlines three characteristics.[6] First, a distinctive capability contributes to superior customer value and offers real benefits to customers. Whatever it is that your customers value, a distinctive organizational capability enables you to provide it. Hampton Inns, for example, has developed a distinctive capability in providing customers moderately priced accommodations with all of the amenities and conveniences travelers want.[7] Take, for example, how Hampton Inns resolved one of travelers' biggest pet peeves—the frustrating task of figuring out how to set the hotel room alarm clock. After testing some 150 clock radios and not finding a single one that met their requirements, they finally designed their own. The result was a custom-designed clock radio manufactured by Timex, whose alarm can be set in three easy steps. (Try to describe some of the organizational processes and routines that you think allow Hampton Inns to continually determine what customers want and how to meet those needs.)

The second characteristic of distinctive organizational capabilities is that they should be difficult for competitors to imitate. Think back to how we described organizational capabilities as a network of organizational routines and processes. Making these capabilities difficult to imitate means balancing a complex array of employee skills and knowledge and harnessing the considerable learning that exists in the organization. It also means recognizing how capabilities cross functional units and how functional units can benefit from each other. If these complex interactions are strategically managed and exploited, it can be

Figure 4.3

Characteristics of Distinctive Organizational Capabilities

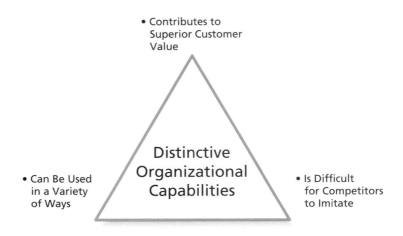

- Contributes to Superior Customer Value

Distinctive Organizational Capabilities

- Can Be Used in a Variety of Ways

- Is Difficult for Competitors to Imitate

difficult for competitors to imitate them, even if they have similar resources and organizational processes and routines. For example, Anheuser Busch (AB) has developed an incredibly accurate approach to finding out what beer lovers are buying as well as when, where, and why they're buying.[8] Its data mining capability—referred to as BudNet—is AB's little-known "jewel" and the primary reason the company's share of the U.S. beer market edged up to over 50 percent from 48.9 percent—a huge gain in a market where a weak economy, lousy weather, and threats of tougher drinking laws kept competitors' sales down. AB uses the data from BudNet to constantly change marketing strategies, to design promotions for particular ethnic groups, and to get early warnings when rivals might have an edge. This capability will be difficult for competitors to imitate.

Finally, a distinctive organizational capability should be able to be used in a variety of ways. The organizational routines and processes (what people in the organization do) developed in one area should be transferable to other areas of the organization. For example, Honda Corporation's capabilities at developing fuel-efficient, reliable, and responsive engines and drive trains has provided it with access to different markets, including automobiles, motorcycles, lawn mowers, snowblowers, tillers, all-terrain vehicles, power generators, and marine outboard engines. As a company ad states, "We are first and foremost, an engineering company. But we're also the world's largest engine manufacturer."[9] Another example of using a capability in a variety of ways can be seen at United Technology Corporation, which believes that its capabilities lie in developing energy-conserving technologies. By transferring knowledge about the principles of energy conservation among its various business divisions, which include Pratt & Whitney (engines), Otis (elevators), Sikorsky Aviation (helicopters), Hamilton Sunstrand (aircraft controls), and Carrier (heaters and air conditioners), the company has been able to dominate most of its markets.[10]

This idea of being able to use organizational capabilities in a variety of ways is also a key to understanding the role that core competencies play in this process. Let's take a closer look at core competencies.

Core competencies, a concept popularized by C. K. Prahalad and Gary Hamel, are the organization's major value-creating skills and capabilities that are *shared* across multiple product lines or multiple businesses.[11] Let's look at an example to help explain this idea. W. L. Gore is a company best known for its Gore-Tex fabrics, which are used in a variety of products, especially outdoor apparel. The fact that it's posted a profit every single year since it was founded in 1958 confirms the fact that the company has developed significant skills and capabilities in product innovation. However, more importantly, the company has shared those critical innovation skills and capabilities across multiple product lines in diverse industries ranging from guitar strings and dental floss to medical devices and fuel

strategic **MANAGERS** *in action*

You've probably heard of Club Méditerranée S.A. (popularly known as Club Med), the Paris-based seller of all-inclusive sea- or ski-vacation packages. After all, brand-recognition surveys show that 92 percent of the U.S. population has heard of Club Med. What you may not know is that CEO Philippe Bourguignon, who engineered Club Med's much-needed turnaround, is now ready to exploit his company's capabilities in helping consumers enjoy their leisure time. His goal is to turn Club Med into an umbrella leisure brand by using what he has learned from operating 150 resorts around the world and transferring those capabilities to fitness clubs and cabarets. He's also proposing a line of cosmetics. Do you think he will be able to capture what's made Club Med successful and transfer those capabilities to these new ventures?

Sources: *Hoover's Online*, **www.hoovers.com**, *March 8, 2004; and J. Levine, "Sun Blocked?" Forbes, May 27, 2002, pp. 143–44.*

Here are some other examples of companies exploiting their core competencies.

Toyota Motor is test flying a prototype single-engine propeller plane. Building on its major value-creating skills and capabilities in product development and manufacturing, the company is hoping to cash in on the growing leisure and short-haul commercial aircraft sectors currently dominated by Cessna and New Piper Aircraft.

Nokia Corporation has taken what it's learned in the cell phone business and is applying it to video games. With the introduction of its N-Gage game in October of 2003, Nokia is taking game playing a step further because its game unit is also a phone, a text messenger, an FM radio, and a digital music player.

Sources: A. Reinhardt, E. Sylvers, and I. M. Kunii, "Nokia's Big Leap," *Business Week*, October 13, 2003, pp. 50–52; and C. Dawson, "Toyota Gets the Urge to Fly," *Business Week*, August 5, 2002, p. 16.

cells. And, in at least one of those industries, guitar strings, it has used this core competency to become the second leading manufacturer.[12]

This process of "sharing" what an organization does best across various organizational units and developing other outlets for creating value from these core skills and capabilities is what distinguishes the concept of core competencies from distinctive capabilities. However, as Figure 4.2 illustrates, core competencies cannot be a source of competitive advantage. However, they can contribute to the development of distinctive capabilities. The major value-creating skills and capabilities (i.e., the core competencies) can become distinctive capabilities *if* they meet the test of what makes capabilities distinctive. Take the example we just looked at, W. L. Gore. If the company's innovation skills (core competency) can contribute to superior customer value, be difficult for competitors to imitate, and can be used in a variety of ways, it would then be one of W. L. Gore's distinctive capabilities.

Whereas an organization's capabilities are the source of its core competencies, these core competencies also contribute to the improvement and enhancement of organizational capabilities. (Note the two-directional arrow in Figure 4.2.) Although this may seem like the puzzling question of "which came first . . . the chicken or the egg," it's actually pretty simple. Organizational capabilities come first—they're the fundamental building blocks for developing core competencies. Every organization has processes and routines to get work done. The major value-creating skills and capabilities—that is, the organization's core competencies—are created out of those routines and processes, accumulated knowledge, and actual work activities. If these core competencies *are* established—and not every organization will be able to do so—they can, in turn, improve and enhance organizational capabilities and also contribute to the development of certain distinctive organizational capabilities. Because core competencies span the organization's various product lines or business units, they are fundamental skills and capabilities that the organization has developed and is able to exploit. Moreover, the distinction between capabilities and competencies isn't really the important thing. Instead, both represent important aspects of managing strategically.

Now for the two remaining boxes in Figure 4.2, which address competitive advantage and performance results. (Refer to page 108.) We previously discussed the concept of competitive advantage in Chapter 2. Recall that it's what sets an organization apart—its competitive edge. Whether the organization has a competitive advantage will impact its performance results, both in the long run *and* the short run. Although it's possible for an organization to enjoy strong performance results in the short run without a significant competitive advantage, there are limits to how long these results can last. Without a sustainable competitive advantage, the organization's long-run success and survival are uncertain. It's important, therefore, that organizational decision makers know where the organization's strengths and weaknesses are in terms of its resources, capabilities, and competencies. Our discussion of strengths and weaknesses is the last topic in describing *what* an internal analysis is.

The Role of Strengths and Weaknesses

The whole reason for doing an internal analysis is to assess what the organization has or doesn't have (resources) and what it can and can't do (capabilities)—in other words, its strengths and its weaknesses. **Strengths** are resources that the organization possesses and capabilities that the organization has developed, both of which can be exploited and developed into a sustainable competitive advantage. Although not every strength has the potential to be a sustainable competitive advantage, an organization's strengths should be nurtured and reinforced as its main competitive weapons. **Weaknesses**, on the other hand, are resources and capabilities that are lacking or deficient and that prevent the organization from developing a sustainable competitive advantage. Organizational weaknesses need to be corrected if they're in critical areas that are preventing the organization from developing a sustainable competitive advantage. However, because most organizations have limited resources to correct problems, strategic decision makers often choose to simply minimize the impact of weaknesses as long as those weaknesses aren't in critical areas—that is, those areas that are crucial for developing a sustainable competitive advantage.

Organizational members at all levels of the organization are grappling with these types of strategic decisions: What are the strengths and weaknesses in my area(s) of responsibility, and how can I strategically manage these areas to high levels of performance? Now that you have a good understanding of *what* an internal analysis, it's time to look at *how* you do one.

Learning Review

- When do organizational capabilities become a source of sustainable competitive advantage?
- What are distinctive organizational capabilities and what characteristics do they have?
- What are core competencies?
- What is the relationship between organizational capabilities and core competencies?
- How do core competencies and distinctive organizational capabilities differ?
- Describe strengths and weaknesses.

HOW TO DO AN INTERNAL ANALYSIS

How do you assess the organization's resources, capabilities, and core competencies? What's involved in the process? In this section, we want to look at three different techniques for analyzing an organization's internal situation. We're first going to look at an approach that views the organization's work—what it's in business to do—as a series of value-creating activities. Then we'll describe an approach that's similar to a financial audit, but, instead of just evaluating financial information, it's used to examine and assess all the internal facets of an organization. The final approach we'll discuss is one that focuses on developing a

Cold Stone Creamery, the nation's fastest-growing ice cream franchise, knows what customers value. And how do they give customers what they want? By custom blending high-quality ice cream with the customer's choice of mix-ins (e.g., Reese's Peanut Butter Cups, mint chips, brownies, fruit, etc.) in an attractive and entertaining atmosphere. Cold Stone fanatics state that Cold Stone isn't just any ice cream shop—it's an experience! Based out of Scottsdale, Arizona, Cold Stone has over 500 stores and plans to open many more. How might corporate strategists use value chain analysis? How might local store owners?

Sources: B. Kiviat, "Hot Ice Cream," Inside Business Time Bonus Section, *September 2003; and* L. Weber, "With Cheers, Stores Try to Make Shopping an Experience," USA Today, September 1, 2003, p. B3.

profile of the organization's capabilities. To conclude this section, then, we'll look at how to classify an organization's strengths and weaknesses.

Value Chain Analysis

Every organization needs customers if it's going to survive. Even not-for-profit organizations must have "customers" who use its services or purchase its products. The premise behind value chain analysis is that customers want (demand) some type of value from the goods and services they purchase or obtain. And just what is it that customers value? **Customer value** arises from three broad categories: the product is unique and different; the product is low priced; or the providing organization has the ability to respond to specific or distinctive customer needs quickly. In order to assess the organization's ability to provide value, strategic decision makers look at how an organization's functional activities contribute to creating customer value. This is where value chain analysis comes in. The **value chain** is a systematic way of examining all of the organization's functional activities and how well they create customer value.

The concept of the value chain was developed by Michael Porter (the same person who created the five forces model used in analyzing an organization's industry and competitive situation) as a tool for identifying ways to create more customer value.[13] As discussed earlier, every organization has specific organizational routines and processes—those work activities that organizational members perform—that allow it to do whatever it's in business to do. Each of these activities creates varying levels of customer value and organizational costs. What strategic decision makers hope is that the customer value created—as evidenced by the products the organization distributes or the services it provides and what customers are willing to "pay" for that value—outweighs the costs of creating that value. In using the value chain, we're assessing the organization's ability to create customer value through its work activities. In other words, what are the organization's strengths and weaknesses in these areas? How did Porter describe these activities? Figure 4.4 shows the nine activities—five primary and four support—that Porter felt were important to assess.

Let's look first at the primary activities, which are those activities that actually create customer value. These include the organizational routines and processes involved in bringing resources into the business (inbound logistics), processing these resources into the organization's goods or services (operations), physically distributing them to customers (outbound logistics), marketing the goods and services to customers (marketing and sales), and servicing customers (customer service). However, it's not enough to know just what these activities *are;* we must judge *how well* the organization is performing these activities. That's what we need to know to assess the organization's strengths and weaknesses. Table 4.1 lists some questions to ask as you assess the primary activities in the value chain.

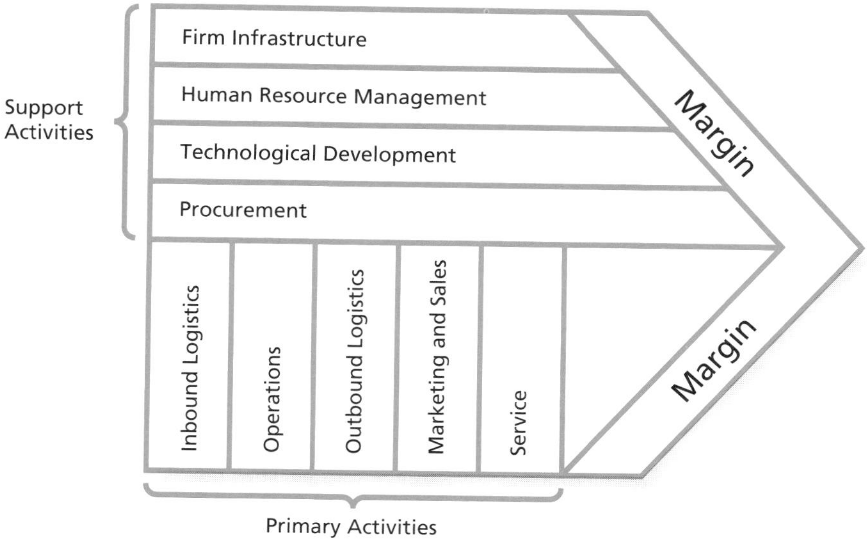

Figure 4.4

Primary and Support Activities in the Value Chain

Source: *Adapted with the permission of The Free Press, a Division of Simon and Schuster from Competitive Advantage: Creating and Sustaining Superior Performance by Michael E. Porter. Copyright © 1985 by Michael E. Porter.*

Table 4.1

Assessing the Primary Activities in the Value Chain

INBOUND LOGISTICS

- Is there a materials control system? How well does it work?
- What type of inventory control system is there? How well does it work?
- How are raw materials handled and warehoused?
- How efficiently are raw materials handled and warehoused?

OPERATIONS

- How productive is our equipment as compared with our competitors?
- What type of plant layout is used? How efficient is it?
- Are production control systems in place to control quality and reduce costs? How efficient and effective are they in doing so?
- Are we using the appropriate level of automation in our production processes?

OUTBOUND LOGISTICS

- Are finished products delivered in a timely fashion to customers?
- Are finished products efficiently delivered to customers?
- Are finished products warehoused efficiently?

MARKETING AND SALES

- Is marketing research effectively used to identify customer segments and needs?
- Are sales promotions and advertising innovative?
- Have alternative distribution channels been evaluated?
- How competent is the sales force? Is its level of motivation as high as it can be?
- Does our organization present an image of quality to our customers? Does our organization have a favorable reputation?
- How brand loyal are our customers? Does our customer brand loyalty need improvement?
- Do we dominate the various market segments we're in?

CUSTOMER SERVICE

- How well do we solicit customer input for product improvements?
- How promptly and effectively are customer complaints handled?
- Are our product warranty and guarantee policies appropriate?
- How effectively do we train employees in customer education and service issues?
- How well do we provide replacement parts and repair services?

Source: *Based on Michael E. Porter,* Competitive Advantage: Creating and Sustaining Superior Performance *(New York: Free Press, 1985).*

What about the support activities in the value chain? These activities support the primary activities as well as each other. Although it may seem that the primary activities are the most critical to the organization because they are the ones that create value, keep in mind that the "performance" of the primary activities wouldn't be possible without the support activities. For instance, if the Haier Group didn't have effective human resources management processes and routines, it wouldn't have employees to assemble the appliances, create the marketing materials, or innovate new products. And if it can't do these things, it won't be creating value for the customer, the customer won't be willing to purchase the product, and organizational performance will suffer. How can you assess strengths and weaknesses in the support activities? Table 4.2 lists some questions to ask in assessing the support activities.

<table>
<tr><td>

Table 4.2

Assessing the Support Activities in the Value Chain

</td><td>

PROCUREMENT
- Have we developed alternate sources for obtaining needed resources?
- Are resources procured in a timely fashion? At lowest possible cost? At acceptable quality levels?
- How efficient and effective are our procedures for procuring large capital expenditure resources such as plant, machinery, and buildings?
- Are criteria in place for deciding on lease-versus-purchase decisions?
- Have we established sound long-term relationships with reliable suppliers?

TECHNOLOGICAL DEVELOPMENT
- How successful have our research and development activities been in product and process innovations?
- Is the relationship between R&D employees and other departments strong and reliable?
- Have technology development activities been able to meet critical deadlines?
- What is the quality of our organization's laboratories and other research facilities?
- How qualified and trained are our laboratory technicians and scientists?
- Does our organizational culture encourage creativity and innovation?

HUMAN RESOURCE MANAGEMENT
- How effective are our procedures for recruiting, selecting, orienting, and training employees?
- Are there appropriate employee promotion policies in place and are they used effectively?
- How appropriate are reward systems for motivating and challenging employees?
- Do we have a work environment that minimizes absenteeism and keeps turnover at reasonable levels?
- Are union–organization relations acceptable?
- Do managers and technical personnel actively participate in professional organizations?
- Are levels of employee motivation, job commitment, and job satisfaction acceptable?

FIRM INFRASTRUCTURE
- Is our organization able to identify potential external opportunities and threats?
- Does our strategic planning system facilitate and enhance the accomplishment of organizational goals?
- Are value chain activities coordinated and integrated throughout the organization?
- Can we obtain relatively low-cost funds for capital expenditures and working capital?
- Does our information system support strategic and operational decision making?
- Does our information system provide timely and accurate information on general environmental trends and competitive conditions?
- Do we have good relationships with our stakeholders including public policy makers and interest groups?
- Do we have a good public image of being a responsible corporate citizen?

</td></tr>
</table>

Source: *Based on Michael E. Porter,* Competitive Advantage: Creating and Sustaining Superior Performance *(New York: Free Press, 1985).*

By assessing the organization's primary and support activities, you get a good picture of its resources and capabilities (i.e., how resources are used in its work routines and processes) and its strengths and weaknesses. To the extent that the organization performs any of these activities more effectively or efficiently than its competitors, it should be able to achieve a competitive advantage. The advantage of the value chain analysis technique is that it emphasizes the importance of customer value and how well an organization performs the primary and support activities in order to create customer value. However, this technique may be somewhat difficult to use in assessing organizational strengths and weaknesses because organizational work activities don't always fit nicely and neatly into the primary and support activities framework. Therefore, some strategic decision makers prefer to use another approach—an internal audit.

Using an Internal Audit

Another approach to assessing organizational strengths and weaknesses is an internal audit of organizational functions. Just as the value chain approach starts with the premise that every organization needs customers and must provide value to those customers to achieve a competitive advantage, the internal audit approach starts with the premise that every organization has certain functions that it must perform. In pursuing a sustainable competitive advantage, these functions may be performed well or performed poorly. We base our identification of strengths and weaknesses on how well these basic organizational functions are performed. You may be familiar with the concept of a financial audit, which is simply a thorough examination of a firm's financial records and procedures. An **internal audit** is a thorough assessment of an organization's internal functional areas. It's

Organizations Need Physicals, Too

Have you ever had a physical exam? If you have, then you know that your past medical history, current health issues or complaints, and lifestyle factors are scrutinized. And, the physical exam may point to the need for additional scrutiny with test results compared to normal ranges. Doesn't this seem to be an appropriate analogy for assessing organizations? Could the concept of a "physical exam" be applied to organizations? Here's a guide to giving your organization a physical exam.

- *Brain function.* This would be the organization's strategy and planning function. How well does your organization's "brain" function? Are the strategies and plans getting through to the rest of the organization? Is the "command center" functioning effectively and efficiently?

- *Nervous system.* You need to check your company's reflexes. Are communication and information technology systems responsive as information is gathered and disseminated from the brain?

- *Eyes, ears, nose, and mouth.* These sense organs respond to the outside world. Are the marketing and sales groups "sensing" customers' needs accurately?

- *Arms, hands, legs, feet, and associated muscle groups.* These body parts convert energy into action. What kind of shape are your operations systems in? Do they acquire materials, make things, and deliver them efficiently and effectively?

- *Lungs, digestive system.* In your body, the lungs and digestive system absorb nutrients and filter waste. Are resources being absorbed efficiently? Are you getting rid of waste efficiently?

- *The heart.* You need to have a strong, highly conditioned heart to keep the rest of the body functioning properly. The organization's heart is its culture, its sense of meaning and purpose. How is the flow of culture throughout your organization? Has it cut off circulation or is it sending out strength-giving nutrients?

Source: J. Mariotti, "Give Your Company a Physical," Industry Week, October 5, 1998, p. 74.

similar to a financial audit, although it obviously focuses on much more than just the financial aspects. Strategic decision makers use the internal audit to assess the organization's resources and capabilities from the perspective of its different functions. Are the necessary resources available so that the people in these functional areas can perform their assigned work activities and how well do they perform these assigned work activities (i.e., what are their capabilities)?

An internal audit should look at six main organizational functions: production–operations, marketing, research and development, financial–accounting, management (which typically includes human resources management and other general management activities), and information systems. Obviously, individual organizations may have unique functions that aren't covered by these categories, or they may not call their functions by these names, but these six are the most common. What should you examine and evaluate in each of these areas? Table 4.3 (see pp. 119–120) lists some key internal audit questions to use in assessing the strengths and weaknesses of each functional area. This assessment concentrates on the availability or lack of critical resources and the level of capabilities (i.e., how efficiently and effectively work is being done) in each functional area.

The internal audit approach is fairly straightforward. The analysis can be tailored to fit whatever distinctive functions an organization might have. For example, in the case of a hotel, an internal audit might cover specific functional areas such as front-desk operations, housekeeping, food services, hospitality and customer service, and bookkeeping. Again, the key to using an internal audit is to determine how well or poorly these organizational functions are being performed and what resources are available to these functional areas for carrying out their work activities.

Learning Review

- Describe what a value chain analysis shows.
- When will a customer find value in a product?
- What are the primary activities in the value chain? The support activities?
- What is an internal audit and what does it look at?
- How is an internal audit different from the value chain analysis?

Capabilities Assessment Profile

The last approach we're going to discuss for doing an internal analysis is a capabilities assessment profile. It's an in-depth evaluation of an organization's capabilities in order to determine strengths and weaknesses. This approach was developed because strategic decision makers had few guidelines for identifying and evaluating their organization's distinctive capabilities.[14] Assessing capabilities is quite complex, because capabilities develop out of the way resources are combined in the organization's basic work processes and routines. They're not as easily identifiable as organizational functions or even the value-creating primary and support activities. However, the complex nature of capabilities also makes it hard for competitors to imitate them, which makes them excellent sources of sustainable competitive advantage. Therefore, we need some guidelines for identifying the organization's distinctive capabilities. That's what the capabilities assessment profile approach provides.

The capabilities assessment actually consists of two phases: (1) identifying distinctive capabilities and (2) developing and leveraging these distinctive capabilities.[15] Because our

Table 4.3

*Important Internal
Audit Questions*

PRODUCTION–OPERATIONS

- Does the organization have reliable and reasonably priced suppliers?
- Are facilities, offices, machinery, and equipment in good working condition?
- Are facilities strategically located close to resources and markets?
- Does the organization have effective inventory control policies and procedures?
- Does the organization utilize quality control procedures? Are these procedures effective?
- How does the organization do on quality assessments?
- Does the organization have an appropriate amount of capacity?
- What is the organization's safety record?
- Does the production–operations process work smoothly and with little disruptions?
- Have production–operations goals been established, and are work activities aimed at achieving these goals?
- Do production–operations employees use appropriate operations planning and controlling tools and techniques?
- Has the organization developed any particular competencies in the areas of production–operations?

MARKETING

- Does the organization segment markets effectively?
- What is the organization's market position or rank?
- Does the organization position itself well against its competitors?
- What is the organization's market share, and has it been increasing or decreasing?
- Does the organization conduct market research, and is this research effective?
- Is market research information used in making marketing decisions?
- Does the organization have an effective sales force?
- Has the organization priced its products and services appropriately?
- How is product quality, and how does it compare with that of competitors?
- Is customer service effective, and how does it compare with competitors?
- Is the advertising strategy effective?
- Are promotion and publicity strategies effective?
- Are customer complaints decreasing, increasing, or stable?
- Are customer complaints handled effectively and efficiently?
- Are present channels of distribution reliable and cost effective?
- Are marketing planning and budgeting effective?
- Do marketing employees use appropriate marketing planning and controlling tools and techniques?
- Has the organization developed any particular competencies in any of the marketing areas?

RESEARCH AND DEVELOPMENT

- Does the organization have adequate R&D facilities?
- Are the R&D employees well qualified?
- Does organizational culture encourage creativity and innovation?
- Is communication between R&D and other organizational units effective?
- Are the organization's products technologically competitive?
- If patents are appropriate, are patent applications increasing, decreasing, or stable?
- Is development time from concept to actual product appropriate?
- How many new products have been developed during the last year (or whatever time period is most appropriate)?
- Does the organization commit more, the same, or less to R&D than its competitors do?
- Do R&D employees use appropriate R&D tools and techniques?
- Has the organization developed any particular competencies in the R&D area?

Table 4.3

Continued

FINANCIAL AND ACCOUNTING

- Is the organization financially strong or weak according to the financial ratio analyses?
- What are the trends in the organization's financial ratios, and how do these compare with industry trends?
- Is the organization able to raise short-term capital?
- Is the organization able to raise long-term capital?
- What is the organization's working capital position? Is it sufficient?
- Are the organization's capital budgeting procedures effective?
- Has the organization established financial goals? Are they appropriate?
- Are dividend payout policies reasonable?
- What type of relationship does the organization have with its creditors and stockholders?
- Is there a match between the organization's sources and uses of funds?
- Do financial–accounting employees use appropriate financial–accounting tools and techniques?
- Has the organization developed any particular competencies in the financial–accounting area?

MANAGEMENT

- Do organization employees manage strategically?
- Are organizational goals clear and measurable? Are they communicated to organizational members?
- Is the organization's structure appropriate?
- What is the organization's culture? Does it support organizational goals and mission?
- Has the organization developed its vision? What about mission(s)?
- Does the organization attract appropriate job applicants?
- Are employee selection procedures effective?
- Does the organization provide employees with appropriate training?
- Are job descriptions and job specifications clear?
- Are jobs effectively designed?
- What is the level of employee morale?
- What is the level of employee turnover?
- Are organizational compensation and reward programs appropriate?
- Are organizational employee discipline and control mechanisms appropriate?
- How does the organization treat its employees?
- What kind of relationships does the organization have with employee groups?
- Does the organization effectively use work teams?
- Are legal guidelines followed in human resource management activities?
- Has the organization developed any competencies in its human resource management activities?
- Has the organization developed any competencies in the management area?

INFORMATION SYSTEMS–INFORMATION TECHNOLOGY

- How does the organization gather and disseminate information? Is it effective and efficient?
- Is the information system used by employees in making decisions?
- Is information updated regularly?
- Is information distributed effectively and efficiently?
- Do employees have access to contribute input to the information system?
- Has the organization made an investment in information technology that's greater than, equal to, or less than competitors?
- Is information technology used effectively and efficiently in all areas of the organization?
- Is the organization's information system secure?
- Is the organization's information system user friendly?
- Are training workshops or seminars provided for users of the information system?
- Are employees in the information systems–information technology area well qualified?
- Has the organization developed any competencies in the information systems–information technology area?

Figure 4.5

*Identifying Distinctive
Organizational Capabilities*

Source: *Based on Kenneth E. Marino,
"Developing Consensus on Firm
Competencies and Capabilities," Academy
of Management Executive, August 1996,
pp. 40–51.*

main interest at this point is analyzing the internal aspects of the organization, we're going to concentrate on phase 1, identifying distinctive capabilities. Phase 2 addresses strategy development issues that are beyond the scope of our discussion of how to do an internal analysis. Figure 4.5 illustrates the steps in phase 1—identifying the distinctive organizational capabilities.

Earlier in the chapter, we described what makes capabilities distinctive. Let's review those characteristics. First, distinctive capabilities should contribute to superior customer value and offer customers real benefits. Next, they should be difficult for competitors to imitate. Finally, distinctive capabilities should be usable in a variety of ways by the organization. This brief reminder about the characteristics of distinctive organizational capabilities is important because they influence what type of information is gathered in a capabilities assessment. In fact, the first step in assessing organizational capabilities—*preparing a current product–market profile*—emphasizes organization–customer interactions. In this step, we identify what we're selling, who we're selling to, and whether we're providing superior customer value and offering the customer desirable benefits. To do this, we need information about specific products and markets; principal competitors in each of these product–market segments; and performance measures, such as sales growth rates, market share, competitive position, contributions to sales and earnings, for each product–market segment.

Once we have a current (and thorough) product–market profile, the next step in the capabilities assessment is *identifying sources of competitive advantage and disadvantage in the main product–market segments.* We want to know why customers choose our products instead of our competitors. This assessment would involve identifying specific cost, product, and service attributes. What are these "attributes" we need to identify? When customers purchase a product (physical good or service), what they're actually purchasing is a bundle of attributes that they believe will satisfy their needs.[16] These attributes vary by product and market. For example, camera customers may be interested in product attributes such as picture clarity, camera speed, camera size, or price. Airline customers might choose a particular airline based on attributes such as safety record, close adherence to arrival–departure schedules, customer service, meal availability, convenience of arrival–departure times, and price. Community arts customers might choose a live theater performance on attributes such as familiarity with the play, actors or actresses starring in the play, or ticket price. Again, in this step we're attempting to identify those attributes that our customers value in our products and what competitive advantages or disadvantages these attributes provide us.

Auto parts manufacturer Accuride struggled as a division of Bridgestone/Firestone. However, when it was purchased by a private-equity firm and freed from bureaucratic corporate constraints, strategic decision makers soon realized that they could profit by becoming the dominant supplier to a few major customers. However, to do so meant understanding the capabilities (and resources) necessary to gain large shares of a buyer's business, which they eventually were able to do. Accuride invested in a new, highly automated manufacturing facility to increase its capacity and thereby reduce production costs. The low costs enabled the company to undercut competitors on prices and terms offered to target customers. By understanding the critical capabilities, Accuride flourished.

Source: P. Rogers, T. Holland, and D. Haas, "Value Acceleration: Lessons from Private-Equity Masters," Harvard Business Review, June 2002, pp. 94–101.

With this information, then, we're ready to pinpoint the organizational capabilities that lead to those sources of competitive advantage and disadvantage. Step 3 involves *describing organizational capabilities and competencies.* To identify those capabilities, you need to closely examine the resources, skills, and abilities of the organization's various divisions. Let's look at an example to help explain this. Suppose that you're a strategic manager at one of the nation's airlines. Your analysis of sources of competitive advantage and disadvantage (step 2) showed that one of the reasons customers choose your airline over competitors is because scheduled flights consistently left on time. In step 3, you'd need to uncover what resources and capabilities led to this competitive advantage. You might find, for example, that consistent departures were the result of a well-trained ground crew who loaded baggage efficiently and effectively; appropriate numbers of customer service representatives who processed passengers quickly; a system of paperless ticketing and boarding passes; and pilots who knew the ins and outs of getting quick control tower clearance for takeoff. This type of intense analysis of the organizational resources and the organizational routines and processes behind the capabilities is an important step. It forces strategic decision makers to really understand what happens (and what has to happen) in order to deliver superior customer value and benefits. Even strategic decision makers in not-for-profit organizations should assess what organizational resources and organizational routines and processes lead to customers' willingness to support, sponsor, and advocate their products and programs. This is probably the most difficult of all the steps in the capabilities profile. Yet, it's also the one that yields the most important information because it gets to the heart of the matter—the most basic aspects of organizational operations and the inherent interactions as an organization's work is performed by organizational members.

What's next? Step 4 involves *sorting these core capabilities and competencies according to their strategic importance.* In other words, which capabilities are most important for building the organization's future? Judging which capabilities are strategically important is a matter of evaluating each one according to three criteria: (1) Does the capability provide tangible customer benefits? (2) Is the capability difficult for competitors to imitate? (3) Can the capability provide wide access to a number of different markets? Do these criteria sound familiar? They should—we described them earlier as the characteristics of a distinctive capability. This analysis will show you how organizational capabilities differ in their level of strategic importance. Those that are most important strategically should be placed at the top of the list and on down. By sorting organizational capabilities according to level of strategic importance, strategic decision makers gain an understanding of their organization's critical strengths and weaknesses. But, there's one more step in a capabilities assessment profile.

Marcelo Claure, CEO of Brightstar Corporation, has a good feel for what has made his company a success. Brightstar, a cellular phone distributor based in Miami, has operations in several South American and Central American countries. When asked for advice he'd give to other entrepreneurs, Claure responded, "build your company around your customers." His definition of customer, however, isn't just the person or organization purchasing products, it's also the person or organization supplying products to Brightstar. Claure has developed good relationships along all points in the distribution system. What do you think of Claure's philosophy?

Source: J. Russell, "Why Brightstar Shines," Hispanic Business, January–February 2004, pp. 14–18.

The final step involves *identifying and agreeing on the key competencies and capabilities*. Based on the ranking of strategic importance, decision makers can easily identify the organization's key competencies and capabilities. What's difficult is agreeing that these *are* the key ones. Obviously, when certain organizational capabilities are selected as more critical to competitive advantage than others, it's likely to affect future resource allocation and organizational support for various organizational units and divisions. Therefore, even though organizational members may be impacted differently, getting agreement on the organization's key capabilities is an important step in capabilities assessment. Without agreement on these critical capabilities, managing strategically for a sustainable competitive advantage will be extremely difficult.

Although the capabilities assessment approach provides a thorough analysis of the organization's important strategic capabilities, it's a complicated process. It's an approach that appears to be most useful to upper-level strategic managers because it forces an assessment of the vast number of underlying organizational capabilities, which, because they reflect the network of organizational routines and processes, don't always fit nicely and neatly into narrowly defined specific functional areas.

Classifying an Organization's Strengths and Weaknesses

Each approach to internal analysis can be used to identify the organization's resources and capabilities. Whether it's from the perspective of analyzing the customer value created by the organization's primary and support activities, from the perspective of auditing the organization's various functional areas, or from the perspective of identifying the organization's distinctive capabilities, we get a broad picture of the organization's resources and work routines and processes. However, that's only half the picture. We have to do more than just *identify* these factors. We've also got to *assess* the organization's strengths and weaknesses in each of these areas. What are its strong points? What are its weak points? What resources and capabilities can be enhanced and exploited for a sustainable competitive advantage? What resources and capabilities are lacking or not being used effectively? Strategic decision makers should make these assessments as they analyze the information about the various internal organizational areas, whether from the value chain approach, internal audit approach, or capabilities process approach. To assess whether resources and capabilities are strengths or weaknesses and whether certain ones could be sources of sustainable competitive advantage, we need some criteria against which to measure them. What criteria can we use to judge a strength or weakness?[17] Figure 4.6 identifies four such criteria.

Figure 4.6

*Criteria to Judge Organizational
Strengths and Weaknesses*

Past Performance Trends

Comparison Against Competitors

Are organizational resources and capabilities strengths or weaknesses?

Specific Goals or Targets

Personal Opinions of Strategic Decision Makers or Consultants

One criterion that could be used to determine whether resources and capabilities are strengths or weaknesses is past performance trends. This criterion could include performance measures such as financial ratios, operational efficiency statistics, employee productivity statistics, or data on adherence to quality control standards. Any organizational area that's measurable could be assessed by looking at the trends. For instance, is market share increasing or decreasing? Are liquidity ratios going up or down? Is the number of product returns increasing or decreasing? Are employee training expenditures reducing product reject rates? For example, in our chapter-opening case, Haier's CEO undoubtedly examines various organizational performance trends before making strategic decisions. Remember how he stressed the importance of product quality. These quantitative measures can be used as indicators of organizational strengths and weaknesses. Although performance trends can show important information about the organization's use of resources and capabilities, it doesn't show us whether performance is up to standards.

Therefore, another criterion to use in assessing organizational strengths and weaknesses is to look at specific performance goals or targets and how actual performance measures up against these. **Organizational goals** are statements of desired outcomes. Every organization should have specific goals at all levels and in all functional areas that state *what* it hopes to do or accomplish within a certain time frame. These goals provide direction by specifying what and how organizational resources and capabilities are used in carrying out the organizational vision and missions. By comparing actual performance in the various functional areas against stated goals, we can assess strengths and weaknesses. However, just looking at how organizational performance measures up to the goals and looking at performance trends isn't enough to help us determine whether these strengths or weaknesses can be used to influence the development of potential sustainable competitive advantage. To do this, we need some comparisons against our competitors—which is another criterion we can use to measure strengths and weaknesses.

By comparing our organization's resources and capabilities against our competitors, we can see how we stack up against those who are battling for the same customers. Remember from Chapter 3 that we look at competitors as part of our *external* analysis. However, as part of the internal analysis, we need to focus not only on *what* our competitors are doing, but *how* they're doing. Getting this information isn't quite as easy as getting our own internal performance information. This information may include such things as surveys and rankings published in external information sources. For example, *Fortune* publishes an annual corporate reputations survey that ranks industry competitors according to what companies are most admired. *Business Week* publishes annual rankings

FOR YOUR information

There's Something About Market Share

One commonly used comparison against competitors is market share. Is it an appropriate measure? Nearly every business is mesmerized by market share—keeping it or increasing it. Conventional wisdom about the importance of market share was that the biggest market share would give a company the biggest revenues and the lowest cost per unit. That approach may have worked in the 1960s through the 1980s. However, the reality of today's environment is that increasing market share may not be the route to continued competitive advantage and profitability. Having the most customers doesn't automatically translate into having the most profits. In fact, one study conducted by a consulting firm found that 70 percent of the time, the company with the largest market share didn't have the highest rate of

return. Strategic decision makers need to address how customers' needs are changing and how they can best meet those changing needs. Maybe *that's* how companies need to measure themselves against their competitors—by how well they are meeting customers' changing needs. What do you think? Do you agree with the premises of this argument regarding the decreased importance of market share? What are the implications for doing an internal analysis? Are there customers an organization might not want? Explain.

Sources: L. Selden and G. Colvin, "Will This Customer Sink Your Stock?" Fortune, September 30, 2002, pp. 127–30; R. Brooks, "Alienating Customers Isn't Always a Bad Idea, Many Firms Discover," Wall Street Journal, January 7, 1999, p. A1; C. Boyd, "When Market Share is a Good Goal," www.mgt.smsu/edu/mgt487/mgtissue/mktshare/goodgoal.htm, December 17, 1998; R. Miniter, "The Myth of Market Share," Wall Street Journal, June 15, 1998, p. A28; and A. Slywotzky and D. J. Morrison, "When Baseball is in Trouble, How GE Makes Money, and Other Insights Into the True Origin of Corporate Profits," Fortune, May 11, 1998, pp. 183–84.

of research and development expenditures. We might also find competitor information in sources such as articles in business or general newsmagazines, other types of public documents such as annual reports or Securities and Exchange Commission filings, industry association newsletters, networking at professional meetings, customer contacts, and even the competitor's Web site. A key consideration for gathering information on your competitors is whether your competitive intelligence methods are ethical. (See *The Grey Zone* ethical issue.) For example, although there's nothing unethical about scouring published sources for competitor information, ethical issues might arise if you decide, for instance,

The Grey Zone

Here are some techniques that have been suggested for gathering competitor information: (1) Pretend to be a journalist writing a story. Call up competitors' offices and interview them. (2) Dig through a competitor's trash. (3) Sit outside a competitor's place of business and count how many customers go in. (4) Get copies of your competitors' in-house newsletters and read them. (5) Call the Better Business Bureau and ask if competitors have had any complaints filed against them and, if so, what kinds of complaints. (6) Have friends call competitors for price lists, brochures, or other marketing information. Do you think these methods are ethical or unethical? Why? What ethical guidelines might you propose for strategic decision makers when doing competitor intelligence?

to rummage through a competitor's trash bins for information or hack into its electronic databases. Although there are no easy answers in these ethical dilemmas, be alert to the perceived "rightness" or "wrongness" of your competitive intelligence gathering methods.[18]

The last criterion for judging organizational strengths and weaknesses is the use of personal or subjective opinions of strategic decision makers or consultants. Sometimes, the best way to assess strong or weak areas is to get the personal opinion of those who are directly involved in the activity. Quantitative performance measures, such as trends or comparisons against standards, don't always capture what's really going on in a particular functional area. Because not every resource or capability may be appropriate for quantitative measurement, qualitative opinions or assessments of organizational members can be useful in determining areas of strength or weakness. Also, if outside consultants are working with any of the organization's divisions or units, what's their opinion? What do they see as strengths or weaknesses? Although this particular criterion is impossible to use in case analysis for this class (unless you're studying a local organization), it's likely to be useful as another way to assess strengths and weaknesses when you're working in an organization and managing strategically.

By now, you should have a fairly good idea of what's involved in actually *doing* an internal analysis and identifying strengths and weaknesses. It's more than simply identifying an organization's internal resources and capabilities. It's also assessing whether those resources and capabilities are sufficient and can be sources of sustainable competitive advantage. Although we've discussed what internal analysis is and how to do one, we haven't yet addressed *why* it's an important part of managing strategically. That's what we're going to cover next.

WHY DO AN INTERNAL ANALYSIS?

Doing an internal analysis is important for two reasons: (1) It's the only way to identify an organization's strengths and weaknesses and (2) it's needed for making good strategic decisions. Let's explain.

As we stated at the beginning of the chapter, an internal analysis is a process of identifying and evaluating an organization's specific characteristics, including its resources, capabilities, and core competencies. The outcome of the process is important information about an organization's specific assets, skills, and work routines and processes. What strengths do we have because of our specific resources and capabilities? What weaknesses are there in our specific resources and capabilities? If we didn't do this analysis, we wouldn't have this critical strategic information. But, this information in and of itself isn't useful. It's how strategic decision makers *use* this information that's important.

With the information from an internal analysis, strategic decision makers can make intelligent judgments about what competitive advantages the organization might currently have, what might potentially be developed into competitive advantages, and what might be preventing competitive advantages from being developed. This internal information, coupled with the information from the external analysis and information about the organizational context, provides the basis for deciding what strategic actions are necessary for sustainable competitive advantage.

- What does a capabilities assessment profile provide?

- Describe the five steps in assessing organizational capabilities.

- How do you judge which organizational capabilities are strategically important?

- What criteria can be used to judge organizational resources and capabilities as either strengths or weaknesses? Describe.

- What are organizational goals? How do they affect the determination of strengths or weaknesses in organizational resources and capabilities?

- Describe the role ethics plays in determining organizational strengths and weaknesses.

- Why is an internal analysis an important part of managing strategically?

- An **internal analysis** is a process of identifying and evaluating an organization's specific characteristics, including its resources, capabilities, and core competencies.

- One important part of the internal analysis is looking at the organization's current vision, mission(s), strategic objectives, and strategies.

- An organization's resources can be financial, physical, human, intangible, and structural–cultural.

- Although an organization's tangible and intangible resources can be a source of competitive advantage if they are unique, they play a more important role in determining an organization's capabilities and core competencies.

- **Organizational capabilities** are the network of organizational routines and processes that determine how efficiently and effectively the organization transforms its inputs (resources) into outputs (products including goods and services).

- **Organizational routines and processes** are the regular, predictable, and sequential patterns of work activities performed by organizational members.

- Creating organizational capabilities isn't simply a matter of assembling resources. Capabilities involve complex patterns of coordination between people and between people and other organizational resources.

- The concept of **dynamic capabilities** suggests that organizations must have the ability to build, integrate, and reconfigure capabilities to address rapidly changing environments.

- Before organizational capabilities can become a source of competitive advantage, they must be truly distinctive.

- **Distinctive organizational capabilities** are the special and unique capabilities that distinguish the organization from its competitors.

- Three characteristics of distinctive organizational capabilities are that they must contribute to superior customer value, they should be difficult for competitors to imitate, and they should be able to be used in a variety of ways.

- The concept of **core competencies**, developed by Prahalad and Hamel, describes the organization's major value-creating skills and capabilities that are *shared* across multiple product lines or multiple businesses.

- This process of sharing what an organization does best is what distinguishes the concept of core competencies from distinctive capabilities.

- Core competencies cannot be a source of competitive advantage. However, they can contribute to the development of distinctive capabilities that lead to a competitive advantage.

- The major value-creating skills and capabilities (the core competencies) can become distinctive capabilities if they meet the test of what distinctive capabilities are.

- Core competencies also contribute to the improvement and enhancement of organizational capabilities. However, capabilities do come first.

- **Strengths** are resources that the organization possesses and capabilities that it has developed, both of which can be exploited and developed into a sustainable competitive advantage.

- **Weaknesses** are resources and capabilities that are lacking or deficient and that prevent the organization from developing a sustainable competitive advantage.

- There are three approaches to doing an internal analysis: value chain analysis, internal audit, and capabilities assessment profile.

- The value chain focuses on **customer value**, which arises from (1) the product being unique and different, (2) the product being low priced, and (3) the organization having the ability to respond to specific or distinctive customer needs.

- The **value chain** was developed by Michael Porter and is a systematic way of examining all of the organization's functional activities and how well they create customer value.

- These organizational activities include the primary activities (those that actually create customer value and include inbound logistics, operations, outbound logistics, marketing and sales, and customer service) and the support activities (those that provide support for the primary activities and include procurement, technological development, human resource management, and firm infrastructure).

- The advantage of the value chain analysis is that it emphasizes the importance of customer value and how effectively the organization creates it. However, the drawback is that this approach may be confusing and complex to use because organizational work activities don't always fit into the primary and support activities framework.

- The **internal audit** is a thorough assessment of an organization's internal functional areas.

- The six main internal functional areas include production–operations, marketing, research and development, financial–accounting, management, and information systems.

- The advantage of the internal audit approach is that it's fairly straightforward and can be tailored to fit whatever distinctive functions an organization might have.

- The capabilities assessment profile is used to identify an organization's distinctive capabilities.

- The steps in a capabilities assessment profile include (1) preparing a current product–market profile, (2) identifying sources of competitive advantage and disadvantage in the main product–market segments, (3) describing organizational capabilities and competencies, (4) sorting these core capabilities and competencies according to their strategic importance, and (5) identifying and agreeing on the key competencies and capabilities.

- The advantage of this approach is that it provides a thorough analysis of the organization's important strategic capabilities. The drawback is that it's a complicated process.

- Identifying strengths and weaknesses is only half the picture. They must be assessed against some criteria.

- Four criteria that can be used to assess organizational strengths and weaknesses include organizational performance measures, **organizational goals** (statements of desired outcomes), comparison against competitors, and personal or subjective opinions of strategic decision makers or consultants.

- Doing an internal analysis is important because it's the only way to identify an organization's strengths and weaknesses, and it's needed for making good strategic decisions.

1. The conventional view that leading brands maintain their market leadership for long periods of time may be inaccurate. Strategic decision makers can no longer assume that they will be able to retain their companies' brand leadership over decades. In fact, studies of brands show that consumers are finding it harder to distinguish among competing products. (a) What type of resources are brands? (b) What are the implications of these statements for internal analysis? (c) Could brands ever be the ultimate competitive weapon? Why or why not? (d) Could a brand ever be a weakness? Explain.

2. Customer loyalty can be a powerful competitive advantage. And customer loyalty is more than repeat purchasing. Customers who are loyal tend to buy more over time and, most importantly, tend to tell others, such as family, friends, and colleagues, about a company. Enterprise Rent-A-Car figured this out early on, and rather than having a complicated and sophisticated customer research program, they focus on two simple questions. The first question asks about the quality of the customer's rental experience. The second asks how likely a customer would be to rent from the company again. What do you think about this view? What organizational capabilities would be necessary to develop customer loyalty? Check out Enterprise's Web site (**www.enterprise.com**). Look at the statements of the company's mission, culture, and founding values. How do these relate to customer loyalty?

3. A study by Fuld & Company, a competitive intelligence firm, found that companies fail to use as much as 70 percent of the online business data that they buy. Why do you think strategic decision makers might not look at all of the available business data? Why are such actions a problem? What recommendations might you have for strategic decision makers regarding business data?

   Source: *"Expensive Unused Data Are Clogging Up Budgets and Decision Making,"* Wall Street Journal, *July 1, 1999, p. A1.*

4. How to ask the right questions is an important skill for strategic decision makers. The following questions might be useful to strategic decision makers:

   - How can we do that? (Don't ask "Why can't we do that?")
   - How else can we do that? What else could we do?
   - Will you help me? Can you explain that to me again?
   - Who, what, why, where, when, how, and how much?
   - Who will do what and by when?

   Would these types of questions be useful in doing an internal analysis? Why or why not?

5. In the cosmetics industry, knowing what and how the various competitors are doing could be important strategic information in developing a sustainable competitive advantage. Suppose that you're a manager at Prescriptives. What types of competitive intelligence information would you want and where would you find it? Create a table that lists this information. Be prepared to support your ideas in class. (You'll probably need to do some outside research—library, Internet, or otherwise—to complete this assignment.)

6. Find five examples of companies' goals. List these goals on a sheet of paper. Then, do some reverse thinking and list what organizational resources and capabilities would be needed to accomplish those goals.

7. Studies of companies that are leaders in achieving exceptional customer profitability have found that such companies become leaders because they follow six steps: (1) Figure out the needs of your most profitable customers. (2) Get creative by imagining competitively superior ways to deliver value to customers. (3) Test and verify your hypotheses. (4) Tell customers how great your value propositions are. (5) Apply the best approaches on a large scale. (6) Start over, even the most successful initiatives need to be revised over time. What do you think of these suggestions? What are the implications for developing core competencies and distinctive capabilities? How could an internal analysis help an organization in this process?

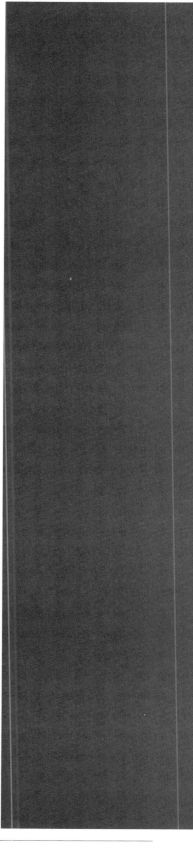

Strategic Management in Action Cases

CASE #1: Higher and Higher

This Strategic Management in Action Case can be found at the beginning of Chapter 4.

Discussion Questions

1. What resources and capabilities does the Haier Group appear to have? Are any of these capabilities distinctive? Explain. What will it take to make its capabilities distinctive?

2. What strengths and weaknesses does the Haier Group appear to have? How could it prevent its strengths from becoming weaknesses?

3. What approach to internal analysis would you suggest that CEO Zhang Ruimin use in assessing his organization's strengths and weaknesses? Why?

4. What do you think of Zhang's goals for his company? What must the company do to exploit its resources and capabilities in order to reach these goals?

CASE #2: Shooting for Success

Using an exceptionally well-executed game plan, the National Basketball Association (NBA) has emerged as the first truly global sports league. The transformation of a once-faltering domestic sport into a global commercial success reflects a keen understanding of resources and capabilities. And much of the credit should go to NBA commissioner David Stern, who has been deliberately building the NBA into a global brand. He says, "Basketball is a universal language, and it's about to bloom on a global basis."

Professional basketball sparked the interest of fans and players around the globe in the mid-1990s, and the NBA cashed in on the game's universal appeal. At one time, if you had asked someone in China what the most popular basketball team was, the answer would have been the "Red Oxen" from Chicago (the Bulls). Today, the NBA's center of attention *comes* from China. Yao Ming, the seven-foot, five-inch centerpiece of the Houston Rockets, has a personality that appeals to fans around the world. But he's not the only global player in the league. Others include the Dallas Mavericks' Dirk Nowitzki, a seven-footer from Germany; Pau Gasol of the Memphis Grizzlies, a native of Spain and also seven feet tall; San Antonio Spurs' guard Tony Parker from France; Denver Nuggets' forward Nene Hilario from Brazil; Orlando Magic guard Gordan Giricek from Croatia; and the newest "import," Darko Milicic, a seven-foot teenager from Serbia, now playing for the Detroit Pistons. What started as a trickle in the 1980s with occasional foreign stars such as Hakeem Olajuwon (Nigeria) and the late Drazen Petrovic (Croatia) has turned into a flood. A record 64 players from 34 countries and territories outside the United States are playing in the NBA.

In addition to the global players now in the U.S. league, the NBA is taking its game global. The league held several pre-season games in Europe, Latin America, and Asia. In addition, Stern predicts that there will be multiple teams in Europe by the end of the decade; developers are starting to build modern arenas to help promote expansion of the game. But today's global appeal didn't come easily.

In the mid-1990s, the league wanted to be a global entertainment leader and had the resources and capabilities to make it happen. However, the 1998–1999 season almost brought it to a crashing end. A brutal contract negotiation with players forced the cancellation of more than one-third of the league's games. The lockout frustrated and angered fans. Stern found the league's many global business initiatives grinding to a halt. Then, there was the issue of the NBA's most celebrated and revered icon, Michael Jordan. His first retirement in 1999 took away one of the league's key draws, both as a player and as a celebrity. From its winning streak, the NBA was suddenly struggling. However, Stern wasn't throwing in the towel.

To address the strategic challenges facing the NBA, Stern looked at what the league had to offer. What it had was consumer familiarity with basketball both domestically and globally, some talented young players, and a recognized image and track record. If those things could be exploited, the NBA might be able to get back in the game.

One of the actions that Stern took was to expand its network of offices globally. Why? The league hoped to reignite the NBA's popularity with global consumers by being visible. Stern explained, "The model is the rock concert. Sell lots of records. Tour occasionally."

Another thing that Stern did was enhance the league's Internet presence through its Web site. Today, some 40 percent of the visitors to the NBA Web site (which includes sites in Spanish, Japanese, and Chinese) log on from outside the United States. The NBA pushes its games and merchandise to fans around the world via their computers.

The league's global appeal is filling its coffers. About 20 percent of all NBA merchandise is now sold outside the United States, which is more than $430 million in annual revenue. Almost 1 million fans pay $10 a month to listen to streaming English or Spanish audio of almost any game on the league's Web site. The NBA built an NBA City theme restaurant in the Dominican Republic and is thinking of opening NBA stores in Asia and Europe. Separate NBA boutiques can be found in big department stores such as El Corte Ingles in Spain. Then, there's the television revenue. Nearly 15 percent of its $900 million in annual TV revenue comes from partners in some 212 countries and territories outside the United States.

Stern and the NBA are definitely taking actions to enhance their resources and capabilities. Whether these are just hoop dreams or can be a reality remains to be seen.

Discussion Questions

1. From this abbreviated description, what resources and capabilities do you think the NBA has? Does the fact that an organization is striving for global success make it more difficult to develop unique resources and distinctive capabilities? Explain.

2. Take each of the three approaches to internal analysis and describe how each could be used in analyzing the strengths and weaknesses of the NBA. Which one do you think is most appropriate for an organization such as the NBA? Support your choice.

3. Look at each of the strategic initiatives implemented by Stern. Are they exploiting the NBA's strengths and minimizing its weaknesses? Explain.

Sources: Information from NBA's Web page, **www.nba.com**, March 10, 2004; D. Eisenberg, "The NBA's Global Game Plan," *Time*, March 17, 2003, pp. 59–63; J. Tyrangiel, "The Center of Attention," *Time*, February 10, 2003, pp. 56–60; J. Tagliabue, "Hoop Dreams, Fiscal Realities," *New York Times*, March 4, 2000, p. B1; and D. Roth, "The NBA's Next Shot," *Fortune*, February 21, 2000, pp. 207–16.

CASE #3: Cooking Up Trouble

From the publication of her first book on entertaining back in 1982 to what is now the media empire called Martha Stewart Living Omnimedia, Martha Stewart has capitalized on what she does best—helping people create a lifestyle in which the ultimate in cooking, decorating, entertaining, and other homemaking arts is emphasized and celebrated. What exactly does Martha Stewart Living Omnimedia do? The company has two primary strategic goals: to provide original "how-to" content and information to as many consumers as possible and to turn customers into "doers" by offering them the information and products they need for do-it-yourself projects. The business is built around core subject areas, including cooking, entertaining, weddings, crafts, gardening, home, holidays, baby and children, and keeping and preserving (clothes, mementos, decorative artifacts, etc.).

From these different subject areas, content is developed for different media, including magazines, books, network television, cable television, newspapers and radio, and the Web. In addition, the core subject areas have evolved into merchandise lines (sheets, towels, table linens, paints, etc.) at Kmart and Sherwin Williams. Martha Stewart herself personified the Martha Stewart brand. It appeared that the company had positioned its resources and capabilities well to exploit sociocultural and demographic trends. Unfortunately, the company would soon find itself facing serious challenges—challenges that would test the company's ability to maintain its competitive advantage.

The trouble began in late December 2001 when Stewart sold all of her shares of stock in a company called ImClone Systems. The regulatory arm of the

Securities and Exchange Commission (SEC) would soon claim that she received a tip from a close friend, ImClone founder Sam Waksal, who also supposedly had been tipped off that the Federal Drug Administration was going to deny the sale of his company's new cancer drug. In June 2002, Waksal was arrested and charged with insider trading and was sentenced in June 2003 to more than seven years in prison for insider trading. Now, the SEC was coming after Stewart. Early in 2004, a jury was seated for Martha Stewart's trial in which prosecutors claimed that Stewart sold her ImClone stock on a "secret tip" and then lied to cover it up. The trial went on for almost six weeks. The judge eventually threw out the securities fraud count against Stewart, but left in the other charges of obstructing the federal government's investigation and lying about her involvement. On March 5, 2004, Stewart was convicted of four counts of conspiracy, obstruction, and making false statements.

The full damage to Martha Stewart Living Omnimedia (and its shareholders and 550 employees) won't be known for some time. Revenues in 2003 had fallen off more than 16 percent to $245 million, the stock price had plummeted, and the company reported its first-ever loss since going public in 1998. The company's board definitely had a tough job ahead of it. One expert stated, "They now face the big task of selling the content and forgetting the person." Stewart was replaced as CEO and stepped down from the board of the company, but retains the title of "founding editorial director, a role that gives her some influence at the company but with less operational authority." She will remain a full-time employee, however, and report to the current CEO Sharon Patrick. They have also started "debranding" the Martha Stewart brand by introducing more products without Stewart's name. The television show and magazine, which both prominently featured Stewart and her name, remain vulnerable. Retail experts are split on whether the Martha Stewart empire can survive this situation. One said, "The brand as we know it is dead. Any brand that's built exclusively around a single personality can't survive something like this. Advertisers are likely to pull away from her magazines and TV shows as they would much rather invest in Oprah's media publishing empire than associate with the Stewart brand now." Others believe that Martha Stewart's fans will forgive her and continue buying the products and watching the shows. What is obvious is that the company's strategic decision makers have an enormous challenge ahead of them to get beyond the scandal and attempt to reassert the power of the Martha Stewart brand.

Discussion Questions

1. What resources and capabilities did Martha Stewart Living Omnimedia appear to have prior to the trial and conviction? Have those resources and capabilities changed? Explain.

2. Do you think an organization can ever regain its competitive advantage from weakened or lost resources or distinctive capabilities? Why or why not? Do you think that Martha Stewart Living Omnimedia will be able to do so? Take both sides of this issue and list reasons why Martha Stewart Living Omnimedia will be able to do so and why it will not. Be prepared to debate one side or the other in class.

3. Would a company that has a reputation for having the "best" product in its industry ever have a need for competitive intelligence information? Why or why not?

4. How could Martha Stewart Living Omnimedia's strategic decision makers use value chain analysis in assessing the company's strengths and weaknesses? How about an internal audit? How about a capabilities assessment profile?

Sources: M. Rose, "Stewart Steps Down from Board but Retains an Influential Role," *Wall Street Journal*, March 16, 2004, p. B6; D. Carpenter, "Guilty Verdict Hasn't Yet Hurt Stewart's Store Sales," *Springfield News Leader*, March 11, 2004, p. 6B; L. Grant, "Stewart Brands See No Change in Sales Rates," *USA Today*, March 11, 2004, p. 3B; T. Howard, "Business Partners Shy From Stewart," *USA Today*, March 9, 2004, p. 1B; G. Farrell, "Lie May Cost Stewart Her Freedom," *USA Today*, March 8, 2004, p. 1B; T. Howard, "Homemaking Empire Tries to Dust Off Image," *USA Today*, March 8, 2004, p. 3B; M. Puente, "Stewart's Image is Tarnished, But For How Long?" *USA Today*, March 8, 2004, p. 5D; P. Bhastnagar, "Martha Inc. Beginning of the End," *CNN Money*, www.cnnmoney.com, March 8, 2004; "Timeline of Martha Stewart Scandal," *USA Today*, March 6, 2004. A. D'Innocenzio, "As a Brand, Stewart May Be Cooked," *Springfield News Leader*, March 6, 2004, p. 7B; T. Howard, "Stewart Empire Takes Hit from 'Challenge' of Trial," *USA Today*, March 5, 2004, p. B2; A. D'Innocenzio, "Is Martha's Image Stained for Good?" *Springfield News Leader*, January 24, 2004, p. 1E; and N. Byrnes, "Propping Up the House That Martha Built," *Business Week*, June 16, 2003, p. 38.

Endnotes

1. Haier American, **www.haieramerica.com**, March 8, 2004; Hoover's Online, **www.hoovers.com**, March 8, 2004; A. Raskin, "When Your Customer Says Jump," *Business 2.0*, October 2003, pp. 62–66; G. Khermouch, B. Einhorn, and D. Roberts, "Breaking into the Name Game," *Business Week*, April 7, 2003, p. 54; "Online Extra: Haier's Aim is to 'Develop Our Brand Overseas,'" *Business Week Online*, **www.businessweek.com**, March 31, 2003; D. J. Lynch, "CEO Pushes China's Haier as Global Brand," *USA Today*, January 3, 2003, p. 1B; and M. Arndt, "Can Haier Freeze Out Whirlpool and GE?" *Business Week*, April 11, 2002, **www.businessweek.com**.

2. D. J. Collis, "Research Note: How Valuable Are Organizational Capabilities," *Strategic Management Journal*, Winter 1994, pp. 143–52.

3. R. M. Grant, "The Resource-Based Theory of Competitive Advantage: Implications for Strategy Formulation," *California Management Review*, Spring 1991, pp. 114–35.

4. Collis, "Research Note."

5. S. G. Winter, "Understanding Dynamic Capabilities," *Strategic Management Journal*, October 2003, pp. 991–95; C. E. Helfat and M. A. Peteraf, "The Dynamic Resource-Based View: Capability Lifecycles," *Strategic Management Journal*, October 2003, pp. 997–1010; S. A. Zahra and G. George, "Absorptive Capacity: A Review, Reconceptualization, and Extension," *Academy of Management Review*, April 2002, pp. 185–203; G. S. Day, "The Capabilities of Market-Driven Organizations," *Journal of Marketing*, October 1994, pp. 37–52; and C. K. Prahalad and G. Hamel, "The Core Competence of the Corporation," *Harvard Business Review*, May–June 1990, pp. 79–91.

6. Day, "The Capabilities of Market-Driven Organizations," p. 39.

7. "An Industry Wake-Up Call," *Time Bonus Section*, March 1, 2004, p. A5; and C. Woodyard, "Hampton Inns Doesn't Hit Snooze on Its Overhaul," *USA Today*, January 28, 2004, p. B5.

8. K. Kelleher, "66,207,897 Bottles of Beer on the Wall," *Business 2.0*, January–February 2004, pp. 47–49.

9. Honda Ad, front inside cover of *Forbes*, July 7, 2003.

10. B. Nelson, "The Thinker," *Forbes*, March 3, 2003, pp. 62–64.

11. Prahalad and Hamel, "The Core Competence of the Corporation."

12. D. Sacks, "The Gore-Tex of Guitar Strings," *Fast Company*, December 2003, p. 46; and A. Harrington, "Who's Afraid of a New Product" *Fortune*, November 10, 2003, pp. 189–92.

13. See M. E. Porter, *Competitive Advantage: Creating and Sustaining Superior Performance*, Chapter 2 (New York: The Free Press, 1985).

14. K. E. Marino, "Developing Consensus on Firm Competencies and Capabilities," *Academy of Management Executive*, August 1996, pp. 40–51.

15. This discussion of the capabilities assessment profile is based on K. E. Marino, *Academy of Management Executive*.

16. P. Kotler, *Marketing Management*, 8th ed. (Upper Saddle River, NJ: Prentice Hall, 1996), p. 195.

17. H. H. Stevenson, "Defining Corporate Strengths and Weaknesses," *Sloan Management Review*, Spring 1967, pp. 51–68.

18. K. Western, "Ethical Spying," *Business Ethics*, September–October 1995, pp. 22–23.

5

Functional Strategies

LEARNING OUTLINE

The Role of Strategies

- *Explain how functional strategies fit into the strategic management process.*
- *Describe what happens after the SWOT analysis is completed.*

Types of Functional Strategies

- *Define functional strategies.*
- *Describe the three basic functions that all organizations perform.*
- *Discuss the various production–operations–manufacturing strategies.*
- *Describe the various marketing strategies.*
- *Explain why high-performance work activities are important.*
- *Discuss the various human resource management strategies.*
- *Describe the three strategic areas in research and development.*
- *List the advantages and disadvantages of being a first mover.*
- *Describe the strategies associated with the different information systems.*
- *Explain the various financial–accounting strategies.*

Now What?

- *Explain the interrelatedness of the functional strategies.*
- *Discuss how the functional strategies are implemented, evaluated, and changed.*
- *Discuss the importance of coordinating the functional strategies with the other organizational strategies.*

The Keys to Driving for Success

Toyota Motor Corporation has done it again! Once again it has proven why it's known worldwide as a leader in innovation, this time by developing and manufacturing a commercially viable (i.e., profitable) hybrid passenger vehicle—another example in a long line of accomplishments for Toyota.[1] This follows Toyota's success in developing a way to make a custom car in five days, which many thought was simply a dream. But Toyota showed it could be done, and it continues to revolutionize the auto industry. How has Toyota been able to achieve such successes?

Assessments of Toyota's business reveal that its successes can be attributed to a well-coordinated mix of functional strategies. The company leaves nothing to chance. For instance, in Toyota's highly efficient and effective manufacturing area, its work activities, connections, and production flows are rigidly scripted, yet extremely flexible. How can a rigid system also be flexible? As Toyota has discovered, it's those very rigid specifications that nourish and preserve flexibility and creativity. Four principles guide Toyota's Production System (TPS). Before we look at these four principles, you need to understand the role that the scientific process plays in Toyota's culture. Any change requires a rigorous problem-solving process with a detailed assessment of the current state of affairs and a plan for improvement. This scientific method is so ingrained at Toyota that the system actually inspires workers and managers to engage in the kinds of experimentation that are the hallmarks of a learning organization.

The four basic rules that guide the TPS are the following. *Rule 1—All work shall be highly specified as to content, sequence, timing, and outcome.* Toyota recognizes and emphasizes the details. Because employees follow a well-defined sequence of steps for a particular job, deviations are instantly obvious. *Rule 2— Every customer–supplier connection must be direct, and there must be an unambiguous yes-or-no way to send requests and receive responses.* An inherent part of this rule is the recognition that customers aren't only external. Every employee is "serving" some "customer," who may be simply the next person in the assembly process. *Rule 3—The pathway for every product and service must be simple and direct.* Every production line at Toyota is set up so every product and service flows along a simple, specified path. However, this doesn't mean that each path is dedicated to only one product. In fact, it's quite the opposite. Each production line at a Toyota plant typically accommodates many products. *Rule 4—Any improvement must be made in accordance with the scientific method, under the guidance of a teacher, at the lowest possible level in the organization.* Toyota explicitly teaches people how to improve and expects them to follow the scientific approach when doing so.

These four rules guide Toyota's employees from the top level to the bottom level. However, as we said earlier, it's not just the production strategies that are the keys to Toyota's success. All its functional strategies contribute. From Toyota's marketing strategies, which showcase the unique features of the company's cars, to its human resource management strategies, which emphasize education and training (e.g., Toyota's Technical Education Network is a partnership with over 50 select vocational and community colleges in the United States that train highly skilled technicians to work on Toyota products), to its research and development strategies (the commercially viable hybrid car and the five-day custom car), Toyota has a firm grasp on its functional strategies.

As our chapter-opening case illustrates, when an organization's functional strategies are managed strategically, it's able to exploit the resources, capabilities, and core competencies found in its various functions. In this chapter, we'll be discussing the role of the functional strategies in managing strategically. First, we're going to explain why we think it's important to look at the functional strategies before the competitive or corporate strategies and then look at what happens after the SWOT analysis. Next, we'll describe the various types of functional strategies—what they are and how they're implemented. Finally, we'll discuss strategy evaluation, making strategic changes, and coordinating functional strategies with the other organizational strategies.

THE ROLE OF FUNCTIONAL STRATEGIES

In this chapter, we actually begin to look at *how* strategic decision makers formulate and implement organizational strategies. We're approaching this step in the strategic management process differently than most other strategic management textbooks by looking at functional strategies first, which, as you'll see, seems to make the most sense.

Strategic Management in Action Process

Although you've studied several aspects of strategic management in action, the whole process still may appear totally confusing! (See Figure 5.1.) Just exactly *how* does it work? Although every organizational situation is different, it's like being faced with a 500-piece three-dimensional puzzle, and you're not quite sure where or how to start. You finally decide that the best approach is to start with pieces from the bottom while keeping in mind the overall goal (i.e., what the completed puzzle looks like). So, you start assembling the puzzle, keeping in mind the completed picture. Yet, the completed picture only serves to provide an overall perspective; it doesn't tell you what it takes to complete the puzzle so it looks like the picture. This approach is also the best way to look at organizational strategies. The organization's top-level decision makers will develop the overall goal of what the organization hopes to achieve (its vision, mission, and strategic objectives) and establish the overall corporate direction (i.e., a picture of the completed "puzzle"). However, by looking at the organization's functional strategies first (i.e., the puzzle pieces), we're able to see how to get to the completed picture. Do keep in mind, though, that the functional strategies *are* developed in light of the organization's vision, mission(s), overall corporate strategies, and competitive strategies.

One situation when it's more logical to discuss corporate strategies first, followed by competitive and then functional strategies, is when an organization is new. In that situation,

Figure 5.1

Strategic Management in Action

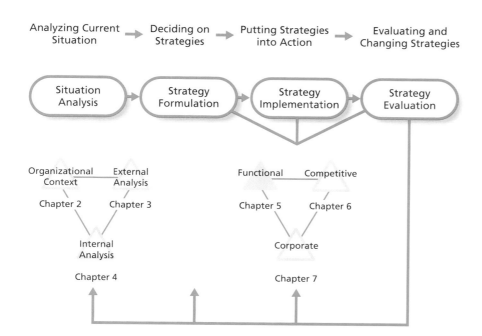

top-level strategists (usually the CEO and the top management team) formulate the overall strategic goal(s) and strategies as the organization begins to carry out its vision and organizational members begin performing their work activities. Over time, as the organization competes in its industry and as organizational members in the various functional areas do their jobs—whether providing current weather information, writing lines of software code, building a new greenways bike path, or selling telecommunications equipment— organizational resources are being used, capabilities are being developed, and, hopefully, distinctive capabilities are beginning to emerge. By managing strategically, organizational members in these various functional areas are working to create sustainable competitive advantage. And, the specific functional strategies being used are supporting the business-level (competitive) and corporate-level strategies. Because you'll most likely be facing strategic situations where the organization or organizational unit is *not* new, it makes sense to look at the organization's functional strategies first as we look at the process of deciding an organization's most appropriate strategies—that is, the ones that will lead to a sustainable competitive advantage.

What happens if the corporate or competitive strategies aren't working and need to be changed to accommodate changes in either the external or internal environments? What if there is no sustainable competitive advantage? Again, strategic decision makers will look to the organization's various functional units and assess what changes need to be made. What *is* and *isn't* working? This is where the information from the SWOT analysis is used.

What Happens After the SWOT Analysis?

After completing the SWOT analysis, decision makers are armed with information about the positive and negative aspects of both the external and internal environments. If the organization's strengths in the various functional units can be exploited as competitive advantages, particularly in light of any relevant external opportunities, the organization may well be on its way to achieving high levels of performance. In addition, if the SWOT analysis points to negative trends in any of the organization's external areas, changes in functional strategies might be needed to counteract these. Also, serious functional

More pizza is sold on Super Bowl Sunday than any other day of the year. Domino's Pizza alone will deliver more than 1.2 million pizzas. Why the increased demand on that one day? Pizza is the one food that seems to meet game-day criteria: It's cheap. It's easy. And it's social. The challenge for the pizza companies is making sure they can meet customers' demands. What are the implications for an organization's functional areas? Could SWOT analysis help? Explain.

Source: B. Horovitz, "Pizza People Prepare Super Bowl Blitz," USA Today, January 16, 2004, p.1B.

weaknesses that might be preventing a competitive advantage from being developed may need to be corrected or minimized.

The SWOT analysis points to the strategic issues organizational decision makers need to address in their pursuit of sustainable competitive advantage and high performance. Many strategic issues concern the level of performance reached (good or bad) in the various functional areas. Even if it's evident from the SWOT analysis that the organization's corporate or competitive strategies need to be changed, strategists will base their decisions on the resources, capabilities, and core competencies found in the functional areas. These important contributions to the organization's performance by the various organizational functions and the strategies being employed are another reason why we're looking at functional strategies first.

Now that we've explained what happens after SWOT analysis and why we're looking at the various functional strategies first, *what* are these strategies and *how* are they implemented in organizations?

Learning Review

- How do the functional strategies fit into the strategic management in action process?
- How does the work done in the functional areas support the creation of a competitive advantage?
- What happens after the SWOT analysis is completed?

TYPES OF FUNCTIONAL STRATEGIES

Each functional area of the organization has strategies for achieving its mission and for helping the organization reach its overall vision. In Chapter 1, we defined an organization's **functional strategies** (or operational strategies) as the short-term goal-directed decisions and actions of the organization's various functional areas. All organizations—even not-for-profit ones—perform three basic functions as they create and deliver goods and services: (1) marketing (assess and establish the demand for the product and then market and deliver the product after it's produced); (2) production and operations (create the product); and (3) financial and accounting (account for payments received for products and provide information on performance results). These three basic functions, especially for businesses, usually are expanded to include six areas: marketing, research and development, production–operations–manufacturing, human resource management, financial–accounting, and information systems–technology. As we pointed out in the last chapter, each organization may have its own uniquely named functional areas, yet the basic work activities that comprise these functions remain the same—acquiring and transforming the organization's resources (inputs) into the organization's outputs (goods or services), which are delivered to the organization's customers. Because they're convenient and familiar, we'll use these six areas as our framework for describing the functional strategies. For each functional area, we'll look at the most common strategies used in that particular area and how these strategies are implemented. In addition, we'll also look at some of the current strategies being used in those functional areas. One thing we need to state up front is that our description of the various functional strategies is intended only as an *overview*. We're not attempting to cover the specifics of these strategies. If you want more information, you'll need to look at other textbooks or more specialized books on a specific functional area.

Production–Operations–Manufacturing Strategies

It takes more than seven years to make the world's most complicated manufactured product—a nuclear-powered, Nimitz-class U.S. Navy aircraft carrier.[2] "Putting together an aircraft carrier is like no other manufacturing task in the world. It is the most technologically challenging and toughest product to manufacture." Each ship costs more than $4 billion and involves more than 47,000 tons of precision-welded steel, more than 1 million distinct parts, 900 miles of wire and cable, approximately 40 million skilled-worker hours, and massive numbers of engineers. Talk about the need for some efficient and effective production–operations–manufacturing strategies!

Although you probably won't be purchasing an aircraft carrier anytime soon, you've obviously purchased and used an incredible number and variety of products and services by this time in your life. In fact, you may have produced some of these yourself—for example, if you've ever grown produce in a garden, built bookshelves out of scrap wood and bricks, or baked a loaf of bread. However, most of the products we consume and use are produced by someone else. The process of creating goods and services in which organizational inputs (resources) are transformed into outputs is called **production**.[3] The production process used to create physical (tangible) products is fairly obvious. However, even the creation and delivery of services requires some type of transformation activities. As our chapter-opening case illustrates, when the various production strategies are well integrated with the other functional areas of the organization and support the overall company objectives, it's possible to create a sustainable competitive advantage. What we'll look at in this section are some of the common strategic choices in the organization's production area. Table 5.1 provides a concise summary of possible production–operations–manufacturing (POM) strategies.

Production Process Strategies

Different organizations use different approaches to transforming their resources into goods and services. The goal of an organization's production process strategies is to find a way to produce products or services that meet (or exceed) customer requirements in light of certain cost and other managerial constraints. Three possible strategies include: (1) process focused, which is organized around processes and appropriate for producing high-variety, low-volume products (e.g., gourmet meals, heart transplants, specialized print jobs, or a cruise ship vacation); (2) product focused, which is organized around products and appropriate for producing high-volume, low-variety products (e.g., steel, paper, light bulbs, or bread); (3) repetitive focused, which falls somewhere between process focused and product focused and which uses standardized component parts in assembling products such as those produced on a typical assembly line (e.g., motorcycles, televisions, or fast food). The process strategy that is most appropriate and important to developing a competitive advantage depends on the volume and variety of products being produced. An organization might also be able to develop a competitive advantage with its specific machinery, equipment, and technology if these things contribute to a production process with lower costs, higher quality, or the ability to better meet customer needs.

Table 5.1

Possible Production–Operations–Manufacturing (POM) Strategies

PRODUCTION PROCESS STRATEGIES
- Process focused
- Product focused
- Repetitive focused

CAPACITY STRATEGIES
- Size of facility
- Efficient use

LOCATION STRATEGIES
- Location selection

WORK DESIGN STRATEGIES
- Job specialization
- Job enlargement
- Job enrichment
- Ergonomics
- Work methods
- Motivation–incentive systems
- Standards–output levels

LAYOUT STRATEGIES
- Fixed position
- Process oriented
- Office
- Retail–service
- Warehouse
- Product oriented

POM MANAGEMENT STRATEGIES
- Aggregate planning techniques
- Just-in-time systems
- Purchasing management procedures
- Inventory management systems
- Materials requirement planning
- Short-term scheduling techniques
- Project management procedures
- Maintenance management

CURRENT POM STRATEGIES
- Value chain management
- Integrated manufacturing
  - Advanced manufacturing technology
  - Total quality management
  - Just-in-time inventory control

Capacity Strategies

The size of a facility and how efficiently facilities are used can be important contributors to the development of competitive advantage. Some strategies associated with production capacity include demand management and capacity management. How do organizations "manage" demand? By employing strategies such as staffing changes (adding or laying off employees), adjusting equipment and processes (purchase, sell, or lease), improving work methods to be more efficient, or redesigning the product. On the other hand, capacity management involves strategies to effectively and efficiently use current facilities, part of which includes determining the break-even point. Also, as part of this strategy, strategic decision makers may have to forecast future capacity requirements to ensure that facilities are up and running when needed.

Location Strategies

One of the most important competitive decisions a company makes is where to locate its operations. Because location significantly influences an organization's costs and revenues, the objective of the location strategy should be to maximize the benefits and minimize the costs of locating in a particular area. For example, General Motors recently decided to locate its first automotive research lab outside the United States in Bangalore, India, for cost and diversity reasons.[4] In choosing appropriate location strategies, decision makers assess factors such as labor costs and availability, proximity to raw materials and suppliers, proximity to markets, state and local government policies and regulations, environmental regulations, utilities, site costs, transportation availability, and quality-of-life issues.

Work Design Strategies

The POM function plays a significant role in work design strategies by determining who can do what, when, and under what conditions. Some of the more common work design strategies include job specialization, job enlargement, job enrichment, ergonomics, work methods, and motivation–incentive systems. Work design also involves establishing performance standards for different jobs and different levels of output for those jobs.

STRATEGIC MANAGEMENT
the global perspective

Canadian company Magna International, the world's seventh largest auto parts supplier, is fast becoming an integral part of some car manufacturers' POM strategies. Magna has turned its European subsidiary, Magna Steyr, into the only parts company in the world to offer car makers fully outsourced engineering and production. The car manufacturer provides Magna the plans for a new model style and a chassis to build on, and Magna Steyr performs the engineering, builds the assembly line, and produces

the car. For example, German manufacturer Bayerisch Motoren Werk (BMW), whose plants were already running at full capacity, turned to Magna to build its small SUV, the X3. It's the first BMW built in a non-BMW plant. BMW said the strategy accelerated production of the car by several months and lowered costs. Could there by any drawbacks to such a strategy for Magna and for the car makers? Discuss.

Source: J. Turrettini, "Made to Order," Forbes, September 1, 2003, pp. 78–80.

Layout Strategies

How a facility is arranged or laid out to do the organization's work has a significant impact on operational efficiency. The objective of this strategy is to develop a layout that's economical and meets the requirements of product design and volume, process equipment and capacity, quality of work life, and building and site constraints. The six potential layouts include the following:

1. The *fixed-position layout* is one in which the product remains stationery and requires workers and equipment to come to the work area. Examples include constructing a bridge, building an apartment building or an aircraft carrier, or containing a burning oil well.

2. The *process-oriented layout* is appropriate for low-volume, high-variety (job shop) products where the focus is on the processes being used to create the product or service. Examples include a medical clinic, cafeteria kitchen, or a job shop that produces temperature-control panels.

3. The *office layout* positions workers, equipment, and workspaces/offices to provide for movement of information. Examples include an insurance company, an advertising agency, or a software design firm.

4. The *retail-service layout* arranges people and equipment according to customer needs and behavior. The objective behind the retail layout is to maximize profitability per square foot of shelf space or floor space. Examples include a grocery store, department store, or office-products store.

5. In the *warehouse layout,* the objective is to find the optimum trade-off between product handling cost and warehouse space. Examples include any type of warehouse or distribution facility.

6. The *product-oriented layout* is organized around a product or group of similar high-volume, low-variety products. In this type of repetitive, continuous production, it's important to have layout arrangements that maximize people and machine utilization. Examples include a meat-packing facility, a TV assembly line, or a furniture manufacturer.

POM Strategies

Other strategies include those associated with actually *managing* the production function. These include strategic decisions about aggregate planning techniques, just-in-time

Designing Desirable Workspaces

Do you study better in some places than in others? What would your ideal study space look like? It used to be that organizational architects were told to squeeze the largest number of workers into the smallest space possible to balance the cost of expensive real estate. However, many organizations today are discovering that workspace design can have a significant impact on what employees do and how they accomplish their work. For example, Nortel Networks' Canadian headquarters is a vast indoor cityscape. The former manufacturing plant was transformed into a unique workplace where departmental "neighborhoods" have their own distinctive décor. Employees can go to the plaza outside the Java.cup café at the corner of 20th and Main streets (yes, there are streets and street signs in the facility) or work out in the fitness facility. Why would an organization go to this type of effort—and expense—to create such a work environment? There are several reasons. First, office and workspace design has become an important recruiting tool. Potential employees judge the look and feel of workspaces and consider it third most important after salary and benefits. Another reason

for designing desirable workspaces is the belief that it will lead to more communal bonds among employees. Fostering this community feeling is conducive to employee interaction, trust, and openness. Finally, workspace design can be used to foster creativity and innovation. When workspaces are open, flexible, and designed for social interaction, employees mingle and move about. The impromptu conversations and "chance encounters" can lead to sharing of information and new insights—all hallmarks of an innovative organization. Can workspace design give an organization a competitive edge? The answer would have to be "not by itself." But having well-designed workspaces can be an important component of an organization's functional strategies. Do some additional research on workspace design. What did you find? How might an organization's functional strategies be impacted by workspace design?

Sources: C. Taylor, "Space Odyssey," Smart Money, June 2002, p. 120; D. Danbom, "It's an Office Feng," Business Finance, March 2002, p. 64; L. Kanter, "Dream Offices," Business Week, November 6, 2000, pp. F18–F28; M. McDonald, "The Latte Connections," U.S. News and World Report, March 29, 1999, pp. 63–66; B. Nussbaum, "Blueprints for Business: Business Week Architectural Record Awards," Business Week, November 3, 1997, pp. 112–16; and "Northern Exposure," Business Week, November 3, 1997, pp. 124–25.

systems, purchasing management procedures, inventory management systems, materials requirement planning techniques, short-term scheduling techniques, project management procedures, and maintenance management. Each of these strategies is aimed at making the organization's production area as effective and efficient as possible. What we want to look at next are some POM strategies currently being used by organizations.

Current POM Strategies

Ideally, an organization's POM strategies create a "seamless, value-creating pipeline endlessly meeting customers' expectations by transforming ideas, raw materials, parts, and subassemblies into finished products and services."[5] Even if our POM strategies can't quite live up to that ideal, research studies do show that an organization's production and manufacturing strategies can make important strategic contributions to organizational performance.[6] What types of POM strategies are today's world-class organizations using to achieve high levels of performance and the development of a sustainable competitive advantage? One is the adoption of a value chain management strategy. **Value chain management** is a process of managing the entire sequence of activities and information flows along the entire value chain from incoming materials to outgoing products. The goal of value chain management is creating a strategy that enables organizations to meet and exceed customers' needs and allows for full and seamless integration along all members of the chain. Figure 5.2 illustrates the six main requirements of a successful value chain management strategy.

Figure 5.2

Six Requirements for Successful Value Chain Management

Another current POM strategy is **integrated manufacturing**, which is a production–operations approach that emphasizes the use of advanced manufacturing technology, total quality management, and just-in-time inventory control. What do these involve? Advanced manufacturing technology strategies involve flexible manufacturing systems and computer-integrated manufacturing. Total quality management strategies involve production principles such as continuous improvement and teaming up with suppliers to improve quality. Just-in-time inventory control strategies entail work practices that reduce lead time and inventory.

No matter the type, size, or location of the organization, value chain management and integrated manufacturing strategies are becoming the blue-ribbon standard for the design of the production–operations function. Our chapter-opening case on Toyota Motor Corporation provides an excellent example of how an organization can achieve successful performance and a competitive advantage through both value chain management and integrated manufacturing strategies.

Learning Review

- Define functional strategies.
- Describe the three basic functions that all organizations perform as they create and deliver goods and services.
- What is production? Why is it important for both physical products *and* intangible services?
- Describe the six basic types of POM strategies.
- How is value chain management important to today's organizations?
- What are the six requirements for a successful value chain management strategy?
- What is integrated manufacturing? What is its importance to strategic management in action?

Marketing Strategies

An organization's marketing function plays a critical role in the pursuit of sustainable competitive advantage. **Marketing** is defined as a process of assessing and meeting individual's or group's wants and needs by creating, offering, and exchanging products of value.[7] The two biggest factors in marketing are the two "Cs"—customers and competitors. An organization's marketing strategies are directed at effectively and efficiently managing these two groups. The main marketing strategies involve segmentation or target market, differentiation, positioning, and marketing mix strategic decisions (the 4 Ps: product, pricing, promotion, and place). Let's look at the most common strategic choices for each of these areas. (See Table 5.2 for a summary.)

Segmentation or Target Market Strategies

Every market consists of potential or actual customers who may differ in one or more ways. These differences can be used to segment a market. Market segments are large identifiable groups within a market. At the most basic level, an organization can choose a marketing strategy to either segment the market or treat it as one homogeneous market. If an organization chooses to segment the consumer market, it can select from several different variables such as geographic (region, city or metropolitan area, population density, and climate); demographic (age, gender, family size, family life cycle, income, occupation, education, religion, race, and nationality); psychographic (social class, lifestyle, and personality); or behavioral (occasions of product use, benefits, user status, usage rate, loyalty status, readiness to buy stage, and attitude toward product). The major segmentation variables for business markets include: demographic (industry type, company size, and location); operating variables (technology, user–nonuser status, and customer capabilities); purchasing approaches (purchasing function organization, power structure, nature of existing relationships, general purchase policies, and purchasing criteria); situational factors (urgency, specific application, and size of order); or personal characteristics (buyer–seller similarity, attitudes toward risk, and loyalty). Once the possible customer segments have been identified, the next step is to determine which ones are the most attractive targets.

Target market selection entails one of five possible strategic approaches. Single-segment concentration means that the organization selects a single segment to target. In selective specialization, the organization chooses to serve a number of equally attractive and appropriate segments that have few or no common characteristics. The product specialization strategy is where the organization concentrates on making a certain product that's sold to several segments. In the market specialization strategy, the organization serves many needs of a particular customer group. Finally, the full market coverage strategy means that the organization is attempting to serve all customer groups with all the products they might need or desire.

Differentiation Strategies

Because the vast majority of product and services marketing takes place in competitive markets, organizations look for ways to differentiate their products from competitors. How? Four differentiation dimensions have been identified: the product itself (features, performance, conformance, durability, reliability, repairability, style, and design); services (delivery, installation, customer training, consulting service, repair, and miscellaneous factors); personnel (competence, courtesy, credibility, reliability, responsiveness, and communication abilities); and image (symbols such as a logo, color identifier, or famous person; written and audiovisual media; atmosphere features such as building design, interior design, layout, colors, or furnishings; and sponsored events or causes). The main differentiators organizations tend to use are features, performance, conformance, durability, reliability, repairability, style, and design.[8]

Table 5.2

Possible Marketing Strategies

SEGMENTATION STRATEGIES
- Geographic
- Demographic
- Psychographic
- Behavioral

TARGET MARKET SELECTION STRATEGIES
- Single-segment concentration
- Selective specialization
- Product specialization
- Market specialization
- Full market coverage

DIFFERENTIATION STRATEGIES
- Product itself
  - Features, performance, conformance, durability, reliability, repairability, style, design
- Services
  - Delivery, installation, customer training, consulting service, repair, miscellaneous factors
- Personnel
  - Competence, courtesy, credibility, reliability, responsiveness, communication abilities
- Image
  - Symbols (logo, color identifier, or famous person)
  - Written and audiovisual media
  - Atmosphere features (building design, interior design, layout, colors, furnishings)
  - Sponsored events or causes

POSITIONING STRATEGIES
- Attribute positioning
- Benefit positioning
- Use–application positioning
- User positioning
- Competitor positioning
- Product category positioning
- Quality–price positioning

MARKETING MIX STRATEGIES

Product
- New-product development
- Product line
- Brand
- Packaging–labeling
- Product life cycle decisions

Pricing
- Markup pricing
- Target–return pricing
- Perceived-value pricing
- Value pricing
- Going-rate pricing
- Sealed-bid pricing
- Geographical pricing
- Price discounts–allowances
- Promotional pricing
- Discriminatory pricing
- Product mix pricing

Promoting
- Advertising
  - Billboards
  - Point-of-purchase displays
  - Symbols and logos
  - Packaging inserts
- Sales promotion
- Public relations
- Personal selling
- Direct marketing

Place
- Channel choice
- Market logistics
- Inventory
- Transportation modes–carriers

CURRENT MARKETING STRATEGIES
- Relationship marketing
  - Financial benefits
  - Social benefits
  - Structural ties
- Mass customization
- Events and activities marketing
- Database marketing

Positioning Strategies

Once an organization has identified potential differentiators, it needs to decide which and how many differences to highlight. In other words, it wants to establish a specific and distinct position in the marketplace. At least seven different positioning strategies exist: attribute positioning (positioning on the basis of certain product attributes), benefit positioning (positioning on the basis of providing certain benefits), use–application positioning (positioning on the basis of a limited use or application), user positioning (positioning on the basis of some customer characteristic), competitor positioning (positioning

Dicky Riegel is president and CEO of a company whose product first appeared in the 1930s and has managed over the years to retain an enviable image in consumers' minds. The company is Airstream, maker of those sleek aluminum trailers that glisten in the light. Those trailers attract a loyal and demanding customer base that cuts across demographic lines. When asked what accounts for the product's mystique, Riegel replied, "Airstreams have an allure. People have an emotional response to them. They also appeal in a very basic way to people's love for the nomadic way of life and to their sense of community. Airstream owners have a very strong sense of belonging." Go to the company's Web site. What strategies do you think the company uses to differentiate and position its product?

Source: *Airstream,* **www.airstream.com**, March 12, 2004; and "Innovating a Classic at Airstream," Harvard Business Review, October 2003, pp. 18–20.

against one or more competitors), product category positioning (positioning on the basis of some product category), and quality–price positioning (positioning on the basis of quality–price strategies). Each of these possible strategies builds upon what the organization views as its most important differentiators in establishing a competitive advantage. The positioning strategies also are important in influencing the development of appropriate marketing mix strategies.

Marketing Mix Strategies

The marketing mix strategies involve the specifics of what *product* is going to be offered to customers, how it will be *priced,* how it will be *promoted,* and where it will be *placed* so customers can get it. These are the 4 Ps often referred to in marketing—that is, product, price, promotion, and place. Let's look at the possible strategies for each.

An organization's *product* strategies involve several aspects. An important one is how the organization approaches new-product development. (New products can include original products, improved products, modified products, or new brands.) Once new-product ideas have been developed, the organization will have different strategies for developing and testing the actual product itself. If the proposed product passes these stages, then the organization must decide how much and what type of market testing to use, requiring the use of different strategies. Strategic product decisions at this point also involve the width, depth, length, and consistency of the product line(s). There also may be strategic choices that involve brand decisions such as whether to use a brand name, a brand sponsor, and what type of brand strategy to pursue. Other product strategies involve packaging and labeling decisions. Once the product is in the market, product strategies concern managing the various stages in the product life cycle (PLC). The PLC concept is a recognition that a product's sales rise and decline, bringing about the need for different strategies for coping with these ups and downs. (See Figure 5.3 for an example of a typical PLC.) As you probably know, the various stages of the PLC might require changes not only in the product strategies, but in the other Ps, as well.

The *pricing* strategy depends on the organization's pricing objectives (survival, maximum current profit, maximum current revenue, maximum sales growth, maximum market skimming, product–quality leadership, or other). It's also influenced by customers' demand for the product, costs of producing and marketing the product, and competitors' prices. Based on these factors, the company can choose from the following pricing strategies: markup pricing (pricing by adding a standard markup), target-return pricing (pricing to achieve a targeted or desired return), perceived-value pricing (pricing based on the customers' perception of value), value pricing (pricing based on charging low price for high-quality products), going-rate pricing (pricing based largely on what competitors are charging), or sealed-bid pricing (pricing based on expectations of how competitors will

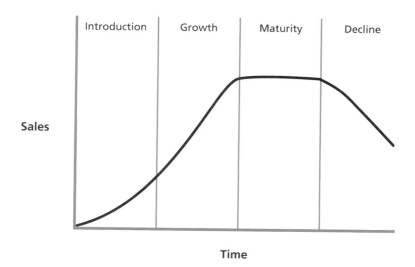

Figure 5.3

Product Life Cycle

bid). Other possible decisions in the pricing strategy include geographical pricing, price discounts and allowances, promotional pricing, discriminatory pricing, or product mix pricing. Also, although an organization may establish what it feels is an effective and efficient pricing strategy, competitive and marketplace dynamics may require increasing or lowering prices, thus creating a need to change the current pricing strategy.

A good overall marketing strategy includes strategies for *promoting* the product. Common strategies for promotion involve the use of the various marketing communication and promotion tools such as advertising (print and broadcast media ads, brochures and booklets, posters and leaflets, billboards, point-of-purchase displays, symbols and logos, packaging inserts, and many others); sales promotion (contests, games, sweepstakes and lotteries; premiums and gifts; sampling; fairs and trade shows; exhibits; demonstrations; coupons; rebates; trading stamps; product tie-ins; and others); public relations (press kits, speeches, annual reports, charitable contributions, sponsorships, community relations, lobbying, events, company magazine, and others); personal selling (sales presentations, sales meetings, incentive programs, samples, and others); and direct marketing (catalogs, mailings, telemarketing, electronic shopping, and TV shopping). What are appropriate choices? It depends on the target audience and the marketing communication objectives. Once these are determined, then the appropriate message, communication channel, promotion budget, and promotion mix strategies can be formulated.

The final aspect of the marketing mix strategies involves specific *place* or distribution strategies. What's involved with the place strategy? One important aspect is the choice of channels for distributing the product or service. Alternatives include the type of intermediary to use (i.e., wholesaler, dealer, direct sales, value-added reseller, mail-order marketer, and so forth) and the number of intermediaries to use (exclusive distribution, selective distribution, or intensive distribution). Another important aspect of the place strategy involves the actual physical distribution of the product, which is also referred to as *market logistics*. Normally, there are four market logistics strategies to decide. The first is determining the strategic approach to be used in processing customer orders. Next, strategic decision makers must determine the warehousing arrangements. Then, decisions about inventory (when to order and how much to order) must be addressed. Obviously, decisions about inventory strategy should be coordinated with the production–operations function so that finished products are available when needed, in the style and design needed, and at an appropriate cost. The final market logistics strategy involves decisions about specific transportation modes and carriers.

A hot and gooey delectable Southern confection. That's the mouth-watering description of Krispy Kreme's original glazed doughnuts. Krispy Kreme, based in Winston-Salem, North Carolina, used to be available mainly in the Southeast. People who grew up with Krispy Kreme and moved away longed to be able to sink their teeth into a Krispy Kreme doughnut. Throughout the years, the company has expanded gradually. However, Krispy Kreme is stepping up its geographic expansion. The company is even opening test stores (called "fresh shops") in select Wal-Mart locations. At what point do a company's products, like Krispy Kreme doughnuts, lose their allure because they become more widely available? That's a problem that Coors beer had. During the 1970s, Coors products were available only in parts of the West. The product developed a cult following among college students in the rest of the country. When it went national in the 1980s, Coors became just another beer. Now, strategic decision makers at Krispy Kreme have to find a way to keep its product's allure alive while continuing to pursue new market opportunities. What are the implications for marketing strategies?

Sources: Reuters, "Krispy Kreme to Open Test Stores in Wal-Marts," USA Today, September 12, 2003; A. Serwer, "The Hole Story," Fortune, July 7, 2003, pp. 52–62; and J. R. Hagerty, "Krispy Kreme at a Krossroads," Wall Street Journal, February 24, 2000, p. B1.

Current Marketing Strategies

Developing effective marketing strategies is getting harder and harder. Why? Customers are becoming more sophisticated and knowledgeable, maybe even cynical, about marketing activities. The number of strategic options for the marketing area is multiplying, making appropriate choices even more difficult. Also, the increasing extent of global markets and global competitors challenges organizational decision makers who must strategically manage the marketing function. How are world-class organizations addressing these marketing strategy challenges? One approach is **relationship marketing**, which is a process of building long-term, trusting, "win–win" relationships with valued customers.[9] This strategy emphasizes the importance of building solid and valuable partnerships with customers. How can organizations do this? Three approaches to building solid and valuable customer relationships have been identified:

1. Adding *financial* benefits to the customer relationship through programs such as frequent buyers, collectors' societies, kids clubs, and so forth. For instance, Harley Davidson sponsors the Harley Owners Group (HOG), whose members pay an annual fee to receive a magazine (*Hog Tales*), an emergency pick-up service, touring guides, theft reward service, discount hotel rates, and so forth.

2. Adding *social* benefits to the financial benefits by bonding with customers and building personalized relationships with them through events such as customer appreciation days. In today's wired world, such customer connections can be virtual. Many organizations have created **online communities**—constantly changing groups of people who collaborate, share ideas, and build relationships online.

3. Adding *structural* ties as well as financial and social benefits through such activities as, for example, supplying customers with special equipment or computer linkages.

A variation of relationship marketing is approaching customers with "one-to-one marketing" or "mass customization."[10] With mass customization, organizations provide customers with products or services based on what they tell you and what else you may know about them. For instance, customers can get personalized vitamins, custom-fit golf clubs, customized textbooks, or any number of custom products. Also, the Internet is proving to be a useful tool in the push towards mass customization. Through well-designed Web sites, companies can communicate with customers and tailor product offerings to

Data Mining

Just like a miner digging for gold, an organization's marketers need to mine their customer data to learn more about their customers and their buying habits. The challenge of data mining is being able to spot the unexpected in the reams of customer information that's collected. There are six basic techniques for data mining. The first is *neural networks,* which attempt to simulate the way the human brain discovers patterns. It involves looking at data and trying to discern possible patterns by thinking the way the customer thinks. The next type of data mining technique is *induction techniques.* In this approach, data miners use a process of reasoning from specific facts to reach a hypothesis. Another technique is using *statistics* by building models that describe the behavior of the data. Then, there's the *visualization technique* that displays

analytical data in ways that most nonexperts can understand. Another technique is *online analytical processing,* which is a more sophisticated and complex display of data, often across several time periods. Finally, *query languages* can be used to provide even more explicit descriptions of data. Many of these techniques can be done through software that makes the data miner's job much easier. What happens to data that are "mined"? Such data can be used to pinpoint which customers are more profitable. They can also help recognize subtle changes in customers' buying habits and patterns. Ultimately, this is the type of information that's needed when designing effective marketing strategies.

Sources: G. Morse, "Hidden Minds: A Conversation with Gerald Zaltman," Harvard Business Review, June 2002, pp. 26–27; L. Bransten, "Looking for Patterns," Wall Street Journal, June 21, 1999, p. R16; "Six Data Mining Techniques," Executive Edge, April–May 1999, p. 10; J. Teresko, "Information Rich, Knowledge Poor," Industry Week, February 1, 1999, pp. 19–24; and P. C. Judge, "What've You Done For Us Lately?" Business Week, September 14, 1998, pp. 140–42.

their unique needs. For example, Amazon.com understands this process well. Let's say, for instance, that you've purchased books from Amazon on mountain climbing. As Amazon gets new books on that subject or related subjects, it will contact you to see if you'd like to order them. To make this marketing strategy work, all the other functions must support and facilitate this close customer connection.

Another current marketing approach is *events and activities marketing.* As media outlets have become more fragmented and as technologies (such as TiVo) now allow TV viewers to skip over ads completely, organizations have had to become more creative in pushing their products.[11] Marketers have moved beyond covert product placement in movies and television shows to outright experiential approaches. For example, Coca-Cola has been testing "teen lounges" in Chicago and Los Angeles where kids can watch music videos, listen to music, play video games, and, of course, buy Coke products. And Coca-Cola scored a mega-marketing hit with the reality show *American Idol.* Coke-related items appeared all over the set—from the red Coke cups sitting in front of the judges to the red couches with the signature white swoop along the back where the contestants sat. As these examples show, strategic decision makers will have to become more creative in their marketing strategies.

The final current marketing strategy we'll discuss is **database marketing**, which uses database technology and sophisticated analytical techniques combined with direct-marketing methods to elicit a desired, measurable response in target groups and individuals. A database marketing system can help strategic decision makers learn customers' buying habits—which products and colors sell best, which time of year is best for selling particular items, and so forth. Having a lot of information about customers can provide an organization a distinct competitive advantage. Many software programs make it possible for organizations to amass detailed profiles of customers and then offer them the things they're likely to buy. For instance, American Express amasses large quantities of customer data and then massages it to pinpoint their best customers, who are then targeted in a more personal way. It "mines" the data (data mining) for critical strategic marketing information.

Table 5.3

Examples of High-
performance Work Practices

• Self-directed work team	• Job rotation
• Problem-solving groups	• Total quality management programs
• Contingent pay	• Information sharing
• Attitude surveys	• Employee suggestions implemented

Source: Based on Brian Becker and Barry Gerhart, "The Impact of Human Resource Management on Organizational Performance: Progress and Prospects," Academy of Management Journal, August 1996, pp. 779–801.

Human Resource Management Strategies

"Our people are our *most* important asset." How often have you heard this statement? More importantly, can human resources management (HRM) strategies be used to establish a sustainable competitive advantage? The answer seems to be "yes, they can." Various studies have concluded that an organization's human resources can be a significant source of competitive advantage.[12] Although an organization's HRM strategies may lead to competitive advantage, do they also have an impact on performance? Other studies have looked at the link between HR policies–practices and performance. Most have shown that certain HR policies and practices—ones referred to as "high-performance work practices"—*can* have a positive impact on firm performance.[13] What are **high-performance work practices**? They're human resource policies and practices that can lead to both high individual and high organizational performance. They include strategies such as comprehensive employee recruitment and selection procedures, incentive compensation and performance management systems, and extensive employee involvement and training. Table 5.3 lists some high-performance work practices that have been identified. These types of HRM strategies can improve the knowledge, skills, and abilities of an organization's current and potential

Table 5.4

Possible Human
Resource Management
(HRM) Strategies

WORK FLOWS	• Type of training
• Organize for efficiency or innovation	• Job-specific or generic training
• Organize for control or flexibility	
• Use specialized or broad job categories	**COMPENSATION**
• Use detailed or loose work planning	• Fixed or variable pay
	• Job-based or individual pay
STAFFING	• Seniority-based or performance-based pay
• Internal or external recruiting	• Who makes pay decisions
• Who makes hiring decisions	
• What's important in hiring	**EMPLOYEE AND LABOR RELATIONS**
• Formal or informal approach	• Top-down or bottom-up communication
	• Interaction with labor unions
EMPLOYEE SEPARATIONS	• Adversarial or cooperative relationship
• How to downsize	
• Hiring freezes	**EMPLOYEE RIGHTS**
• Support for terminated employees	• Use discipline as control or learning
• Preferential or nonpreferential rehiring	• Protect organization's or employees' rights
	• Formal or informal ethics program
PERFORMANCE APPRAISAL	
• Customized or uniform approach	**CURRENT HRM STRATEGIES**
• Purpose of appraisal	• View of human resources
• Multipurpose or focused approach	• Family-friendly benefits
• Use multiple inputs or one input	
• Appraisal instruments used	
TRAINING AND DEVELOPMENT	
• Buy or develop skills	
• Individual or team-based training	

The Human Capital Index

The Human Capital Index was a comprehensive global study of over 2,000 firms conducted by consulting firm Watson Wyatt Worldwide. The study showed that "superior human capital practices are not only correlated with financial returns, they are, in fact, a leading indicator of increased shareholder value." But that finding wasn't the most interesting thing to come out of the study. More importantly, the researchers were able to identify which HR practices were the main contributors to increasing a company's market value and which detracted from the company's market value. They categorized these HR practices into six dimensions.

- *Total Rewards and Accountability*—rewarding employees for good work and refusing to accept subpar performance. These particular practices had a dramatic impact on shareholder value—accounting for a 16.5 percent increase in shareholder value.

- *Collegial, Flexible Workplace*—great leadership and a less hierarchical culture that encourages employee contributions. These particular practices were responsible for a 9 percent increase in shareholder value.

- *Recruiting and Retention Excellence*—investing time in the recruitment and selection process and establishing a reputation as a great place to work. These particular practices increased shareholder value by 7.9 percent.

- *Communications Integrity*—creating an environment where employees can and will share their knowledge. These particular practices were responsible for a 7.1 percent increase in shareholder value.

- *Focused HR Service Technologies*—using new technology for the fundamentals of HR (improving accuracy, service, and cost effectiveness) paid off in a 6.5 percent increase in shareholder value.

- *Prudent Use of Resources*—some HR practices that conventional wisdom says are good were found to be associated with a decrease in market value of almost 33.9 percent. These included 360-degree reviews, longer-term developmental training (i.e., preparing people for their next job instead of the current one), and implementing HR technologies with no specific goal in mind.

This comprehensive research provides proof that superior HR practices can drive financial results. As the study concludes, "There's no question that it pays to manage people right."

Source: *Watson Wyatt's* Human Capital Index, 2001–2002 Survey Report *(Washington, DC, 2001).*

employees, increase their motivation, reduce loafing on the job, and enhance retention of quality employees while encouraging nonperformers to leave the organization.

Regardless which HRM strategies are used, they should be closely aligned with other functional strategies to ensure that the right numbers of the appropriately skilled people are in the right place at the right time and that the workforce is being used effectively and efficiently. Let's look at some of the strategic HR options covering such areas as work flows, staffing, employee separations, performance appraisal, training and development, compensation, employee relations, and employee rights.[14] Table 5.4 lists some common HRM strategies used in each of these areas.

Work Flows

Work flow is the way an organization's work activities are organized so that the vision, mission(s), and objectives are effectively and efficiently accomplished. What are the strategic choices? Primarily, they're choices about ways to organize work activities—things such as organizing for efficiency or innovation; organizing for control or flexibility; using specialized and narrow job descriptions or broad job categories; and using detailed work planning or loose work planning. Inherent in these different approaches are strategic decisions about the use of typical HR tools such as job analysis, job design, job descriptions, and job specifications. However, work-flow strategies also encompass contemporary human resource practices such as boundaryless organizations, self-managed work teams, contingent

The Grey Zone

Pharmacists working for major drug store chains are often expected to push products—even ones that have been shown to have serious risks associated with their use, such as ma huang or ephedra. In one particular organization (that will remain anonymous for obvious reasons), an all-out marketing campaign to push ephedra-based products distressed one pharmacist enough that he went to his manager with concerns about selling the products. The pharmacist's concerns were ignored, and the marketing promotion turned out to be one of the most successful that the company ever ran. What do you think of this situation? Do you think the organization's actions were acceptable? Why or why not? Are there other possible strategic actions the organization could have used? How can decision makers weigh the ethical costs and benefits of strategic decisions? When an employee expresses concern over a strategic decision, should the organization respond? What guidelines might you suggest for such situations?

workers, and flexible work schedules. Of course, these decisions should be coordinated with the work activities required by the organization's other functions.

Staffing

Once strategic decisions about work flow have been made, it's time to be sure there are appropriately skilled people to perform the work. Staffing decisions involve strategic choices in the following areas: whether to use internal or external recruitment; who will make hiring decisions—the HR department or the supervisor; what's important in hiring—the "fit" of the applicant with the organizational culture or the applicant's technical qualifications and skills; and whether a formal or informal hiring and socialization approach is taken.

Employee Separations

Whereas staffing strategies deal with getting people *into* the organization, employee separation strategies involve people *leaving* the organization, whether voluntarily or involuntarily. You've experienced employee separation if you've ever had a summer job and left at the end of summer to return to school. Some strategic choices in terms of employee separation include downsizing by using voluntary inducements to encourage early retirement or using layoffs; implementing a hiring freeze to avoid layoffs or recruiting employees as needed even if this means other employees may be laid off; whether to provide support for terminated employees or let them fend for themselves; and whether to use a preferential or non-preferential rehiring process.

Performance Appraisal

Your professor appraises your "work performance" using tests, in-class assignments, case analyses, or group projects. The work performed by an organization's employees also needs to be evaluated to determine whether assigned duties are being completed efficiently and effectively. This is done through performance appraisal. An appropriately designed performance appraisal system should help the organization achieve two things: employee performance improvement and employee development. Some strategic choices in terms of performance appraisal include using customized or uniform appraisals; using employee appraisal data for developmental or control purposes; deciding whether appraisals will be multipurpose (i.e., used for training, selection, pay decisions, or promotion) or more narrowly focused (such as for pay decisions only); and whether to have an appraisal system that uses multiple inputs or supervisory input only.

Training and Development

Employee training and development plays a critical role in meeting the challenges of the continuously changing marketplace. An organization's employees need skills to perform their jobs today *and* in the future. That's the role of HR training and development strategies. What strategic alternatives are there? One that influences the organization's entire training approach is whether we intend to "buy" skills by hiring experienced employees (usually at a higher wage) or "develop" skills by training employees (who lack skills but who can usually can be hired at a lower wage). Also, will we use individual or team-based training? Will we use on-the-job training or external training? Will training be job specific or generic skill training (such as leadership development, problem-solving skills, listening skills, and so forth)?

Compensation

Because employees expect to be compensated for their work, it's important to have appropriate compensation strategies. An organization's compensation system directly impacts how it attracts, retains, and motivates organizational members. If we want to attract and keep good people, we've got to have a good compensation system in place. In addition, though, the organization's choice of compensation strategies will impact overall labor costs, which in turn impacts financial performance. So, decision makers have to weigh these two variables—attracting and keeping good people versus what it costs to do so. What strategic choices do we have in strategically managing the compensation system? One decision involves whether to have a system of fixed salaries and benefits or one that uses variable pay components. Another strategic decision revolves around whether to use job-based pay (paying on the basis of the job an individual has) or individual-based pay (paying on the basis of an individual's contributions to the organization). We also must decide whether to use a seniority-based system (compensating on the basis of years with the organization) or a performance-based system (compensating on the basis of performance). Finally, we must decide whether to centralize or decentralize pay decisions.

Employee and Labor Relations

Although it might seem odd to be talking about employee relations *strategies,* the interactions an organization has with its employees can affect how committed they are to the organization and its goals. "Good employee relations involves providing fair and consistent treatment to all employees so that they will be committed to the organization's goals."[15] What are the strategic alternatives? One decision concerns how the organization chooses to communicate with its employees. Is it a strictly top-down or bottom-up system of

strategic **MANAGEMENT** *in action*

UPS, the world's largest package delivery company, is a popular target for many job seekers. Why? Its pay and perks. Although driver trainees must survive a nerve-wracking month of instruction and field training—including mastering the high-tech clipboards, written exams, and road safety tests—they willingly do it because the result is a top-dollar blue-collar job. After 30 months on the job, a U.S. driver can earn up to $70,000 or more a year. Senior drivers get up to nine weeks paid annual leave. The company picks up 100 percent of medical insurance premiums. And pensions are generous—drivers retiring after 25 years can get up to $30,000 a year. But it is a tough and physically demanding job. Drivers often get in and out of their truck more than 100 times a day. They're lifting heavy packages, which can be hard on the back and the knees. And the hours can be long, because drivers must make sure that deliveries are made, no matter what.

Source: G. Strauss, "UPS' Pay, Perks Make It a Destination Job for Many," USA Today, October 14, 2003, p. 1B.

communication and feedback? Another strategic choice—usually described as labor relations—has to do with the organization's interactions with employee unions. Will we actively avoid or suppress employee union organization efforts or work closely with employee unions as the employees' representatives? In addition, labor negotiations are likely to be affected by the labor relations strategic approach the organization adopts. The final decision in terms of employee relations strategies addresses how the organization will approach its overall relationship with its employees. Will we take an adversarial approach to employee interactions or will we attempt to address employees' needs? The strategic choices we make here will influence our willingness to implement HR programs, policies, and systems (including such contemporary workplace practices as family-friendly programs, employee assistance programs, employee recognition programs, and so forth) that have the potential to support and strengthen all employee–organization interactions. In other words, it establishes the whole basis for how we're going to treat our employees.

Employee Rights

The final HRM strategies we're going to discuss concern employee rights; that is, the relationship an organization has with its employees, specifically, employee–management rights and disciplinary strategies. What are the strategic options? One is the approach the organization uses to get appropriate work behavior. Is discipline used as a way to control employee behavior and reduce mistakes or do we encourage appropriate behavior in the first place in order to reduce mistakes? After all, disciplinary measures aren't the only way to encourage appropriate work behavior. Another strategic decision involves whose rights will be protected—the organization's or the employees'. Not surprisingly, there are many instances when the rights of the employer and the rights of the employee are in conflict. How will these situations be strategically managed? That depends upon the employee rights strategies being used. Finally, we need to decide how our organization is going to address ethics. Will we rely on informal ethical standards or have explicit ethical codes, standards, and enforcement procedures?

Current HRM Strategies

The HRM strategies an organization uses are a pretty good reflection of how it views its *human* resources and the role they're perceived to play in organizational performance. The traditional, often adversarial approach to employees isn't likely to lead to a sustainable competitive advantage. There are many examples of organizations that view their employees as partners, working together to accomplish the organization's vision, missions, and goals. For example, at Southwest Airlines (SWA), employees are encouraged to have fun and be playful on the job. Flight attendants often dress up in outrageous outfits on Halloween and other holidays. Stories abound of how flight attendants hide in the plane's overhead storage bins, only to yell "surprise" at the first passenger to open it up. When co-founder Herb Kelleher was still CEO, he was known to dress in costume and show up to entertain the crowd on certain flights. Even on today's flights, if a passenger is being particularly difficult, he or she might find a plastic cockroach in their drink. Of course, the added "garnish" will be pointed out to the individual before they've had an opportunity to drink out of the cup. All these zany antics are in fun, but SWA is serious about fostering a friendly work environment so that customer service can flourish. In fact, Kelleher himself once said, "What we are looking for (in potential hires), first and foremost, is a sense of humor. We look for attitudes. We'll train you on whatever you need to do, but the one thing we can't do is change inherent attitudes in people."[16] Has the company's people focus paid off? Even during the difficult years of the early twenty-first century, it was the only airline to consistently make a profit. And it continues to receive awards for outstanding customer service.

Another current HRM strategy concerns how organizations address employees' work–life balance issues. In the 1980s, organizations began to realize that employees don't leave their families and personal lives behind when they come to work. To deal with the realities that employees have lives outside the office, and that they may have personal problems and family commitments to attend to, organizations are making their workplaces more family-friendly by offering **family-friendly benefits**, which are benefits that accommodate employees' needs for work–life balance. These family-friendly benefits can include a wide range of work and family programs such as on-site child care, summer day camps, flexible work schedules, approved leaves for school functions, and even job sharing. Organizations that believe that "people are our most important asset" are implementing these kinds of HR strategies to accommodate their employees.[17]

Many organizations are committed to developing and implementing strong HRM strategies. Reinforcing what we stated earlier, researchers studying the link between an organization's HRM systems and strategies and its performance are finding that, indeed, certain HRM strategies can positively impact a firm's performance.[18] That's a pretty good reason to look at developing appropriate strategies in the HRM area.

Learning Review

- What is marketing, and what are the two biggest factors in marketing?
- Describe the possible segmentation or target market strategies.
- What are the four possible differentiation dimensions?
- Why is positioning important to the marketing strategies?
- Describe the marketing mix strategies.
- How does the product life cycle affect the choice of marketing strategies?
- Describe the marketing strategies being currently used by organizations.
- Describe high-performance work practices. Why do you think these practices lead to high performance?
- What strategic choices are there in work flow?
- Describe possible strategic choices in the following HR areas: staffing, employee separations, performance appraisal, training and development, compensation, employee and labor relations, and employee rights.
- What types of current HRM strategies are organizations pursuing?

Research and Development Strategies

Remember when a "mouse" referred to a little gray, furry rodent? Now, however, when a "mouse" comes up in conversation, it's usually in reference to the hand device used in point-and-click computer technology. How did this man-made mouse come into existence and become a standard feature on most desktops in homes and offices? Some organization's research and development (R&D) strategies obviously played a significant role. Without R&D, we wouldn't have the scientific breakthroughs, product innovations, or process improvements used in today's world. An organization's R&D strategies should reflect its philosophy about innovation, which we defined earlier in Chapter 2 as the process of taking a creative idea and turning it into a product or process that can be used or sold. R&D is how innovation is realized in organizations. In today's fast-changing markets, rapid innovation can lead to a sustainable competitive advantage. What R&D strategies might an organization implement? Here we will examine three strategic areas of R&D: R&D emphasis, R&D timing, and specific product and process development strategies. A summary of these strategies is provided in Table 5.5.

Table 5.5

Possible Research and Development (R&D) Strategies

R&D EMPHASIS	**How?**
• Basic scientific research	• Formal or informal process
• Product development	• Use prototypes, product tests, design
• Process development	reviews, or test markets
	• How to implement new design
R&D TIMING	• How to evaluate success of new design
• First mover	
• Follower	**CURRENT R&D STRATEGIES**
	• Employee suggestion systems
PRODUCT AND PROCESS DEVELOPMENT	• Innovative culture
Who?	
• Separate R&D department	
• Cross-functional team	
• Some combination	

R&D Emphasis

One strategic decision that has to be made is *what* an organization is going to emphasize in its R&D activities. There are three possible alternatives. (See Figure 5.4.) The first is an emphasis on basic scientific research. This R&D strategy requires the heaviest commitment in terms of resources because it involves the nuts-and-bolts work involved with scientific research. In some industries (e.g., genetic engineering, computer hardware, or pharmaceuticals), an organization's expertise in basic research can be the key to a sustainable competitive advantage. However, not every industry requires this level of basic scientific research for organizations to achieve high performance levels. That leads us to the second strategic alternative, which is an emphasis on product development. Many organizations depend on their product development strategies for continued growth in sales and profits. This strategy also requires a significant resource commitment, but not in those work activities associated with basic scientific research. We'll address some specific product development strategies later in this section. The third strategic alternative that an organization might pursue is an emphasis on process development. This strategy involves looking for ways to improve and enhance the organization's work processes. We'll also describe some specific process development strategies later in this section.

R&D Timing

Another strategic choice is the R&D timing an organization uses. Some organizations want to be the first to introduce or use innovations, whereas other organizations are content to follow or mimic the innovations. An organization that's first to bring a new product innovation to the marketplace or to use a new process innovation is called a **first mover**. Being a first mover has certain strategic advantages and disadvantages, as shown in Table 5.6. Some organizations pursue these pioneering strategies. By doing so, they hope to develop a sustainable competitive advantage. Other organizations have been able to develop a sustainable competitive advantage by being the followers in the industry. They let the first movers pioneer the innovations and then simply copy their offerings or processes. Which R&D timing strategy an organization chooses to pursue depends on its overall innovation philosophy and approach as well as its specific resources and capabilities.

The R&D emphasis and R&D timing strategies an organization chooses will influence its choice of product and process development strategies. We need to look at some specific approaches to these two R&D activities.

Figure 5.4

Possible R&D Emphasis

> (Basic Scientific Research)　(Product Development)　(Process Development)

To be More Innovative, Get Rid of R&D

You know how important innovation is to an organization's development of a competitive advantage. We've discussed it at various points so far in the text. However, what if to win with innovation, you had to eliminate your organization's R&D efforts? What would you think of that? Some companies in the most innovation-intensive industries (where product life cycles are short and the need for breakthrough products is critical) have pioneered a radically different approach to innovation. How? By engaging the innovation talents of individuals who are not employees. These innovation "superstars" champion the innovation

process and are often hired on a project-by-project basis. What this innovative approach to innovation does is nurture "outside-the-box," breakout thinking. In industries from entertainment to toys to pharmaceuticals, innovation superstar free agents are changing the face of product development. What do you think about this strategic approach to innovation? Do you think it would work in all types of organizations? Explain. Do you think an organization could ever totally eliminate its R&D function? Why or why not?

Sources: J. Greene, J. Carey, M. Arndt, and O. Port, "Reinventing Corporate R&D," Business Week, September 22, 2003, pp. 74–76; G. Donnelly, "A P&L for R&D," CFO, February 2000, pp. 44–50; and C. E. Lucier and J. D. Torsilieri, "To Win With Innovation—Kill R&D," Strategy & Business, Third Quarter 1999, pp. 8–12.

ADVANTAGES	DISADVANTAGES
• Reputation for being innovative and an industry leader • Cost and learning benefits resulting from moving along experience curve first • Control over scarce assets preventing competitors from having access to them • Opportunity to begin building customer relationships and customer loyalty	• Uncertainty over exact direction technology and market will go • Risk of competitors imitating innovations (free-rider effect) • Financial and strategic risks • High development costs

Table 5.6

First Mover Advantages–Disadvantages

Product and Process Development Strategies

Given the dynamics of today's marketplace, it's important for organizations to develop new products. The approaches used to do this are its product development strategies. However, innovation isn't important just for product development, it's also vital with regards to how the organization manufactures and markets these products. The strategic alternatives in implementing product and process development revolve around *who* and *how*.

The *who* choices address who's going to be responsible for developing new ideas. Will it be a separate R&D department of scientists and engineers who have total responsibility for creating and implementing new products and processes? Will it be a **cross-functional team**, which is a group of individuals from various functional departments who work together on product or process development, or will it be something in between these two options? More and more organizations are using some type of development team for product and process innovations. And, it appears that these teams are better at developing new ideas when they include individuals from all the work areas involved with R&D efforts. But, exactly *how* does the R&D effort get done?

The *how* of R&D involves the actual sequence of activities from idea generation to implementation and evaluation. An organization must make several strategic choices as it *does* R&D. Some of these choices include:

- Will we use a formal or informal process for generating ideas for product and process design?
- Will we use prototypes, and how extensively will we use them?

the global perspective

China is influencing another area of global business—industrial design. The country now has more than 200 design schools that graduate almost 8,000 students a year. Chinese students are also attending some of the best U.S. and European graduate programs in design. And these designers are beginning to have an impact on the R&D strategies of many large global organizations. For instance, Germany's Siemens AG Information and Communications Unit and Sweden's AB Electrolux have used young Chinese designers to create products tailored to China's domestic market. Even Chinese companies are using the local designers. For example, TCL International Holdings Ltd. was able to triple its share of the Chinese mobile phone market because designers came up with splashy gem-studded designs that appealed to local tastes.

Source: F. Balfour and D. Roberts, "China's Dream Team," *Business Week*, September 1, 2003, pp. 50–51.

- Will we use product tests, and what type will we use?
- Will we use design reviews in determining manufacturing cost and quality aspects?
- Will we use test markets, and how extensively will we use them?
- How will we implement the new product design or process design?
- How will we evaluate the success of the R&D process?

The selected strategic approach will depend on the organization's overall innovation philosophy and whether innovation is a significant source of competitive advantage for the organization. Of course, these decisions must be coordinated with the marketing and production–operations strategies.

Current R&D Strategies

What types of R&D strategies are today's organizations using in their attempts to develop a sustainable competitive advantage? To answer this, let's look at a couple of organizations who appear to be strategically managing their R&D strategies.

Where do good ideas come from? Employee suggestion systems can be a good source of process design improvements. For example, at the Autoliv Steering Wheel-Airbag factory in Columbia City, Indiana, employee suggestions have improved efficiency and overall productivity and were a major reason behind the facility's being named one of *Industry Week*'s "Best Manufacturing Plants of 2003."[19] These suggestions translated into significant cost savings for the company. Although not every employee suggestion has been feasible, this organization has found employee suggestions to be good sources of ideas for process R&D innovations as well as a boost to employee morale.

What about product design? Hewlett-Packard (HP) is widely regarded as an organization that's strong in the area of product design and development. The company has become the dominant player in the laser printer market by consistently developing higher quality and more reliable products at affordable prices. How does it do this? One critically important aspect is HP's culture. Its culture encourages risk taking and innovation by product design teams. If product designers come up with something new or different, they're supported even if the product idea never makes it out of design. Also, the company supports its product development people by giving them whatever resources they need to do their jobs. As this example shows, an organization's culture plays a vital role in the success of its R&D strategies. The more that the culture supports innovation, the more likely it is that the R&D strategies will lead to a sustainable competitive advantage.

Table 5.7

Possible Information Systems Strategies

SYSTEM TECHNOLOGY
- Manual-based
- Computer-based
- Combination

TYPES OF INFORMATION SYSTEMS
- Transaction processing system
- Office automation system
- Knowledge work system
- Management information system
- Decision support system
- Executive support system

CURRENT INFORMATION SYSTEMS STRATEGIES
- Information technology
- Business intelligence applications
- Information vulnerability and protection
- Internet

Information Systems Strategies

How would you like to do your job as a student (study, write papers, take tests, etc.) without information? It would be pretty tough, wouldn't it? You'd probably agree that information affects how effectively and efficiently organizational members do their work. Without information, the payroll clerk doesn't know what deductions to make from paychecks; the sales representative doesn't know what prices to quote a potential customer; or the plant manager doesn't know how this month's product quality levels compared with last month's. It's essential to have information to make decisions and to carry out work duties. How do organizational members get information? That's what an information system does. An **information system** is a set of interrelated components used with collect, process, store, and disseminate information to support decision making, analysis, and management control in organizations.[20] Let's look at two strategic decisions associated with the organization's information system. These are the choice of system technology and the choice of information system type. Table 5.7 summarizes possible information systems strategies.

System Technology

The choice of system technology is fairly simple—the information system can either be manual or computer based. A manual system uses pencil-and-paper technology to collect, store, process, and disseminate information. A computer-based system relies on computer hardware and software technology to do the same. As prices have fallen and computing power has risen, many organizations have moved to more extensive use of computer-based information systems. However, some organizations still collect all or some information manually. Which approach an organization uses depends on how important information is to developing a sustainable competitive advantage. For instance, is it critical that strategic decision makers have rapid access to information from all functional areas of the organization? Is it critical that organizational members have rapid access to information to help them do their jobs effectively and efficiently? Is it critical that organizational units share information? Is information a significant resource in our industry? Is having current

strategic **MANAGEMENT** *in action*

Harrah's Entertainment, the Las Vegas-based gaming company, is fanatical about customer service, and for good reason. Company research showed that customers who were satisfied with the service they received at a Harrah's casino increased their gaming expenditures by 10 percent, and those who were extremely satisfied increased their gaming expenditures by 24 percent. Harrah's was able to discover this important customer service–expenditures connection because of its incredibly sophisticated information system. All employees were made aware of this information so they truly understood their vital role in providing outstanding customer service.

Sources: G. Loveman, "Diamonds in the Data Mine," *Harvard Business Review, May 2003, pp. 109–13;* and L. Gary, "Simplify and Execute: Words to Live By in Times of Turbulence," *Harvard Management Update, January 2003, p. 12.*

Table 5.8 *Types of Information Systems and Their Characteristics*

Types of System	Information Inputs	Processing	Information Outputs	Users
ESS	Aggregate data; external, internal	Graphics; simulations; interactive	Projections; responses to queries	Senior managers
DSS	Low-volume data; analytic models	Interactive; simulations; analysis	Special reports; decision analyses; responses to queries	Professionals; staff managers
MIS	Summary transaction data; high-volume data; simple models	Routine reports; simple models; low-level analysis	Summary and exception reports	Middle managers
KWS	Design specifications; knowledge base	Modeling; simulations	Models; graphics	Professionals; technical staff
OAS	Documents; schedules	Document management; scheduling; communication	Documents; schedules; mail	Clerical workers
TPS	Transactions; events	Sorting; listing; merging; updating	Detailed reports; lists; summaries	Operations personnel; supervisors

Source: Management Information Systems, *4th. ed.* by Laudon/Laudon © 1986. Reprinted by permission of Prentice-Hall, Inc., Upper Saddle River, NJ.

information a critical success factor in our industry? All these factors will influence an organization's strategic choice of a computer-based or manual system.

Types of Information Systems

An organization's information system isn't just one single system, because no single system can provide all the information needed. Instead, an organization likely will have many different types of information systems serving different organizational levels and functions. We need to briefly explain the six different strategic choices of types of information systems. Table 5.8 summarizes the characteristics of each of these systems.

The first type of information system, a transaction processing system (TPS), is used for tracking work being done in the organization's basic functional areas. Examples include payroll, reservation systems, sales order tracking and processing, and plant scheduling.

The next type of information system is an office automation system (OAS) and includes all the documents, schedules, and mail generated by an organization's clerical workers. Examples include letters, invoices, press releases, newsletters, or contracts. More and more, this type of information gathering and exchange is being done with word processing, electronic mail, and desktop publishing software.

Another type of information system is a knowledge work system (KWS). This information system is used primarily by an organization's knowledge workers, such as engineers, analysts, designers, attorneys, scientists, or doctors. The KWS provides ways to promote and use new knowledge and innovation. Examples include product design graphics (such as computer-aided design or CAD), legal database search, virtual reality simulations, or financial data analysis.

The next type of information system is the management information system (MIS), which is used by an organization's managers for planning, controlling, and decision making. The MIS typically summarizes and reports on the organization's basic functional activities. It's different from the TPS because it's not designed to report day-to-day activities, but to summarize a series of time periods (week, month, quarter, or year). Examples include summary sales reports, cost comparisons from different products, or employee training expenditures for the quarter.

Information technology is supposed to help, not hurt, an organization's performance. The example described here, although a few years old, still illustrates that having a successful information system strategy isn't always as easy as it seems.

Even behind a scary mask, there's a smile on a kid's face who gets Hershey's candy in a trick-or-treat bag. Yet, during Halloween of 1999—the biggest candy event of the year—Hershey Foods Corporation was trying to correct delivery foul-ups caused by a newly installed information system. New technology brought online in mid-summer 1999 caused significant problems in the company's ordering and distribution system. The computer system was supposed to automate and modernize all activities from taking candy orders to loading pallets on trucks, but it didn't work as planned. The impact was felt all the way from corporate headquarters to food distributors and retailers. Hershey's third-quarter EPS (earnings per share) dropped 16 percent and industry experts said that Hershey may have missed as much as $100 million in sales in the fourth quarter of 1999 because of the information systems problems.

Sources: "Cyberwoes Gum Up Hershey Sales," Springfield News-Leader, October 30, 1999, p. 9A; and E. Nelson and E. Ramstad, "Hershey's Biggest Dud Has Turned Out to Be New Computer System, Wall Street Journal, October 29, 1999, p. A1.

Another type of information system that's also used by managers and other professionals for decision making is a decision support system (DSS). The DSS is different from both the KWS and MIS because it allows for more powerful data analysis and also allows decision makers to change the assumptions and information to see what impact those changes have on the outcomes. In addition, a DSS is typically designed so that users can work with it directly—that is, the user initiates and controls the information inputs and outputs. These types of information systems are unique to different situations, but some examples might include a financial portfolio analysis with "what-if" scenarios, production facility optimization analysis, evaluation of potential well drilling sites, or defense contract analysis.

The final type of information system is an executive support system (ESS). This type of system would be used by an organization's upper-level managers to aid in making unstructured, comprehensive, broad, and complex decisions. An ESS wouldn't be used to help solve specific problems, but rather to provide a generalized approach for looking at a broad array of organizational issues. For instance, an ESS might be designed to help track competitors' actions or to assess the impact of proposed investment tax changes on company earnings.

What role do information and information systems play in managing strategically? It depends on how important it is to have the right types of information when, where, and how organizational members need it. Choosing an appropriate information systems strategy—that is, the system technology and the type(s) of information systems—involves some important decisions. Let's look at some current information systems strategies being used by organizations.

Current Information Systems Strategies

As we discussed in Chapter 2, the information revolution is one of the most important driving forces in today's business context. How an organization collects, uses, and disseminates information ultimately will affect its ability to develop a sustainable competitive advantage. We're seeing four areas where current information systems (IS) strategies are focused: information technology, business intelligence, information vulnerability and protection, and the Internet.

Information technology is ever changing. Bar codes and electronic data information sharing (EDI) were once the cutting edge in information technology. Now we have "smart tags" on products that send out radio frequency signals so employees know where products are at all times. Wal-Mart, for example, has made a major commitment to this RFID (radio-frequency identification) technology by asking its top 100 suppliers to start using smart tags by 2005. Even the U.S. Department of Defense has told its 43,000 suppliers that they will be required to use this information technology.[21] As new information technologies appear, strategists must decide what and how much they're willing to invest in these new technologies. It's a decision that obviously should be based on whether strategists believe the technology can contribute to the development of a sustainable competitive advantage.

The second area in which we're seeing significant changes in information system strategies is business intelligence (BI) software. BI software helps organizations recognize and capture important relationships and connections in the information gathered by their information systems. With this information, then, strategists can make better decisions. For example, an information technology consultant brought in to study Schneider National, one of the largest truckload carriers in the United States, found that "They were drowning in data but starving for information." The company now uses BI software to show managers hidden costs and benefits in their work areas.[22]

If the terrorist attacks on 9/11 weren't enough to make strategic decision makers recognize the importance of protecting their information, then maybe the estimated $12 billion that cyberattacks cost businesses worldwide in 2003 alone will get their attention. Protecting critical information is a vital information system strategy for today's organizations.[23] Addressing information vulnerability usually requires a combination of hardware and software solutions and, even more importantly, making sure employees understand the importance of protecting information they're collecting, using, and disseminating. That may be the hardest part of all; hardware and software only work effectively if people use them correctly.

Finally, we can't leave this discussion of current information system strategies without mentioning the continuing pervasiveness of the Internet. There's hardly an industry that hasn't experienced its power (positively *or* negatively). The instantaneous availability and interactivity of Web sites gives organizations a powerful tool for collecting, processing, storing, and disseminating information. An organization's decision makers should carefully evaluate the role of the Internet in its information systems strategies.

Financial–Accounting Strategies

The last functional area we're going to look at involves the organization's financial–accounting strategies. These strategies concern choices about how financial and accounting data are collected and used. We'll look at four broad areas: evaluating financial performance, financial forecasting and budgeting, financing mix, and financial management decisions.[24] Possible financial–accounting strategies are summarized in Table 5.9.

Evaluating Financial Performance

How do we evaluate an organization's financial performance? By looking at the financial statements and evaluating the information found there. These financial statements include specific pieces of information about the organization's operations. The typical financial statements are the income statement, the balance sheet, and a cash flow statement. By themselves, the financial statements only show results. To evaluate financial performance, we have to look more closely at the statements. Financial ratios, calculated with information from the financial statements, are the principal tool for financial analysis. The financial ratios standardize financial information so that comparisons can be made from time period to time period or of the organization to its industry. The strategic choices in terms of evaluating financial performance revolve around how often to do it and how much analysis to do. Quite often, this is dictated by law and not entirely open to individual choice. However, even if financial analysis isn't legally required, the fact remains that an organization needs some mechanism for evaluating financial performance. Without this information, strategic decision makers would have little knowledge of how the organization is performing, at least from a financial and quantitative standpoint.

Table 5.9

*Possible Financial–
Accounting Strategies*

EVALUATING FINANCIAL PERFORMANCE
- How often
- How much analysis

FINANCIAL FORECASTING AND BUDGETING
- Percentage of sales forecast
- Discretionary financing needed model
- Sustainable rate of growth model
- Types of budgets used and how often

FINANCIAL MIX
- Financial structure
- Capital structure
- Short-term vs. long-term

OTHER FINANCIAL MANAGEMENT DECISIONS
- Capital budgeting choices
- Stock dividend policy

- Capital budgeting
- Cash flow management
- Working capital management and short-term financing
- Cash and marketable securities management
- Accounts receivable and inventory management
- Use of term loans or leases

CURRENT FINANCIAL–ACCOUNTING STRATEGIES
- Controlling costs
- Compliance
- New financial performance measures
- Valuing intangible assets

Financial Forecasting and Budgeting

These two processes are important ones in the organization's financial area because they are the ways an organization's financial resources are planned and allocated. Financial forecasting is used to estimate an organization's future financial needs. Once forecasts are developed, then decision makers can plan and budget according to the forecasts. The most popular type of financial forecast is the percent of sales method, which involves estimating the potential level of an expense, asset, or liability as a percentage of the sales forecast. The resulting numbers, then, provide the basis for operational planning and budgeting. Other forecasting models decision makers might use include the Discretionary Financing Needed (DFN) model, which predicts changes in assets, liabilities, and owners' equity based on predicted changes in sales or the sustainable rate of growth calculation, which represents the rate at which an organization's sales can maintain its current financial ratios without having to sell new common stock. The strategic choices for the budgeting process are quite simple and concern the specific types of budgets used and how often they're used.

Financing Mix

The financing mix strategies concern decisions about the organization's financial structure and capital structure. **Financial structure** refers to the mix of all items found on the right-hand side of the organization's balance sheet. **Capital structure** refers to the mix of the long-term sources of funds used by the organization. How do decision makers determine the optimum financing mix? It depends on how the organization wants to divide its total fund sources between short- and long-term components (maturity composition) and the proportion of total financing the organization wants from permanent sources. Answers to these two questions will affect the choice of financing mix strategies. Other factors that influence an organization's choice of financial structure are its debt capacity, whether it has reached its optimum or target amount of debt, the stage in the business cycle, and the amount of risk the organization faces. All these factors will affect the types and maturities of an organization's financing options.

Other Financial Management Decisions

Other strategic decisions involve financial management choices about capital budgeting, stock dividend policy, capital budgeting and cash flow management, working capital

Building Better Budgets

Budgeting is often viewed as the most despised task in organizations. Employees say it's a meaningless exercise that is only slightly related to the organization's overall objectives, is extremely time-consuming, and, once completed, has little to do with the realities of conducting business. However, budgeting is an important financial and accounting strategy. How can an organization's budgeting system be improved? Here are some suggestions for effective budgeting:

- Establish a link between what the organization does and what it spends money on.
- Think about what the organization measures. Are the important things being funded?
- Get agreement outside the financial department about what the organization's measures should be.

- Link compensation to budget goals.
- Don't forecast in a vacuum; encourage discussion among all functional areas.
- Reduce the number of budget line items.
- Reduce the time the process takes.
- Give employees the flexibility to meet their budget targets.
- Don't be bound by calendar-based or fiscal-year-based forecasts.
- Understand that technology can't solve all the budget-planning challenges. It's only a tool!

Sources: J. Hope and R. Fraser, "Who Needs Budgets?" Harvard Business Review, February 2003, pp. 108–15; T. Leahy, "The Top 10 Traps of Budgeting," Business Finance, November 1, 2001, pp. 20–26; T. Leahy, "Necessary Evil," Business Finance, November 1999, pp. 41–45; and R. N. Anthony, J. Dearden, and N. M. Bedford, Management Control Systems, 5th ed. (Homewood, IL: Irwin, 1984), Chapters 5–7.

management and short-term financing, cash and marketable securities management, accounts receivable and inventory management, and the use of term loans and leases. For each of these financial areas, decision makers must choose what to use and how to implement it. For instance, are we going to pay shareholder dividends or not? If so, are we going to try to maintain some standardized payout amount or vary it? Or, for instance, what's the organization's strategy for maintaining sufficient cash flow? In each of these financial management areas, strategic choices must be made.

Current Financial–Accounting Strategies

Some important current strategies in the financial–accounting function include the following: controlling costs, compliance, new financial performance measures, and valuing intangible assets. The first area—controlling costs—isn't really a new strategy. Strategic decision makers have always looked for ways to control costs. But in today's environment, controlling costs, especially SG&A (selling, general, and administrative), continues to be an important strategy.

With the passage of the Sarbanes-Oxley Act of 2002, financial–accounting executives face several compliance issues, especially as they relate to financial controls and financial reporting. One requirement of the law is that executives and auditors must evaluate their company's internal financial controls. And company CEOs and CFOs must certify that the controls work. Although such extreme measures are probably justified in light of the many financial–accounting scandals at Enron, Worldcom, and other organizations, experts believe that the costs of compliance are likely to be high. In fact, some believe they could total $7 billion a year.[25] However, regardless the cost, financial reporting and financial control compliance are issues that will affect strategic choices in the financial– accounting area.

Another area of current financial–accounting strategies involves suggested new measures of financial performance. One interesting possibility is that the Financial Accounting Standards Board (FASB) is considering a proposal to eliminate operating income, net income, and perhaps even earnings per share as standard measures of company performance.[26]

It's a problem that few—okay none—of us will ever face. A $52 billion pile of cash. That's the difficult problem that Microsoft faces. First, let's get some perspective on the magnitude of $52 billion: It exceeds the annual gross output of Romania. Microsoft could mail every U.S. household a check for almost $500. And, if all those dollars were stretched end to end, they'd equal over 10 round trips to the moon.

What does a company do with that much cash? And how can strategic decision makers ensure that they're making the best strategic choices regarding the disposition of such a cash horde? Although it might be easy to just tell

Microsoft to spend it on acquiring a company or raising shareholder dividend payments, those may not be the most appropriate decisions, especially considering that Microsoft would likely be reluctant to go on a buying spree after its tangle with the U.S. Justice Department and given that it wants to maintain some financial flexibility. It seems like a nice problem to have, but there are still some tough strategic decisions to make—even with $52 billion in cash.

Sources: On July 20, 2004, Microsoft announced the largest one-time corporate dividend in history. On December 2, 2004, it will pay out $32 billion to shareholders. It also plans to double the annual dividend to 32 cents per share and buy back $30 billion worth of its own stock over the next four years. P. R. La Monica, "Hey Bill! Go Buy Something," CNNMoney, **www.cnnmoney.com**, February 26, 2004; and J. Greene, "Microsoft's $49 Billion 'Problem,'" Business Week, August 11, 2003, p. 36.

Instead, the proposed "new" income statements would include the following items: business activities, financing, and other gains and losses. Another measure that some financial analysts have begun to use is enterprise value, or EV.[27] EV simply measures how much capital it would take to buy an entire public company. It's the sum of a company's stock market capitalization plus its net debt. Stock market capitalization is a company's total shares multiplied by its stock price. Net debt is a company's total debt minus its cash and marketable securities holdings. Whether either of these new measures ever becomes an accepted part of the financial–accounting area remains to be seen. However, in terms of strategic choices, strategists need to be aware of these and other possible new approaches.

Finally, we want to look at a current challenge in the area of financial–accounting strategies—valuing intangible assets. Our current system of financial measurement is fairly inadequate when assessing intellectual capital and other intangible assets. These intangible resources are subjective and hard to define. Even an asset, such as an organization's computer system, that seems relatively straightforward, is complicated by intangible measurement issues such as compatibility, usage, and bandwidth. To address this glaring weakness in financial–accounting measures, three organizations (*Forbes* magazine, Ernst & Young Center for Business Innovation, and the Wharton Research Program on Value Creation in Organizations) teamed together to jointly research and develop the first practical audit of intangible assets.[28] The team developed the Value Creation Index (VCI), a measurement tool that incorporates the relative importance of each key organizational value driver. What are these value drivers? The team's thorough research uncovered eight organizational functions ranked in order from most important to least important: innovation; ability to attract talented employees; strategic alliances; quality of major processes, products, or services; environmental performance; brand investment; technology; and customer satisfaction. You may be asking yourself why this is such a big deal. The importance of this VCI is that if these truly are the keys behind increasing organizational value, we've identified strategic initiatives that can improve both corporate performance and market value. It represents an important step in unlocking the challenge of measuring intangible assets.

Learning Review

- Describe the three R&D activities that organizations can emphasize.
- What are the advantages and disadvantages of being the first mover?
- Why are product and process development strategies important?

- What is a cross-functional team, and how might it be used?
- What is an information system, and what are the two strategic decisions associated with an organization's information system?
- Why is financial performance evaluation an important functional strategy?
- Describe the other choices in financial–accounting strategies.

NOW WHAT?

Even though it may seem you've been introduced to all aspects of an organization's functional strategies, we still need to look at a couple of issues. First, what's involved with implementing these strategies? Next, how do we evaluate the functional strategies, and what do we do if they aren't working as well as we'd planned? Finally, how do we coordinate these strategies with the other organizational strategies?

Implementing the Various Functional Strategies

Implementing strategies very simply means *doing* them. What comes to mind is the marketing slogan from the well-known athletic shoe marketer, "Just Do It." Implementing the functional strategies involves five aspects: processes, activities, budgets, structure, and culture. What this means is: What are we going to do? How are we going to do it? Who's going to do it? When are we going to do it? Where are we going to do it? At the functional level, these five aspects are relatively narrow in scope and definition because each functional area has its own specific work to do in contributing to the overall organizational goals. However, this doesn't mean that there's no coordination among the various functions. Quite the contrary! Coordinating the various functions is one of the keys to strategically managing at this level. This coordination is important because of the inherent interdependence and interactions of the various functional areas and their contribution to the organization "doing" what it's in business to do—whether that's manufacturing baseball gloves, designing Web pages, selling insurance, or building houses. What does this mean for implementation?

Managing the organization's various functional areas as separate "chimneys" or "silos" might keep an organization from exploiting its key resources and capabilities and being able to develop them into a sustainable competitive advantage. And, as the functional strategies are implemented through the assorted work processes and activities unique to each area, it's important to foster an organizational environment in which all areas are working toward fulfilling the organization's vision, missions, and goals. Implementation at the functional level includes both the specific use of certain processes, activities, structure, budget, and culture *and* the coordination of the various functional units.

Evaluating Strategies and Making Changes

How do we know whether the organization's functional strategies are working and what do we do if they're not? If you go back and look at Figure 5.1 on page 139, you'll see that the processes of evaluating and changing strategies are parts of strategic management in action. Strategy evaluation at the functional level involves using specific performance measures— quantitative *and* qualitative—for each functional area. For instance, how many product coupons were redeemed from the seasonal sales promotion program; how many and what types of problems have been encountered since the new management information system was put in place; or what's the manufacturing product reject rate? Like any evaluation process, the actual performance measures must be compared against some standard. These standards are the strategic goals established in each functional area. For instance, if the goal of a new employee safety awareness program was to decrease employee disability claims, did this happen? Was the HRM strategy successful? If the rate of employee disability claims didn't go down, then we'd try to determine what happened and why. Maybe the safety information wasn't communicated clearly or maybe the manufacturing unit was behind in its work and employees were being rushed to complete the work and ended up being careless. Strategy evaluation involves looking at what *was* done, what was *supposed* to be done, assessing any variances, and trying to determine what happened. If actual performance didn't measure up to standards and if we think a change in a functional strategy is needed, then what? At this point, it depends on how critical the strategy is to the accomplishment of other organizational goals and whether it's something we can control and change. If we determine that the functional strategy is important and controllable, we'd look once again to the first steps in strategic management in action—that is, analyzing the current situation and then formulating appropriate strategies. Any changes in functional strategies would then be implemented and after a certain period of time, evaluated, and changed, if necessary.

Coordinating with Other Organizational Strategies

Not only is it important for the functional strategies to be coordinated with each other, it's important that they be coordinated with the other organizational strategies. Each organizational level—functional, business, corporate—needs to coordinate with and support the others in order to develop sustainable competitive advantages.[29] Strategic choices made at the business (competitive) and corporate levels do affect and are influenced by the functional strategies being implemented. Depending on what corporate and competitive strategies are being pursued, certain functional areas might be more important in carrying out those strategies. Then, it would be important for the resources, capabilities, and core competencies in those areas to be more fully developed and exploited. This strategic coordination and interdependency reflects the fact that an organization is a *system* with interrelated and interdependent units.

In addition, if strategic changes are made at the other levels, changes in functional strategies might be warranted. For example, say that the organization decides to start selling its products in a foreign market. What's it going to take to implement this major strategy? It will take formulating and implementing numerous functional strategies—marketing strategies, HRM strategies, production–operations strategies, and so forth—to implement this change.

As you can see, the functional strategies play an important role in executing the vision, missions, and goals of the organization. That's why they need to be coordinated with the other levels of strategies and changed to accommodate changes in those strategies. As we stated at the beginning of this chapter, it's important for an organization's functional strategies to be managed strategically so that its resources, capabilities, and core competencies can be developed into sustainable competitive advantage. Think back to the chapter-opening case. The strategic decision makers at Toyota have created a system in which the functional level strategies have been finely tuned and are contributing to the company's success. The effectiveness and efficiency of the strategies implemented at the functional levels have had a significant impact on the success of the corporate and business strategies as well as on current and future revenues.

Learning Review

- How are the functional strategies implemented?
- Why do the functional strategies need to be evaluated?
- Why is it important for the functional strategies to be (a) coordinated with each other and (b) coordinated with the other organizational strategies?

- By looking at the organization's functional strategies first, we're able to see how the strategic management process really works.

- The functional strategies, however, are developed in light of the organization's vision, mission, overall corporate strategies, and competitive strategies.

- When an organization is brand new, it makes sense to discuss corporate strategies first because no resources, capabilities, or competencies have been developed in the functional areas.

- After completing the SWOT analysis, strategic decision makers can identify positive and negative aspects of the external and internal environments.

- The SWOT analysis points to strategic issues decision makers need to address in their pursuit of sustainable competitive advantage and high performance levels.

- Even if it's evident from the SWOT analysis that the organization's corporate or competitive strategies need to be changed, strategists will base their decisions on the resources, capabilities, and competencies found in the functional areas.

- The organization's **functional strategies** (or operational strategies) are the short-term goal-directed decisions and actions of the organization's various functional units.

- The three basic functions (marketing, production–operations, and financial–accounting) are typically expanded to six (marketing, research and development, production–operations, human resource management, financial–accounting, and information systems–technology).

- Each organization will have its own uniquely named functional areas, but the basic work activities that comprise these functions remain the same.

- Each functional unit of the organization has strategies for achieving its own mission and for helping the organization reach its overall vision.

- The process of creating goods and services in which organizational inputs (resources) are transformed into outputs is called **production**.

- The strategies for the production function include choices about production process, capacity, location, work design, layout, and production and operations management.

- Current production–operations strategies include **value chain management**, which is a process of managing the entire sequence of activities and information flows along the entire value chain from incoming materials to outgoing products, and **integrated manufacturing**, which is a production–operations approach that emphasizes the use of advanced manufacturing technology, total quality management, and just-in-time inventory control to create a streamlined flow of materials, people, and work activities for transforming inputs into outputs.

- **Marketing** is the process of assessing and meeting individual's or a group's wants and needs by creating, offering, and exchanging products of value.

- Strategies for the marketing area include choices about segmentation or target market, differentiation, positioning, and marketing mix.

- One current marketing strategy is **relationship marketing**, which is a process of building long-term, trusting, "win–win" relationships with valued customers.

- As a type of relationship marketing, many organizations have created **online communities**—constantly changing groups of people who collaborate, share ideas, and build relationships online.

- A variation of relationship marketing is mass customization in which organizations provide customers with personalized products or services.

- Another current marketing approach is events and activities marketing in which organizations market their products through experiential activities rather than relying on traditional advertising or covert product placement.

- Another current marketing strategy is **database marketing**, which uses database technology and sophisticated analytical techniques combined with direct-marketing methods to elicit desired measurable responses in target groups and individuals.

- In the area of human resource management, **high-performance work practices**, are human resource policies and practices that can lead to both high individual and high organizational performance.

- Strategies in the HRM area include choices about **work flow** (the way an organization's work activities are organized so that the vision, missions, and objectives are effectively and efficiently accomplished), staffing, employee separations, performance appraisal, training and development, compensation, employee-labor relations, and employee rights.

- Current HRM strategies revolve around viewing employees as partners, working together to accomplish the organization's vision, missions, and goals and providing employees with **family-friendly benefits**, which are benefits that accommodate employees' needs for work–life balance.

- Strategies in the research and development area include strategic choices about R&D emphasis, R&D timing, and specific product and process development issues (which revolve around *who* and *how* decisions).

- One particular strategic choice in terms of R&D timing is whether to be a **first mover**, which is an organization that's first to bring a new product innovation to the marketplace or to use a new process innovation.

- One R&D "who" strategy involves whether to use a **cross-functional team**, which is a group of individuals from various functional departments who work together on product or process development.

- Current R&D strategies involve using employee suggestion systems and having an organizational culture that supports innovation.
- Strategies in the information systems function include choices about system technology and what types of information systems to use.
- An **information system** is a set of interrelated components used to collect, process, store, and disseminate information to support decision making, analysis, and management control in organizations.
- The six different types of information systems include transaction processing systems, office automation systems, knowledge work systems, management information systems, decision support systems, and executive support systems.
- Current strategies in the information systems area are focused on information technology, business intelligence, information vulnerability, and the Internet.
- Strategies in the financial–accounting area include choices about evaluating financial performance, financial forecasting and budgeting, financing mix, and other financial management decisions.
- The financing mix strategies concern decisions about the organization's **financial structure** (the mix of all items found on the right-hand side of the organization's balance sheet) and **capital structure** (the mix of long-term sources of funds used by the organization).
- Current strategies in the financial–accounting area include controlling costs, compliance, new financial performance measures, and valuing intangible assets.
- Once the strategic choices are made in each functional area, the strategies must be implemented.
- Functional strategy implementation involves five aspects: processes, activities, budgets, structure, and culture.
- At the functional level, these five aspects are relatively narrow in scope and definition because each functional area has its own specific work to do in contributing to the overall organizational goals.
- Although implementation involves the specific use of these aspects, it also involves the coordination of the various functional units.
- Strategy evaluation at the functional level involves using specific performance measures for each functional area.
- The actual performance measures must be compared against some standard (the goals established for the strategies in each functional area).

Strategic Management in Action

- If actual performance isn't up to standards, what happens next depends on how critical the strategy is to the accomplishment of other organizational goals and whether it's something we can control and change.

- The functional strategies need to be coordinated with the other organizational strategies. Strategic choices made at the business (competitive) and corporate levels do affect and are influenced by the functional strategies being implemented.

- Depending on what corporate and competitive strategies are being pursued, certain functional areas might be more important in carrying out those strategies.

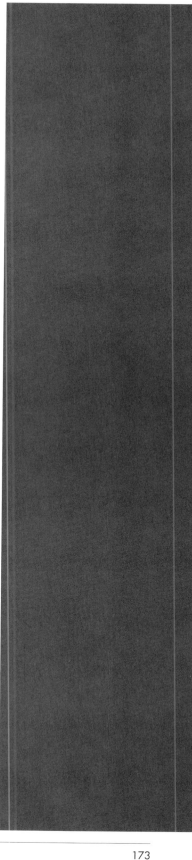

1. The skirts, shirts, and jackets we wear today aren't a whole lot different than what was worn a decade ago. However, the ways they're produced have been transformed by a forced infusion of information technology. When American apparel makers learned to view their product not as pieces of fabric sewn together but as a process of harnessing information along a chain that runs from the factory floor to the retail counter, they were able to improve their performance. Strategic factors such as bar coding, computer systems and software, high-tech distribution centers, and uniform standards have played a role in this reinvention of the clothing industry. How would each of these factors affect a clothing manufacturer's functional strategies in production–operations, research and development, marketing, human resource management, financial–accounting, and information systems?

2. Jack Welch, former CEO of General Electric, was noted for his managerial skills and abilities. The secret to his success was described as not a series of brilliant insights or bold gambles, but a fanatical attention to detail. What do you think this statement means? What are the implications for strategically managing an organization's functional strategies?

3. A federal law called the Economic Espionage Act of 1996 protects businesses from having their highly confidential product information stolen. Theft of intellectual property by trusted insiders (employees or contractors) happens frequently. One study estimated that intellectual property loss by U.S. companies amounted to over $250 billion annually. Many types of organizations in many types of industries are vulnerable. What are the implications for the way an organization's functional strategies are formulated and implemented? Think about each functional area that might be affected.

4. Many organizations are putting customer service activities online and making them available 24/7 (24 hours a day, 7 days a week). What would be the advantages of this strategic approach? What disadvantages might there be? How could strategic decision makers address the disadvantages?

5. Corporate sponsorships of special events and programs (sports programs, entertainment attractions, festivals and fairs, medical–education–social causes, and the arts) are a unique type of marketing strategy. The number of such sponsorships is decreasing. Do some research on corporate sponsorships. Find five examples of companies using corporate sponsorships. Describe these examples in a brief paper. What types of corporate sponsorships are these companies doing? Given the nature of the company's industry, why do you think they chose the sponsorship they did? Do you think these corporate sponsorships are an effective and efficient marketing strategy? Why or why not?

6. How important is a fun workplace to employees? Many experts say that being recognized as a fun place to work can be an important competitive edge when recruiting in a tight labor market. Fun-loving firms indicate that incorporating humor and fun in the workplace reduces stress, increases job satisfaction, stimulates creativity, and increases productivity. Research the topic of fun and humor in the workplace. What are the pros and cons of this strategic choice? Make a bulleted list of your findings. Be prepared to debate the topic (from either side) in class.

7. "Why do companies spend billions of dollars on information technology systems that fail to respond to the needs of those who use them?" This complaint isn't unique. What are the implications for designing effective information systems strategies? Be specific.

8. Revenue management (also called yield management) is proposed as a strategic tool that can help strategists make better decisions. Drawing from the fields of operations research, economics, finance, and marketing, revenue management uses a disciplined approach to forecasting demand for products or services, figuring out how to most efficiently provide them, and using price as a lever to influence demand and generate as much revenue as possible. Research the topic of revenue management. Make a bulleted list of its key points.

9. Customer service would appear to be an important strategic goal of any organization. Yet, surveys of customer satisfaction by the University of Michigan conclude that customer service is lacking. Research the topic of customer service. Then, in a short paper, describe which functional strategies might have to change and how they need to change to improve customer service.

10. Every year, *Fortune* magazine honors the 100 best companies to work for. Get the latest list. (The list is usually published in January.) What are the top 10 companies on the list? Select three of these companies to research. What types of functional strategies are these three companies using? What could other companies learn from the strategies being used by these companies?

Strategic Management in Action Cases

CASE #1: The Keys to Driving for Success

This Strategic Management in Action Case can be found at the beginning of Chapter 5.

Discussion Questions

1. What do you think are the keys to Toyota's success?

2. Do you think production or marketing would be most important to Toyota? Support your choice.

3. Is strategy coordination important to Toyota? Explain.

4. Go to the company's Web site (**www.toyota. com**). Describe what examples of functional strategies you find there.

CASE #2: Fishing Fantasies

The most popular tourist destination in Missouri isn't what you might expect. It's not the Gateway Arch in St. Louis, nor is it Harry Truman's home in Independence. Instead, you'd have to travel to the southwest corner of the state to Springfield to Bass Pro Shops Outdoor World. More than 4 million people visit this store annually. Although most visitors are hunting, fishing, and outdoors enthusiasts, many come just to see the incredible sights and to experience the retail atmosphere of the store. There's a four-story waterfall, rifle and archery ranges, a putting green, and an indoor driving range. Visitors can get their hair cut at the barbershop and then arrange to have a lure made from their hair clippings. They can grab a latté at the coffee shop or eat a full meal at Hemingway's Blue Water Café, whose showpiece is a 30,000-gallon saltwater aquarium. And then there are the incredible wildlife displays throughout the store—many of which have become popular photo spots for visitors. However, despite all of these fascinating attractions, the heart (and soul) of the store is still the row after row of guns, decoys, tents, rods, reels, lures, campers, clothing, and other sports and outdoors equipment and apparel. One enormous wing of the store showcases boats—speedboats, houseboats, pontoon boats, fiberglass boats, and aluminum boats. There's something for everyone to experience and enjoy.

Johnny Morris, founder of Bass Pro, was born and raised in Springfield. He opened the original store in 1972 in a small corner of his father's liquor store. From that humble beginning, the company has grown to be a dominant player in the sports and outdoors market. Morris's operating philosophy is never allowing the customer to have a dull moment. His retailing approach has been one of excitement and entertainment. The design of the flagship (the "granddaddy") store—and ultimately, all the other stores—was developed from trips to other popular retailing destinations to understand their appeal. One visit to L. L. Bean in Freeport, Maine, was particularly memorable. Morris felt that if that store could draw well over 3.5 million visitors a year to the middle of nowhere, then he could do that, and better, in Springfield. The retailing success that is Bass Pro Shops has been duplicated now in 26 different locations from Islamorada, Florida, to Oklahoma City to Baltimore to Las Vegas. And the company continues to look for new opportunities. Its newest store announcement was for a waterfront location in a new retail development in downtown Branson, Missouri, another popular tourist destination.

Although the stores are vital parts of Bass Pro's strategies, they aren't the only way that customers can purchase any of Bass Pro's thousands of items. The company's catalogs and online ordering are important parts of its operations as well. Bass Pro's catalog, which was launched in 1974, was its first step to achieving national recognition. Through the catalogs, many customers became fiercely loyal to the brand. In addition to these retailing strategies, Bass Pro also sponsors several TV and radio programs and runs a luxurious resort in the Ozark Mountains.

Discussion Questions

1. What examples of functional strategies do you see in this case? Label your examples and be specific in describing them.

2. As a company grows, what challenges might it face in replicating in different locations what's made it successful? How might these challenges be addressed?

3. Go to the Bass Pro Web site (**www.basspro. com**) and check out the information on the company. What is its mission? What other examples of functional strategies do you see?

(*Sources:* Bass Pro, **www.basspro.com**, March 14, 2004; K. Culp, "Bass Pro 'Granddaddy' Spawns New Generation," *Springfield News-Leader,* March 14, 2004, p. 1A; E. McDowell, Adventures in Retailing," *New York Times,* March 20, 1999, p. B1; and author's personal experiences visiting the "granddaddy" store in Springfield, Missouri.)

CASE #3: Cleaning Up

Whirlpool Corporation is the number one home appliance maker in the United States and ranks second in the world behind Sweden's AB Electrolux. The company has nearly 50 manufacturing and technology research centers in 13 countries and sells its products in more than 170 countries. Chairman and CEO David Whitwam oversees the $12 billion company and has built a global organization that knows how to capitalize on its strengths.

If there's one word that captures the essence of Whirlpool's strategic approach, it's innovation. In fact, the company's vision states, "Bringing innovation and quality to Every Home . . . Everywhere." Whirlpool believes that innovative thinking comes from anyone and anywhere within the company. To show how serious it is about innovation, Whirlpool launched a worldwide effort in 1999 to instill innovation as a core competency throughout the company. And innovation is evident in many different areas of the company.

In an industry known for producing boring, white boxes, Whirlpool has taken a different approach. Its artfully designed toasters, roasters, washing machines, dishwashers, and other eye-catching appliances are setting it apart from competitors and winning over customers. This intense commitment to product innovation can be seen in the company's Insperience Studio in the Buckhead neighborhood in Atlanta. Insperience was designed as a soft-sell showcase for the company's Whirlpool and KitchenAid brand products. It's a place where customers, interior designers, and home builders can learn about the company's products without feeling pressured. But it's more than that. It's also a place where salespeople hone their skills and a laboratory where the company's product designers actually see up close how customers interact with appliances. And Whirlpool takes that human–appliance bond seriously. Whirlpool aims to understand how customers interact with appliances and to apply that knowledge to building branded products that "stand for something." This philosophy was a counterattack against the "sea of white" that had characterized the appliance industry during the 1980s and 1990s. During that time, appliance companies' main goal had been to make appliances cheaper and cheaper. Customers came to perceive them as commodities, with little or no brand loyalty. Whitwam said, "Nobody (the customers) knew one from the other, so they just made their purchase decision on price." And he was determined to change that by focusing on selling to customers, not to the appliance dealers. That's when Whirlpool recommitted itself to innovation—in all areas throughout the organization.

To underscore the importance of innovative thinking, employees worldwide are encouraged to submit ideas and are routinely given money to develop business plans for their ideas. As an example, David Swift, head of North American operations says, "We've got a product in development now that came from a line worker at one of our plants in Ohio. It's a laundry product, and it could be a big one."

But innovation isn't only for the products. You can also see it in how Whirlpool does its work. For instance, the company was named one of *Business Week's* Web Smart 50 for its information technology project that linked every factory and sales operation together with suppliers and key retail partners. The company's investment in e-business software has helped it cut inventories from 15 percent of sales to 12 percent.

Discussion Questions

1. What examples of functional strategies do you see in this case? Be specific.

2. How has the emphasis on innovation affected functional strategies being implemented by Whirlpool? Give examples.

3. How are the functional strategies being used by Whirlpool contributing to the company's other strategies?

4. The company's Web site (**www.whirlpool.com**) is a treasure trove of information about the company's philosophies and strategies. Go to the Web site. What other types of functional strategies are described there? What do you think of Whirlpool's strategic philosophy and initiatives?

(**Sources:** Whirlpool, **www.whirlpool.com**, March 14, 2004; Hoover's Online, **www.hoovers.com**, March 14, 2004; M. Hudson, "Human–Appliance Bond Not Taken Lightly," *Springfield News-Leader,* March 14, 2004, p. 3E; M. Arndt, "The Web Smart 50—Whirlpool," *Business Week,* November 24, 2003, p. 98–99 and S. Kirsner, "Are You Insperienced?" *Fast Company,* July 2003, p. 32.)

Strategic Management in Action

Endnotes

1. E. Eldridge, "Ford Borrows from Toyota's Blueprints for New Hybrid Escape," *USA Today*, March 10, 2004, p. 6B; J. Teresko, "Asia: Yesterday's Fast Followers, Today's Global Leaders," *Industry Week*, February 2004, pp. 22–29; A. Taylor III, "The Americanization of Toyota," *Fortune*, December 8, 2003, pp. 165–70; B. Bremner and C. Dawson, "Can Anything Stop Toyota?" *Business Week*, November 17, 2003, pp. 114–22; R. Meredith and J. Fahey, "The 'Ooof' Company," *Forbes*, April 14, 2003, pp. 72–80; S. Spear and H. K. Bowen, "Decoding the DNA of the Toyota Production System," *Harvard Business Review*, September–October 1999, pp. 96–106; R. L. Simison, "Toyota Finds Way to Make a Custom Car in 5 Days," *Wall Street Journal*, August 6, 1999, p. A4; and D. Bartholomew, "Lean vs. ERP," *Industry Week*, July 19, 1999, pp. 24–30.

2. P. Siekman, "Build to Order: One Aircraft Carrier," *Fortune*, July 22, 2002, pp. 180B–180J.

3. Information for this section on production–operations–manufacturing is based on J. Heizer and B. Render, *Operations Management*, 7th ed. (Upper Saddle River, NJ: Prentice Hall, 2004).

4. T. Purdum, "GM Taps India for IT and R&D," *Industry Week*, February 2004, p. 57.

5. D. Drickhamer, "Ties that Bind," *Industry Week*, January 2004, p. 49.

6. J. W. Dean, Jr. and S. A. Snell, "The Strategic Use of Integrated Manufacturing: An Empirical Examination," *Strategic Management Journal*, June 1996, pp. 459–80.

7. Information for this section on marketing is based on P. Kotler, *Marketing Management*, 11th ed. (Upper Saddle River, NJ: Prentice Hall, 2002); and P. Kotler and G. Armstrong, *Principles of Marketing: An Introduction*, 7th ed. (Upper Saddle River, NJ: Prentice Hall, 2005.)

8. See D. A. Garvin, "Competing on the Eight Dimensions of Quality," *Harvard Business Review*, November–December 1987, pp. 101–109.

9. P. F. Nunes and F. V. Cespedes, "The Customer Has Escaped," *Harvard Business Review*, November 2003, pp. 96–105; J. Griffin, "Divide and Prosper," *IQ Magazine*, March–April 2003, pp. 32–33; and N. Paley, "Romancing Your Customers," *Sales & Marketing Management*, March 1996, pp. 30–32.

10. J. Lardner, "Your Every Command," *U.S. News & World Report*, July 5, 1999, pp. 44–46; "Mass Customization Becomes the New Marketing Mantra," *Wall Street Journal*, April 29, 1999, p. A1; D. Peppers, M. Rogers, and B. Dorf, "Is Your Company Ready for One-to-One Marketing?" *Harvard Business Review*, January–February 1999, pp. 151–60; and J. H. Gilmore and B. J. Pine II, "The Four Faces of Mass Customization," *Harvard Business Review*, January–February 1997, pp. 91–101.

11. D. Foust and B. Grow, "Coke: Wooing the TiVo Generation," *Business Week*, March 1, 2004, pp. 77–80; R. Grover, T. Lowry, G. Khermouch, C. Edwards, and D. Foust, "Can Mad Ave. Make Zap-Proof Ads?" *Business Week*, February 2, 2004, pp. 36–37; T. Howard, "Real Winner of 'American Idol': Coke," *USA Today*, September 9, 2002, p. 6B; and D. Eisenberg, "It's an Ad, Ad, Ad, Ad World," *Time*, September 2, 2002, pp. 38–41.

12. R. Batt, "Managing Customer Services: Human Resource Practices, Quit Rates, and Sales Growth," *Academy of Management Journal*, June 2002, pp. 587–97; J. Pfeffer, *The Human Equation: Building Profits By Putting People First*, (Boston: Harvard Business School Press, 1998); A. A. Lado and M. C. Wilson, "Human Resource Systems and Sustained Competitive Advantage: A Competency-Based Perspective," *Academy of Management Review*, October 1994, pp. 699–727; J. Pfeffer, *Competitive Advantage Through People* (Boston: Harvard Business School Press, 1994); and P. M. Wright and G. C. McMahan, "Theoretical Perspectives for Strategic Human Resource Management," *Journal of Management*, 17 (1991), pp. 295–320.

13. "Human Capital: A Key to Higher Market Value," *Business Finance*, December 1999, p. 15; M. A. Huselid, "The Impact of Human Resource Management Practices on Turnover, Productivity, and Corporate Financial Performance," *Academy of Management Journal*, June 1995, pp. 635–72.

14. Information for this section was based primarily on L. R. Gomez-Mejia, D. B. Balkin, and R. L. Cardy, *Managing Human Resources* (Upper Saddle River, NJ: Prentice Hall, 1995).

15. Ibid., p. 464.

16. B. P. Sunoo, "How Fun Flies at Southwest Airlines," *Personnel Journal*, June 1995, p. 62.

17. F. Hansen, "Truths and Myths about Work/Life Balance," *Workforce*, December 2002, pp. 34–39; and S. D. Friedman and J. H. Greenhaus, *Work and Family—Allies or Enemies*? (New York: Oxford University Press, 2000).

18. B. Becker and B. Gerhart, "The Impact of Human Resource Management on Organizational Performance: Progress and Prospects," *Academy of Management Journal*, August 1996, pp. 670–87; J. T. Delaney and M. A. Huselid, "The Impact of Human Resource Management Practices on Perceptions of Organizational Performance," *Academy of Management Journal*, August 1996, pp. 949–69; J. E. Delery and D. H. Doty, "Modes of Theorizing in Strategic Human Resource Management: Tests of Universalistic, Contingency, and Configurational Performance Predictions," *Academy of Management Journal*, August 1996, pp. 802–35; M. A. Youndt, S. A. Snell, J. W. Dean, Jr., and D. P. LePak, "Human Resource Management, Manufacturing Strategy, and Firm Performance," *Academy of Management Journal*, August 1996, pp. 836–66; M. J. Koch and R. G. McGrath, "Improving Labor Productivity: Human Resource Management Policies Do Matter," *Strategic Management Journal*, May 1996, pp. 335–54; Huselid, "The Impact of Human Resource Management Practices"; and J. B. Arthur, "Effects of Human Resource Systems on Manufacturing Performance and Turnover," *Academy of Management Journal*, June 1994, pp. 670–87.

19. "Best Plant Winners: Taking the High Road," *Industry Week*, October 29, 2003, p. 33–35.

20. The information in this section is based on K.C. Laudon and J. P. Laudon, *Essentials of Management Information Systems* (Upper Saddle River, NJ: Prentice Hall, 1995).

21. I. Sager, "Keeping Closer Track of K-Rations," *Business Week*, November 3, 2003, p. 9.

22. E. Brown, "Slow Road to Fast Data," *Fortune*, March 18, 2002, pp. 170–72.

23. C. Tkaczyk, "Crushing Bugs," *Fortune*, September 15, 2003, p. 48; T. Reason, "Stopping the Flow," *CFO*, September 2003, pp. 97–99; and S. Baker, "Where Danger Lurks," *Business Week*, August 25, 2003, pp. 114–18.

24. Information for this section is based on A. J. Keown, D. F. Scott, Jr., J. D. Martin, and J. W. Petty, *Basic Financial Management*, 7th ed. (Upper Saddle River, NJ: Prentice Hall, 1996).

25. D. Henry and A. Borrus, "Honesty is a Pricey Policy," *Business Week*, October 27, 2003, pp. 100–101.

26. T. Reason, "Goodbye to Net Income?" *CFO*, November 2003, p. 22.

27. R. Barker, "A Better Way to Size Up a Company," *Business Week*, October 6, 2003, pp. 154–56.

28. G. Baum, C. Ittner, D. Larcker, J. Low, T. Siesfeld, and M. S. Malone, "Introducing the New Value Creation Index," *Forbes ASAP*, April 3, 2000, pp. 140–43.

29. D. Nath and D. Sudharshan, "Measuring Strategy Coherence Through Patterns of Strategic Choice," *Strategic Management Journal*, January 1994, pp. 43–61.

6

Competitive Strategies

LEARNING OUTLINE

What Is Competitive Advantage and How Do We Get It?

- *Explain the importance of competitive advantage.*
- *Describe how an organization's competitors can be determined.*
- *Discuss how resources, capabilities, and core competencies lead to competitive advantage.*
- *Explain the relationship between competitive advantage and competitive strategies.*

What Are the Competitive Strategies?

- *Describe Miles and Snow's adaptive strategies.*
- *Describe Abell's business definition framework and his competitive strategies.*
- *Describe Porter's generic competitive strategies.*
- *Explain what it means to be "stuck in the middle."*
- *Describe an integrated low-cost differentiation strategy.*
- *Explain Mintzberg's generic competitive strategies.*

Implementing, Evaluating, and Changing Competitive Strategy

- *Describe how an organization implements, evaluates, and changes its competitive strategies.*
- *Explain what role functional strategies play in an organization's competitive strategies.*
- *Discuss the various competitive postures and actions an organization can take.*

They've Got Game

With one of the world's most recognizable slogans (Just Do It) and brand logos (the swoosh), you wouldn't think that Nike would have to worry about the competition. However, in the athletic apparel industry, where consumer tastes are fickle and the intensity of rivalry high, even Nike needs effective competitive strategies.[1]

Nike, the company, reflects the brash confidence of its founder and CEO Phil Knight. He still believes, as one of his company's most controversial Olympic ads once stated, "You don't win silver. You lose gold." With that type of attitude, it's no wonder that 9 of the 10 top-selling basketball shoes are Nike and that Nike is the world's number one athletic apparel company with 40 percent of the U.S. athletic footwear market. How does Nike play the game?

One thing that Nike understands well is the power of a competitive spirit, which continues to be a guiding force in the way the company does business. This competitive spirit, instilled by the late Bill Bowerman, Knight's mentor and track coach at the University of Oregon, has characterized the company's culture from the early days. The company (then called Blue Ribbon Sports) began with a handshake between Knight and Bowerman when they decided to import cheap, high-tech Japanese "Tiger" shoes to challenge Adidas, the industry leader. Even then, Knight was not afraid to go after someone, even the industry leader. And this competitive spirit influences strategic actions in other areas. For instance, when Foot Locker (one of Nike's biggest retailers), upset by Nike's hard-nosed marketing tactics, trimmed orders and slashed prices, Nike struck back by cutting shipments to the company on some of its top sellers. The move had serious consequences (Nike's U.S. sales fell 5 percent and its stock price plummeted), but it also brought Foot Locker back to the bargaining table. Later, an analyst said, "Nike knew its actions were going to have a negative impact, but they did it anyway," because it knew it would prevail at the end. Even the company's name reflects this competitive spirit; Nike is the name of the Greek goddess of victory.

Another thing that Nike understands well is marketing. Knight has been called the "most powerful person in sports" even though he's never played professional sports or owned a professional sports team. What he's done, though, is rewrite the rules of sports marketing. When he signed a young basketball player by the name of Michael Jordan, an endorsement relationship began that even today remains the gold standard. And Nike continues to go after the new sports geniuses. For instance, when basketball phenom LeBron James was garnering attention, Nike signed him to an endorsement contract, beating out rivals Reebok and Adidas. The company has also signed Freddy Adu, a teenage soccer prodigy viewed as America's first potential breakthrough soccer star. And you can't discuss Nike's marketing prowess without mentioning the company's legendary ads. Nike has always taken chances in its advertising by sounding off on social and political issues in sports. Knight says he knows that he risks offending people but believes "the publicity and notoriety are worth it."

Not only is the company on the cutting edge in its marketing, it continues to take risks with its products. One of Nike's newest strategies is going after more specialized markets such as skateboarding and golf. And it has developed a new collection of casual and sporty street apparel. Whether the company can exploit its brand power in these new markets remains to be seen. But one thing is for sure—this company's got game!

As the chapter-opening case points out, competition is a given for all organizations, regardless of their size, type, geographic location, or even reputation. Even not-for-profit organizations compete for resources and customers. A small, local community theater faces competition from other entertainment options—both local and global—just as Google (the Internet search company) faces competition from Yahoo!, Mamma.com, AlltheWeb, and other Internet search services. How can organizations cope with competition and still achieve strategic goals? By formulating and implementing appropriate competitive strategies. For instance, that's exactly what Nike did when it decided to exploit its brand name in new markets. The company was betting that this decision would turn out to be a savvy and brilliant competitive move that would lead to increased sales and profits and an even more enviable competitive position in the marketplace. In this chapter, we're going to look at the various competitive strategies—what they are and how they're implemented, evaluated, and changed. (Figure 6.1 illustrates how competitive strategies fit into the overall strategic management in action process.) First, we're going to start off by reviewing competitive advantage and then discussing the competitive environment.

Figure 6.1

Strategic Management in Action

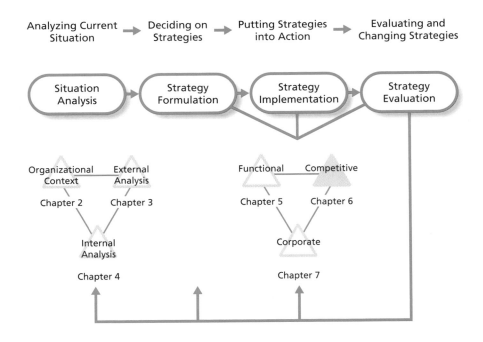

WHAT IS COMPETITIVE ADVANTAGE AND HOW DO WE GET IT?

As we've said in earlier chapters, competitive advantage is a key concept in strategic management—getting it and keeping it is what managing strategically is all about. Remember that **competitive advantage** is what sets an organization apart—its competitive edge. In other words, the organization does something that others can't or does it better than others do. Or, competitive advantage might arise from having something that other competitors don't. Competitive advantage is what an organization's competitive strategies are designed to exploit. Other organizations are also attempting to develop competitive advantage and to attract customers. Thus, an organization's competitive advantage can be eroded easily (and often quickly) by competitors' actions. Because competitive advantage implies that there are other competitors, we first need to look at the competitive environment to better understand the conditions under which competitive advantage is pursued.

Understanding the Competitive Environment

Competition is everywhere. Very few industries or organizations haven't experienced some form or degree of competition. In fact, some strategic management researchers have described the current business competitive environment as one of **hypercompetition**, which is a situation with very intense and continually increasing levels of competition.[2] Is hypercompetition the only way to describe today's competitive environment? Fortunately, no, although it's obvious that the current competitive environment *is* changing and will continue to change. To understand the competitive environment, we first have to understand *what* competition is and then look at *who* our competitors are.

What Is Competition?

Competition is when organizations battle or vie for some desired object or outcome—typically customers, market share, survey ranking, or needed resources. Although individuals and even teams also compete for desired objects or outcomes, our primary interest is competition as it relates to organizations. The intensity of competition (i.e., how seriously organizations battle for customers or resources) varies depending on several factors, which we described in Chapter 3 in our discussion of current rivalry in Porter's five forces model. What types of competition might an organization face? This can be answered by looking at *who* our competitors are.

Who Are Our Competitors?

One approach proposes defining an organization's competitors according to an industry perspective or a market perspective.[3] Figure 6.2 illustrates each of these perspectives.

The industry perspective identifies competitors as organizations that are making the same product or providing the same service. For example, there's the oil industry, the supermarket industry, the automobile industry, the credit card industry, or the dental health care industry. The competitors in these industries are producing the same or highly similar types of products or services. (To make sure you understand this concept, take a minute and try to name some of the competitors in these industries.) In addition, industries can be described according to the number of sellers and whether the products or services are similar or different. The number of sellers and the level of product–service differentiation will affect how intensely competitive the industry is. The most intense competition will be under situations of pure competition (see Figure 6.2) in which there are many sellers and no differentiation exists among the sellers.

The market perspective says that competitors are organizations that satisfy the same customer need. So, for example, if the customer need is entertainment, competitors might

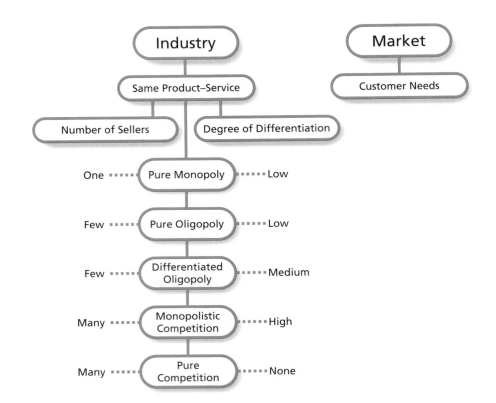

Figure 6.2

Industry and Market Approaches to Defining Competitors

range all the way from video game manufacturers to theme parks to movie theaters to the local community symphony orchestra. If the customer need happens to be athletic apparel, then competitors would be Nike, Reebok, Adidas, or even Hanes. From the market perspective, the intensity of competition depends on how well the customer's need is understood or defined and how well different organizations are able to meet that need.

Another approach to defining *who* competitors are is to use the strategic groups concept. We talked about strategic groups in Chapter 3 in our discussion of current rivalry in

The Grey Zone

The dry cleaning industry continues to debate the high cost of being green; that is, recognizing the impact of strategic actions on the natural environment. A vast majority of dry cleaners in the United States still use a number of toxic chemicals in the dry cleaning process that are linked to cancer, nervous system disorders, and other health hazards. "Green" cleaners that use water and biodegradable detergents have been available for almost 15 years. However, few existing businesses have been willing to switch to this new process because this form of "wet" cleaning takes longer, increases labor costs, and can easily lead to clothes shrinkage or other quality problems. What if you were a strategic decision maker in this industry? Do you think a competitor who chose to go green could survive? How might you deal with this ethical dilemma of wanting to "do the right thing" yet needing to stay in business?

Sources: *Environmental Protection Agency*, **www.epa.gov**, *March 15, 2004; and B. J. Feder, "Cleaning Up the Dry Cleaners,"* New York Times, *February 15, 2000, p. C1.*

- Price
- Quality
- Level of vertical integration
- Geographic scope
- Product line breadth–depth
- Level of diversification
- R&D expenditures
- Market share
- Profits
- Product characteristics
- Any other relevant strategic factor

Porter's five forces model. Remember that a **strategic group** is a set of firms competing within an industry that have similar strategies, resources, and customers.[4] Within a single industry, you might find few or several strategic groups, depending on what strategic factors are important to different groups of customers. For instance, two strategic factors often used in grouping competitors are price (low to high) and quality (low to high), because these are usually important to customers. Competitors would then be "grouped" according to their price–quality strategies with those following the same or similar approaches in the same strategic group. Keep in mind that the strategic dimensions used to determine an organization's competitors are different for every industry and can be different even for different industry segments. Table 6.1 lists some possible strategic dimensions that might be used to distinguish strategic groups. An example illustrating some of the strategic groups in the cosmetics industry is shown in Figure 6.3. Note in this example that

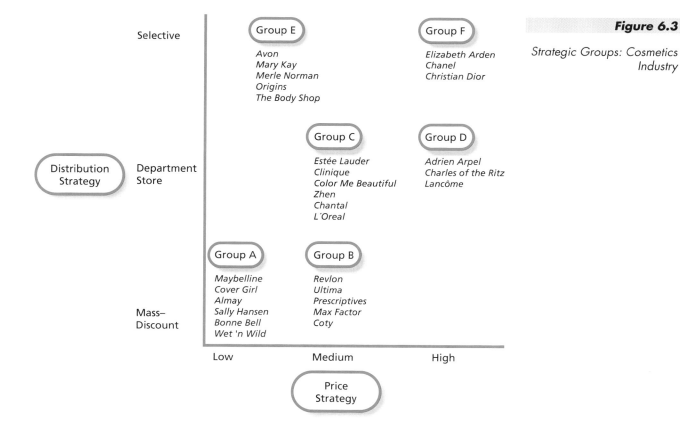

Figure 6.3

Strategic Groups: Cosmetics
Industry

the strategic factors for grouping the competitors aren't price and quality, but are instead price and distribution strategy, two factors that are important to this particular industry.

The strategic groups approach is important to understanding *who* competitors are because your most relevant competitors are those in your strategic group. Although competition might, and often does, come from organizations in other strategic groups, your main competitive concern is those organizations in your own strategic group. The intensity of competition from this perspective depends on how effectively each competitor has developed a sustainable competitive advantage and on the competitive strategies and competitive actions being used by each of the competitors in the strategic group.

Although the strategic groups approach is frequently used to define an industry's competitors, you should also be aware that there has been some controversy about whether specific, identifiable strategic groups even exist.[5] These questions generally concern *what* factors are used to define a strategic group and *how* these factors are chosen and used to separate specific and identifiable groups. Despite these concerns, the strategic groups concept remains a useful approach to determining *who* an organization's competitors are.

No matter how we define our competitors, the fact remains that there *are* other organizations struggling to secure customers, resources, and other desired outcomes. Each of those organizations has resources and capabilities it's attempting to exploit. That's what we want to look at next—the role that resources and capabilities play in competitive advantage.

The Role of Resources and Distinctive Capabilities in Gaining Competitive Advantage

What makes some organizations more successful—however you choose to measure success—than others? Why do some professional basketball teams consistently win championships or draw large crowds? Why do some organizations have consistent and continuous growth in revenues and profits? Why do some colleges, universities, or departmental majors experience continually increasing enrollments? Why do some organizations appear consistently on lists ranking "the best," "the most admired," or "the most profitable"? Every organization has resources and capabilities to do whatever it's in business to do. However, not every organization is able to effectively exploit the resources or capabilities it has or obtain the resources or capabilities it needs but doesn't have. It's a classic case of "the haves" and "the have-nots" and "the can dos" and "the can't dos." Some organizations are able to put it all together and develop those distinctive organizational capabilities that can provide them with a sustainable competitive advantage. Other organizations never quite get to that point.

Organizations will develop strategies to exploit their current resources and capabilities or to vie for needed-but-not-owned resources and capabilities in order to pursue and attain desired outcomes such as customers, market share, resources, or even perhaps, in the case of a college football team, a national championship. They do this while other organizations (few or many) are doing exactly the same thing. Competitive advantage, by its very nature, implies that we're trying to gain the edge on others. As organizations fight for a sustainable competitive advantage, the stage for competition—intense, moderate, or mild—is set.

From Competitive Advantage to Competitive Strategies

As organizations attempt to create a sustainable competitive advantage, they're looking for ways to set themselves apart. How an organization chooses to do this is what **competitive**

the global perspective

Butterfly farming is big business in Costa Rica. It's the largest butterfly supplier in the world, exporting more than 300,000 pupae a year. Who buys butterflies? The main customers include zoos, natural history museums, and other tourist attractions. Even some innovative hotels and restaurants have opened butterfly exhibits. And releasing butterflies at weddings has replaced the traditional throwing of rice or bird seed. At one business, Butterfly Paradise, increasing competition forced owner Mario Polsa to branch out into handicrafts such as mounted, encased butterflies that can be displayed on desks or walls. As in any intensely competitive situation, successful organizations look for some competitive edge.

Sources: *Costa Rica Entomological Supply,* **www.butterflyfarm.com.cr**, March 15, 2004; Butterfly Paradise, **www.westnet.com/costarica/go/ mariposas3.html**, *March 15, 2004; and J. Dulude, "Butterflies Aren't Free," Latin Trade, March 2000, pp. 32–34.*

strategy is all about. The choice of competitive strategy is a choice of how an organization or business unit is going to compete in its particular industry or market. What's the choice of competitive strategy based on? It's based on the competitive advantage(s) that the organization has been able to develop. For example, Nike's competitive strategy was based on what it saw as its competitive advantage—its competitive spirit and its marketing and innovation capabilities. As an organization refines and sharpens its competitive advantage (whether found in unique resources or distinctive capabilities), the basis for its competitive strategy is established. What we need to look at next, then, are the various competitive strategies.

Learning Review

- Is competition an issue for all organizations? Discuss.
- What is competitive advantage?
- Define competition. Define hypercompetition. What influences the level of competition among organizations?
- Compare and contrast the industry and marketing perspectives of defining competitors.
- Why is the concept of strategic groups important to identifying an organization's competitors?
- Describe factors that can be used for grouping competitors.
- What role do resources and distinctive capabilities play in gaining competitive advantage?
- Define competitive strategy. What's the connection between competitive advantage and competitive strategy?

WHAT ARE THE COMPETITIVE STRATEGIES?

Although it may seem that there are an endless number of competitive strategies, the ways an organization competes are actually quite limited. In this section, we want to look at some specific competitive strategy alternatives. We'll look first at the traditional approaches to defining competitive strategies. Then, we'll discuss some contemporary perspectives on competitive strategies.

Traditional Approaches to Defining Competitive Strategy

Attempts to describe, explain, and categorize specific competitive strategies that organizations use has been a favorite challenge of strategy researchers. Three popular approaches include Miles and Snow's adaptive strategies (1978), Abell's business definition framework (1980), and Porter's generic competitive strategies (1980).[6] We're going to look at each approach to see what it says about the strategies organizations use to compete.

Miles and Snow's Adaptive Strategies

Miles and Snow's approach is based on the strategies organizations use to adapt to their uncertain competitive environments. According to their approach, four strategic postures are possible: prospector, defender, analyzer, and reactor. What competitive actions are involved with each?

The **prospector strategy** is one in which an organization continually innovates by finding and exploiting new product and market opportunities. A prospector's competitive strength is its ability to survey a wide range of rapidly changing environmental conditions, trends, and situations and to create new products and services to fit this dynamic environment. The prospector's competitive strategy is to continually innovate, develop, and test new products and services. Prospectors are constantly on the lookout—prospecting—for new directions to pursue. This constant search for innovation creates uncertainties for the prospector's competitors; they never know what's going to happen next or what to expect from the prospector. If the prospector can develop new products or services that the market desires and is willing to pay for, it will have a sustainable competitive advantage. What's an example of an organization that's using the prospector competitive strategy? In the broadcast television industry, the Fox Broadcasting Network and MTV are good examples of organizations using the prospector strategy. Both are noted for their innovative television network programming and willingness to pursue new directions. They've been able to tap into changing societal attitudes and interests (e.g., Fox's *American Idol* and MTV's *The Osbournes*) and develop television programs that appeal to these changes. And they're willing to constantly "push the envelope" in developing new products. Their competitive advantage stems from their ability to assess environmental trends and continually create new and innovative programs.

STRATEGIC MANAGEMENT
the global perspective

It's hot! Cholula hot sauce, originally made in Chapala, Guadalajara, in western Mexico, is threatening the dominance of McIlhenny Company's Tabasco sauce. When executives at José Cuervo, the Mexico City-based tequila company, heard about Cholula in the early 1990s, they bought the license and began marketing it in Mexico. Then, the company decided to take the product north to the United States, where specialty food shops and restaurants tried it and liked customers' reactions. Based on its initial successes, Cuervo chose to make an all-out assault on Tabasco. It hired a spokesman, a well-known Houston chef, and sent him on a 12-city tour to create Cholula-enhanced dishes. The company ran advertisements in trade magazines and put coupons in newspaper inserts. Sales of Cholula have taken off. Although Tabasco has about a 25 percent share of the hot sauce market, Cholula is coming on strong. If you were a strategic decision maker at Cuervo, what would you do at this point? What if you were a strategic decision maker at Tabasco?

Sources: *Hoover's Online*, **www.hoovers.com**, March 15, 2004; and C. Poole, *"Watch Out, Tabasco,"* Latin Trade, February 2000, pp. 29–30.

The **defender strategy** is characterized by the search for market stability and producing only a limited product line directed at a narrow segment of the total potential market. Defenders have well-established businesses that they're seeking to protect (i.e., to "defend"). They'll do whatever it takes to aggressively prevent competitors from coming into their turf. A defender will be successful with this strategy as long as its primary technology and narrow product line remain competitive. Over time, defenders are able to carve out and maintain niches within their industries that competitors find difficult to penetrate. Cleveland-based Lincoln Electric would be a good example of a company using a defender strategy. It's a leading manufacturer of welding products, which account for most of its revenues. The company vigorously protects its product lines and market share against competitors by providing outstanding customer service and aggressively matching price cuts.

The **analyzer strategy** is one of analysis and imitation. Organizations using this strategy thoroughly analyze new business ideas before jumping in. Analyzers also watch for and copy the successful ideas of prospectors. They compete by following the direction that prospectors pioneer. Even before blindly jumping in, though, analyzers will systematically assess and evaluate whether this move is appropriate for them. For example, consumer products company Unilever uses the analyzer strategy for its Suave shampoo and skin care product line. Unilever markets its lines by matching the packaging, smell, and feel of rival's products. Another example of this strategy is COSMI Corporation, which makes and mass markets inexpensive education, entertainment, and business software. Its chief corporate officer describes the company as an "imitator, not an innovator" and says that he'd rather leave being first in the market to the "Microsofts of the software world and come out with simpler versions of whatever proves successful."[7]

Finally, the **reactor strategy** is characterized by the lack of a coherent strategic plan or apparent means of competing. Reactors simply react to environmental changes and make adjustments only when finally forced to do so by environmental pressures. Oftentimes, reactors are unable to respond quickly to perceived environmental changes because they either lack the needed resources or capabilities or they're not able to exploit their current resources and capabilities. Obviously, this is *not* a preferred or recommended competitive strategy for developing a sustainable competitive advantage. In fact, the reactor strategy can be thought of as a "default" strategy, almost a nonstrategy position. Some examples of organizations that have used the reactor strategy at one time—willingly or unwillingly—include Sears, Sizzler International Inc. (the steakhouse chain), and Digital Equipment Corporation. In each of these instances, the organization lagged significantly behind its competitors in products or services offered and had no consistent strategic direction. Without significant strategic changes, a reactor will always be in a weak competitive position.

Table 6.2 summarizes the characteristics of each of Miles and Snow's competitive strategies. Strategy research using the Miles and Snow typology verifies that these four competitive strategies are theoretically sound and appropriate for describing how organizations are competing.[8]

Abell's Business Definition Framework

Another approach suggested for describing the competitive strategies used by organizations is the business definition framework developed by Derek Abell. According to Abell, a business can be defined using three dimensions: (1) customer groups—*who* we're going to serve; (2) customer needs—*what* customer need we're attempting to meet; and (3) technology or distinctive competencies—*how* we're going to meet that need. As you can see, this approach strongly stresses understanding *customers,* not an *industry,* when developing an appropriate and effective competitive strategy.

Based on these three dimensions, Abell's classification scheme proposed that a business could be defined by its competitive scope (i.e., broad or narrow markets) and by the

The Copycat Economy

Have you seen the Swiffer WetJet? How about ReadyMop? When Procter & Gamble (P&G) introduced its Swiffer WetJet mop, they thought they had a breakthrough product that was sure to be a winner and charged a premium price for it. But not long after Swiffer's debut, Clorox Company brought out its copycat product, ReadyMop, an action that forced P&G to cut its price in half. And this scenario has been repeated continuously in other industries with other products. The situation has been described as the "copycat economy." Whereas a hot new idea used to mean years of fat profits, rivals now move into markets almost instanta-neously. The question for strategic decision makers is "How do you make money in such an environment, especially when demand is flat?" Unfortunately, there are no easy answers. For some industries, product upgrades are the answer. In other industries, companies have to continuously pump out cutting-edge products that fetch premium prices, no matter for how short a time. Others are finding that they have to continually fine-tune product formulas and designs. And finally, some companies have gone the opposite way by focusing research on fewer products, tenaciously defending patents, and vigorously promoting well-established brands with heavy marketing. Find other examples of copycat products (goods or services). How has the initial player responded to the competitive challenge? What strategies are the copycats using? Can you think of other possible strategic responses that either player might use?

Source: P. Engardio and F. Keenan, "The Copycat Economy," Business Week, August 26, 2002, pp. 94–96.

Table 6.2

Characteristics of Miles and Snow's Adaptive (Competitive) Strategies

Strategy	Characteristics
Prospector	• Organization seeks innovation • Demonstrated ability to survey dynamic environment and develop new products–services to fit the changing environment • Frequently and continually innovating, developing, and testing new products–services • Competitors are uncertain about prospector's future strategic decisions and actions
Defender	• Searches for market stability • Produces only a limited product line for a narrow segment of total potential market • Seeks to protect (defend) its well-established business • Does whatever is necessary to aggressively prevent competitors from entering their turf • Can carve out and maintain niches within its industry that competitors find difficult to penetrate
Analyzer	• Strategy of analysis and imitation • Thoroughly analyzes new business ideas (products, services, markets) before deciding to jump in • Watches for and copies the promising and successful ideas of prospectors
Reactor	• Lacks coherent strategic plan • Simply reacts to environmental changes • Makes strategic adjustments only when finally forced to do so • Unable to respond quickly to environmental changes because resources–capabilities are lacking or are not developed or exploited properly

Source: Based on R. E. Miles and C. C. Snow, Organizational Strategy, Structure, and Process (New York: McGraw-Hill, 1978).

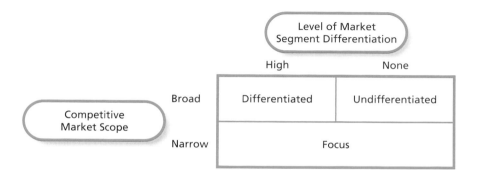

Figure 6.4

Abell's Competitive Strategies

Source: Based on J. J. Chrisman, C. W. Hofer, and W. R. Boulton, "Toward a System for Classifying Business Strategies," Academy of Management Review, 13, no. 3 (1988), pp. 413–28.

extent of competitive differentiation of its product or service offerings (i.e., how differentiated products and services are). The various combinations of these dimensions formed the basis for Abell's three possible competitive strategies: differentiated, undifferentiated, and focus. Figure 6.4 illustrates these three strategies.

Abell's differentiated strategy describes businesses that compete in broad markets and use different competitive weapons to serve the various market segments in which they compete. The undifferentiated strategy also describes businesses with broad competitive scopes, but these businesses use only one common competitive weapon for serving each segment; that is, there's no differentiation in products or services. The focus strategy is used by businesses that compete in a narrow market and also use only one common competitive weapon.

Abell's strict marketing emphasis limits his business definition framework as a widely used or general approach to describing organization's competitive strategies. However, it does provide clues to two important aspects of competitive strategy—competitive scope and the level of product differentiation.

Learning Review

- What is the organization adapting to in Miles and Snow's adaptive strategies approach?
- Describe each of Miles and Snow's four adaptive strategies.
- What are the three dimensions Abell proposed for defining a business?
- Describe Abell's three competitive strategies.

Porter's Generic Competitive Strategies

Yes, we're once again discussing the same Porter who developed the five forces model (external analysis) and the value chain (internal analysis)—analytical tools that are part of the strategic approach he developed for explaining how organizations create and exploit a sustainable competitive advantage. Why are these important to our discussion of competitive strategies? According to Porter, strategic decision makers need this information before choosing an appropriate competitive strategy.

What's an "appropriate" competitive strategy? In Porter's approach, it's one based on an organization's competitive advantage, which, according to Porter, can come from only one of two sources: having the lowest costs in the industry or possessing significant and desirable differences from competitors.[9] Another factor that's important to competitive advantage in Porter's approach is the scope of the product–market in which the organization wishes to compete—that is, broad (all or most market segments) or narrow (only one segment or few segments). The mix of these factors provides the basis for Porter's generic

Figure 6.5

Porter's Generic Competitive
Strategies

Source: Adapted with the permission of
The Free Press, a Division of Simon and
Schuster from Competitive Strategy:
Techniques for Analyzing Industries and
Competitors by M. E. Porter. Copyright ©
1980 by The Free Press.

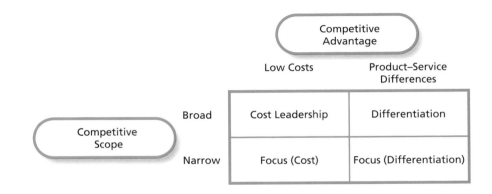

competitive strategies. These include cost leadership, differentiation, and focus (cost and differentiation). Figure 6.5 shows the configurations of these four possible strategies. At this point, you may be wondering why Porter called these strategies "generic." The term simply refers to the fact that they can be pursued by any type or size organization in any type or size industry. We're going to provide more detail on Porter's strategies because they're well known and have been used numerous times in research on organization's competitive strategies.

The **cost leadership strategy** is one in which an organization strives to have the lowest costs in its industry and produces products or services for a broad customer base. This strategy is also sometimes called the low-cost strategy. The main goal of the cost leader is to have *the* lowest costs in the industry. Notice that the emphasis here is on *costs*, not *prices*. In other words, the cost leader is striving to have the lowest total unit costs in the industry. Because the cost leader does have the lowest costs in the industry, it can potentially charge the lowest prices and still earn profits. Although every organization should attempt to keep costs low—that's just smart strategic management—the cost leader is choosing to *compete* on the basis of having the lowest costs. What are the advantages of having the lowest costs? Having the lowest costs means that the cost leader can charge a lower price than its competitors and still earn significant profits. It also means that when competitive rivalry heats up and competitors begin to compete ferociously on price (i.e., a price war breaks out), the cost leader is in a better position to withstand it and continue earning profits.

What does it take to successfully pursue the cost leadership strategy? Everything the cost leader does—every strategic decision and every strategic action—is aimed at keeping costs as low as possible. Efficiency in all areas of operations is the main objective, and all functional strategies and distinctive capabilities are directed at that. The cost leader isn't going to have deep and wide product lines. Providing product or service variations is expensive, and the cost leader has chosen to compete on the basis of low costs, not on being different than competitors. The cost leader will market products aimed at the "average" customer. Little or no product frills or differences will be available. The cost leader organization isn't going to have fancy artwork on the walls at corporate headquarters or plush office furniture. It's unlikely that you'd see a cost leader with an elaborate high-tech, multimedia interactive Web site *unless* it was determined that this would be an extremely cost-effective and efficient way to reach masses of potential customers. In fact, being a cost leader doesn't mean ignoring the latest advances in technology. Quite the opposite. If new and improved technology can pave the way to further lowering costs, the cost leader will jump on it. For instance, Payless ShoeSource, the shoe retailer with over $2.7 billion in annual sales, has a modern automated warehouse in Topeka, Kansas, where the corporate headquarters is located. Out of this warehouse, which spans 17 acres under one roof, Payless' approximately 4,800 stores can be restocked with styles and sizes on as little as a day's notice.[10] Because Payless competes in an intensely competitive industry (discount-priced shoes), the cost savings associated with such speed-to-market is critical. Another example of an organiza-tion pursuing a cost leadership strategy is Google.[11] The Web search firm handles more than 200 million page views a day, but handles those Internet queries with 12,000 cheap computer servers. If one goes down, Google junks it and brings a replacement online. Google doesn't have any expensive hardware service contracts or an in-house repair depart-ment. Then, there's the ultimate low-cost leader—Wal-Mart. As the world's largest retailer, you'd expect business operations befitting such a corporate icon, but you'd be wrong. At Wal-Mart's headquarters, office furnishings are modern, but plain. Employees take out their own trash. There's no free coffee or soda. And the bathrooms on corporate jets have curtains, not doors.[12] By focusing on efficient, cost-effective performance rather than on image, Wal-Mart has been able to prosper in a cutthroat, competitive industry. Other char-acteristics of cost leaders include strict attention to production controls; rigorous use of budgets; little product differentiation—just enough to satisfy what the mass market might demand; limited market segmentation—products or services are aimed at the mass market; emphasis on productivity improvements; and resources, distinctive capabilities, and core competencies are found in manufacturing and materials management.

What are the drawbacks of the cost leadership strategy? The main danger is that com-petitors might find ways of lowering costs even further, taking away the cost leader's cost advantage. The cost leader's competitive strategy is successful as long as it can maintain its cost advantage. Another drawback of this strategy is that competitors might be able to eas-ily imitate what the cost leader is doing and erode the cost advantage. Finally, a drawback of the cost leadership strategy is that the cost leader, in its all-out pursuit of lowering costs, might lose sight of changing customer tastes and needs. In other words, it doesn't matter

FOR YOUR
information

Customers as Collaborators

As organizations look for ways to differentiate themselves, they must recognize that the new economy is radically changing the way they must deal with customers. C. K. Prahalad (who together with Gary Hamel proposed that businesses need to identify their core competencies) is now saying that businesses are going to have to recognize that "consumers are going to drive the firm." What does he mean? His premise is that a product is no more than an "artifact around which customers have experiences." Because the company can only make the product and can't dictate the customer's experience, that gives customers power. However, because of the Internet, this switch isn't as threatening as it may first seem. The Internet makes it possible to reach customers in new ways, and strategic decision makers can use this tool to offer customers an engaging experience. Ideally, that experience would offer enough choices to allow customers to shape their own path. The goal would be to tap into customers' talents, shape their expectations, and encourage communities to form around the product. A company that can do this can absorb customers' knowledge of the product and their sug-gestions for making it better. In this approach, customers are no longer simply purchasers of the product, but become collaborators on product design and development. Prahalad and his co-researcher Venkatram Ramaswamy suggest four ways to harness customers' competencies. These include: (1) encourage active dialogue (e.g., Amazon.com and its book recommendations and reviews); (2) mobilize customer communities (e.g., eBay, Yahoo!, E*Trade); (3) manage customer diversity (gear products–services to customers' varying skill levels, such as Microsoft's Hotmail service); and (4) cocreate personalized experiences (e.g., online florists who let customers cus-tomize floral arrangements, vases, and colors). Smart companies must draw customers in and keep them coming back. What's your interpretation of this idea of customers as collaborators? Can you find other examples? What are the implications for competitive strategy choices?

Sources: F. Andrews, "Regarding Customers as Business Collaborators," New York Times, February 9, 2000, p. C10; and C. K. Prahalad and V. Ramaswamy, "Co-opting Customer Competence," Harvard Business Review, January–February 2000, pp. 79–87.

how cost efficiently you can produce or market a product or service if there's no customer demand and no one willing to purchase it even at rock-bottom prices.

The **differentiation strategy** is a strategy in which the organization competes on the basis of providing unique (different) products–services with features that customers value, perceive as different, and are willing to pay a premium price for. The main goal of the differentiator is to provide products or services that are truly unique and different in the eyes of the customers. The differentiator is competing on the basis of being different and unique. If the differentiator is able to do this, it can charge a premium price because customers perceive that the product or service is different and that it uniquely meets their needs. This premium price provides the profit incentive to compete on the basis of differentiation.

What does it take to be a successful differentiator? Every strategic decision and action is designed to set the organization apart from its competitors. All the differentiator's distinctive capabilities, resources, and functional strategies are aimed at isolating and understanding specific market segments and developing product features that are valued by customers in these various segments. The differentiator is going to have broad and wide product lines—that is, many different models, features, price ranges, and so forth. In fact, *how* the differentiator chooses to differentiate is practically endless. Differentiators can use countless variations of market segments and product features. What's important to the differentiator is that the customer *perceives* the product or service as different and unique and worth the extra price. Because the differentiation strategy can be expensive, the differentiator also needs to control costs to protect profits, but not to the extent that it loses its source of differentiation. Remember that the differentiator is competing on the basis of being unique, not on the basis of having the lowest costs. For example, Gap Inc. has developed a strong competitive advantage by marketing a wide variety of fashions in different formats.[13] It sells casual clothes in a multitude of styles, colors, and features at its flagship Gap stores. In addition, at its Old Navy stores Gap sells, amidst 1950s Chevies and merchandise piled in old freezers, hip clothes with lower price points that appeal to a broader market. However, Gap isn't selling just a physical product. It's marketing attitude and status. Its ability to differentiate its products has given this clothing company a great brand. Gap's differentiation strategy obviously has been successful.

Differentiators often differentiate themselves along as many dimensions as possible and segment the market into many niches. In addition, the differentiator works hard to establish **brand loyalty**, which describes a situation in which customers consistently and repeatedly seek out, purchase, and use a particular brand. Brand loyalty can be a very powerful

strategic **MANAGEMENT** *in action*

William Wrigley Jr. Co., the Chicago-based chewing gum company, is facing some real competitive challenges. Even though it controls a commanding 50 percent share of the U.S. gum market on the strength of decades-old brands, its challenge is attracting the huge youth market, which consumes the bulk of gum and candy in the United States. Kids have gravitated to nongum products, especially mints such as Altoids, Mentos, and Tic Tacs. In addition, other gum makers have introduced super-strong mint gums such as Dentyne Ice and Ice Breakers. To combat these competitive pressures, Wrigley didn't just stick to its old products. The company introduced its own

Eclipse mint gum, its first new product in years. In addition, it revamped old standbys such as Juicy Fruit and Big Red with new youth-oriented advertisements and Internet tie-ins. Look for examples of other differentiation strategies Wrigley is using. Evaluate Wrigley's product displays in stores. Check out its Web site (**www.wrigley.com**). Do you think Wrigley is on the right path? What does this example tell you about the differentiation strategy?

Sources: Wrigley, **www.wrigley.com**, March 15, 2004; J. Ginsburg, "Not the Flavor of the Month," Business Week, March 20, 2000, p. 128; and J. Raymond, "Chewed Out by Mints," Newsweek, November 1, 1999, p. 62.

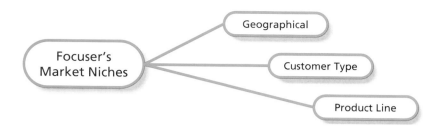

Figure 6.6

Possible Market Niches

competitive weapon for the differentiator. Not surprisingly, the differentiator's unique resources and distinctive capabilities tend to be in marketing and research and development.

What are the drawbacks of the differentiation strategy? One is that the organization must remain unique in customers' eyes, which may be difficult depending on competitors' abilities to imitate and copy successful differentiation features. If the product loses its uniqueness in customers' eyes, they won't be willing to pay the premium price just to have the differentiated product. Another drawback is that customers might become more price sensitive, and the product differences might become less important. In this instance, also, the organization might find that its competitive advantage based on being different and unique no longer works.

The **focus strategy** is when an organization pursues either a cost or differentiation advantage but in a limited (narrow) customer group or segment. A focuser concentrates on serving a specific market niche. What's a market niche based on?[14] Figure 6.6 shows that there are three broad ways to segment specialized market niches: (1) geographical, (2) type of customer, or (3) product line segment. A geographical niche can be defined in terms of region or locality. For example, Midwest Air Group serves 25 Midwestern cities from hubs in Kansas City, Omaha, and Milwaukee.[15] By focusing on this particular geographic area, the company has been able to build a significant customer base. A customer niche focuses on a specific group of customers. For instance, Christine Columbus is a mail-order catalog that offers items specifically for women travelers.[16] In this specialized niche, customers can find products tailored to their unique needs. Finally, a product line market niche would focus on a specific and specialized product line. Rhino Records, for example, has built a successful business producing and marketing CDs based on past pop music hits and videos and DVDs of classic TV series and cult movies. The company's collections of pop music and culture created a new market niche.[17] All of these organizations have chosen to compete on the basis of some specific and narrow niche.

What's involved with the focus strategy? As stated earlier, the focuser can pursue either a cost or differentiation advantage. A cost focuser competes by having lower costs than the overall industry cost leader in specific and narrow niches. For example, Minimoves Inc. found a lucrative niche by handling small shipments that fell below big moving company minimums and that were too costly and inconvenient for homeowners to box and ship themselves. The company has been able to successfully pursue a cost focus advantage because the big moving companies can't use their low-cost advantages with these small-sized shipments.[18] The cost focus strategy also can be successful if an organization can produce complex or custom-built products that don't lend themselves easily to cost efficiencies by the industry's overall cost leaders. The differentiation focuser can use whatever forms of differentiation the broad differentiator might use—product features, product innovations, product quality, customer responsiveness, or whatever. The only difference, however, is that the focuser is specializing in one or a few segments instead of all market segments. For example, a New York company called T-Ink is a leader in a specialized field—conductive ink technology. Its inks, which can make things light up or create sound, have been used in products from Hasbro's Clue Fx game to Fisher-Price Sesame Street posters to McDonald's Happy Meal boxes.[19]

This middle would be a good place to be stuck! For most consumers, the delicious frosting middle is the appeal of chocolate sandwich cookies. What company do you think founded this market? If you said Oreos, you'd be wrong. Hydrox debuted in 1908 and Oreos in 1912. Yet, over the years, Oreos' (now a product of Kraft Foods) popularity and market power became so overwhelming that Hydrox languished in obscurity—never able to be a low-cost leader or a differentiator. However, Kellogg Company (which purchased Keebler Foods, maker of Hydrox, in 2001) is hoping to change all that. Kellogg changed Hydrox's name to Keebler Droxies, reformulated the cookie's flavor, and redesigned the package to be more kid oriented. Will these strategic changes be enough to pull the cookie with the tastefully delicious middle out of being stuck in the middle? What do you think?

Source: P. Lukas, "Oreos to Hydrox: Resistance is Futile," Fortune, March 15, 1999, pp. 52–54.

What are the advantages of the focus strategy? One distinct advantage is that the focuser knows its market niche well. The focuser can stay close to customers and respond quickly to their changing needs—often much quicker than organizations pursuing a broad market. By effectively and efficiently responding to customers' needs, the focuser can, in turn, develop strong brand loyalty. This brand loyalty can be hard for other competitors to overcome. Also, if the focuser can provide products or services that the broad competitors can't or won't, then it will have the niche all to itself.

What are the drawbacks of the focus strategy? One drawback is that the focuser often operates at a small scale, making it difficult to lower costs significantly. However, with technological advancements such as flexible manufacturing systems, this drawback isn't as critical as it once was. In other words, as information and computer technology have become more affordable, focusers have discovered that economies (cost efficiencies) don't necessarily have to come from large-scale production runs. Many times, the focuser can be just as efficient running small batches as the large-scale competitor can be running large batches. Another drawback is that the niche customers might change their tastes or needs. Because it's often difficult for a focuser to change niches easily and quickly, this could be a serious problem. In addition, any technological changes that might impact the niche can have a similar effect. Finally, there's always the threat of the broad differentiator taking notice of the focuser's market niche, especially if the focuser is enjoying a significant level of success, and moving in to offer products–services to those customers. In other words, the focuser is subject to being "outfocused" by its competitors—large and small.

The final aspect of Porter's generic competitive strategies that we need to discuss is the concept of being **stuck in the middle**, which happens when an organization isn't successfully pursuing either a low cost or a differentiation competitive advantage. An organization becomes stuck in the middle when its costs are too high to compete with the low-cost leader or when its products and services aren't differentiated enough to compete with the differentiator. As you can imagine, being stuck in the middle isn't a preferred or profitable strategic direction. Becoming "unstuck" means making consistent strategic decisions about what competitive advantage to pursue and then doing so by aligning resources, distinctive capabilities, and core competencies.

Learning Review

- Why are Porter's competitive strategies called "generic"?
- According to Porter, what are the two types of competitive advantage?
- What role does competitive scope play in Porter's approach to competitive strategies?

- Describe the cost leadership (low-cost leader) strategy. Be sure to note the characteristics of a cost leader and the advantages and disadvantages of this strategy.

- Describe the differentiation strategy. Be sure to note the characteristics of a differentiator and the advantages and disadvantages of this strategy.

- How is a focus strategy different from the other two generic competitive strategies?

- Describe the low-cost focus strategy. Describe the differentiation focus strategy.

- What are the advantages and drawbacks of a focus strategy?

- What does it mean to be stuck in the middle? How would an organization get unstuck?

Contemporary Perspectives on Competitive Strategy

Although the traditional approaches to describing an organization's competitive strategies are widely used, particularly Porter's generic competitive strategies framework, some of the contemporary perspectives provide an expanded, and more realistic, description of *what* competitive strategies organizations are using. In this section, we want to look at two contemporary perspectives. First, we'll look at an integrated low-cost differentiation strategy. Finally, we'll discuss a generic strategies framework proposed by Henry Mintzberg as a better way to take into account the increasing complexity of the competitive environment.

Integrated Low-Cost Differentiation Strategy

Porter's original work on competitive advantage and competitive strategies maintained that an organization couldn't simultaneously pursue a low-cost and a differentiation advantage. To do so meant the risk of being stuck in the middle and not successfully developing or exploiting either competitive advantage. You had to do one or the other.[20] Despite strong empirical support for Porter's strategy framework,[21] several strategy researchers began to question this "mutual exclusivity" of the low-cost and differentiation strategies.[22] Instead of having to pursue *either* low cost *or* differentiation, was it possible that organizations could pursue both strategies simultaneously and successfully? Strategy research evidence is starting to show that organizations *can* successfully pursue an integrated low-cost differentiation strategy.[23]

What is an **integrated low-cost differentiation strategy**? It's one in which an organization develops a competitive advantage by simultaneously achieving low costs and high levels of differentiation. What are some examples of organizations that have implemented such a strategy successfully? One is Dell, which has succeeded in an intensely competitive market by providing high-quality products and services while undercutting IBM, Gateway, and other PC makers in price.[24] What's Dell's secret? It's been able to keep its costs low and its level of differentiation high by developing and exploiting a competitive advantage that's based on a disciplined, extremely low-cost corporate culture, while still being able to provide high-quality products and services. Other organizations such as Southwest Airlines, Anheuser-Busch, and McDonald's also have been able to successfully pursue this hybrid competitive strategy. What makes an integrated low-cost differentiation strategy possible?

The answer is technology. Successfully establishing sources of differentiation can be expensive. When creating, manufacturing, and marketing a wide range of quality products or services, it's often difficult to keep costs as low as possible. Yet, the widespread availability and increasing affordability of computer and information technology has made it easier for organizations to pursue product and service differentiation and yet keep their costs low.

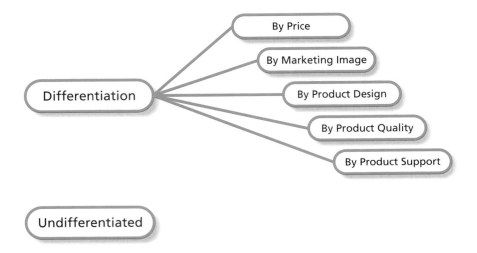

Figure 6.7

Mintzberg's Generic Competitive Strategies

Technological advancements such as flexible manufacturing systems, just-in-time inventory systems, and integrated information systems have opened the door for competing on the basis of having low costs *and* being unique. However, keep in mind that just because these technological advancements are available doesn't mean that every organization that uses them will be able to successfully pursue an integrated low-cost differentiation strategy. It still takes strict attention to keeping costs as low as possible and providing products and services with enough desirable features for the marketplace.

Mintzberg's Generic Competitive Strategies

Henry Mintzberg has developed an alternative typology of competitive strategies that he felt better reflected the increasing complexity of the competitive environment.[25] He proposed six possible competitive strategies, as shown in Figure 6.7.

Differentiation by price is a modification of Porter's cost leadership strategy. Mintzberg argued that having the lowest costs didn't provide a competitive advantage by itself, but that the advantage came from the fact it allowed the organization to charge below-average market prices. Therefore, an organization pursuing this strategy was instead differentiating on the basis of price. Differentiation by marketing image described a competitive strategy in which an organization attempted to create a certain image in customers' minds. Organizations following this competitive strategy used their marketing image as a potent competitive weapon. The competitive strategy of differentiation by product design can be used to describe organizations that competed on the basis of providing desirable product features and design configurations. An organization that followed this competitive strategy would attempt to give customers a wide selection of product features and different designs. Differentiation by quality described a strategy in which organizations competed by delivering higher reliability and performance at a comparable price. In this strategy, superior product quality was pursued as the organization's competitive advantage. The competitive strategy of differentiation by product support emphasized the customer support services provided by the organization. In this strategy, competitive advantage would be sought through providing an all-encompassing bundle of desired customer support services. Finally, the undifferentiated strategy described situations in which an organization had no basis for differentiation or when it deliberately followed a copycat strategy.

What's the verdict on Mintzberg's alternative generic competitive strategies typology? It appears that his approach has merit.[26] Research on his strategy typology shows it has strong conceptual clarity and descriptive power. Although it will probably never replace the popularity of Porter's competitive strategies, Mintzberg's typology does seem to capture

198   Strategic Management in Action

New Points of Differentiation

Successful companies must realize that points of differentiation between themselves and competitors aren't just limited to products or services. Indeed, a company has the opportunity to differentiate itself at any point where it comes in contact with customers. How? By examining the *consumption chain*, or a customer's entire experience with a product or service. Here are some questions to guide this mapping process:

- How do people become aware of their need for your product or service?
- How do consumers find your products being offered?
- How do consumers make their final selections?
- How do customers order and purchase your product or service?
- How is your product or service delivered?
- What happens when your product or service is delivered?
- How is your product installed?
- How is your product or service paid for?
- How is your product stored?
- How is your product moved around?
- What is the customer really using your product for?

- What type of help do customers need as they use your product?
- What about returns or exchanges?
- How is your product repaired or serviced?
- What happens when your product is disposed of or no longer used?

Once you've mapped these issues, you can begin to analyze your customer's experience. The goal is to gain insights into your customers as you look at the context surrounding their consumption chains. Do this by asking what, where, who, when, and how questions. For instance: What are customers doing at each point in the consumption chain? What problems might they be experiencing? Where are your customers at each point in the consumption chain? Where else would they like to be? Who is with the customer at any point in the consumption chain? Do these other people have influence over the customer? When are customers at any point in the consumption chain? How are customers' needs being addressed? How else might you take care of their needs and concerns? By mapping the consumption chain and analyzing customers' experiences, organizations can uncover many possible points of differentiation.

Sources: W. Chan Kim and Renee Mauborgne, "Creating New Market Space," *Harvard Business Review*, January–February 1999, pp. 83–93; and I. C. MacMillan and R G. McGrath, "Discovering New Points of Differentiation," *Harvard Business Review*, July–August 1997, pp. 133–45.

the essence of competitive strategies being used by organizations in today's complex and dynamic competitive climate. As such, it provides an alternative way to describe organizations' competitive strategies.

A Brief Recap of the Various Approaches to Describing Competitive Strategies

What is our conclusion about *what* competitive strategies an organization might use? Undoubtedly, Porter's generic competitive strategy framework remains the most popular approach to describing how organizations compete. Current business books and periodicals continue to use cost leadership and differentiation to describe the strategies organizations are using to compete. However, if these two competitive strategies are approached as mutually exclusive, Porter's generic strategy typology probably isn't highly relevant or realistic in light of today's competitive environment. On the other hand, if the integrated low-cost differentiation strategy is seen as a legitimate extension of Porter's basic generic strategies, then his framework would appear to be appropriate and suitable for describing an organization's competitive strategies.

This doesn't mean, however, that the other competitive strategy perspectives discussed earlier aren't conceptually sound or appropriate for describing competitive strategies. Mintzberg's typology, with its emphasis on mirroring today's dynamic competitive environment, seems to have appealing promise as an approach to describing what competitive strategies an organization might pursue. Even Miles and Snow's adaptive strategies can be appropriate choices for describing different organizational competitive approaches.

No matter how you describe them, the main thing to remember about *what* competitive strategies an organization has at its disposal is that its competitive strategy should exploit the competitive advantage(s) the organization has developed. Without a competitive advantage that's been developed from its resources or distinctive capabilities, it will be extremely difficult for the organization to compete successfully in any given situation.

Learning Review

- What is the integrated low-cost differentiation strategy and how does it contradict the concept behind Porter's generic competitive strategies?
- What makes the integrated low-cost differentiation strategy possible? Explain.
- Describe each of the competitive strategies in Mintzberg's generic strategy typology.
- What is the main point to remember about *what* competitive strategy an organization might choose to implement?

IMPLEMENTING, EVALUATING, AND CHANGING COMPETITIVE STRATEGY

Look back at the chapter-opening case. What type of competitive strategy did Nike appear to be pursuing? How can you tell? You'll probably note such things as its competitive culture, its marketing expertise, and its willingness to move into new markets. The competitive strategy an organization is using can be seen by what's actually being done or implemented. Strategy implementation is critical. If a strategy is not implemented, then it's nothing more than an idea. And, if you remember the entire strategic management process model, once a strategy is implemented, it must be assessed or evaluated, and modified if needed. In this section, we want to look at how organizations' competitive strategies are implemented, evaluated, and changed.

Implementing Competitive Strategy

How does Abercrombie & Fitch keep current styles in its stores? How does Payless ShoeSource restock its stores within a day's notice? Obviously, employees, facilities and equipment, work activities, and work systems have to be in place to facilitate such accomplishments. (Think in terms of resources, distinctive capabilities, and core competencies.) This is what implementation is all about. Because an organization's resources and capabilities are developed and used within its various functional areas, it shouldn't come as a surprise that the organization's functional strategies play a significant role in implementing competitive strategy. That's what we're going to look at first. Then we'll discuss the competitive postures or actions an organization might take as it implements its overall competitive strategy.

The Role of Functional Strategies

The challenge in implementing the organization's competitive strategy is to create and exploit a sustainable competitive advantage. As we've discussed many times, competitive

Table 6.3 Requirements for Porter's Generic Competitive Strategies

Generic Strategy	Commonly Required Skills and Resources	Common Organizational Requirements
Overall cost leadership	Sustained capital investment and access Process engineering skills Intense supervision of labor Products designed for ease of manufacture Low-cost distribution system	Tight cost control Frequent, detailed control reports Structured organization and responsibilities Incentives based on meeting strict quantitative targets
Differentiation	Strong marketing abilities Product engineering Creative flair Strong capability in basic research Corporate reputation for quality or technological leadership Long tradition in the industry or unique combination of skills drawn from other businesses Strong cooperation from channels	Strong coordination among functions in R&D, product development, and marketing Subjective measurement and incentives instead of quantitative measures Amenities to attract highly skilled labor, scientists, or creative people
Focus	Combination of the above policies directed at the particular strategic target	Combination of the above policies directed at the particular strategic target

Source: Adapted with permission of The Free Press, a Division of Simon & Schuster Inc. From Competitive Strategy: Techniques for Analyzing Industries and Competitors by Michael E. Porter. Copyright © 1980, 1988 by The Free Press.

advantage comes from the organization's ability to use its resources to develop capabilities that, in turn, may become distinctive. This happens through the functional strategies being used.

The functional strategies play a dual role in the implementation of competitive strategy. First of all, whatever resources are currently available or being procured and whatever distinctive capabilities are currently in place or being developed will influence what competitive strategy is most feasible and likely to lead to a sustainable competitive advantage. In other words, the initial choice of an appropriate competitive strategy depends on what organizational resources and capabilities are currently in place or being acquired and developed through the functional strategies. For instance, each of Porter's generic competitive strategies requires certain skills, resources, and organizational requirements in order to successfully attain a sustainable competitive advantage. Table 6.3 lists these suggested requirements for the generic competitive strategies. However, functional strategies also play another role. Once the organization's competitive strategy is determined, the resources, capabilities, and competencies found in the various functional areas are *how* the competitive strategy is implemented.

We won't repeat all the possible variations of the functional strategies here (see Chapter 5), but keep in mind that the functional strategies being used should align with whatever competitive advantage—and, of course, competitive strategy—is being pursued. This means that, for instance, if we've chosen to compete on the basis of having the lowest costs, then the functional strategies being used should support and reinforce that strategy. Cost efficiencies would be pursued in all operational areas, but particularly in the functional areas of manufacturing and materials management. Financial strategies would support the quest for operational efficiency, including such things as investing in technology if that could contribute to lowering costs. All organizational resources, distinctive capabilities, and core competencies would be directed at attaining the goal of having the industry's

PepsiCo CEO Steve Reinemund is proposing some changes in his company. To better serve customers' increasing interest in taking control of their health, Reinemund's goal is that 50 percent of his company's new products be nutritious in some way. The company recently divided its products into three categories: Fun-for-You, which includes indulgent products, such as Doritos and Mountain Dew; Better-for-You, which includes products with fewer calories and less fat, such as Baked Lays and Diet Pepsi; and

Good-for-You, which includes products with high nutritional content, such as Quaker Oatmeal and Tropicana Orange Juice. What changes, if any, do you think the company will need to make in its competitive strategies? How about the functional strategies that support the company's competitive strategies?

Source: A. Klingbeil, "PepsiCo Seeks Niche among Health Foods," Springfield News-Leader, August 10, 2003, p. 4E.

lowest costs. Likewise, if the organization chose to compete on the basis of both low costs and differentiation, then its functional strategies should reflect that choice or it will never be able to develop a sustainable competitive advantage. To summarize, the functional strategies—that is, how the organization develops and exploits its resources, distinctive capabilities, and core competencies—influence both *what* competitive strategy is most appropriate and *how* that strategy is implemented.

It should be fairly obvious by now that an organization's functional strategies play a critical role in the implementation of its competitive strategy. Without developing and exploiting the organization's resources, capabilities, and competencies—which happen through the functional strategies being used—there will be no hope of developing a sustainable competitive advantage. As we've said from the beginning, developing a sustainable competitive advantage is the whole intent of managing strategically. If the organization doesn't have or can't develop a sustainable competitive advantage, it's going to have a tough time competing and continuing in business. What we're going to discuss next are the types of competitive postures or actions an organization might use as it implements its competitive strategy.

Competitive Postures and Actions

Once an organization's competitive strategy is implemented through specific functional decisions and actions, the real fun begins! The very notion of "competitive" strategy means that the organization is going to be competing "against" other organizations, vying for customers, market share, or other desired objects or outcomes. What happens in this competitive "dance" is that organizations use certain postures, actions, and tactics in the ongoing battle to keep or acquire whatever object or outcome they're after. What are these competitive postures and actions?

The competitive postures and actions that organizations use are typically described using an old military and sports analogy: offensive and defensive moves. Why? Because that's what organizations are doing when they compete: They're going after competitors' positions or they're defending their own position. **Offensive moves** are when an organization attempts to exploit and strengthen its competitive position through attacks on a competitor's position. What are some offensive moves an organization might use?[27] A frontal assault is when the attacking firm goes head-to-head with its competitor and matches the competitor in every possible category, including price, promotion, product features, and distribution channel. This competitive move can be an effective way to gain market share from weaker competitors. It's also a good way to slice away rivals' competitive advantages. Another offensive tactic is to attack competitors' weaknesses. How? An organization might concentrate on geographic areas where its competitor is weak. Or it might begin serving customer segments that a competitor is ignoring or where the competitors' offerings are weak. The organization might introduce new product models or product features to fill gaps its competitors aren't serving. What this offensive tactic entails is attacking wherever the competitor has specific weaknesses. Another offensive tactic is to use an all-out attack on competitors by hitting them from both the product *and* the market segment side. Needless to say, this all-out competitive attack requires significant resources and capabilities. Another type of offensive move is to avoid direct, head-on competitive challenges by maneuvering around competitors and subtly changing the rules of the game. How? The most typical way is that the organization attempts to create new market segments that competitors aren't serving by introducing products with different features. This competitive action cuts the market out from under the competitor and forces the competitor to play catch-up. Finally, another possible offensive tactic is to use "guerilla" attacks—small, intermittent, seemingly random assaults on competitors' markets. For instance, an organization might use special promotions, price incentives, or advertising campaigns to lure away competitors' customers.

Offensive moves are good ways to attack competitors and strengthen your own competitive position. What happens when *your* organization is the one being attacked or threatened with attack? That's where the defensive competitive moves come in.

Defensive moves describe when an organization is attempting to protect its competitive advantage and turf. Defensive moves don't increase an organization's competitive advantage, but can make that competitive advantage more sustainable.[28] Let's look at some defensive moves an organization might use. One is to prevent challengers from attacking by not giving them any areas to attack. For instance, an organization could offer a full line of products in every profitable market segment, keep prices low on products that most closely match competitors' offerings, use exclusive agreements with dealers to block competitors from using them, protect technologies through patents or licenses, or use any other number of possible preventive strategic actions. Again, the intent of this particular defensive move is to make sure competitors don't have any holes or weaknesses to attack. Another possible defensive move is to increase competitors' beliefs that significant retaliation can be expected if competitive attacks are initiated. How could an organization signal the market that it's serious about retaliating if attacked? Public announcements by managers to "protect" market share are important. Also, strong responses to competitors' moves are important. Doing things such as matching price cuts or matching promotion incentives signals competitors that you aren't going to sit back and let them steal away your customers. Competitive counterattacks are particularly critical if the markets or segments being attacked are crucial to the organization. However, these types of retaliatory actions should be approached cautiously, particularly in instances where the attacker is a new entrant to the market. Why? Research has shown that the typical *new* entrant doesn't pose a serious threat and aggressive retaliation can be expensive.[29] The final type of defensive move involves lowering the incentive for a competitor to attack. If a potential attacker is led to believe that the expectations of future profits are minimal, chances are it won't want to challenge the current leader. For instance, an organization might use media announcements to highlight problems in the industry or it might deliberately keep prices low and continually invest in cost-lowering actions. All of these competitive moves make it less attractive for a competitor to launch an attack.

Evaluating and Changing Competitive Strategy

As with any other strategy, the responsibility of managing strategically doesn't stop once the competitive strategy is implemented. The organization's competitive moves, actions, and responses being carried out through the various functional strategies need to be

One of the biggest competitive battles is shaping up in your local grocery store's meat case. The nation's meatpackers are trying to turn their anonymous meat products into coveted national brand names. Hormel, Tyson, Cargill, and ConAgra are selling precooked steaks, chops, roasts, and chickens under their company's own logos. Considering that consumers are often too busy to cook meats for long periods of time during the day, these products may prove to be popular. But the competitive struggle to be the packages thrown in the customer's shopping cart is just beginning!

Source: S. Kilman, "Branding Beef," *Wall Street Journal,* February 20, 2002, p. A1.

monitored and evaluated for performance effectiveness and efficiency. What are the results of the various strategies? Are they having the intended effect? Are we successfully exploiting our competitive advantage? Why or why not? These are the types of questions that need to be asked when evaluating the competitive strategy. Because most organizations' competitive strategies are targeted at increasing sales revenues, market share, or profitability, data on these particular performance areas would be needed to determine the impact of the competitive strategies. Likewise, not-for-profit organizations should assess the results of their competitive strategies even though they're not focused on revenues, market share, or profitability. For instance, strategy evaluation might address such areas as did the number of plasma and blood donors increase; did the number of contributors to the church building fund go up or did the average donation amount increase; or did governmental funding of the community drug outreach program increase? No matter what type of organization or what type of competitive strategy is being used, it's important to measure its impact.

It's not enough, however, just to measure the results of the competitive strategy. What if results aren't as high as expected, or what if they're better than expected? Then what? Part of the evaluation of the competitive strategy is also to determine what happened and why. We do this by trying to pinpoint areas of competitive weakness. Has the market changed and we haven't? Are the organization's numerous resources and capabilities being used effectively and efficiently so that the needed and crucial competitive advantage is being developed and exploited? Which ones are and which ones aren't? As you can see, the evaluation of the competitive strategy turns out to be an assessment of the organization's various functional areas and the activities being performed there. If the evaluation of an organization's competitive strategy shows that it isn't having the intended impact or hasn't resulted in desired levels of performance, it may need to be changed. However, a change in the organization's competitive strategy isn't something that organizations want to do frequently. Why? Remember that each competitive strategy entails the development of specific resources, distinctive capabilities, and core competencies. To change the competitive strategy would mean modifying or redeveloping the organization's resources and capabilities. This is difficult and expensive. However, this doesn't, and shouldn't, mean that an organization would *never* change its basic competitive approach. What it does mean, though, is that this type of major strategic change should be approached realistically and intelligently.

Although changing the organization's basic competitive strategy isn't highly likely, modifying the organization's competitive actions *is.* Many of the stories in the popular business press are about changes organizations are making in their competitive actions. As competitors battle for desired outcomes or objects, they'll try one thing. If that doesn't work, they'll try something else. That's the reality of the competitive struggle that's taking place. As we stated at the beginning of the chapter, competition is a given for all sizes and types of organizations. It's a game that the players are trying to win. Organizations improve their chances of doing so if they choose a competitive strategy that exploits their competitive advantage.

- Why is strategy implementation critical?

- Describe the role(s) that functional strategies play in implementing the organization's competitive strategy.

- What are offensive moves? Describe the offensive competitive actions an organization might use.

- What are defensive moves? Describe the defensive competitive actions an organization might use.

- Why should the competitive strategy be evaluated? How is it evaluated?

- Why is it unlikely that an organization's fundamental competitive strategy will be changed frequently and continually?

- What types of competitive changes are likely to be made?

- **Competitive advantage**, what sets an organization apart, is a key concept in strategic management.

- An organization's competitive advantage can be eroded easily (and often quickly) by competitors' actions.

- Because competitive advantage implies that there are other competitors, we need to look at the competitive environment.

- Competition is everywhere. **Competition** is organizations battling or vying for some desired object or outcome—typically customers, market share, survey ranking, or needed resources.

- Some describe the current business environment as **hypercompetition**, a situation with very intense and continually increasing levels of competition.

- The level of intensity of competition depends on factors described in the current rivalry section of Porter's five forces model.

- An organization's competitors can be described from the industry perspective, market perspective, or strategic groups perspective.

- The industry perspective says that competitors are organizations that are making the same product or providing the same service.

- The market perspective says that competitors are organizations that satisfy the same customer need.

- The strategic groups perspective says that competitors are those organizations in your **strategic group**—a group of firms competing within an industry that have similar strategies, resources, and customers.

- Some possible dimensions to identify strategic groups include price, quality, product line breadth–depth, market share, geographic scope, and so forth.

- Every organization has resources and capabilities to do whatever it's in business to do, although not every organization can effectively exploit those resources or capabilities.

- **Competitive strategy** is a choice of how an organization or business unit is going to compete in its particular industry or market.

- The traditional approaches to defining competitive strategy are Miles and Snow's adaptive strategies, Abell's business definition, and Porter's generic strategies.

- Miles and Snow's approach is based on the strategies organizations use to successfully adapt to their uncertain competitive environments.

- Their **prospector strategy** is one in which an organization continually innovates by finding and exploiting new product and market opportunities.

- Their **defender strategy** is characterized by the search for market stability and producing only a limited product line directed at a narrow segment of the total potential market.

- The **analyzer strategy** is one of analysis and imitation.

- The **reactor strategy** is characterized by the lack of a coherent strategic plan or apparent means of competing.

- Research has shown Miles and Snow's typology to be theoretically sound and appropriate for describing how organizations compete.

- Abell's business definition framework is heavily marketing focused and proposes defining a business using three dimensions: customer groups (who), customer needs (what), and technology or distinctive competencies (how).

- The various combinations of competitive scope and extent of competitive differentiation of products and services provide the basis for Abell's three possible competitive strategies: differentiated, undifferentiated, and focus.

- Abell's strict marketing emphasis limits his business definition framework as a widely used and general approach to describing competitive strategies.

- Porter's generic competitive strategies are based on the assumption that competitive advantage comes from only one of two possible sources: having the lowest costs in the industry or possessing significant and desirable differences from competitors.

- Porter called his competitive strategies generic because they can be pursued by any type or size organization in any type or size industry.

- The mix of type of competitive advantage and competitive scope provides the basis for Porter's competitive strategies.

- The **cost leadership strategy** is one in which an organization strives to have the lowest costs in its industry and produces products or services for a broad customer base.

- The **differentiation strategy** is one in which the organization competes on the basis of providing unique (different) products or services with features that customers value, perceive as different, and are willing to pay a premium price for.

- A differentiator works hard to establish **brand loyalty**, a situation in which customers consistently and repeatedly seek out, purchase, and use a particular brand.

- The **focus strategy** is when an organization pursues either a cost or differentiation advantage in a limited (narrow) customer group or segment. A focuser concentrates on serving a specific market niche. This approach has advantages and disadvantages.

- Porter also identified the concept of **stuck in the middle**, which describes an organization that isn't successfully pursuing either a low cost or differentiation competitive advantage.

- Two contemporary perspectives on competitive strategy are the integrated low-cost differentiation strategy and Mintzberg's competitive strategy typology.

- The **integrated low-cost differentiation strategy** is a strategy in which an organization develops a competitive advantage by simultaneously achieving low costs and high levels of differentiation.

- This competitive strategy is possible because of technological advancements such as flexible manufacturing systems, just-in-time inventory systems, and integrated information systems.

- Henry Mintzberg's competitive strategy typology was developed to better reflect the increasing complexity of the competitive environment.

- Mintzberg's six possible competitive strategies include differentiation by price, marketing image, product design, quality, product support, and undifferentiation.

- The challenge in implementing the organization's competitive strategy is to create and exploit a sustainable competitive advantage.

- Competitive strategy implementation is done through the functional strategies. Whatever competitive strategy is selected, certain resources and capabilities will be required to implement it.

- In addition, competitive strategy implementation involves various competitive actions. **Offensive moves** are competitive actions taken when an organization attempts to exploit and strengthen its competitive position through attacks on a competitor's position. **Defensive moves** are competitive actions taken when an organization is attempting to protect its competitive advantage and turf.

- The organization's competitive strategy must be evaluated to make sure it's doing what it's intended to do.

- It's highly unlikely that an organization would continually change its competitive strategy because each competitive strategy requires certain resources, capabilities, and competencies.

- Instead, the organization may change the functional strategies that are being used to implement the competitive strategy and it may change the competitive actions (both offensive and defensive) it's also using to implement the competitive strategy.

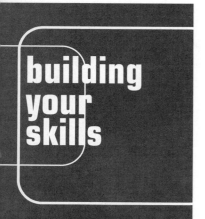
1. A patent is a legal property that allows its holder to prevent others from employing this property for their own use for a specified period of time. A patent protects an invention and is valid for up to 20 years from the date of filing a patent application. Research patents and the patent application process. (You might want to access the U.S. Patent & Trademark Office Web site at **www.uspto.gov**.) How many types of patents are there? What other interesting information about patents did you find? Would patents play any role in an organization's choice of competitive strategy? Explain.

2. Scented candles are a $2-billion-a-year industry, and that sales figure continues to increase. Three leading industry players are Yankee Candle Company (**www.yankeecandle.com**), Illuminations (**www.illuminations.com**), and Wicks and Sticks (**www.wicksnsticks.com**). What competitive actions are these companies using? How are these competitors similar? How are they different? Suppose that an industry newcomer bursts onto the scene. What do you think a newcomer will need to do—that is, what competitive strategy approach—to establish itself as a viable competitor? What will the established competitors need to do?

3. Product comebacks. Long-established brand names are finding it necessary to update their competitive strategies in order to keep up with a continually and rapidly changing economy. For instance, Volvo has moved away from emphasizing safety to advertisements that appeal to younger customers. Find five examples of brands or products that have been "shocked" back to life. Describe what each company has done (is doing) to implement the product comeback. What are the implications for competitive strategy?

4. Competition is a whole lot like war. What can strategic decision makers learn from military strategists? Sun-Tzu, the great Chinese military strategist wrote *The Art of War*, sometime between 480 and 221 B.C. Could his warfare strategies be used in battling competitors? Here's one interpretation of some of these strategies:

   - Don't start what you shouldn't begin.
   - The impossible is impossible.
   - Don't attack a tank with a peashooter.
   - Attack what isn't defended.
   - If you can't attack, defend.
   - Illusion creates confusion.
   - Do what they don't expect.
   - Rather than assuming they won't attack, position yourself so they can't attack.
   - The unprepared can be defeated.
   - The unknowing can be outsmarted.
   - Do not challenge unless you have the means to win.
   - Do not fight unless you're determined to win.

   What do you think of these "strategies?" What implications do you see for an organization's competitive strategy?

5. Henry Ford once said, "Competition whose motive is merely to compete, to drive some other fellow out, never carries very far. The competitor to be feared is one who never bothers about you at all, but goes on making his own business better all the time. Businesses that grow by development and improvement do not die. But when a business ceases to be creative, when it believes it has reached perfection and needs to

do nothing but produce—no improvement, no development—it is done."[30] Are his thoughts still valid in today's environment? Explain.

6. Most organizations face an intensely competitive environment. With this type of competitive pressure, strategic managers might be tempted to engage in unethical competitive actions and activities to keep ahead of competitors. Do some research to find four examples of what you think are unfair competitive moves. Write a short paper explaining the examples you've found, why you think they're unfair, and what you'd do about it.

7. Select an industry that you know about or that you're interested in. (You might want to select an industry where you're concentrating your postgraduation job search.) Do a strategic groups analysis, covering as many of the potential competitors as you can. Determine what strategic dimensions would be most appropriate for grouping competitors. Then, group competitors according to your strategic dimensions. Be sure to put your analysis on a chart showing the strategic dimensions and the various strategic groups. Write up a brief explanation (one to two pages) of what you did, how you did it, and why you did what you did.

8. Interbrand Corporation is a global design and marketing consultant known for its brand surveys. Go to the company's Web site (**www.interbrand.com**) and check out the latest global brand survey. Pick three companies from the top 10 global brands. Research those companies and describe their competitive strategies (using any of the approaches we've discussed). Do you think the value of those companies' brands contribute to their ability to create a sustainable competitive advantage? Explain.

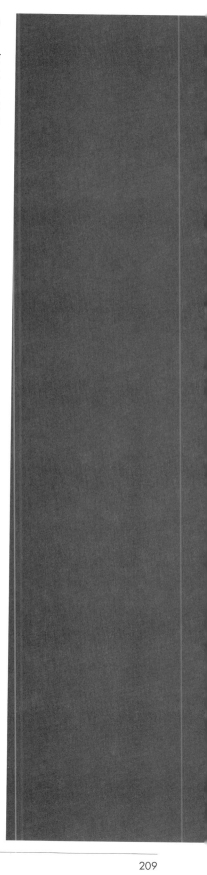

CASE #1: They've Got Game

This Strategic Management in Action Case can be found at the beginning of Chapter 6.

Discussion Questions

1. Describe what you think Nike's competitive strategy is using Miles and Snow's framework, Abell's framework, and Porter's framework. Explain each of your choices.

2. What competitive advantage(s) do you think Nike has? Have its resources, capabilities, or core competencies contributed to its competitive advantage(s)? Explain.

3. Do Nike's functional strategies support its competitive strategy? Explain.

4. What do you think Nike is going to have to do to maintain its strong competitive position?

CASE #2: Pretty in Brown

The package-delivery industry has become an all-out war between the two main competitors: UPS and FedEx. Right now, the battle appears to be going in UPS's favor. Smaller, flashier FedEx has been described as a "collection of marketers with trucks and planes," whereas UPS has been described as "industrial engineers with a collection of trucks and planes." In 2003, UPS earned $2.9 billion on sales of $33.5 billion. FedEx earned $431 million on sales of $16.3 billion. Founded in 1907, UPS practically owns the business of economical ground delivery of packages to any address in the United States and is striving to do the same around the world.

UPS once considered itself a trucking company with technology. Now it's eyeing a future far beyond just simple package delivery and considers itself more a technology company with trucks. For example, in one building at the company's sprawling 4-million-square-foot facility at the Louisville (Kentucky) International Airport, repair technicians are working on faulty laptops, cell phones, printers, and digital projectors. In another building, workers are packaging sports apparel for distribution. And in yet another building, UPS employees are packaging digital cameras with CD-ROMs, straps, and operating instructions. These work tasks are all part of the company division known as UPS Supply Chain Solutions and represent UPS's aggressive moves for new business

and deeper, more lucrative relationships with companies. But UPS isn't ignoring its roots as a package delivery company. At that same facility, itself a modern marvel of automation and technology, "countless cameras, scales, and scanners photograph, weigh, and monitor every package while belts, tracks, and chutes miraculously pilot the lot of them—with no package getting closer than 18 inches to the next—to their outgoing gates." And that's just the first step in the process of delivering more than 13 million packages and documents per business day throughout the United States and to more than 200 countries.

To efficiently and effectively run this part of the business, UPS has a fleet of about 88,000 motor vehicles and more than 575 jets. But it takes more than just resources to do what UPS does. Over the years, UPS had developed a successful business model in which uniformity and efficiency were the strategic factors behind the 340 precise methods of correct package delivery. For instance, its legendary operations training encompassed everything from training drivers to hold their keys on a pinky finger so they didn't waste time fumbling in their pockets for the keys to asking employees to clean off their desks at the end of the day so they can have an efficient start in the morning. These strategic factors weren't going to change. Instead, the company began looking at how to build on its key resources, capabilities, and competencies using a new tool—technology. The company has a vast electronic tracking system whose anchor is the smart label that's found on every package. This label contains exhaustive details about the parcel from its class of service to its destination. And the label can be scanned from any angle, a plus for people and packages on the go. Other technologies include the Delivery Information Acquisition Device, the brown tablet PDA that customers sign when receiving a delivery. All UPS drivers carry one for capturing and transmitting parcel pickup and delivery data. And once a package gets to the warehouse, the information flow doesn't stop. UPS loaders scan labels on the incoming packages with a wearable scanner device. A Bluetooth transmitter sends the tracking information to a terminal, which is then transmitted via a Wi-Fi network to the company's database. The goal is to get information from the customer to the driver to the warehouse to the Web and back to the customer as quickly as possible.

As UPS declares on its Web site, it's not just in the delivery business, it's in the customer satisfaction business. Meeting and exceeding customer needs will continue to be the company's driving force.

Discussion Questions

1. Describe UPS's competitive strategy using Miles and Snow's framework, Abell's framework, and Porter's framework. Explain each of your choices.

2. What competitive advantage(s) do you think UPS has? Have its resources, capabilities, and core competencies contributed to its competitive advantage(s)? Explain.

3. Do UPS's functional strategies support its competitive strategy? Explain.

4. What do you think UPS is going to have to do to maintain its strong competitive position?

(*Sources:* C. Salter, "Surprise Package," *Fast Company,* February 2004, pp. 62–66; M. Benjamin, "Out of the Box," *U.S. News & World Report,* January 26, 2004, pp. EE2–EE10; J. Freund, "How Brown Gets Around," *Wired,* October 2003, p. 42; C. Haddad and C. Tierney, "FedEx and Brown Are Going Green," *Business Week,* August 11, 2003, pp. 60–62; and "A Big Question for Big Brown: An Interview with CEO Michael Eskew," *Money,* June 2002, pp. 49–50.)

CASE #3: Picture Perfect

Snapshots. You probably have photo albums filled with them. They capture historic moments and provide visual links to the past—to that brief moment in time when the photo was snapped. Photographs play an important role in telling stories, whether that story is personal, part of a report for your boss, or part of a news story that you're reading. With a database of over 70 million photographs and an estimated 30,000 hours of film, Seattle-based Getty Images, Inc. (**www.gettyimages.com**) is in the business of providing stock photos to all kinds of customers around the world. The stock photo business is probably one you're not too familiar with.

When you read a magazine or newspaper (or even textbooks), where do the photos come from? Unless they're custom-shot photos, they're probably from stock photo companies. These companies purchase photos from numerous professional photographers around the world, organize those photos into categories, and sell the photos to customers (creative and design professionals, other businesses, and consumers). In the "old" way of doing business, it often took days, even weeks, for customers to get a photo. They'd have to look through pages and pages of expensively produced color catalogs, trying to find that perfect image for the project on which they were working. If they couldn't find it, they might have to pay a photo researcher at an image company to search through thousands of photos to help them find just what they were looking for. After numerous phone calls and selecting that perfect image, a package would show up at the customer's door with the chosen image. It would be on a square of film that would have to be digitized and eventually returned to the stock agency. And if you were working late at night or rushing to meet a deadline, you were out of luck! It was a truly inefficient and cumbersome process. Mark Getty, cofounder and executive chairman of Getty Images, knew there had to be a better way, especially given the capabilities offered by the Internet. In 1998, the company shifted gears. The goal was to digitize all archived images, build one massive database, and sell images exclusively online. And that's exactly what they've done.

Getty Image's integrated Web site can be accessed anywhere, anytime by customers. Using a keyword search, customers receive a series of relevant images. Customers can immediately download a rough image for free and see what it looks like in a page layout. Buying a final image is simple—enter a credit card number and download the image.

Although there aren't many competitors in this industry (the other three main ones are Associated Press, Corbis, and Reuters), the competitive challenge for Getty Images is that every other competitor offers the same product. Maintaining its position as a leader and innovator in the visual-content market will be a challenge for the company and will require a concentrated focus on providing customers what they want.

Discussion Questions

1. Describe the competitors in this industry from the industry perspective and from the market perspective. Do you think the concept of strategic groups would be appropriate given that there are four main competitors in the industry? Explain.

2. What, if any, competitive advantage do you think Getty Images has?

3. Competitive strategy is a choice of how an organization is going to compete in its industry or market so that it can develop a sustainable competitive advantage. Given the nature of this industry, what competitive strategy would be most likely to allow an organization to develop a sustainable competitive advantage? Explain your choice. Is this what Getty is doing? Explain.

4. What insights about the company's competitive advantage, competitive strategy, or other functional strategies can you find on its Web site? Describe.

(*Sources:* B. Acohido, "The Getty Family Is Back in Business," *USA Today,* March 15, 2004, p. 1B; and C. Dahle, "Image Isn't Everything," *Fast Company,* June 2000, pp. 346–57.)

Endnotes

1. B. Stone, "Nike's Short Game," *Newsweek*, January 26, 2004, pp. 40–41; J. Ewers, "A Designer Swooshes In," *U.S. News & World Report*, January 26, 2004, pp. EE12–EE13; S. Holmes, "Nike's New Advice? Just Strut It," *Business Week*, November 3, 2003, p. 40; M. McCarthy, "Nike Laces Up Converse Deal," *USA Today*, July 10, 2003, p. 1B; M. McCarthy, "Wake Up Consumers? Nike's Brash CEO Dares to Just Do It," *USA Today*, June 16, 2003, p. 1B; and M. McCarthy, "Rivals Scramble to Topple Nike's Sneaker Supremacy," *USA Today*, April 3, 2003, p. 1B.

2. R. A. D'Aveni, "Coping With Hypercompetition: Utilizing the New 7S's Framework," *Academy of Management Executive*, August 1995, pp. 45–60.

3. P. Kotler, *Marketing Management*, 5th ed. (Upper Saddle River, NJ: Prentice Hall, 2000), pp. 220–23.

4. See Michael E. Porter, *Competitive Strategy* (New York: Free Press, 1980), Chapter 7.

5. D. Dranove, M. Peteraf, and M. Shanley, "Do Strategic Groups Exist? An Economic Framework for Analysis," *Strategic Management Journal*, November 1998, pp. 1029–44; and J. B. Barney and R. E. Hoskisson, "Strategic Groups: Untested Assertions and Research Proposals," *Managerial and Decision Economics*, 11 (1990), pp. 187–98.

6. D. J. Ketchen, Jr., "An Interview with Raymond E. Miles and Charles C. Snow," *Academy of Management Executive*, November 2003, pp. 95–118; D. E. Abell, *Defining the Business: The Starting Point of Strategic Planning* (Upper Saddle River, NJ: Prentice Hall, 1980); M. E. Porter, *Competitive Strategy: Techniques for Analyzing Industries and Competitors* (New York: Free Press, 1980); and R. E. Miles and C. C. Snow, *Organizational Strategy, Structure, and Process* (New York: McGraw-Hill, 1978).

7. D. Fenn, "Money Rules," *Inc.*, April 2001, p. 94.

8. D. F. Jennings and S. L. Seaman, "High and Low Levels of Organizational Adaptation: An Empirical Analysis of Strategy, Structure, and Performance," *Strategic Management Journal*, July 1995, pp. 459–75; J. Tan and R. J. Litschert, "Environment–Strategy Relationship and Its Performance Implications: An Empirical Study of the Chinese Electronics Industry," *Strategic Management Journal*, January 1994, pp. 1–20; D. H. Doty, W. H. Glick, and G. P. Huber, "Fit, Equifinality, and Organizational Effectiveness: A Test of Two Configurational Theories," *Academy of Management Journal*, December 1993, pp. 1196–1250; D. Dvir, E. Segev, and A. Shenhar, "Technology's Varying Impact on the Success of Strategic Business Units Within the Miles and Snow Typology," *Strategic Management Journal*, February 1993, pp. 155–62; S. M. Shortell and E. J. Zajac, "Perceptual and Archival Measures of Miles and Snow's Strategic Types: A Comprehensive Assessment of Reliability and Validity," *Academy of Management Journal*, December 1990, pp. 817–32; S. A. Zahra and J. A. Pearce II, "Research Evidence on the Miles-Snow Typology," *Journal of Management*, December 1990, pp. 751–68; and D. C. Hambrick, "Some Tests of the Effectiveness and Functional Attributes of Miles and Snow's Strategic Types," *Academy of Management Journal*, March 1983, pp. 5–26.

9. M. E. Porter, *Competitive Advantage* (New York: Free Press, 1985); and M. E. Porter, *Competitive Strategy* (New York: Free Press, 1980).

10. Hoover's Online, **www.hoovers.com**, March 15, 2004; and M. B. Grover, "The Odd Couple," *Forbes*, November 18, 1996, pp. 178–81.

11. Hoover's Online, **www.hoovers.com**, March 15, 2004; and R. Karlgaard, "The Cheap Decade," *Forbes*, March 31, 2003, p. 37.

12. "The Frugal Life of the Wal-Mart Muckety-Muck," *Business 2.0*, May 2002, p. 22.

13. C. Y. Coleman, "Gap Profit Rose 32%," *Wall Street Journal*, February 25, 2000, p. B4; S. Perman, "Mend That Gap," *Time*, February 14, 2000, pp. 60–62; L. Lee, "A Savvy Captain for Old Navy," *Business Week*, November 8, 1999, pp. 133–34; and L. Lee, "Clicks and Mortar at Gap.Com," *Business Week*, October 18, 1999, pp. 150–52.

14. Porter, *Competitive Strategy*, p. 46.

15. Hoover's Online, **www.hoovers.com**, March 15, 2004.

16. Hoover's Online, **www.hoovers.com**, March 15, 2004; H. Page, "For Women Only," *Entrepreneur*, May 1996, p. 42; and M. O. Ray, "Catalog Focuses on Women Travelers," *Marketing News*, February 26, 1996, p. 12.

17. Hoover's Online, **www.hoovers.com**, March 15, 2004; and M. Warshaw, "Master the Future," *Success*, October 1996, pp. 28–29.

18. Hoover's Online, **www.hoovers.com**, March 15, 2004; and "Think Small," *Wall Street Journal*, April 25, 1996, p. A1.

19. M. Burke, "Touchy Circuits," *Forbes*, March 29, 2004, p. 82.

20. Porter, *Competitive Advantage*, p. 17.

21. C. Campbell-Hunt, "What Have We Learned About Generic Competitive Strategy? A Meta-Analysis," *Strategic Management Journal*, March 2000, pp. 127–54; R. B. Robinson and J. B. Pearce, "Planned Patterns of Strategic Behavior and Their Relationship to Business Unit Performance," *Strategic Management Journal*, 9, no. 1 (1988), pp. 43–60; D. Miller and P. H. Friesen, "Porter's Generic Strategies and Performance: An Empirical Examination With American Data," *Organization Studies*, 7 (1986), pp. 37–55; G. G. Dess and P. S. Davis, "Porter's Generic Strategies as Determinants of Strategic Group Membership and Organizational Performance," *Academy of Management Review*, 21 (1984), pp. 467–88; and D. Hambrick, "An Empirical Typology of Mature Industrial Product Environments," *Academy of Management Journal*, 26 (1983), pp. 213–30.

22. S. Kotha and B. L. Vadlamani, "Assessing Generic Strategies: An Empirical Investigation of Two Competing Typologies in Discrete Manufacturing Industries," *Strategic Management Journal*, January 1995, pp. 75–83; H. Mintzberg, "Generic Strategies: Toward a Comprehensive Framework," *Advances in Strategic Management*, Vol. 5 (Greenwich, CT: JAI Press, 1988), pp. 1–67; C. W. L. Hill, "Differentiation versus Low Cost or Differentiation and Low Cost," *Academy of Management Review*, July 1988, pp. 401–12; J. J. Chrisman, C. W. Hofer, and W. R. Boulton, "Toward a System for Classifying Business Strategies," *Academy of Management Review*, July 1988, pp. 413–28; and P. Wright, "A Refinement of Porter's Generic Strategies," *Strategic Management Journal*, vol. 8, no. 1, 1987, pp. 93–101.

23. C. W. L. Hill and G. R. Jones, *Strategic Management Theory*, 3d ed. (Boston: Houghton Mifflin Company, 1995), pp. 178–79; S. Cappel, P. Wright, M. Kroll, and D. Wyld, "Competitive Strategies and Business Performance: An Empirical Study of Select Service Businesses," *International Journal of Management*, March 1992, pp. 1–11; D. Miller, "The Generic Strategy Trap," *Journal of Business Strategy*, January–February 1991, pp. 37–41; and R. E. White, "Organizing to Make Business Unit Strategies Work," *Handbook of Business Strategy*, 2d ed., edited by H. E. Glass (Boston: Warren, Gorham, and Lamont, 1991), pp. 24.1–24.14.

24. F. Andrews, "Dell, It Turns Out, Has a Better Idea Than Ford," *New York Times*, January 26, 2000, p. C12; D. P. Hamilton, "Dell Surpasses Compaq in U.S. Sales," *Wall Street Journal*, October 25, 1999, p. A3; W. J. Holstein, "No Place Like Home," *U.S. News & World Report*, September 27, 1999, pp. 44–45; and

M. Treacy and F. Wiersma, "How Market Leaders Keep Their Edge," *Fortune*, February 6, 1995, p. 90.

25. Mintzberg, 1988.

26. Kotha and Vadlamani, 1995.

27. The information in this section is based on various articles in L. Fahey, ed., *The Strategic Management Reader* (Upper Saddle River, NJ: Prentice Hall, 1989), pp. 178–205.

28. The information on this section is based on Porter, *Competitive Advantage*, pp. 482–512.

29. W. T. Robinson, "Marketing Mix Reactions to New Business Ventures," *The PIMSletter on Business Strategy*, no. 42 (Cambridge, MA: Strategic Planning Institute, 1988), p. 9.

30. "Newsworthy Quotes," *Strategy & Business*, first quarter 1999, p. 155.

7

Corporate Strategies

STRATEGIC MANAGEMENT IN ACTION CASE #1

A Little Bit of Magic

Maybe Sears CEO Alan J. Lacy could use a little bit of magic to solve his company's retailing woes.[1] The company continues to be battered by mass merchandisers such as Wal-Mart, Kohl's, and Target and by mall chain stores such as J.C. Penney and Foot Locker. Add to that changing consumer demographics and the uncertain economic situation and you can see why a little retailing magic may be needed.

Although Sears is still struggling to find its place in today's retailing environment, the company has been a cornerstone of American retailing from its beginnings in 1886 as a mail-order merchandiser. By 1925, the company had opened its first retail stores, which soon surpassed catalog sales in revenues. The company also began offering Allstate auto insurance in 1931. The company continued to grow and prosper until the 1970s, which proved to be a tough period for all retailers. During that challenging period, Sears chose to further diversify by acquiring Coldwell Banker (the real estate sales company) and Dean Witter Reynolds (the stock brokerage) in 1981. It also launched the Discover credit card in 1985. However, its retail market share continued to fall, and Sears stumbled from one retail strategy to another, trying to find the right combination to turn things around. Finally, in 1993, the company decided to refocus its attention on retailing and sold its stake in Coldwell Banker and spun off the Dean Witter and Discover businesses. It also transferred ownership of the famed Sears Tower in downtown Chicago to a trust to cut its debt load. Then, in 1995, the company spun off its Allstate insurance business. However, the company still couldn't find the right retailing format to combat the growing power of Wal-Mart, Target, Home Depot, Best Buy, and other retailers. After a few years of retailing format flip-flops and struggles, several corporate executives, including the CEO, left the company. Lacy, who assumed the title of CEO in October 2000, has tried to bring some direction to the company ever since.

One of the first things Lacy did was restructure the company by closing select hardware stores, full-line stores, and tire and battery shops. In addition, Sears dropped certain product lines, including installed floor coverings, cosmetics, bicycles, and custom window treatments. Then, in 2002, the company laid off about 22 percent of its workforce. In May 2002, the company bought catalog retailer Lands' End for almost $2 billion. Lands' End executives now head Sears' women's apparel business, its design business, and its Internet and catalog sales. However, it has not been an easy transition; the Lands' End people had never operated retail stores and were accustomed to a target market composed of white, affluent baby boomers, unlike Sears' typical customers, of which one in three is Hispanic or African American.

Other corporate changes that Lacy initiated included acquiring the Structure men's brand from Limited Brands in September 2003; selling its huge credit card business to Citigroup in November 2003 for about $6 billion; and selling its National Tire & Battery chain in December 2003. But the company still faces serious challenges. "It's crucial for Sears to get its stores in shape quickly. It has spent the last two decades starting businesses outside of retail operations—and then getting rid of them. For the past five years, Sears has repeatedly restructured and cut costs in its retail business, promising an eventual payoff in rising sales." But those payoffs haven't occurred yet. Has Lacy finally gotten it right? If so, maybe he won't need magic after all. If not, magic probably wouldn't be the answer anyway!

Deciding the optimal mix of businesses and the overall direction of the organization are key parts of corporate strategy. It involves looking at all aspects of the organization—including resources, distinctive capabilities, core competencies, and competitive advantage(s)—and choosing how best to capitalize upon what the organization has or how to compensate for what it doesn't have in light of critical environmental trends and changes. Examples of corporate strategy in the chapter-opening case are shown by the decisions that strategic managers at Sears made as they moved into and out of various businesses. They didn't, and couldn't, know how those strategic changes would turn out, but they *did* know that the convergence of certain environmental threats and opportunities coupled with their organization's strengths and weaknesses had to be addressed. Although not every organization will face the risks that Sears did, the fact remains that strategic decision makers must look at the broad and long-term strategic issues facing their organizations; that is, they must address the organization's corporate strategies.

In this chapter, we're going to examine all aspects of corporate strategy. First, we'll look at how it differs for single- and multiple-business organizations. In addition, we explore the role of corporate strategy and how it's related to the other types of organizational strategies we've discussed in previous chapters. Then, we'll get into a comprehensive discussion of the various types of corporate strategies that organizations might choose to implement. Finally, we'll talk about what's involved with evaluating and changing corporate strategies.

A BRIEF OVERVIEW OF CORPORATE STRATEGY

Before we get into the actual nuts and bolts of corporate strategy, it would be helpful first to look at some basic information about it. What is it and how is it related to the other types of organizational strategies?

What Is Corporate Strategy?

We first defined **corporate strategy** back in Chapter 1 as that strategy concerned with the broad and long-term questions of what business(es) the organization is in or wants to be in and what it wants to do with those businesses. Because an organization exists for some purpose (its vision and missions), carrying out that purpose means strategic managers must make decisions about the best courses of action or best direction for the organization to take. This is the essence of corporate strategy—determining the overall direction that will enable the organization to best fulfill its purpose and achieve its strategic goals through the business(es) it chooses to be in. One aspect of corporate strategy that affects how an organization can best fulfill its purpose and achieve its strategic goals is whether the organization is in a single business or in multiple businesses.

Single- and Multiple-Business Organizations

A **single-business organization** is one that operates primarily in one industry. A **multiple-business organization** is one that operates in more than one industry. For instance, Coca-Cola can be considered a single-business organization because it competes primarily in the beverage industry. Even though it has multiple products, multiple markets, and multiple outlets, it is still primarily a beverage company. In contrast, Coke's biggest competitor, PepsiCo, is an example of a multiple-business organization. Its business units include its snack food business (Frito Lay), its beverage business (Pepsi, Diet Pepsi, and its other beverages), its prepared foods business (Quaker Foods North America), and its international business (PepsiCo International). PepsiCo also once had a restaurant unit, which included Taco Bell, Pizza Hut, and KFC, but chose to spin off this business unit—now known as YUM! Brands—in early 1997. PepsiCo follows a corporate strategy in which it operates in more than one industry; that is, it operates as a multiple-business organization. Also, look back at the chapter-opening case. Sears would be an example of a company that had been a multiple-business organization because it was operating in different industries—insurance, credit cards, stock brokerage, and so forth, but has returned to being a single-business organization by refocusing on its retail operations. Why is this distinction between single- and multiple-business organizations important? It's important because it influences the organization's overall strategic direction, what corporate strategy is used, and how that strategy is implemented and managed.

Another general aspect of corporate strategy that should be considered is its relationship to the other organizational strategies. What role does corporate strategy play and how is it related to the functional and competitive strategies?

Relating Corporate Strategy to Other Organizational Strategies

Whereas the corporate strategy establishes the overall direction that the organization hopes to go, the other organizational strategies—functional and competitive—provide the means for making sure the organization gets there. A good analogy would be a cargo ship headed across the Pacific Ocean with its load of containers filled with athletic shoes. The ship's captain sets off in a general direction toward the chosen destination, Seattle. However, the ship doesn't sail by itself. It needs resources—that is, the crew, the equipment, the fuel, the navigation tools, and so on—and it needs capabilities—that is, the work activities necessary to operate a ship. If a significant development arises, perhaps a fierce storm, the ship's crew knows what to do and how to respond. They take actions to keep the ship headed in the chosen direction. An organization's corporate strategy is much the same. It's used to steer the organization in a certain direction, but the other strategies provide the means for making sure that direction is followed and ensuring that significant changes are understood and managed. What are these "means"? As we've discussed in earlier chapters, the means for moving the organization in the strategic direction it wants to go are the resources, distinctive capabilities, core competencies, and competitive advantage(s) being developed and used in the organization's functional and competitive strategies. For example, if the organization's goal is to increase market share, it needs appropriate functional and competitive strategies that support and enhance its competitive edge so it can attract customers. Otherwise, it's likely to find that it can't achieve its goal of increasing market share. Figure 7.1 shows how corporate strategy fits into the overall strategic management in action process.

Figure 7.1

*Strategic Management
in Action*

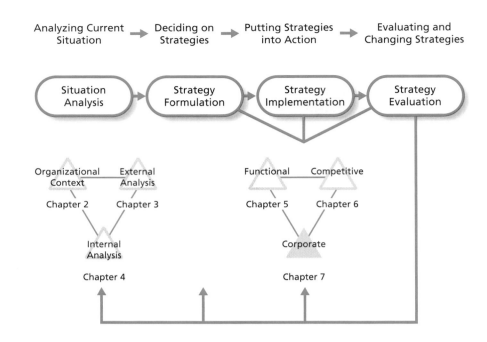

Each organizational strategy plays a significant role in whether the organization does what it's in business to do and whether it achieves its strategic goals. Coordinating these organizational strategies is critical to managing strategically. The corporate strategy can't be implemented effectively or efficiently without the support from the resources, capabilities, and competencies being developed and used in the competitive and functional strategies. And, the competitive and functional strategies that are implemented must support the organization's overall strategic direction and its corporate strategy. In what overall directions can an organization go? That's what we're going to look at next.

What Are the Possible Corporate Strategic Directions?

Strategic decision makers can choose from three corporate strategic directions: (1) moving the organization ahead, (2) keeping the organization where it is, and (3) reversing the organization's decline. What does each of these mean?

Moving ahead means that the organization's strategic managers hope to expand the organization's activities or operations—that is, to grow. How? By looking at the various corporate growth strategies and choosing one (or more) that is appropriate given the characteristics and objectives of the particular situation. Choosing to keep the organization where it is means not moving ahead, but also not falling behind. This, very simply, is an organizational stability strategy. Finally, reversing the organization's decline describes situations in which the organization has problems and may be seeing a weakening in one or more performance areas. These situations are typically addressed by using organizational renewal strategies.

Now you know the three corporate strategic directions: organizational growth, organizational stability, and organizational renewal. In the rest of this chapter, we're going to discuss specific corporate strategies that can be used to move the organization in these broad directions and how these corporate strategies are implemented, evaluated, and changed.

- What is corporate strategy?
- How are the organization's vision and mission(s) related to its corporate strategy?
- Contrast single-business and multiple-business organizations.
- How is corporate strategy related to the other organizational strategies?
- Which organizational strategy is most important? Explain.
- Describe each of the three corporate strategic directions.

ORGANIZATIONAL GROWTH

Organizational growth is a desirable goal for an organization. The pursuit of growth appeals to business and not-for-profit organizations alike. For instance, universities will develop new degree programs or change old ones to attract more customers (students) and more resources (e.g., state funds, alumni donations, books, buildings, equipment, and so forth). Or, for example, McDonald's announces that it's opening additional outlets in various countries throughout Southeast Asia. Also, in the chapter-opening case, Sears added the Lands' End and Structure brands to its fashion portfolio. All of these strategic decisions and actions involve ways for an organization to grow.

What exactly do we mean by organizational growth? A **growth strategy** involves the attainment of specific growth objectives by expanding an organization's activities or operations. What growth objectives might organizations pursue? The typical ones for business organizations include increases in sales revenues, profits, or other financial or performance measures. However, even not-for-profit organizations have growth objectives; for instance, increasing the number of clients served or patrons attracted, broadening the geographic area of coverage, or even perhaps increasing the number of programs offered. To reach these growth objectives, organizations use specific growth strategies, which we'll look at next.

Growth Strategies

If an organization's strategic managers have decided that moving the organization ahead is the direction they want the organization to go, they have specific growth alternatives from which to choose, as shown in Figure 7.2. Let's look at each in more depth.

Figure 7.2

Possible Growth Strategies

Figure 7.3

Concentration Options

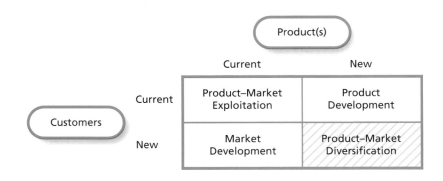

Concentration

The **concentration strategy** is a growth strategy in which the organization concentrates on its primary line of business and looks for ways to meet its growth objectives through expanding its activities or operations in this core business. When a single-business organization grows by adding products or opening new locations, it's using the concentration strategy. As long as desired growth objectives—increases in sales, profits, or other measures of growth—are achieved with this strategy, most organizations will choose to continue with it.

Exactly *how* might an organization use the concentration strategy, particularly when attempting to increase sales and profits? Three concentration options, shown in Figure 7.3, reflect the various combinations of current product(s) and market(s), and new product(s) and market(s).[2]

The product–market exploitation option describes attempts by the organization to increase sales of its current product(s) in its current market(s). How? By using its functional (particularly, marketing and advertising) and its competitive strategies. It might use incentives to get current customers to buy more. Or, it might advertise other uses for the product. For instance, that's what the Church and Dwight Company, Inc. did to increase sales of its Arm & Hammer baking soda. Just think of the numerous ways, beyond baking, that consumers are encouraged to use baking soda—as an air freshener, a cleaner, a deodorant, and so forth. L.L. Bean, the catalog company, is using product–market exploitation as it expands its clothing lines, updates its Web site, and adds more retail stores—all in an attempt to sell more products to current customers. Of course, organizations have numerous other ways to get current customers to use more of the current product.

Using the product development option, organizations create new products for use by its current market (customers). What is a "new" product? New products may include improved or modified versions of existing products. In addition, new features, options, sizes, and ingredients are often used in developing new products for current customers. For example, Kodak markets film for every conceivable type of camera, light, or photo situation. Each new product development is designed to increase sales to its current customers. Another example of product development can be seen at Hershey Corporation when it added new candies that were not chocolates, including Jolly Rancher and Good and Plenty, to sell to its current customers. Another example of product development is Apple's iPod digital music player, which has gone through different product variations to extend its sales reach.

In contrast, the market development option describes when an organization sells its current products in new markets. What are "new" markets? It might be additional geographic areas or it might be market segments not currently served by the organization. For instance, luxury retailer Tiffany's is reaching out to a new market with affordable indulgences for younger consumers. Several items such as its sterling silver Heart Tag charm bracelets and necklaces have generated new sales and new customers. And many skin care

Americans' expanding waistlines have led dining outlets to offer a vast array of low-carb products. In addition, dozens of other companies now provide products that are sturdier and more generously cut. For example, Lane Home Furnishing's Comfort King recliner can accommodate a person who weighs up to 300 pounds. Omron Healthcare's new blood pressure monitor has a larger cuff than standard models for a more accurate reading on people with larger arms. And Goliath Casket makes large-sized coffins. Can you find other examples of how businesses are tapping into this new market using product or market development?

Source: "Livin' Large," USA Weekend, March 5–7, 2004, p. 14.

companies are going after an important new market—men. Although department stores have sold expensive men's skin care products for years, the skin care companies are now going mainstream with these products by selling them at drugstores and discount retailers. These are examples of market development—current products aimed at a new market.

To summarize the concentration strategy, remember that the organization looks for ways to grow in its core business by different combinations of product(s) and market(s). The focus is finding ways to meet organizational growth objectives by concentrating on its core business.

The remaining option shown in Figure 7.3—product–market diversification—isn't a concentration option because it involves expanding both into new products and new markets. And once a single-business organization that has concentrated on its core business chooses to move into a business with new products *and* new markets, it becomes a multiple-business organization because it's now operating in a different industry. We'll discuss this concept of diversification more thoroughly in a later section.

The advantage of the concentration strategy is that the organization becomes very good at what it does. The strategic managers know the industry and their competitors well. The organization's functional and competitive strategies can be fine-tuned to ensure the development of a sustainable competitive advantage because the strategic managers know what customers want and how they can provide it. Everyone in the organization can concentrate on the primary business and on developing and exploiting the unique resources, distinctive capabilities, and core competencies that are critical to success in this market.

The main drawback of the concentration strategy is that the organization is vulnerable to industry and other external shifts. This risk can be minimized by remaining alert to significant trends and changes, but strategic managers need to be willing to adjust the organization's direction should it become necessary. After all, you could be the best buggy whip manufacturer in the world and still not have customers beating down your door for your product. Perhaps an even more relevant example of the risks of the concentration strategy might be the fate suffered by the Royal Typewriter Company when personal computers became the standard equipment for offices and demand for typewriters plummeted. Royal unwisely chose to concentrate on producing typewriters, and, as a result, it doesn't exist anymore. If an organization implements its concentration strategy blindly without understanding the opportunities and threats facing the industry, *not* achieving its growth objectives may be the least of its problems!

Although the concentration strategy may seem ideal for small organizations, large organizations also can use this strategy. In fact, large organizations often start off using the concentration strategy and continue to use it to pursue growth. For example, Beckman Coulter, Inc., a Fullerton, California-based organization with annual revenues of over $2.2 billion, has successfully used the concentration strategy to become one of the world's largest medical equipment and diagnostics companies.[3] The company has grown by

Many luxury retailers are extending their brands into the children's market. Not only are these companies looking to expand sales now, they are hoping to create future loyal customers. For example, Coach, a high-end retailer of leather bags and accessories, unveiled a line of kids' outerwear and accessories in November 2003, with items ranging from hat-and-mitten sets to scarves and slippers. Burberry miniaturized its classic trench and duffle coats and also brought out its trademark plaid in a line of umbrellas and boots for the young set. And Polo Ralph Lauren sells one-of-a-kind christening gowns as well as children's denim clothes and turquoise and silver jewelry. What do you think of these strategies? You may recognize the potential advantages, but what might be some possible drawbacks to such a strategy?

Source: L. Grant, "Upscale Retailers Go Miniature to Draw Kids into Brand Loyalty," USA Today, September 25, 2003, p. 3B.

continually innovating new products and processes in this industry. Another example of a large organization that has successfully used the concentration strategy is Bose Corporation of Framingham, Massachusetts. The company's innovative audio products have helped make it the world's number one audio equipment manufacturer with annual sales of more than $1.6 billion.[4] Again, this organization has grown because of product innovations concentrated in its primary industry.

If the organization isn't able to meet its growth objectives through concentrating on its primary industry, however, it will begin to look at other corporate growth strategies, such as vertical integration, to meet those goals.

Vertical Integration (Forward and Backward)

The **vertical integration strategy** is an organization's attempt to gain control of its inputs (backward), its outputs (forward), or both. In backward vertical integration, the organization gains control of its inputs or resources by becoming its own supplier. For example, Anheuser-Busch owns businesses in grain processing and beverage containers and lids. In forward vertical integration, the organization gains control of its outputs (products or services) by becoming its own distributor, such as through an outlet store or maybe through franchising. For example, Apple Computer has over 80 retail stores to distribute its products.

The vertical integration strategy is considered a growth strategy because the organization is expanding its activities and operations. However, because it is expanding into industries connected to its primary business, a single-business organization that implements a vertical integration strategy would still be considered a single-business organization. It, very simply, is taking another path to meeting its organizational growth objectives by controlling different points along the value chain.

Studies of vertical integration strategies have shown mixed results in terms of whether the strategy helped or hurt performance. Some of the problems associated with vertical integration include poor performance, higher costs, and a higher risk of bankruptcy.[5] However, studies have also confirmed some of the advantages associated with vertical integration, such as better control of costs, more efficient use of inputs, protection of proprietary technology, and creation of barriers to entry to keep out competitors, to name a few.[6] What should we believe? Is the vertical integration strategy an appropriate one to help an organization achieve its growth objectives? In general, we can say that the benefits of vertical integration slightly outweigh the costs associated with it.[7] Table 7.1 summarizes these costs and benefits.

What are some examples of organizations using the vertical integration strategy to meet growth objectives? Oil companies, such as Exxon–Mobil and BP–Amoco, have long used vertical integration strategies. All have varying business operations in the oil

Benefits	Costs	Table 7.1
• Reduced purchasing and selling costs • Improved coordination among functions and capabilities • Protect proprietary technology	• Reduced flexibility as organization is locked into product(s) and technology • Difficulties in integrating various operations • Financial costs of acquiring or starting up	Major Benefits and Costs of Vertical Integration

exploration, refining, distributing, and selling functions—all the way from oil well to gas pump. Another example of vertical integration from a completely different industry is The Walt Disney Company and its valued collections of animated cartoons, fictional characters, and other media properties. Disney controls both the programming content *and* the distribution systems to get their media content to the public. For example, Disney has had its Disney Channel for a number of years. That's not all they do, however! Disney also has outlets for distributing (selling) all the consumer products associated with its media characters—that is, the Disney retail stores and the theme parks and resorts where consumers can purchase stuffed animals, clothing, trinkets, jewelry, videos, and any number of other Disney-branded products.

Horizontal Integration

Whereas vertical integration involves an organization remaining in the same industry but supplying its own inputs (resources) or distributing its own outputs (products or services), the **horizontal integration strategy** involves expanding the organization's activities and operations by combining with other organizations in the same industry doing the same things it is—that is, combining with competitors. This growth strategy keeps the organization in the same industry and provides a means of expanding market share and strengthening competitive position. Is it legal? Obviously, in the United States, the Federal Trade Commission (FTC) and Department of Justice assess the impact of such proposed combinations on the level of competition. They evaluate whether antitrust laws will be violated. And globally, the European Union has been quite active in approving or rejecting proposed horizontal growth strategies, especially those with a potential impact on its member countries. If domestic or global regulators perceive that competition is likely to decrease or if the ultimate consumer will be unfairly impacted, combining operations with competitors probably will not be allowed. In industries as diverse as pharmaceuticals, oil, software, and car manufacturing, companies using the horizontal integration strategy have come under FTC scrutiny. However, despite this potential roadblock, many organizations have used the horizontal integration strategy to grow.

strategic MANAGERS *in action*

Stan Sigman, president and CEO of Atlanta-based Cingular, caught a big fish in early 2004 when his company won the bidding war for AT&T Wireless. Cingular, the industry's number two mobile phone service provider, made the winning bid of more than $40 billion for the number three competitor, AT&T, by beating out British-based Vodafone Group PLC, which dropped out of the heated bidding war. The combined company created the nation's largest cellular subscription base with more than 46 million potential subscribers. Sigman said, "This combination is expected to create customer benefits and growth prospects neither company could have achieved on its own and will mean better coverage, improved reliability, enhanced call quality, and a wide array of new and innovative services for consumers." What do you think of this horizontal integration strategic move? What are the potential advantages and drawbacks for the companies *and* for consumers?

Source: Associated Press, "Agreement: Cingular to Acquire AT&T Wireless," USA Today, February 27, 2004.

For example, women's apparel retailer Chico acquired The White House, which also sells women's fashions. Teen retailer Alloy bought its top rival, Delia's. Carnival Cruise Lines beat out Royal Caribbean's bid for Princess Cruises, a move that gave Carnival more capacity than its two biggest competitors combined. Another example of the horizontal integration strategy can be seen around the snow-covered mountains of Colorado. Vail Resorts Inc., the nation's number two ski resort operator, wanted to grow by combining with other ski areas, including Breckenridge, Keystone, and Arapahoe Basin. The FTC expressed concern about the competitive impact from the proposed combination and asked that the Arapahoe Basin property be divested. Even today, however, the company continues to grow by acquiring other ski resort properties.

Horizontal integration is an appropriate corporate growth strategy as long as (1) it enables the company to meet its growth objectives, (2) it can be strategically managed to attain a sustainable competitive advantage, *and* (3) it satisfies legal and regulatory guidelines.

Diversification

We introduced the concept of diversification earlier in our discussion of the concentration growth strategy. When an organization chooses to go into different products *and* different markets, it is diversifying. The **diversification strategy** is a corporate growth strategy in which an organization expands its activities and operations by moving into a different industry. There are two major types of diversification: related and unrelated. **Related (concentric) diversification** is diversifying into a different industry, but one that's related in some way to the organization's current operations. **Unrelated (conglomerate) diversification** is diversifying into a completely different industry from the organization's current operations. Any move into a different industry—related or unrelated—automatically makes an organization a multiple-business organization because it's no longer operating in just one industry. Let's look more closely at each of the two types of diversification.

How can diversification—a term which means "different"—ever be related? In other words, how is a different industry "related" to the one an organization is currently in? An organization using related diversification to achieve its growth objectives is looking for some type of strategic "fit" into which it can transfer its resources, distinctive capabilities, and core competencies to the new industry and apply those in such a way that a sustainable

FOR YOUR
information

Growing Outside the Core

A five-year study of corporate growth strategies of 1,850 companies concluded that the most sustainable, profitable growth comes "when a company pushes out the boundaries of its core business into an adjacent space" and that the most successful companies "profitably outgrow their rivals by developing a formula for expanding those boundaries in predictable, repeatable ways." The authors of the study were able to identify six types of adjacent spaces that successful companies used to outperform their competitors. These six adjacencies were as follows: expand along the value chain (one of the most difficult adjacent spaces to grow into); grow new products and services; use new distribution channels; enter new geographic markets; address new customer segments, often by modifying a proven product or technology; and moving into the "white space" with a new business built around a strong capability that is difficult for competitors to imitate (the rarest adjacent space and the hardest to implement). How does this concept of adjacent spaces relate to the concepts of growth that we've discussed?

Source: C. Zook and J. Allen, "Growth Outside the Core," Harvard Business Review, December 2003, pp. 66–74.

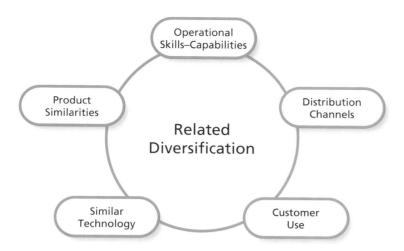

Figure 7.4

Types of Related
Diversification

competitive advantage results. This search for strategic "synergy" very simply is the idea that the performance of combined operations will be much greater than the performance of each unit separately. (Another way of viewing this is the old saying that 2 + 2 can equal 5.) How does synergy happen? It happens through the interactions and interrelatedness of the combined operations and the sharing of resources, capabilities, and core competencies. A good illustration of synergy can be seen in a statement made by Steve Perry, lead singer of Journey (the successful rock music group from the 1980s), when the band got back together in 1996, "Individually, none of us made the music as magically as we collectively make it together."[8] That's what synergy is all about—the combined operations are more "magical" than what each unit could do separately. Figure 7.4 illustrates the various ways that an organization might transfer resources, capabilities, and core competencies to achieve synergy as it moves into a related industry.

What organizations have used a related diversification strategy? One example is Apple Computer, which is in a variety of businesses, from music (iTunes Music Store and iPod), movies (Pixar Animation Studios), and home-entertainment hubs (software and wireless networking technologies) to retail shops (Apple Stores) and, of course, its desktop computers. Another example is Altria Group (formerly Philip Morris Companies). Its subsidiaries include Philip Morris USA, Philip Morris International, Kraft Foods, SABMiller (South African Breweries and Miller Brewing Company), and a financial services business. All of these industries are different, but obviously share many common characteristics, which allows Altria to exchange resources, capabilities, and competencies. As with any strategic action, there's no guarantee that related diversification will always succeed at helping an organization reach its strategic goals. Here's an example of a related diversification that *didn't* work. Anheuser-Busch entered the snack food industry with its Eagle Snacks business unit because it felt that it could exploit certain marketing synergies (distribution channels, customer use, product similarities) it had developed as the market leader in the beer business and transfer those resources and capabilities to the snack food industry. However, it was never able to develop a sustainable competitive advantage against industry leader Frito Lay (a business unit of PepsiCo) in this intensely competitive market. As a result, the company shut down the Eagle Snacks unit in 1996. Anheuser-Busch had already sold its baseball team, the St. Louis Cardinals, in 1995. However, the company is still an example of a related diversified company because, even though its primary business is beer, it has retained its theme parks businesses, including Sea World, Busch Gardens, and others.

What about unrelated diversification? This growth strategy involves the organization moving into industries in which there is absolutely no strategic fit to be exploited. Why

Japanese giant Sony Corporation is a good global example of related diversification. It's in a variety of businesses, from consumer electronics to entertainment assets. Its Playstation 2 game console dominates the game console market with about 70 percent of global sales. It's also the world's number one consumer electronics firm with a host of products ranging from PCs, televisions, digital cameras, and Walkman stereos to semiconductors. Then, there's its entertainment businesses, which include Epic and Columbia (recorded music and video) and Columbia TriStar (motion pictures, DVDs, and TV programming). Although its various businesses encompass different industries, Sony has been able to exploit a number of strategic synergies. Explain whether you think being a global business makes it more or less difficult to achieve these all-important strategic synergies.

Sources: *Hoover's Online*, **www.hoovers.com**, *March 21, 2004; and S. Levy, "Sony's New Day," Newsweek, January 27, 2003, pp. 50–53.*

would an organization choose to be in industries where there were no possible strategic relationships or potential synergies? Most often, an organization will use this approach when its core industry and related industries don't offer enough growth potential. For the organization to pursue and achieve its growth goals, it has to look elsewhere. Also, some organizations might choose unrelated diversification if their specialized resources, capabilities, and core competencies can't be easily applied to other industries outside its core business. This would obviously limit the options for growth. That's why an organization in this situation might look at the unrelated diversification strategy.

Because of the challenges of strategically managing such entirely different businesses, few companies use this growth strategy. However, some organizations do use it. For instance, Fortune Brands is a crazy quilt of businesses producing market-leading products such as Jim Beam bourbon, Absolut vodka, Moen faucets, Aristokraft and Schrock cabinets, DeKuyper cordials, Titleist golf balls, Swingline staplers, and Master Lock padlocks. Another example is Lancaster Colony Corporation, which makes and markets Marzetti salad dressing, Dee Zee truck running boards and Protecta truck bed liners, Colony and Fostoria glassware, and Candle-lite candles and potpourri. Finally, another example from the global arena is the Charoen Pokphand Group, headquartered in Bangkok, Thailand. Its widely diverse businesses include agricultural business operations (feed production, animal breeding, meat processing, shrimp farming, and so forth), industrial operations (production of petrochemicals, leather goods, toys, telecommunications equipment, motorcycles, beer, and so forth), and investment properties and investment holdings (real estate and other types of financial investments).[9]

What is our conclusion about the usefulness of the diversification strategy? Is it an effective growth strategy for organizations? Research studies of organizations using the diversification strategy have shown that, for the most part, related diversification is superior to unrelated diversification.[10] If an organization can develop and exploit the potential synergies in the resources, capabilities, and core competencies of its diversified operations, then it's likely to create a sustainable competitive advantage. However, achieving these desired synergies isn't by any means easy. The ability to strategically manage these diverse businesses and develop a sustainable competitive advantage—no matter how related the different industries might be—is crucial. Also, even though organizations' unrelated diversification efforts haven't fared as well in performance measures according to certain research studies, the unrelated diversification strategy probably can be just as valuable a growth strategy as the related one. Once again, it depends on how effectively the diverse operations are strategically managed as a sustainable competitive advantage is sought.[11]

- Define growth strategy.
- What types of growth objectives might business (for-profit) organizations have? What about not-for-profit organizations?
- What are the various corporate growth strategies?
- Describe the concentration strategy. (Look at the ways organizations can use it, its advantages and drawbacks, and what types of organizations might use it.)
- What is the vertical integration strategy? How is it a growth strategy?
- What are some of the benefits and costs associated with the vertical integration strategy?
- Describe the horizontal integration strategy. When is it an appropriate growth strategy?
- What is the diversification strategy? Describe the two major types of diversification.
- Explain the concept of synergy and how it relates to the diversification strategy.
- Is diversification an effective growth strategy for organizations? Explain.

International

Strategic decision makers will undoubtedly have to deal with international issues as they manage strategically. An organization's corporate strategies likely involve looking for ways to grow by taking advantage of the potential revenues–profits offered by global markets or by protecting the organization's core operations from global competitors.[12] One thing we need to clarify up front about international growth is that it's possible for an organization to "go international" as it pursues growth using any of the other strategies. That is, if an organization chooses to vertically integrate, it could be done globally as well as domestically. If a related diversification strategy is being implemented, it could involve combining the operations of organizations in different countries as well as those in the home market. You need to understand some specific international growth issues, however, and that's why we've also included it as a specific growth strategy.

The first issues we need to examine in relation to the international growth strategy are the advantages and drawbacks of international expansion, which are summarized in Table 7.2. Essentially, the advantages and drawbacks of international growth boil down to the fact that it provides significant opportunities for organizations to create and exploit sustainable competitive advantages, but their ability to do so is not easily achieved. Although international expansion—of markets or organizational resources and capabilities—is a common strategic approach, it, like everything else we've discussed, must be managed strategically to contribute to the development of a sustainable competitive advantage.

Advantages	Drawbacks
• Could lower operational costs	• Poses greater economic, strategic, and financial risks
• Provides a way to supplement or strengthen domestic growth	• Process of managing strategically becomes more complex and challenging
• Contributes to achieving benefits of economies of scale	• Finding similarities in markets or operational capabilities is more difficult
• Becomes a stronger competitor both domestically and internationally	• Capturing and exploiting advantages is not easy or automatic

Table 7.2

Advantages and Drawbacks of International Expansion

Figure 7.5

Approaches to International
Expansion

Source: *From Strategic Management:
Competitiveness and Globalization by Hitt,
Ireland, Hoskisson. Copyright © 1997 by
permission of South-Western College
Publishing, a division of International
Thomson Publishing Inc., Cincinnati, Ohio,
45227.*

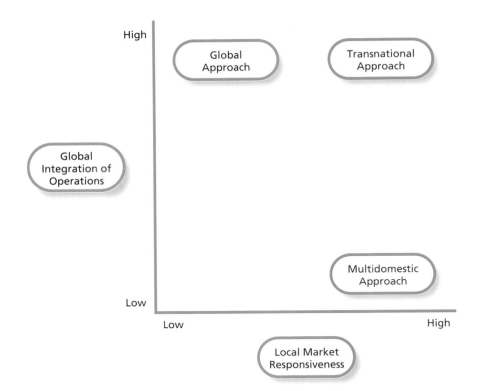

Another international growth issue that must be resolved is the general approach the organization is going to take as it goes international. The organization has three choices when going international: (1) multidomestic, (2) global, or (3) transnational.[13] Each approach entails a unique configuration of two factors: the need for the organization to respond to local needs and differences (i.e., the organization's competitive strategy is to pursue a differentiation advantage) and the need for it to globally integrate and standardize operations (i.e., the organization's competitive strategy is to pursue a low cost advantage). These combinations are shown in Figure 7.5. In the **multidomestic approach** (high local market responsiveness and low global integration of operations), the organization would implement its global expansion strategy by decentralizing operational decisions and activities to each country in which it's operating and by tailoring its products and services to each market. This approach is designed with a differentiation advantage in mind. The **global approach** (low local market responsiveness and high global integration of operations) would involve the organization providing more standardized products—not tailored to each specific country—and using significantly integrated operations. This approach is designed to help develop a low-cost advantage. Finally, in the **transnational approach** (high local market responsiveness and high global integration of operations), the organization wants to achieve both global efficiency through globally integrating operations *and* product differentiation through tailoring products and services to the local market. The choice of approach to global growth hinges on the organization's desired competitive advantage.

The final issue we need to discuss in relation to the organization's international expansion strategy is the various ways an organization begins to do so. The five ways to do this are exporting, importing, licensing, franchising, and direct investment. In *exporting*, the organization manufactures products in its home country and then transports those products to other countries to be sold there through an existing distribution channel. *Importing* involves selling products at home that are made in another country. *Licensing* is an arrangement in which a foreign licensee buys the rights to manufacture and market a company's product in that country for a negotiated fee. In *franchising*—which is mainly used by service providers—the company sells franchisees in the foreign country limited rights to use its brand name in return for a lump-sum payment and a share of the franchisee's profits. In *direct investment*, the organization actually owns assets such as a manufacturing facility or a sales office in the foreign country.

What are some examples of the international growth strategy? Toymakers Mattel and Hasbro pushed into overseas markets, something they hadn't done because many toys popular in the U.S. market simply didn't appeal to other global customers. However, as American culture continues to spread, these companies are finding their products more in demand. Hasbro is selling its Transformers and Playskool toys whereas Mattel is succeeding with its Little People line.[14] MTV Networks is another company growing in the global marketplace by tailoring its programming to specific markets. MTV is available in over 70 million homes in the United States, but over 100 million in Southeast Asia. It's continuing to expand into China and Russia. Then there's Domino's Pizza, which recently opened its 2,500th international restaurant. These international stores have achieved 39 consecutive quarters of same-store sales growth. How? Domino's "careful balance of central control and local flexibility."[15] The company knows what makes a Domino's pizza a Domino's pizza, but they also understand what makes a pizza Japanese, Indian, or British. Finally, another example of a different international experience altogether is the challenge that Newell Rubbermaid Inc., the U.S.-based manufacturer of plastic household and other consumer products, faced as it attempted to enter foreign markets.[16] The company's strategic decision makers soon discovered that its products would have to be tailored to each foreign market—something it hadn't wanted or planned to do. Whereas most Americans preferred Rubbermaid's storage containers in neutral blues and almond colors, consumers in southern Europe preferred red containers, and customers in Holland wanted white. Also, in markets outside the United States, Rubbermaid faced consumer resistance to plastic furniture and cleaning tools. Even though Rubbermaid has a strong brand name and a reputation for quality in the United States, customers in other parts of the world tended to perceive that plastic products were cheap and cheaply made. As Rubbermaid's experience in international expansion illustrates, even given the vast growth opportunities presented by foreign markets, there are still significant strategic challenges associated with growing globally.

You've now been introduced to all the types of corporate growth strategies an organization can use to pursue its growth objectives: concentration, vertical integration, horizontal integration, diversification, and international. What we need to look at next are the mechanisms that organizations use to implement these growth strategies.

strategic MANAGERS *in action*

Samsung may not be a well-known corporate name. However, CEO and vice chairman Yun Jong Yong is leading a company that's thriving by defying conventional wisdom. How? First of all, Samsung focuses on high-tech electronics hardware, not software. In fact, the South Korean company is emerging as a market leader in a variety of technology markets, from big-screen televisions and microwave ovens to LCD displays and flash memory devices. Its closest rival, Sony Corporation, is well aware of Samsung's progress. Sony's president, Kunitake Ando says, "I ask for a report on what Samsung is doing every week." Another strategic approach that Yun has implemented is a continued focus on Samsung making

everything itself. It does not outsource manufacturing, but instead builds huge new factories and does its own manufacturing. And, Samsung remains diversified and vertically integrated instead of focusing on a few core competencies. Yun believes that if you "stay at the forefront of core technologies and master the manufacturing, you control your future." Whether his strategy works in the long run remains to be seen. But Samsung is betting billions that its strategy can and will work, even in the challenging consumer electronics industry.

Source: C. Edwards, M. Ihlwan, and P. Engardio, "The Samsung Way," Business Week, June 16, 2003, pp. 56–64.

Implementing Growth Strategies

As we've just seen, organizations have specific corporate strategy alternatives they can use to pursue growth objectives, if that's the overall direction strategic managers have decided to pursue. However, as we've discussed in previous chapters, just choosing an appropriate strategic alternative is only part of the picture. That strategy must be implemented. For corporate growth strategies, implementation options are (1) mergers–acquisitions, (2) internal development, and (3) strategic partnering.

Mergers–Acquisitions

One way that an organization can implement the growth strategies is by "purchasing" what it needs to expand its operations. These purchases are done through mergers and acquisitions. You might think that mergers and acquisitions are synonymous, but they're not. Both describe situations in which an organization combines its operations with another's, but each involves a different approach. A **merger** is a legal transaction in which two or more organizations combine operations through an exchange of stock and create a third entity. Mergers usually take place between organizations that are similar in size and are usually "friendly"—that is, a merger is usually acceptable to all the concerned parties. On the other hand, an **acquisition** is an outright purchase of an organization by another. The purchased organization is completely absorbed by the purchasing organization. Acquisitions usually are between organizations of unequal sizes and can be friendly or hostile. Friendly acquisitions are ones in which the combination is desired by the respective organizations. When an organization being acquired doesn't want to be acquired, it's often referred to as a **hostile takeover**. In fact, the target of a hostile takeover often will take steps to prevent the acquisition. Table 7.3 lists possible defensive maneuvers a takeover target might use to scare off the acquiring organization.

How popular are mergers and acquisitions for implementing organizations' growth strategies? Research has shown that their popularity seems to go in cycles.[17]

Keep in mind that a merger or acquisition could be used by an organization when implementing *any* of the growth strategies—concentration, vertical integration, horizontal integration, diversification, or international. The main distinguishing feature of mergers–acquisitions as a way to implement growth strategies is that the organization is "buying" its expanded activities and operations. We want to look next at another mechanism for implementing the growth strategies.

Internal Development

In **internal development**, the organization chooses to expand its operations itself by creating and developing the new business activities from the ground up. In this approach, strategic decision makers believe that they have the necessary resources, distinctive capabilities, and core competencies to "start from scratch." Using internal development, strategic managers choose to internally provide the resources and develop the capabilities needed to meet the desired growth objectives rather than dealing with the risks, aggravations, and

Table 7.3

Possible Defensive Mechanisms Used by Hostile Takeover Targets

- Buys up (repurchases) its stock
- Looks for a friendly merger partner, often referred to as a *white knight*
- Takes on significant amounts of long-term debt that become due and payable if it's acquired, often referred to as a *cyanide pill*
- Calls in government regulators to initiate an antitrust suit
- Staggers the terms (time frames) its board members serve
- Gives current shareholders the right to purchase additional stock at a substantial discount, often called a *poison pill*

General Electric believes that there are growing opportunities in the airport security market. Rather than develop their own expertise in this area, GE's strategic decision makers chose to purchase security firms. GE made its first acquisition in 2002 when it purchased Ion Track, a company that makes devices used to screen carry-on baggage for bombs. To further build on its expertise in this area, in 2004, GE purchased InVision Technologies, the leading manufacturer of bomb detectors that scan passengers' checked bags, for $900 million in cash. One analyst says, "These acquisitions are a win–win situation for both companies" because GE's brand, size and credibility teamed with the acquired companies' technologies should make "an appealing mix to potential customers." Why do you think GE chose acquisitions as its way to grow?

Source: G. Stoller, "GE to pay $900M for Security Firm Invision," USA Today, March 16, 2004, p. 3B.

challenges of combining two or more different organizations. This doesn't mean that there aren't risks, aggravations, and challenges associated with starting a new business. In fact, there are! But, again, with internal development, strategic managers believe that the best way for the organization to expand its operations to achieve growth objectives is to do it themselves.

When would purchasing (mergers or acquisitions) be preferable, and when would doing it yourself (internal development) be preferable? Research has shown that the choice depends on (1) the new industry's barriers to entry, (2) the relatedness of the new business to the existing one, (3) the speed and development costs associated with each approach, (4) the risks associated with each approach, and (5) the stage of the industry life cycle.[18] These factors are summarized in Table 7.4.

Although both mergers–acquisitions and internal development continue to be popular ways to implement the growth strategy, organizations are using some newer approaches. These approaches fall under the category of "strategic partnering," which we'll look at next.

Strategic Partnering

Is it possible for an organization to exploit the benefits of combining operations with other organization(s) to pursue growth objectives while also minimizing the challenges and risks of buying a business or developing one from scratch? Welcome to the world of strategic partnering! Exactly what is **strategic partnering**? It's a situation in which two or more organizations establish a legitimate relationship (partnership) by combining their resources, distinctive capabilities, and core competencies for some business purpose. It's an umbrella term that covers a variety of situations, from loose relationships among partnering organizations to formal legal arrangements among the strategic partners. These cooperative arrangements can be used to implement any of the growth strategies. For instance, an organization may decide to strategically partner with one of its suppliers or

Use Merger–Acquisition When:	Use Internal Development When:	**Table 7.4**
• Maturity stage of industry life cycle • High barriers to entry • New industry not closely related to existing one • Unwilling to accept time frame and development costs of starting new business • Unwilling to accept risks of starting new business	• Embryonic or growth stage of industry life cycle • Low barriers to entry • New industry closely related to existing one • Willing to accept time frame and development costs of starting new business • Willing to accept risks of starting new business	*Mergers–Acquisitions or Internal Development*

distributors (vertical integration), or it may develop a strategic relationship with one of its competitors (horizontal integration) or with an organization in a related industry (related diversification). Rather than buying or internally developing what's needed to expand its operations, an organization's strategic decision makers instead might choose to develop a strategic partnership. The three main types of strategic partnerships are: (1) joint ventures, (2) long-term contracts, and (3) strategic alliances.

In a **joint venture**, two or more separate organizations form a separate independent organization for strategic purposes. In this cooperative arrangement, the strategic partners will typically own equal shares of the new joint venture. A joint venture is often used when the partners do not want to or cannot legally join together permanently. Instead, the partners create this separate entity to perform whatever business activity they're joining together to do. These business activities range from product development to manufacturing or marketing a product or service. Also, a joint venture is a popular partnering method in global growth strategies because it can minimize the financial and political–legal constraints that plague mergers–acquisitions and internal development. For example, a long-running joint venture is the New United Motor Manufacturing Company (NUMMI) formed by General Motors and Toyota in 1984. This joint venture was created to help introduce a new automobile production system into the United States and is still in operation.[19] Another example of a joint venture is the strategic partnership between French hair care and cosmetics group L'Oreal SA and Swiss food group Nestlé SA to develop cosmetic nutritional supplements. The new company, called Laboratoires Inneov, is headquartered in France and makes products aimed at improving the quality of skin, hair, and nails by supplying nutrients essential to their care.[20] Finally, Clorox Company and Procter & Gamble created a joint venture to develop such products as garbage bags and plastic wraps. Both companies provided employees and manufacturing equipment to the venture.[21]

Another type of strategic partnership arrangement is a **long-term contract**, a legal contract between organizations covering a specific business purpose. Long-term contracts typically have been used between an organization and its suppliers. They're often viewed as a variation of vertical integration without the organization having to buy the supplier or internally develop its own supply source. Instead, in this way, the organization locks a supplier into a long-term relationship in which both partners understand the importance of developing resources, capabilities, and core competencies for a sustainable competitive advantage. The organization benefits by having an assured source of supplies that meets its cost and quality expectations. The supplier benefits by having an assured outlet for its supplies. The partners in a long-term contract often find that it's in their best interests to share resources, capabilities, and core competencies in order for both to capture the potential benefits. Again, that's the attraction of the long-term contract as a strategic partnership. The partners recognize and accept that they must work together in order for both to profit.

The last type of strategic partnership we're going to discuss is the **strategic alliance** in which two or more organizations share resources, capabilities, or competencies to pursue some business purpose. You might be thinking that this sounds very similar to a joint venture. In the case of a strategic alliance, however, a separate entity is not formed. Instead, the partnering organizations simply share whatever they need to in order to do whatever they want to do. Most often, strategic alliances are pursued to encourage product innovation, bring stability to cyclical businesses, expand product line offerings, or to cement relationships with suppliers, distributors, or competitors. For example, PepsiCo and Lipton joined together to jointly sell canned iced tea beverages. PepsiCo brought to the alliance its marketing strengths in canned beverages and Lipton brought its recognized tea brand and customer base. Although each organization could have attempted this on its own, the hurdles to developing a sustainable competitive advantage would have been much higher. By combining their strengths, the two partners have dominated this product line. Another example of a strategic alliance would be the partnership arrangement between industrial giants

Why Alliances Make Sense

Companies worldwide are finding ways to build bridges to each other. Although these resulting alliances may not always work, they often make more sense than acquisitions. Here are some reasons why alliances make sense: flexibility and informality of arrangements promote efficiencies; provide access to new markets and technologies; entail less paperwork when creating and disbanding projects; risks and expenses are shared by multiple parties; independent brand identification is kept and can be exploited; working with partners possessing multiple skills can create major synergies; rivals can often work together harmoniously; alliances can take on varied forms from simple to complex; dozens of participants can be accommodated in alliance arrangements; and antitrust laws can protect R&D activities. Do alliances make strategic sense? One expert says that, "The future of business is that fewer companies will succeed by going it alone." What do you think?

Sources: R. D. Ireland, M. A. Hitt, and D. Vaidyanath, "Alliance Management as a Source of Competitive Advantage," Journal of Management, 28, no. 3 (2002), pp. 413–46; E. Krell, "The Alliance Advantage," Business Finance, July 2002, pp. 16–23; D. Sparks, "Partners," Business Week, October 25, 1999, pp. 106–12; and D. Brady, "When Is Cozy Too Cozy?" Business Week, October 25, 1999, pp. 127–30.

Honda Motor and General Electric. The two are teaming up to produce an engine to power a new generation of smaller, lower-cost business jets.[22] As you can see, each partner in a strategic alliance can reap the benefits of expanded operations by contributing to the alliance its unique resources, capabilities, or core competencies.

Strategic partnering arrangements are growing in popularity among organizations.[23] Keep in mind that the intent of all of these types of strategic partnerships—joint venture, long-term contract, and strategic alliance—is to gain the benefits of expanding business operations (growth) while minimizing the drawbacks of buying or internally developing the means to expand. Strategic partnerships should be approached with the same careful preparation and diligence as an acquisition–merger or an internally developed business. There's no guarantee that the hoped-for strategic benefits will be realized using these arrangements, and there's no doubt that trust among all strategic partners is a critical component to making these arrangements successful.[24]

We have now discussed all the ways that an organization can implement its growth strategies. We will next look at the situation when the organization's strategic managers decide that the best organizational direction is to stay as is.

Learning Review

- How can international growth be used in all the other growth strategies?
- Describe the advantages and drawbacks of international expansion.
- Compare and contrast the three approaches an organization can take as it goes global.
- What are the five main ways an organization can pursue global expansion?
- What is a merger? An acquisition? A hostile takeover?
- When are mergers and acquisitions preferable for implementing growth strategies?
- What is internal development? When is it preferable for implementing growth strategies?
- What is strategic partnering?
- Compare and contrast the three types of strategic partnerships.

ORGANIZATIONAL STABILITY

Although it may seem inconceivable that an organization would want to stay as it is, there are times when its resources, distinctive capabilities, and core competencies are stretched to their limits and expanding operations further might risk the organization's competitive advantage. It's at times like these that the organization's strategic managers may decide that it's best for the organization to stay where it is. The **stability strategy** is one in which the organization maintains its current size and current activities and business operations.

When Is Stability an Appropriate Strategic Choice?

When might strategic managers decide that the stability strategy is the most appropriate direction for the organization? One situation might be that the industry is in a period of rapid upheaval with several key industry and general external forces drastically changing, making the future highly uncertain. At times like this, the strategic managers might decide that the prudent course of action is to sit tight and wait to see what happens. This doesn't mean that organizational resources and capabilities would be allowed to deteriorate. Quite the contrary! In order to stabilize and maintain the organization's current position, it's important to keep up levels of investment and commitment in the various business functions or units. The stability strategy doesn't mean slipping backwards, but it also doesn't mean moving ahead. It's simply stabilizing at the current level of operations.

Another situation in which strategic managers might pursue the stability strategy is if the industry is facing slow or no growth opportunities. In this instance, the strategic managers might decide to keep the organization operating at its current levels before making any strategic moves into new industries. This period of stability would allow them time to analyze their strategic options, such as diversification, vertical integration, or even perhaps horizontal integration to address the disadvantages of being in a low- or no-growth industry.

An organization's strategic managers might also choose a stability strategy if it has just completed a frenzied period of growth and needs to have some "down" time in order for its resources and capabilities to build up strength again. For instance, Staples Inc., the office-supply retailer, believed that it was important to open as many stores as possible and proceeded to open 1,500 stores in the United States over a 15-year period, outnumbering its closest rival by more than 400 stores. However, the company pulled back on its store-expansion plans in order to better manage activities and operations at its current level.

STRATEGIC MANAGEMENT
the global perspective

The global beer industry is changing. Beer consumption in the United States and Europe is declining for several reasons, including tougher drunk-driving laws and the growing popularity of wine, wine coolers, and malt-based drinks. At the same time, a number of competitors are flooding the market with new brands, from low-carb beers to Italian and Czech imports. CEO Anthony Ruys of Dutch brewer Heineken wants to push his company out of its "play-it-safe" corporate culture, but is facing external challenges that make it difficult to do so. Do some research on the beer industry. Do you think a stability strategy might be appropriate given the state of the industry? Why or why not?

Source: J. Ewing and G. Khermouch, "Waking Up Heineken," Business Week, September 8, 2003, pp. 68–72.

Strategic Management in Action

Once managers feel they've been able to make the current stores as competitive as possible, they'll look to once again start expanding.

Stability might also be an appropriate strategy for large firms in a large industry that's in the maturity stage of the industry life cycle. In this situation, if profits and other performance results are satisfactory *and* if strategic decision makers are relatively risk averse, they may choose to "stay as they are" rather than pursuing growth.

Finally, whereas most strategic managers in large organizations prefer pursuing growth (and often are rewarded for doing so), many small business owners may follow a stability strategy indefinitely. Why? Because they may feel that their business is successful enough just as it is and that it adequately meets their personal goals.

Although there may be other times when a stability strategy is the most appropriate organizational direction, these are the most common situations. One thing we need to emphasize about the stability strategy is that it typically should be a short-run strategy. Because industry and competitive conditions continue to change while an organization stabilizes, it's important for strategic managers to get the organization's resources, capabilities, and core competencies aligned and strengthened once again so it doesn't lose its competitive position or competitive advantage.

Implementing the Stability Strategy

There's not much to implementing the stability strategy. It primarily involves *not* expanding or increasing the organization's activities or operations. In other words, during stability, the organization won't be doing such things as putting new products out on the market, developing new programs, or adding production capacity. This doesn't mean that organizational resources, capabilities, and core competencies don't change during periods of stability—they just don't expand. In fact, organizations often use the period of stability to assess operations and activities and strengthen and reinforce those that need it. The stability period essentially gives the organization an opportunity to "take a breather" and prepare itself for the return to pursuing growth and the strategic challenges associated with it. For example, at Geon Company, one of the largest global producers of polyvinyl chloride (PVC) resins, the stability strategy was designed to "put it into a position to succeed" in a fiercely competitive market.[25] Once Geon had strengthened its resources, capabilities, and core competencies, it was ready to grow once again, and the company used its position as a leading producer of PVC compounds to set up a merger with M. A. Hanna, forming what is now known as PolyOne Corporation.

As a possible direction for an organization to go, stability can be an appropriate choice. Again, it's important to remember that stability probably should be a short-run strategy. If the organization becomes too complacent, it's susceptible to losing its competitive position. And, if during its period of stability, the organization finds significant organizational weaknesses or that its performance, however measured, is declining, then it may be necessary for the organization to look at a different strategic direction altogether—organizational renewal. That's the next topic we'll discuss.

ORGANIZATIONAL RENEWAL

The popular business periodicals frequently report about organizations that aren't meeting their strategic objectives or whose performance is declining. It's obvious that strategic managers in these organizations have *not* done an effective job of managing strategically and have been *not* been able to develop or exploit a sustainable competitive advantage. The organization is in trouble and something needs to be done or it can't achieve high levels of success; maybe even in the worst-case scenario, it won't survive. Given these circumstances, the organization's situation can be described as declining, and it's important for the

Figure 7.6

Possible Causes of
Corporate Decline

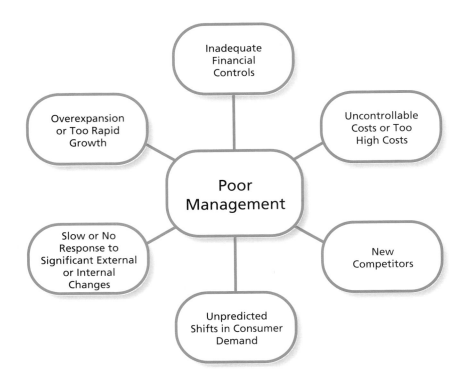

strategic managers to implement strategies that reverse the decline and put it back on a more appropriate path to successfully achieving its strategic goals. The strategies that are used to accomplish this are called **renewal strategies**. In this section, we will discuss two organizational renewal strategies—retrenchment and turnaround—and how these strategies are implemented. Before we get into a discussion of these specific renewal strategies, however, we need to look at some of the possible causes of corporate decline and at indicators of possible decline.

We can say that, generally speaking, an organization's strategic managers don't deliberately make ineffective or inappropriate strategic decisions to cause the organization to decline. However, strategic decisions they do make or strategies they do implement may create conditions that keep the organization from developing or exploiting a sustainable competitive advantage. Without this competitive advantage, it's going to be difficult for an organization to meet its strategic goals and have desirable performance results. What leads to this situation? Figure 7.6 shows the main causes of corporate decline that researchers have identified.[26] As you can see, the main reason behind corporate decline is poor management. In fact, all other causes of decline can be traced back to poor management as well. If strategic managers are inept or incompetent or they don't strategically manage all aspects of the organization, then organizational performance is likely to suffer. And, strategic decisions to overexpand or expand too rapidly indicate poor management judgment. In addition, if the organization has inadequate financial controls or if costs are out of control or too high to be competitive, then strategic managers aren't being effective. Likewise, there's no excuse for not anticipating new competitors or shifts in consumer demand. Strategic managers don't have crystal balls that give them all the answers, but they should—as we discussed in Chapter 3—systematically scan and evaluate the external environment for significant changes and trends. There's no excuse for strategic managers not to be aware of what's happening in their external environment. That's simply poor management! Finally, managers who are slow to respond or who never respond to significant changes in their external and internal situations are doing a poor job of managing strategically. Inertia can be a kiss of death in the competitive environment that most organizations face!

Table 7.5

*Signs of Potential
Performance Decline*

- Excess numbers of personnel
- Unnecessary and cumbersome administrative procedures
- Fear of conflict or taking risk
- Tolerating work incompetence at any level or in any area of the organization
- Lack of clear vision, mission, or goals
- Ineffective or poor communication within various units and between various units

Can strategic managers tell when performance declines might be imminent? Are there certain signals to look for? Yes, there are some signs that the organization might have problems that would require the eventual implementation of renewal strategies.[27] These are listed in Table 7.5. Again, if everyone in the organization is managing strategically and focused on developing and exploiting the organization's competitive advantage, then performance declines shouldn't happen. However, we know that this scenario of perfect strategic management isn't likely or probably even realistic. Even the best-managed organizations sometimes find that performance isn't what was expected and performance results aren't meeting strategic goals. If the organization's overall performance—however it's measured—is declining, then organizational renewal strategies may need to be implemented.

Renewal Strategies

The two main organizational renewal strategies are retrenchment and turnaround. Both are designed to halt the organization's declining performance and return it to more desirable performance levels. Let's look at each more closely.

Retrenchment

The **retrenchment strategy** is a common short-run strategy designed to address organizational weaknesses that are leading to performance declines. In a retrenchment situation, an organization doesn't necessarily have negative financial returns. Although it may have had some time periods when revenues didn't cover expenses, this isn't the typical sign that an organization needs to retrench. Instead, the usual situation in retrenchment is that the organization hasn't been able to meet its strategic goals. Revenues and profits aren't negative but may be declining, and the organization needs to do something to reverse the slide or it soon may face significant performance declines leading to severe financial problems.

The term *retrenchment* is a military term that describes situations when a military unit "goes back to the trenches" in order to stabilize, revitalize, and prepare for entering battle again. That's pretty descriptive of what organizations must do in retrenching. The organization's strategic managers must stabilize operations, replenish or revitalize organizational resources and capabilities, and prepare to compete once again. At a later point, we'll discuss how retrenchment strategies are implemented.

What happens if the organization's circumstances are more serious? What if the organization's profits aren't just declining, but instead there *aren't* any profits, only losses? And, what if other performance results are also significantly low or maybe negative? This type of situation calls for a more drastic strategic response.

Turnaround

The **turnaround strategy** is an organizational renewal strategy that's designed for situations in which the organization's performance problems are more serious. This organization has to be "turned around" or its very survival may be in jeopardy. Some well-known companies that have used a turnaround strategy include Sears, Kmart, Chrysler, Motorola, Mitsubishi, Cray, Intuit, and Apple. In each of these instances, the organization faced severe external and internal pressures and had to make strategic changes in order to remain a viable entity. There's no guarantee that a turnaround strategy will accomplish the desired results and make the organization a strong competitor once again, but without it, the organization is doomed to fail.

How are retrenchment and turnaround strategies implemented? What tools can strategic managers draw on to renew the organization's performance? That's what we want to look at next.

Learning Review

- What is a stability strategy?
- Why might an organization choose a stability strategy?
- Describe how a stability strategy is implemented.
- Why is it important that a stability strategy be a short-run strategy?
- What are renewal strategies?
- Describe the causes of corporate decline.
- Why is poor management the root problem of almost all organizational decline?
- What are some signs that declining performance might be imminent?
- Describe the two organizational renewal strategies.

Implementing Renewal Strategies

Implementing both organizational renewal strategies is primarily dependent on two strategic actions: cutting costs and restructuring. A retrenchment strategy typically does not involve as extensive a use of these actions as a turnaround strategy does. The retrenchment strategy may in fact require only selected cost cutting to get organizational performance back on track. We need to look more closely at these strategic actions.

Cost Cutting

In Chapter 6, we discussed the concept of having low costs or even having the *lowest* costs in the industry as a source of competitive advantage. However, cost cutting as a response to declining performance has little to do with developing a sustainable competitive advantage. Instead, the need to cut costs is approached as a tactic to bring the organization's performance results back in line with expectations. Strategic managers want to avoid severely cutting costs in those critical areas they feel the organization needs to retain or exploit a competitive advantage, however weak that advantage may be. What the organization's strategic managers are trying to do when they cut costs is revitalize the organization's performance (retrenchment) or save the organization (turnaround).

Cost cutting can be across-the-board cuts (implemented in all areas of the organization) or selective cuts (implemented in selected areas). Obviously, in a turnaround strategy, the cuts need to be more extensive and comprehensive.

How will organizations try to cut costs? Strategic decision makers will evaluate to see if there are any redundancies, inefficiencies, or waste in work activities (i.e., in the organization's capabilities) that could be eliminated. They'll also look to see if there are resources that could be eliminated or used more efficiently. For example, UPS found that it could cut costs by over $200,000 annually by changing the light bulbs in the "Exit" signs in its buildings to a lower wattage. That might not seem like a significant amount to an organization whose revenues are in the billions of dollars, but keep in mind that this is just one small cost cut with savings that could be redirected to resources or capabilities that UPS needs for a sustainable competitive advantage or savings that could be applied directly to the bottom line. Either way, the company comes out ahead!

Cost-cutting efforts have paid off in a big way in an organization you wouldn't normally think of—the United States Mint. Henrietta Holsman Fore, head of the U.S. Mint, implemented several changes that are saving the government some serious cash. For example, the amount of time to produce a coin from raw material to final product has been reduced to 62 days—a decline of 80 percent. She also noticed that the agency was spending a lot of money on the pallets used to transport the coins. When she asked why the pallets weren't being reused after shipments were complete, she found that there was no method to track them, so they were often lost. Now, each pallet is numbered and entered into a computer database at every step of the coin-transport process. Not only has this change cut costs, the Mint can now better track coin shipments. During her tenure, the Mint has cut coin production costs by 20 percent and the agency has made money—it returned over $1 billion to the U.S. Treasury in fiscal year 2003. Fore is the first business person to head the agency and says, "Having outside business eyes look at the operation can be very helpful. We're looking at private industry models and seeing what we can learn from them."

Source: B. Hagenbaugh, "Head of U.S. Mint Mines New Ideas to Cut Costs," *Springfield News-Leader*, September 21, 2003, p. 6E.

Generally, if additional cuts are needed to keep performance from declining further, strategic managers may have to look at reducing and eliminating certain work activities or even entire departments, units, or divisions. We'll discuss this type of more severe cost cutting when we get into the restructuring section and look at downsizing as a an implementation option.

Restructuring

Other strategic actions an organization might take as it implements a retrenchment or turnaround strategy involve restructuring its operations. An organization can restructure its operations in a number of ways. In many instances, restructuring involves refocusing on the organization's primary business(es) as it sells off, spins off, liquidates, or downsizes. In fact, organizational refocusing has been found to be the most beneficial form of restructuring an organization can do.[28] Let's look closer at the various ways that an organization can restructure and refocus itself.

One possible strategic action that the organization might take is to sell off one or more of its business units. Frequently, when an organization finds that a business unit isn't performing up to expectations or doesn't fit in with the organization's long-run direction, strategic managers will choose to sell it. The process of selling off a business to someone else where it will continue as an ongoing business is called **divestment**. To whom might an organization sell the business unit? Three possible types of buyers include independent investors, other companies, and the management of the business unit being divested. An example of a divestment to independent investors would be when Investcorp Bank sold Jostens, the largest U.S. supplier of class rings and yearbooks, to a unit of Credit Suisse First Boston. Investcorp's strategy has been to buy out-of-favor companies and hold them for three to seven years, waiting for them to return to popularity and profitability and then selling them for a profit.[29] An example of a divestment to another company is DreamWorks SKG's sale of its music unit, DreamWorks Records, to Universal Music Project. Keep in mind from our earlier discussion of ways to implement corporate growth strategies that one way for organizations to grow is through acquisition. Those acquisitions have to come from somewhere. When one company is acquiring, it means another company has to be selling.

Another possibility for restructuring the organization is to remove a business unit through a **spin-off**, which typically involves setting up the business unit as a separate business through a distribution of shares of stock. For example, Viacom spun off its Blockbuster unit to stockholders after not being able to find a buyer for the company.[30]

H. J. Heinz Company is pretty good at repackaging its products. After all, look at the wide selection of ketchup colors and flavors. The company's strategic managers decided that they needed to repackage the whole company. They decided to spin off their most sluggish units—pet food products, seafood, baby food, and soups, but keep their ketchup, condiments, sauces, frozen foods, and convenience meals. CEO William R. Johnson said that they made the move to "improve its focus." What do you think is meant by this statement? What are the implications for the company's future strategic direction?

Source: J. Eig and R. Frank, "Heinz Spins Off Sluggish Units," Wall Street Journal, June 14, 2002, p. B4.

What happens if there's no buyer for a business unit or if there's no possibility of spinning off the business unit? The only strategic option at that point might be **liquidation**, which is shutting down a business completely. A business unit that's liquidated will not continue as an ongoing, viable business. There may be ways to sell off the business's assets, but that's the only revenue an organization could see from liquidating a business unit. For instance, severe financial problems led textile maker Pillowtex Corporation to liquidate and sell off its plants and other assets. As you can well imagine, liquidation is often the strategic action of last resort. It may be the only option if a turnaround strategy hasn't had the intended effects.

Part of an organization's cost-cutting or restructuring efforts might involve **downsizing**, which is an organizational restructuring in which individuals are laid off from their jobs. Although downsizing can be a quick way to pare costs, simply cutting the number of employees without some type of strategic analysis of where employee cuts might be most beneficial is dangerous.[31] For the organization to be competitive when it eventually emerges from retrenchment or turnaround—if and when that happens—it's important that downsizing be done for the right reasons. In fact, research has shown that downsizing efforts can improve stockholder wealth when they're done for strategic purposes.[32] How can strategic managers ensure their downsizing actions are effective? Table 7.6 lists some recommendations.[33]

The final option we want to discuss for restructuring the organization is the one of last resort: bankruptcy. **Bankruptcy** is the failure of a business and involves dissolving or reorganizing the business under the protection of bankruptcy legislation. It's typically the result of years of significant performance declines where other restructuring or cost-cutting actions have had little effect or have not been implemented effectively. What happens when an organization "goes bankrupt"?

Business bankruptcies were dramatically changed with the passage of the Bankruptcy Reform Act of 1979.[34] This legislative change encouraged firms to reorganize (Chapter 11 bankruptcy) rather than liquidate their assets (Chapter 7 bankruptcy). Therefore, the aftermath of bankruptcy depends on which type of bankruptcy filing is used. An organization in Chapter 7 bankruptcy will have its assets liquidated by the court with the proceeds used

Table 7.6 *Recommendations for Making Downsizing Effective*	• Communicate openly and honestly about needed actions • Clarify goals and expectations before, during, and after downsizing • Eliminate unnecessary work *activities* rather than making across-the-board cuts in *people* • Outsource work if it can be done more inexpensively and more effectively elsewhere • Provide whatever assistance is appropriate to downsized individuals • Counsel, communicate with, and seek input from those employees not downsized • Ensure that those individuals remaining after downsizing know they are a valuable and much-needed organizational resource

to pay off outstanding debts. An organization in Chapter 11 bankruptcy reorganizes its debts and is protected from creditors collecting on their debts until such time that it can emerge from bankruptcy. Although bankruptcy may not be a preferred strategic action, if an organization's turnaround strategy hasn't been effective, it may be the *only* option open to the organization. One other aspect associated with going bankrupt that strategic decision makers should be aware of is the result of fallout from the recent corporate financial scandals. Legislators have debated overhauling business bankruptcy legislation, but so far no final action has been taken on this issue.

We need to clarify a couple of issues regarding the alternatives for implementing organizational renewal strategies. One issue is that these strategic actions typically aren't used one at a time and by themselves. Instead, it's often necessary to use some combination of these alternatives as the organization struggles to regain or develop a sustainable competitive advantage. In fact, most organizations faced with the need to retrench or to do serious restructuring (needed for a turnaround) will look at a coordinated long-run program of strategic actions. Another issue is that while we chose to discuss restructuring and cost-cutting actions in relation to retrenchment and turnaround strategies, organizations *don't* have to be pursuing just these strategies to implement these actions. Strategic managers may choose to use selected cost-cutting or restructuring actions (such as divesting selected business units) even during periods of organizational growth if these strategic actions are viewed as contributing to the organization's development or exploitation of a competitive advantage. That's the important key: Is the organization's competitive advantage(s) enhanced and strengthened with these actions?

You've now been introduced to all the possible corporate strategic directions: organizational growth, organizational stability, and organizational renewal. You should also be familiar with the various options for implementing these strategies. What we need to look at next is how strategic managers evaluate the corporate strategies and make any needed changes.

Learning Review

- What two strategic actions are used in implementing the renewal strategies?
- How could the organization use cost cutting in retrenching? In turnaround?
- Describe organizational restructuring actions.
- What is divestment?
- What are the three possible types of buyers for a business unit?
- How is a spin-off different from divestment?
- Describe liquidation.
- What is downsizing, and how can strategic managers ensure that their downsizing efforts are effective?
- Describe bankruptcy.
- What's the difference between Chapter 7 and Chapter 11 bankruptcy?
- Why are most organizational renewal strategies used in combination?

EVALUATING AND CHANGING CORPORATE STRATEGY

The organization's corporate strategy has been implemented. The competitive strategy and various functional strategies are aligned with the overall direction that strategic managers have chosen for the organization and are being implemented. How do you know it's all working as it should? How do you know whether the corporate strategy has been successful? How could the corporate strategy be evaluated? That's what we're going to discuss in this section.

Evaluating Corporate Strategies

Evaluation is an important part of the entire strategic management process. Without evaluation, strategic managers wouldn't have a clue as to whether the implemented strategies—at any level of the organization—were working. We've discussed the specifics of evaluating the functional and competitive strategies in earlier chapters. Now we need to look at how the corporate strategy is assessed and evaluated. It shouldn't come as a surprise that the tools used in evaluating corporate strategy tend to be broader and encompass the overall performance of the organization rather than just focusing on narrow functional areas. We will look at four main evaluation techniques: (1) corporate objectives or goals; (2) efficiency, effectiveness, and productivity measures; (3) benchmarking; and (4) portfolio analysis.

Corporate Objectives or Goals

The corporate objectives or goals indicate the desired results or targets that strategic managers have established. Although each functional area and each business unit also have goals that are being pursued, the corporate objectives tend to be broader, more comprehensive, and more long run than these others. However, remember that success in meeting the goals at the functional and competitive (business) levels determines whether the corporate goals are met. In other words, the attainment of functional and competitive goals is how the organization ultimately achieves its corporate goals. If the functional and competitive targets aren't being reached, it's impossible for the organization to reach its corporate goals. Again, this simply reflects the inherent interaction and interdependence among the organization's various strategy levels.

What types of corporate goals or objectives might an organization have? Figure 7.7 lists some of the more common organization-wide goals. For a publicly held corporation,

Figure 7.7

Types of Corporate Goals

The Grey Zone

An organization's goals often include being a good corporate citizen by emphasizing ethical and socially responsible decisions and actions. What happens when an organization's values are continually on public display? That's the situation executives at Wal-Mart, the world's largest retailer, face. Wal-Mart, by virtue of its enormous size and reach, has played an unwanted role of national conscience enforcer. Don Soderquist, former senior vice chairman said it best, "The watchword for all of our people is 'Do what is right.' That's what we really preach and teach and we want, but there's so much gray." For instance, handguns were booted off the shelves in 1994, but the company sells hunting rifles as part of its strategy to create a dominant sporting goods department for males. Alcohol isn't sold in traditional Wal-Mart stores, but is sold in its Superstores in locations where it's legal. Wal-Mart clearly articulates its role as an "agent" for the consumer. The company views its job as finding out what customers want and getting those products into stores at the lowest possible cost. What are the ethical implications of this "public display" phenomenon for an organization measuring its performance to see if corporate strategies are effective? *Can* corporate morality be "practical"? *Should* it be practical? Explain your position.

Source: B. Saporito, "Wrestling With Your Conscience," Time, November 15, 1999, pp. 72–73.

maximizing stockholder wealth ranks right at the top of its goals. Why? As the company's legal owners and in exchange for providing capital, the stockholders expect an appropriate return on their investment. However, even not-for-profit, government, and privately held organizations need corporate goals to guide decision making. Don't forget that the goals should reflect the organization's vision, missions, and the overall direction it intends to go.

How are goals used in evaluating corporate strategy? They become the standards against which actual performance is measured. Say, for instance, that a corporate goal is to increase the organization's market share by 1 percent. The evaluation would see if this result happened. It's helpful for corporate goals to be quantified, but that may not always be possible. This doesn't mean that nonquantifiable areas shouldn't be evaluated. Sometimes a qualitative (subjective) assessment can be just as useful in evaluating corporate performance as can a quantitative one. Also, we need to remember that not every organization is expanding operations—that is, not every organization is pursuing growth. Organizations that are using the stability strategy or renewal strategies will have goals that reflect those organizational directions. In these situations, the attainment of those objectives should be evaluated as well.

Efficiency, Effectiveness, and Productivity Measures

Three specific organizational measures that deserve special attention are efficiency, effectiveness, and productivity. Why? They represent the organization's ability to use its limited resources strategically in achieving high levels of corporate performance.

Efficiency is the ability of the organization to minimize the use of resources in achieving organizational goals. **Effectiveness** is the organization's ability to complete or reach goals. **Productivity** is a specific measure of how many inputs it took to produce outputs and is typically used in the production–operations–manufacturing area. It's measured by taking the overall output of goods and services produced, divided by the inputs needed to generate that output.

Although these organizational measures aren't easy to calculate or evaluate, strategic decision makers should attempt to gauge how efficient, effective, and productive the organization is. They should be concerned with getting activities completed so that goals are attained (effectiveness) and doing so efficiently and productively. Because total organizational performance is a result of the interaction of a vast array of work activities at many different levels and in different areas of the organization, these three measures can serve as appropriate assessments of how well or how successfully the organization works *and* how well it's doing at going in the desired corporate direction (growth, stability, or renewal).

Benchmarking

Benchmarking is the search for the best practices from other leading organizations (competitors or noncompetitors) that are believed to have contributed to their superior performance. Whereas the actual process of benchmarking may be useful for implementing strategy, the specific "benchmarks" or best practices can be a standard against which to measure corporate strategy performance. In Chapter 2, we discussed that a world-class organization strives to be the best in the world at what it does. With the benchmarks, an organization's strategic managers can evaluate whether the organization is being strategically managed as a world-class organization and where improvements are needed. Is the overall organizational performance up to the standards of the best in the world? For example, Southwest Airlines studied Indy 500 pit crews, who can change a race car tire in under 15 seconds, to see how their gate crews could make their gate turnaround times even faster. Why benchmark against Indy pit crews? Southwest felt they were the best in the world at incredibly fast turnaround and, as Southwest's strategic managers reasoned, you don't make money sitting on the ground. You've got to have quick ground turnaround time and get the planes back in the air flying passengers to the next location. The benchmark or best practice was a standard against which to measure one aspect of corporate performance.

Portfolio Analysis

The last approach to evaluating corporate performance we're going to look at is portfolio analysis. What's in an organization's "portfolio"? The answer would be the organization's various business units. If the organization has only one business unit, then portfolio analysis would be useless because there's no evaluation or comparison of specific businesses. (We should mention that some single businesses that have multiple brands use portfolio analysis to evaluate those brands, but that's not our focus here.) However, if the organization has multiple business units—in the same or different industries—then portfolio analysis can be used to evaluate corporate performance.

Portfolio analysis is done with two-dimensional matrices that summarize internal and external factors. We're going to focus on three main portfolio analysis approaches: (1) the BCG matrix, (2) the McKinsey–GE stoplight matrix, and (3) the product–market evolution matrix.

The BCG matrix (also known as the growth–share matrix) was created by the Boston Consulting Group as a way to determine whether a business unit was a cash producer or a cash user. It's a simple, four-cell matrix. (See Figure 7.8.) The X axis is a measure of the business unit's relative market share. In a very general sense, market share is a proxy for the business unit's internal strengths and weaknesses. Relative market share is defined as the ratio of a business unit's market share compared with the market share held by the largest rival in the industry. If the ratio is greater than 1.0, then the business unit is said to have high relative market share. If it's less than 1.0, then the business unit has low relative market share. (Note that only if a business unit is the market leader in its industry it will have a

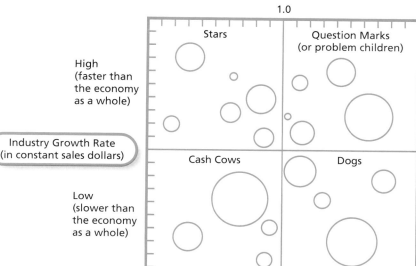

relative market share greater than 1.0.) Some analysts have concluded that this 1.0 figure is too restrictive and have recommended using lower figures such as .75 or even .50.

The *Y* axis is a measure of the industry growth rate. Likewise, in a very general sense, industry growth rate is a proxy for the external opportunities and threats facing the business unit. We want to know whether this industry is growing faster than the overall economy as a whole. If it is, then industry growth rate is evaluated as high. If it's not growing faster, the industry growth rate is low.

Each of the organization's business units would be assessed according to these guidelines and placed in the appropriate cell on the matrix. On the sample BCG matrix shown in Figure 7.8, the circles represent an organization's various business units. The size of the circle corresponds to the size of the business unit, using some measure such as the business unit proportion of total corporate revenues. You can tell from the matrix the relative size of the organization's various business units—some are bigger and some are smaller. The business units are plotted on the matrix according to their scores on relative market share and industry growth rate.

A business unit with low relative market share and low industry growth rate is classified as a *dog*. According to the BCG analysis, a dog offers few growth prospects and in fact may require significant investments of cash just to maintain its position. The strategic recommendation for a business unit evaluated as a dog often is to exit that industry by either divesting or liquidating. However, a strategy of harvesting—that is, gradually letting the business unit decline in a controlled and calculated fashion and using any excess cash flows to support other, more desirable business units—may be an option *if* the business unit is profitable. A business unit with low relative market share and high industry growth rate is classified as a *question mark*. The question marks are low in competitive strengths, but they're in an industry where there's a lot of potential. The recommendation for a business unit evaluated as a question mark is that those with the weakest or most uncertain long-term potential should be divested. Why? Meeting the cash needs of too many business units may spread organizational resources too thinly and result in none being able to achieve star status. However, question marks are easy to sell because of the attractiveness of the industries. Those question marks with more potential should be infused with cash to attempt to turn them into market leaders. A business unit with high relative market share and high industry growth rate is classified as a *star*. Stars are the leading business units in an organization's portfolio. Depending on how competitive the industry is, stars may take significant cash resources to maintain their market leadership position or they may take little cash if they're in an industry where competitive rivalry isn't high. The recommendation for a business unit evaluated as a star is to maintain its strong position while taking advantage of the significant growth opportunities in the industry. Finally, a business unit with high relative market share but low industry growth rate is a *cash cow*. Cash cows are strong cash providers. The positive cash flows from cash cows should be used to support stars and those question marks with potential.

Although the BCG matrix is relatively simple to use, its simplicity is both its biggest advantage and its biggest drawback. The reliance on relative market share and industry growth rate to evaluate a business unit's performance and future potential is an extremely limited view. The fact that the BCG matrix is easy to use and understand is the main reason for its continued popularity as a portfolio assessment tool.

The McKinsey–GE stoplight matrix was developed by McKinsey and Company for General Electric. This nine-cell matrix (shown in Figure 7.9) provides a more comprehensive analysis of a business unit's internal and external factors. In this matrix, the *X* axis is defined as business strength–competitive position. What's included in this analysis? It's more than just relative market share! It includes an analysis of the internal resources and capabilities that are believed by strategic managers to be important for success in this

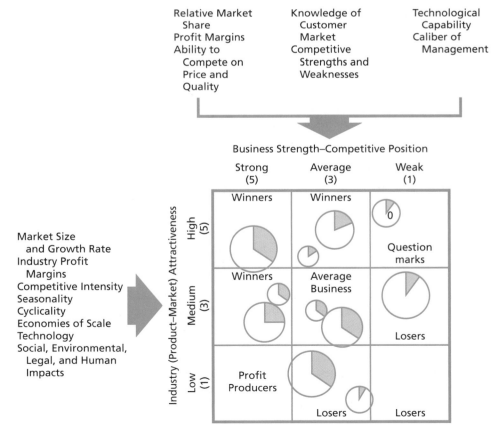

Figure 7.9

McKinsey–GE Stoplight Matrix

Source: *Adapted from Strategic Management in GE, Corporate Planning and Development, General Electric Corporation. Used by permission of General Electric Company.*

Strategic Management in Action

business. For instance, it might include an analysis of economies of scale, manufacturing flexibility, workforce morale, product quality, company image, and so forth—whatever strategic managers think the business needs to be good at to be competitive. The evaluation scale used in this analysis typically ranges from 1 (very weak) to 5 (very strong). The Y axis is defined as industry attractiveness, which again provides a much broader analysis than the BCG's industry growth rate. Industry attractiveness may include such factors as average industry profitability, number of competitors, ethical standards, technological stability of the market, market growth rate, and so forth. Again, strategic managers would use a measurement scale from 1 (very unattractive) to 5 (very attractive) to evaluate the industry a business unit is in. An organization's business units would be plotted on the matrix using these two measures.

As with the BCG matrix, the number of circles on the McKinsey matrix corresponds to the number of business units. In this instance, however, the size of the circle corresponds to the relative size of the industry and the shaded wedge corresponds to the market share held by the organization's business unit. With this matrix, we have a little more information to judge a business unit's position. How should strategic managers evaluate the placement of the business units on the matrix?

The three cells in the lower right-hand corner of the matrix are evaluated as *losers*. These business units have weak competitive position–low industry attractiveness; weak competitive position–medium industry attractiveness; and average competitive position–low industry attractiveness. In the original GE stoplight matrix, these cells were colored "red," indicating that the organization should stop investing in these business units. The three cells in the upper left-hand corner of the matrix are described as *winners*. These business units are evaluated as strong competitive position–high industry attractiveness; strong competitive position–medium industry attractiveness; and average competitive position–high industry attractiveness. As you can probably guess, these cells were colored "green," indicating that the organization should invest in and grow these business units. Finally, the three cells along the diagonal in the matrix are evaluated as question marks (weak competitive position–high industry attractiveness), average businesses (average competitive position–medium industry attractiveness), and profit producers (strong competitive position–low industry attractiveness). These cells were colored "yellow," indicating caution in strategic decisions about these business units. Obviously, the profit producers would be milked for their cash flows with the cash going to support the winners and those question marks with potential to turn into winners.

The McKinsey matrix overcame the problem of simplistic analysis that plagued the BCG matrix tool. However, its main drawback is the subjectivity of the analysis. Because the factors to measure competitive position and industry attractiveness were created by an organization's decision makers, and also because these individuals then rated business units on these factors, there was a risk that the analysis might be too subjective. Another drawback (also shared by the BCG matrix) is that the performance analysis is static. It's similar to what accountants often say about an organization's balance sheet—that it's a snapshot of the performance of business units at one point in time. Unless a series of "snapshots" are taken, strategic managers would have no way to interpret whether or not a business unit's performance is improving or declining. So even though the McKinsey matrix was an improvement over the BCG matrix, it still had its shortcomings.

The product–market evolution matrix was developed by C.W. Hofer and is based on the product life cycle, which serves as the Y axis. The X axis (internal analysis of the business unit) is the competitive position as used in the McKinsey matrix. This matrix is shown in Figure 7.10.

Also, like the McKinsey matrix, the size of the circles corresponds to the relative size of the industry, and the shaded wedge corresponds to the market share of that business unit. Business units are placed on the matrix according to their individual evaluation on

Figure 7.10

Product–Market Evolution Matrix

Source: *John Pearce and Richard Robinson, Strategic Management, 5th ed. (Burr Ridge: IL, Richard D. Irwin, 1994), p. 278.*

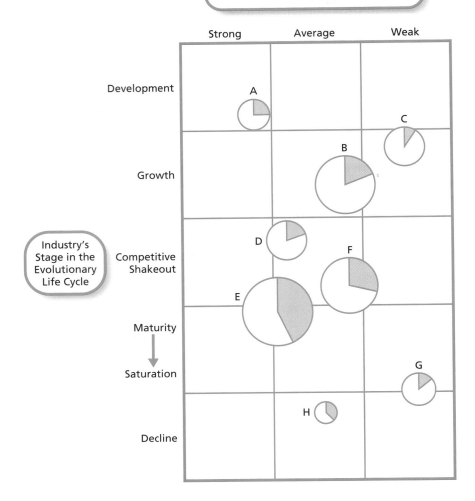

competitive position and stage in the product life cycle. Once all business units are plotted on the matrix, strategic managers have an indicator of the range of business units in various stages of the product life cycle. Say, for instance, that most of the organization's business units were positioned in the maturity or even decline stages. Then the strategic managers should be looking at ways to balance the organization's portfolio with some business units in earlier stages of the life cycle in order to provide long-run potential.

Although Hofer's product–market evolution matrix attempts to provide some semblance of the dynamic nature of an organization's business units by using the product life cycle, it still suffers from the same subjectivity biases as the McKinsey matrix. In addition, many products don't fit nicely and neatly into the industry life cycle, so this particular evaluation tool also has drawbacks that limit its usefulness.

As an evaluation tool, the portfolio matrices do provide a way to assess the performance of the organization's various business units. With this evaluation, an organization's strategic decision makers have information for deciding what to do with the various business units. Should they be supported and strengthened? Should they be sold? Do we need to start looking for businesses to acquire? Because each portfolio analysis technique suffers

Strategic Management in Action

from serious drawbacks, they should be used with caution or at least in conjunction with other strategy evaluation measures.

What happens after evaluating the corporate strategy? If the evaluation indicates that performance results aren't as strategic managers had hoped, then strategic changes are in order.

Changing Corporate Strategies

If the evaluation of corporate strategies shows that they aren't having the intended results—growth objectives aren't being attained, organizational stability is causing the organization to fall behind, or organizational renewal efforts aren't working—then changes are obviously needed. Strategic managers then have to decide whether to act and, if they do, what actions they should take.

If it's determined that changes are needed, they might look at changing the functional and competitive strategies that have been implemented. Perhaps some modifications to those will be enough to bring about the desired results. On the other hand, strategic managers might decide that more drastic action is needed and the corporate direction should be changed. If so, changes might also be necessary in the way the corporate strategy is being implemented. For example, when Microsoft's strategic decision makers realized that the Internet had dramatically altered the world of computing, they did a complete about-face and changed the corporate direction with an all-out focus on this area. What did this corporate strategic change involve? Several actions! Microsoft acquired various Internet and Web start-up companies, reshuffled administrative duties, redesigned software already under development, and basically did what it had to in order to build up its commitment to this new corporate direction.[35] Notice how, in this example, the corporate strategy change affected the organization's functional and competitive strategies as well.

An organization's corporate strategy is important to establishing the overall direction the organization wants to go. As the chapter-opening case illustrated, strategic managers have to understand both the opportunities–threats and the strengths–weaknesses facing the organization in order to design appropriate strategies—ones that will develop or exploit the resources, distinctive capabilities, and core competencies the organization has in its various business units in order to realize a sustainable competitive advantage. Each level of the organization's strategies is linked through this all-encompassing effort to develop a sustainable competitive strategy. Each plays a different, but important, role in this process.

Learning Review

- Why is it important to evaluate corporate strategies?
- What are the four ways to evaluate corporate strategies?
- How would objectives and goals be used in evaluating corporate strategy?
- Differentiate among efficiency, effectiveness, and productivity. How would each be used to evaluate corporate strategy?
- What is benchmarking? How could it be used to evaluate corporate strategy?
- What is an organization's portfolio?
- How is portfolio analysis important as an evaluation tool?
- Describe each of the portfolio analysis matrices including how it's used, the cells in the matrix, and its advantages and drawbacks.
- Why might an organization's corporate strategy need to be changed?
- How might an organization's corporate strategy be changed?

- An organization's **corporate strategy** describes that strategy concerned with the broad and long-term questions of what business(es) the organization is in or wants to be in and what it wants to do with those businesses.

- Deciding on a corporate strategy involves looking at all aspects of the organization, including the other types of strategies and choosing how best to capitalize on what the organization has or how to compensate for what it doesn't in light of critical environmental trends and changes.

- One aspect of corporate strategy that's important to understand is whether the organization is a **single-business organization** (operates primarily in one industry) or a **multiple-business organization** (operates in more than one industry).

- Each of the various types of organizational strategies plays a significant role in whether the organization does what it's in business to do and whether it achieves its strategic goals.

- Coordinating these organizational strategies is critical to managing strategically.

- The corporate strategy can't be implemented effectively or efficiently without the support provided by the organizational resources, capabilities, and core competencies that are developed and used as the competitive and functional strategies are implemented.

- In addition, the competitive and functional strategies that are implemented should support the organization's overall strategic direction as reflected by its choice of corporate strategy.

- The possible corporate strategic directions include moving the organization ahead, keeping the organization where it is, and reversing the organization's decline.

- The corporate strategies associated with these directions are growth, stability, and renewal.

- A **growth strategy** is a corporate strategy that involves the attainment of specific growth objectives by expanding an organization's activities or operations. The five main growth strategies are: concentration, vertical integration, horizontal integration, diversification, and international growth.

- In the **concentration strategy**, the organization concentrates on its primary line of business.

- Possible ways for an organization to concentrate include product–market exploitation (current products–current customers), product development (new products–current customers), and market development (current products–new customers). The new products–new customers option is actually product–market diversification, not concentration.

- In the **vertical integration strategy**, the organization attempts to gain control of its inputs (backward vertical integration) or its outputs (forward vertical integration) or both.

- In **horizontal integration**, the organization expands by combining with other organizations in the same industry (i.e., competitors).

- The **diversification strategy** is a growth strategy in which the organization expands by moving into a different industry.

- Diversification can either be **related diversification** (diversifying into a different industry but one that's related in some way to the organization's current operations) or **unrelated diversification** (diversifying into a completely different industry that has no relationship to the current industry).

- International growth is the last strategic growth option an organization might use.
- It is possible for an organization to "go international" as it concentrates, vertically integrates, horizontally integrates, or diversifies.
- There are three general approaches to international growth.
- The **multidomestic approach** is one in which the organization decentralizes operational decisions and activities to each country in which it is operating and tailors its products and services to each market in order to be highly differentiated.
- The **global approach** is one in which the organization provides more standardized products and uses significantly integrated operations in order to be highly efficient.
- The **transnational approach** is one in which the organization hopes to be both efficient and differentiated by globally integrating operations and tailoring products and services to local markets.
- An organization might choose to pursue global expansion by exporting, importing, licensing, franchising, or direct investment.
- The three main options for implementing corporate growth strategy are mergers and acquisitions, internal development, and strategic partnering.
- A **merger** is a legal transaction in which two or more organizations combine operations through an exchange of stock, but only one organization entity will remain.
- An **acquisition** is an outright purchase of an organization by another. If the organization being acquired doesn't want to be acquired, then it is known as a **hostile takeover**.
- In **internal development**, the organization chooses to expand its operations itself by creating and developing the new business activities from the ground up.
- The choice of internal development or mergers–acquisitions would depend on the new industry's barriers to entry, the relatedness of the new business to the existing one, the speed and development costs associated with each approach, the risks associated with each approach, and the stage of the industry life cycle.
- The **strategic partnering** approach describes a situation in which two or more organizations establish a legitimate relationship (partnership) by combining their resources, capabilities, and core competencies for some business purpose. There are three types of strategic partnerships.
- One type of strategic partnership is a **joint venture** in which two or more separate organizations form a separate, independent organization for strategic purposes.
- Another type of strategic partnership is a **long-term contract** in which two or more organizations establish a long-term legal contract covering a specific business purpose.
- The final type of strategic partnership is the **strategic alliance** in which two or more organizations share resources, capabilities, or core competencies to pursue some business purpose.
- The **stability strategy** is a corporate strategy in which an organization maintains its current size and current activities and business operations. The stability strategy is typically a short-run strategy, although small businesses may pursue it long term.

- The stability strategy might be an appropriate choice if the organization's industry is in a period of rapid upheaval, if the industry is facing slow or no growth opportunities, and if the organization has just completed a frenzied period of growth.

- The stability strategy doesn't mean that organizational resources, capabilities, and core competencies don't change; they just don't expand.

- When organizations aren't meeting their strategic objectives or when performance results are declining, organizational renewal strategies are needed.

- The main reason behind organizational decline is poor management. In fact, all of the other causes of decline (inadequate financial controls, uncontrollable costs or too high costs, new competitors, unpredicted shifts in consumer demand, slow or no response to significant external or internal changes, and overexpansion or too rapid growth) can be traced to poor management.

- A **renewal strategy** is designed to stop an organization's decline and put it back on a more appropriate path to achieving its strategic goals. The two main types of renewal strategies are retrenchment and turnaround.

- The **retrenchment strategy** is a short-run strategy designed to address organizational weaknesses that are leading to performance declines.

- The **turnaround strategy** is designed for situations in which the organization's problems are more serious as reflected by its performance measures.

- Both organizational renewal strategies are implemented through cost cutting and restructuring.

- Cost cutting might be across the board or selective.

- Restructuring involves various actions to refocus the organization.

- **Divestment** is a restructuring action that involves selling off a business unit to someone else where it will continue as an ongoing business.

- A **spin-off** is a restructuring action in which a business unit is set up as a separate business through a distribution of shares of stock.

- **Liquidation** is a restructuring action in which a business unit is shut down completely.

- **Downsizing** is a restructuring action in which individuals are laid off from their jobs.

- The restructuring option of last resort is **bankruptcy** in which a business has failed and is either dissolved or reorganized under the protection of bankruptcy legislation.

- These organizational renewal strategies aren't typically used one at a time and by themselves. It's often necessary for the organization to use some combination of these alternatives as it struggles to regain or develop a competitive advantage.

- In addition, organizations don't necessarily have to be pursuing renewal in order to implement some of these actions. Strategic decision makers may choose to use cost cutting or restructuring at other times, especially if these strategic actions are viewed as contributing to the organization's development or exploitation of a competitive advantage.

- Once the corporate strategy has been implemented, it should be evaluated and changed if necessary. There are four main evaluation techniques.

- One evaluation technique is comparing results against corporate objectives or goals (such as increased market share, increased earnings, strong customer satisfaction, etc.).

- Another evaluation technique involves measuring **efficiency** (the ability of an organization to minimize the use of resources in achieving organizational goals), **effectiveness** (the ability to complete or reach goals), and **productivity** (a specific performance measure typically used in the production–operations–manufacturing area that looks at how many inputs it took to produce outputs).

- **Benchmarking** is another evaluation technique that involves searching for the best practices from other leading organizations (competitors or noncompetitors) that are believed to have contributed to their superior performance.

- Finally, the organization could use portfolio analysis in which it evaluates the performance of the businesses in its portfolio.

- The three main portfolio analysis approaches are the BCG Matrix, the McKinsey–GE stoplight matrix, and the product–market evolution matrix.

- If the evaluation of corporate strategies shows that the strategy isn't having the intended results—growth objectives aren't being attained, organizational stability is causing the organization to fall behind, or organizational renewal efforts aren't working—it may be time to make some changes.

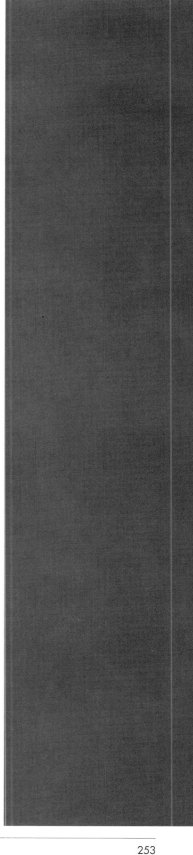

building your skills

1. What were the five largest mergers–acquisitions last year? Make a list of the merger–acquisition partners. What reasons were given for the merger–acquisition? What do you think of each of these strategic actions? Do you think they made strategic sense? Explain.

2. Using the Internet (company's Web site, Hoover's Online, or other Web sites), research each of the companies listed below and answer the following questions:

   a. What corporate strategy(ies) does the company appear to be following? Explain your choice.

   b. Evaluate the company's performance using financial and any other measures you choose.

   c. What changes might you recommend to the company's strategic direction? Explain why you did or did not recommend changes.

   Companies
   Cemex (**www.cemex.com**)
   United Technologies (**www.utc.com**)
   Unilever (**www.unilever.com**)
   Toshiba (**www.toshiba.com**)
   Smith Corona (**www.smithcorona.com**)

3. A company growing at an annual rate of 35 percent will double in size in just two years. A company growing at an 18 percent rate will double in size in four years. A company growing by 12 percent will double in size in six years. Persistent long-term growth is most achievable in moderate rates. Do you agree? Why or why not?

4. Globalization is here to stay. Has it been beneficial for the United States? Here are some of its pluses and minuses:

Pluses of Globalization	Minuses of Globalization
Productivity grows more quickly.	Millions of people have lost jobs due to production shifts abroad.
Global competition and cheap imports keep a lid on prices, holding down inflation.	Millions fear losing their jobs.
An open economy spurs innovation.	Workers face pay-cut demands from employers.
Export jobs often pay more.	Service and white-collar jobs are increasingly vulnerable to moving offshore.
Unfettered capital flows give U.S. access to foreign investment and keep interest rates low.	U.S. employees can lose their comparative advantage.

   What do you think of these statements of globalization pluses and minuses? Do you think globalization is good for a country? Explain.

5. Find examples of each of the types of corporate strategy (i.e., each of the types of growth strategies, stability strategy, and each of the types of renewal strategies). Describe your examples. Be sure to provide your citation information.

6. "The acid test for any corporate strategy is that the company's businesses must not be worth more to another owner." Do you agree with this statement? Explain.

7. Can corporate growth have a downside? Explain. How might these drawbacks be addressed?

8. Research on corporate "bloopers" by Professor Sidney Finkelstein pinpointed reasons why smart executives made bad decisions.[36] Some of these reasons included the following: CEO identifies too closely with his or her company; CEO is too distracted by involvement in personal and social causes; CEO and executive team are so overconfident and aggressive that it's hard to trust them; CEO believes all problems are public relations related and can be handled by putting a "good spin on it"; and CEO missed clear market signals. Find three examples of bad decisions made by executives. Do any of your examples fit under the reasons listed above? What could other organizations learn from these mistakes? What are the implications for an organization's corporate strategy?

9. Companies often grow by doing one or more of the following: boosting capital spending on new technologies, launching new products, entering new markets, increasing marketing, and bolstering R&D.[37] Find an example of each of these. Describe what the company did. Were any strategic goals listed? If so, what was the goal? How might strategic decision makers evaluate the effectiveness of their company's growth strategy?

Strategic Management in Action Cases

CASE #1: A Little Bit of Magic

This Strategic Management in Action Case can be found at the beginning of Chapter 7.

Discussion Questions

1. What examples of corporate strategies do you see in this situation? Explain.

2. What strategic challenges must Lacy deal with?

3. When an organization frequently changes its strategic direction, what problems can arise? (Think in terms of its functional and competitive strategies.)

4. What do you think of Lacy's current strategic initiatives?

5. What corporate strategy evaluation measures might you suggest that the company use? Explain your choices.

6. Update the information on Sears: revenues, profits, number of stores, strategic initiatives.

CASE #2: Time for Bread

From the heartland of America comes bread baked with heart. Panera Bread Company, based in a suburb of St. Louis, operates and franchises more than 550 bakery–cafés in over 35 states under the Panera Bread and St. Louis Bread Company brands. Panera was originally founded in 1981 when CEO Ron Shaich co-founded Au Bon Pain Company, which operated bakery–cafés on the East Coast and internationally.

In late 1993, Shaich met the owners of St. Louis Bread Company, which had 19 bake shops doing about $1 million in lunch business a year. He sensed an opportunity, seeing it as "our gateway into the suburban marketplace and backward into a manufacturing business." Shaich and his management team were looking for a concept that combined Au Bon Pain's quality food with the potential for a broader appeal. After studying the business inside and out, they decided to sell Au Bon Pain Company and purchase the St. Louis Bread Company. Their goal—turn the concept into a national brand under the Panera Bread name.

The management team at Panera (which is Latin for "time for bread") spent considerable time trying to figure out what this new business should look like. They looked at restaurants, coffeehouses, and even retailers in an attempt to understand what it would take to be successful. One thing they discovered was that consumers were tired of the boring sameness of dining-out choices. Shaich said, "Customers are rejecting fast food. They want something better, something special." The new owners knew they would have to eliminate that perception by paying careful

attention to the details. They also used what they had learned from running Au Bon Pain—quality makes a real difference. In Panera's case, that meant making fresh dough every single day in 14 locations and trucking it to the cafés for baking.

Today, Panera is a leader in the quick-casual restaurant business. Its locations, of which more than 70 percent are owned by franchisees, sell custom sandwiches made with artisan breads. And customers can get soups and salads with their sandwiches. After they've eaten, customers also can buy bread, bagels, pastries, and gourmet coffees to go. They've built significant customer loyalty by concentrating on the quality of their fresh-baked breads and other ingredients. In opening new locations, Panera targets suburban areas where real estate tends to be less expensive, the competition tends to be less intense, and their target customers live. The company appears to have tapped into a consumer phenomenon called "trading up," in which middle-class consumers decide to buy better quality new-luxury goods in a few categories that are important to them. Panera's premium sandwiches, bread, and pastries fit into this category. Maybe it really is Panera's "time for bread!"

Discussion Questions

1. What corporate, competitive, and functional strategies is it going to take for Panera to realize its goal of turning the concept into a national brand under the Panera Bread name? Be as specific as possible.

2. How would you recommend Shaich and his management team evaluate whether the company is accomplishing its corporate strategy?

3. *Business Week* listed Panera Bread as one of the hot growth companies of 2003. It's been opening new locations at a pace of about 100 per year since 2002. What problems might arise if the company grows too fast? How might they know if they were growing too fast?

4. The company depends heavily on franchising to fuel its growth. What advantages and drawbacks might that present?

5. What other examples of "trading up" can you think of? What strategic risks are there to such a trend? How can Shaich ensure that Panera doesn't fall victim to those risks?

(*Sources:* P. O'Connell, "The Middle Class's Urge to Splurge," *Business Week Online,* **www.businessweek.com**, December 3, 2003; M. J. Silverstein and N. Fiske, *Trading Up: The New American Luxury* (New York: Penguin Group, 2003); C. Hymowitz, "Panera CEO's Recipe: Learn from the Past, Anticipate the Trends," *Wall Street Journal,* June 10, 2003, p. B1; A. Barrett and D. Foust, "Hot Growth Companies," *Business Week,* June 9, 2003, p. 74–76; J. Suhr, "Panera Knows How to Make the Dough," *Springfield News-Leader,* March 29, 2003, p. 5B; and L. Tischler, "Vote of Confidence," *Fast Company,* December 2002, pp. 110–12.)

CASE #3: Fast Company

What comes to mind when you think of NASCAR? Fast cars, roaring engines, the smell of gasoline, and beer-guzzling spectators? That's the image that Brian France, NASCAR chairman and CEO, wants to change. But will that change keep the company on the fast track or cause a spin out?

NASCAR (National Association for Stock Car Auto Racing) was founded in 1948 by Brian's grandfather, Bill France Sr., as a place for ex-moonshine runners to show off their driving skills. During the early years, France Sr. tirelessly promoted the sport with the help of racetrack owners who wanted to make their stock car races official. The sport grew rapidly in the 1950s and 1960s. Racetrack owners responded by upgrading their facilities and building new paved tracks to replace the older dirt tracks. In 1971, NASCAR signed R.J. Reynolds Tobacco Company as a major sponsor and held the first Winston 500 race in Talladega, Alabama. The first televised race—the Daytona 500—aired on CBS in 1979. Cable sports network ESPN began airing races in 1981. And in 2000, NBC, Fox, and Turner Broadcasting paid the company $2.4 billion for the NASCAR circuit's broadcasting rights until 2006. The untimely deaths of drivers Adam Petty in 2000 and Dale Earnhardt in 2001 only served to heighten the appeal of the sport as exciting and dangerous.

Today, NASCAR is one of the fastest-growing spectator sports in the United States. It runs about 90 races a year in 25 states through three racing circuits: Busch, Craftsman Truck, and the Nextel Cup (formerly the Winston Cup) series. The Nextel Cup alone, with big-name drivers such as Jeff Gordon, Dale Earnhardt Jr., Kyle Petty, and Michael Waltrip, draws more than 7 million race fans each year. Despite the company's success—as a private company, its revenues are estimated at over $3 billion—France realizes that changes may be necessary. The company's top management team has a goal of "making the sport grow in a way that invigorates your hard-core fans and makes it attractive to people who might want to sample racing." And those changes won't be easy. It's a balancing act between managing what's made you successful and managing change.

What are some of these changes? A major one dealt with car and driver safety requirements, especially after the death of Dale Earnhardt. But does making the sport "safer" make it less appealing to the fans who come to experience vicariously in the stands or on television the speed, the danger, and the excitement of going really really fast in a crowd of cars? Other changes the company made included more late-afternoon and night races and the addition of a foreign automaker, Toyota, to the Craftsman Truck series. And it's evaluating a change in the points system whereby drivers' series rankings and earnings are determined—something that hasn't changed since 1975.

What about the company's decision to go after new fans? Kyle Petty, a racing legend, feels that it only makes sense. He said, "If NASCAR feels like they have the Southern white male segment of the market wrapped up, then where are they going to go? They're going to have to go after a Hispanic market. They're going to have to go after a black market. They're going to have to go after an upscale market." NASCAR's ability to do so not only impacts whether it can attract new fans, but also affects its ability to attract new corporate sponsors and advertisers, important contributors to the company's revenues. Making these changes run smoothly won't be easy.

Discussion Questions

1. What strategic challenges do you think Brian France might face as he guides his company? Using what you know about managing strategically, how might he respond to these challenges?

2. Look at the goal the top management team has for the company. What are the implications for corporate strategy? How about for the other strategy levels (functional and competitive)?

3. The success of NASCAR depends on its ability to satisfy the advertisers—sponsors, the drivers, and the customers. What are the implications for the company as it formulates appropriate strategies?

4. What corporate strategy evaluation tools might you recommend for NASCAR? Explain your choices.

5. Update what is happening with NASCAR. What strategic changes has the company made? What impact do these changes appear to be having?

(*Sources:* T. Lowry, "The Prince of NASCAR," *Business Week*, February 23, 2004, p. 90–96; R. Underwood, "Joe Redneck, Meet Eustace Tilly," *Fast Company*, December 2003, p. 36; C. Jenkins, "The Changing Face of NASCAR," *USA Today*, August 29, 2003, p. 1E; and Hoover's Online, **www.hoovers.com**, March 21, 2004.

Endnotes

1. Sears, **www.sears.com**, March 21, 2004; Hoover's Online, **www.hoovers.com**, March 21, 2004; B. Dorfman and E. Kaiser, "Sears CEO Sees Expansion in 2005," *Reuters News Service*, **www.forbes.com**, March 19, 2004; A. Merrick, "Sears Orders Fashion Makeover from the Lands' End Catalog," *Wall Street Journal*, January 28, 2004, p. A1; A. Tsao, "Web Synergies Pay Off," *Business Week Online*, November 3, 2003; R. Berner, "Sears: The Silent Partner Who's Making Himself Heard," *Business Week*, August 11, 2003, p. 38; and R. Berner, "The Struggle in Store for Sears," *Business Week Online*, July 24, 2003.

2. The discussion of these concentration strategy options has been slightly modified from information found in P. Kotler, *Marketing Management* (Upper Saddle River, NJ: Prentice Hall, 2000), pp. 74–75.

3. Beckman Coulter, **www.beckmancoulter.com**, March 21, 2004; and B. Upbin, "What Have You Invented for Me Lately?" *Forbes*, December 16, 1996, pp. 330–34.

4. Bose, **www.bose.com**, March 21, 2004; and W. M. Bulkeley, "How an MIT Professor Came to Dominate Stereo Speaker Sales," *Wall Street Journal*, December 31, 1996, p. A1.

5. R. A. D'Aveni and A. V. Illinitch, "Complex Patterns of Vertical Integration in the Forest Products Industry: Systematic and Bankruptcy Risk," *Academy of Management Journal*, 35 (1992), pp. 596–625; J. B. Quinn, T. L. Doorley, and P. C. Paquette, "Technology in Services: Rethinking Strategic Focus," *Sloan Management Review*, 31, no. 2 (1990), pp. 79–87; R. E. Miles and C. C. Snow, "Organizations: New Concepts for New Forms," *California Management Review*, 28, no. 3 (1986), pp. 62–73; K. R. Harrigan, "Strategies for Intrafirm Transfers and Outside Sourcing," *Academy of Management Journal*, 28 (1985), pp. 914–25; K. R. Harrigan, *Strategies for Joint Ventures* (Lexington, MA: Heath & Lexington Books, 1985); R. P. Rumelt, "Diversification Strategy and Profitability," *Strategic Management Journal*, 3 (1982), pp. 359–70; and R. P. Rumelt, *Strategy, Structure and Economic Performance* (Cambridge, MA: Harvard University Press, 1974).

6. J. T. Mahoney, "The Choice of Organizational Form: Vertical Ownership versus Other Methods of Vertical Integration," *Strategic Management Journal*, 13 (1992), pp. 559–84; M. K. Perry, "Vertical Integration: Determinants and Effects," in R. Schmalansee and R. D. Willig, eds., *Handbook of Industrial Organization* (New York: Elsevier Science, 1989), vol. 1, pp. 185–255; G. R. Jones and C. W. L. Hill, "Transaction Cost Analysis of Strategy-Structure Choice," *Strategic Management Journal*, 9 (1988), pp. 159–72; M. H. Riordan and D. E. M. Sappington, "Information, Incentives, and Organizational Mode," *Quarterly Journal of Economics*, 102 (1987), pp. 243–63; M. K. Perry and R. H. Groff, "Resale Price Maintenance and Forward Integration into a Monopolistically Competitive Industry," *Quarterly Journal of Economics*, 100 (1985), pp. 1293–1311; S. C. Salop and D. T. Scheffman, "Raising Rivals' Costs," *American Economic Review*, 73 (1983), pp. 267–71; K. R. Harrigan, *Strategies for Vertical Integration* (Lexington, MA: Heath & Lexington Books, 1983); F. M. Westfield, "Vertical Integration: Does Product Price Rise or Fall?," *American Economic Review*, 71 (1981), pp. 334–46; M. A. Porter, *Competitive Strategy: Techniques for Analyzing Industries and Competitors* (New York: Free Press, 1980); M. K. Perry, "Forward Integration by Alcoa: 1888–1930," *Journal of Industrial Economics*, 29 (1980), pp. 159–70; O. E. Williamson, "The Vertical Integration of Production: Market Failure Considerations," *American Economic Review*, 61 (1971), pp. 112–23; J. M. Vernon and D. A. Graham, "Profitability of Monopolization by Vertical Integration," *Journal of Political Economy*, 79 (1971), pp. 924–25; J. S. Bain, *Barriers to New Competition* (Cambridge, MA: Harvard University Press, 1956); and G. J. Stigler, "The Division of Labor Is Limited by the Extent of the Market," *Journal of Political Economy*, 59 (1951), pp. 185–93.

7. R. D'Aveni and D. J. Ravenscraft, "Economies of Integration versus Bureaucracy Costs: Does Vertical Integration Improve Performance," *Academy of Management Journal*, October 1994, pp. 1167–1206.

8. The Associated Press, "Journey Back With New Album, Tour Plans," *Springfield News-Leader*, January 21, 1997, p. 5B.

9. F. Balfour, "Promises Aren't Enough," *Business Week Asia Online*, May 28, 2001; and E. A. Gargan, "From Chickens to Chemicals," *New York Times*, November 14, 1995, p. D1.

10. L. E. Palich, G. R. Carini, and S. L. Seaman, "Internationalization as a Moderator in the Diversification–Performance Relationship: An Empirical Assessment," *Academy of Management Proceedings on CD-Rom*, August 1996; I. Goll and R. B. Sambharya, "Corporate Ideology, Diversification and Firm Performance," *Organization Studies*, 16, no. 5 (1995), pp. 823–46; C. C. Markides and P. J. Williamson, "Related Diversification, Core Competencies, and Corporate Performance," *Strategic Management Journal*, 15 (1994), pp. 149–165; H. Singh and C. A. Montgomery, "Corporate Acquisition Strategies and Economic Performance," *Strategic Management Journal*, 8, no. 4 (1987), pp. 377–86; K. Palepu, "Diversification Strategy, Profit Performance, and the Entropy Measure," *Strategic Management Journal*, 6, no. 3 (1985), pp. 239–55; D. J. Lecraw, "Diversification Strategy and Performance," *Journal of Industrial Economics*, 33, no. 2 (1984), pp. 179–98; R. A. Bettis, "Performance Differences in Related and Unrelated Diversified Firms," *Strategic Management Journal*, 2, no. 4 (1981), pp. 379–93; R. Rumelt, "Diversification Strategy and Profitability"; and H. I. Ansoff, *Corporate Strategy* (New York: McGraw-Hill, 1965).

11. L. Palich, G. R. Carini, and S. L. Seaman, 1996; R. B. Sambharya, "The Combined Effect of International Diversification and Product Diversification Strategies on the Performance of U.S.-based Multinational Corporations," *Management International Review*, 35, no. 3 (1995), pp. 197–218; V. L. Blackburn, J. R. Lang, and K. H. Johnson, "Mergers and Shareholder Returns: The Roles of Acquiring Firms' Ownership and Diversification Strategy," *Journal of Management*, December 1990, pp. 769–82; B. W. Keats, "Diversification and Business Economic Performance Revisited: Issues of Measurement and Causality," *Journal of Management*, March 1990, pp. 61–72; and A. Seth, "Value Creation in Acquisitions: A Re-examination of Performance Issues," *Strategic Management Journal*, February 1990, pp. 99–115.

12. J. Birkinshaw, A. Morrison, and J. Hulland, "Structural and Competitive Determinants of a Global Integration Strategy,"

Strategic Management Journal, 15 (1995), pp. 637–55; J. F. Bolt, "Competitors: Some Criteria for Success," Business Horizons, January–February 1988, pp. 34–41; and B. S. Chakravarthy and H. V. Perlmutter, "Strategic Planning for a Global Business," Columbia Journal of World Business, Spring 1985, pp. 3–10.

13. C. A. Bartlett and S. Ghosal, Managing Across Borders: The Transnational Solution (Boston: Harvard Business School Press, 1989); and S. Ghoshal, "Global Strategy: An Organizing Framework," Strategic Management Journal, 8 (1987), pp. 425–440.

14. F. Arner and C. Palmeri, "Overseas Adventure for U.S. Toys," Business Week, November 3, 2003, p. 12.

15. J. Esty, "One Pizza, United . . . but Open to Interpretation," Fast Company, February 2004, p. 32.

16. R. Narisetti, "Can Rubbermaid Crack Foreign Markets?" Wall Street Journal, June 20, 1996, p. B1.

17. D. Henry, "Mergers: Why Most Big Deals Don't Pay Off," Business Week, October 14, 2002, pp. 60–70; M. Arndt, "How Companies Can Marry Well," Business Week, March 4, 2002, p. 28; L. Capron, "Historical Analyses of Three Waves of Mergers and Acquisitions in the United States: Triggering Factors, Motivations, and Performance," Academy of Management Proceedings on CD-Rom, August 1996; and M. H. Lubatkin and P. J. Lane, "Psst . . . the Merger Mavens Still Have It Wrong," Academy of Management Executive, February 1996, pp. 21–39.

18. P. Haspeslagh and D. Jemison, Managing Acquisitions (New York: Free Press, 1991); E. R. Biggadike, Corporate Diversification: Entry, Strategy, and Performance (Cambridge, MA: Division of Research, Harvard Business School, 1983); G. S. Yip, "Diversification Entry: Internal Development versus Acquisition," Strategic Management Journal, 3 (1982), pp. 331–45; M. S. Salter and W. A. Weinhold, Diversification Through Acquisition: Strategies for Creating Economic Value, (New York: Free Press, 1979); and H. L. Ansoff, Corporate Strategy (New York: McGraw-Hill, 1965).

19. "Happy 20th Birthday, NUMMI," Industry Week, March 2004, p. 15.

20. "L'Oreal, Nestle Team Up on Product Line," Springfield News-Leader, June 26, 2002, p. 6B.

21. "Clorox, P&G to Form Joint Venture," Wall Street Journal, November 15, 2002, p. A10.

22. C. Woodyard, "Honda, GE Build New Jet Engine," USA Today, February 17, 2004, p. 1B.

23. R. D. Ireland, M. A. Hitt, and D. Vaidyanath, "Alliance Management as a Source of Competitive Advantage," Journal of Management, 28, no. 3 (2002), pp. 413–46; E. Krell, "The Alliance Advantage," Business Finance, July 2002, pp. 16–23; C. Ellis, "Making Strategic Alliances Succeed," Harvard Business Review, July–August 1996, pp. 8–9; C. M. Brown, "Partnering for Profit," Black Enterprise, June 1995, p. 43; R. Maynard, "Striking the Right Match," Nation's Business, May 1995, pp. 18–28; Roundtable Discussion, "Strategic Partnering," Chief Executive, November 1995, pp. 52–62; D. E. Gumpert, "Business 2000: Partnerships for Success," Inc., December 1995, pp. 133–46; N. Templin, "More and More Firms Enter Joint Ventures with Big Competitors," Wall Street Journal, November 1, 1995, p. A1; N. S. Levinson and M. Asahi, "Cross-National Alliances and Interorganizational Learning," Organizational Dynamics, Autumn 1995, pp. 50–63; and J. Bleeke and D. Ernst, "Is Your

Strategic Alliance Really a Sale?" Harvard Business Review, January–February 1995, pp. 97–105.

24. S. Parise and A. Casher, "Alliance Portfolios: Designing and Managing Your Network of Business–Partner Relationships," Academy of Management Executive, November 2003, pp. 25–39; Ireland, Hitt, and Vaidyanath, "Alliance Management as a Source of Competitive Advantage"; M. Kotabe and K. S. Swan, "The Role of Strategic Alliances in High Technology New Product Development," Strategic Management Journal, 16 (1995), pp. 621–36; J. B. Barney and M. H. Hansen, "Trustworthiness: Can It Be a Source of Competitive Advantage?" Strategic Management Journal, 15, Special Issue (1994), pp. 175–203; and C. W. L. Hill, "Cooperation, Opportunism, and the Invisible Hand: Implications for Transaction Cost Theory," Academy of Management Review, 15, 1990, pp. 500–13.

25. M. A. Verespej, "Stability before Growth," Industry Week, April 15, 1996, pp. 12–16.

26. See C. Siafter, Corporate Recovery: Successful Turnaround Strategies and Their Implementation (Hammondsworth, England: Penguin Books, 1984); R. C. Hoffman, "Strategies for Corporate Turnarounds: What Do We Know About Them?" Journal of General Management, 14 (1984), pp. 46–66; D. Schendel, G. R. Patton, and J. Riggs, "Corporate Turnaround Strategies: A Study of Profit Decline and Recovery," Journal of General Management, 2 (1976), pp. 1–22; and J. Argenti, Corporate Collapse: Causes and Symptoms (New York: McGraw-Hill, 1976).

27. P. Lorange and R. T. Nelson, "How to Recognize—and Avoid—Organizational Decline," Sloan Management Review, Spring 1987, pp. 41–48.

28. C. C. Markides, "Diversification, Restructuring, and Economic Performance," Strategic Management Journal, February 1995, pp. 101–18; W. W. Lewis, "Strategic Restructuring: A Critical Requirement in the Search for Corporate Potential," in M. L. Rock and R. H. Rock, eds., Corporate Restructuring (New York: McGraw-Hill, 1990), pp. 43–55; and "Shifting Strategies: Surge in Restructuring is Profoundly Altering Much of U.S. Industry," Wall Street Journal, August 12, 1985, p. 1.

29. The Associated Press, "Ring-Maker Jostens Sold to Credit Suisse First Boston Unit," USA Today, www.usatoday.com, June 19, 2003.

30. M. McCarthy, "Viacom Plans Blockbuster Spinoff for Shareholders," USA Today, February 11, 2004, p. IB.

31. G. D. Bruton, J. K. Keels, and C. L. Shook, "Downsizing the Firm: Answering the Strategic Questions," Academy of Management Executive, May 1996, pp. 38–45; and W. McKinley, C. M. Sanchez, and A. G. Schick, "Organizational Downsizing: Constraining, Cloning, and Learning," Academy of Management Executive, August 1995, pp. 32–44.

32. D. L. Worrell, W. M. Davidson, and V. M. Sharma, "Layoff Announcements and Stockholder Wealth," Academy of Management Journal, 34 (1991), pp. 662–78.

33. Numerous articles have been written on organizational downsizing. Here are some of the most informative: A series of articles on "The Downsizing of America" can be found in the New York Times, March 1996; S. Greengard, "Don't Rush Downsizing: Plan, Plan, Plan," Personnel Journal, November 1993, pp. 64–72; W. F. Cascio, "Downsizing: What Do We Know? What Have We Learned?" Academy of Management Executive, February 1993,

p. 96; K. S. Cameron, S. J. Freeman, and A. K. Miskra, "Best Practices in White-Collar Downsizing: Managing Contradictions," *Academy of Management Executive*, August 1991, pp. 57–73; R. Henkoff, "Cost Cutting: How To Do It Right," *Fortune,* April 9, 1990, pp. 40–49; and D. A. Heenan, "The Downside of Downsizing," *Journal of Business Strategy,* November–December 1989, pp. 18–23.

34. Y. Chen, J. F. Weston, and E. I. Altman, "Financial Distress and Restructuring Models," *Financial Management*, Summer 1995, pp. 57–75; J. P. Sheppard, "Strategy and Bankruptcy: An Exploration into Organizational Death," *Journal of Management*, 20, no. 4 (1994), pp. 795–833; and C. M. Daily,

"Bankruptcy in Strategic Studies: Past and Promise," *Journal of Management*, 20, no. 2 (1994), pp. 263–295.

35. J. Markoff, "Tomorrow, the World Wide Web," *New York Times*, January 16, 1996, p. C1; and K. Rebello, "Inside Microsoft," *Business Week*, July 15, 1996, pp. 56–67.

36. S. Finkelstein, *Why Smart Executives Fail and What You Can Learn from Their Mistakes* (New York: Penguin Books, 2003); and J. Merritt, "The ABCs of Failure," *Business Week*, June 9, 2003, p. 126.

37. M. Arndt, S. Hamm, S. Rosenbrush, and C. Edwards, "Signs of Life," *Business Week*, July 14, 2003, pp. 32–34.

8

Strategic Management in Other Organization Types

LEARNING OUTLINE

Small Businesses and Entrepreneurial Ventures

- *Differentiate between a small business and an entrepreneurial venture.*

- *Explain why small businesses and entrepreneurial ventures are important.*

- *Describe how the strategic management process is used in small businesses and entrepreneurial ventures.*

- *Discuss the special strategic issues facing small businesses and entrepreneurial ventures.*

Not-for-Profit and Public Sector Organizations

- *Define not-for-profit organization and public sector organization.*

- *Describe the various types of not-for-profit organizations.*

- *Describe how the strategic management process is used in not-for-profit and public sector organizations.*

- *Discuss the special strategic issues facing not-for-profit and public sector organizations.*

- *Describe the unique strategies developed by not-for-profit organizations.*

The Sky's the Limit

It's been described as the future "checker cab of the skies." Eclipse Aviation of Albuquerque, New Mexico, aims to change the face of aviation with its Eclipse 500 aircraft.[1] Founded by Vern Raburn, (a former Microsoft executive who was president of Microsoft's consumer products division), Eclipse Aviation's CEO is an air buff and a pilot. His company is using revolutionary propulsion, manufacturing, and electronics systems to produce aircraft that cost less than a third of today's small jet aircraft and that are significantly safer and easier to operate. In addition, these jets will have the lowest cost of ownership ever achieved in a jet aircraft. Eclipse's goal is to make air travel "personal" by making it possible for passengers to move directly between cities on a quick, affordable, and convenient basis rather than having to rely on the big airlines' scheduled services. That dream is embodied in the Eclipse 500, the company's twin-engine microjet. This six-seater will be able to go about 400 miles per hour and will have a flight range of approximately 1,500 miles.

What has made Eclipse's dream possible is a handful of technological breakthroughs, the most critical being an engine that has the highest thrust-to-weight ratio of any commercial jet on the market. Also, in building the aircraft, Eclipse has pioneered the use of innovative manufacturing processes that speed production and lower costs. For instance, technologies such as friction stir welding, which replaces more than 60 percent of the rivets in assembling the aircraft, dramatically reduces assembly time while producing stronger (and safer) joints on the aluminum aircraft. That aluminum skin is also an innovation that will save manufacturing costs. Raburn also chose to merge navigation and weather systems into digital displays and to replace the units that control the plane's flaps and gears with computers that do it at a fraction of the weight. Estimated operating costs for the jet are just 56 cents per mile, compared with $1.75 per mile for the Cessna CJ1, the plane's closest competitor. And at a selling price of $1 million, the Eclipse costs about a fourth of what the CJ1 does.

Bringing the Eclipse 500 to life has been the result of several partnerships with other organizations. For instance, Avidyne Corporation of Lincoln, Massachusetts, is supplying avionics and integrated electronics for the jet. Some other partners include Autronics, a division of Curtiss-Wright, which will supply the aircraft's computer system, and Crossbow Technology, which will provide the attitude and heading reference system. However, not all of Eclipse's initial partners are still partners. The plane's engines originally were to be supplied by Williams International, but Eclipse dropped them as a supplier in late 2002 after discovering reliability and power problems with the engine during test flights of the first preproduction plane. Pratt & Whitney has since become the engine supplier. And supplier BAE Systems was dropped in late 2003 when it could not meet its commitments to Eclipse.

Assembly of the Eclipse 500 began in May 2004, with the first test flights scheduled for the end of 2004 and most of 2005. The delivery of the first Eclipse 500 jets to customers will begin in 2006. Vern Raburn's vision of helping bring corporate jets to the masses seems to be opening up lots of opportunities where, perhaps, the sky's the limit.

The story of Eclipse Aviation's progress from vision to actual flight illustrates how strategic management and managing strategically can be applied and are important in unique types of organizations. Vern Raburn's recognition of environmental opportunities, his strategic plan for targeting a mass aviation market, and the venture's use of strategic partnerships are all examples of strategic management in action in an entrepreneurial venture. Although we may have a tendency to think of competitive advantage, internal and external analysis, strategy formulation, and strategy implementation as important concepts for large business organizations, the fact is that strategic management is important for all types and sizes of organizations. Although we've used examples of not-for-profit and other types of organizations in previous chapters as we discussed various strategy topics, in this chapter we want to focus exclusively on what it means to manage strategically in these unique types of organizations—that is, organizations that aren't your large business corporations. Why do we need to look at these organizations separately? The best answer is that these organizations may face unique types of challenges and issues when managing strategically. Yet, it's still important for them to think and manage strategically.

In this chapter, we'll examine three "other" types of organizations: small businesses and entrepreneurial ventures, not-for-profits, and public sector organizations. First, we'll look at small businesses and entrepreneurial ventures. What role does strategic management play in these organizations, how is it used, and what types of unique strategic issues do these organizations specifically have to deal with both in the initial start-up phase and as they grow? Then, we'll look at the broad category of not-for-profit organizations, including public sector organizations. Again, we'll examine the role strategic management plays, how it's used, and the unique issues that strategic decision makers in these organizations might have to deal with.

SMALL BUSINESSES AND ENTREPRENEURIAL VENTURES

In this section, we want to look at the process of managing strategically in small businesses and entrepreneurial ventures. Before we can do that, however, we need to know what these organization types are, how they're the same, and how they're different.

What Is a Small Business and What Is an Entrepreneurial Venture?

Although you may think these two organizational types are the same, there *are* some important differences that might influence the process of managing strategically and strategic decisions and actions. Let's look first at what a small business is.

What constitutes a "small" business? There is no universally accepted definition of a small business, but most definitions use some measure of number of employees or annual revenues. Also, the Small Business Administration (SBA), an agency of the U.S. government that provides assistance and loans to small businesses, has different definitions for a small business depending on what industry it's in. For instance, the cutoff point for a "small" business in the office machinery manufacturing industry is 1,000 employees, whereas in the confectionery wholesalers industry, it's 100 employees.[2]

We're going to define a **small business** as one that is independently owned, operated, and financed; has fewer than 100 employees; doesn't engage in any new marketing or innovative practices; and has relatively little impact on its industry.[3]

The whole idea of entrepreneurship involves the discovery of opportunities and the resources to exploit them.[4] We're going to define an **entrepreneurial venture** as a business that is characterized by innovative strategic practices and that has profitability and growth as its main goals.[5] Obviously, some definitional and actual overlap exists between small businesses and entrepreneurial ventures, but we're going to look at them as two different organizational types. A small business isn't necessarily entrepreneurial in nature just because it's small. To be entrepreneurial means being innovative and seeking out new opportunities—being willing to take risks. Although entrepreneurial ventures may start small, they do pursue growth. Some new small firms may grow, but many will remain small businesses.

To summarize, small businesses and entrepreneurial ventures differ in a number of ways, primarily with regards to their perspective on growth and innovation. These differences are summarized in Table 8.1.

At this point, you may be asking yourself why we're emphasizing small businesses and entrepreneurial ventures as "special" types of organizations. The fact is that both small businesses and entrepreneurial ventures play an important role in the global economy.

Why Are These Types of Organizations Important?

Using any number of sources, you can find statistics on how many small businesses there are, how many workers they employ, and how much of the gross national economic output they're responsible for. The headlines boast the facts: small businesses represent over 99 percent of all employers, employ 51 percent of all private workers, account for 51 percent of the nonfarm private-sector output, and are responsible for virtually all new jobs.[6] The importance of small businesses and entrepreneurial ventures can be shown in three areas: job creation, the number of new start-ups, and innovation.

Job Creation

How important are small businesses and entrepreneurial ventures to job creation? Statistics collected by the SBA show that small firms generate 60 to 80 percent of all net new jobs annually.[7] And, the creation of jobs by small businesses is expected to continue into the future as new firms start small and grow.[8]

Small Business	Entrepreneurial Venture
• Independently owned, operated, and financed • Fewer than 100 employees • Doesn't emphasize new or innovative practices • Little impact on industry	• Innovative strategic practices • Strategic goals are profitability and growth • Seeks out new opportunities • Willingness to take risks

Table 8.1

Characteristics of Small Business versus Entrepreneurial Venture

The Number of New Start-ups

Entrepreneurship is, and continues to be, important to every industry sector in the United States and in other global economies. The number of new start-ups continues to be high, probably for a couple of reasons. First, continual changes in the external environment—competition, technology, customer desires, and so forth—provide a fertile climate for small businesses and entrepreneurial ventures because these organizations are often better able to respond quickly to changing conditions than are larger, more bureaucratic, and less flexible organizations. Second, many of the cost advantages that large organizations traditionally had because of their size (i.e., economies of scale) have been eroded and diminished by advances in technology. This means that small businesses and entrepreneurial ventures can compete against the larger organizations and aren't at a disadvantage because of their small size.

How many new start-ups are there? In 1970, some 264,000 new businesses were launched.[9] In 1995, almost 600,000 new businesses were started. The latest figures show over 550,000 new business formations in 2002.[10] Add these new start-ups to the large number of small businesses already operating (estimated at 5.4 million employer firms), and you can begin to understand the economic importance of small business and entrepreneurial ventures.

Innovation

Finally, you can understand the importance of small businesses and entrepreneurial ventures when you see their role in innovation. Innovation is a process of creating, changing, experimenting, transforming, and revolutionizing. As we know from our earlier definition, innovation is one of the key distinguishing characteristics of entrepreneurial ventures. The "creative destruction" process of innovation leads to technological changes and employment growth.[11] Entrepreneurial firms are an essential source of new and unique ideas that might otherwise go untapped.[12] Statistics back up this assertion. New entrepreneurial organizations generate 24 times more innovations per research and development dollar

Global Entrepreneurship Monitor (GEM)

What about entrepreneurial activity outside the United States? How extensive is it and what kind of impact has it had? An annual assessment of global entrepreneurship called the Global Entrepreneurship Monitor (GEM) studies the impact of entrepreneurial activity on economic growth in various countries. The GEM 2003 Report covered 40 countries that were divided into five groups based on their level of entrepreneurial activity. These five groups, ranked from the most entrepreneurial (Group A) to least entrepreneurial (Group E), were as follows:

Group A: Chile, Korea, New Zealand, Uganda, Venezuela

Group B: Brazil, China, India, Mexico

Group C: Argentina, Australia, Canada, Denmark, Finland, Hong Kong, Hungary, Iceland, Ireland, Slovenia, Spain, Singapore, Thailand, United Kingdom, United States.

Group D: Belgium, Germany, Greece, Israel, Italy, Norway, South Africa, Sweden, Switzerland

Group E: Chinese Taipei (Taiwan), Croatia, France, The Netherlands, Japan, Russia, Poland

Why are these findings important? The GEM researchers point to three consequences that they found entrepreneurial activity can have for a country: the absolute scope of effort devoted to entrepreneurial activities, the impact on job creation, and the relationship between entrepreneurial activity and national economic growth.

Source: "Global Entrepreneurship Monitor: 2003 Executive Report," GEM Consortium, www.gemconsortium.org, March 24, 2004.

strategic MANAGERS *in action*

Jay Sorensen is the founder of Java Jacket. In 1991, he pulled into a drive-through gourmet coffee bar in Portland and then spilled the coffee in his lap as he drove away. He thought to himself that there had to be a better way. So he started playing around with some embossed paper towels. Eventually, he talked to some paper converters about making insulated sleeves from waffle-textured chipboard that could be placed around the paper coffee cups.

Jay believed that coffee-to-go wasn't a fad, so he proceeded to pursue his invention—an insulated paper sleeve for coffee cups. It proved to be a good decision. Today, his company's annual revenues are estimated at between $4 million and $5 million.

Sources: C. Canabou, "Fast Talk," *Fast Company*, February 2004, p. 45; and Hoover's Online, **www.hoovers.com**, March 24, 2004.

spent than do *Fortune* 500 organizations, and they account for over 95 percent of new and "radical" product developments.[13] And a study by the SBA's Office of Advocacy found that small firms represented 40 percent of the highly innovative firms in a 2002 sample (as opposed to 33 percent in 2000).[14]

There's no doubt that small businesses and entrepreneurial ventures play a significant role in the U.S. economy and the global economy. And their economic importance will continue. That's why we need to look at what it means to manage strategically in these types of organizations. Both types of business organizations face unique strategic challenges. Before we look at these unique issues, though, we need to discuss how the strategic management process might be used in small businesses and entrepreneurial ventures.

The Strategic Management Process in Small Businesses and Entrepreneurial Ventures

Developing and exploiting a sustainable competitive advantage is important for small businesses and entrepreneurial ventures, just as it is for large, single-business or multiple-business organizations. As we've discussed numerous times in previous chapters, securing a sustainable competitive advantage means developing those organizational resources and capabilities that result in distinctive capabilities and core competencies that competitors can't duplicate and that provide customers with products–services they desire. Getting to that point isn't easy no matter what size or type organization. Again, that's the intent behind managing strategically—using the strategic management process to identify and assess the important internal and external factors that influence appropriate strategic choices and decisions. What are "appropriate" strategic choices and decisions? They're those that lead to developing or exploiting a sustainable competitive advantage. What's different or unique about the way that strategic managers in small businesses and entrepreneurial ventures do this? Let's look more closely at the strategic management process in small businesses and entrepreneurial ventures.

Value of Strategic Planning

The first thing we need to address is whether strategic decision makers in these organizations should actually do strategic planning. What's the value of strategic planning for these types of organizations? Research on the value of general planning and the value of pre-start-up planning in particular has shown mixed results. Several studies have shown positive links between planning and business performance.[15] Others have found no such relationship between planning and performance or have shown that the relationship depends on the industry.[16] What's our conclusion? Despite the contradictory findings, we

Benefits	Drawbacks
• Positive impact on organizational performance • Positive impact on long-run success and survival • More complete knowledge of strategic issues facing the organization • Forces strategic managers to identify and assess external and internal factors • Positive influence on product–service innovation	• Takes time and resources to complete • Strategic manager may not know how to do it or may lack skills to do it • Plans are just that—plans. Implementation is the important thing • Too much planning can be harmful if by the time an opportunity is investigated fully, it no longer exists

believe that the benefits to be gained from strategic planning in small businesses and entrepreneurial ventures *do* outweigh the drawbacks of doing so. Table 8.2 summarizes the benefits and drawbacks of strategic planning for these organizations. If we conclude that strategic planning *is* important, how should it be done?

The Overall Approach to the Strategic Planning Process

Most researchers generally agree that the strategic planning process in small organizations should be far less formal than that in large organizations.[17] If the process becomes too formal, rigid, and cumbersome for the strategic decision makers, a small business or entrepreneurial venture can lose much of the flexibility that's often crucial to its competitive success. In fact, the value of strategic planning for small businesses and entrepreneurial ventures lies more in the "doing"—that is, in the process itself—not in the outcome of the process, a formal strategic "plan." Most of the value of the strategic planning process comes from its emphasis on analyzing and evaluating the external and internal environments, steps that are important to effective strategic planning.

Learning Review

- What is a "small" business?
- How is an entrepreneurial venture defined?
- How are small businesses and entrepreneurial ventures different?
- Why are small businesses and entrepreneurial ventures important to the U.S. and global economies?
- Is strategic planning valuable to small businesses and entrepreneurial ventures? Explain.
- Why should the strategic planning process be more informal in small businesses and entrepreneurial ventures?

External and Internal Environmental Analysis

Strategic decision makers in small businesses and entrepreneurial ventures need to know what's happening both externally and internally for a couple of reasons. One reason is that many aspects of an organization's external environment have been shown to influence performance, particularly in new entrepreneurial ventures.[18] Even for established small businesses, however, external analysis could provide crucial information for developing or exploiting a sustainable competitive advantage. Another reason it's important to do an external analysis is to have information about changes and trends in customer expectations,

Trend Spotting

The skill of observing. Do you have it? Can you pick up on what people think is "hot" or popular? Faith Popcorn, an author and well-known trend spotter, actually says that you don't have to be a pro to be good at it. In fact, professionals may be constrained from recognizing emerging trends by rigid organizational structures and their past successes. So, how can you become more in tune with what's happening and hone your skills at trend spotting? Here are some suggestions:

1. Remember that valuable information is everywhere around you. Look for it everywhere and anywhere. Read magazines you don't normally read. Watch television shows or movies that you personally might not be interested in. Go to places. Do things. Talk to people. Information is the bread and butter of a good trend spotter.

2. File that information away. If your memory isn't as good as it should be, use note cards. What you write down doesn't have to be long and complex. It could be something as simple as "avocado seems to be a hot color," "teens seem to be flocking to organized fitness programs," or whatever.

3. Determine whether the fads seem to be part of deeper, wider trends that can be good sources of entrepreneurial opportunity. You can do this by assessing whether the fad seems to have staying power, whether the fad is a reflection of a change in people's attitudes or behaviors, and whether you see the fad in more than a few places.

4. Test your ideas about trends on intelligent friends of various ages and incomes. Bounce your ideas off of them. What do they say? Make sure, however, that these people will be honest with you.

5. Don't expect trends to jump out at you. After all, if they were easy to spot, everyone would be doing it. You have to be alert, be open to new and unusual possibilities, and be willing to work at it. Don't worry if you miss a trend. After all, there will always be more.

Why is the ability to spot trends so important? Find three examples of small businesses or entrepreneurial ventures that seem to have tapped into popular trends and describe what they've done. Are there any drawbacks to trend spotting? Explain.

Sources: K.G. Salwen, "Thinking About Tomorrow: An Interview with David Birch," Wall Street Journal, May 24, 1999, p. R30; and R. Furchgott, "Trend-Spotting: Anyone Can Play," Business Week Enterprise, March 2, 1998, pp. ENT12–ENT16.

competitors and their actions, economic factors, technological advances, and other marketplace features.[19] As we discussed in Chapter 3, the information from the external analysis provides an indication of the various opportunities and threats in the external environment. If no external analysis is done, then it's impossible to know the positive or negative changes and trends that are occurring. The same thing holds true for an internal analysis. If employees don't assess the organization's strengths and weaknesses, then it's difficult to know what strategic decisions and actions are needed to help develop or exploit the organization's competitive advantage. In other words, what resources, capabilities, and core competencies does the organization have and not have? Remember from our discussion in Chapter 4 that identifying these things is the whole purpose behind an internal analysis. Although it may be difficult for a small business owner or entrepreneur to be totally objective in analyzing strengths and weaknesses, such an analysis is necessary.

Environmental analysis is so important to small businesses and entrepreneurial ventures for one final reason, and it has to do with a concept called the "boiled frog phenomenon," which is a classic psychological experiment.[20] In the experiment, when a live frog is dropped in a boiling pan of water, it reacts instantaneously and jumps out. However, if a live frog is dropped into mild water that's gradually heated to the boiling point, the frog fails to react and dies. The same concept can be applied to small businesses and entrepreneurial ventures. Research has shown that in small businesses, when negative changes in organizational performance are gradual, a serious response to do something about it is never triggered or isn't triggered until it's too late.[21] Therefore, employees need to analyze

STRATEGIC MANAGEMENT

the global perspective

Rob McEwen, chairman and CEO of Toronto-based Goldcorp, Inc., literally struck gold on the Internet. His company owned an underperforming gold mine in northwestern Ontario, and he needed new ideas on where to dig. He decided to try something different by issuing an extraordinary challenge to the world's geologists. In his Goldcorp Challenge, he placed all of the data on his company's Red Lake mine online and challenged geologists to see if they could tell him the likely location of the next 6 million ounces of gold. And he turned it into a contest, offering the winner a prize of $105,000. McEwen knew that the contest entailed big risks, but he also knew

that continuing to do things the same old way had even greater risks. McEwen felt that if he could find the gold faster, he could really improve the value of his company. The external response was immediate; more than 1,400 scientists, engineers, and geologists from 50 countries downloaded the company's information and started their virtual exploration. Did it pay off? Absolutely. The company drilled four of the five top targets identified by the winning teams and "hit gold" on all four.

Sources: *Hoover's Online*, **www.hoovers.com**, March 24, 2004; and L. Tischler, "He Struck Gold on the Net (Really)," Fast Company, June 2002, pp. 40–44.

both the external and internal environments in order to detect subtle, but potentially damaging, changes in their organization's competitive advantage. They don't want to be like the frog that waits too long to jump out of the boiling water.

Strategy Choices

Small businesses and entrepreneurial ventures will have most of the same strategy choices as large firms, but there are some differences. Let's look at the three different strategy levels to see what these differences are.

At the functional level, strategies for the various functional areas have to be decided. For instance, what production and operations strategies will the organization use? What human resource management strategies will be used? What financing strategies will be adopted? Look back at the chapter-opening case. What types of production–operations and research and development strategies did Eclipse Aviation use? The main difference in the functional strategies of small businesses and entrepreneurial ventures and large businesses is the extent or range of the possible strategies. Small size doesn't mean that the functional strategies aren't used. It just means that these organizations are limited in terms of the resources and capabilities that are available to implement their strategies.

The competitive strategy choices for small businesses and entrepreneurial ventures often are limited to focus (either low-cost or differentiation) strategies because of their small size and narrow competitive scope. It would be extremely difficult, even with technological advances, for a small-sized organization to compete head-to-head in a broad market with a large organization on the basis of low costs, and probably even on differentiation. However, small businesses and entrepreneurial ventures can compete successfully in narrow market niches by developing a low-cost, differentiation, or integrated competitive advantage. Which one strategic decision makers choose to develop or exploit depends on the resources, capabilities, and core competencies present in the functional areas of the organization.

Finally, it may seem strange to talk about "corporate" strategies for a small business or entrepreneurial venture, especially if you think of corporate strategy as encompassing a portfolio of businesses. However, strategic decision makers in these businesses do need a strategy that addresses the broad, overall direction the organization is going to go. The possible strategic directions are the same as for a large organization: Is it going to grow, stabilize, or reverse a decline by renewing? Again, however, there are limits to the range of strategic options available to small businesses and entrepreneurial ventures in each of these directions. For example, most entrepreneurial ventures will choose to grow using the concentration strategy because vertical integration, horizontal integration, or diversification may not be financially or operationally feasible. Organization renewal actions may be limited to cost cutting and simple restructuring activities. Although the strategic options at the broad, corporate level may be limited, strategic decision makers in these organizations still need to determine the strategic direction they'd like the organization to go.

One final point we need to stress about the strategy choices for small businesses and entrepreneurial ventures is that the whole process comes down to the strategic decision makers choosing what business to be in, the competitive advantages needed to be successful in that business, and the strategies necessary to get there. This encompasses the whole range of strategic activities, from developing or exploiting organizational resources, capabilities, and core competencies to building or exploiting a sustainable competitive advantage from these in order to move the firm in the desired direction.

Strategy Evaluation and Control

The evaluation and control phase of the strategic management process for small businesses and entrepreneurial ventures is similar to that in large organizations. The organization's strategies might be evaluated by measuring the attainment of goals at the various levels. Strategy evaluation might also include an assessment of certain performance trends and a comparison of the organization to its competitors. The organization's strategic decision makers want to know (and *need* to know) whether the implemented strategies are having the intended effect. If not, why not, and what changes might be necessary? The main difference between the strategy evaluation efforts of large and small organizations would be the extent of evaluation.

The Grey Zone

How far should a business go in exploiting its competitive advantage? Chipotle Mexican Grill, a Denver-based chain of some 300 restaurants, was pushing the limits with its advertising. The company's ads showed a foil-wrapped package of Mexican food, looking very much like a package of marijuana wrapped for shipment. The ad's copy read, "Usually when you roll something this good, it's illegal." The only other words in small print in a bottom corner of the ad were "Gourmet burritos. Addictive flavor." There was also a Chipotle logo in the bottom corner. The ads ran in Chicago and Denver editions of *The Onion,* a newspaper known for its satirical views and commentaries. One other twist to this story is that the controlling stockholder of the Chipotle chain is McDonald's Corporation. Do these ads sound like an appropriate strategic choice? When does a business cross the line between humor and bad taste? Should the fact that Chipotle's majority stockholder is a successful family-oriented company play any role in the choice and evaluation of strategies? Explain. Are there ethical guidelines that you might propose?

Source: "Fast Food for the Munchies," Business Week, February 21, 2000, p. 10.

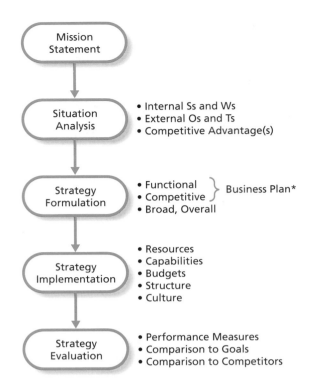

*Business plan is typically needed when business is first starting up.

All in all, the strategic management process in small businesses and entrepreneurial ventures is very similar to that used in larger organizations. Figure 8.1 illustrates this process. As we stated earlier, the main differences will be in terms of "how much" the small business or entrepreneurial venture can do these things. Because of their limited resources and capabilities, strategic decision makers in the small business or entrepreneurial venture often find that their strategic options and actions are limited. As we've already stated, however, this doesn't mean that they don't —or shouldn't—do these things; it just means they don't have the range or extent of alternatives to choose from.

Specific Strategic Issues Facing Small Businesses and Entrepreneurial Ventures

Although the strategic management process for small business and entrepreneurial ventures is virtually identical to that for larger organizations, these smaller organizations do face some unique strategic issues, including global international opportunities and challenges, human resource management issues, and innovation and flexibility considerations. Let's take a closer look at each.

Global Opportunities and Challenges

International markets offer small companies many opportunities for long-term growth and profitability.[22] Just because an organization is small doesn't mean it can't pursue global growth. In fact, small organizations are as capable of entering the same markets as larger firms.[23] Size only limits the number of markets a small organization can serve. However, small businesses and entrepreneurial ventures face certain challenges when going global. What kinds of challenges?

One has to do with external factors such as understanding the cultural, economic, and legal–political factors of the country(ies) in which the organization wishes to do business. It's not easy to get this information, but it's important for strategic decision makers to know the ins and outs of doing business in a particular country.

The other challenges associated with going international have to do with internal factors—that is, with the organization's resources and capabilities. Strategic decision makers want to make sure that the organization's resources and capabilities are adequate for doing business on an international scale. They don't want to jeopardize any competitive advantages they may have developed domestically. However, if these competitive advantages can be transferred to other countries, there are prime opportunities for enhancing the organization's growth and profitability.

Human Resource Management Issues

One of the most valuable resources and competitive advantages a small organization has is its employees. Yet, research indicates that recruiting, motivating, and retaining employees is one of the biggest problems for small organizations.[24] Human resource management (HRM) issues are among the most significant ones for small businesses and entrepreneurial ventures. A large organization typically enjoys a wider range of HR strategy options than does a smaller organization in terms of recruiting, selecting, training, appraising, and compensating employees. However, just because small businesses and entrepreneurial ventures don't have the wide range of HR strategies doesn't mean they should just forget them. Quite the opposite! Strategic decision makers should recognize how important human resources are and commit whatever time and resources are necessary to develop appropriate strategies for attracting and keeping good people. It's an investment that small businesses and entrepreneurial ventures can't ignore.

Innovation and Flexibility Considerations

One of the primary advantages that small businesses and entrepreneurial ventures can develop is being flexible and innovative.[25] Because large organizations are usually concerned with producing large quantities of products in order to take advantage of economies of scale, they often can't be as flexible as small organizations. Their resource commitments often prevent them from responding to new and quickly changing markets as effectively as small, nimble businesses can. Therefore, strategic decision makers need to capitalize on this flexibility advantage and be aware of and open to environmental changes (another good reason for doing an external analysis while managing strategically).

---

strategic **M A N A G E R S** *in action*

Zingerman's Deli is an institution in Ann Arbor, Michigan. Opened in 1982 by Ari Weinzweig and Paul Saginaw, their deli–bakery–café-restaurant business has prospered because they understand the business's product, customers, and employees. Their business principles include the following:

- Customer service is what earns the profits, because no one really needs what we sell.

- Customers who get a great product but poor service won't be as loyal as those who get an okay product but great service.

- Getting complaints by listening to people shows you care—and that's a good thing.

- Employees who are rewarded, respected, and well cared for will treat customers the same way.

These two guys understand the strategies it takes to be successful. What do you think of their business principles? How might these principles affect strategy choices? Do you think these could be applied to other businesses? Explain.

Source: D. Kiley, "Zingerman's Took the Road Less Traveled to Success," USA Today, October 1, 2003, p. 5B.

Also, small businesses and entrepreneurial ventures have the potential, more so than large organizations, to come up with real innovations. Why? Larger organizations tend to concentrate on improving products they already have in order to justify large capital expenditures on facilities and equipment. Small businesses and entrepreneurial ventures are in a better position to develop innovations in technology, markets, products, and ideas. Economist Joseph Schumpeter referred to this process in which existing products, processes, ideas, and businesses are replaced with better ones as **creative destruction**. Small businesses and entrepreneurial ventures are the driving force of change in the process of creative destruction. Developing and exploiting a sustainable competitive advantage may mean that strategic managers at small businesses and entrepreneurial ventures need to be on the lookout for ways to "creatively destruct"!

Learning Review

- Why is environmental analysis (both external and internal) important to small businesses and entrepreneurial ventures?
- How do strategic choices for small businesses and entrepreneurial ventures differ from larger organizations?
- Describe the strategic management process for small businesses and entrepreneurial ventures.
- What is the boiled frog phenomenon? How does it apply to small businesses and entrepreneurial ventures?
- Describe the specific strategic issues that face small businesses and entrepreneurial ventures.
- What is creative destruction? Why is it important to small businesses and entrepreneurial ventures?

NOT-FOR-PROFIT AND PUBLIC SECTOR ORGANIZATIONS

In this section, we're going to look at managing strategically in public sector (governmental) organizations and in other types of not-for-profit organizations. We'll start off by defining these organizational types and looking at how they're different from for-profit organizations. Then, we'll discuss the details of the strategic management process for these types of organizations and finish up with a discussion of some special strategic issues with which these organizations might have to contend.

What Are Not-for-Profit Organizations and What Are Public Sector Organizations?

One thing we need to clarify up front is that public sector organizations *are* not-for-profit organizations, also. However, we're defining them separately because of their unique importance to our economic system. Before we define public sector organizations, let's look first at what a not-for-profit organization is.

A **not-for-profit organization** is an organization whose purpose is to provide some service or good with no intention or goal of earning a profit and, as such, has met the requirements of Section 501(c)(3) of the U.S. Internal Revenue Service tax code as a tax-exempt organization. Note that "not-for-profit" doesn't mean "no revenue." Just because a not-for-profit (NFP) organization has no intention of earning a profit doesn't

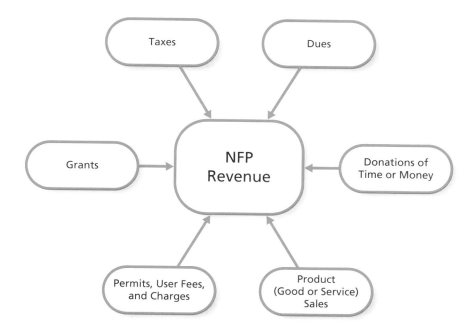

Figure 8.2

*Revenue Sources for
Not-for-Profit Organizations*

mean that it doesn't need some source of income. An organization can't exist without some means of covering the expenses associated with providing a good or service. Where can an NFP's revenues come from? Figure 8.2 lists the typical sources of revenue: taxes; dues; donations; product sales; permits, fees, and charges; and grants. In many instances, an NFP gets its revenues from a combination of these sources. What happens if an NFP's revenues actually *exceed* its expenses? Because an NFP can't earn a profit and retain its not-for-profit status, usually it will use any excess of revenues over expenses to improve those goods or services it's providing or to reduce the price of those goods or services. Also, it's not uncommon for an NFP to set aside a specified amount of funds in some type of reserve accounts to be used when revenues *don't* meet expenses.

Just as business (for-profit) organizations aren't all alike, neither are NFPs! There are a number of different types of not-for-profit organizations. We've already mentioned one type, the public sector organization, which we'll discuss more fully later. What are some other types of NFPs? The main ones include educational (public schools, colleges, and universities); charitable (United Way, American Cancer, Society, Children's Miracle Network, etc.); religious (churches, synagogues, and other religious associations); social service (Junior League, American Red Cross, Camp Fire, Habitat for Humanity, Big Brothers-Big Sisters, Mothers Against Drunk Drivers, etc.); cultural and recreational (theaters, museums, dance troupes, symphonies, parks, zoos, and other arts or recreation-oriented organizations); health service (hospitals, medical clinics, and other health-care-related organizations); professional membership associations (American Bar Association, Academy of Management, etc.); cause related (Save the Whales, Republican or Democratic National Parties, Nature Conservancy, American Association of Retired Persons, etc.); and foundations (Rockefeller Foundation, Bill and Melinda Gates Foundation, college or university alumni foundations, Foundation for the Health and Safety of American Firefighters, etc.). Figure 8.3 summarizes the various types of not-for-profit organizations.

The other main type of NFP is the public sector organization. A **public sector organization** is a not-for-profit organization created, funded, and regulated by the public sector or government. Public sector organizations include governmental units, offices, departments, agencies, and divisions at all levels—federal, state, and local. Public sector organizations provide those public services that a society needs to exist and operate, such as police

Figure 8.3

Types of Not-for-Profit Organizations

protection, paved roads and other transportation needs, recreation facilities, care and help for needy and disabled citizens, laws and regulations to protect and enhance life, and so forth.

Both public sector organizations and other types of NFPs are important to society. These organizations provide many of society's essential needs that either can't be or shouldn't be provided by for-profit businesses. For example, most individual citizens couldn't afford to pay for private police protection, but instead rely on the government to provide this protection; the American Cancer Society provides funds for cancer research and to help educate people about cancer and its causes; and any child born with birth defects is eligible for help from the March of Dimes. Many of the services and goods that NFPs provide are important to the quality of life in society. NFPs also play a significant role in maintaining an economic, social, and political system that encourages, facilitates, and protects the development and continued existence of for-profit organizations. Although the vast array of laws and regulations may seem overly cumbersome and meaningless at times, most have been enacted with society's best interests in mind. Finally, NFPs are an important economic activity. Figure 8.4 shows that these organizations (both public and other types of NFPs) provide a significant portion of the gross national product. In addition, NFPs employ a large number of individuals who, in turn, have income to pay taxes and to spend on goods and services.

You may not have realized the wide variety of not-for-profit organizations, understood the extent of what NFPs did, or recognized the economic significance of these types of organizations. Not-for-profit and public sector organizations *are* important to our society as well as to other societies around the world. Strategically managing these organizations would also appear to be a necessity. That's what we want to look at next—how the strategic management process is used in NFPs.

Figure 8.4

Employment (2002 Figures)	Public Sector	Not-for-Profits
Number (in thousands)	20,970	10,200
Percent of total employment	15.7%	6.9%
Gross Domestic Product (2002 Figures)		
Amount	$1.7 trillion	$639.2 billion
Percent of total GDP	16.3%	6.1%

Sources: *Nonprofit information from highlights of* Nonprofit Almanac and Desk Reference, *Independent Sector Organization,* **www.independentsector.org**, *2003; and U.S. Census Bureau* Statistical Abstract of the United States, *2003, pp. 279, 312, 385, and 438.*

The Strategic Management Process in Not-for-Profit and Public Sector Organizations

Because these types of organizations aren't struggling to "make a profit," you may think that managing strategically isn't necessary or maybe even possible. However, developing and exploiting a sustainable competitive advantage *is* an important task for strategic decision makers. Why? Because NFPs are also competing for resources and customers! For example, the American Heart Association competes with other social service, health service, and charitable and religious organizations for volunteers. A local community theater or symphony competes with other community arts organizations and with "entertainment" businesses for customers, volunteers, and corporate and private donations. A state university is competing with countless other organizations for state funds, employees, and "customers" (that's you and the rest of your fellow students!). That means an NFP also needs to develop and exploit a competitive advantage—something that sets it apart and gives it a competitive edge. So, the strategic management process is clearly needed by these organizations.

Unfortunately, most of the research on the strategic management process and organizational strategy actions and decisions has taken place in for-profit organizations. Yet, strategy researchers have recognized the need to look at strategic management concepts and techniques in not-for-profit organizations.[26] As in for-profit organizations, there does appear to be a positive link between strategic planning efforts in NFPs and organizational performance measures.[27] So, what *does* the strategic management process involve for not-for-profit and public sector organizations?

External and Internal Environmental Analysis

Both external and internal analyses can reveal important information for strategically managing NFPs. Not-for-profits are facing increasingly dynamic environments just as business organizations are. The external analysis provides an assessment of the positive and negative environmental trends and changes that might impact the NFP's strategic decisions and actions, just as it does for for-profit organizations. For example, economic trends are likely to influence the amount of tax revenues or the level of private and corporate donations an NFP or public sector organization might expect. Changing societal attitudes toward respect for others and individual responsibility can influence the willingness of individuals to volunteer or to make contributions to a particular cause. A new community arts organization (a new "competitor") can affect the program offerings and revenues of other community arts organizations. Even a long-running governmental monopoly such as

The U.S. Army is well aware that it has to understand demographic and sociocultural trends when designing its recruitment strategies. For example, more than 90 percent of the Army's target market is online at least once a week. So what better way to reach them than by designing a Web site that is sleek, loud, and action oriented and that features soldiers carrying big guns. The Army also has to tap into what's hot. When a professor at West Point saw how obsessed his students were with computer games, the Army decided to create a computer game that could be used for recruiting. It then realized that it would be important to "play to its audience." How? By sponsoring a NASCAR driver and putting up elaborate displays at every race to attract the largely white, working-class audience packed with potential recruits. To reach African Americans, they designed the "Taking it to the Streets" tour with an "Army of One" Hummer fitted with a basketball hoop and blaring hip-hop music. To reach Latinos, they're customizing a Hummer H2 with tricked-out rims. Will these new strategies work? Army recruiters are hoping so. What other external trends can you think of that might impact military organizations' strategies?

Source: T. Mucha, "Operation Sign 'Em Up," Business 2.0, April 2003, pp. 44–45.

the U.S. Postal Service faces competition from technological advances such as e-mail, fax machines, and overnight package delivery services. It should be quite evident that strategic decision makers need to analyze the external factors to assess the positive and negative impacts of changes and trends on strategic decisions and actions. The NFPs face opportunities and threats just as for-profit organizations do.

The internal analysis provides an assessment of the organization's resources and capabilities and its strengths and weaknesses in specific areas. What resources and capabilities does it have? Which ones are inadequate or absent? With this information, strategic decision makers can see what distinctive capabilities, core competencies, and competitive advantage(s) the NFP might have or might need to develop. The functional areas of an NFP are probably not named the same as those of a for-profit organization, but the process of analyzing the functional areas *is* similar. Even in an NFP, the product or service must be produced and delivered to the "customer," and revenues must be accounted for in some way. What the internal analysis shows, as we well know, is how efficient and effective the organization is at doing these things. An internal audit would be an appropriate tool for assessing an NFPs resources and capabilities and where the organization's strengths and weaknesses are.

What happens after we have the information from the SWOT analysis? If you remember, this information is used to assess various strategy options and choices for creating or exploiting a competitive advantage.

Learning Review

- What is a not-for-profit organization?
- Do not-for-profit organizations need revenue? How about profits? Explain.
- Describe the typical sources of revenues for not-for-profit organizations.
- What are the main types of not-for-profit organizations?
- What is a public sector organization, and what does it provide?
- Why are public sector organizations and other types of NFPs important?
- Explain how not-for-profits "compete."
- How would strategic managers in an NFP do an external analysis? An internal analysis?

Welcome to the world of e-government in the United States! Public agencies at all levels of government are putting an increasing variety of services online. As local, state, and federal agencies go online, millions of dollars are being saved on staffing and mailing expenses. However, delivering services at lower costs is only one benefit of online government services. There's also the convenience factor. For instance, motorists in Alabama, Alaska, Arizona, Michigan, and other states can register a car and get new license plates via their home computer anytime, day or night. Residents of Georgia can purchase hunting, fishing, and boating licenses on the Internet. Parking tickets can be paid online in Boston, Indianapolis, and Seattle. College students even can apply for financial aid on the U.S. Department of Education Web site. But wait, there's more!

E-government initiatives are even going global. When the European Commission (the governing body of the European Union) established its eEurope 2002 Action Plan, it established aggressive targets for moving government services and information to the Web. The EC chose 20 common government services, including income taxes, car registration, building permits, and so forth, and challenged its member nations to put them online. Currently, 55 percent of services are online.

Yet, with all the progress in online government services, there's still a long way to go. Despite the advantages associated with going online, the biggest drawback may be the widespread lack of Internet access for many citizens. Often, those individuals lacking access are society's poorest and most disadvantaged. Government decision makers will have to address this as they look at future e-government initiatives.

Sources: Cisco Corporation, "E-Government Blooms in Europe," IQ Magazine, May–June 2003, p. 13; and A. Borrus, "Click Here to Pay Your Parking Ticket," Business Week, January 17, 2000, pp. 76–78.

Strategy Choices

The idea that NFPs and public sector organizations have strategic choices may seem odd. After all, NFPs aren't "selling" anything and aren't competing with other organizations, and they certainly aren't motivated to be efficient and effective in developing a competitive advantage because they don't have to make a profit to stay in business. These statements are definitely *not* true! Strategic managers at NFPs face similar constraints of limited resources, competition for customers and resources, performance measurement, and long-run survival, just as strategic managers at for-profit organizations do. Thus, at some point, an NFPs strategic decision makers must make some decisions about strategies the organization is going to use to fulfill its vision and mission(s). The strategic options are similar in many respects to those available to businesses. Let's look first at the functional strategies.

At the functional level, the NFP or public sector organization must have strategies that allow it to do what it's set up to do—whether that's collecting taxes; imprisoning or rehabilitating convicted felons; developing and showcasing community art, dance, and music; or providing regional home health care assistance to elderly individuals. Every NFP or public sector organization must have resources and capabilities to perform whatever service or to provide whatever good(s) it's set up to do. As we know from earlier discussions, the functional strategies are the various ways an organization might choose to do these things. The main difference between the functional strategies of business organizations and NFPs is that not-for-profits don't have a wide variety of strategic alternatives from which to choose because of scarce and limited resources or because of external constraints. Whereas scarce and limited resources affect both public sector organizations and other types of not-for-profits, external constraints are most common in public sector organizations, particularly in functional areas such as purchasing or employee hiring–firing. These constraints may limit strategic decision makers' discretion in choosing appropriate and feasible functional strategies.

Competition doesn't cease to exist just because an organization isn't profit oriented. As we stated earlier, not-for-profits and public sector organizations *do* compete for resources (financial and human) and customers (clients, users, members, etc.) just like business organizations do. These NFPs are competing with each other and, in many instances, with business organizations for these resources and customers. Very little research has been done on specific competitive strategies that NFPs and public sector organizations use. One study of community arts organizations did show that these organizations competed on the basis of keeping costs low, being different, or focusing on a specific niche—in other words, Porter's cost leadership, differentiation, and focus strategies.[28] Another study of competitive strategies of religious organizations focused on explaining how these organizations compete and elaborated specific strategic management issues facing these organizations.[29] However, even without a significant amount of research on specific competitive strategies in NFPs and public sector organizations, we do know that these organizations must develop and exploit a sustainable competitive advantage to ensure their continued existence. How strategic decision makers choose to do that is the essence of their organization's competitive strategy.

Finally, not-for-profits and public sector organizations face the same types of corporate strategy choices as do businesses: Should the organization grow, and what are its options for growth? Does the organization need to stabilize its operations? Or, does it need to correct declining performance and renew itself? The main difference between corporate strategies for business organizations and for NFPs and public sector organizations is the limited range of strategic options. For instance, concentration is a frequently used growth strategy for NFPs, but diversification would be rare, if not nonexistent. However, strategic managers at Rotary International had to use a turnaround strategy to address its declining performance. Strategic actions involved cost cutting, restructuring, and reestablishing good relationships with member chapters throughout the United States. Even if strategic alternatives are somewhat limited, NFPs and public sector organizations *do* look at ways to grow, stabilize, or renew. They're faced with the same kinds of broad, comprehensive, and long-run strategic decisions that for-profit organizations face.

Strategy Evaluation and Control

As we've said many times before, formulating and implementing a strategy is only part of managing strategically. Once the strategy has been implemented, strategic decision makers must evaluate whether the strategy had the intended effect and, if it didn't, to take corrective action. Even though we know that strategy evaluation and control are important, this is the part of the strategic management process that's probably the most difficult for not-for-profit and public sector organizations. Why? Primarily because clearly stated performance standards (typically, goals and objectives) aren't easy to develop for these types of organizations. Without clearly stated goals, strategy evaluation and control become more difficult. In these organizations, there's not one simple performance measure, like profit, that's used for business organizations. Instead, strategic managers may have to look at several measures of strategic performance. For example, what are some ways that a church's strategic performance could be measured? One measure might be whether member contributions increased. Another might be the increase (or decrease) in the number of members. The fact that strategic decision makers may have to look for different performance measures makes the process of strategy evaluation and control more cumbersome and difficult. Also, because it's often easier for strategic managers of not-for-profit organizations to measure the resources coming into the organization (inputs) than the services or goods being provided (outputs), they often tend to focus more on the resources coming into the organization than on how the resources are being used—that is, how the organization is performing.[30] Again, this reflects the difficulties associated with developing appropriate ways to evaluate and control the strategies.

IRS Rule Affects Not-for-Profit Organizations

An Internal Revenue Service regulation requires many not-for-profit groups to provide detailed financial information. Colleges, universities, hospitals, publicly supported charities, and other tax-exempt organizations now must provide, on request, copies of their financial filings. These forms, filed annually with the IRS, include information about executive salaries and other sensitive information. Before the IRS rule went into effect, tax-exempt organizations only had to make their financial forms available for public "inspection" at their offices. A former IRS official said, "The new rules, backed by significantly increased penalties, will lead to sharply increased scrutiny and a higher level of accountability for the nation's nonprofit organizations." Organizations that post their documents on the Internet in a prescribed format will be exempt from these rules. How might these rules benefit not-for-profits? Other stakeholders? What drawbacks might there be to the rules? How might these rules affect strategy formulation, implementation, and evaluation in not-for-profits?

Source: T. Herman, "Nonprofit Groups Ordered to Open Their Books," Wall Street Journal, April 9, 1999, p. A2.

However, even given the difficulties associated with strategy evaluation and control in these organizations, strategic decision makers must assess the strategies being used to see if they're doing what was intended. Without some performance measure or other type of evaluation measure, it would be difficult to assess the appropriateness of functional, competitive, and corporate strategies.

Specific Strategic Issues Facing Not-for-Profit and Public Sector Organizations

Because of their unique purposes and designs, not-for-profit and public sector organizations often must deal with some specific strategic issues that other types of organizations do not. The issues we'll discuss include the misperception that strategic management isn't needed in or can't be applied to these types of organizations, the challenges of managing multiple stakeholders, and some specific strategies that not-for-profits have developed in response to environmental pressures.

Misperception About the Usefulness of Strategic Management

You'd probably agree that strategic management is useful and necessary in for-profit organizations. Somehow, when "profit" is involved, the benefits of the process are clear. However, many people question the usefulness of the strategic management process for not-for-profits. Also, many not-for-profit managers themselves aren't aware of what managing strategically is and why it's important. They don't understand why and how strategic management should be used. Some of these managers even go so far as to say that management, in general, isn't needed. Their rationale: We're not a business, so why should we be worried about managing the organization like a business?

Of course, we're aware that these types of attitudes are simply misperceptions about strategic management and its purposes. As we've stated numerous times, managing strategically to develop a sustainable competitive advantage is a task that *all* strategic decision makers face. The caseload manager at a local Social Security Administration office and even the executive director of a community ballet school should be concerned with managing strategically. Tasks such as developing an organizational vision and mission(s), analyzing

What would happen if a not-for-profit organization suddenly had more money that it knew what to do with it? That's the nice "problem" the Salvation Army found itself facing when the late Joan Kroc, widow of McDonald's founder Ray Kroc, bequeathed it at least $1.5 billion. A Salvation Army spokesperson said that the charity is not aware of a larger gift by an individual to a single charity, although there have been larger gifts to not-for-profit organizations (Microsoft founder Bill Gates and his wife Melinda, for instance, donated $6 billion to his own foundation.) In announcing the donation, Salvation Army National Commander W. Todd Bassett said, "This blends beautifully with Joan's desire to see the lives of people strengthened, enriched, and made full." What were the plans for the money? It will be used to build and operate more than two dozen community centers across the country modeled after the one in Kroc's hometown of San Diego. What strategic challenges would such a gift present to a not-for-profit organization? How would you recommend an organization that received such a gift use strategic management to help it use it wisely?

Source: T. A. Fogarty, "Joan Kroc Leaves Salvation Army $1.5 Billion," USA Today, January 21, 2004, p. 2B.

positive and negative external trends, assessing internal resources and capabilities, and designing appropriate programs and services are all key aspects of managing strategically.

Fortunately, these misperceptions about the usefulness of strategic management for not-for-profit organizations are changing, albeit slowly. As academic research and even media reports on successful strategic management outcomes in these types of organizations continue to appear, these misperceptions will continue to change. However, it's still an issue that not-for-profit and public sector organizations face.

Multiple Stakeholders

We know that strategic decision makers in business organizations must cope with multiple stakeholders. However, this issue is magnified in not-for-profit organizations, and particularly in public sector organizations. Public sector organizations are best described as the government—at all levels—doing its work. This means that public sector organizations are closely intertwined with politics and the political process. Strategic managers in public sector organizations may find that their plans and strategies are ignored by political leaders who may be interested only in getting reelected. In addition, in the United States, our fundamental assumption about government is that individual citizens *are* the government—government of the people, by the people, and for the people, as our Constitution so eloquently states. Public sector organizations, then, are "owned" by all citizens, and strategic managers may find that their decisions and actions are more closely monitored. Public sector managers also may find their actions scrutinized by oversight agencies such as courts, legislative bodies, and political commissions. They may find their strategic decisions "second guessed" by individuals who feel they have the right to voice their opinions.

Just as strategic managers in public sector organizations face multiple and often conflicting stakeholder demands, strategic managers in other types of not-for-profit organizations may find themselves dealing with multiple stakeholders who have different agendas to push. For instance, think of a public school superintendent and the various stakeholder groups he or she must consider when making decisions and taking actions, or think of the executive director of a local Red Cross organization and the many stakeholders that might influence strategic decisions and actions. The challenge of coping with these multiple stakeholders is compounded if the not-for-profit organization relies on these different stakeholders for revenues. You can begin to imagine how difficult this might be! Multiple stakeholders do represent a unique strategic issue with which NFP and public sector decisions makers have to deal.

FOR YOUR information

Making Not-for-Profits Better

A major new study of charitable organizations shows that they could become more productive by making five changes in the way they operate. What are these five changes?

1. *Reduce funding costs.* Become more efficient in raising funds.

2. *Distribute holdings faster.* Most foundations give away the legal minimum of 5 percent of their assets annually, but by increasing payout rates, not-for-profits could deliver an additional $30 billion a year to social service needs.

3. *Reduce program service costs.* Identify performance benchmarks and then find ways to meet those standards more efficiently and effectively.

4. *Trim administrative costs.* Most not-for-profits run lean operations, making it somewhat difficult to further reduce administrative costs. However, look for areas where costs can be reduced.

5. *Improve effectiveness.* Effectiveness (achieving goals) doesn't have to be sacrificed to make the organization more efficient. Hire talented managers and give them the freedom to create organizations that are both efficient *and* effective.

Source: B. Bradley, P. Jansen, and L. Silverman, "The Nonprofit Sector's $100 billion Opportunity," Harvard Business Review, May 2003, pp. 94–103.

Unique Strategies Developed by Not-for-Profit Organizations

Because not-for-profit organizations often rely on variable and unpredictable revenue sources, many have developed some unique strategies to cope with changing environmental conditions—both external and internal. Three of these strategies are: (1) cause-related marketing, (2) marketing alliances, and (3) strategic piggybacking.

Many not-for-profit organizations are participating in cause-related marketing activities. **Cause-related marketing** is a strategic practice in which a for-profit business links up with a social cause that fits in well with the company's product or service. For instance, Avon Products, Inc. (the cosmetics company) developed the Avon Breast Cancer Crusade (**www.avoncrusade.com**). Its mission has been to provide women, particularly those who are medically underserved, with direct access to breast cancer education and early detection screening services. The Avon Breast Cancer Crusade in the United States is one of several Avon-sponsored programs in countries around the world that support women's health. These programs, known as the Avon Worldwide Fund for Women's Health, have raised over $165 million to serve women's health needs. The company saw this as a way to fund a good cause that was meaningful to its target customers. Cause-related marketing can, and does, benefit not-for-profit organizations through public exposure and corporate donations, but the primary intent of the strategy is to enhance the image of the supporting company.[31] Although cause-related marketing may be designed for the strategic advantage of the sponsoring corporation, NFPs can also benefit from the marketing link, and many have chosen to participate in these types of activities.

Some not-for-profits have taken cause-related marketing a step further and have actively pursued and initiated alliances between themselves and corporate partners. These **not-for-profit marketing alliances** are strategic partnerships between a not-for-profit organization and one or more corporate partners in which the corporate partner(s) agrees to undertake a series of marketing actions that will benefit both the NFP and the corporate partner(s).[32] These marketing alliances are an extension of cause-related marketing, with the main difference being that the not-for-profit organization is the one that proposes and initiates the alliance. Figure 8.5 illustrates the three different types of these marketing alliances.

Figure 8.5

Types of NFP Marketing
Alliances

Source: Based on Alan R. Andreason,
"Profits for Nonprofits: Find a Corporate
Partner," Harvard Business Review,
November–December 1996, p. 49.

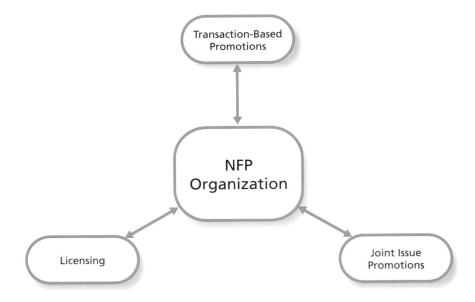

The transaction-based promotion is an alliance in which the corporate partner donates a specific amount of cash, food, or equipment in direct proportion to sales revenues, typically up to a certain limit. For example, American Express's Charge Against Hunger is an example of this type of not-for-profit marketing alliance. In this program, American Express donates three cents (up to a total of $5 million annually) to Share Our Strength, a hunger-relief program, every time someone uses an American Express card between November 1 and December 31 of any year.

The joint-issue promotion is an alliance in which the partners agree to tackle a social problem through actions such as advertising and distributing products and promotional materials. For example, *Glamour* magazine and Hanes Hosiery teamed up with the National Cancer Institute, the American College of Obstetricians and Gynecologists, and the American Health Foundation to distribute health materials and magazine articles about breast cancer to young women between the ages of 18 and 39.

The last type of not-for-profit marketing alliance involves licensing names and logos of not-for-profits in return for a fee or percentage of revenues. For example, the Arthritis Foundation allowed McNeil Consumer Products, a division of Johnson & Johnson, to market a line of pain relievers called "Arthritis Foundation Pain Relievers." In return, the Foundation receives a minimum of $1 million annually to fund research. Another good example of licensing you might be more familiar with is the licensing of a university's name and logo for use on clothing and other types of merchandise. In return for allowing its name and logo to be used, the university or college receives licensing fees. In fact, some universities generate significant funds through these licensing arrangements.

These marketing alliances can be an excellent way for not-for-profits to cope with the uncertainties of revenue sources. However, strategic decision makers *do* need to ensure that the marketing alliance doesn't waste scarce organizational resources, reduce other types of donations, bring about restricted flexibility in decision making, or establish partnerships with unethical or questionable corporate partners.

The last unique NFP strategy we want to look at is **strategic piggybacking**. This is a term that describes the development of a new activity that would generate revenue for the not-for-profit organization.[33] For instance, when the Special Olympics organization sells clothing and other related merchandise, it's generating revenue through strategic piggybacking. A community symphony may decide to sell cookbooks or other types of merchandise to supplement revenue from symphony memberships. One cautionary note regarding strategy piggybacking is that the Internal Revenue Service watches these activities very closely. If an NFP engages in a business "not substantially related" to its exempt purposes, it may jeopardize its tax-exempt status. Obviously, the strategic managers would want to monitor these activities closely.

Learning Review

- What kinds of strategic choices do decision makers at not-for-profit and public sector organizations face?

- Describe how functional, competitive, and corporate strategies might be used in NFPs and public sector organizations.

- What types of strategy evaluation and control issues do strategic decision makers at NFPs face?

- How would you address the misperceptions that strategic management isn't useful for or isn't needed in not-for-profit and public organizations?

- What types of challenges do NFPs face in dealing with multiple stakeholders? How can these challenges be addressed?

- Describe cause-related marketing.

- How are marketing alliances different from cause-related marketing efforts?

- What are the three different types of not-for-profit marketing alliances?

- What is strategic piggybacking? What are its benefits and drawbacks?

- Strategic management is important for all types and sizes of organizations.

- Strategic managers of small businesses and entrepreneurial ventures and of not-for-profit organizations face some unique challenges in managing strategically.

- A small business and entrepreneurial venture are different types of organizations.

- A **small business** is one that is independently owned, operated, and financed; has fewer than 100 employees; doesn't engage in any new marketing or innovative practices; and has relatively little impact on its industry.

- An **entrepreneurial venture** is a business that is characterized by innovative strategic practices and has profitability and growth as its main goals.

- The primary difference between these two types of organizations is their differing perspective on growth and innovation.

- Small businesses and entrepreneurial ventures are important to every industry sector and play a significant role in the global economy.

- One factor that establishes the economic importance of small businesses and entrepreneurial ventures is the number of new jobs created by these types of organizations.

- Another fact that establishes their importance is the number of new start-ups, which continues to increase because continual changes in the external environment provide a fertile climate for small businesses and entrepreneurial ventures to flourish because these organizations are often better able to respond quickly to changing conditions than are larger organizations.

- The number of new start-ups is also increasing because many of the cost advantages that large organizations traditionally had because of size are being eroded and diminished by advances in technology.

- The total number of small businesses and entrepreneurial ventures also reflects their economic importance.

- Another factor that establishes the importance of entrepreneurial ventures is their impact on innovation. Entrepreneurial ventures are an essential source of new and unique ideas that might otherwise go untapped.

- It's important that the strategic management process be used in small businesses and entrepreneurial ventures.

- Generally speaking, the benefits to be gained from strategic planning in these organizations outweigh the drawbacks of doing so.

- Most researchers generally agree that the strategic planning process in small organizations and entrepreneurial ventures should be far less formal than that found in large organizations.

- The process shouldn't become too formal, rigid, or cumbersome or you risk the flexibility that's often crucial to a small business's competitive success.

- The value of strategic planning for small businesses and entrepreneurial ventures lies more in the "doing" than in the "outcome."

- The strategic management process in small businesses and entrepreneurial ventures involves external and internal environmental analysis, strategy choices, and strategy evaluation and control.

- External and internal environmental analyses play an important part in assessing the opportunities, threats, strengths and weaknesses of the organization.

- Also, the boiled frog phenomenon has been shown to be relevant to small organizations.

- Strategic decision makers at small businesses and entrepreneurial ventures have similar strategy choices as far as functional, competitive, and corporate strategies as larger organizations do. The main difference is the range or extent of possible strategies.

- A small organization often will not have as many strategic options as the larger organization.

- Strategy evaluation and control is similar to that used in large organizations. Again, the main difference will be in terms of the magnitude or extent of evaluation that can be done.

- Some of the special strategic issues facing small businesses and entrepreneurial ventures include global–international opportunities and challenges, human resource management issues, and innovation and flexibility considerations.

- The other types of special organizations include not-for-profit and public sector organizations.

- A **not-for-profit organization** is one that has met the requirements of Section 501(c)(3) of the U.S. Internal Revenue Service tax code because its purpose is to provide some good or service with no intention or goal of earning a profit.

- The wide variety of NFPs include educational, charitable, religious, social service, cultural and recreational, health service, professional membership associations, cause related, and foundations.

- **Public sector organizations** are also not-for-profit and are defined as organizations that are created, funded, and regulated by the public sector or government.

- Both not-for-profit and public sector organizations are important to society.

- The strategic management process in NFPs has not been well researched, but we know that managing strategically is important for these organizations.

- The strategic management process for these types of organizations involves external and internal environmental analysis, strategy choices (functional, competitive, and corporate), and strategy evaluation and control.

- Some specific strategic issues facing not-for-profit organizations include the misperception about the usefulness of strategic management, multiple stakeholders, and some unique strategies used by NFPs in response to the variable and unpredictable revenue sources.

- The unique strategies used by NFPs include **cause-related marketing** (a strategic practice in which a for-profit businesses links up with a social cause that fits in well with the company's product or service), **not-for-profit marketing alliances** (strategic partnerships between a not-for-profit organization and one or more corporate partners in which the corporate partner agrees to undertake a series of marketing actions that will benefit both the NFP and the corporate partner); and **strategic piggybacking** (the development of a new activity that would generate revenue for the not-for-profit organization).

building your skills

1. The American Lung Association (**www.lungusa.org**) is facing some serious strategic challenges. First established to combat the lung disease tuberculosis (TB), the organization has done such an effective job helping to educate individuals about TB and to eradicate the disease that the ALA no longer has an identity or a cause to rally people around. Its well-known annual Christmas Seal campaign, the organization's revenue generator, is losing its pull because a new generation of donors has more "attractive" causes to support. Log on to the organization's Web site and familiarize yourself with its mission and activities. You might even want to contact the local chapter for more information. With the information you get, do a brief SWOT analysis. Then, come up with some strategies that the ALA could use to make itself more appealing to potential donors.

2. *Judo strategy* is a term being used to describe what it takes to successfully compete in today's dynamic context.[34] A successful judo practitioner needs three things: rapid movement, flexibility, and leverage. Write a paper that addresses the following issues:

   a. What do you think each of these characteristics refers to in relation to competing in today's dynamic context?

   b. What impact might these three characteristics have as strategic decision makers in entrepreneurial ventures and small businesses strategically manage their businesses?

   c. Find two examples of entrepreneurial ventures or small businesses (check out *Business 2.0, Fast Company, Inc.,* or other sources) that you feel fit the characteristics of a judo strategy. Describe what they're doing and why you think they're good examples of a judo strategy.

3. In order to cope with dwindling budgets and growing maintenance backlogs, many state parks are becoming entrepreneurs. How? In Ohio, for example, campers who don't own their own gear or who don't want to haul their gear around can rent cots, coolers, cook stoves, and even teepees at many of the state parks. In New York, the state park system now serves Coke products as its "official" soft drink thanks to a $2 million alliance with the Coca-Cola Company. Many park administrators around the United States believe that they don't have any choice but to pursue revenues on their own. Park attendance is up, but overall state park budgets have decreased by an estimated 22 percent since 1980, and funds for capital improvements and maintenance have declined 68 percent. One analyst says, "Entrepreneurial fund raising is the wave of the future for state parks and someday, national parks." What type of not-for-profit strategy would you call these activities by parks? What conflicts might these types of "entrepreneurial" activities raise for strategic decision makers at state parks? What recommendations would you make for strategically managing in the environment that state parks face?

4. Trends can be a powerful source for entrepreneurial ideas. However, how do you know when something is really a trend and not simply a fad? For instance, think of the "clear" colas. Why did these turn out to be a fad? Do some research on trends and fads. Write up a report that includes suggestions for strategic decision makers about understanding trends and fads.

5. The Sierra Club (**www.sierraclub.org**) is a well-known environmental organization. In fact, it's the world's largest grass-roots environmental organization, with over 700,000 members and a multimillion-dollar budget. What is the Sierra Club's mission? What stakeholders do you think the Sierra Club might have to contend with? What are its strategic goals and policies? If you were the Club's president, how would you use the strategic management process to help you strategically manage this not-for-profit organization? Be specific.

6. An article on small business growth strategies in *Entrepreneur* magazine stated, "A good growth strategy is in focus with what the business owner has in mind for the company. In other words, the best growth strategy is a well-planned one."[35] What's your interpretation of this statement? On a piece of paper, make two columns with one listing reasons why this statement is a good description of growth strategy for small businesses and entrepreneurial ventures and the other listing some reasons why it isn't a good description. Be prepared to debate both sides in a class discussion.

7. A survey of professionals who help troubled companies cited the top reasons why most businesses fail.[36] Reasons included the following: too much debt, inadequate leadership, poor planning, failure to change, inexperienced management, and not enough revenue. What are the implications of each of these for managing strategically? How could strategic management help prevent or resolve each?

Strategic Management in Action Cases

CASE #1: The Sky's the Limit

This Strategic Management in Action Case can be found at the beginning of Chapter 8.

Discussion Questions

1. Would you call Eclipse Aviation a small business or an entrepreneurial venture? Explain your choice.

2. What examples of managing strategically do you see in this case? Be specific.

3. What strategic challenges might Eclipse Aviation face as it moves beyond the idea stage into actual production and marketing of its aircraft?

4. Which part of the strategic management process is most important to small businesses and entrepreneurial ventures? Explain your answer.

CASE #2: Finding Its Way

The United Way of America (UWA) has been described as "a mutual fund for charitable causes." That's because its some 1,400 local chapters support thousands of community agencies, especially in the areas of health and human services. Funding recipients have ranged from the American Cancer Society, Big Brothers–Big Sisters, and The Salvation Army to local organizations devoted to addressing local needs. And the UWA has been quite successful in carrying out its vision: to improve people's lives by mobilizing the caring power of communities. The latest available figures show that the United Way raised over $4 billion during 2002 and 2003. Despite its important role in helping local chapters address critical needs, the UWA itself has had to work through some problems.

One issue that never seems to go away is the competition for donors' dollars. Many deserving organizations depend on donations from individuals and businesses. Coupled with a sluggish economy that has slowed down donations in general, you can see the difficulties UWA and its local branches face when it comes to funding. Then, there was the organizational scandal in the 1990s. William Aramony, who had served as United Way's president for 22 years, resigned under charges that he had diverted organizational funds to finance a lavish lifestyle, including limousine transportation, trips on the Concorde jet, exotic vacations, and expensive gifts for a teenage mistress. He was convicted in 1996 of mail, wire, and tax fraud and served a seven-year prison sentence. The negative publicity surrounding that whole situation had a significant impact on activities and programs at UWA headquarters and at local chapters. However, through the able leadership of Elaine Chao, it was able to move beyond those problems and stabilize donations and programs. After Chao resigned in 1996, Betty Beene came in as the new president. She led a brand-awareness campaign designed to stress the important benefits that local United Way chapters brought to their communities. However, Beene soon came under fire from local chapters when she suggested a national pledge-processing center and national performance standards. After she stepped down in January 2001, current president and CEO Brian Gallagher came on board. He has some ideas for "a better way to make a difference."

Gallagher's approach is to deal with systemic community issues such as homelessness and racism with leadership and activism, as well as with money. He believes the goal should be to show corporations and the general public that their donations really do make a difference. His main strategy for doing this is by converting the organization from a simple money collector and dispenser of cash into a community problem-solver. How? He's proposing that "local United Way chapters work with communities to devise strategies for dealing with specific problems, such as crime or hunger." Then, funds would be directed to those organizations and charities that target those issues. His idea is meeting some resistance from local chapters and charities that feel they may be left out. However, Gallagher responds that he's interested in identifying critical issues and coming up with strategies to fix them, "not making sure that all agencies have financial support."

Discussion Questions

1. What evidence of strategic management, if any, do you see in this organization? Explain.

2. What types of constraints do you think strategic decision makers at UWA face?

3. What should an external analysis for UWA include? Be specific. With what stakeholders might UWA have to be concerned?

4. What types of strategic evaluation and control would you recommend that UWA use? Be specific.

5. Using what you know about strategic management, how would you suggest that Gallagher proceed with his vision for changing UWA?

(*Sources:* United Way, **national.unitedway.org**, March 26, 2004; Hoover's Online, **www.hoovers.com**, March 26, 2004; and D. Little, "A Better Way to Make a Difference?" *Business Week*, March 18, 2002, pp. 66–68.)

CASE #3: Don't Get Stung

Beeswax candles, lip balm, soaps, and baby oil. These are just a few of the unique personal care products manufactured by Burt's Bees, Inc. of Durham, North Carolina. And sell they do—to the tune of some $50 million in 2003.

Burt's Bees was founded in 1984 when Roxanne Quimby met reclusive beekeeper Burt Shavitz in rural Maine. They began making candles, furniture polish, and lip balm from beeswax, which was obviously in great abundance thanks to Burt's bees. Roxanne and Burt began selling their products at craft fairs throughout New England. Sales took off, and they soon had to move their factory from Roxanne's kitchen to an abandoned schoolhouse and then to three trailers parked on her front lawn. When sales hit the $3 million mark in 1993, Roxanne and Burt realized that they had outgrown the rural Maine landscape, where future growth would be restricted by high taxes and unskilled labor. However, fast-paced urban life wasn't at all appealing to them. To maintain that simple down-home atmosphere that was so important to the company, Roxanne looked at different locations and eventually settled the company in Durham, North Carolina, a hub of cosmetics manufacturing.

Roxanne is the current president and CEO, having bought out Burt, who still lives in his turkey coop in rural Maine. Roxanne and Burt's commitment to a simple lifestyle always was reflected in the way they ran their business. Roxanne says that living off the land was actually good training for running a business, especially a start-up, because you're always undercapitalized and looking for ways to survive. But after the move to North Carolina, Quimby got more serious about the business of Burt's Bees. She auto- mated manufacturing and recruited an experienced management team. These changes helped the company achieve sales of some $50 million in 2003.

As the company grew, however, Quimby grew more and more dissatisfied with her lifestyle of commuting between her home in rural Maine and the business in North Carolina. Although the success of Burt's Bees allowed her to be able to support her passion of saving forest land in Maine, she finally made the decision to steer a new course. At the end of 2003, she sold a controlling stake in Burt's Bees for more than $175 million to AEA Investors, a private equity firm. She plans to donate half the proceeds to a land trust to establish a national park in northern Maine and is considering a run for Maine's governorship in 2006.

Discussion Questions

1. Would you describe Burt's Bees as an entrepreneurial venture or a small business? Explain.

2. What examples of strategic management can you identify in this case? Be specific.

3. What strategic challenges might arise when a business has a CEO whose passion isn't the business but some social and political cause? What potential advantages and drawbacks might there be?

4. Update the information on Burt's Bees. What are current sales? What new products do they have?

(*Sources:* Burt's Bees, **www.burtsbees.com**, March 26, 2004; Hoover's Online, **www.hoovers.com**, March 26, 2004; S. Donovan, "Roxanne Quimby: How I Did It," *Inc.*, January 2004, pp. 76–78; L. Adamson, "Roxanne Quimby for Governor!" *Fast Company*, December 2003, pp. 112–15; and J. Sloane, "From Maine to Mainstream," *Fortune*, October 16, 2000, pp. 312[J]–312[N].)

Endnotes

1. Eclipse Aviation, **www.eclipseaviation.com**, March 24, 2004; D. Jones, "Helping Bring Corporate Jets to the Masses," *USA Today*, March 8, 2004, p. 1E; A. Webb, "Eclipse to Start Work on Jets," *Albuquerque Journal*, March 6, 2004; H. Kestin, "The Plane Truth," *Inc.*, June 2002, pp. 64–74; M. Stibbe, "The Checker Cab of the Skies?" *Business 2.0*, May 2002, p. 26; and R. Karlgaard, "Business Travel Battleground," *Forbes*, May 13, 2002, p. 45.

2. Title 13 (Business Credit and Assistance), Chapter 1 (Small Business Administration), Part 121 (Small Business Size Regulations) of the Code of Federal Regulations. Revised as of January 1, 2001, found on the U.S. Small Business Administration's Web site, **www.sba.gov**, March 24, 2004.

3. T. L. Hatten, *Small Business: Entrepreneurship and Beyond* (Upper Saddle River, NJ: Prentice Hall, 1997), p. 5; and J. W. Carland, F. Hoy, W. R. Boulton, and J. C. Carland, "Differentiating Entrepreneurs from Small Business Owners: A Conceptualization," *Academy of Management Review*, 9, no. 2 (1984), pp. 354–59.

4. L. W. Busenitz, "Research on Entrepreneurial Alertness," *Journal of Small Business Management*, October 1996, pp. 35–44.

5. Carland et al., "Differentiating Entrepreneurs from Small Business Owners."

6. "United States Business Facts," U.S. Chamber of Commerce Statistics and Research Center, **www.uschamber.org**, March 24, 2004.

7. "Frequently Asked Questions," Office of Advocacy, U.S. Small Business Administration, **www.sba.gov/advo**, March 24, 2004; and P. Coy, "Small Business: Right Place, Right Time," *Business Week*, October 13, 2003, pp. 82–88.

8. "The Third Millennium: Small Business and Entrepreneurship in the 21st Century," Office of Advocacy, U.S. Small Business Administration, **www.sba.gov/advo**, March 24, 2004.

9. *Statistical Abstract of the United States*, 1993.

10. "Small Business Economic Indicators for 2002," Office of Advocacy, U.S. Small Business Administration, **www.sba.gov/advo**, March 24, 2004.

11. "The Third Millennium: Small Business and Entrepreneurship in the 21st Century."

12. P. Almeida and B. Kogut, "The Exploration of Technological Diversity and Geographic Localization in Innovation: Start-up Firms in the Semiconductor Industry," *Small Business Economics*, 9, no. 1 (1997), pp. 21–31.

13. R. J. Arend, "Emergence of Entrepreneurs Following Exogenous Technological Change," *Strategic Management Journal*, January 1999, pp. 21–31.

14. S. Jones, "Small Businesses Are Still Innovative, Study Says," *Springfield Business Journal*, February 16–22, 2004, p. 25.

15. C. Schwenk and C. B. Shrader, "Effects of Formal Strategic Planning on Financial Performance in Small Firms: A Meta-Analysis," *Entrepreneurship Theory and Practice*, 17, no. 3 (1993), pp. 53–64; J. Bracker, B. Keats, and J. Pearson, "Planning and Financial Performance Among Small Firms in a Growth Industry," *Strategic Management Journal*, 9 (1988), pp. 591–603;

J. Bracker and J. Pearson, "Planning and Financial Performance of Small, Mature Firms," *Strategic Management Journal*, 7 (1986), pp. 503–22; R. Ackelsberg and P. Arlow, "Small Businesses Do Plan and It Pays Off," *Long Range Planning*, 18, no. 3 (1985), pp. 61–67; C. Orpen, "The Effects of Long-range Planning on Small Business Performance," *Journal of Small Business Management*, January 1985, pp. 16–23; R. Robinson and J. Pearce, "Research Thrusts in Small Firm Strategic Planning," *Academy of Management Review*, 9 (1984), pp. 128–37; P. Wood and R. LaForge, "The Impact of Comprehensive Planning on Financial Performance," *Academy of Management Journal*, 22 (1979), pp. 516–26; R. Robinson, "Forecasting and Small Business: A Study of the Strategic Planning Process," *Journal of Small Business Management*, 17, no. 3 (1979), pp. 19–27; P. Karger and R. Mali, "Long Range Planning and Organizational Performance," *Long Range Planning*, 8, no. 6 (1975), pp. 61–64; D. Herold, "Long Range Planning and Organizational Performance: A Cross-validation Study," *Academy of Management Journal*, 15 (1972), pp. 91–102; and H. I. Ansoff, H. I. Ansoff, J. Avner, R. G. Brandenburg, F. E. Portner, and R. Radosevich, "Does Planning Pay? The Effect of Planning on Success of Acquisition in American Firms," *Long Range Planning*, 3, no. 2 (1970), pp. 2–7.

16. C. B. Shrader, C. Mulford, and V. Blackburn, "Strategic and Operational Planning, Uncertainty, and Performance in Small Firms," *Journal of Small Business Management*, October 1989, pp. 45–60; R. Robinson and J. Pearce, "The Impact of Formalized Strategic Planning on Financial Performance in Small Organizations," *Strategic Management Journal*, 4 (1983), pp. 197–207; W. Lindsay, W. R. Boulton, W. M. Lindsay, S. G. Franklin, and L. W. Rue, "Strategic Planning: Determining the Impact of Environmental Characteristics and Uncertainty," *Academy of Management Journal*, 25 (1982), pp. 500–509; R. Hogarth and S. Makridakis, "Forecasting and Planning: An Evaluation," *Management Science*, 27, no. 2 (1981), pp. 115–38; M. Leontiades and A. Tezel, "Planning Perceptions and Planning Results," *Strategic Management Journal*, 1 (1980), pp. 65–76; R. Kudla, "The Effects of Strategic Planning on Common Stock Returns," *Academy of Management Journal*, 23 (1980), pp. 5–20; R. Fulmer and L. Rue, "The Practice and Profitability of Long-Range Planning," *Managerial Planning*, May–June 1974, pp. 1–7; and S. Thune and R. House, "Where Long Range Planning Pays Off," *Business Horizons*, 13, no. 4 (1970), pp. 81–87.

17. T. J. Callahan and M. D. Cassar, "Small Business Owners' Assessment of Their Abilities to Perform and Interpret Formal Market Studies," *Journal of Small Business Management*, October 1995, pp. 1–9; C. B. Shrader, et al., "Strategic and Operational Planning, Uncertainty, and Performance in Small Firms"; L. R. Smeltzer, G. L. Fann, and V. N. Nikolaisen, "Environmental Scanning Practices in Small Businesses," *Journal of Small Business Management*, July 1988, pp. 56–62; S. W. McDaniel and A. Parasuraman, "Practical Guidelines for Small Business Marketing Research," *Journal of Small Business Management*, January 1986, pp. 1–9; and S. W. McDaniel and A. Parasuraman, "Small Business Experience With and Attitudes Toward Formal Marketing Research," *American Journal of Small Business*, Spring 1985, pp. 1–6.

18. S. Shane and L. Kolvereid, "National Environment, Strategy, and New Venture Performance: A Three Country Study," *Journal of Small Business Management*, April 1995, pp. 37–50.

19. A. Bhide, "The Questions Every Entrepreneur Must Answer," *Harvard Business Review*, November–December 1996, pp. 120–30; S. I. Mohan-Neill, "The Influence of Firm's Age and Size on Its Environmental Scanning Activities," *Journal of Small Business Management*, October 1995, pp. 10–21; T. J. Callahan and M. D. Cassar, "Small Business Owners' Assessment of Their Abilities to Perform and Interpret Formal Market Studies"; J. Masten, G. B. Hartmann, and A. Safari, "Small Business Strategic Planning and Technology Transfer: The Use of Publicly Supported Technology Assistance Agencies," *Journal of Small Business Management*, July 1995, pp. 26–37; and A. Shama, "Marketing Strategies During Recession: A Comparison of Small and Large Firms," *Journal of Small Business Management*, July 1993, pp. 62–72.

20. S. D. Chowdhury and J. R. Lang, "Crisis, Decline, and Turnaround: A Test of Competing Hypotheses for Short-Term Performance Improvement in Small Firms," *Journal of Small Business Management*, October 1993, pp. 8–17.

21. Ibid.

22. J. L. Calof, "The Impact of Size on Internationalization," *Journal of Small Business Management*, October 1993, pp. 60–69; and P. C. Wright, "The Personal and the Personnel Adjustments and Costs for Small Businesses Entering the International Market Place," *Journal of Small Business Management*, January 1993, pp. 83–93.

23. Calof, "The Impact of Size on Internationalization."

24. S. P. Deshpande and D. Y. Golhar, "HRM Practices in Large and Small Manufacturing Firms: A Comparative Study," *Journal of Small Business Management*, April 1994, pp. 49–56.

25. See Hatten, *Small Business: Entrepreneurship and Beyond*, pp. 17–18.

26. K. Ascher and B. Nare, "Strategic Planning in the Public Sector," in *International Review of Strategic Management*, Vol. 1, ed. D. E. Hussey (New York: John Wiley and Sons, 1988), pp. 297–315; M. S. Wortman, Jr., "Strategic Management in Nonprofit Organizations: A Research Typology and Research Prospectus," in *Strategic Management Frontiers*, ed. J. H. Grant (Greenwich, CT: JAI Press, 1988), pp. 425–42; J. W. Harvey and K. F. McCrohan, "Strategic Issues for Charities and Philanthropies," *Long Range Planning*, December 1988, pp. 44–55; D. Harvey and J. D. Snyder, "Charities Need a Bottom Line, Too," *Harvard Business Review*, January–February 1987,

pp. 14–22; I. Unterman and R. H. Davis, *Strategic Management of Not-for-Profit Organizations*, (New York: Praeger, 1984); J. M. Stevens and R. P. McGowan, "Managerial Strategies in Municipal Government Organizations," *Academy of Management Journal*, 26, no. 3 (1983), pp. 527–34.

27. A. Howard and J. Magretta, "Surviving Success: An Interview with the Nature Conservancy's John Sawhill," *Harvard Business Review*, September–October 1995, pp. 108–18; P. V. Jenster and G. A. Overstreet, "Planning for a Non-Profit Service: A Study of U.S. Credit Unions," *Long Range Planning*, April 1990, pp. 103–11; and G. J. Medley, "Strategic Planning for the World Wildlife Fund," *Long Range Planning*, February 1988, pp. 46–54.

28. M. Coulter, "Competitive Strategies of Community Arts Organizations," working paper from a research study of community arts organizations in the Midwest, 1996.

29. K. D. Miller, "Competitive Strategies of Religious Organizations," *Strategic Management Journal*, May 2002, pp. 435–56.

30. R. M. Kanter and D. V. Summers, "Doing Well While Doing Good: Dilemmas of Performance Measurement in Nonprofit Organizations and the Need for a Multiple-constituency Approach," in *The Nonprofit Sector: A Research Handbook*, ed. W. W. Powell (New Haven, CT: Yale University Press, 1987).

31. See, for example, G. Smith and R. Stodghill II, "Are Good Causes Good Marketing?" *Business Week*, March 21, 1994, pp. 64–65; G. Levin, "Green Marketing Gets Cautious," *Advertising Age*, July 5, 1993, p. 4; "Cause-Related Marketing," *Inc.*, July 1991, p. 72; and "Marketing: Cause-Related Marketing," *Wall Street Journal*, February 19, 1987, p. B1.

32. A. R. Andreason, "Profits for Nonprofits: Find a Corporate Partner," *Harvard Business Review*, November–December 1996, pp. 47–59.

33. R. P. Nielsen, "Piggybacking Strategies for Nonprofits: A Shared Costs Approach," *Strategic Management Journal*, May–June 1986, pp. 209–11; R. P. Nielsen, "Piggybacking for Business and Nonprofits: A Strategy for Hard Times," *Long Range Planning*, April 1984, pp. 96–102; and R. P. Nielsen, "SMR Forum: Strategic Piggybacking—A Self-Subsidizing Strategy for Nonprofit Institutions," *Sloan Management Review*, Summer 1982, pp. 65–69.

34. D. B. Yoffie and M. A. Cusumano, "Judo Strategy: The Competitive Dynamics of Internet Time," *Harvard Business Review*, January–February 1999, pp. 71–81.

35. L. Beresford, "Growing Up," *Entrepreneur*, July 1996, pp. 124–28.

36. "Keys to Failure," *Business Week*, August 25, 2003, p. 14.

Appendix 1

HOW TO DO A COMPREHENSIVE CASE ANALYSIS

Case analysis is a major component of the strategic management course at many schools. In this part of the book, we want to look at how to do a comprehensive case analysis so that when it's time for you to do one, you'll feel comfortable with what's involved. One thing you need to understand is that a comprehensive case analysis is not like the end-of-chapter cases that you may have completed as you read the chapters in this textbook; that is, no discussion questions appear at the end of the case to guide you as to which issues to look at. Instead, you'll be using what you've learned by reading and studying the various aspects of strategic management in action to analyze the case.

What Is a Case?

A case is simply a story about a company and the strategic issues its strategic decision makers face. In order to identify and address those issues, you put yourself in the position of being one of those decision makers. You analyze the information that's provided about the company in the case. In some cases, your professor may provide you with additional information that's not specifically provided in the case. Based on your analysis of this information, you should be able to identify the major strategic issues facing the company and formulate the strategic alternatives you think would best address those issues. Going through the process of analyzing a case can be a wonderful way to "practice" the skills of being a strategic decision maker, especially if you remember to put yourself in the role of being that decision maker by asking the following questions: *What information do I have? What information do I need? Based on my analysis of that information, what do I need to do now?* Given this, what specifically should a case analysis include?

What Should a Case Analysis Include?

A case analysis typically includes six parts: external analysis, internal analysis (including financial analysis), strategic issues, strategic alternatives, recommendations, and implementation. Let's look at what's included in each of these areas.

External Analysis

The external analysis section includes a description of the opportunities and threats found in the specific and general external environmental sectors. The specific sector includes the industry and competitive forces. The general sectors include economic, demographic, sociocultural, political–legal, and technological forces. In Chapter 3, we discussed how to do an external analysis and what to look for in each of these sectors. Based on your analysis of these sectors, then, you should describe *what* opportunities and threats you see in each area and explain *why* you see these as opportunities and threats.

Internal Analysis

The internal analysis section includes a description of the strengths and weaknesses found in the organization's internal functional areas, which typically include production–operations, marketing, human resource management, research and development, information systems, and financial–accounting. The internal analysis may also include an assessment of other internal organizational aspects, such as strategic managers (top management team, board of directors, and others), organizational culture, and organizational structure. In Chapter 4, you learned how to do an internal analysis and what you should look for in each of these areas. Based on your analysis of these internal areas, then, you should describe *what* strengths and weaknesses you see in each area and explain *why* you see these as strengths and weaknesses.

The internal analysis section also usually includes a thorough financial analysis. An organization's financial data represent the results or outcomes of its past or current strategies. Strategic decision makers must and do use some form of financial analysis to make good decisions. In preparing your financial analysis, be sure to examine and analyze any financial information that's included in the case material such as exhibits, tables, graphs, appendices, and so forth.

The financial analysis should cover three parts: (1) ratio analysis and comparison to industry trends and company trends and an explanation of what is happening in the ratios (see Exhibit 1 for a description of the four major categories of ratios); (2) graphs and charts outlining the company's sales, profits, and other important financial and performance measures; and (3) a statement of the company's overall financial condition (weak, fair, or strong) and written support of how you came to that conclusion.

Strategic Issues

Once you've completed the SWOT analysis, you're ready to identify the critical strategic issues facing the company. What are "typical" issues? They're critical weaknesses that need to be corrected, opportunities that the company wants to take advantage of with its strengths, distinctive competencies the company wants or needs to develop from its strengths, or possibly threats the company wants to steer away from or buffer against. In describing the strategic issues, focus on describing *what* the issue is as well as *why* you see it as an issue. Supporting "why" you see something as an issue should come from the information you've included in your SWOT analysis.

Strategic Alternatives

Once you've identified the critical strategic issues, you'll need to develop strategic alternatives to address those issues. How many alternatives do you need to develop? For each issue, you should propose at least two alternatives that address that issue. In fact, some issues may have only two alternatives—to change or to stay as is. However, other issues may have numerous alternatives that could be proposed to resolve them.

What should your description of each alternative include? One approach is to describe what, how, who, when, and where. *What* is the strategic alternative being proposed? The possible strategic alternatives are the functional, competitive, and corporate strategies we discussed in Chapters 5, 6, and 7. *How* will the alternative be done? This is an important

Exhibit 1 *Financial Ratios*

Category	Ratio	How Calculated	What It Measures
Liquidity	Current ratio	$\dfrac{\text{Current assets}}{\text{Current liabilities}}$	A measure of the organization's ability to meet short-term obligations
	Acid test	$\dfrac{\text{Current assets minus inventories}}{\text{Current liabilities}}$	A more accurate measure of liquidity when inventories turn over slowly or are more difficult to sell
Leverage	Debt ratio	$\dfrac{\text{Total debt}}{\text{Total assets}}$	Indicates what percentage of an organization's assets are financed by debt
	Debt–equity ratio	$\dfrac{\text{Total debt}}{\text{Total equity}}$	Indicates the organization's use of equity compared with its use of debt
	Times interest earned	$\dfrac{\text{Profits before interest and taxes}}{\text{Total interest charges}}$	Measures how many times the organization can cover its interest payments with its gross operating income
Activity	Inventory turnover	$\dfrac{\text{Sales}}{\text{Inventory}}$	A measure of efficiency that indicates how many times the organization has "sold" its inventory
	Total asset turnover	$\dfrac{\text{Sales}}{\text{Total assets}}$	A measure of how efficiently the organization is using its total assets to generate sales
	Fixed asset turnover	$\dfrac{\text{Sales}}{\text{Fixed assets}}$	A measure of how efficiently the organization is using its fixed assets to generate sales
Profitability	Profit margin	$\dfrac{\text{Net profit (after taxes)}}{\text{Sales}}$	Indicates the percentage of profit being generated from each dollar of sales
	Return on assets (ROA) (also called return on investment, or ROI)	$\dfrac{\text{Net profit (after taxes)}}{\text{Sales}}$	Indicates the rate of return an organization is generating from its assets
	Return on equity	$\dfrac{\text{Net profit (after taxes)}}{\text{Sales}}$	Indicates the rate of return the organization is earning for its shareholders

part of describing your proposed alternative; you should explain in detail—step-by-step—what needs to happen in this alternative. *Who* will be responsible for doing the alternative? What individuals or groups will be involved in the alternative? *When* will the alternative need to be done? Is it something that needs to happen immediately, in the short run, or is it more long term? And finally, *where* will the alternative need to be done? Think in terms of the location(s) where the alternative will take place.

Recommendations

Once you've developed your issues and proposed strategic alternatives, you're ready to make some choices. Which alternatives are you choosing and why? Which alternatives are you rejecting and why? You can choose as many of your alternatives to "resolve" your issue as you want, as long as they're not mutually exclusive. You want to also explain how your chosen alternative(s) will resolve the strategic issue.

Implementation

One drawback of case analysis is that you can't really put your proposed ideas into action. To overcome this limitation, however, your case analysis should provide a description of what changes would have to take place if your chosen strategies were implemented. One approach to describing implementation involves describing the proposed changes in organizational structure, the proposed changes in organizational culture, and the source of funding for implementing the chosen strategies. In other words, how would the organization's structure and culture have to change if this alternative were implemented, and where would the money come from to implement the alternative?

The format for a case analysis that we just described—external analysis, internal analysis, strategic issues, strategic alternatives, recommendations, and implementation—is just one approach. Keep in mind that your professor may have another specific format for you to follow other than the approach that's described here.

FINDING INFORMATION TO DO A CASE ANALYSIS

Doing a case analysis involves getting and evaluating information. Where do you find the information to do a case analysis? The obvious place to start is the written case itself. You'll first want to read through the case to familiarize yourself with the company and the situation. Then, go back through the case and start noting certain statements and whether they describe internal or external factors. For instance, does the information relate to marketing, production–operations, or research and development? Or, does the information seem to describe external sectors such as industry–competition, demographics, the economy, and so forth? It may take you a couple of times reading through the case to be able to determine the categories under which the information might eventually fit. And, keep in mind that not every piece of information included in the written case is going to be important to your analysis. But you won't be able to determine that unless you've studied the case by reading through it more than once.

If your professor allows, you might also want to look at other sources of information about the company and the external environment it's facing (i.e., company Web sites, government Web sites, company and industry reference sources, and even general business and news periodicals). One precaution, however, is that you need to stay within the same time frame as the case. For instance, if your case ends in 2003, you couldn't use news events that happened in 2004, because those events wouldn't have happened yet. To get the most educational benefit from doing a case analysis, you have to "arm" yourself with the information the company's strategic decision makers would have had and address the case under those conditions. However, keep in mind that your professor may ask you to update the case, which you would do by finding current information on the company, the industry, and the general external environment.

What then? Once you have your information, you're ready to evaluate it by identifying strengths, weaknesses, opportunities, and threats. The SWOT analysis should help you in identifying the relevant strategic issues facing the company and serve as the basis for formulating appropriate strategic responses to the issues.

PRESENTING CASE ANALYSIS INFORMATION

You've completed your analysis of the case information. Now what? You'll need to present the information in a written format, as an oral presentation, or maybe both. What do you need to know about presenting information as a written report or as an oral presentation?

Written Case Analysis

Your written report should cover the six areas of a case analysis. This information could be presented in a bulleted item format or in a paragraph format. Your professor will tell you what he or she prefers. Either way, label your case sections clearly and carefully check your spelling and grammar. If you have used information from another source, you will need to cite that information. Again, your professor will tell you the citation format (e.g., in the text itself, at the end of the report, or some other way) he or she prefers. Also, you should include

Exhibit 2

Suggestions for Good Oral Presentations

- Get the audience's attention immediately by opening with, for instance, an interesting piece of information about the company, an audience participation survey, video clips, or examples of the company's products.
- Present all the required parts. Your professor will let you know what these are.
- Provide explanations of your analysis, but don't provide so much detail that you lose your audience.
- As each person starts his or her part, state your name and what you will be covering.
- Use good transitions between speakers.
- Stay within the allotted time frame.
- Use visuals to present information when appropriate. For example, audience members likely will better understand financial and other quantitative information when it is presented in a visual format.
- Make sure visuals have no grammatical or spelling errors.
- Make your visuals simple and attractive.
- Display examples or samples of the company's products, if appropriate.
- Make good eye contact with different members of the audience—you don't want to always look at your professor.
- Practice the presentation before actually doing it.
- Enjoy giving your presentation, or at least act like you're enjoying it. If you act bored or uninterested, your audience is likely to respond in the same way.
- Vary the tone of your voice so it doesn't sound like you're speaking in a monotone.
- Don't use "umm" or "uhh" as you speak.
- Wear appropriate business–professional dress.
- Use note cards or a professional-looking folder to hold your typed notes.
- If using a PowerPoint presentation, do not talk to the computer screen in front of you or to the display screen behind you.
- Be sure to turn off cell phones, beepers, or pagers.

a cover page with pertinent information. You may even want to include a table of contents if your report is lengthy. Pay careful attention to what your professor outlines as the specific requirements for a written case analysis and follow those requirements to the letter!

Oral Presentation

You may also be required to present your case analysis information in an oral presentation. Again, your professor may have specific requirements for an oral presentation. Be sure that you prepare your materials in accordance with those specific requirements. Exhibit 2 offers some suggestions for good oral presentations.

Appendix 2
COMPREHENSIVE
CASES FOR ANALYSIS

In this section, you'll find five comprehensive cases for analysis. These cases—which include McDonald's, Starbucks, Southwest Airlines, Ford Motor Corporation, and Dell—cover a range of industries and strategic issues to consider. Although a significant amount of information is provided, you may want to find and use additional outside information, if your professor allows you to do so. After gathering your information, use the guidelines outlined in Appendix 1 for doing a comprehensive case analysis, unless your professor has specific directions for you to follow. I hope you have as much fun reading and analyzing these cases as I did writing them!

Mary Coulter

McDonald's Corporation

The Golden Arches of the McDonald's Corporation, which had lost a lot of their luster, are finally beginning to shine again. McDonald's, one of the world's best-known and most valuable brands, ranks eighth out of 100 brands in the Global 2003 Brand Scoreboard compiled by Interbrand Corporation and *Business Week*. As the world's number one fast-food company with more than $17 billion in sales and systemwide sales of over $42 billion for 2003, it has more than 30,000 locations in more than 100 countries. Approximately 30 percent of these locations are company owned; the rest are run by franchisees. The company that was founded on the premise of providing food and an atmosphere to make people smile saw nothing but frowns during 2001 and 2002.

WHAT HAPPENED?

For decades, McDonald's had been at the forefront of the fast-food industry. It was the best known of the fast-food chains, and it changed the way Americans ate (issues of healthy eating aside). And millions of Americans got their first taste of work life at a McDonald's. McDonald's prided itself on its consistent product and restaurant experience. Customers knew what to expect—they knew they would have the same food and restaurant experience at a McDonald's in downtown Detroit as they would at one in rural Arkansas. However, the brand, which was once synonymous with good service and consistently high product quality, was becoming known for slow, surly service and poor product quality. In a national survey of nearly 50,000 frequent eaters on 70 fast-food chains, McDonald's ranked last. As one of the researchers said, "Most consumers have a pretty low perception about food at McDonald's." And the chain had not launched a blockbuster product since 1983 when Chicken McNuggets were introduced. As if these problems weren't enough, the industry itself was dealing with major challenges during this time period. A price war with a "how-low-can-you-go" approach was taking a toll on all fast-food restaurants. Savvy consumers looking for value recognized that they could get a really cheap meal by purchasing a full-size burger or sandwich for a dollar and stopped buying the value meal deals, which typically require a purchase of the more-profitable fries and soft drink.

All these factors had a profound negative effect on the company's bottom line. In 2002 alone, same-store sales were down 1.5 percent in the United States and down 2 percent worldwide. In January 2003, the company announced its first quarterly loss ever since going public in 1965. During a three-year period from 2001 to early 2003, the price of this once-proud blue chip stock had slid 60 percent to a low of $13.50 at one point.

What had gone wrong? The problems could be traced to several strategic missteps under the leadership of former CEO Jack M. Greenberg. First, several new product launches didn't catch on. For example, the adult-targeted Arch Deluxe sandwich bombed and the Grilled Chicken Flatbread sandwich was only offered for a limited period of time. The chain also suffered serious execution problems when it tried to improve operations but failed miserably. Greenberg launched the Made For You food preparation system, which was designed to reduce waste and produce a better-tasting product. The company also tried customizing orders without increasing wait times, but that didn't work either. The designers of the preparation system somehow ignored the fact that cooking individual orders takes longer, thus jeopardizing speedy service. The franchise operators blamed corporate executives for the problems, saying that the remodeled kitchen design was faulty. The corporate executives blamed the franchise operators, saying that they needed to hire more people and provide better training.

Another strategy Greenberg thought would help the chain overcome the challenges of the increasingly competitive burger industry was expanding into the nonburger business. McDonald's Corp. purchased Boston Market, Donatos Pizzeria, and Chipotle Mexican Grill and took a minority stake in the London-based Pret A Manger sandwich shops. In addition, corporate executives discussed "expanding the company beyond food by trying a bunch of retailing experiments." They could pursue such a strategy because McDonald's is unique in the fast-food industry in that it owns much of its real estate or has it locked up in long-term leases, which means that it has more control over what it can do with its land. One of those retail experiments was with a mortgage finance company in which computers were installed in some restaurants to provide information about home ownership. Even though McDonald's had access to millions of customers daily, retail experts cautioned the company against trying to sell products that strayed too far from its core target market—families with children.

Despite all these strategic "fixes," corporate performance continued to deteriorate. In late 2001, the company announced a major restructuring of U.S. operations, cutting some 700 corporate jobs. When performance failed to improve in 2002, another 600 corporate employees were laid off and some underperforming units closed. It had become increasingly clear that it was time for a drastic change.

The first step in that change was the ouster of Greenberg and the naming of Jim Cantalupo as chairman and CEO on January 1, 2003.

THE STRATEGIC CHALLENGE

Cantalupo took over a company that was facing serious problems. He had to fix things and fix them fast or risk the company's ability to ever regain its prominence as an industry leader and corporate icon. It would be a difficult challenge! However, if anyone was up to the challenge of leading the company into the future, it would appear to be Jim Cantalupo. After 30 years working his way up the corporate hierarchy to the position of controller and eventually head of international operations—at one point he had even worked with the legendary late founder Ray Kroc—Cantalupo knew McDonald's business inside out. A term often used by long-term corporate employees is "having ketchup in your veins," and Cantalupo definitely did. He knew this business and this industry. However, when he was publicly passed over for the CEO post in 1998 upon the naming of Greenberg to the position, Cantalupo chose to leave the company and retire. With the decision to replace Greenberg, Cantalupo was called out of retirement to become CEO and to help move the company forward. His hands-on, back-to-basics leadership style would be what the company needed to correct its strategic missteps.

Several experts, including industry executives, business analysts, corporate consultants, and consumers, offered—with a nod to David Letterman—the top 10 things McDonald's needed to do to get its house in order: fix the food; serve it hot; lose the lines; clean up the place; don't ignore grown-ups; get relevant; get smarter about sideline businesses; give R&D more freedom to innovate; fix the ads; and get back to the basics.

Other experts and analysts outlined more broad and strategic changes that the company needed, including the following:

- *Split off the fast-casual partner brands.* Some experts estimated that these other restaurants had caused the company to lose over $120 million and had distracted it from its core business.

- *Say goodbye to the cooking system.* Even though operators had shelled out $50,000 per unit for the new kitchens, the system only marginally improved quality, while slowing down service.

- *Drop restaurant renovation plans.* The $300 million cost, which originally was almost $1 billion, was still too much at this time and wouldn't resolve the important problems.

- *Focus on the food.* Somehow and somewhere the products had lost their unique flavor and taste, and that needed to be regained as quickly as possible.

- *Execute more corporate layoffs.* Although painful, the company needed to continue restructuring to become more efficient.

- *Close underperforming stores.* They're a drag on corporate performance and may be cannibalizing other outlets.

- *Dump the distractions.* Retailing experiments and product extensions such as coffee shops and cafés aren't what McDonald's needed to be focusing on.

- *Reexamine the Disney connection.* Although the marketing deal between Disney and McDonald's had had its share of winners, Disney hasn't produced a smash kids movie for a while.
- *Remake the marketing.* The company's advertising had lost its way and needed work.
- *Think healthier.* Consumers' attitudes were changing and the company needed to respond.

However, Cantalupo had his own plans for restoring the luster to the Golden Arches. Those plans included *improving the basics* in order to pull the company out of the bottom of the heap in consumer surveys; *rekindling the relationship with franchisees* who had struggled as the company missed the mark again and again and again; *coming up with something new* by creating can't-miss new products; and *stop cannibalizing sales* of profitable outlets by shutting down poorly performing stores and beefing up locations with more potential.

McDONALD'S TODAY

Cantalupo's obsession with the basics—fast service, hot food, and clean restaurants—is relentless. He's been known to walk into McDonald's restaurants unannounced and, after looking around, to hand the store manager a score card that just happens to be printed on the back of his business card. And many times, the score on the scorecard is frank and critical. He says, "When I see something wrong, someone's gonna hear about it." But individual store operations wasn't the only area where Cantalupo focused his strategic efforts.

New Product Development

McDonald's had always been an innovator in developing new fast-food products. From the Big Mac to breakfast items to Chicken McNuggets, the company had been successful in understanding changing consumers' tastes and coming up with new formats and new products. However, product introductions during Greenberg's tenure had not done well at all because they were poor product concepts that were poorly executed. Cantalupo's first push was to "beef up" (pun intended) the company's salad offerings. Although McDonald's had been selling salads for more than a decade, they had never really been a hit with consumers. The initial salad products were simply unappetizing lettuce sold in containers displayed in countertop refrigerators. The company had tried something new when it introduced McSalad Shakers, a salad offered in a cup-like container. But once again, these weren't very popular with consumers. In April 2003, the company introduced its new line of Premium Salads. Premium Salads are made to order and blend iceberg lettuce with other, more nutritional greens and can be topped with warm grilled or crispy chicken. Customers have a choice of four Newman's Own dressing flavors. The new salads, and the marketing to promote them, were designed to appeal to health-conscious women who had been avoiding McDonald's. Kay Napier, senior vice president of marketing, said, "A lot of women were still coming to McDonald's and eating but weren't satisfied with the food offerings, or they were coming and buying food for their kids and not buying food for themselves." This salad line has been a resounding success. Sales of the salads have skyrocketed and, in turn, helped boost sales of other products. Happy Meal sales were the strongest they'd been in two years and sales of grilled chicken sandwiches also rose once the salads were launched.

Another popular new product has been the McGriddles breakfast sandwich, which launched in June 2003. The McGriddles breakfast sandwich, which is not the healthiest item, and not intended to be, consists of two syrup-drenched pancakes acting as top and bottom "buns" holding eggs, cheese, sausage, and bacon in three different combinations. The product has sold so well that it's now second only to the sausage McMuffin with egg as the most popular breakfast item.

Not counting the McGriddles, McDonald's has become quite serious about promoting healthier product choices. They've enlisted the services of Bob Greene, the personal trainer who has worked with Oprah Winfrey. It's testing new healthier, adult "Go Active" meals that offer a salad, an exercise booklet, and a pedometer meant to encourage walking. It also introduced a taco version of its premium salads. And, in December, 2003, it introduced an all-white-meat Chicken McNugget. Yet, not everything has been positive from a healthy eating perspective. The promised removal of artery-clogging trans fat from its french fries has yet to happen.

Store Operations and Customer Service

This area needed serious improvements. Although some progress had been made, a survey of restaurant drive-through operations in mid-2003 showed that McDonald's had tumbled from 4th place to 12th overall. And in a specific measure of order accuracy, the company fell to 19th place out of 25 restaurants studied.

McDonald's past global success had been, in part, due to its standardized and uniform operations. The McDonald's operations manual dictated every move made inside one of its restaurants. There were rules governing how many hamburger patties to a pound (10), how long to toast a bun (17 seconds), and how much sanitizer to use when cleaning the milkshake machine. Yet, somewhere along the way, the fundamentals had lost their importance. Customers complained of dirty restaurants and warm (sometimes even cold) food. And the worst part was that no one seemed to care. At one of Cantalupo's first meetings with executives in the home office, he made one thing clear: The focus would be on fixing McDonald's first before worrying about the pizza, chicken, and Mexican chains. He cut back the number of new store openings in 2003 to 500, from 1,250 in 2002, because he wanted to ensure that existing stores had time and space to improve. He said, "If you're confused about what this is about, let me make it clear: This is about our customers."

In addition to his own personal ratings of stores he visits, Cantalupo decided it was time to start grading the restaurants on a scale everyone could understand. Former CEO Greenberg's attempt at getting more customer feedback, a $1 billion information network called Project Innovate that was designed to provide real-time sales data from the company's 31,000 plus restaurants to headquarters in Oak Brook, Illinois, wasn't working. Michael Roberts, head of McDonald's U.S. operations, wanted more customer feedback, because massive amounts of sales data weren't what he needed when customers were upset with lousy food, slow service, sloppy stores, and rude employees. It didn't take long for Cantalupo to drop Project Innovate in favor of anonymous reviews of service using a hard-number scoring system. Mystery diners from outside survey firms now rate restaurants on their speed of service; food temperature, presentation and taste; cleanliness of the counter, tables, and condiment islands; and on other factors, including whether counter employees smile at customers. The results are posted on an internal McDonald's Web site so owners can compare their stores with regional averages. They can pinpoint problems and take action. "People know what's being measured, and it certainly helps to focus their minds," says one corporate executive.

Cantalupo also sent 900 operations experts out into the field restaurants, with each person visiting stores multiple times to help them fine-tune operations. McDonald's Corp. also conducted day-long seminars where store managers shared tips with each other and where corporate kitchen experts educated the managers about topics such as how to position crew members to shave precious seconds off average service times.

After surveys revealed that changes to popular products, such as the sauce on the Big Mac, had not gone over well with customers, Cantalupo ordered a comprehensive product review. He appointed a team of chefs and selected franchisee operators to review the products, and they made several changes. They restored the more expensive ingredients in the Big Mac sauce and changed the salt-and-pepper seasoning in the beef patties. They also changed the bun recipes to enhance the sweet, caramelized flavor and lengthened the toasting time to enhance the look and feel of the product. Cantalupo said, "Everyone wants to say that our turnaround was about the salads. But it isn't. It was hundreds of things—with formulations, times and temperatures, the Big Mac sauce. Our food tastes better today. It's one of the reasons we're doing so well."

Other changes included improving customer wait time by making the outdoor menu boards more "idiot proof" with more pictures and fewer words. An LED display also confirms what customers say so there's no confusion about the order. Also, premium sandwiches have been repackaged in boxes, rather than wrappers. And the boxes are color coded by sandwich to improve speed and accuracy.

Marketing

The company's marketing was another area that needed to be fixed. Surveys showed that its ads were hitting the mark with little kids, but alienating teenagers and young adults. The "I'm lovin' it" ads left consumers uncomfortable with the unfamiliar message. However, McDonald's executives have decided to stick with the ads and use them globally as a single brand message, a first for the company. Its advertising expenditures in 2003 were nearly $710 million, up 9.6 percent from 2002.

Other marketing changes being proposed include a redesign of the company's packaging, especially its cups, french-fry holders, and the to-go bags. Happy Meals are getting a makeover as well. In the United States, the company is adding 1 percent milk and Apple Dippers; in Italy, fruit cups are being added; and in Spain, Dannon low-fat yogurt is being added. The company will also be pursuing opportunities to align the brand more with popular music, sports, fashion, and entertainment outlets.

Although the company had made changes in its marketing, problems still existed. In addition to the surveys described earlier, the company got some disturbing news from a mid-2003 marketing survey of repeat customers. Many ate at McDonald's simply because they had no better alternative. And, for the first time in 15 years, more people disliked the brand than liked it. So there's still work to be done.

Beyond Burgers

Some of McDonald's past attempts to expand outside of fast food hadn't been as successful as hoped. In 1991, Sears closed all 47 free-standing McKids stores (which sold kids' clothing and toys) because of poor performance. And test marketing of huge, high-tech vending machines—described as really tiny convenience stores—outside some McDonald's in Washington D.C. didn't work. They were shut down because they attracted lots of attention, but didn't generate much business. The biggest question mark, though, was the company's fast-casual dining brands, which still, for the most part, were losing money.

After deliberating several months about what to do with the company's outside partner brands, the company's executives decided in the fourth quarter of 2003 to sell a couple of divisions: the Boston Market chicken restaurants outside the United States and the Donatos Pizzeria chain, which they sold back to its founder. The company also chose to exit its domestic joint venture with Fazoli's Italian Restaurants. They chose, however, to keep the Chipotle Mexican Grill chain and the U.S. Boston Market chicken restaurants and to retain its minority investment in Pret a Manger in all locations except Japan. Cantalupo said the moves were "consistent with the company's new priority to do fewer things better" in order to boost long-term growth in sales and profits. To accommodate the divestments, the company took mostly non-cash charges of 23 to 28 cents a share.

Despite its stated desire to narrow its focus, McDonald's announced plans in November 2003 to globally relaunch its marginally successful McKids line, which it did in spring 2004. But this time, instead of just kids' clothing and toys, the line expanded to include interactive videos and books. The McKids line isn't sold at McDonald's stores, but at Wal-Mart, Toys R Us, and Target. The company also signed licensing agreements for the McKids brand name with Mattel, Hasbro, and Creative Designs.

Taking Care of Its People

McDonald's commitment to its employees has been a focus since Ray Kroc founded the company in 1955. Its belief is that "only satisfied people can satisfy our customers." This philosophy has continued throughout its history.

Take good care of those who work for you, and you will float to greatness on their achievements.—Ray Kroc, Founder and Chairman of the Board, 1955–1977.

We are not going to give in to a hollow concept of bigness, because people make a company—not a balance sheet or a listing on the New York Stock Exchange.—Fred Turner, Chairman of the Board, 1977–1990.

We have to recognize that we have to empower our management teams and our crews to do what's necessary to take the best care of our customers.—Michael Quinlan, Chairman of the Board, 1990–1999.

For McDonald's to achieve its goal of being the world's best quick-service restaurant, it realized the importance of providing the best experience for all McDonald's employees. These beliefs have been formalized into its People Vision and its People Promise.

McDonald's People Vision:
We Aspire to Be the Best Employer in Each Community Around the World.

McDonald's People Promise:
To the 1.5 million people who work at McDonald's in 119 countries around the world, and to all future employees, we want you to know that: We Value You, Your Growth, and Your Contributions. This is our People Promise.

The company has won several awards worldwide for its employment practices. It was named Brazil's Best Employer in the Retail Industry for the third year in a row by a leading business magazine. The company's focus on training, employee development, and opportunities for advancement were key factors in receiving this award. McDonald's Sweden was named Best Competence Company by a leading Swedish university, again because of its commitment to employee training and career development. And in 1999, the Australian National Training Association named McDonald's Australia as the Employer of the Year, the third consecutive year for the honor.

Doing Business Responsibly

McDonald's commitment to social responsibility is an important part of its heritage. Jim Cantalupo says, "More than ever, we are focused on and committed to doing the right thing for the local communities in which we operate and for the customers we serve. This philosophy of doing good and giving back has always been at the heart and soul of the McDonald's business." This commitment can be seen in four areas: community, environment, marketplace, and people.

Its community commitment means that it supports local schools, youth sports, and other community programs. For example, one of its most widely known programs, the Ronald McDonald House charity, provides health care and help to children and families around the world. Its environmental commitment is reflected in its long-standing support of environmental protection. McDonald's has developed innovative programs for recycling, resource conservation, and waste reduction. The company's marketplace commitment involve working with suppliers and expert advisers to improve animal handling practices, helping to preserve the effectiveness of antibiotics, ensuring the safety and quality of products and restaurant environments, and promoting the protection of workers' healthy, safety, and human rights. Finally, its people commitment is expressed in its People Vision and People Promise and extends further to integrating diversity in business operations and planning.

INDUSTRY CHARACTERISTICS

The restaurant industry is an interesting one. The industry has a lot of growth potential because an increasing portion of consumers' food dollars is being spent on eating out. According to the U.S. Department of Agriculture, consumption of food away from home accounted for 46.1 percent of total food expenditures in 2002 (the latest data available). With the increase in dual-income families, single-parent families, and numerous moderately priced restaurant choices, dining out is often the most convenient option. But it's the casual dining sector that's profiting most from this trend. It continues to gain market share from fast-food chains, probably because an aging population prefers full-service restaurants. In addition, fast-food chains have to deal with consumers' demands for healthier food alternatives. Not only will this help attract customers, it's important for deflecting potential obesity-related lawsuits.

Another trend impacting the fast-food industry is the rapidly fragmenting market of different ethnicities that have made once-exotic foods such as sushi and burritos everyday meal options. In addition, quick meals of all kinds can be found in many locations, including supermarkets, convenience stores, and even vending machines.

In late 2003, burger companies were startled by the first case of mad-cow disease found in the United States. McDonald's profits previously had been hurt by this food-safety issue in its global restaurants, but this was the first time it was faced with the potential fall-out from this threat domestically.

WHAT NOW?

Grappling with a tired brand, a glut of restaurants, and increasing societal concerns about obesity, Cantalupo had his work cut out for him. However, he was able to spark a turnaround. He said, "It's clear to me that we have turned the corner and are embarking on 2004 with a stronger playbook. Our Plan to Win is driving results and we are gaining momentum." This Plan to Win has played a primary role in the company's new strategic direction. What is it?

> McDonald's strategies for achieving sustainable, profitable growth are customer driven, goal oriented, and are designed to increase restaurant visits and grow brand loyalty among new and existing customers, and further build our financial strength. (excerpted from the Plan to Win).

The Plan to Win is built upon three components of success.

The first is operational excellence. The company pursued this by implementing a consistent restaurant-specific review and measurement process that included mystery diners. It also made changes to increase the speed of service, including better organizing the kitchen, front-counter, and drive-through areas and simplifying the restaurant environment by eliminating certain sizes and slow-selling items. In addition, it made a commitment to reemphasize hospitality, accuracy, and cleanliness through new employee training and incentive programs.

The second component for success is leadership marketing, which it is doing by reconnecting with customers using a hip and contemporary global marketing direction. It chose to use a global brand message in advertising, packaging, and restaurant experiences. The "I'm lovin' it" campaign was designed to be more than a global marketing effort. It reflected an attitude that employees were to embrace and display as they served customers.

The final component for success is innovation. The company is refocusing its efforts on being an innovator. Its goal is to feature a variety of value, premium, and wholesome product options and to deliver the right products at the right price to customers.

In addition to its Plan to Win, the company has been working hard to improve individual restaurant profitability by leveraging economies of scale and by being more efficient. To this end, it has expanded the use of labor-saving equipment and streamlined processes. Corporate financial highlights can be found on its Web site (**www.mcdonalds.com**).

Where does McDonald's go from here? The company seems to have reversed its downward slide, but faces continuing challenges. Its goals for 2005 and beyond include annual systemwide sales and revenue growth of 3 percent to 5 percent, annual operating income growth of 6 percent to 7 percent, and annual return on incremental invested capital in the high teens. Achieving these returns will be a challenge for Cantalupo and the entire McDonald's organization.

Epilogue

On April 19, 2004, Jim Cantalupo died unexpectedly of an apparent heart attack in Orlando, Florida, where almost 12,000 McDonald's franchisees had gathered for a worldwide convention. The company's board met and quickly named Charlie Bell, the company president as CEO. Bell was Cantalupo's right-hand man and one of the most forceful proponents of change at McDonald's. He faces the difficult task of keeping the momentum going in the company's remarkable turnaround. As if dealing with these issues wasn't enough, just 16 days after being named Cantalupo's replacement, Bell underwent successful colorectal cancer surgery in early May.

(*Sources:* McDonald's, **www.mcdonalds.com**, April 8, 2004; Hoover's Online, **www.hoovers.com**, April 8, 2004; Standard & Poor's NetAdvantage, **www.netadvantage.standardandpoors.com**, April 8, 2004; B. Horovitz and T. Ankner, "McDonald's Absorbs Another Blow," *USA Today,* May 7, 2004, p. 3B; J. Zich, "McDonald's CEO Cantalupo Restored Luster of Its Arches," *USA Today,* April 20, 2004, pp. 1A+; D. Kruger, "You Want Data With That?" *Forbes,* March 29, 2004, pp. 58–60; The Associated Press, "McDonald's Happy Meals Get New Items, Make-Over," *USA Today,* March 19, 2004; S. Leung, "McDonald's Makeover," *Wall Street Journal,* January 28, 2004, p. B1; B. Horovitz, "McDonald's CEO Could Be One to Copy or One to Console," *USA Today,* December 23, 2003, p. B1; The Associated Press, "McDonald's Sells Donatos, Narrows Focus," *USA Today,* December 16, 2003; T. Howard, "Survey: Not All Viewers Lovin' It," *USA Today,* November 24, 2003; B. Horovitz, "McDonald's Ventures Beyond Burgers to Duds, Toys," *USA Today,* November 14, 2003, p. 6B; The Associated Press, "Drive-Thru Survey Bags McDonald's," *USA Today,* September 30, 2003; The Associated Press, "McDonald's Testing Healthier, Adult 'Go Active' Meal," *USA Today,* September 18, 2003; P. Gogoi, "Saving Mickey D's Bacon," *Business Week,* August 25, 2003, p. 46; "The Top 100 Brands," *Business Week,* August 4, 2003, p. 72; N. Pachetti, "Back in the Kitchen," *Money,* July 2003, pp. 44–45; T. Howard, "McDonald's Salads Lure Women," *USA Today,* June 16, 2003; B. Horovitz, "CEO May Reveal Plans to Restore Luster to Golden Arches," *USA Today,* May 5, 2003; P. Gogoi and M. Arndt, "Hamburger Hell," *Business Week,* March 3, 2003, pp. 104–108; B. Horovitz, "McDonald's Plans Big Overhaul for Image," *USA Today,* February 7, 2003; B. Horovitz, "Ten Things McDonald's Must Do to Get Its House in Order," *USA Today,* December 12, 2002; B. Horovitz, "Burger Wars Heat Up as Consumers Devour Value," *USA Today,* November 11, 2002, p. 4B; J. Forster, "You Deserve A Better Break Today," *Business Week,* September 30, 2002, p. 42; J. Forster, "Thinking Outside the Burger Box," *Business Week,* September 16, 2002, pp. 66–67; and D. Stires, "Fallen Arches," *Fortune,* April 29, 2002, pp. 74–76.)

Starbucks Corporation

If a steaming cup of aromatic specialty gourmet coffee is your thing, you've undoubtedly heard of Starbucks Corporation. Starbucks is the world's number one specialty coffee retailer with more than 7,500 coffee shops in more than 30 countries of which licensees operate over 2,800. Starbucks coffee shops and kiosks are located in shopping centers, airports, office buildings, bookstores, supermarkets, and as stand-alone stores. Can Starbucks' managers keep the company's growth percolating along?

INDUSTRY AND COMPETITORS

The coffee industry is an interesting one. Coffee has been consumed since the fifteenth century when traveling Arabian merchants and herbalists peddled it. Although it was first used as an essential component in religious ceremonies, it soon spread from the clergy to the masses, and coffee production and trade became, and remain, a very serious business. Coffee is now one of the most valuable primary commodities in the world—second only to oil in terms of dollar trade worldwide—and more than 20 million people around the world earn their living from it.

In the United States, total coffee consumption per capita (not just coffee drinkers) has held fairly steady, going up some years and declining slightly in others. Exhibit 1 provides a summary of the total cups consumed per capita since 1995. Another survey done by the National Coffee Association found that 54 percent of the adult population of the United States drink coffee daily and 25 percent drink coffee occasionally. The average consumption among coffee drinkers is 3.1 cups of coffee per day. The survey also reported that over 18 percent of the coffee drinkers in the United States drink gourmet coffee beverages daily. Consumption has been increasing in the gourmet specialty coffee segment, although not as quickly as it once had.

The specialty coffee segment is popular, and its interests are supported and advocated by the Specialty Coffee Association of America (**www.scaa.org**), which was founded in 1982. Members of the SCAA include retailers, roasters, roaster–retailers, producers, exporters, importers, and manufacturers of coffee equipment and other allied products. It is now the world's largest trade association with almost 2,500 members. Its goal is to "improve the industry on a global level and from a 'seed to cup' perspective to ensure specialty coffees are available long into the twenty-first century." The SCAA is particularly focused on "the establishment of coffee quality standards and certified professional skills."

Year	Cups Consumed
1995	1.67
1996	1.69
1997	1.84
1998	1.63
1999	1.89
2000	1.66
2001	1.72
2002	1.64

Source: *United States Department of Agriculture*, **www.usda.gov**, *"U.S. Coffee Consumption," April 8, 2004.*

Exhibit 1

U.S. Consumption of Coffee: Cups Per Capita, Per Day

Exhibit 2

*Facts About the Specialty
Coffee Segment*

DAILY CONSUMPTION OF SPECIALTY COFFEE AMONG ADULTS:

1999	9% of adult population
2000	9% of adult population
2001	14% of adult population
2002	13% of adult population

DOLLAR SIZE OF MARKET (2002)

Coffee Cafés (beverage retailers with seating)	$4.5 billion
Coffee Kiosks (beverage retailers without seating)	$0.78 billion
Coffee Carts (mobile beverage retailers)	$0.25 billion
Coffee Bean Roasters–Retailers (roasting on premise)	$1.10 billion
Total Café Segment Sales	$6.63 billion
Other Bean Sales	$1.77 billion
TOTAL MARKET SIZE	$8.40 billion

Source: *Specialty Coffee Association of America,* **www.scaa.org**, *April 12, 2004.*

Specialty coffee, sometimes called gourmet or premium coffee, is defined as a coffee that has no defects and has a distinctive flavor in the cup. The term was coined by Erna Knutsen in a 1974 issue of *Tea & Coffee Trade Journal* as a way to describe beans of outstanding flavor produced by special microclimates. Specialty coffees are made from exceptional beans grown only in ideal coffee-producing climates and tend to feature distinctive flavors shaped by the unique characteristics of the soil that produced them.

The proliferation of cafés and gourmet coffee retailers in the 1990s has made specialty coffee one of the fastest-growing food-service markets in the world, netting revenues of some $8.4 billion in 2002 in the United States alone. Other facts about the specialty coffee segment are shown in Exhibit 2.

Other interesting and fun facts about coffee from the SCAA include:

- A cup of specialty coffee costs about 24 cents, making it cheaper than bottled water.

- Every day, Americans drink more than 300 million cups of coffee, 75 percent of which are home brewed.

- It takes approximately 42 coffee beans to make an average serving of espresso.

- More than half of Americans (66 percent) drink coffee away from home.

One concern that has plagued the coffee industry is conflicting reports about the safety of coffee consumption. Based on medical studies in the 1970s and 1980s, it was thought that drinking too much coffee, especially caffeinated coffee, could be harmful, which led people to cut back on consumption. However, a recent study by Harvard and Brigham and Young researchers found that study participants who regularly drank coffee had a significantly reduced risk of onset of Type 2 diabetes when compared with non-coffee-drinking study participants. Despite the contradictory advice, drinking a cup of coffee continues to be an important part of many people's daily routines.

Other factors affecting the industry are the increasing consumption of bottled water and the consumption habits of 18- to 35-year-olds, who regularly drink carbonated caffeine soft drinks (i.e., soda). The Beverage Marketing Corporation reported in April 2004 that bottled water now ranks as the second largest commercial beverage category in the United States on a volume basis. It has surpassed beer, coffee, and milk to become one of America's favorite drinks. And in the carbonated soft drink market, industry giants Coca-Cola and Pepsi continue to seek growth by introducing new flavored line extensions of existing products, such as Sprite Remix and Mountain Dew LiveWire. These products are specifically designed to appeal to the teen and young adult market.

The success of Starbucks has been beneficial for all coffee distributors in the United States by encouraging innovation in the industry. Competition in the specialty gourmet coffee segment comes from other large global chains as well as from small local and regional gourmet coffee stores. In addition, other coffee and baked goods chains and coffee sold by consumer-products companies can be considered competitors. Who are some of these competitors?

Among gourmet coffee providers, illycaffé (**www.illy.com**) may be one of Starbucks' strongest competitors globally, because it is well positioned in the premium sector. illycaffé is the number two Italian espresso coffee manufacturer. Being a single-product company, illycaffé differentiates its packages of espresso coffee only by weight (from 3 kilograms for professional consumption and from 125 to 150 grams for individual consumption), form (ground coffee, beans, or other), and type (regular or decaffeinated). illycaffé estimates its coffee produces almost 5 million cups of espresso each day. And Italy's leading producer of coffee beans, Luigi Lavazza S.P.A., offers more than 350 varieties of roasted coffee beans for sale in 70 countries. Lavazza (**www.lavazza.it**) makes coffee for home use, institutional customers, and restaurants.

BAB, Inc. (**www.babholdings.com**), which is based in Chicago, franchises and licenses about 200 specialty restaurants in 30 states and 3 foreign countries. BAB's flagship store, Big Apple Bagels, offers bagels, spreads, sandwiches, soups, and gourmet coffee. It also owns Brewster's Coffee, which serves gourmet and specialty coffee along with sandwiches and snacks.

Another competitor is New World Restaurant Group, Inc. (**www.nwrgi.com**), based in Golden, Colorado. The company is one of the largest bagel shop operators in the United States. Its brands include Einstein Brothers Bagels, Noah's Bagels, Manhattan Bagel, and Chesapeake Bagel Bakery. The company's almost 750 locations offer fresh-made bagels and spreads, sandwich items, and coffee. It also operates two coffee shop chains: New World Coffee and Willoughby's Coffee & Tea. The New World Coffee neighborhood shops (**www.newworld-coffee.com**) offer different varieties of fresh roasted coffee, Italian-style beverages, and an extensive selection of breakfast and dessert items. Currently, there are fewer than 30 of these locations in the northeastern United States.

Switzerland-based Nestlé SA (**www.nestle.com**) is the world's number one food company and the world leader in coffee with its Nescafé brand and in bottled water with its Perrier brand. Nestlé is a formidable player that other competitors must keep an eye on. Any strategic moves that it makes may necessitate strategic responses or changes on the part of industry competitors.

Other potential competitors include:

- Au Bon Pain (**www.aubonpain.com**)
- AFC Enterprises (**www.afce.com**)—includes the brands Cinnabon and Seattle's Best Coffee.
- Allied Domecq, PLC (**www.allieddomecqplc.com**)—includes the brand Dunkin' Donuts, which sells over 1.8 million cups of coffee daily
- Churchill Coffee Company (**www.churchillcoffee.com**)

- Diedrich Coffee (**www.diedrich.com**)
- Farmer Brothers (**www.easycoffee.com**)
- Green Mountain Coffee (**www.greenmountaincoffee.com**)
- Kraft Foods (**www.kraftfoods.com**)—markets the Maxwell House and Sanka brands
- Panera Bread (**www.panerabread.com**)
- Peets (**www.peets.com**)
- Procter & Gamble (**www.pg.com**)—markets the Folger's brand
- Sara Lee (**www.saralee.com**)
- Tully's Coffee Corporation (**www.tullys.com**)

STARBUCKS—THE COMPANY

"We aren't in the coffee business, serving people. We are in the people business, serving coffee." That's the philosophy of Howard Schultz, chairman and chief global strategist of Starbucks Corporation. It's a philosophy that shapes the company's goals, strategies, and future.

The first Starbucks, which opened in Seattle's famous Pike Place Market in 1971, was founded by Gordon Bowker, Jerry Baldwin, and Ziv Siegl. The company was named for the coffee-loving first mate in the book *Moby Dick,* which also influenced the design of Starbucks' distinctive two-tailed siren logo. Schultz, a successful New York City businessperson, first walked into Starbucks as a sales representative for a Swedish kitchenware manufacturer. He was hooked immediately. He knew that he wanted to work at this company, but the owners weren't easily convinced. Schultz finally joined the company as director of retail operations and marketing in 1982 and pushed for the company to grow, but the owners weren't really interested in making Starbucks big. While on a business trip to Milan a year after joining the company, Schultz walked into an espresso bar and right away knew that this concept could be successful in the United States. He said, "There was nothing like this in America. It was an extension of people's front porch. It was an emotional experience. I believed intuitively we could do it. I felt it in my bones." However, Starbucks' owners wouldn't really give it a try, so Schultz left the company in 1985 to start his own small chain of espresso bars in Seattle and Vancouver called Il Giornale. Two years later when Starbucks' owners finally wanted to sell, Schultz raised $3.8 million from local investors to buy them out. That small investment has made Schultz a very wealthy person indeed!

At first, only yuppies went to Starbucks. After all, at $3.50 for a latte, customers had to be convinced that it was worth it. But considering the company's success, they obviously did find it worth the price. Starbucks now brings in a much wider demographic, from older people to younger people to people of different ethnic backgrounds. And what do they get at a Starbucks? Some of the finest coffee available commercially, custom preparation, and the Starbucks ambiance—the music, the comfy chairs, the smells, and, of course, the hissing steam. Today, the company has over 7,500 company-operated and licensed stores worldwide. What does Starbucks actually do?

The company purchases and roasts high-quality whole bean coffees and sells them along with fresh, rich-brewed coffees; Italian-style espresso beverages; cold, blended beverages; a variety of complementary food items; coffee-related accessories and equipment; a selection of premium teas; and a line of compact discs. It also produces and sells bottled Frappuccino® and Starbucks DoubleShot™ coffee drinks and a line of premium ice creams. The company has two operating segments—United States and International, each of which includes a division comprising the company-operated retail stores and a division called Specialty Operations.

Company-Operated Retail Stores

In 2003, Starbucks opened 602 new company-operated stores, which gave it 3,779 company-operated stores in the United States, 373 in the United Kingdom, 316 in Canada, 40 in Australia, and 38 in Thailand at the end of fiscal 2003. This division accounted for approximately 85 percent of total net revenues in 2003.

Because their size and format can vary, these stores are located in a variety of settings, including downtown and suburban retail centers, office buildings, and university campuses. Although Starbucks selectively locates in suburban malls, it focuses on stores that have convenient access for pedestrians and drivers. In 2003, the retail sales mix by product type was 78 percent beverages, 12 percent food items, 5 percent whole bean coffees, and 5 percent coffee-making equipment and accessories.

Starbucks' goal for its retail operations is to become the leading retailer and brand of coffee in each of its target markets by selling the finest quality coffee and related products and by providing superior customer service, thus building a high degree of customer loyalty. Its strategy for achieving this goal has been to expand its retail business by increasing market share in existing markets, primarily by opening additional stores and by opening stores in new markets where an opportunity exists to become the leading specialty coffee retailer.

Specialty Operations

The Specialty Operations division develops the Starbucks brand outside the company-operated retail store environment through a number of different channels. These channels include licensing arrangements, food-service accounts, and other strategic initiatives related to the company's core business. Revenues from this division accounted for approximately 15 percent of total net revenues in 2003.

At the end of 2003, Starbucks had 1,422 licensed or franchised stores in the United States and 1,257 international licensed stores. In 2003, Starbucks licensed the first stores in Chile, Peru, and Turkey. In addition to the new stores it licensed in 2003, Starbucks also now has 76 franchised Seattle's Best Coffee retail stores from its acquisition of Seattle Coffee Company from AFC Enterprises. It also has a licensing arrangement with Kraft Foods to market and distribute Starbucks whole bean and ground coffees to grocery stores and warehouse club stores. And it has licensed the rights to produce and distribute Starbucks branded products with two companies: Pepsi-Cola (Frappuccino® and DoubleShot™ coffee drinks) and Dreyer's Grand Ice Cream (Starbucks Ice Cream). In April 2004, Starbucks announced it was developing a line of premium coffee liqueurs with the Jim Beam unit of Fortune Brands. The product will be sold in bars, restaurants, and liquor stores, but not in its retail store locations. Experts believed that this new product partner was a close, logical brand extension.

In its food-service business, Starbucks sells whole bean and ground coffees (Starbucks®, Seattle's Best Coffee®, and Torrefazione Italia®) brands to institutional food-service companies that service hotels, restaurants, airlines, business and industry, education, health care, and other retail accounts. Starbucks is also the only premium national brand coffee actively promoted by SYSCO Corporation's national distribution network. SYSCO just happens to be the largest food-service distributor in North America.

Starbucks has also developed other strategic initiatives to enhance its core business. It markets a selection of premium tea products since its acquisition of Tazo, LLC in 1999. The company also maintains a Web site where customers may purchase, register, or reload a Starbucks stored-value card as well as apply for a Starbucks Card Duetto™ Visa®, which is a first-of-its-kind card that combines the functionality of a credit card with the convenience of a reloadable Starbucks card. Within two months of its introduction in 2003, the Duetto Card was recognized by *Business Week* as one of the "Best Products of 2003." The company's original Starbucks Card was launched in late 2001 as a way to save customers time waiting in line. In the first month of the program, customers purchased 2.3 million cards worth $32 million. Since then, they've purchased another 11.3 million cards. Although hard-number comparison is difficult, industry experts rate the Starbucks card as one of the most successful launches of its kind. It accounts for 1 out of every 10 transactions at stores, and about one-third of cardholders reload the cards to use again. That level of return business suggests that Starbucks has transformed a relatively "dumb" pre-paid convenience card into a smart device that identifies its most loyal customers, who undoubtedly will return.

One of the company's most interesting brand extensions has been music. The sale of music at Starbucks began when a store manager (Timothy Jones) made tapes for his store. These tapes proved to be so popular that the company licensed compilations for sale. Schultz had to be talked into this product and recalls, "I began to understand that our customers looked to Starbucks as kind of editor. It was like . . . we trust you. Help us choose." In addition to selling its private-label CDs, the company launched the Hear Music Café in Santa Monica, California, in March 2004. There, customers can listen to more than 250,000 online songs on headphones for free. After sampling selections, if they choose to buy, they can walk up to a music "bar" and order a custom CD with any variation of songs and have it delivered to their table when it's completed. The company expanded the service to 10 stores in Seattle in April 2004 and will roll out the concept to 2,500 stores over the next two years.

Although it may seem that all of Starbucks' brand extensions have prospered, that's not the case. For example, the *Joe* magazine launched in 1999 by Starbucks and *Time* lasted three issues. Five Starbucks restaurants, opened in 1998, have been closed. And a carbonated coffee beverage called Mazagran, developed with PepsiCo, never made it to market.

In 2003, total Specialty Operations revenue was allocated as follows: worldwide retail store licensing, approximately 39 percent; grocery and warehouse club sales, approximately 25 percent; equity investees, approximately 1 percent; food-service accounts, approximately 27 percent; and other strategic initiatives, approximately 8 percent. This division's strategy continues to be reaching customers where they work, travel, shop, and dine by establishing relationships with prominent third parties that share the company's values and commitment to quality.

Mission Statement and Guiding Principles

The company's mission statement (found on its Web site) is as follows:

> To establish Starbucks as the premier purveyor of the finest coffee in the world while maintaining our uncompromising principles while we grow.

In conjunction with the mission statement, company employees use six guiding principles (found on the company's Web site) to measure the appropriateness of their decisions:

- Provide a great work environment and treat each other with respect and dignity.
- Embrace diversity as an essential component in the way we do business.
- Apply the highest standards of excellence to the purchasing, roasting, and fresh delivery of our coffee.
- Develop enthusiastically satisfied customers all the time.
- Contribute positively to our communities and our environment.
- Recognize that profitability is essential to our future success.

In addition to its corporate mission statement, Starbucks has developed an environmental mission as a framework for employee decision making. This mission is as follows:

Starbucks is committed to a role of environmental leadership in all facets of our business.

Starbucks is an unusual company in that it strives to mix capitalism with social responsibility. Schultz says, "What I'm most proud of over the last 15 years is that Starbucks has integrated a social conscience in all parts of our business. That's one reason we've done so well." And the company's commitment to ethical and socially responsible ways of doing business has been recognized publicly as it was once again named to *Business Ethics* list of the "100 Best Corporate Citizens" and was included on the Dow Jones Sustainability Index in 2003. Starbucks also was the first company to receive the Colombian government's Order of the Grand Cross medal, an honor awarded for its work in local coffee communities. Previous recipients of this award have included the Spanish government and a branch of the United Nations.

STARBUCKS—THE PEOPLE

Howard Schultz is the visionary and soul behind Starbucks Corporation. He's been described as "very directed and dogged and a decent person also." Former Senator Bill Bradley, who is now a member of the company's board of directors, says, "Howard is consumed with his vision of Starbucks. That means showing the good that a corporation can do for its workers, shareholders, and customers." Schultz's dream from the beginning was to create something that never really existed in the United States—the café experience, which for centuries has been a hallmark of European society. In pursuing this dream, he has created an American institution. Starbucks is possibly the most dynamic new brand and retailer to be conceived over the last two decades.

From day one, Schultz's focus has been on growth. He says, "We're in the second inning of a nine-inning game. We are just beginning to tap into all sorts of new markets, new customers, and new products." And many of his ideas about how to continue growing are unconventional. For instance, he refuses to franchise. "I look at franchising as a way of accessing capital and I will never make the tradeoff between cheap money and losing control over our stores." Instead, Starbucks has funded expansion through its own cash flow (at the end of fiscal 2003, it had over

Exhibit 3

List of Executive Officers

• Howard Schultz	Chairman, chief global strategist
• Orin C. Smith	President, chief executive officer
• Jim Donald	President, Starbucks North America
• Paula Boggs	EVP, general counsel and secretary
• Michael Casey	EVP, chief financial officer, chief administrative officer
• E.R. (Ted) Garcia	EVP, Supply Chain and Coffee Operations
• David A. Pace	EVP, Partner Resources
• Deidra Wager	EVP, Starbucks Coffee Company
• Jim Alling	SVP, Marketing, North America
• Troy Alstead	SVP, Starbucks Coffee International
• Martin Annese	SVP, Northeast, U.S. Retail
• Michael Bessire	SVP, Central, U.S. Retail
• David Chichester	CTO, Starbucks Coffee Japan
• Brian Crynes	SVP, chief information officer
• Christine Day	SVP, North American Administration
• Margie Giuntini	SVP, North America Partner Resources
• Julio Gutierrez	SVP, president, Latin America
• Willard (Dub) Hay	SVP, Coffee
• Buck Hendrix	SVP, International Supply Chain Operations
• Wanda J. Herndon	SVP, Worldwide Public Affairs
• Gregg S. Johnson	SVP, Retail Stores - U.S.A.
• Dorothy Kim	SVP, Global Logistics & Procurement, Supply Chain Operations
• Chet Kuchinad	SVP, Total Pay
• David Landau	SVP, deputy general counsel, Law & Corporate Affairs
• Kathie Lindeman	SVP, Operations, Development and Global Business Systems
• Mark Lindstrom	SVP, Southwest, U.S. Retail
• Pedro Y. K. Man	SVP, president, Asia Pacific
• Kenneth F. Meyers	SVP, Human Resources, Starbucks Coffee International
• Colin Moore	SVP, president, Starbucks Coffee Canada
• Dave Olsen	SVP, Culture and Immersion
• Steven Schickler	SVP, Seattle Coffee
• Launi Skinner	SVP, Northwest, U.S. Retail
• Richard Soderberg	SVP, Global Manufacturing, Supply Operations
• Marc Stolzman	SVP, Finance, Starbucks Coffee International
• Sandra Taylor	SVP, Corporate Social Responsibility
• Mark Wesley	SVP, Store Development and Asset Development
• Howard Wollner	SVP, Store Concepts
• Thomas Yang	SVP, Marketing, Starbucks Coffee International

$300 million in cash), not by selling stock or taking on debt. Starbucks also does not advertise on national television because Schultz believes it would diminish the brand.

In 2000, Schultz stepped aside as CEO to pursue a new role—chairman and chief global strategist. Orin Smith, the company's chief operating officer, took over as CEO. The move freed Schultz from the routine tasks of running a multi-billion-dollar corporation and turned over the critical issues, such as driving same-store sales, to Smith, who has been with the company since 1990. A list of the company's executive officers is shown in Exhibit 3.

Schultz's most important ideas about running a business, however, are those dealing with its people. "We know that our people are the heart and soul of our success." Its more than 74,000 employees worldwide serve over 25 million customers each week. That's a lot of opportunities to either satisfy or disappoint the customer. The experiences customers have in the stores ultimately affect the company's all-important brand image. And Starbucks has created a unique relationship with its people, because they are the link to that unique relationship with customers. The company has made a commitment to both its full-time and part-time partners (employees). Those who work more than 20 hours per week receive stock options and health-care benefits. Schultz says, "The most important thing I ever did was give our partners bean stock (Starbucks stock options). That's what sets us apart and gives a higher-quality employee, an employee that cares more." Even as the company continues to grow, it's unlikely to lose its touchy-feely culture, which comes directly from Schultz himself and fosters a cultlike zeal. In 2003 and 2004, Starbucks was recognized on *Fortune* magazine's "Best Places to Work" list again and ranked number nine on *Fortune* magazine's "Most Admired Companies" list in 2003 and number eight in 2004.

At company headquarters in Seattle, the scent of exotic African coffee beans drifts through the offices. And you won't see a necktie, much less a suit. The door to Schultz's office is always open. As one visitor said, "It feels like a small business, but is anything but."

STARBUCKS—THE FINANCIALS

The year 2003 was a record in many ways for Starbucks. Some of the company's performance accomplishments included the following: It attained net revenues and net earnings. For the 12th consecutive year, it attained increases in comparable store sales of 5 percent or higher. It reached a total of 34 international markets. Complete financial information can be found on the company's Web site at **www.starbucks.com**.

THE FUTURE

What does the future hold for Starbucks Corporation? How can the company remain "relevant" to its customers? How can Starbucks achieve its goal of establishing itself as the most recognized and respected brand in the world? Right now, the company continues to grow at an eye-popping rate. Revenues continue to increase at a rate of over 20 percent a year. Same-store sales rose 11 percent in November and December 2003. Its stock price was up 56 percent in 2003. More than 25 million people visit a Starbucks each week. But the company continues to focus on bigness. It has constructed additional coffee-roasting facilities (the third and fourth respectively) in Nevada and Amsterdam. It's also focusing on helping coffee growers improve their crops to meet Starbucks' exacting standards and growing demand. In 2004, it plans on opening more stores with drive-thru windows and opening 1,300 new stores worldwide. Schultz suggests that Starbucks eventually may have close to 25,000 stores (McDonald's has more than 30,000). Although the company could grow faster, it closely monitors and controls growth to make sure that quality is maintained. An analyst at Morgan Stanley estimates that the company can more than double its U.S. outlets without impeding growth. However, the "saturation point" is probably a little over three stores for every 100,000 residents nationwide.

Global issues will continue to be important to Starbucks as well. The company needs to ensure a continued adequate supply of coffee. And in China, an imitator, Shanghai Xing Ba Ke coffee shops (loosely translated as Shanghai Starbucks), which has 29 stores, is creating confusion. The Xing Ba Ke shops do differ from Starbucks in that they have waiters and higher prices, but they plan to open an additional 30 to 50 stores over the next two years. Although Starbucks prefers to handle such disputes amicably, it is considering legal action. And not-so-stellar performance in its other global locations is presenting a real challenge. Unlike the United States, Starbucks faces big rivals in both Europe and Asia. Here in the United States, Wal-Mart wanted to talk business, but Starbucks has resisted for now, and no agreement has been reached. However, Wal-Mart is quietly testing its own coffee bar concept called Kicks Coffee Café.

(*Sources:* Starbucks' Web site, **www.starbucks.com**, April 14, 2004; Hoover's Online, **www.hoovers.com**, April 14, 2004; Standard & Poor's NetAdvantage, **www.netadvantage.standardandpoors.com**, April 14, 2004; Specialty Coffee Association of America, **www.scaa.org**, April 14, 2004; C. Stetkiewicz and M. Weinraub, "Starbucks and Jim Beam to Brew Up Coffee Liqueur," *USA Today,* April 9, 2004, p. B1; "Bottled Water Now Number-Two Commercial Beverage in U.S., Says Beverage Marketing Corporation," Beverage Marketing Corporation, **www.beveragemarketing.com**, April 8, 2004; "Coffee Consumption in the United States," Coffee Research Organization, **www.coffeeresearch.org**, April 8, 2004; J. Graham, "Starbucks to Put Digital Music on Its Menus," *USA Today,* March 15, 2004, p. B1; A. Serwer, "Hot Starbucks to Go," *Fortune,* January 26, 2004, pp. 60–74; Harvard School of Public Health, "Long-Term Coffee Consumption Significantly Reduces Type 2 Diabetes Risk," *Science Daily,* **www.sciencedaily.com**, January 6, 2004; C. Adler, "Copied Coffee," *Fortune,* September 29, 2003, p. 48; M. Krantz, "Not a Johnny-Come-Latte," *USA Today,* September 9, 2003, p. B1; R. Howe, "At Starbucks, the Future Is in Plastic," *Business 2.0,* August 2003, pp. 56–63; S. Holmes, I. M. Kunii, J. Ewing, and K. Capell, "For Starbucks, There's No Place Like Home," *Business Week,* June 9, 2003, p. 48; and "How Much Starbucks Is Too Much?" *Business 2.0,* July 2002, p. 35.)

Southwest Airlines

Simple, fun, and *profitable.* These three words sum up Southwest Airlines. Yet, behind these words lies the heart and soul of the company's strategies that have helped it achieve an enviable record in the intensely competitive airline industry—31 consecutive years of profitability, even during the challenging period following the 9/11 terrorist attacks. As Southwest continues to grow, can it maintain its commitment to simplicity, fun, and profitability?

BACKGROUND

Southwest Airlines began service in June of 1971 with three planes flying between three Texas cities: Houston, Dallas, and San Antonio. Herb Kelleher, the colorful character who co-founded the company and serves as its current chairman, recalls, "A lot of people figured us for road kill at that time." Why? Because the company's strategic approach was unlike anything the other major airlines were doing at that time. The state of air service in the early 1970s could best be described as high airfares, inconvenient flight schedules, complicated ticketing, and long and inconvenient flying experiences (from driving to the airport, parking, and finally reaching your destination). Southwest wanted to change that. It began with a simple notion—get your passengers to their destinations when they want to get there, on time, at the lowest possible fares, and make sure they have a good time doing it. To deliver this type of service, Southwest's strategy was to fly short-haul routes where the fares were competitive with driving. In these short-haul markets, speed and convenience would be essential to marketplace success. Therefore, Southwest's overall strategy was to minimize total travel time for customers, including ticketing and boarding and providing service out of airports convenient to doing business or vacationing in a city. Simple, yet effective. A timeline of Southwest's history is shown in Exhibit 1.

As you can see, Southwest has had a busy and impressive corporate history. The company has earned the respect of other airline competitors as well as other businesses around the world.

CURRENT OPERATIONS

Southwest Airlines bills itself as the nation's low-fare, high-customer-satisfaction airline. It primarily serves short- and medium-haul routes with single-class service targeted at business and leisure travelers. Its approach has been to focus primarily on point-to-point, rather than hub-and-spoke, service in markets. This point-to-point system provides for more direct nonstop flights for customers and minimizes connections, delays, and total trip time. Approximately 79 percent of Southwest's customers fly nonstop, with an average passenger trip length of about 730 miles. Despite the tough challenges facing all the airlines in 2003—the Iraq War, the SARS outbreak, high fuel costs, a weak economy, and terrorism-related concerns—it was another year of accomplishments for Southwest, including its 31st consecutive year of profitability (an airline-industry record) and continued leadership in customer satisfaction as it once again received the fewest customer complaints of all airlines. Several strategic factors can be identified as the keys to Southwest's success.

Exhibit 1

Timeline for Southwest Airlines

1971	Passenger service commences between Dallas, Houston, and San Antonio.
1974	The year of the 1 millionth passenger!
1976	Service begins to other Texas cities: Austin, Corpus Christi, El Paso, Lubbock, and Midland-Odessa.
1977	The year of the 5 millionth passenger and listing of the stock on the NYSE as LUV (for Dallas's Love Field, its base of operations).
1978	Herb Kelleher, cofounder, is named interim president, CEO, and chairman of the board.
1979	Self-ticketing machines are introduced in 10 cities. Service begins between Dallas and New Orleans—the first city outside Texas to be added.
1982	Kelleher is named permanent president, CEO, and chairman. Service is expanded to San Francisco, Los Angeles, San Diego, Las Vegas, and Phoenix.
1984	The fourth consecutive year that Southwest is ranked number one in customer satisfaction ranking.
1986	Fifteenth anniversary celebration of low fares, good times, and high spirits!
1987	The sixth consecutive year Southwest is awarded the Best Customer Satisfaction record of any continental U.S. airline.
1988	The company wins the Triple Crown of airlines: Best On-Time Record, Best Baggage Handling, and Fewest Customer Complaints.
1990	Company reaches the $1 billion revenue mark.
1992	Company wins the first *annual* Triple Crown—something no other airline has done.
1993	Service begins to the east coast.
1994	Ticketless travel is launched.
1996	The company's impressive record for the Triple Crown continues—it wins its fifth one!
2001	Southwest officially turns 30 years old and introduces its new Canyon Blue exterior color scheme. Kelleher steps down as president and CEO.
2003	Because of the success of the internet and a decrease in calls, Southwest decides to close three of its reservation centers in Dallas, Little Rock, and Salt Lake City.

Low-Cost Advantage

Historically, Southwest has enjoyed a significant cost advantage compared to the other big traditional carriers, and low operating costs continue to be one of Southwest's competitive strengths. How does Southwest keep its costs low? One important element is its use of a single type of aircraft—the Boeing 737—which allows for simplified scheduling, operations, and maintenance. The planes have identical configurations, making it easy for crews to operate, maintain, and service them. The company's fleet of planes is also young and well maintained. At the end of 2003, Southwest had 388 Boeing 737 aircraft and planned to expand their fleet by a net 29 new jets in 2004. The company also has outfitted its current and future fleet with fuel-saving, performance-enhancing blended winglets (appendages on the wings). These winglets extend the flight range, save fuel, and reduce engine maintenance costs and takeoff noise.

Another operational strategy that has allowed Southwest to keep costs low includes the use of automated processes. Early on, Southwest recognized the benefits to be gained from automation. It was the first airline to offer a ticketless travel option (in 1994), eliminating the need to process and then print a paper ticket. When increased security requirements were put in place after 9/11, Southwest relied on automation to facilitate the implementation of those requirements. Automation also has made the company more efficient in how it services customers, who now have plenty of ways to acquire boarding passes and who don't have to wait in lines at ticket and gate counters. Baggage tags are computer generated, as are boarding passes, and customers can access both at multiple points in the airport. In 2004, Southwest began offering customers the ability to check their bags using rapid check-in kiosks and to obtain transfer boarding passes at the time of check-in. Customers can also check in and get their boarding passes online at Southwest's Web site. Not only do such options benefit the customer, they benefit the company as well, because fewer employees are needed to provide these services.

The company's Web site has allowed it to cut costs in other ways as well. It was the first airline to establish a home page on the Internet. Now, southwest.com is the number one airline Web site for sales and revenues. In 2003, approximately 54 percent of passenger revenues were derived from the company's Web site, with only 15 percent being booked through travel agents. The Web site has been so successful that Southwest was able to consolidate its reservations operations from nine to six centers. Also, more than 4 million people subscribe to the weekly Click'n Save e-mails.

Southwest also has chosen to operate out of conveniently located satellite or downtown airports, which are typically less congested than other airlines' hub airports, because they are usually located quite a distance from a city's main business district. This operating strategy allows for high asset utilization because gate turnaround is quick (currently, Southwest's turnaround time is approximately 25 minutes), and the planes can get back in the air transporting more customers to their destination. As Kelleher used to point out, you don't make any money sitting on the ground. Quick turnaround also means that the company doesn't need as many aircraft or gate facilities.

Legendary Customer Service

Southwest gives customers what they want—great service at low prices. In August of 2003, the U.S. Bureau of Transportation Statistics reported that Southwest carried more domestic originating passengers in May than any other airline, the first time a low-fare airline had done so. And not only is Southwest attracting large numbers of passengers, they're keeping them happy. The American Customer Satisfaction Index ranked Southwest first among airlines for highest customer service satisfaction in 2003. This honor is in addition to Southwest's continual ranking at the top (for 13 consecutive years) of the Transportation Department's Air Travel Consumer Report for receiving the fewest customer complaints. The company recently formalized its dedication to customer satisfaction by adopting a comprehensive plan called Customer Service Commitment, which outlines actions the company is taking to promote the highest quality of customer service. In fact, the company's mission establishes the foundation for its commitment to serving customers. The mission (as stated on Southwest's Web site) is as follows:

> The mission of Southwest Airlines is dedication to the highest quality of Customer Service delivered with a sense of warmth, friendliness, individual pride, and Company Spirit.

The mission statement affects the way Southwest employees do their work. It emphasizes the company's strong desire to serve its customers and provides guidance to employees when they have to make service-related decisions. In fact, employees are continually reminded that Southwest is in the customer service business—and its business just happens to be airline transportation. The goal is not only getting customers from point A to point B, but doing so in a way that is simple and fun for the customers and profitable for the company.

Southwest currently offers approximately 2,800 daily flights to 59 airports in 58 cities in 30 states throughout the United States. The large number of flights and

- Received 202,357 resumes and hired 908 new employees.
- Served 52.6 million cans of soda, juices, and water; 8.7 million alcoholic beverages; 3 million bags of pretzels, 85 million bags of peanuts, and 31.7 million other snacks.
- Purchased 1.1 billion gallons of jet fuel.
- Moved 236 million pounds of cargo and mail.
- Shortest daily flight: Austin and Houston (152 miles).
- Longest daily flight: Baltimore–Washington and San Jose (2,438 miles).

Source: *Southwest Airlines,* **www.southwest.com**, *April 14, 2004. © Southwest Airlines Co. All rights reserved.*

expansive route system offer customers convenience and reliability with lots of options to get where they want when they want to go. With its combination of low fares, convenient and frequent schedules, and friendly customer service, Southwest dominates the majority of the markets it serves. It consistently ranks first in market share in approximately 90 percent of its top 100 markets. Southwest's top 10 airports include: Las Vegas, Phoenix, Baltimore-Washington, Houston Hobby, Chicago Midway, Dallas (Love Field), Oakland, Los Angeles (LAX), Nashville, and San Diego. Exhibit 2 lists some other fun facts about Southwest Airlines.

SOUTHWEST'S CULTURE AND PEOPLE

A major reason behind Southwest's success is its culture and its people. Southwest has one of the most unique cultures of all major U.S. corporations. It's a high-spirited, often irreverent culture, much like its legendary co-founder Herb Kelleher. At company headquarters, the walls are covered with more than 10,000 picture frames containing photos of employees' pets, of Herb dressed like Elvis or in drag, of flight attendants in mini-skirts, and caricatures of Southwest planes gnawing on competitors' aircraft. There are teddy bears and pink flamingoes. There's cigarette smoking, lots of laughter, and no neckties anywhere. On the flights, flight attendants have been known to dress up as the Easter Bunny or with Halloween masks on those respective holidays. They've hidden in the overhead baggage compartments and jumped out at passengers who first opened them. However, no matter how fun and goofy it may get, no one at Southwest loses sight of the fact that the focus is on customers. This was plainly evident in the challenging weeks after 9/11 when the laughter stopped. And it didn't take a memo from company headquarters to tell the employees how to handle themselves during this difficult period. Employees understood that the normal gags played on passengers and the jokes and Halloween costumes were inappropriate. However, in the spring of 2002, passengers began to indicate through e-mails and comments that they were once again ready for Southwest's brand of fun. But even then, the employees were sensitive to customers' concerns and toned it down when the mood wasn't right.

Southwest recognizes that its success is due to its people and emphasizes that its people are its most valuable asset. The company is extremely concerned about its employees and seeks to provide fun and challenging jobs. It also takes care of its employees. Southwest was the first U.S. airline to offer a profit-sharing plan (in 1974). Today, employees own approximately 10 percent of the company's stock. Southwest's employees are known for their commitment to the company and to the Southwest spirit, which isn't surprising considering that the company has a reputation as a great place to work. An April 2003 issue of *Fortune* magazine identified Southwest as the employer of choice among college students. And the number of resumes it receives every year (over 202,000 in 2003) is further proof that Southwest is perceived as a great place to work. At the end of 2003, Southwest had almost 33,000 employees: 33 percent in flight operations; 6 percent in maintenance; 49 percent in ground, customer, and fleet service; and 12 percent in management, marketing, accounting, and office support positions.

The company, of course, wants the best of the best. Job applicants endure a rigorous interview process that can take as long as six weeks. Once hired, about 20 percent of new hires fail to make it through the training period. "We don't keep them if they don't fit into our culture. A lot of people think we're just relaxed, loosey-goosey, but we have a lot of discipline." Those employees who do make it are provided the support they need to succeed. Southwest has always had the approach of trusting employees and empowering them to effectively make decisions as they perform their jobs.

Many people assume that Southwest's outstanding relationship with its people is because it's nonunion, but nothing could be further from the truth. More than four out of five employees at Southwest (approximately 81 percent) are union members. However, when other heavily unionized airlines were laying off employees and asking for sizable pay cuts from their employees, Southwest was negotiating new contracts with higher compensation and enriched benefits. The company is proud of its reputation as a great place to work, and acknowledges that its people are wonderful. Southwest wants to honor them, to treat them with respect, and to reward their productivity. However, Southwest also understands the importance of maintaining its low-cost structure. If that is lost, the company's future could be jeopardized.

FINANCIAL HIGHLIGHTS

To achieve 31 consecutive years of profitability in an industry that's known to be intensely challenging and competitive is quite an accomplishment. During 2003, the company's passenger load factor was 66.8 percent. (Load factor is a measure of production or utilization of capacity used by transportation companies. It's calculated by dividing revenue passenger miles by available seat miles.) Other highlights of Southwest's financial performance are provided in Exhibit 3. Complete financial information can be found on the company's Web site at **www.southwest.com**.

COMPANY AWARDS AND RECOGNITIONS

When you do outstanding work, you get recognized, and Southwest Airlines is no exception. Here are a few of the company's many awards from 2003:

- One of the most admired companies in *Fortune* magazine's annual ranking of Most Admired Companies in 2003 *and* 2004. In fact, it has ranked in the top 10 for the last six years—a distinction shared only by three other corporate icons: Berkshire Hathaway, General Electric, and Microsoft.
- Cited by *Business Ethics* magazine as one of the 100 Best Corporate Citizens in America.

Exhibit 3 *Selected Financial Highlights-Southwest Airlines*

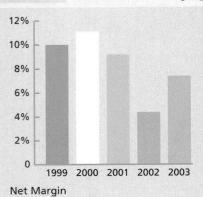

Net Margin

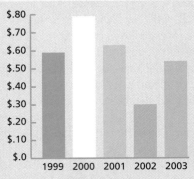

Net Income Per Share, Diluted
*Excludes cumulative effect of change
in accounting principle of $.03.

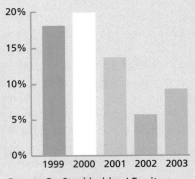

Return On Stockholders' Equity

Consolidated Highlights

(Dollars In Millions, Except Per Share Amounts)	2003	2002	Change
Operating revenues	$5,937	$5,522	7.5%
Operating expenses	$5,454	$5,105	6.8%
Operating income	$483	$417	15.8%
Operating margin	8.1%	7.6%	0.5pts
Net income	$442	$241	83.4%
Net margin	7.4%	4.4%	3.0pts
Net income per share–basic	$.56	$.31	80.6%
Net income per share–diluted	$.54	$.30	80.0%
Stockholders' equity	$5,052	$4,422	14.2%
Return on average stockholders' equity	9.3%	5.7%	3.6pts
Stockholders' equity per common share outstanding	$6.40	$5.69	12.5%
Revenue passengers carried	65,673,945	63,045,988	4.2%
Revenue passenger miles {RPMs} (000s)	47,943,066	45,391,903	5.6%
Available seat miles {ASMs} (000s)	71,790,425	68,886,546	4.2%
Passenger load factor	66.8%	65.9%	0.9pts
Passenger revenue yield per RPM	11.97¢	11.77¢	1.7%
Operating revenue yield per ASM	8.27¢	8.02¢	3.1%
Operatiing expenses per ASM	7.60¢	7.41¢	2.6%
Size of fleet at yearend	388	375	3.5%
Number of Employees at yearend	32,847	33,705	(2.5)%

Strategic Management in Action

- Listed by *Hispanic* magazine on the Hispanic Corporate 100.
- Named the Best Low Cost Airline in the *Official Airline Guide* Airline of the Year awards.
- Named Airline of the Year by *Air Transport World* magazine.
- Cited for Best Customer Service, Best Bonus Promotion, and Best Award Redemption of any frequent flyer program by *Inside Flyer* magazine.
- Listed on the Experts' List of the World's Most Socially Responsible Companies by *Global Finance* magazine.

THE AIRLINE INDUSTRY AND MAJOR COMPETITORS

The airline industry is one of the most intensely competitive industries. Many external factors influence the profitability of each competitor. Uncertainties facing the industry in 2004 included fuel prices; the rate of economic recovery in the United States, and the resulting rate of growth in customer demand; and continued vulnerability to exogenous events that had the potential to adversely affect air travel. Other characteristics of the airline industry that make it especially fragile include the following:

- It is tremendously capital intensive.
- There are enormous fixed costs.
- It is fuel intensive, and with alternative energy sources unlikely, is subject to global political events.
- It is labor intensive.
- There is no product inventory or shelf life—an unfilled seat on a flight can't be put in inventory and sold later.
- It is quite cyclical because much of passenger travel demand is discretionary.
- It is heavily regulated and taxed.

Competitors are also nipping at Southwest's wings. Although several have tried in the past to duplicate Southwest's formula, with little success, some new competitors have caught the attention of Southwest's management team: JetBlue and AirTran, both of which are strong, innovative, and low cost. AirTran, based in Orlando, has been growing fast, operating primarily out of its Atlanta base. JetBlue with its high-profile CEO has managed to generate a lot of buzz with its cool new Airbus A320s outfitted with DirecTV at every seat. JetBlue is still considerably smaller than Southwest (it has about 50 aircraft with 100 more on order) and doesn't yet directly compete with any of Southwest's routes. However, JetBlue has been able to keep its costs below Southwest's and has managed to achieve the second best on-time performance and second lowest customer complaint record in the Department of Transportation's rankings. Southwest is well aware that it needs to keep its eye on both JetBlue and AirTran. In addition, two of the major carriers are once again attempting to go after the low-fare market by using a "low-cost airline within an airline concept." Delta's Song and United's Ted are providing Southwest with another set of challenges, although analysts don't believe that either one presents a viable competitive threat. As one analyst said, "These are Band-Aid fixes. The mainline carriers have to address their fundamental cost issues."

THE FUTURE

Southwest Airlines has been an anomaly among airlines. Its performance has consistently been among the industry's best. However, Southwest has some serious challenges as it seeks to maintain its competitive leadership position. Although its costs remain low, severe cost pressures in the last half of 2003 led the company to implement some aggressive measures to improve productivity. These measures included no longer paying commissions on flights booked by traditional travel agents, consolidating its reservations operations centers, and motivating employees to continue to look for innovative ways to better run the business. Even though Southwest continues to have some of the lowest costs in the industry, its costs have been climbing. A key metric used in the airline business is cost per available seat mile (CASM). In 1995, Southwest's was 7.07 cents; today, it's up to 7.6 cents. However, the big carriers all have CASMs of between 9 cents and 13 cents and haven't been able to close the gap on Southwest. Yet, JetBlue's was 6.08 cents, although its CASM, too, has been increasing. Keeping costs under control and keeping its culture alive are the key challenges facing Southwest as it continues to expand and to reinforce its role as a leading prime-time industry player.

(*Sources:* Southwest Airlines, **www.southwest.com**, April 17, 2004; Hoover's Online, **www.hoovers.com**, April 17, 2004; Standard & Poor's NetAdvantage, **www.netadvantage.standardandpoors.com**, April 17, 2004; L. Miller, "Low-Cost Airlines Do Job Better, Report Finds," *Springfield News Leader,* April 5, 2004, p. 5B; T. Pack, "Low-Cost Rivals Rocking Airlines' World," *Springfield News Leader,* April 4, 2004, p. 1E; A. Serwer, "Southwest Airlines: The Hottest Thing in the Sky," *Fortune,* March 8, 2004, pp. 86–91; W. Zellner and M. Arndt, "Look Who's Buzzing the Discounters," *Business Week,* November 24, 2003, p. 48; W. Zeller and M. Arndt, "Holding Steady," *Business Week,* February 3, 2003, pp. 66–67; R. Suskind, "Humor Has Returned to Southwest Airlines After 9/11 Hiatus," *Wall Street Journal,* January 13, 2003, p. A1; and G. Donnelly, "Recruiting Retention," *CFO,* March 2000, pp. 68–76.)

Ford Motor Corporation

As the world's number two producer of cars and trucks, Ford Motor Corporation should be sitting on top of the world. However, the first few years of the twenty-first century have not been pleasant ones for Ford. The company has been plagued by falling sales and declining market share, a hazardous industry price war, and an uncertain future. Chairman and CEO William Clay Ford Jr. (who prefers to be called Bill) has an uphill battle convincing dealers, employees, and Wall Street analysts that he can deliver on his bold pledge to earn $7 billion in operating profits by mid-decade.

HISTORY

With much sentimental fanfare and hoopla, Ford Motor celebrated its 100-year anniversary in June 2003. In the early 1900s, Ford Motor "began a manufacturing revolution with its mass production assembly lines." From the production of the first Model T in 1908 to the 500hp GT racer with a price tag of $150,000 introduced in 2004, Ford has had some fabulous successes in product design. The Mustang, which turned 40 in 2004, is one of its best ever. The car made Ford Motor rich as it ignited Detroit's obsession with the baby boomer market, a preoccupation that continues even today. The company sold 1 million Mustangs in 24 months, an incredible product launch for a new model, even by today's standards. Then, there was the Ford Explorer, the first sport utility vehicle (SUV) designed for the consumer market. It proved to be extremely popular and started a product craze that other car manufacturers soon had to follow as consumers clamored for more. Other big product successes for Ford Motor include the popular and best-selling Taurus and the F-Series pickup. But it's also had some notable failures as well. For example, there was the Pinto and its exploding gas tank. And we can't forget the Edsel back in 1958–1960, a car with an unusual design that never really caught on with consumers. More recently was the Firestone tires–Ford Explorer fiasco, which many believe was the tipping point behind the company's recent struggles.

In 1998, when Bill became chairman of the company (a position in which he wouldn't be heavily involved with the "strategy stuff"), Ford Motor was riding high. Sales and market share were strong, and the company was well positioned to exploit its strengths. However, the CEO at that time, Jacques Nasser, had grand plans to transform Ford from a simple car manufacturer to a consumer brand company. He planned to take the company into Internet activities, car retailing, repair shops, and even junkyards. Unfortunately, all these ventures backfired and, perhaps even more damaging, distracted Ford executives from their core business of designing, building, and selling cars. Then, the Firestone tire recall spun out of control. With the company's worldwide operations floundering, the board of directors and Bill Ford fired Nasser in October 2001. Not long after, Bill Ford took on the additional responsibility of CEO, a position he was reluctant to assume. However, as the great grandson of founder Henry Ford and the fourth generation of his family to lead the company, Bill accepted his responsibility to carry on the family tradition.

The burden is now on Bill to fix the company and drive it into its second century. His family's firm is in crisis, having lost close to $6.4 billion in 2001 and 2002. Although the company posted a profit of $495 million in 2003, that's still a far cry from the $7 billion level that Bill has pledged the company's profits will be by mid-decade. Making that goal even more difficult to achieve is an incredibly challenging industry that's going through some dramatic changes.

INDUSTRY AND COMPETITORS

The global car industry is one characterized by price wars, fierce competition, fickle customers, worldwide manufacturing overcapacity, and declining demand for cars in the mature U.S. and European markets. In addition, more market segments and new products are intensifying competition. And new technology continues to drive rapid change in products and processes. The once-dominant U.S. car manufacturers continue to be challenged by strong, smart, and aggressive global competitors. In fact, in June 2003, it was announced that during the first three months of 2003, Ford Motor had been displaced by Toyota as the world's number two automaker, as Toyota surpassed Ford in global unit sales. This was bitter news for Ford, which has ranked second behind General Motors since 1931. Although Ford retained its number two ranking based on year-end sales for 2003, the mid-year accomplishment by Toyota confirms that it is a competitor to be reckoned with. And Toyota and the other Japanese car companies are preparing an all-out assault on the European market—a market that has been dominated by the U.S. car companies.

Consumer demand for cars, particularly in the U.S. and European markets, seems to follow the state of the economy. During good economic times, consumers are more willing to open their wallets and buy cars and other expensive products. However, when there's uncertainty—be it economic, social, global, or political—consumers are more hesitant to buy new cars. Therefore, to stimulate demand, car companies use incentives such as rebates, no money down, and free financing for extended time periods to pull customers into dealers' showrooms. Although these incentives can be good for consumers, they tend to have a disastrous effect on the bottom lines of car companies. For example, widespread discounting in the first half of 2003 led General Motors to make only $18 per vehicle and Ford to lose $197. But not every competitor's profits suffered during the same time period, Toyota made an operating profit of about $2,000 per vehicle. Because of the intense competition in the industry, when one car company introduces an incentive, the others must follow suit or risk losing potential buyers. However, sometimes the financial stakes are just too high. For example, General Motors stunned the industry in the summer of 2003 when it offered current GM owners a loyalty discount of up to $1,000 if they bought or leased a new GM car or truck. The discount was in addition to its zero percent financing offer and other cash incentives, which totaled up to $4,000 on many vehicles. After much deliberation, Ford Motor chose not to match this incentive, believing that it wasn't in their best interests in the short run or even in the long run. This is just one example of the types of competitive challenges that car companies face in today's market.

Another area where the U.S. car manufacturers are facing serious challenges from the strong Japanese competitors is in terms of costs and efficiency. Both Ford's and General Motor's factories are less efficient than those of the Japanese. Exhibit 1 lists how long it takes each major car manufacturer to build a car, a manufacturing statistic dominated by the more efficient Japanese car makers. And the Japanese manufacturers have used flexible manufacturing systems for a number of years. These systems allow multiple models to be built on the same assembly line and enable faster product changeovers. (Remember from Chapter 5 our discussion of Toyota's success at developing a way to make a custom car in five days.) Although Ford Motor has committed to transforming its assembly plants into lean and flexible centers of manufacturing excellence, it's still playing a game of catch-up.

Car Company	Hours per Vehicle	Improvement from Year Earlier	
Nissan	16.83	6.1%	**Exhibit 1**
Mitsubishi	21.33	2.2	
Toyota	21.83	3.1	*How Long It Takes to Build A Car**
Honda	22.27	−12.6	
General Motors	24.44	6.4	
Industry Average	25.23	5.0	
Ford Motor	26.14	2.7	
DaimlerChrysler	28.04	9.0	

*Statistics from 2003

Source: Based on D. Kiley, "U.S. Automakers Increasing Efficiency, Report Says," USA Today, June 19, 2003, p. B1.

FORD MOTOR COMPANY TODAY

Bill Ford's goal from the day he took over as CEO has been to turn around the company and to renew its strategic competitiveness and profitability. It has not been an easy journey, but the company continues to make progress toward this goal. Bill has had to make several tough strategic changes in this turnaround effort. He's cut 35,000 jobs, closed factories, and refocused the company on its core business. With demand for cars declining, there is no guarantee that the company's long-term revitalization will be successful. However, Ford Motor, under the able leadership of Bill Ford Jr., continues to progress toward restoring the company to global prominence.

Manufacturing Strategies

Ford's goals in manufacturing have been cost cutting, plant closings, factory flexibility, and quality improvements. And the company has made progress in these areas, although it still must continue to improve. It has put in place a number of manufacturing strategies and processes that maximize operational quality and efficiency.

During 2003, Ford Motor achieved cost reductions of $3.2 billion. Part of those cost savings came from the company's quality improvement and waste elimination methodology called Consumer-driven 6-Sigma. Since the implementation of this quality improvement program, Ford Motor has completed more than 9,500 projects that have saved a total of $1.7 billion worldwide, including $731 million in 2003 alone. These quality improvements also led to a dramatic reduction in the number of car recalls and drove down warranty spending by 18 percent.

Another new manufacturing strategy that Ford Motor implemented throughout North America and in all business units in 2003 was Team Value Management, a process designed to bring together cross-functional teams to improve value and quality. Working collaboratively with suppliers, these teams assessed the gaps between actual and industry benchmark costs and areas where performance improvements could lead to significant cost savings. Through their combined efforts, the cross-functional teams were able to achieve record total material cost reductions.

The transformation of the company's assembly plants into flexible manufacturing systems continues. Three more U.S. plants were scheduled to have these systems in place by the end of 2004. And by the end of the decade, all of the European and 75 percent of the North American assembly plants are to have these flexible systems in place. One thing that is necessary for flexible manufacturing systems to work is common vehicle architectures (body frames). And this is an area where Ford Motor

Exhibit 2

*Sales by Product
(Vehicle) Type*

	2003	2002
	(Percent of Total)	
Cars		
Medium	20%	21%
Small	15	16
Premium	8	8
Large	2	2
Trucks		
SUV	27%	25%
Full-size pickup	14	13
Bus/van	8	9
Compact pickup	4	4
Medium/heavy duty	2	2

Source: *Hoover's Online,* **www.hoovers.com***, April 18, 2004.*

has encountered customer opposition, especially with regards to its luxury cars. Customers don't want a Jaguar body frame that's shared with a less-expensive car model. Therefore, in its Premier Automotive Group (Ford's luxury car group, which includes Jaguar, Aston Martin, Volvo, and Land Rover), each car division will have its own exclusive body frame. It's a costly choice, because each unique architecture costs $1 billion or more, but company executives felt that using common architecture for these cars was too risky and they wanted to ensure that the luxury brands' images were protected.

Marketing

Great automotive products have always been the foundation of Ford Motor's success. Some of the company's auto brands include Ford, Jaguar, Lincoln, Mercury, Volvo, Aston Martin, and Jaguar. Exhibit 2 shows the company's sales by product (vehicle) type.

In 2003, the company had several successful product launches, including the Ford Focus C-MAX in Europe and the Ford F-150, the Ford Freestar, and the Mercury Monterey in North America. In 2004, 40 new products were scheduled to be introduced worldwide. By mid-decade, the company's goal was to launch more than 150 new products, by far the most of any similar time period in the company's history.

One of the company's guiding principles is a commitment to products and customers; it is stated very simply as "We will offer excellent products and services." Ford Motor understands how important strong customer relationships and innovative, high-quality, high-value products are to its business and its ultimate success. In 2002, Ford tied with General Motors for first place in the Sales Satisfaction Index according to a J.D. Power and Associates study. The company also showed twice the rate of improvement over the industry average on this measure. In addition, it exceeded the industry average on J.D. Power and Associate's Customer Service Index, which focuses on service experiences during the first three years of vehicle ownership. In 2003, the company won 10 of 16 possible awards in R. L. Polk's consumer loyalty study, including the Highest Overall Loyalty to Make award, which went to the Ford division. Ford's large and loyal customer base is something the company is proud of and wants to retain.

Ford Motor's more than 28,000 dealers are an important part of the success of Ford Motor's marketing efforts. Together, the dealers and the company must provide customers (current and potential) with products and a buying and service experience that meets and exceeds their expectations. It's a relationship that hasn't always been pleasant. However, Bill has said that he believes Ford's dealer network in North America is the best in the industry. And he is committed to working together more closely as partners and providing dealers with outstanding new products and trucks so everyone experiences a successful and profitable outcome.

Ford Motor's luxury car division (the Premier Automotive Group, or PAG) has established itself as a formidable competitor. In fact, in 2003, Ford sold more luxury cars in the United States than any other manufacturer. The PAG division had an operating profit of $164 million in 2003, a significant improvement over the $897 million loss in 2002. However, the company has to walk a fine line as it balances the need to protect the luxury brands' images while continuing to find ways to cut costs and be more efficient. Mark Fields, head of this division, is looking for ways to share costs that he believes customers won't detect or won't mind. For instance, he believes that few customers will care if a Jaguar and a Land Rover have identical navigation systems and sound systems or if they both use state-of-the-art Volvo safety equipment. The PAG division also can access basic car parts (brake pads, window-lift motors, fasteners, etc.) from Ford's global parts sourcing to take advantage of bulk-purchase savings.

Despite the success being enjoyed by the luxury car segment, the company's European division (Ford of Europe) is still experiencing major problems, and the expected turnaround has yet to materialize. Shrinking sales and declining market share in Europe have made it difficult to earn a profit. Ford Europe sells almost 300,000 fewer cars annually in Western Europe than it did a decade ago. And the fixed costs associated with excess capacity in its European facilities are huge, offsetting even the most diligent cost-cutting efforts. Ford Europe has done a lot of things right. They've made their factories more efficient and flexible. More than $1.3 billion in costs have been eliminated, and internal productivity data show a 15.8 percent improvement from 1999 to 2002. They're also counting on new products with better margins and higher-quality interiors to boost sales. However, the division is still losing money and is barely hanging on to market share. Analysts say that Ford has lagged rivals for so long that its image is badly tarnished. It missed the market for new-generation diesel cars by launching its first model six years after the segment boomed, and its minivan product was seven years behind competitors. And now, the already brutal competition is going to intensify as the Japanese automakers prepare for a European assault. To hold onto their slim market share, Ford and Fiat are having to resort to profit-eroding discounts.

In addition to its automotive products, Ford's other divisions include Ford Motor Credit and The Hertz Corporation. Ford Motor Credit is the leading auto finance company in the United States and Hertz is the world's number one car rental firm. In addition, the company has a controlling (33 percent) stake in Mazda. It is seeking buyers for Th!nk, its electric car division.

Employees

With a little over 327,000 employees worldwide, Ford Motor is committed to its people. The company has an experienced and stable management team and a dedicated and talented workforce. It understands that its future success depends on its people. As it says in its Code of Basic Working Conditions, "The diverse group of men and women who work for Ford are our most important resource." The Code outlines important, universal values that serve as the cornerstone of the company's relationship with employees. Some highlights from the Code (found on company's Web site) include the following:

- Child Labor: We will not use child labor . . .
- Compensation: We will promote our employees' material well-being by providing compensation and benefits that are competitive and comply with applicable law.
- Forced Labor: We will not use forced labor, regardless of its form. We will not tolerate physically abusive disciplinary practices.
- Freedom of Association and Collective Bargaining: We recognize and respect our employees' right to associate freely and bargain collectively . . .
- Harassment and Discrimination: We will not tolerate harassment or discrimination . . .
- Health and Safety: We will provide and maintain for all employees a safe and healthy working environment . . .
- Work Hours: We will comply with applicable law regulating hours of work.

In an attempt to cut costs, the company has reduced the size of its workforce during the last three years. Part of these workforce reductions came from layoffs, as well as through attrition and early retirement incentives. One of the major problems facing Ford Motor is its $25 billion in unfunded pension and health-care liabilities. This commitment will continue to have an impact on the company's ability to meet its profitability goals.

Company Values

With its long and exceptional heritage, Ford Motor believes strongly in the values that have guided the company over the years. Its vision and mission statements and statement of values (as found on the company's Web site) are as follows:

Our Vision:	To become the world's leading consumer company for automotive products and services.
Our Mission:	We are a global family with a proud heritage passionately committed to providing personal mobility for people around the world. We anticipate consumer need and deliver outstanding products and services that improve people's lives.
Values:	*Our business* is driven by our consumer focus, creativity, resourcefulness, and entrepreneurial spirit.
	We are an inspired, diverse team. We respect and value everyone's contribution. The health and safety of our people are paramount.
	We are a leader in environmental responsibility. Our integrity is never compromised and we make a positive contribution to society.
	We constantly strive to improve in everything we do. Guided by these values, we provide superior return to our shareholders.

Employees are also guided by the company's business principles in how they make decisions and do their jobs. These principles can be found on the company's Web site.

Financial

Bill and his executive team are aware that the company's financial health is a long way from being where it once was and where it needs to be. Complete financial information can be found on the company's Web site (**www.ford.com**).

Bill Ford—The Person

"One thing about being a CEO is there is always somebody mad at you, and there is always a crisis somewhere in the world." This statement by Bill Ford not long after taking on the position of CEO pretty much sums up the reality of the job. Although Bill had worked in the company for a number of years, he never intended to take on the responsibility as the company's chief strategist and decision maker. When Nasser was ousted, the board of directors believed that Bill, despite being a rookie CEO, brought a lot of strengths to the position. Those strengths included the credibility of his name and his leadership style of marshaling forces and getting people to work together to find solutions and move forward. In addition, those who had worked with him called him a good listener who elicits opinions and feedback. He wants honesty from those around him and doesn't care the least bit about formal corporate hierarchy—something that the traditional bureaucracy at Ford (like all the other U.S. car makers) had to adapt to. Bill doesn't think twice about meeting alone with executives who are several layers below his direct reports. He also sometimes drops in on an assembly line and frequently buys lunch in the cafeteria where he'll question employees and listen intently to what they're saying. Bill has also been described as a natural "bridge builder" who's quite down to earth. This is an important skill, because he has had to reassure uneasy dealers and establish good relations with the United Auto Workers Union. But he's also not a pushover and has been described at times as being too stubborn.

One of his major challenges is trying to strike a balance between the short term and the long term. He says, "I've been pushed by several strong people, some inside and some outside the company, who say, 'Hey, if you really want to get your cost down, just cut your capital expenditure.' I won't do it. I will not cut our product. I'm trying to build this company for the long term, so even if that would make us look like heroes in the short term, I refuse to do it." In mid-summer 2003, he assembled a team of the company's brightest thinkers to help him establish a strategic vision for the company. He said, "It's taking a critical look at us today, and then anticipating where the world's going to be in 10 or 20 years, and asking 'Are we aligned to get there?'" And there are no sacred cows—everything is up for discussion, from whether Ford should continue to make its own engines to whether it's even operating in the right countries.

One other thing that Bill Ford is best known for is his commitment to environmental responsibility. Although the company has backed off its headline-grabbing promise in 2000 to improve the fuel economy of its SUVs by 25 percent in five years, Bill insists his commitment to the environment hasn't wavered. In fact, he likes to point out his pet project—an eco-friendly manufacturing plant opening in Dearborn in 2004. Bill acknowledges, ". . . it's tough to push a green agenda as long as gasoline is cheaper than bottled water in this country." But Ford Motor must decide if it is serious about developing cleaner, more efficient engines. It is already four years behind Toyota and Honda in bringing hybrid electric vehicles to showrooms. The company is slated to introduce its Ford Escape Hybrid, a mainstream SUV with a full hybrid-electric engine, at the end of 2004. And it also will begin selling a fuel cell-powered version of the Ford

Focus in the commercial fleet market. According to Bill, who's still intent on greening his company, these small steps are just the beginning of the company's overall commitment to improve fuel economy and reduce greenhouse gases and other emissions.

FORD MOTOR—THE FUTURE

Bill Ford Jr. has a lot at stake: his personal reputation, his family's fortune, and the company his great grandfather founded. He says, "This is everything. It's heritage. It's children's future . . . Failure is not an option." And his company has a lot of strategic issues to address.

First and foremost is how to deal with the intensifying competition in the automotive industry globally and especially in the mature European and North American markets where dramatic growth will not come from sales volume. The company must also address the ongoing challenges of improving efficiency and manufacturing excellence while at the same time coping with the rapid changes in technology (both in terms of product and process). And the company must decide where to place its bets globally. It must find ways to make the European division more competitive and profitable. Ford Motor also continues to lose heavily in South America. It is also way behind other automakers in expanding to China. Although it began building vans there in 1997, it only began producing sedans in January 2003 in a $98 million joint venture with Changhan Automotive, China's fourth-largest car company. But General Motors and Chrysler have had operations in China for years. The company does have plans in place to be much more aggressive in emerging markets, including expansions of its manufacturing capacity in China, Thailand, and the Philippines, but once again they're having to play catch up. As Bill Ford Jr. says in his shareholder's letter in the 2003 Annual Report, "Our goal is to be the best automotive company in the world." Will it accomplish that goal?

(*Sources:* Ford Motor, **www.ford.com**, April 19, 2004; Hoover's Online, **www.hoovers.com**, April 19, 2004; Standard & Poor's NetAdvantage, **www.netadvantage.standardandpoors.com**, April 19, 2004; J. R. Healey, "Ford's Famous Filly Turns 40," *USA Today,* April 16, 2004, p. B1; K. Kerwin, "Ford Learns the Lessons of Luxury," *Business Week,* March 1, 2004, pp. 116–17; A. Traylor III, "The Americanization of Toyota," *Fortune,* December 8, 2003, pp. 165–70; G. Edmondson and K. Kerwin, "Can Ford Fix This Flat?" *Business Week,* December 1, 2003, pp. 50–51; R. Banham, "The Right Price," *CFO,* October 2003, pp. 66–72; J. Muller, "Bill Ford's Next Act," *Forbes,* June 23, 2003, pp. 74–80; K. Naughton, "Bill Ford's Rainy Days," *Newsweek,* June 16, 2003, pp. 38–40; A. Traylor III, "And It's Toyota by a Nose!" *Fortune,* June 9, 2003, p. 34; and B. Morris, "Can Ford Save Ford?" *Fortune,* November 18, 2002, pp. 52–63.)

Dell

"We're clearly tracking ahead of $60 billion. We'll continue to grow and we are well ahead of the original plan laid out a few years ago . . . We're a growth company and we have aggressive ambitions." That statement by Chairman Michael Dell provides a clear statement of what this company's intentions are. As the world's number one direct-sale computer vendor, Dell wants to position itself to achieve its goals despite the intense industry and competitive challenges it faces.

INDUSTRY AND COMPETITORS

Dell dominates the PC market. Exhibit 1 provides a summary of market share held by the main competitors in the personal computer, server, and handheld PDA markets. However, the PC industry is still feeling the effects of its worst slowdown ever. Desktop computers are a commodity product with generic box computers taking the place of brand names. The uncertain economy has meant that companies are using their old computer systems longer and bankrupt tech companies have flooded the market with barely used PCs. And competitors, especially Hewlett-Packard, have become very aggressive in their pricing. These characteristics have made the PC market uncertain in terms of supporting future growth. One analyst said, "Dell is the best-positioned company, but in a no-revenue-growth industry."

Given the fact that 80 percent of its sales come from the maturing PC market and in response to the changing dynamics of that market, Dell unveiled plans in the fall of 2003 to make a major push into the consumer electronics market by selling flat-panel TVs and MP3 players as well as opening an online music-downloading store. But slowing PC sales isn't the only reason Dell made this move. It also recognized that entertainment is increasingly digital. Music, movies, and photos are

	Company	Share
Personal Computers	Dell	15%
	Hewlett-Packard	14
	IBM	6
	NEC	3
	Toshiba	3
	Others	59
Servers	Dell	29%
	Hewlett-Packard	28
	IBM	20
	Sun	16
	Fujitsu	5
	Others	1
Handheld PDAs	Palm	38%
	Hewlett-Packard	15
	Sony	11
	Dell	5
	Others	31

Exhibit 1

Tech Industry Market Share

Source: *Based on Y. Oda and T. Sekiguichi, "Branching Out,"* Time, *October 6, 2003, p. 50.*

becoming an extension of the PC. Although it's one of the few companies with the power to alter markets, Dell's move into consumer electronics isn't without risks. Dell has focused mainly on businesses—corporate customers account for about 85 percent of its revenues. Selling in consumer markets is different than selling in corporate markets, and business-oriented tech companies haven't had much success crossing over into consumer markets. In addition, Dell faces strong entrenched competitors (e.g., Sony and Mitsubishi) that aren't just going to roll over and play dead. Another big challenge Dell faces is that most consumers usually want to see what a TV's picture looks like before buying it. But Dell's customers can buy only through Dell's catalogs or Web site, so they obviously won't be able to see the picture firsthand except at the company's few mall kiosks.

LOOKING INSIDE DELL

Dell has prospered by selling PCs directly to customers over the phone and the Internet. It is following a path similar to that followed by a few other companies—specifically, McDonald's, Southwest Airlines, and Wal-Mart—that have perfected a formula and repeated and reapplied it for decades. Can Dell do what these other corporate successes have done and ensure that its future is as bright as its past? Michael Dell, founder and current chairman of the board, is hoping to position the company to do just that.

History

In 1983, as a freshman pre-med biology major at the University of Texas in Austin, Michael Dell was taking in $80,000 a month by reselling surplus IBM hardware from his dorm room. He dropped out of school, much to his parent's dismay, to start PC's Limited, the forerunner of Dell, the company that would soon hold the biggest share of the domestic PC market. Exhibit 2 lists other important dates in Dell's history.

Key Aspects of the Dell Formula

Dell's business model is based on super-efficient manufacturing and direct sales. The one thing that Dell does better than any other competitor is efficiently make and deliver computers. Nobody makes computer hardware more efficiently than Dell. It

Exhibit 2 *Important Dates in Dell's History*	1984	With $1,000 and an unprecedented idea, Michael Dell founds PC's Limited, the forerunner of Dell.
	1988	IPO (initial public offering) of Dell stock—3.5 million shares at $8.50 each.
	1993	Dell becomes one of the top five computer companies worldwide. Starts selling in Japan.
	1996	Customers begin buying Dell computers over the Internet at **www.dell.com**.
	1997	Dell opens a production and sales center in Xiamen, China.
	1999	Dell grabs the top spot in the U.S. PC market.
	2001	Dell overtakes Compaq in worldwide PC and U.S. server sales. Loses both market leads when Compaq announces plans to merge with Hewlett-Packard.
	2002	Dell reclaims top spots in both worldwide PC and U.S. server sales
	2003	Drops "Computer" from its name and is now known simply as Dell.
	2004	Michael Dell hands over job of CEO to Kevin Rollins, the COO and president. Michael Dell retains title of Chairman of the Board.

manages to keep costs low and inventory at a minimum. In 2002, operating costs were just 10 percent of Dell's revenues. By the end of fiscal year 2004, that figure had fallen to 9.7 percent and was even lower—9.6 percent—during the last three quarters. In comparison, operating costs were 21 percent at Hewlett-Packard, 25 percent at Gateway, and 46 percent at Cisco. There are no unnecessary costs at Dell. This almost "sacred" mandate of the Dell direct business model is based on no inventory, no middlemen to eat into profits, and no agenda other than giving customers what they want at irresistible prices.

On the manufacturing side, Dell has no warehouses to store parts and takes delivery of parts only when it has customers' orders that need them. It has, on average, seven hours of inventory, versus the weeks of inventory other manufacturers have. In its manufacturing facilities, parts and products zip by overhead on conveyors so the right items get to the right places at the right time. The walls at one factory are lined with framed certificates of patents (more than 550) given mostly for manufacturing processes. Dell has done everything from innovating a method of using wireless networks in the factories to finding a way to configure manufacturing stations that are four times as productive as a standard assembly line. This ability to invent and reinvent business processes is a capability that Dell has that its competitors do not. In addition, each PC or product is built by one person and can be traced back to that person if something goes wrong. Such an approach creates significant individual responsibility and helps keep product quality high.

In its marketing, Dell's goal has been product leadership, which it defines as "bringing to market exactly what customers want, when they want it, for the best value in the industry." One important way Dell has been able to achieve this is through its strategy of direct customer interaction through the Web or by phone, or in the case of corporate sales, by using a direct sales force. By cutting out retailers—the middlemen—Dell not only saves both time and money, but it has the ability to really focus on customers.

Customers order directly from the company and provide a lot of information during that transaction. Customers tell Dell exactly what they want and need and Dell translates those needs into products and services. In this industry particularly, a company's ability to understand and act on customer needs is critical, because those expectations can and frequently do change. And Dell has proved its abilities to respond to customers. In addition to its direct sales, Dell has launched trials of a Dell "store within in a store" at some big-name retailing chains such as Sears. After a successful trial period, the company is also making its limited number of mall-based kiosks permanent. Dell's experiments with other forms of selling haven't always panned out. For instance, the company's push in 1994 to sell through Wal-Mart's Sam's Clubs, Staples USA, and CompUSA failed because customers got better deals over the phone directly with Dell, leaving retailers stuck with unsold stock and quite unhappy. In this latest round of experimenting with nondirect sales, Best Buy chose not to carry Dell because it considers the company a competitor. And computer superstore CompUSA also chose not to allow Dell kiosks in its stores, perhaps because of its earlier experiences with Dell. In addition to all its other marketing strategies, Dell regularly measures how it's doing from the customer's perspective. Some customer performance measures include how easy it is to contact the company, the accuracy with which orders are filled, whether deliveries are on time, overall product quality, whether problems are resolved the first time, and whether customers are treated with respect and courtesy. And the company must be doing something right; it received more than 100 awards in 2003 for product and service quality and reliability. One of these awards—being ranked first in a survey of corporate technology customers in customer satisfaction and in overall service and support among hardware vendors—was a particularly notable accomplishment. An example of how Dell listens to its customers can be seen in its decision in November 2003 to stop routing corporate customers to a technical support call center in India. A company spokesperson said, "Customers weren't satisfied with the level of support they were receiving, so we're moving some calls around to make sure they don't feel that way anymore."

In the research and development area, Dell doesn't believe in spending a lot of money. It doesn't invest in product development and has no proprietary technology. Dell's strategy has been to leave the costs and risks of innovating to others. Rivals say that approach handicaps Dell's ability to move away from PCs. Hewlett-Packard's CEO Carly Fiorina says, "Dell is a great company, but they are a one-trick pony." Dell's executives would disagree, however, because inventing the "Next Big Thing" isn't their goal. Instead, their focus is on building the "Current Big Thing" better than anyone else. Dell's strategic approach has been to apply its super-efficient techniques to the right products at the right time and is based on its belief that all technologies follow a similar pattern; that is, when a tech product first comes to market, it's a high-priced, high-margin item made differently by each company. As the technology standardizes and parts makers flourish, manufacturing costs drop and the technology starts becoming a commodity. Dell has been able to pinpoint when to jump in at that certain junction between standardization and commoditization when it can exploit its simplicity and efficiency advantages. Kevin Rollins, president and CEO, says, "Our business model excels in that transition." That ability to know when to enter a new market at just the right time has been described as a master surfer knowing when and how to ride that perfect wave.

Dell employs about 46,000 individuals worldwide and recognizes the important role its people play in the company's continued growth and financial success. However, after massive layoffs in the summer of 2001 and an employee survey that revealed that half would leave if they had the chance, Michael Dell and Kevin Rollins vowed to address the criticisms. They understand the importance of employee loyalty and want to prevent an exodus of executives. One area the company is working on is trying to bring better balance between employees' work lives and their personal lives. It has been working with managers to ensure that they respond to their employees' needs both inside and outside the workplace. Managers are also in the middle of a deliberate, multiyear effort to improve and expand their leadership skills. As Michael and Kevin state in the 2004 Annual Report, "This is a critical means to building and inspiring champions at every level of the organization, and realizing all of Dell's vast potential for customers and other stakeholders."

Dell's financial performance reflects the success of its other strategies. Fiscal year 2004 was the most successful year ever. Product shipments grew 26 percent. Revenue increased 17 percent even while total sales in the rest of the industry declined. Financial highlights are shown in Exhibit 3. Complete financial information can be found on the company's Web site.

Michael Dell—the Leader

Michael Dell is an enigma. He is the founder and leader of the world's number one direct-sale computer vendor, yet he is extremely shy and has no oversized ego

Exhibit 3

Operating Results (in millions, except per-share data)

FISCAL-YEAR ENDED	JAN. 30, 2004	JAN. 31, 2003	CHANGE
Net revenue	$ 41,444	$ 35,404	17.1%
Gross margin	7,552	6,349	18.9
Operating income	3,544	2,844	24.6
Net income	2,645	2,122	24.6
Income per common share			
Basic	1.03	0.82	25.6
Diluted	1.01	0.80	26.3
Weighted average shares			
Basic	2,565	2,584	
Diluted	2,619	2,644	
Total cash and investments	11,922	9,905	
Total assets	19,311	15,470	
Long-term debt	505	506	
Total stockholders' equity	6,280	4,873	

Source: *Dell Fiscal 2004 in Review, p. 2.* © Dell Inc. All rights reserved.

Exhibit 4

Fun Facts about Michael Dell

- His only business-related course in college before dropping out was macroeconomics.
- He was a Dr. Seuss fan as a kid.
- He owned a BMW at age 16, purchased with the money he made from a business that targeted newspaper subscriptions at newlyweds.
- At age 27, he was the youngest ever CEO of a *Fortune* 500 company. He was a billionaire at age 31. By age 34, he was richer than Bill Gates at the same age.
- Dell, the company, was profitable on day one.
- Says that when he dropped out of college to start the company, "My parents were very upset until I showed them my first financial statement."

Source: *Based on D. Jones, "Dell: Take Time to Build," USA Today, October 10, 2002, p. 6B.*

Exhibit 5

Michael Dell's Management
Principles

- Be direct.
- Leave the ego at the door.
- No excuses.
- No easy targets.
- No victory laps.
- Worry about saving money, not saving face.

Source: *Based on A. Park and P. Burrows, "What You Don't Know about Dell," Business Week, November 3, 2003, p. 79.*

to speak of. (See some other fun facts about Michael Dell in Exhibit 4.) As one writer said, "Michael Dell does not lead by force of personality. He doesn't have tough-guy charisma . . . or folksy charm." Yet, the way Michael Dell manages his company has helped make it the success it is. Dell also never feared hiring brilliant people who added to his strengths and balanced his weaknesses. His management approach, as summarized in Exhibit 5, is simple and direct—much like the business model he created for his company. He believes that the status quo is never good enough. Also, when something is done successfully, the praise is short-lived because

Dell believes it's necessary to analyze what could have been done better. Just as crucial is his belief that once a problem has been uncovered that it be dealt with quickly and directly. Another of Dell's beliefs is that every product should be profitable from day one. He expects his managers to be able to provide information on everything from product growth patterns to the average number of times a part has to be replaced in the first 30 days. "It's this combination of reaching for the heights of perfection while burrowing down into every last data point that competitors have been unable to imitate."

Michael Dell's management style has influenced the culture that is Dell. It's a culture that stresses winning with integrity by continuously improving and encouraging personal responsibility. A big part of Dell's culture is reflected in an initiative called the "Soul of Dell," which was launched in 2001 after the difficult period following the employee layoffs. The Soul of Dell, a statement of the values and beliefs which define its shared global culture, can be summed up in the phrase "performance with integrity." This culture of performance with integrity unites the employees and establishes the expectations that they understand and adhere to corporate values and to the laws of countries within which Dell does business. Several key characteristics comprise the Soul of Dell and provide the foundation for Dell's corporate Code of Conduct. Those characteristics, as outlined on the company's Web site, include the following:

- Trust—We keep our commitments to each other and to our stakeholders.
- Integrity—We do the right thing without compromise.
- Honesty—We are open and honest in our communications with each other and about our business performance.
- Judgment—We think before we act and consider the consequences of our actions.
- Respect—We treat people with dignity and value their contributions; we maintain fairness in all relationships.
- Courage—We speak up for what is right and report wrongdoing when we see it.
- Responsibility—We accept the consequences of our actions. We admit our mistakes and quickly correct them.

In July 2004, Michael Dell handed over the job of CEO to company president and COO Kevin Rollins. Rollins is an operations expert who has largely run the day-to-day business dealings of the company since the late 1990s. Those who know Rollins best say that he has an eye for detail and absorbs information quickly. "He's an aggressive competitor with great strategic instincts."

Current Strategic Initiatives

As Dell rolled out its line of consumer electronics, Kevin Rollins said, "How many new products can Dell add to its portfolio? Where does it end? We think there's a somewhat limitless number of products and services we could get into." By doing what it does best—finding that right moment to enter a tech product market—Dell intends to continue growing. Although the company has about $12 billion in cash and other investments on hand, it's not looking to grow through acquisitions. The company's goal of hitting $60 billion in revenue by mid-decade isn't dependent on growing by acquiring. Instead, it believes the greatest growth potential is from opportunities in countries such as England and China. In China alone, product shipments were up 60 percent in 2003, and it has become Dell's fourth-largest market.

Growth is also coming from its printer business, first introduced in March 2003. Since that time, more than 2 million of its printers have been shipped.

THE FUTURE OF DELL

What will Dell's third decade be like? Will it be able to continue to achieve the levels of success it has enjoyed? Will the strategies that have worked in the past be appropriate for the future? These are the challenges facing Michael Dell, Kevin Rollins, and the other employees of Dell.

(*Sources:* Dell, **www.dell.com**, April 24, 2004; Hoover's Online, **www.hoovers.com**, April 24, 2004; Standard & Poor's NetAdvantage, **www.netadvantage.standardandpoors.com**, April 24, 2004; M. Slagle, "Dell Says It's on Track to Meet $60 Billion Goal," *USA Today,* April 9, 2004, p. 6B; M. Kessler, "Dell Founder Passes Torch to New CEO," *USA Today,* March 5, 2004, p. 5B; The Associated Press, "Dell Ends Indian Tech Support for Corporate Customers," *USA Today,* November 25, 2003, p. 2B; M. Kessler, "New Products, Markets Boost Dell's Profit," *USA Today,* November 14, 2003, p. 3B; A. Park and P. Burrows, "What You Don't Know about Dell," *Business Week,* November 3, 2003, pp. 76–84; C. B. Thomas, "Dell Wants Your Home," *Time,* October 6, 2003, pp. 48–50; K. Maney, "Dell to Dive Into Consumer Electronics Market," *USA Today,* September 25, 2003, p. B1; "Last Man Standing: Interview with Michael Dell," *SmartMoney,* July 2003, pp. 36–37; K. Jones, "The Dell Way," *Business 2.0,* February 2003, pp. 60–66; G. McWilliams and A. Zimmerman, "Dell Plans to Peddle PCs Inside Sears, Other Large Chains," *Wall Street Journal,* January 30, 2003, p. B1; K. Maney, "Dell Business Model Turns to Muscle as Rivals Struggle," *USA Today,* January 20, 2003, p. B1; D. Jones, "Dell: Take Time to Build," *USA Today,* October 10, 2002, p. 6B; and A. Park, F. Keenan, and C. Edwards, "Whose Lunch Will Dell Eat Next?" *Business Week,* August 12, 2002, pp. 66–67.)

Index

J

J. Crew, 7
James, LeBron, 182
Java Jacket, 267
Jemal, Michael, 106
Job-based pay, 155
Johnson, William R., 240
Johnson & Johnson, 3
Johnston, Jerry, 26
Joint-issue promotion, 284
Joint venture, 232
Jordan, Michael, 132, 182
Jostens, 239
Judo strategy, 288
Jung, Andrea, 1

K

Kanter, Rosabeth Moss, 58
Kashi Company, 69
Kazaa, 29
Keebler Droxies, 196
Keebler Foods Company, 69
Kelleher, Herb, 156
Kellogg Company, 69, 196
Kinko's, 8, 36
Kmart, 4, 83, 109, 237
Knight, Phil, 181–182
Knowledge, 38
Knowledge hoarding, 58
Knowledge work system
    (KWS), 162
Kodak, 220
Kohl's Corporation, 65–66
Kraft, 84
Krispy Kreme, 150
Kroc, Joan, 282
Kroger Company, 8
KWS, 162

L

Labor relations, 155–156
Laboratoires Inneov, 232
Lacy, Alan J., 215–216
Lancaster Colony
    Corporation, 226
Lane Home Furnishing, 221
Laws and regulations, 85, 86
Layout strategies, 143
Learning organization, 51–53
Legislation, 86
Lend Lease Corporation, 16
Levels of strategies, 7
Levi Strauss, 20
Licensing, 228
Licensing (NFPs), 284
Lincoln Electric, 189
Lipton, 232
Liquidation, 240
L.L. Bean, 220
Lo, Anthony, 11
Location strategies, 142
Long-term contract, 232
Longevity, 9
L'Oreal SA, 1–2, 232
Low-carb products, 221
Low-cost strategy, 192

M

M.A. Hanna, 235
Magna International, 143
Magna Steyr, 143
Magnatune, 30
Management information system
    (MIS), 162
Managing strategically, 31
Market development, 220–221
Market logistics, 149
Market niche, 195
Market segments, 146
Market share, 125
Market specialization strategy, 146
Marketing, 146
Marketing mix strategies, 148–149
Marketing strategies, 146–151
    database marketing, 151
    differentiation strategies, 146
    events and activities
        marketing, 151
    marketing mix strategies, 148–149
    mass customization, 150–151
    positioning strategies, 147–148
    relationship marketing, 150
    segmentation (target market)
        strategies, 146
Markup pricing, 148
Martha Stewart Living Omnimedia,
    133–134
Maruti Udyog, 82
Mass customization, 150–151
Matching, 5
Mattel, 229
Maytag, 3
McDonald's Corporation, 16, 50, 84,
    100, 197
McEwen, Rob, 270
McKinsey-GE stoplight matrix, 246–247
McNeil Consumer Products, 284
Merger, 230
Mergers-acquisitions, 230, 231
Microsoft, 3, 30, 107, 167, 193, 249
Midwest Air Group, 195
Miles, R. E., 188, 190
Miles and Snow's adaptive strategies,
    188–189, 190
Mintzberg, Henry, 198
Mintzberg's alternative generic
    competitive strategies,
    198–199
MIS, 162
Mission, 48
Mitsubishi, 237
Morris, Johnny, 176
Motorola, 237
Movie business, 40
MTV Networks, 188, 229
Multidomestic approach, 228
Multiple-business organization, 217
Music industry, 29–30
mvp.com, 75

N

NAFTA, 86
Napster, 29, 30
NASCAR, 257–258

National Basketball Association (NBA),
    132–133
National Cancer Institute, 284
Navistar International Corporation, 73
NBA, 132–133
Nestlé, 17, 232
Neural networks, 151
New business environment, 37–53
    critical success factors, 44–53.
        See also Critical
        success factors
    drivers, 37–44
New product development, 148
Newell Rubbermaid Inc., 229
Nike, 181–182
Nissan, 16
Noble Fiber Technologies, 87
Nokia, 112
Nortel Networks, 144
North American Free Trade Agreement
    (NAFTA), 86
Not-for-profit and public sector
        organizations, 274–285
    cause-related marketing, 283
    competitive strategies, 280
    corporate strategies, 280
    definitions, 274–276
    economic contributions, 277
    external analysis, 277–278
    functional strategies, 279
    internal analysis, 278
    IRS filings, 281
    marketing alliances, 283–284
    stakeholders, 282
    strategic management, 281–282
    strategic piggybacking, 284–285
    strategy evaluation/control, 280
Not-for-profit marketing alliances,
    283–284
NUMMI, 232

O

OAS, 162
Occupational Safety and Health Act, 86
Occupational Safety and Health
        Administration (OSHA), 85
Odland, Steve, 27
Offensive moves, 202–203
Office automation system (OAS), 162
Office layout, 143
Oil companies, 222–223
Old Navy, 66
Olive Garden, 73
Omron Healthcare, 221
1-800-Flowers, 20
One-to-one marketing, 150
Online analytical processing, 151
Online communities, 150
Open system, 67
Opportunities, 66. See also
        External analysis
Oreo, 196
Organizational capabilities, 108–111
Organizational change, 42
Organizational culture, 160
Organizational environments, 67–69
Organizational goals, 124
Organizational growth, 219–233. See also
        Growth strategies